FRAMED!

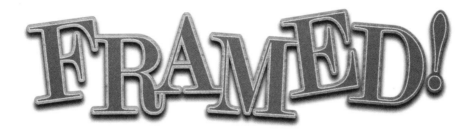

Other *Baby Blues®* Books from Andrews McMeel Publishing

Guess Who Didn't Take a Nap?
I Thought Labor Ended When the Baby Was Born
We Are Experiencing Parental Difficulties . . . Please Stand By
Night of the Living Dad
I Saw Elvis in My Ultrasound
One More and We're Outnumbered!
Check, Please . . .
threats, bribes & videotape
If I'm a Stay-At-Home Mom, Why Am I Always in the Car?
Lift and Separate
I Shouldn't Have to Scream More Than Once!
Motherhood Is Not for Wimps
Baby Blues®: Unplugged
Dad to the Bone
Never a Dry Moment
Two Plus One Is Enough
Playdate: Category 5
Our Server Is Down
Something Chocolate This Way Comes

Treasuries

The Super-Absorbent Biodegradable Family-Size Baby Blues®
Baby Blues®: Ten Years and Still in Diapers
Butt-Naked Baby Blues®
Wall-to-Wall Baby Blues®
Driving Under the Influence of Children

Baby Blues

FRAMED!

A *Baby Blues*® Treasury by Rick Kirkman & Jerry Scott

Andrews McMeel
Publishing, LLC

Kansas City

Framed! copyright © 2006 by Baby Blues Partnership. All rights reserved. Printed in the United States of America. No part of this book may be used or reproduced in any manner whatsoever without written permission except in the case of reprints in the context of reviews. For information, write Andrews McMeel Publishing, LLC, an Andrews McMeel Universal company, 4520 Main Street, Kansas City, Missouri 64111.

06 07 08 09 10 BAM 10 9 8 7 6 5 4 3 2 1

ISBN-13: 978-0-7407-6194-2
ISBN-10: 0-7407-6194-3

Library of Congress Control Number: 2006924333

www.andrewsmcmeel.com

Find *Baby Blues* on the Web at
www.babyblues.com.

──── **ATTENTION: SCHOOLS AND BUSINESSES** ────

Andrews McMeel books are available at quantity discounts with bulk purchase for educational, business, or sales promotional use. For information, please write to: Special Sales Department, Andrews McMeel Publishing, LLC, 4520 Main Street, Kansas City, Missouri 64111.

To Trish, for all you do. Thanks.

—J.S.

For Becca, Lesley, Monica, and Jen. Words can't express the depth of our thanks.

—R.K. and S.K.

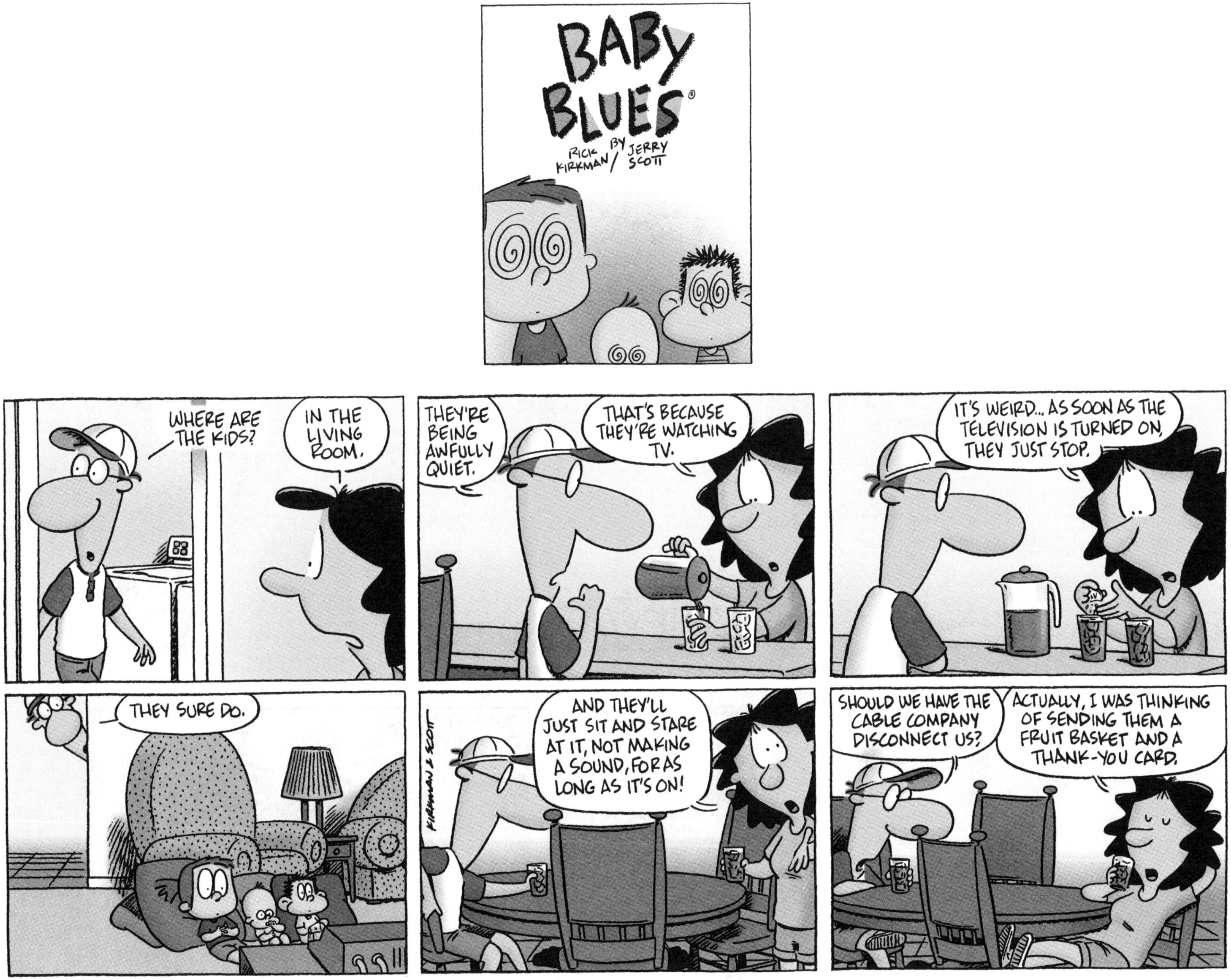
BABY BLUES®
BY RICK KIRKMAN / JERRY SCOTT
WHERE ARE THE KIDS?
IN THE LIVING ROOM.
THEY'RE BEING AWFULLY QUIET.
THAT'S BECAUSE THEY'RE WATCHING TV.
IT'S WEIRD... AS SOON AS THE TELEVISION IS TURNED ON, THEY JUST STOP.
THEY SURE DO.
AND THEY'LL JUST SIT AND STARE AT IT, NOT MAKING A SOUND, FOR AS LONG AS IT'S ON!
SHOULD WE HAVE THE CABLE COMPANY DISCONNECT US?
ACTUALLY, I WAS THINKING OF SENDING THEM A FRUIT BASKET AND A THANK-YOU CARD.
KIRKMAN & SCOTT

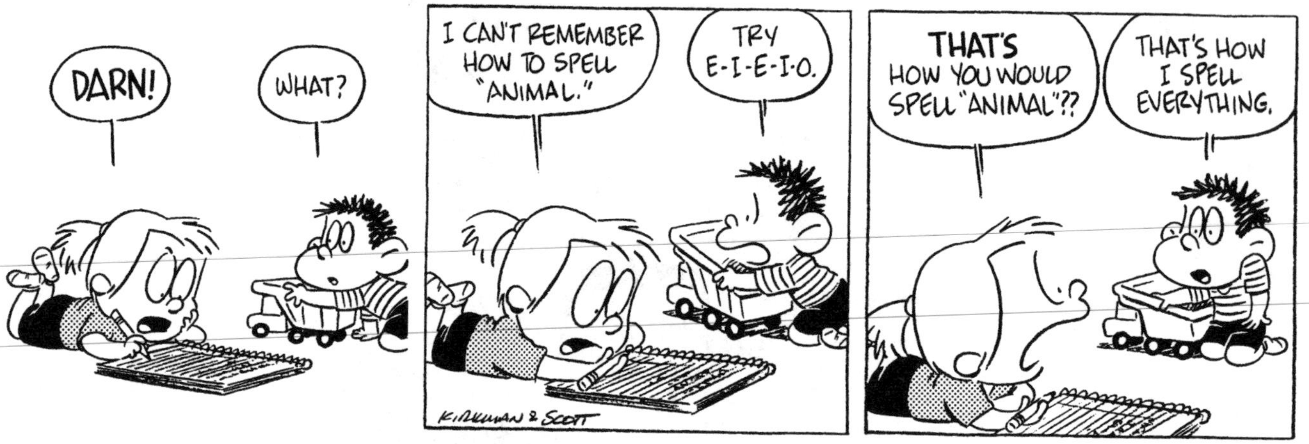
DARN!
WHAT?
I CAN'T REMEMBER HOW TO SPELL "ANIMAL."
TRY E-I-E-I-O.
THAT'S HOW YOU WOULD SPELL "ANIMAL"??
THAT'S HOW I SPELL EVERYTHING.
KIRKMAN & SCOTT

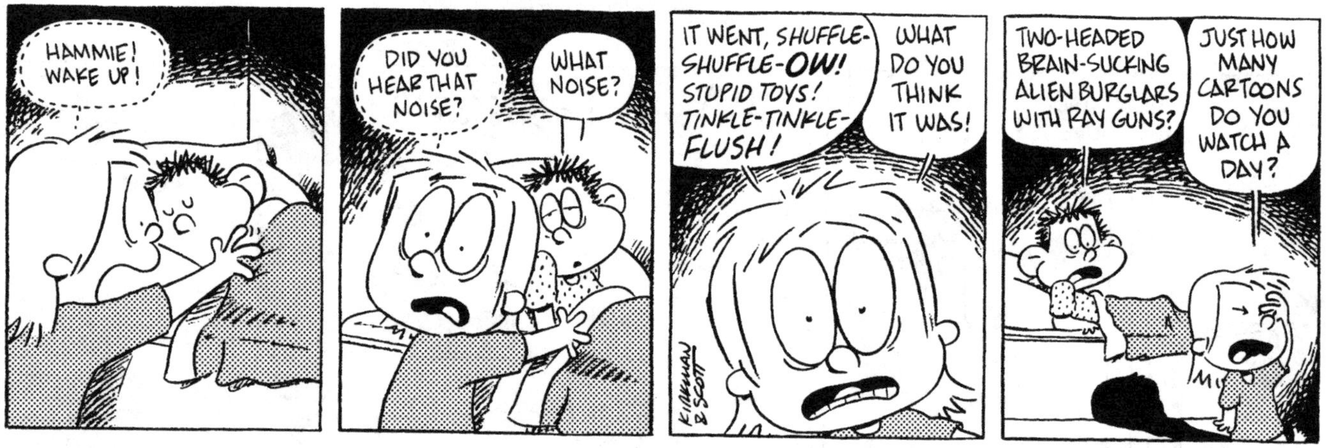
HAMMIE! WAKE UP!
DID YOU HEAR THAT NOISE?
WHAT NOISE?
IT WENT, SHUFFLE-SHUFFLE-OW! STUPID TOYS! TINKLE-TINKLE-FLUSH!
WHAT DO YOU THINK IT WAS!
KIRKMAN & SCOTT
TWO-HEADED BRAIN-SUCKING ALIEN BURGLARS WITH RAY GUNS?
JUST HOW MANY CARTOONS DO YOU WATCH A DAY?

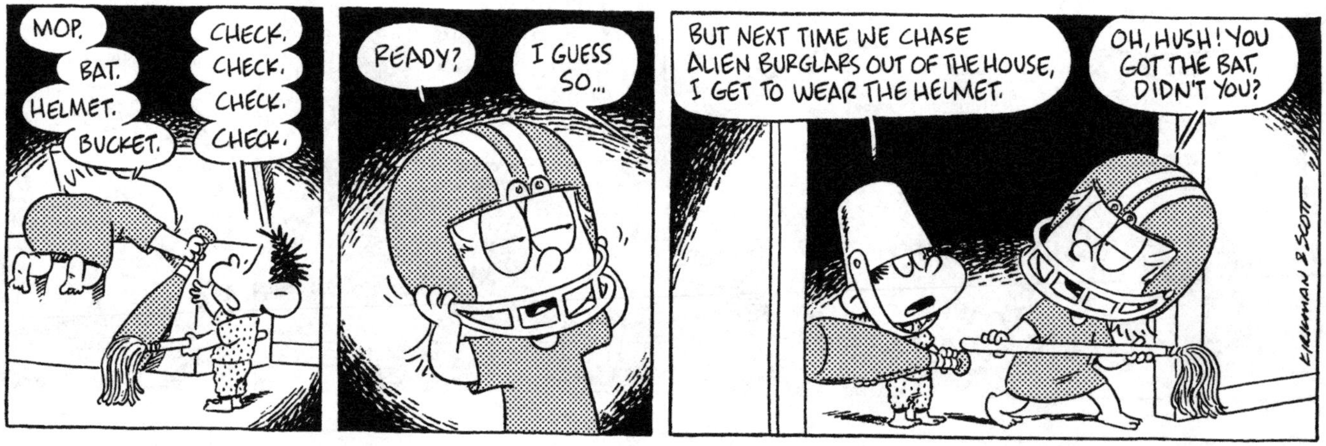
MOP.
CHECK.
BAT.
CHECK.
HELMET.
CHECK.
BUCKET.
CHECK.
READY?
I GUESS SO...
BUT NEXT TIME WE CHASE ALIEN BURGLARS OUT OF THE HOUSE, I GET TO WEAR THE HELMET.
OH, HUSH! YOU GOT THE BAT, DIDN'T YOU?
KIRKMAN & SCOTT

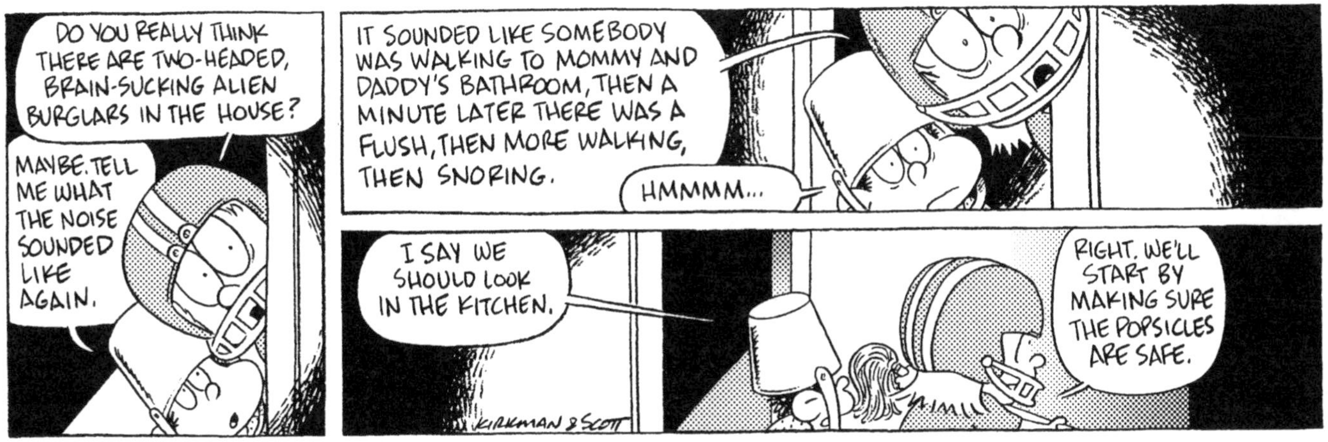
DO YOU REALLY THINK THERE ARE TWO-HEADED, BRAIN-SUCKING ALIEN BURGLARS IN THE HOUSE?
MAYBE. TELL ME WHAT THE NOISE SOUNDED LIKE AGAIN.
IT SOUNDED LIKE SOMEBODY WAS WALKING TO MOMMY AND DADDY'S BATHROOM, THEN A MINUTE LATER THERE WAS A FLUSH, THEN MORE WALKING, THEN SNORING.
HMMMM...
I SAY WE SHOULD LOOK IN THE KITCHEN.
RIGHT. WE'LL START BY MAKING SURE THE POPSICLES ARE SAFE.
KIRKMAN & SCOTT

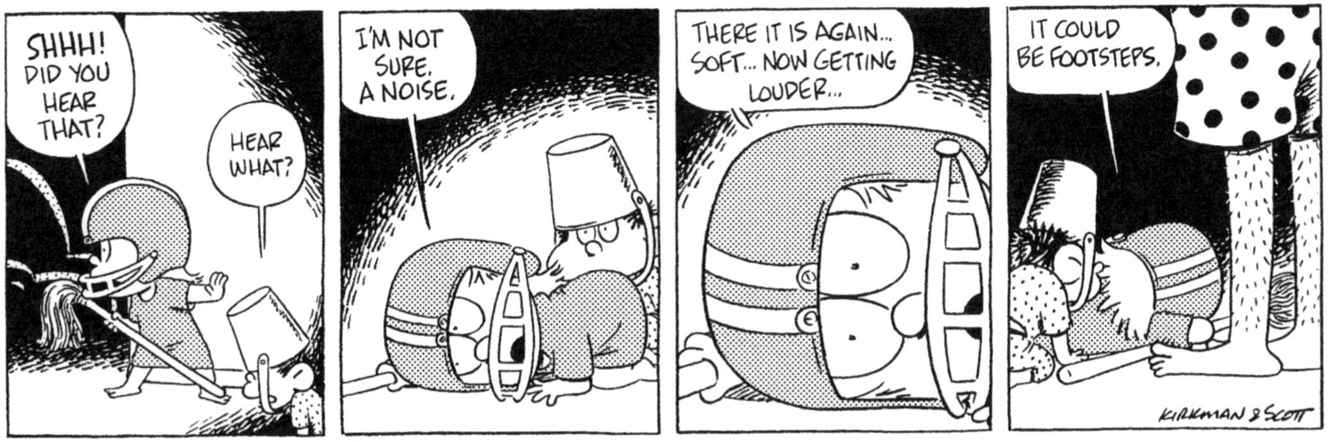
SHHH! DID YOU HEAR THAT?
HEAR WHAT?
I'M NOT SURE. A NOISE.
THERE IT IS AGAIN... SOFT... NOW GETTING LOUDER...
IT COULD BE FOOTSTEPS.
KIRKMAN & SCOTT

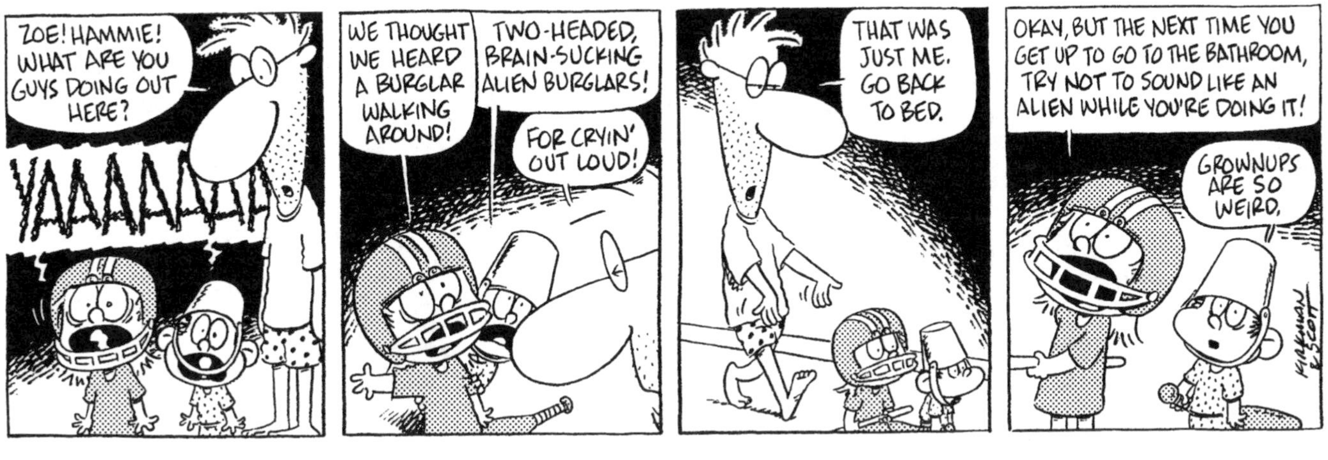
ZOE! HAMMIE! WHAT ARE YOU GUYS DOING OUT HERE?
YAAAAAAA
WE THOUGHT WE HEARD A BURGLAR WALKING AROUND!
TWO-HEADED, BRAIN-SUCKING ALIEN BURGLARS!
FOR CRYIN' OUT LOUD!
THAT WAS JUST ME. GO BACK TO BED.
OKAY, BUT THE NEXT TIME YOU GET UP TO GO TO THE BATHROOM, TRY NOT TO SOUND LIKE AN ALIEN WHILE YOU'RE DOING IT!
GROWNUPS ARE SO WEIRD.
KIRKMAN & SCOTT

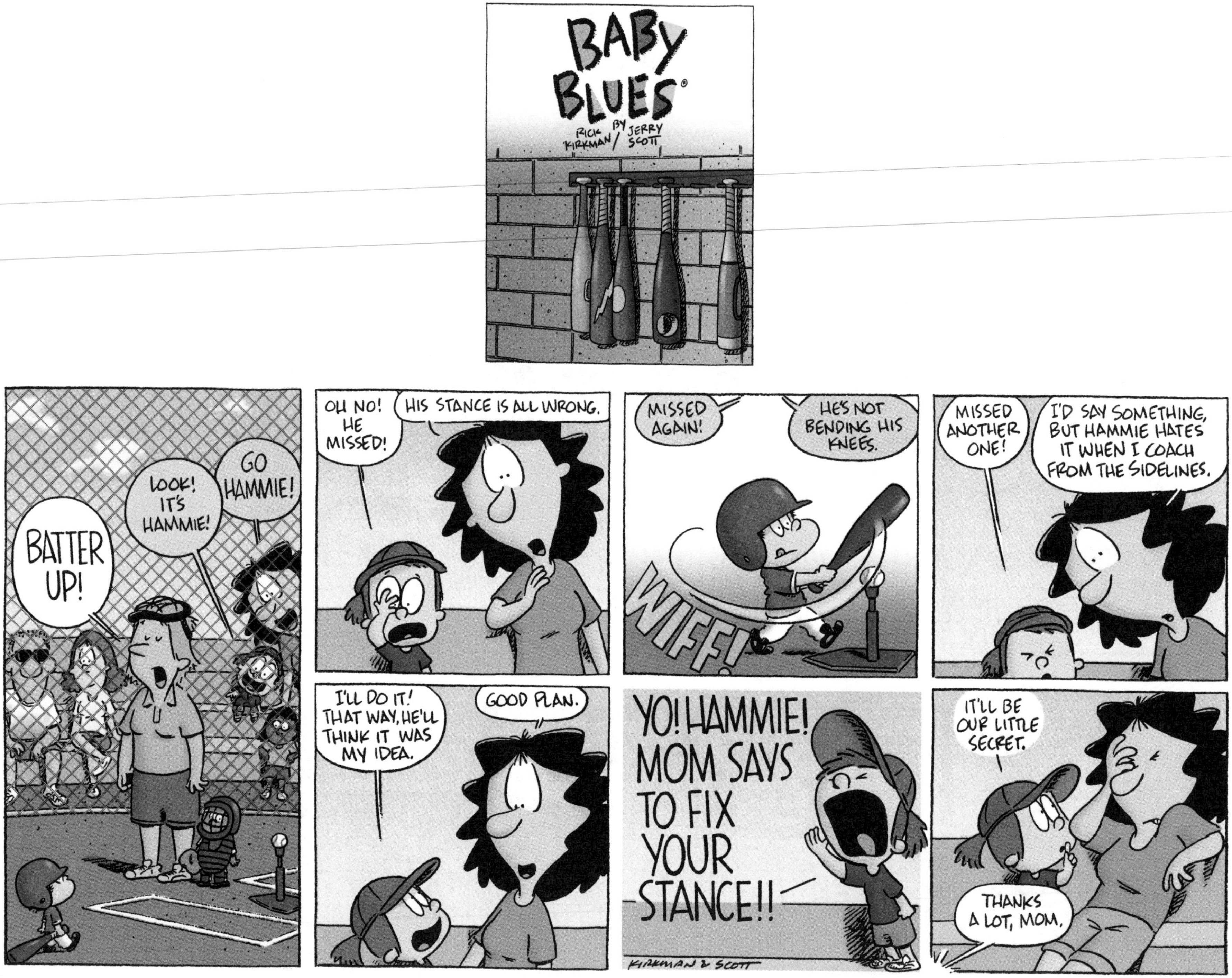
BABY BLUES®
BY RICK KIRKMAN / JERRY SCOTT
BATTER UP!
LOOK! IT'S HAMMIE!
GO HAMMIE!
OH NO! HE MISSED!
HIS STANCE IS ALL WRONG.
MISSED AGAIN!
HE'S NOT BENDING HIS KNEES.
WIFF!
MISSED ANOTHER ONE!
I'D SAY SOMETHING, BUT HAMMIE HATES IT WHEN I COACH FROM THE SIDELINES.
I'LL DO IT! THAT WAY, HE'LL THINK IT WAS MY IDEA.
GOOD PLAN.
YO! HAMMIE! MOM SAYS TO FIX YOUR STANCE!!
KIRKMAN & SCOTT
IT'LL BE OUR LITTLE SECRET.
THANKS A LOT, MOM.

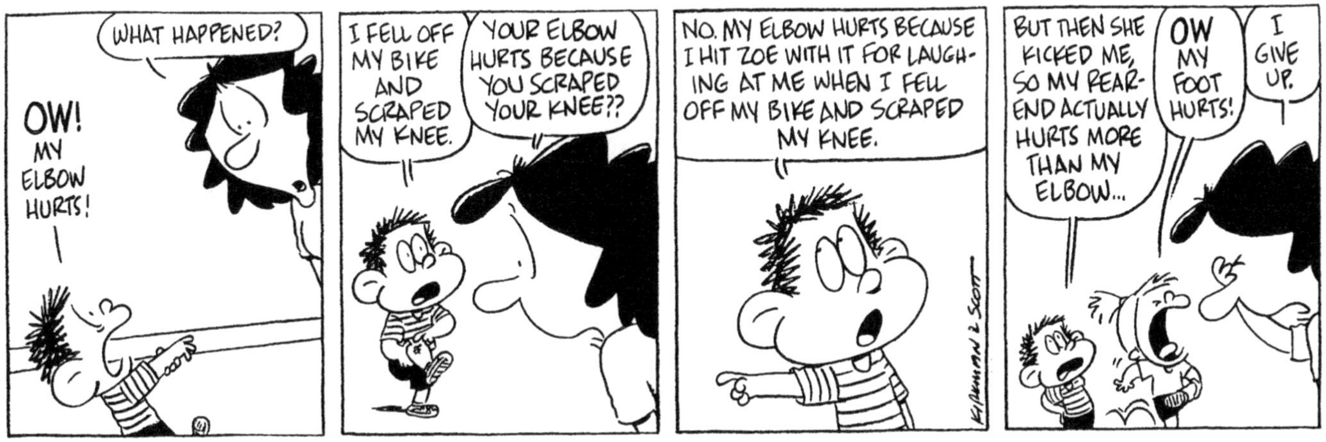
WHAT HAPPENED?
OW! MY ELBOW HURTS!
I FELL OFF MY BIKE AND SCRAPED MY KNEE.
YOUR ELBOW HURTS BECAUSE YOU SCRAPED YOUR KNEE??
NO. MY ELBOW HURTS BECAUSE I HIT ZOE WITH IT FOR LAUGHING AT ME WHEN I FELL OFF MY BIKE AND SCRAPED MY KNEE.
BUT THEN SHE KICKED ME, SO MY REAR-END ACTUALLY HURTS MORE THAN MY ELBOW...
OW MY FOOT HURTS!
I GIVE UP.

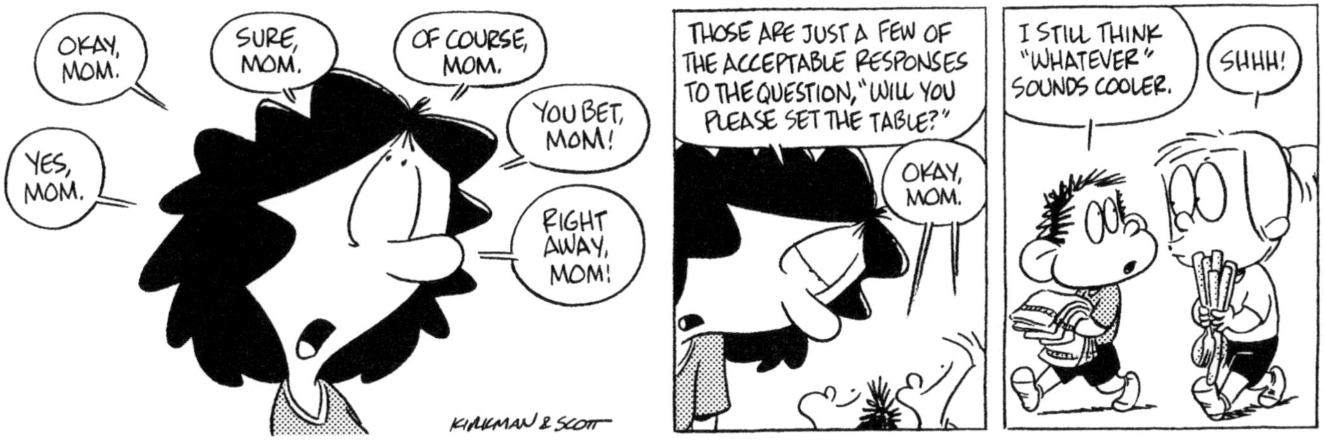
OKAY, MOM.
SURE, MOM.
OF COURSE, MOM.
YES, MOM.
YOU BET, MOM!
RIGHT AWAY, MOM!
KIRKMAN & SCOTT
THOSE ARE JUST A FEW OF THE ACCEPTABLE RESPONSES TO THE QUESTION, "WILL YOU PLEASE SET THE TABLE?"
OKAY, MOM.
I STILL THINK "WHATEVER" SOUNDS COOLER.
SHHH!

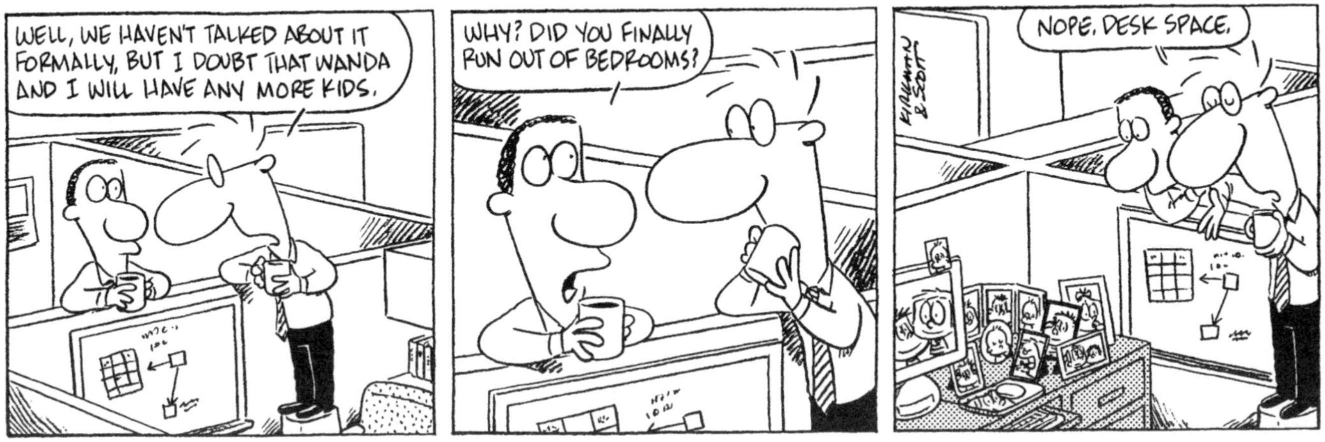
WELL, WE HAVEN'T TALKED ABOUT IT FORMALLY, BUT I DOUBT THAT WANDA AND I WILL HAVE ANY MORE KIDS.
WHY? DID YOU FINALLY RUN OUT OF BEDROOMS?
NOPE. DESK SPACE.

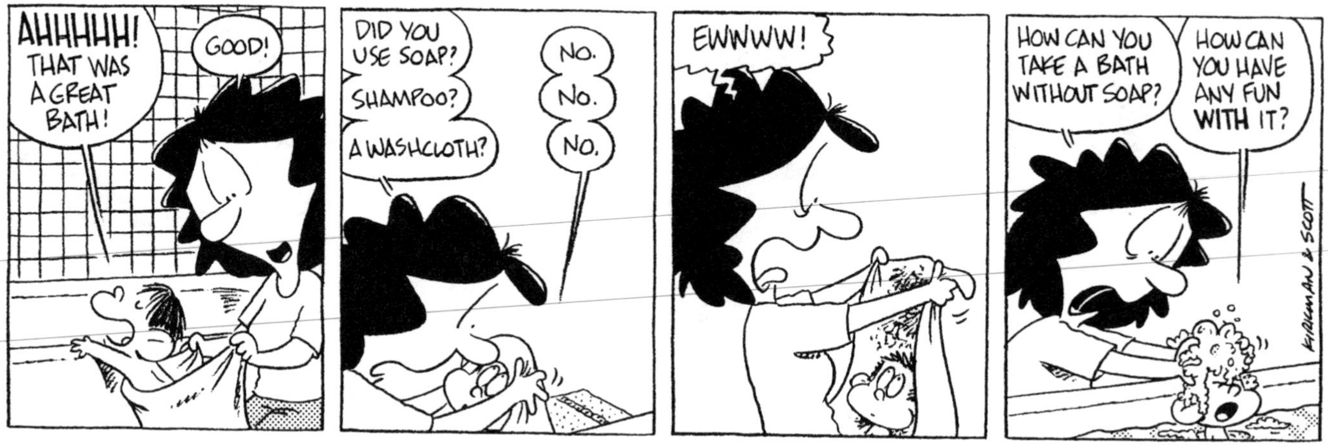
AHHHHH! THAT WAS A GREAT BATH!
GOOD!
DID YOU USE SOAP?
NO.
SHAMPOO?
NO.
A WASHCLOTH?
NO.
EWWWW!
HOW CAN YOU TAKE A BATH WITHOUT SOAP?
HOW CAN YOU HAVE ANY FUN WITH IT?
KIRKMAN & SCOTT

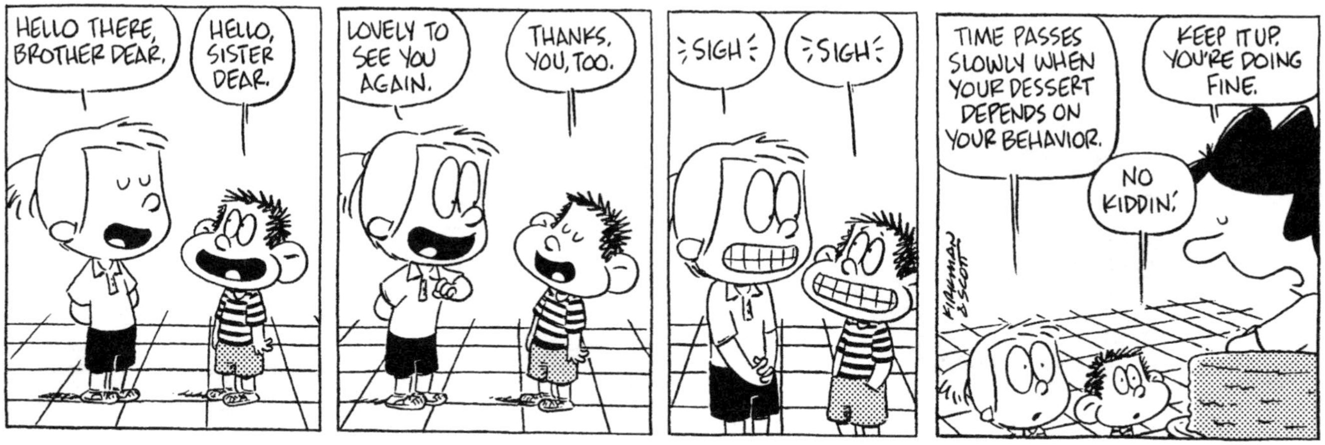
HELLO THERE, BROTHER DEAR.
HELLO, SISTER DEAR.
LOVELY TO SEE YOU AGAIN.
THANKS. YOU, TOO.
SIGH
SIGH
KIRKMAN & SCOTT
TIME PASSES SLOWLY WHEN YOUR DESSERT DEPENDS ON YOUR BEHAVIOR.
KEEP IT UP. YOU'RE DOING FINE.
NO KIDDIN'.

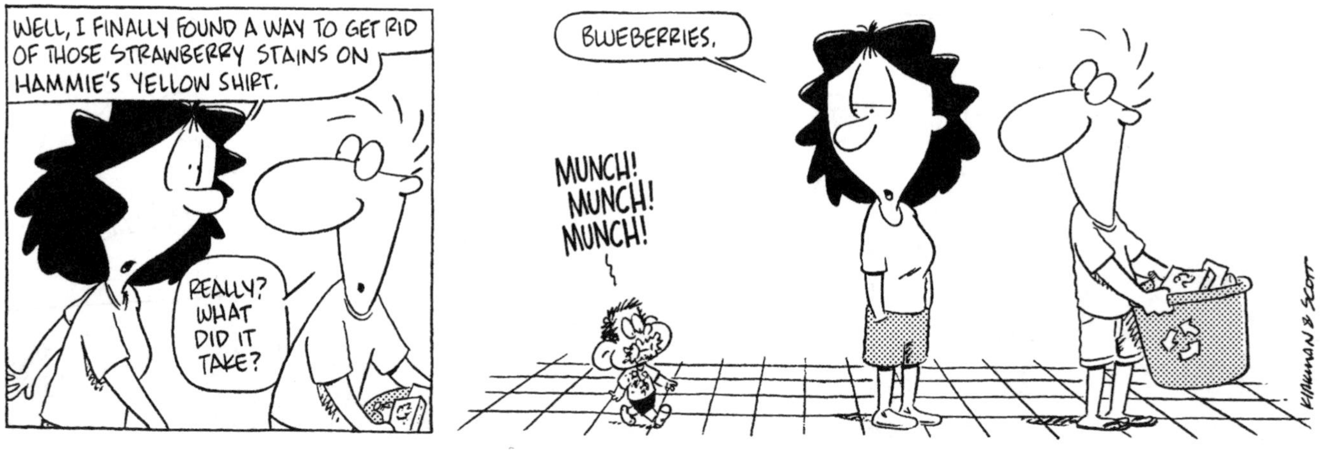
WELL, I FINALLY FOUND A WAY TO GET RID OF THOSE STRAWBERRY STAINS ON HAMMIE'S YELLOW SHIRT.
REALLY? WHAT DID IT TAKE?
BLUEBERRIES.
MUNCH! MUNCH! MUNCH!
KIRKMAN & SCOTT

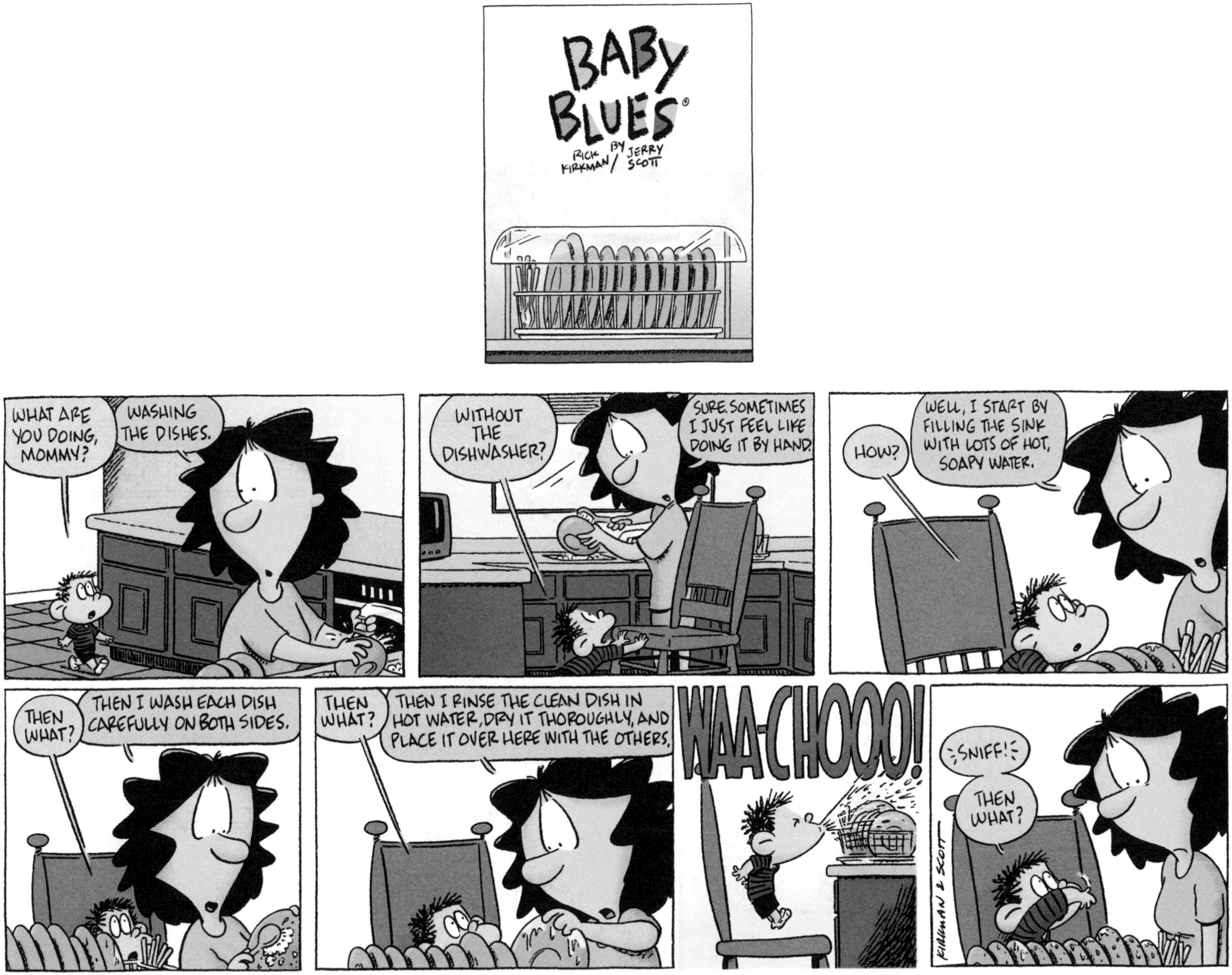
BABY BLUES®
BY RICK KIRKMAN / JERRY SCOTT
WHAT ARE YOU DOING, MOMMY?
WASHING THE DISHES.
WITHOUT THE DISHWASHER?
SURE. SOMETIMES I JUST FEEL LIKE DOING IT BY HAND.
HOW?
WELL, I START BY FILLING THE SINK WITH LOTS OF HOT, SOAPY WATER.
THEN WHAT?
THEN I WASH EACH DISH CAREFULLY ON BOTH SIDES.
THEN WHAT?
THEN I RINSE THE CLEAN DISH IN HOT WATER, DRY IT THOROUGHLY, AND PLACE IT OVER HERE WITH THE OTHERS.
WAA-CHOOO!
KIRKMAN & SCOTT
SNIFF!
THEN WHAT?

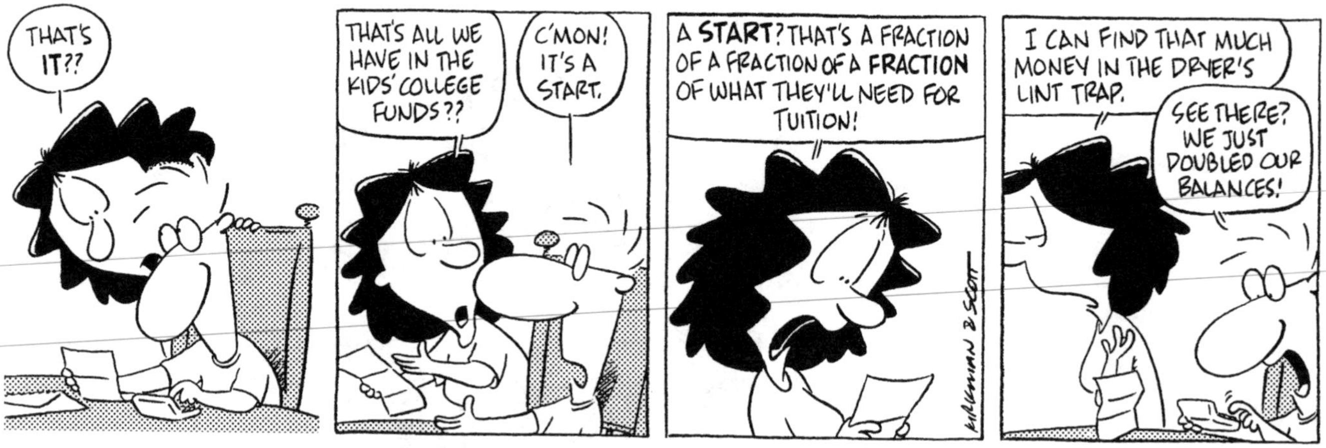
THAT'S IT??
THAT'S ALL WE HAVE IN THE KIDS' COLLEGE FUNDS??
C'MON! IT'S A START.
A START? THAT'S A FRACTION OF A FRACTION OF A FRACTION OF WHAT THEY'LL NEED FOR TUITION!
I CAN FIND THAT MUCH MONEY IN THE DRYER'S LINT TRAP.
SEE THERE? WE JUST DOUBLED OUR BALANCES!
KIRKMAN & SCOTT

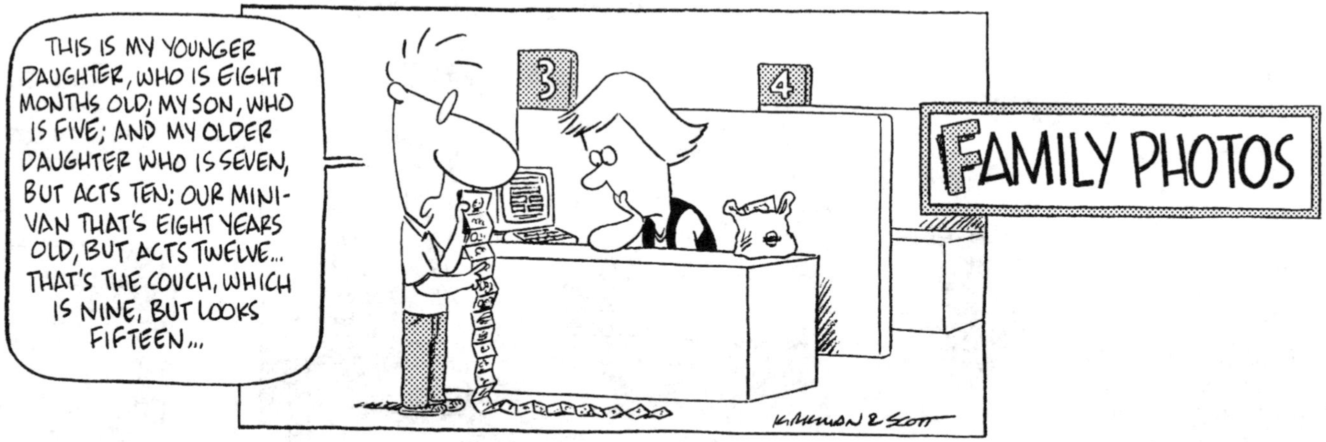
FAMILY PHOTOS
THIS IS MY YOUNGER DAUGHTER, WHO IS EIGHT MONTHS OLD; MY SON, WHO IS FIVE; AND MY OLDER DAUGHTER WHO IS SEVEN, BUT ACTS TEN; OUR MINI-VAN THAT'S EIGHT YEARS OLD, BUT ACTS TWELVE... THAT'S THE COUCH, WHICH IS NINE, BUT LOOKS FIFTEEN...
3
4
KIRKMAN & SCOTT

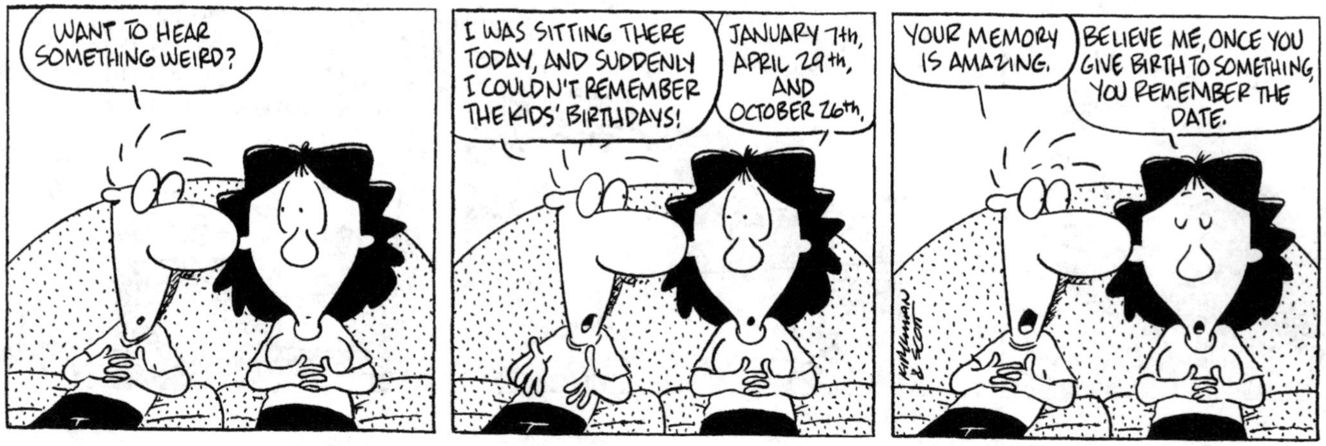
WANT TO HEAR SOMETHING WEIRD?
I WAS SITTING THERE TODAY, AND SUDDENLY I COULDN'T REMEMBER THE KIDS' BIRTHDAYS!
JANUARY 7th, APRIL 29th, AND OCTOBER 26th.
YOUR MEMORY IS AMAZING.
BELIEVE ME, ONCE YOU GIVE BIRTH TO SOMETHING, YOU REMEMBER THE DATE.
KIRKMAN & SCOTT

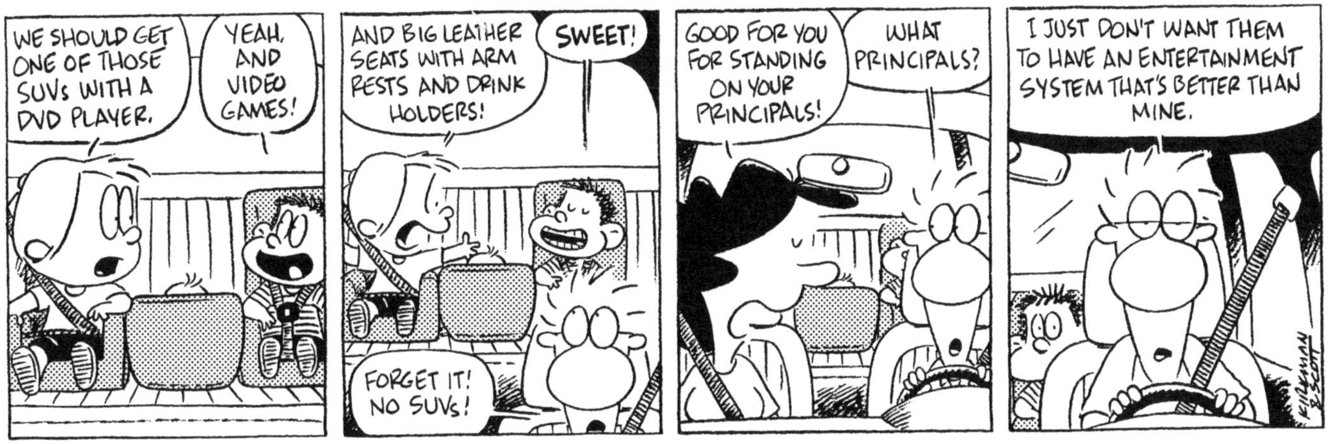
WE SHOULD GET ONE OF THOSE SUVs WITH A DVD PLAYER.
YEAH, AND VIDEO GAMES!
AND BIG LEATHER SEATS WITH ARM RESTS AND DRINK HOLDERS!
SWEET!
FORGET IT! NO SUVs!
GOOD FOR YOU FOR STANDING ON YOUR PRINCIPALS!
WHAT PRINCIPALS?
I JUST DON'T WANT THEM TO HAVE AN ENTERTAINMENT SYSTEM THAT'S BETTER THAN MINE.
KIRKMAN & SCOTT

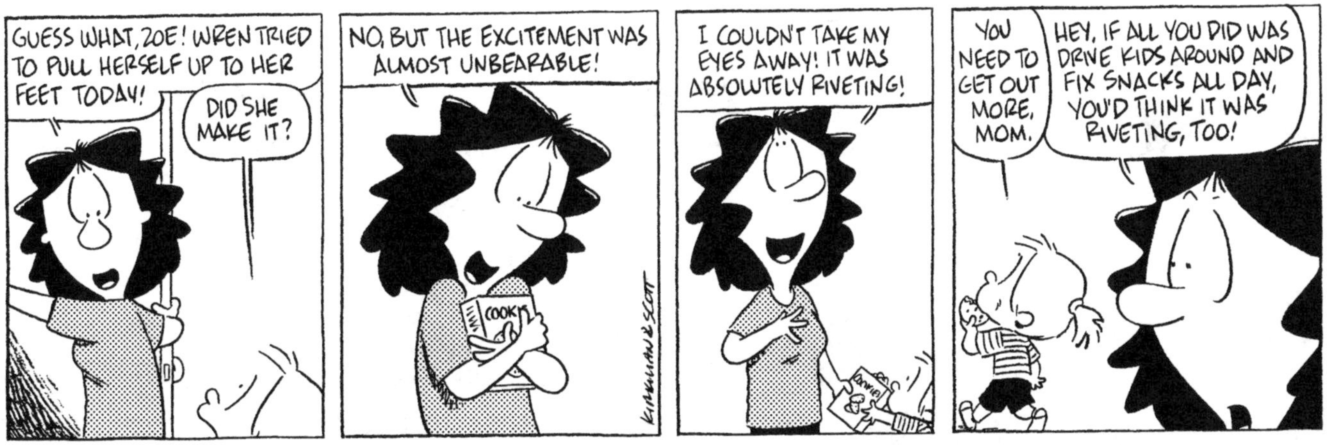
GUESS WHAT, ZOE! WREN TRIED TO PULL HERSELF UP TO HER FEET TODAY!
DID SHE MAKE IT?
NO, BUT THE EXCITEMENT WAS ALMOST UNBEARABLE!
COOK
KIRKMAN & SCOTT
I COULDN'T TAKE MY EYES AWAY! IT WAS ABSOLUTELY RIVETING!
YOU NEED TO GET OUT MORE, MOM.
HEY, IF ALL YOU DID WAS DRIVE KIDS AROUND AND FIX SNACKS ALL DAY, YOU'D THINK IT WAS RIVETING, TOO!

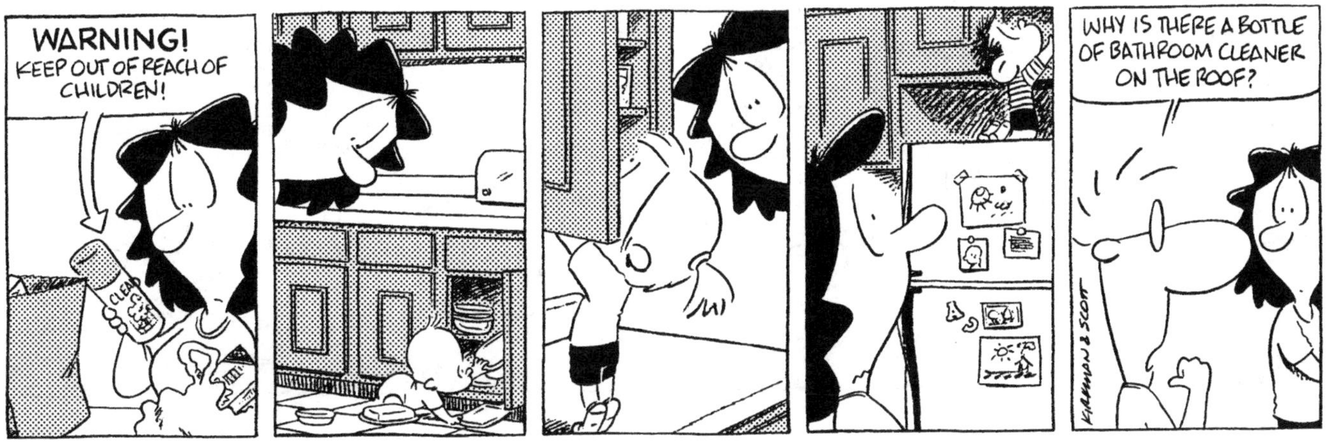
WARNING! KEEP OUT OF REACH OF CHILDREN!
CLEAN
WHY IS THERE A BOTTLE OF BATHROOM CLEANER ON THE ROOF?
KIRKMAN & SCOTT

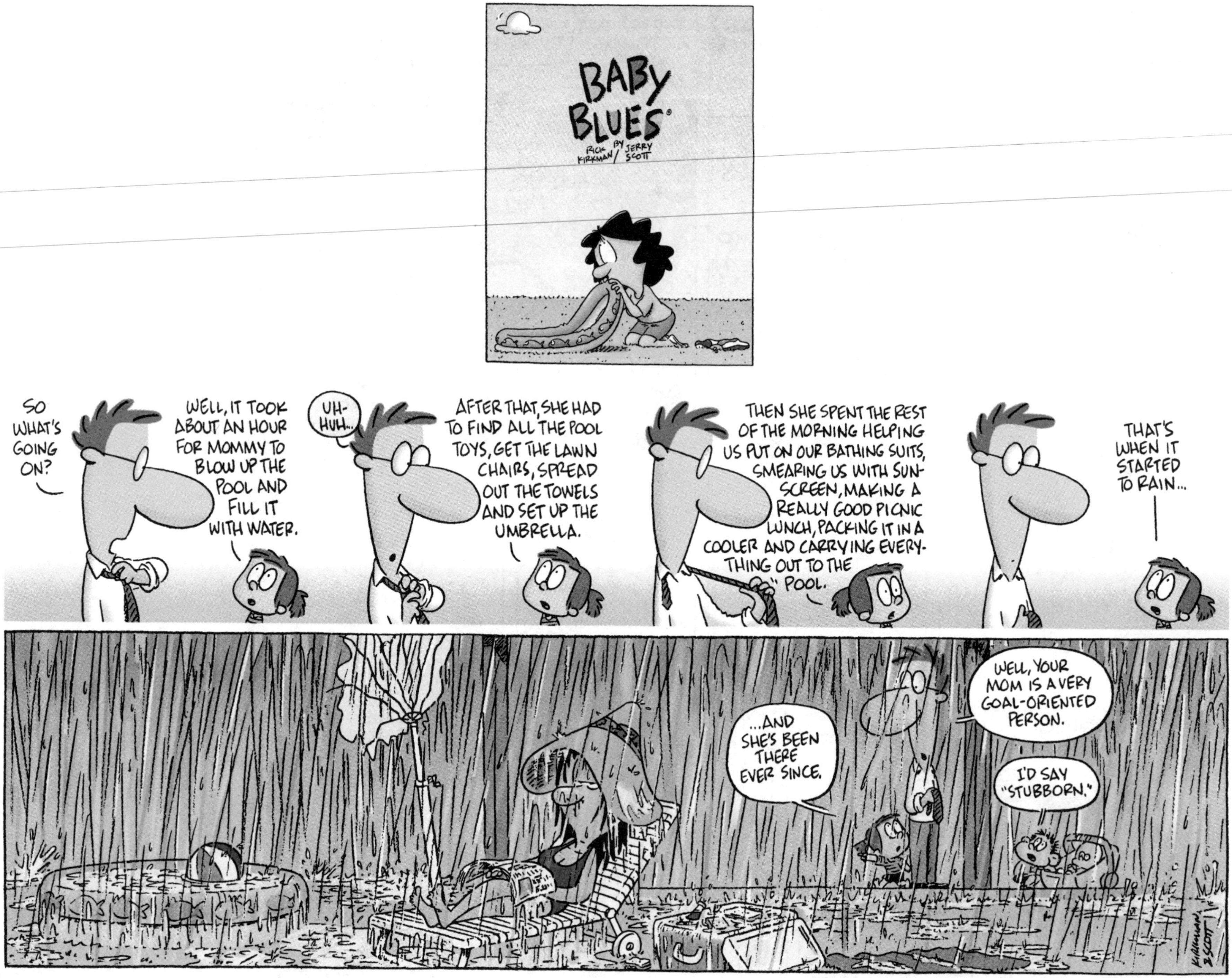
BABY BLUES®
RICK KIRKMAN / BY JERRY SCOTT
SO WHAT'S GOING ON?
WELL, IT TOOK ABOUT AN HOUR FOR MOMMY TO BLOW UP THE POOL AND FILL IT WITH WATER.
UH-HUH...
AFTER THAT, SHE HAD TO FIND ALL THE POOL TOYS, GET THE LAWN CHAIRS, SPREAD OUT THE TOWELS AND SET UP THE UMBRELLA.
THEN SHE SPENT THE REST OF THE MORNING HELPING US PUT ON OUR BATHING SUITS, SMEARING US WITH SUN-SCREEN, MAKING A REALLY GOOD PICNIC LUNCH, PACKING IT IN A COOLER AND CARRYING EVERY-THING OUT TO THE POOL.
THAT'S WHEN IT STARTED TO RAIN...
...AND SHE'S BEEN THERE EVER SINCE.
WELL, YOUR MOM IS A VERY GOAL-ORIENTED PERSON.
I'D SAY "STUBBORN."
KIRKMAN & SCOTT

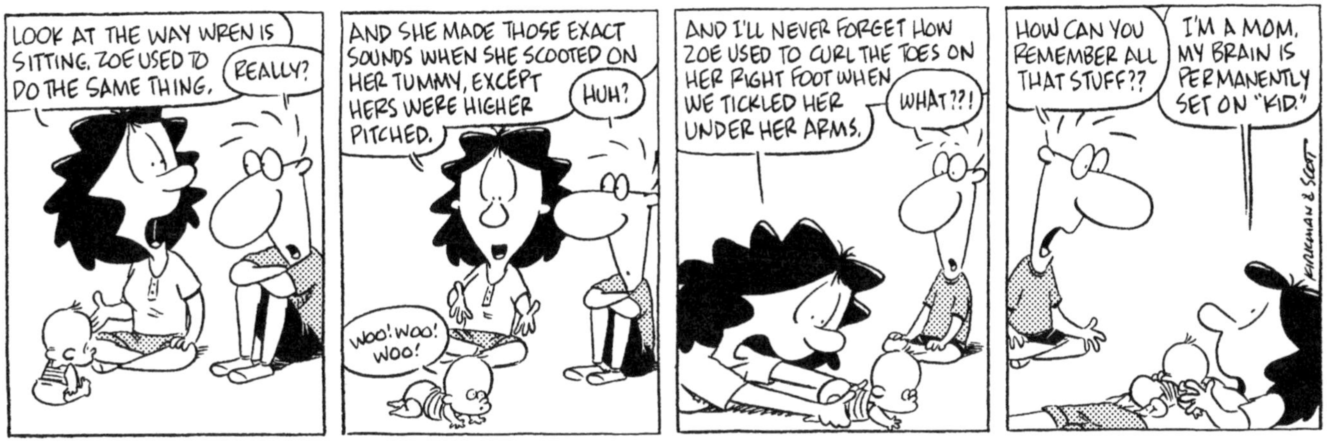
LOOK AT THE WAY WREN IS SITTING. ZOE USED TO DO THE SAME THING.
REALLY?
AND SHE MADE THOSE EXACT SOUNDS WHEN SHE SCOOTED ON HER TUMMY, EXCEPT HERS WERE HIGHER PITCHED.
HUH?
WOO! WOO! WOO!
AND I'LL NEVER FORGET HOW ZOE USED TO CURL THE TOES ON HER RIGHT FOOT WHEN WE TICKLED HER UNDER HER ARMS.
WHAT??!
HOW CAN YOU REMEMBER ALL THAT STUFF??
I'M A MOM. MY BRAIN IS PERMANENTLY SET ON "KID."
KIRKMAN & SCOTT

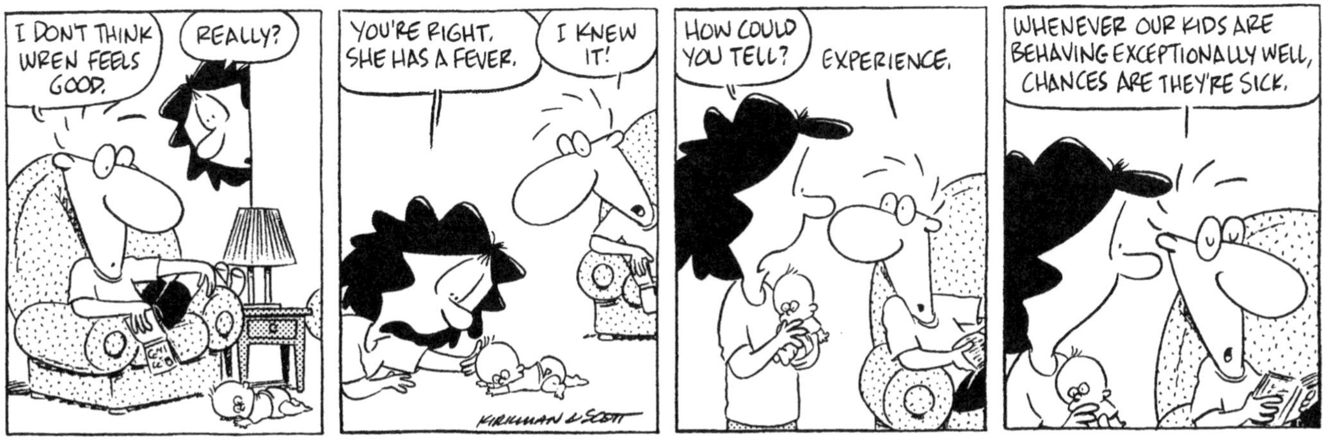
I DON'T THINK WREN FEELS GOOD.
REALLY?
YOU'RE RIGHT. SHE HAS A FEVER.
I KNEW IT!
KIRKMAN & SCOTT
HOW COULD YOU TELL?
EXPERIENCE.
WHENEVER OUR KIDS ARE BEHAVING EXCEPTIONALLY WELL, CHANCES ARE THEY'RE SICK.

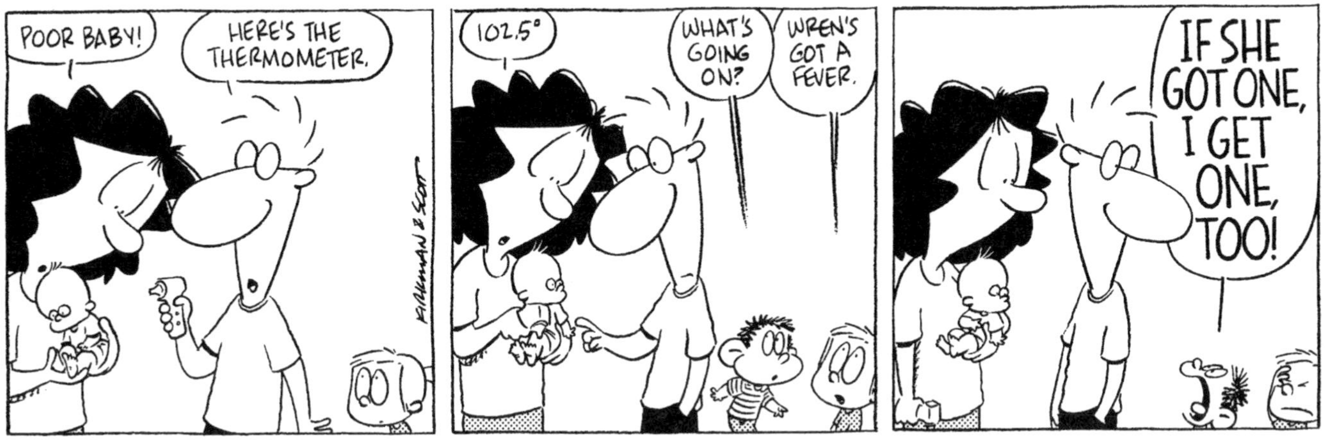
POOR BABY!
HERE'S THE THERMOMETER.
KIRKMAN & SCOTT
102.5°
WHAT'S GOING ON?
WREN'S GOT A FEVER.
IF SHE GOT ONE, I GET ONE, TOO!

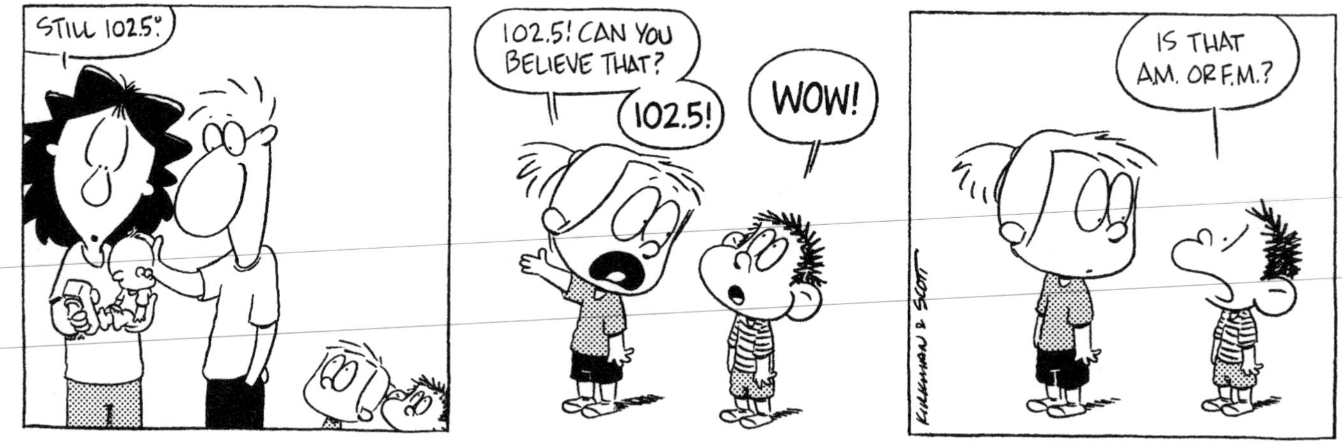
STILL 102.5°.
102.5! CAN YOU BELIEVE THAT?
102.5!
WOW!
IS THAT AM. OR F.M.?
KIRKMAN & SCOTT

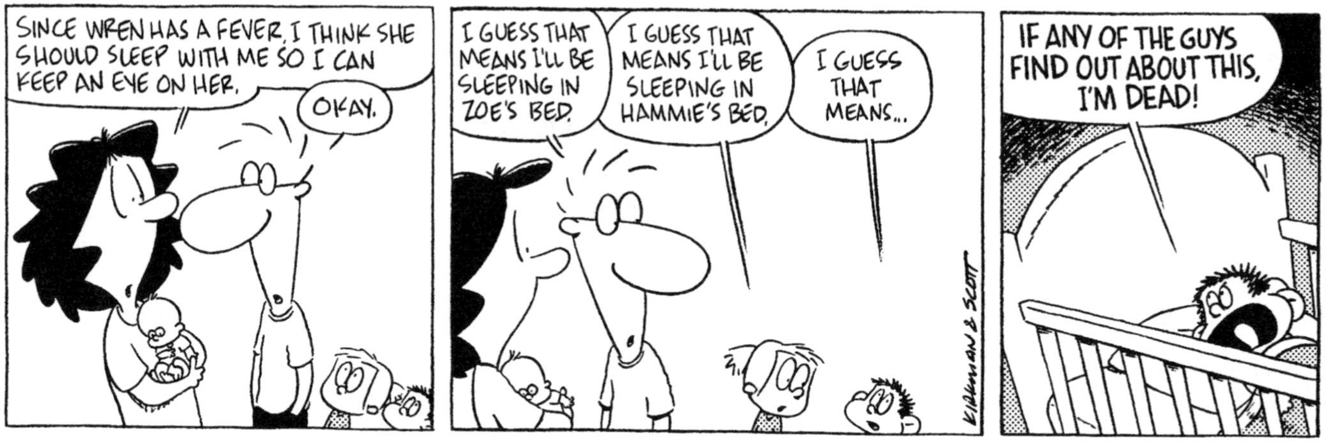
SINCE WREN HAS A FEVER, I THINK SHE SHOULD SLEEP WITH ME SO I CAN KEEP AN EYE ON HER.
OKAY.
I GUESS THAT MEANS I'LL BE SLEEPING IN ZOE'S BED.
I GUESS THAT MEANS I'LL BE SLEEPING IN HAMMIE'S BED.
I GUESS THAT MEANS...
IF ANY OF THE GUYS FIND OUT ABOUT THIS, I'M DEAD!
KIRKMAN & SCOTT

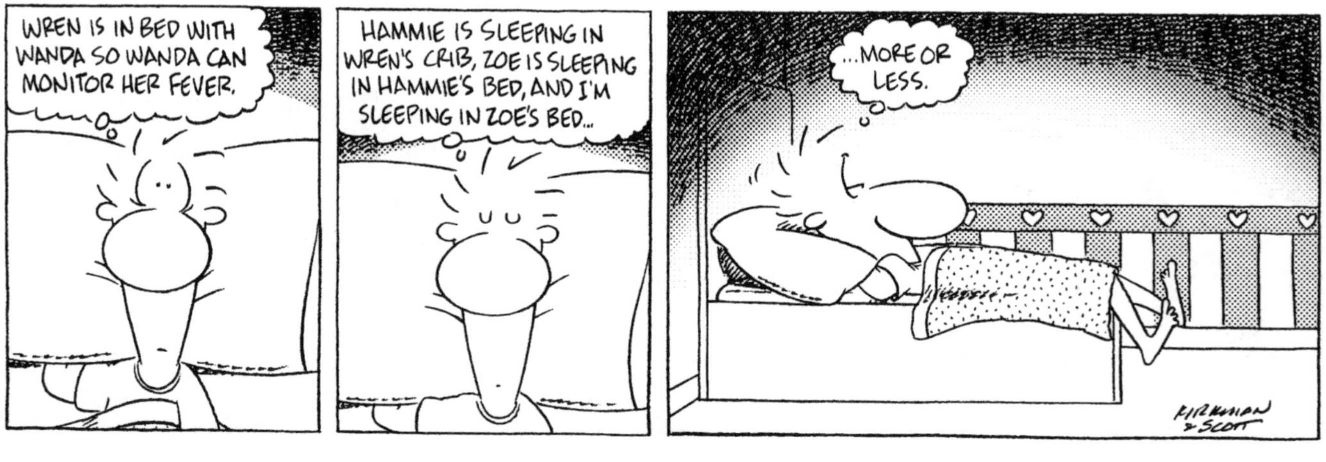
WREN IS IN BED WITH WANDA SO WANDA CAN MONITOR HER FEVER.
HAMMIE IS SLEEPING IN WREN'S CRIB, ZOE IS SLEEPING IN HAMMIE'S BED, AND I'M SLEEPING IN ZOE'S BED...
...MORE OR LESS.
KIRKMAN & SCOTT

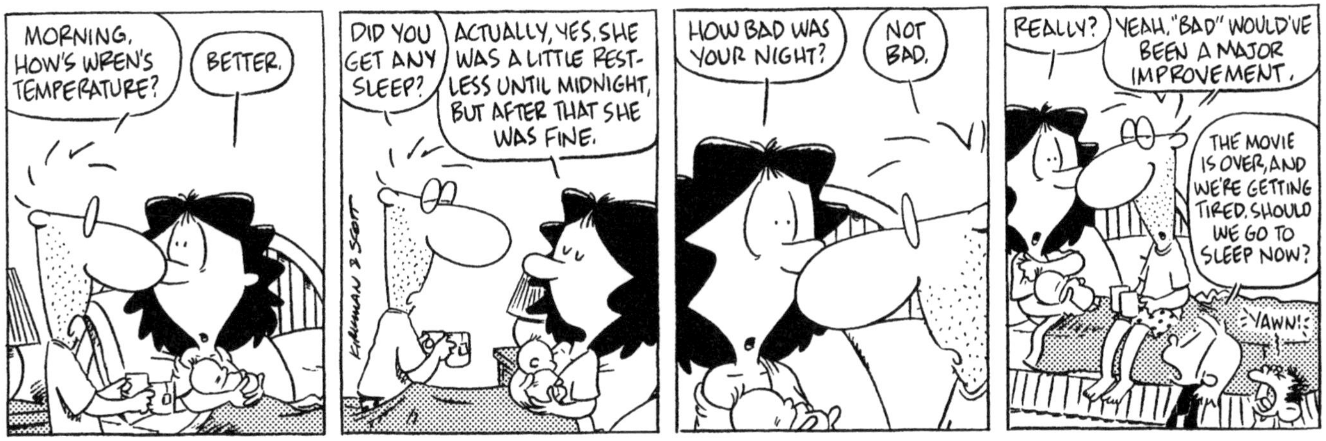
MORNING. HOW'S WREN'S TEMPERATURE?
BETTER.
DID YOU GET ANY SLEEP?
ACTUALLY, YES. SHE WAS A LITTLE RESTLESS UNTIL MIDNIGHT, BUT AFTER THAT SHE WAS FINE.
KIRKMAN & SCOTT
HOW BAD WAS YOUR NIGHT?
NOT BAD.
REALLY?
YEAH. "BAD" WOULD'VE BEEN A MAJOR IMPROVEMENT.
THE MOVIE IS OVER, AND WE'RE GETTING TIRED. SHOULD WE GO TO SLEEP NOW?
YAWN!

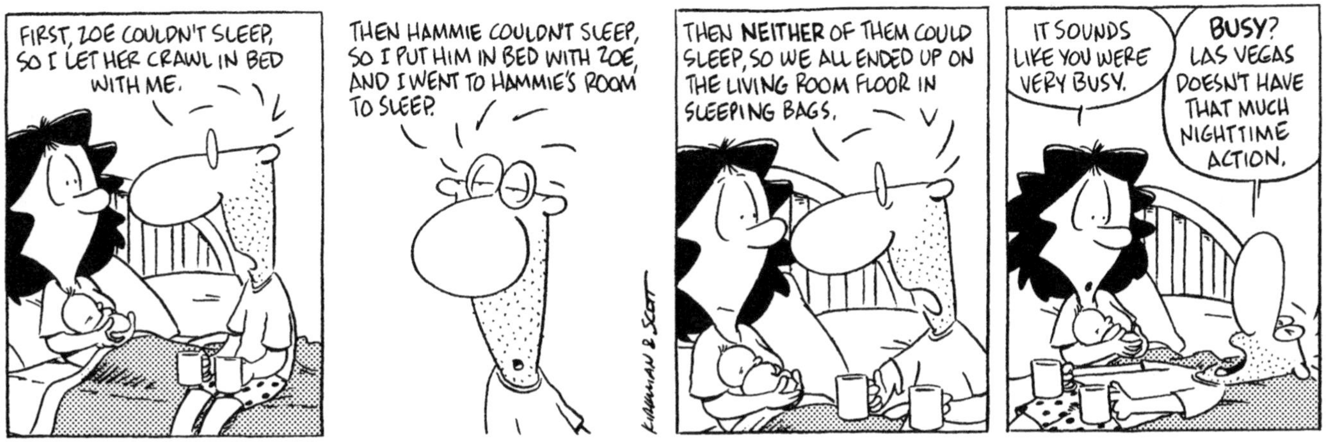
FIRST, ZOE COULDN'T SLEEP, SO I LET HER CRAWL IN BED WITH ME.
THEN HAMMIE COULDN'T SLEEP, SO I PUT HIM IN BED WITH ZOE, AND I WENT TO HAMMIE'S ROOM TO SLEEP.
KIRKMAN & SCOTT
THEN NEITHER OF THEM COULD SLEEP, SO WE ALL ENDED UP ON THE LIVING ROOM FLOOR IN SLEEPING BAGS.
IT SOUNDS LIKE YOU WERE VERY BUSY.
BUSY? LAS VEGAS DOESN'T HAVE THAT MUCH NIGHTTIME ACTION.

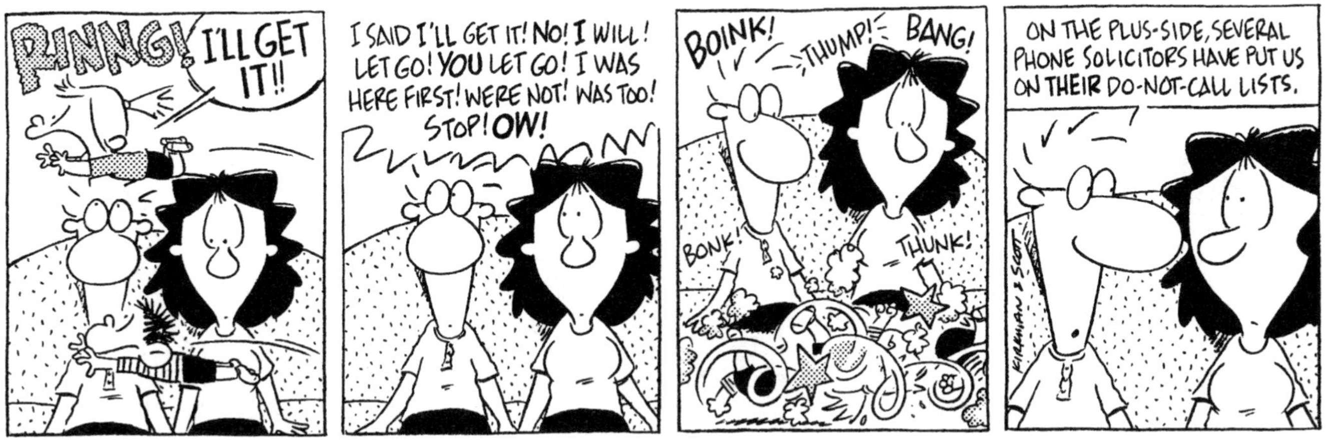
RINNG!
I'LL GET IT!!
I SAID I'LL GET IT! NO! I WILL! LET GO! YOU LET GO! I WAS HERE FIRST! WERE NOT! WAS TOO! STOP! OW!
BOINK!
THUMP!
BANG!
BONK!
THUNK!
ON THE PLUS-SIDE, SEVERAL PHONE SOLICITORS HAVE PUT US ON THEIR DO-NOT-CALL LISTS.
KIRKMAN & SCOTT

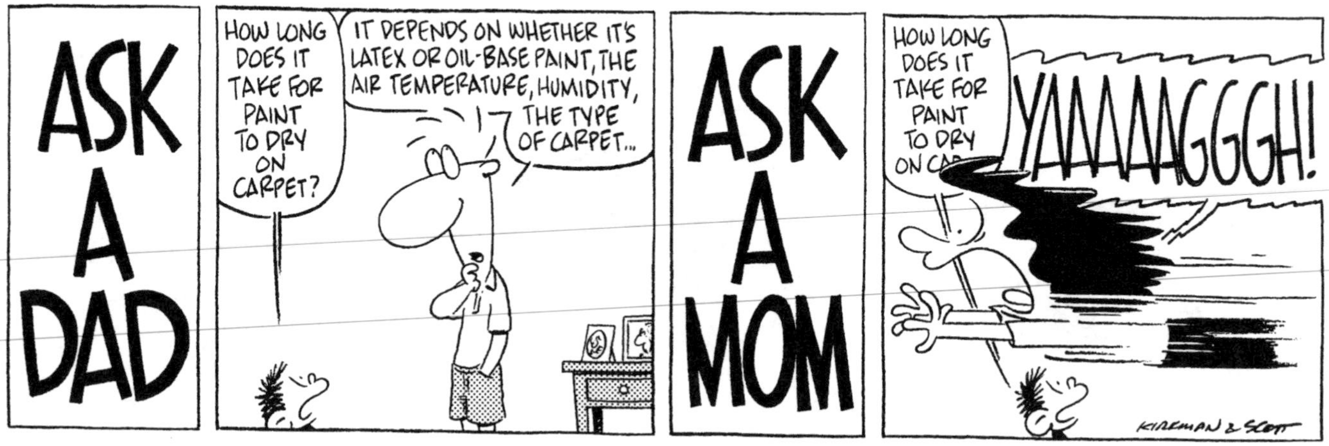
ASK A DAD
HOW LONG DOES IT TAKE FOR PAINT TO DRY ON CARPET?
IT DEPENDS ON WHETHER IT'S LATEX OR OIL-BASE PAINT, THE AIR TEMPERATURE, HUMIDITY, THE TYPE OF CARPET...
ASK A MOM
HOW LONG DOES IT TAKE FOR PAINT TO DRY ON CA
YAAAAAGGGH!
KIRKMAN & SCOTT

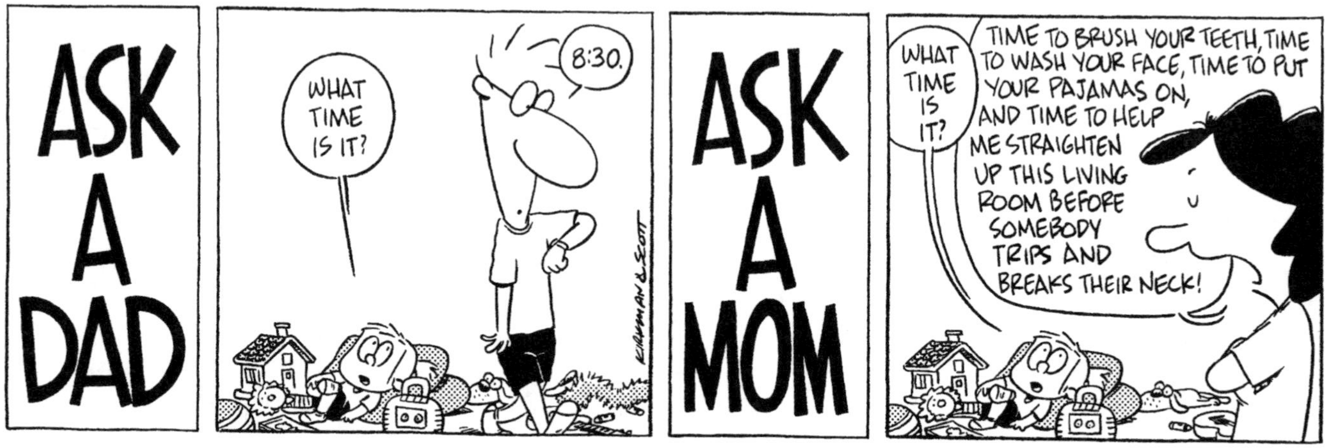
ASK A DAD
WHAT TIME IS IT?
8:30.
KIRKMAN & SCOTT
ASK A MOM
WHAT TIME IS IT?
TIME TO BRUSH YOUR TEETH, TIME TO WASH YOUR FACE, TIME TO PUT YOUR PAJAMAS ON, AND TIME TO HELP ME STRAIGHTEN UP THIS LIVING ROOM BEFORE SOMEBODY TRIPS AND BREAKS THEIR NECK!

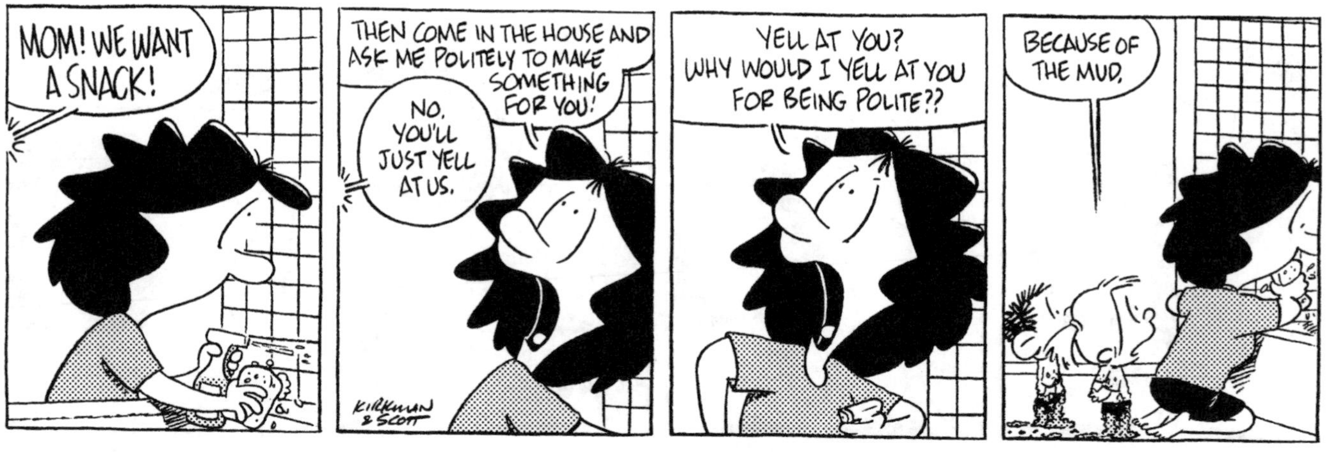
MOM! WE WANT A SNACK!
THEN COME IN THE HOUSE AND ASK ME POLITELY TO MAKE SOMETHING FOR YOU!
NO. YOU'LL JUST YELL AT US.
KIRKMAN & SCOTT
YELL AT YOU? WHY WOULD I YELL AT YOU FOR BEING POLITE??
BECAUSE OF THE MUD.

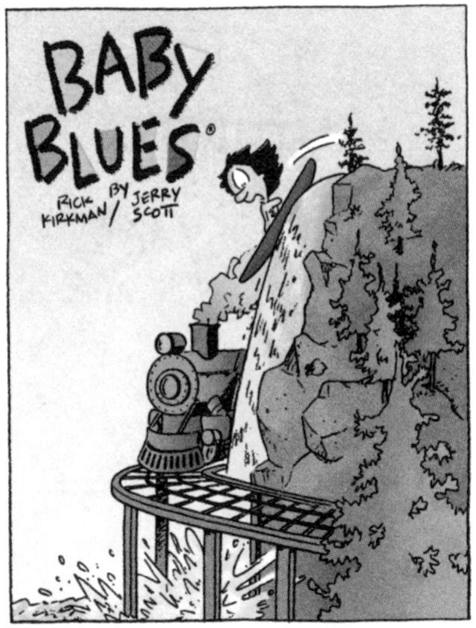
BABY BLUES®
BY RICK KIRKMAN / JERRY SCOTT

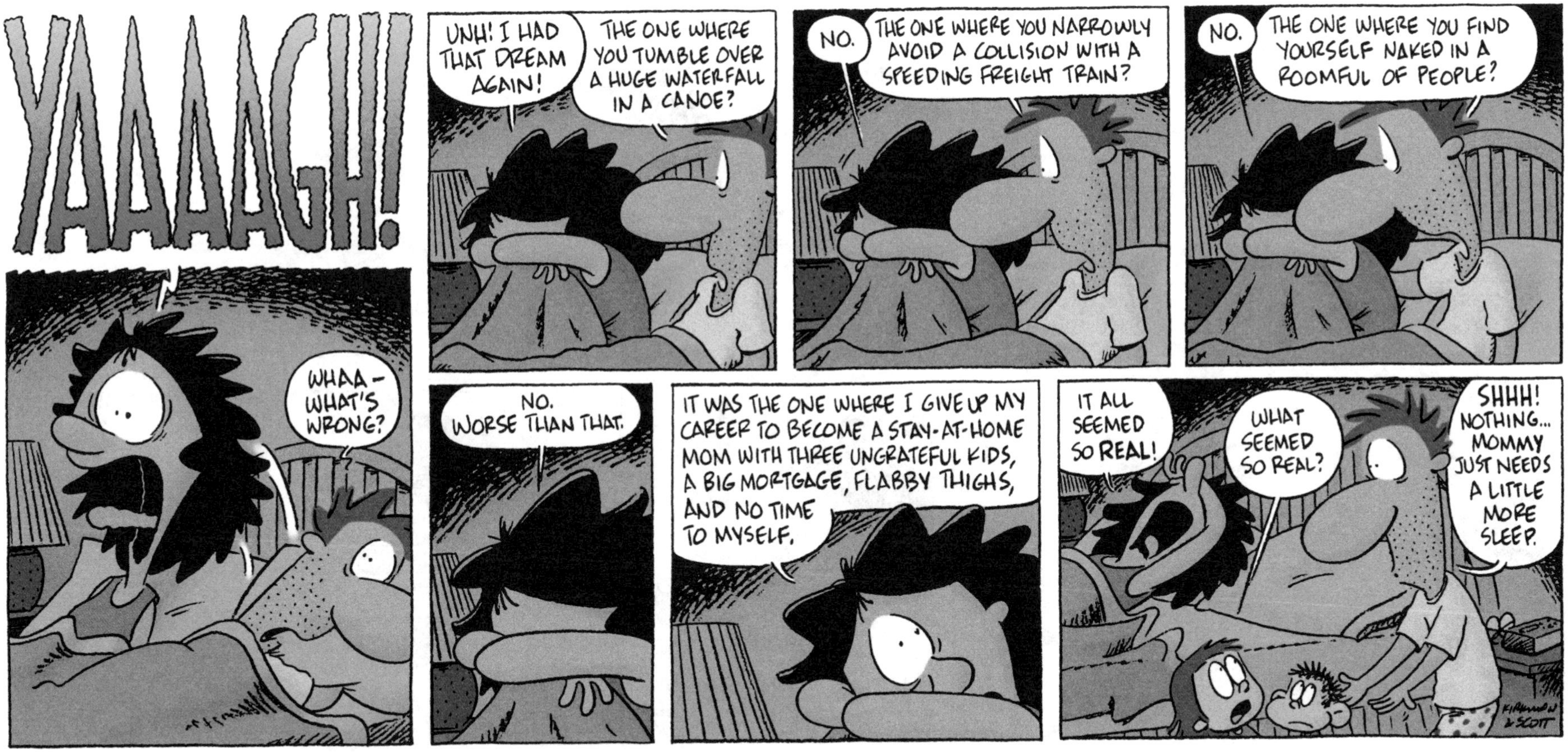
YAAAAGH!
WHAA-WHAT'S WRONG?
UNH! I HAD THAT DREAM AGAIN!
THE ONE WHERE YOU TUMBLE OVER A HUGE WATERFALL IN A CANOE?
NO.
THE ONE WHERE YOU NARROWLY AVOID A COLLISION WITH A SPEEDING FREIGHT TRAIN?
NO.
THE ONE WHERE YOU FIND YOURSELF NAKED IN A ROOMFUL OF PEOPLE?
NO. WORSE THAN THAT.
IT WAS THE ONE WHERE I GIVE UP MY CAREER TO BECOME A STAY-AT-HOME MOM WITH THREE UNGRATEFUL KIDS, A BIG MORTGAGE, FLABBY THIGHS, AND NO TIME TO MYSELF.
IT ALL SEEMED SO REAL!
WHAT SEEMED SO REAL?
SHHH! NOTHING... MOMMY JUST NEEDS A LITTLE MORE SLEEP.
KIRKMAN & SCOTT

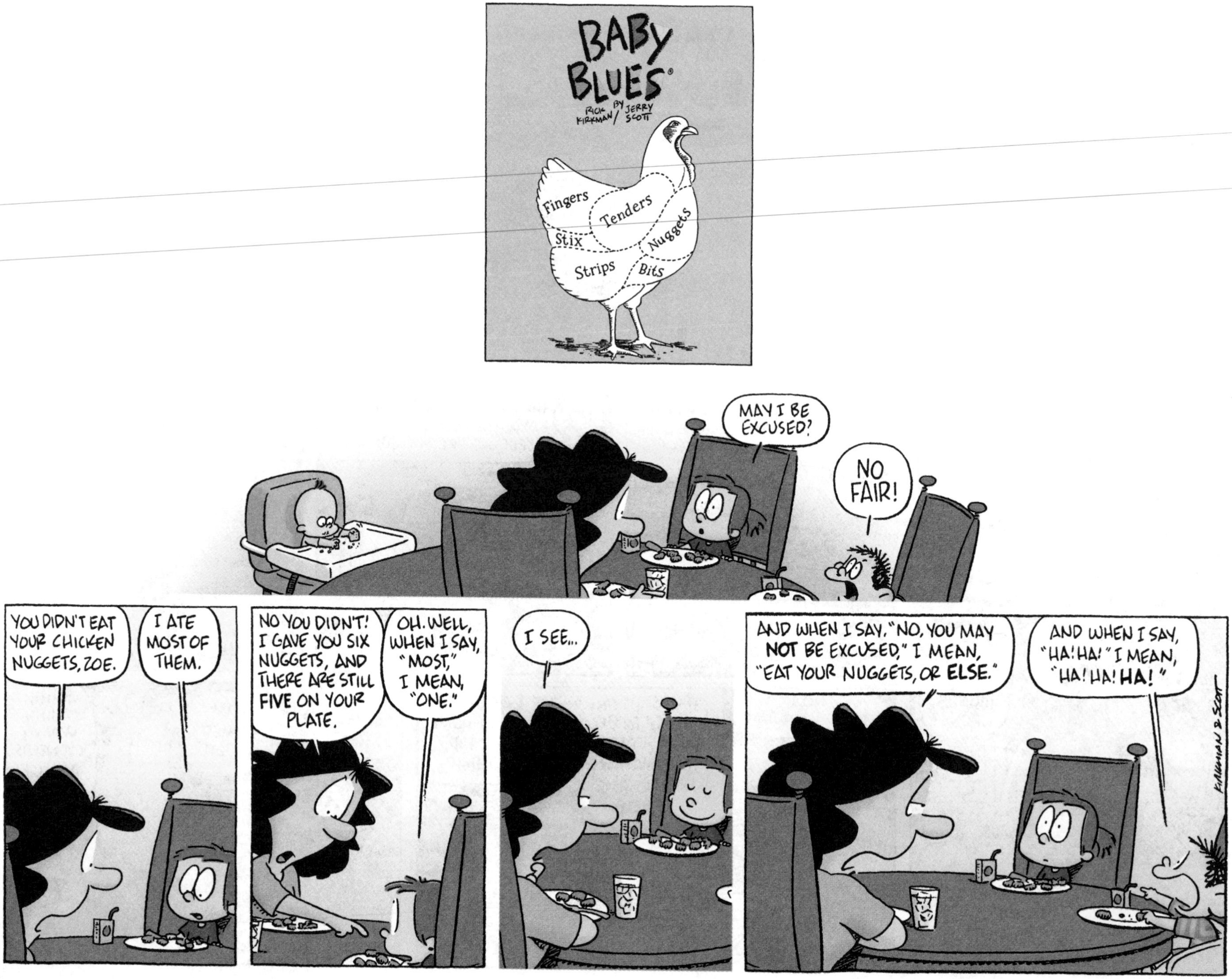
BABY BLUES®
BY RICK KIRKMAN / JERRY SCOTT
Fingers
Tenders
Stix
Nuggets
Strips
Bits
MAY I BE EXCUSED?
NO FAIR!
YOU DIDN'T EAT YOUR CHICKEN NUGGETS, ZOE.
I ATE MOST OF THEM.
NO YOU DIDN'T! I GAVE YOU SIX NUGGETS, AND THERE ARE STILL FIVE ON YOUR PLATE.
OH. WELL, WHEN I SAY, "MOST," I MEAN, "ONE."
I SEE...
AND WHEN I SAY, "NO, YOU MAY NOT BE EXCUSED," I MEAN, "EAT YOUR NUGGETS, OR ELSE."
AND WHEN I SAY, "HA! HA!" I MEAN, "HA! HA! HA!"
KIRKMAN & SCOTT

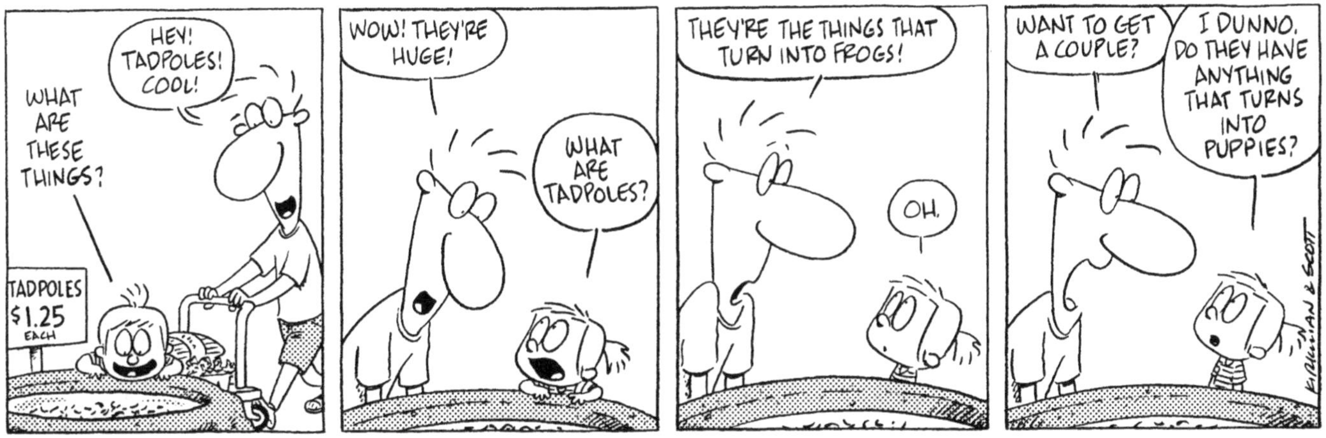
HEY! TADPOLES! COOL!
WHAT ARE THESE THINGS?
TADPOLES $1.25 EACH
WOW! THEY'RE HUGE!
WHAT ARE TADPOLES?
THEY'RE THE THINGS THAT TURN INTO FROGS!
OH.
WANT TO GET A COUPLE?
I DUNNO. DO THEY HAVE ANYTHING THAT TURNS INTO PUPPIES?
KIRKMAN & SCOTT

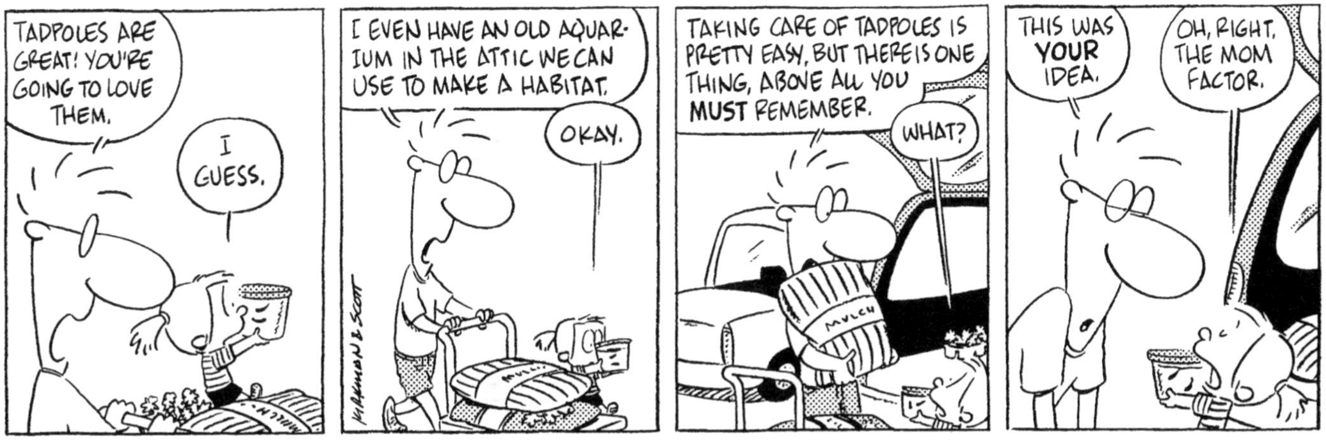
TADPOLES ARE GREAT! YOU'RE GOING TO LOVE THEM.
I GUESS.
I EVEN HAVE AN OLD AQUARIUM IN THE ATTIC WE CAN USE TO MAKE A HABITAT.
OKAY.
KIRKMAN & SCOTT
TAKING CARE OF TADPOLES IS PRETTY EASY, BUT THERE IS ONE THING, ABOVE ALL YOU MUST REMEMBER.
WHAT?
MULCH
THIS WAS YOUR IDEA.
OH, RIGHT. THE MOM FACTOR.

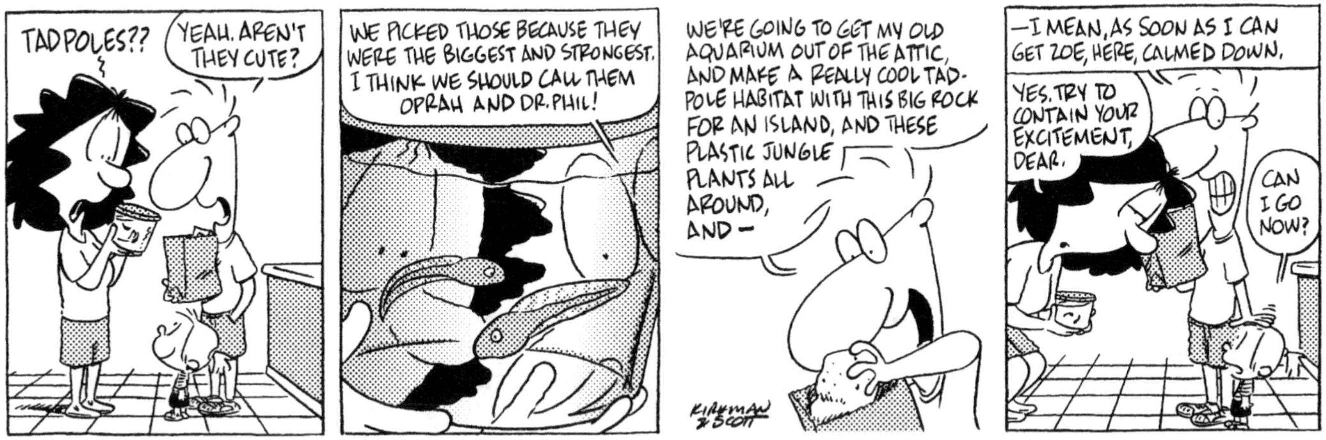
TADPOLES??
YEAH. AREN'T THEY CUTE?
WE PICKED THOSE BECAUSE THEY WERE THE BIGGEST AND STRONGEST. I THINK WE SHOULD CALL THEM OPRAH AND DR. PHIL!
WE'RE GOING TO GET MY OLD AQUARIUM OUT OF THE ATTIC, AND MAKE A REALLY COOL TADPOLE HABITAT WITH THIS BIG ROCK FOR AN ISLAND, AND THESE PLASTIC JUNGLE PLANTS ALL AROUND, AND —
KIRKMAN & SCOTT
—I MEAN, AS SOON AS I CAN GET ZOE, HERE, CALMED DOWN.
YES. TRY TO CONTAIN YOUR EXCITEMENT, DEAR.
CAN I GO NOW?

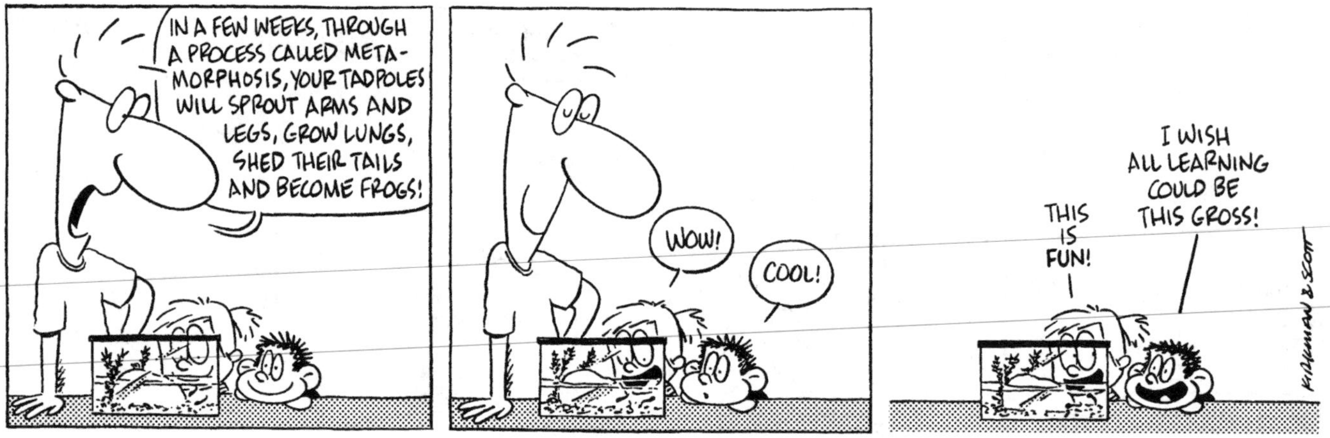
IN A FEW WEEKS, THROUGH A PROCESS CALLED METAMORPHOSIS, YOUR TADPOLES WILL SPROUT ARMS AND LEGS, GROW LUNGS, SHED THEIR TAILS AND BECOME FROGS!
WOW!
COOL!
THIS IS FUN!
I WISH ALL LEARNING COULD BE THIS GROSS!
KIRKMAN & SCOTT

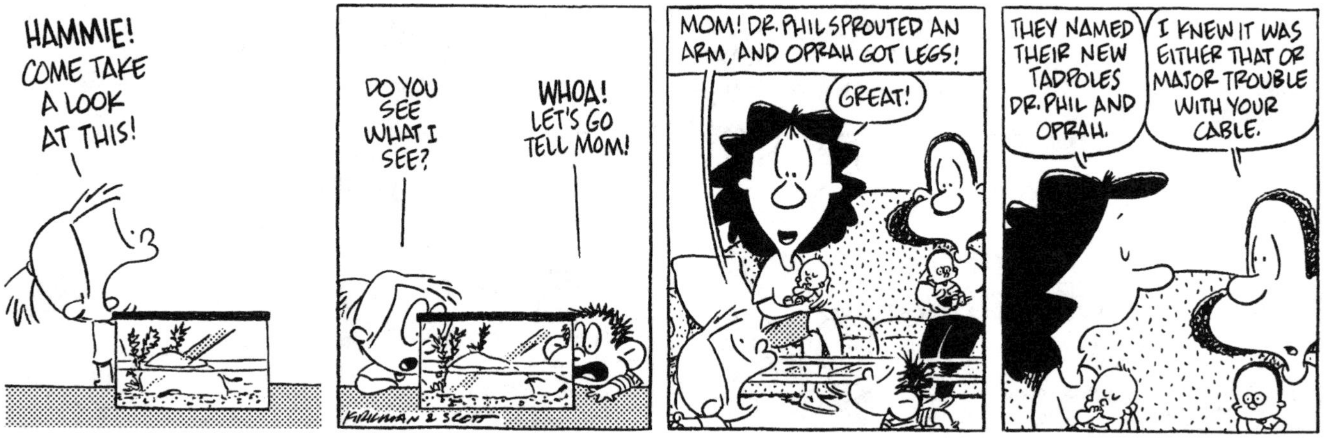
HAMMIE! COME TAKE A LOOK AT THIS!
DO YOU SEE WHAT I SEE?
WHOA! LET'S GO TELL MOM!
KIRKMAN & SCOTT
MOM! DR. PHIL SPROUTED AN ARM, AND OPRAH GOT LEGS!
GREAT!
THEY NAMED THEIR NEW TADPOLES DR. PHIL AND OPRAH.
I KNEW IT WAS EITHER THAT OR MAJOR TROUBLE WITH YOUR CABLE.

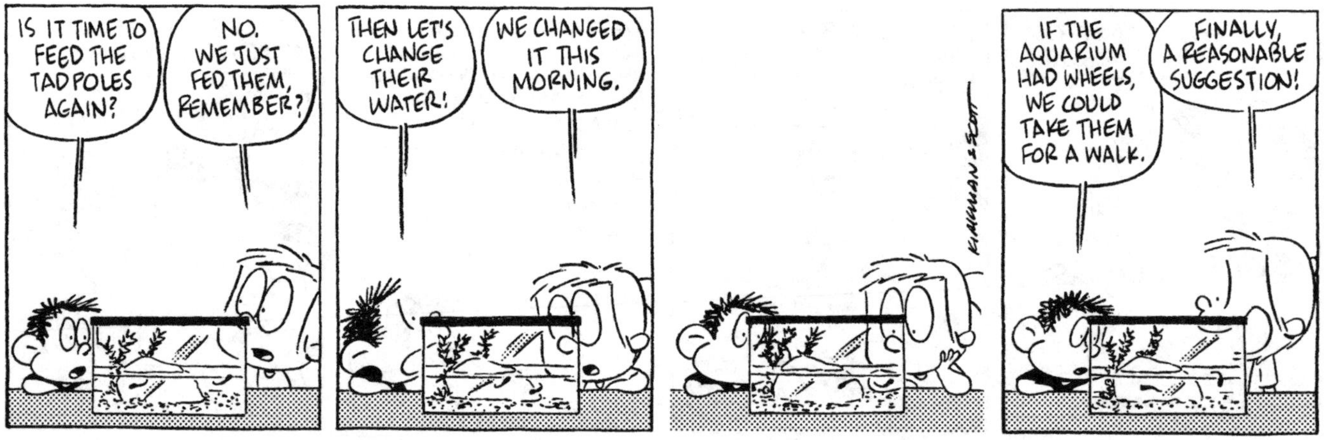
IS IT TIME TO FEED THE TADPOLES AGAIN?
NO. WE JUST FED THEM, REMEMBER?
THEN LET'S CHANGE THEIR WATER!
WE CHANGED IT THIS MORNING.
KIRKMAN & SCOTT
IF THE AQUARIUM HAD WHEELS, WE COULD TAKE THEM FOR A WALK.
FINALLY, A REASONABLE SUGGESTION!

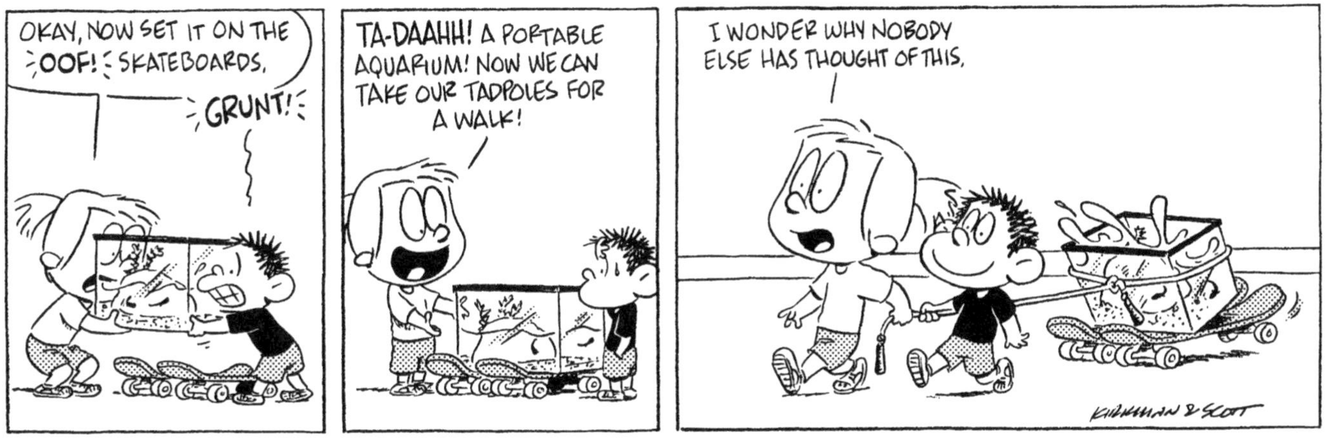
OKAY, NOW SET IT ON THE
OOF! SKATEBOARDS.
GRUNT!
TA-DAAHH! A PORTABLE AQUARIUM! NOW WE CAN TAKE OUR TADPOLES FOR A WALK!
I WONDER WHY NOBODY ELSE HAS THOUGHT OF THIS.
KIRKMAN & SCOTT

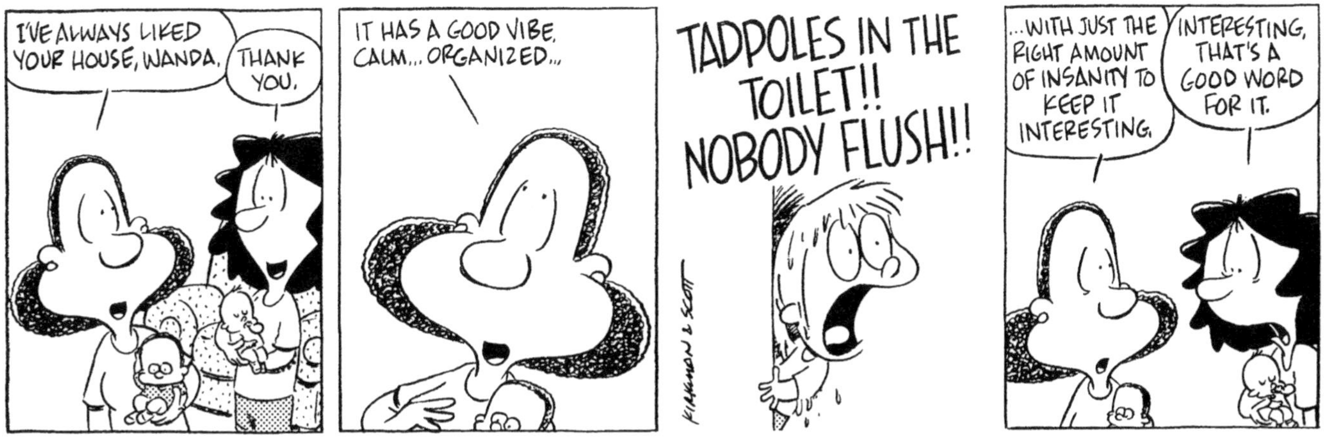
I'VE ALWAYS LIKED YOUR HOUSE, WANDA.
THANK YOU.
IT HAS A GOOD VIBE. CALM... ORGANIZED...
KIRKMAN & SCOTT
TADPOLES IN THE TOILET!! NOBODY FLUSH!!
...WITH JUST THE RIGHT AMOUNT OF INSANITY TO KEEP IT INTERESTING.
INTERESTING. THAT'S A GOOD WORD FOR IT.

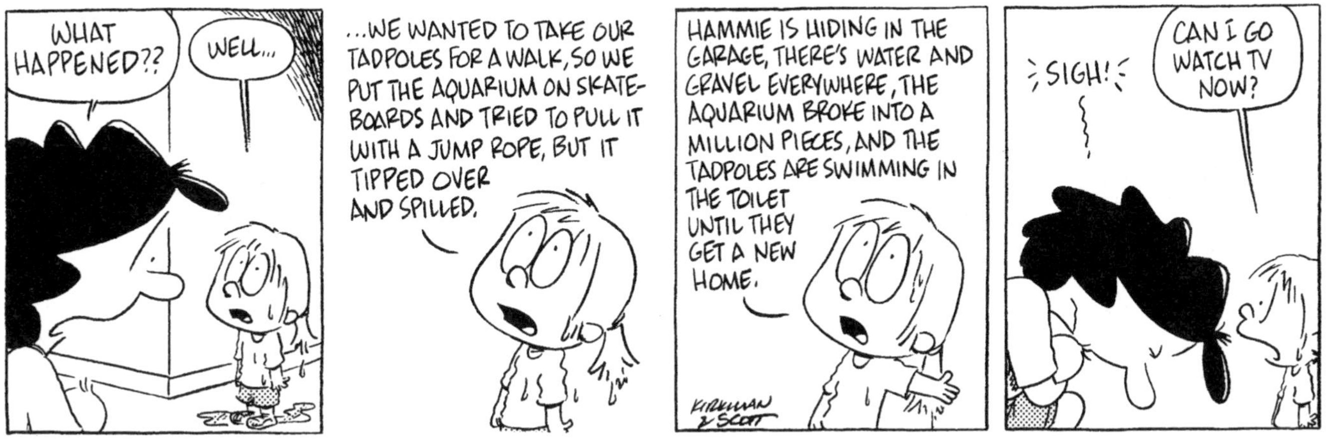
WHAT HAPPENED??
WELL...
...WE WANTED TO TAKE OUR TADPOLES FOR A WALK, SO WE PUT THE AQUARIUM ON SKATEBOARDS AND TRIED TO PULL IT WITH A JUMP ROPE, BUT IT TIPPED OVER AND SPILLED.
HAMMIE IS HIDING IN THE GARAGE, THERE'S WATER AND GRAVEL EVERYWHERE, THE AQUARIUM BROKE INTO A MILLION PIECES, AND THE TADPOLES ARE SWIMMING IN THE TOILET UNTIL THEY GET A NEW HOME.
KIRKMAN & SCOTT
SIGH!
CAN I GO WATCH TV NOW?

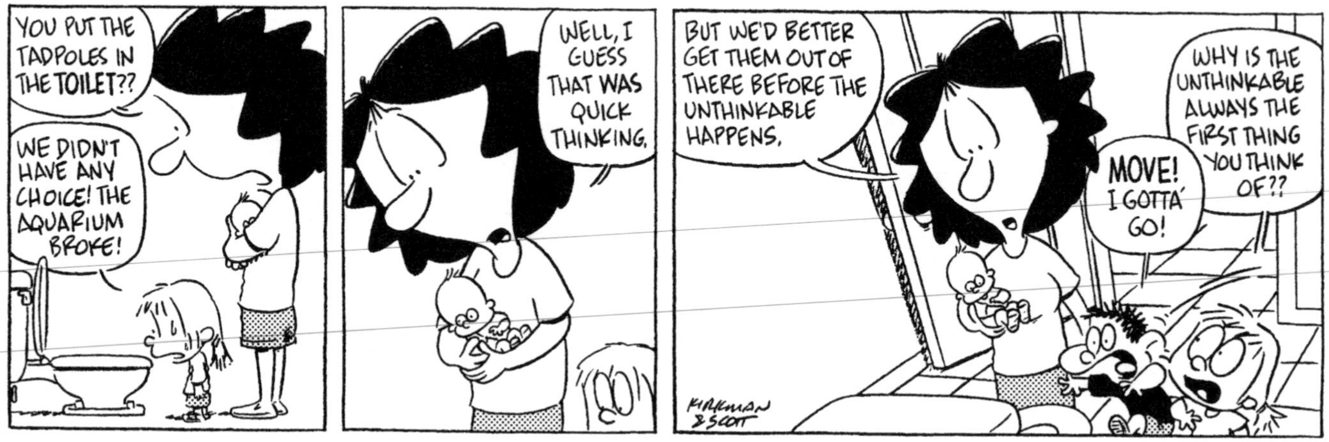
YOU PUT THE TADPOLES IN THE TOILET??
WE DIDN'T HAVE ANY CHOICE! THE AQUARIUM BROKE!
WELL, I GUESS THAT WAS QUICK THINKING.
BUT WE'D BETTER GET THEM OUT OF THERE BEFORE THE UNTHINKABLE HAPPENS.
WHY IS THE UNTHINKABLE ALWAYS THE FIRST THING YOU THINK OF??
MOVE! I GOTTA' GO!
KIRKMAN & SCOTT

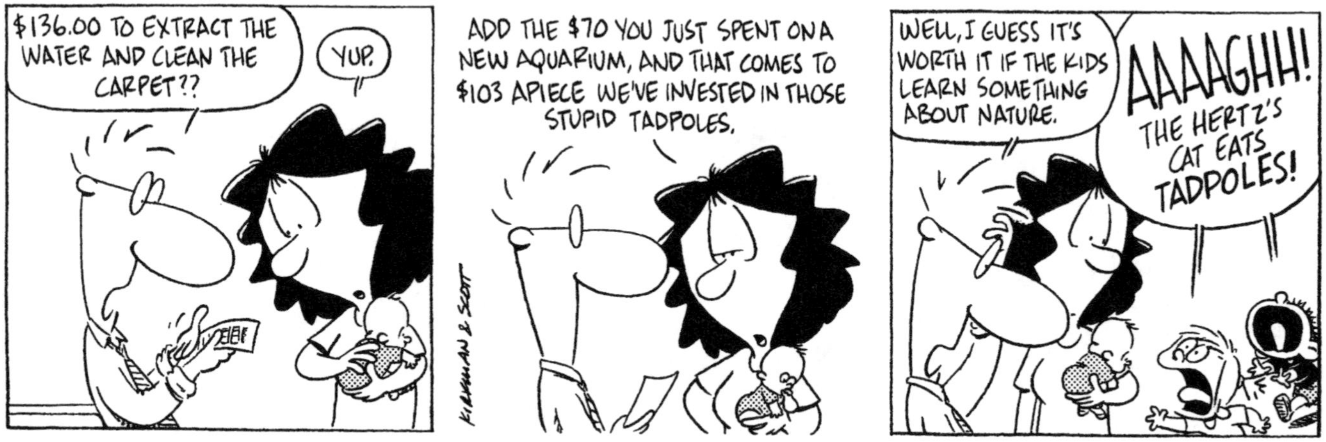
$136.00 TO EXTRACT THE WATER AND CLEAN THE CARPET??
YUP.
ADD THE $70 YOU JUST SPENT ON A NEW AQUARIUM, AND THAT COMES TO $103 APIECE WE'VE INVESTED IN THOSE STUPID TADPOLES.
WELL, I GUESS IT'S WORTH IT IF THE KIDS LEARN SOMETHING ABOUT NATURE.
AAAAGHH! THE HERTZ'S CAT EATS TADPOLES!
KIRKMAN & SCOTT

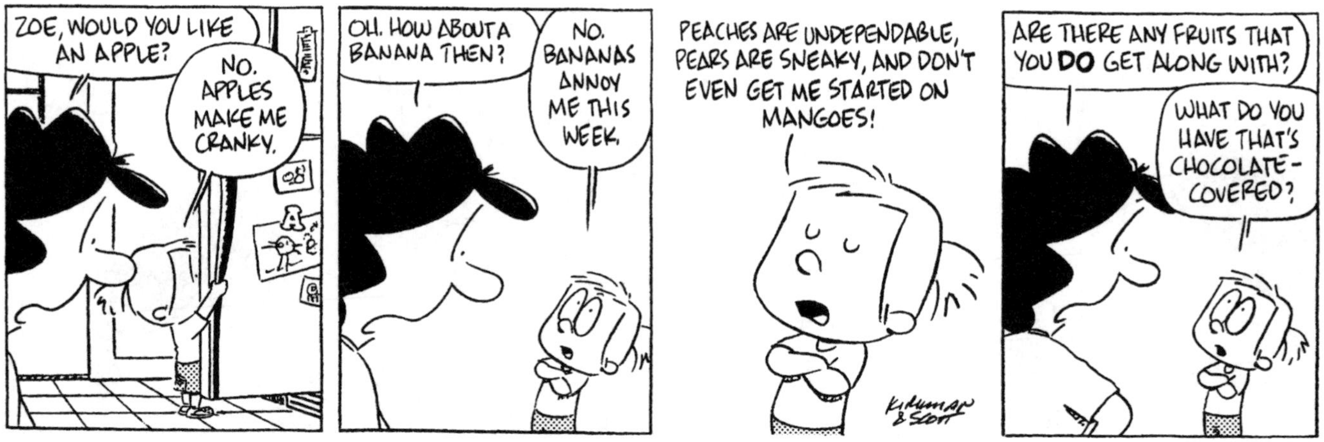
ZOE, WOULD YOU LIKE AN APPLE?
NO. APPLES MAKE ME CRANKY.
OH. HOW ABOUT A BANANA THEN?
NO. BANANAS ANNOY ME THIS WEEK.
PEACHES ARE UNDEPENDABLE, PEARS ARE SNEAKY, AND DON'T EVEN GET ME STARTED ON MANGOES!
ARE THERE ANY FRUITS THAT YOU DO GET ALONG WITH?
WHAT DO YOU HAVE THAT'S CHOCOLATE-COVERED?
KIRKMAN & SCOTT

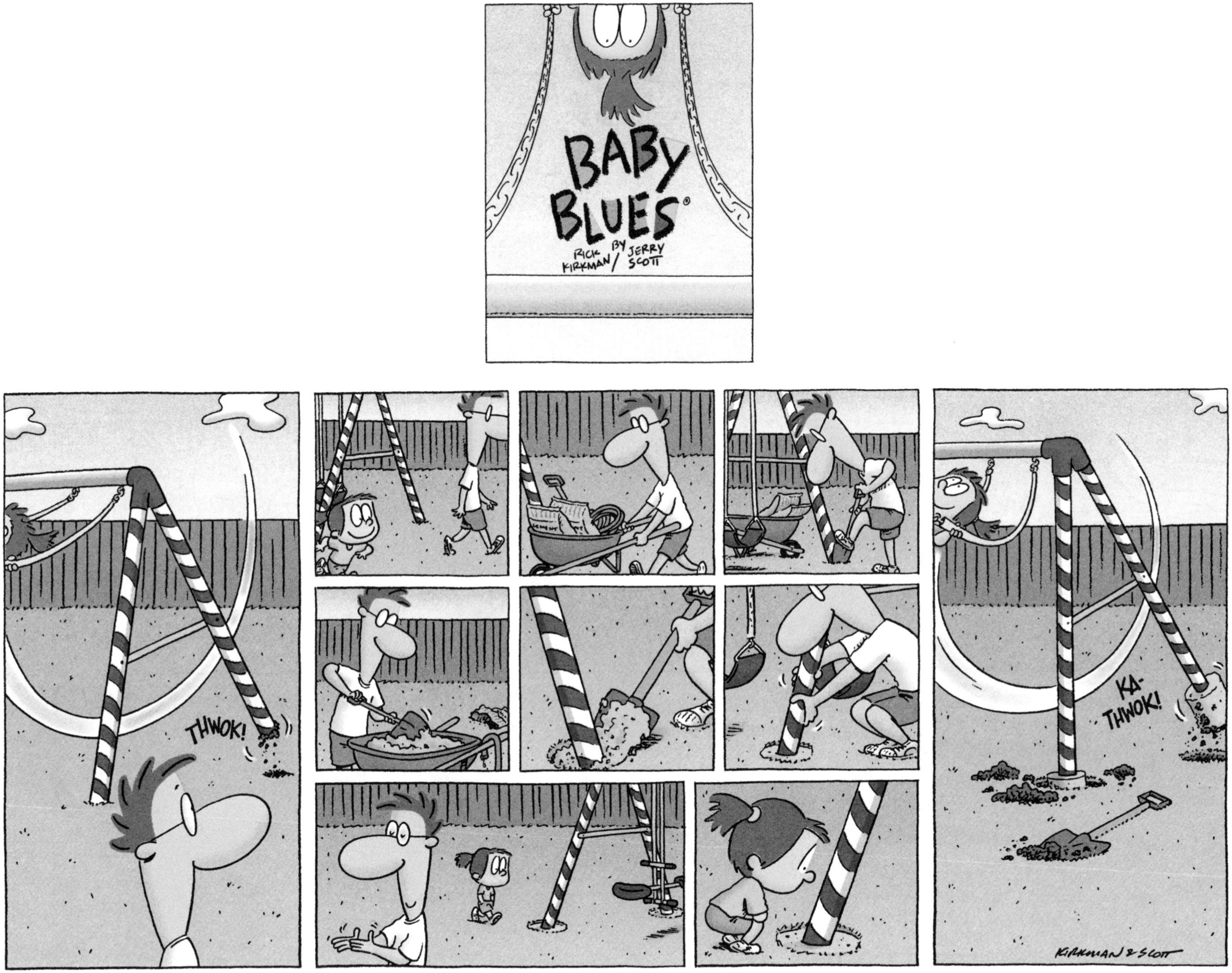
BABY BLUES®
BY RICK KIRKMAN / JERRY SCOTT
THWOK!
KA-THWOK!
KIRKMAN & SCOTT

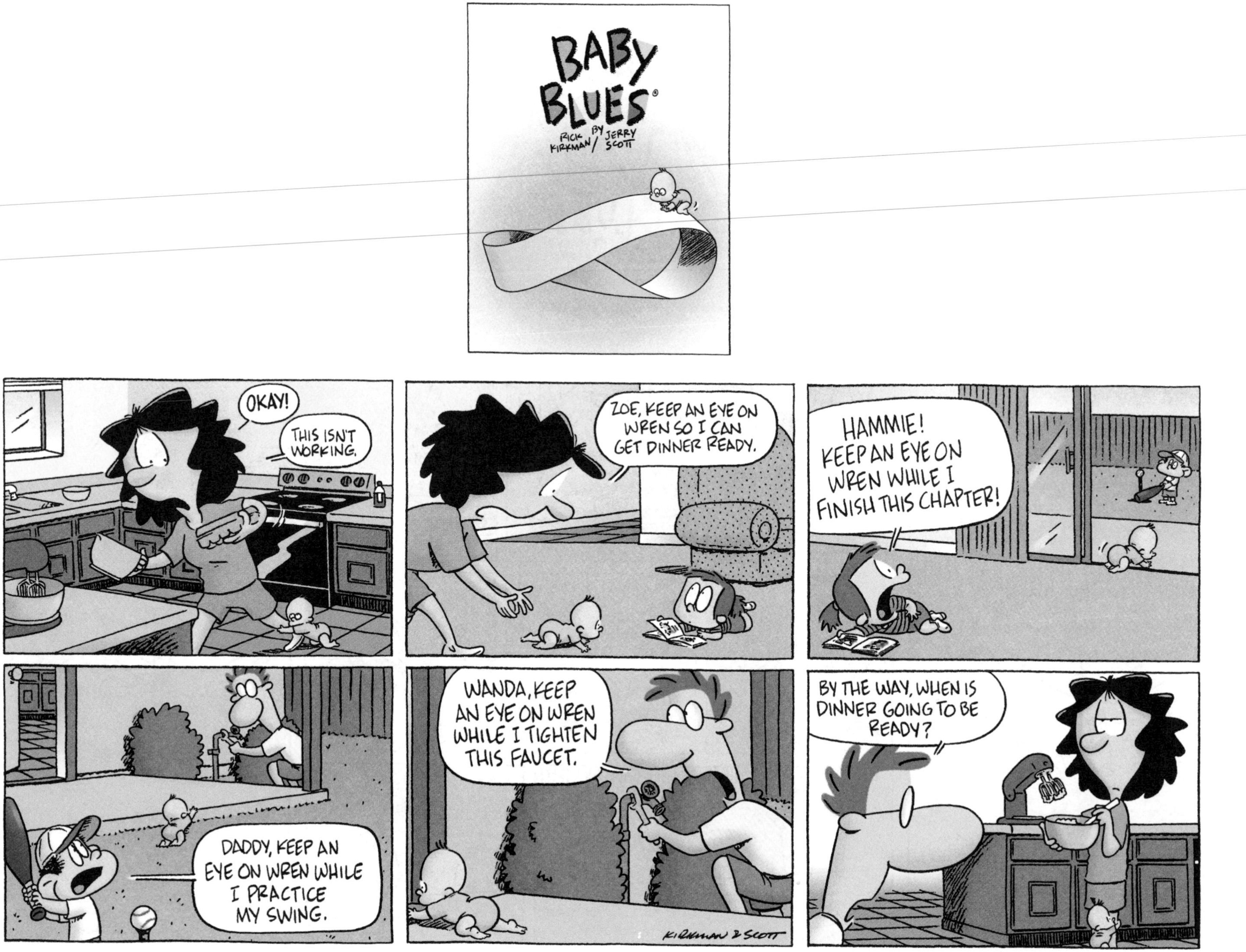
BABY BLUES®
BY RICK KIRKMAN / JERRY SCOTT
OKAY!
THIS ISN'T WORKING.
ZOE, KEEP AN EYE ON WREN SO I CAN GET DINNER READY.
HAMMIE! KEEP AN EYE ON WREN WHILE I FINISH THIS CHAPTER!
DADDY, KEEP AN EYE ON WREN WHILE I PRACTICE MY SWING.
WANDA, KEEP AN EYE ON WREN WHILE I TIGHTEN THIS FAUCET.
KIRKMAN & SCOTT
BY THE WAY, WHEN IS DINNER GOING TO BE READY?

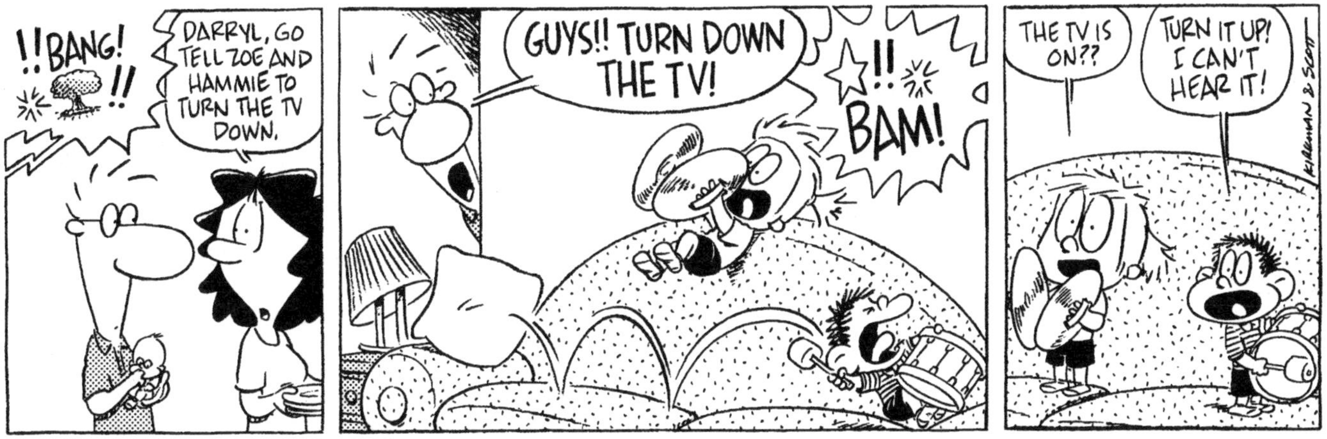
!! BANG! !!
DARRYL, GO TELL ZOE AND HAMMIE TO TURN THE TV DOWN.
GUYS!! TURN DOWN THE TV!
!! BAM!
THE TV IS ON??
TURN IT UP! I CAN'T HEAR IT!
KIRKMAN & SCOTT

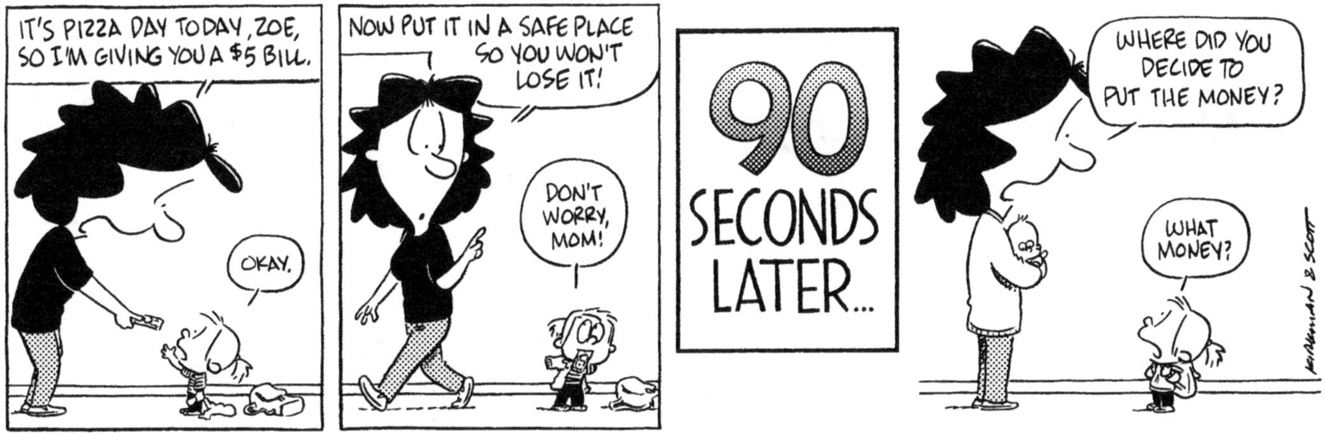
IT'S PIZZA DAY TODAY, ZOE, SO I'M GIVING YOU A $5 BILL.
OKAY.
NOW PUT IT IN A SAFE PLACE SO YOU WON'T LOSE IT!
DON'T WORRY, MOM!
90 SECONDS LATER...
WHERE DID YOU DECIDE TO PUT THE MONEY?
WHAT MONEY?
KIRKMAN & SCOTT

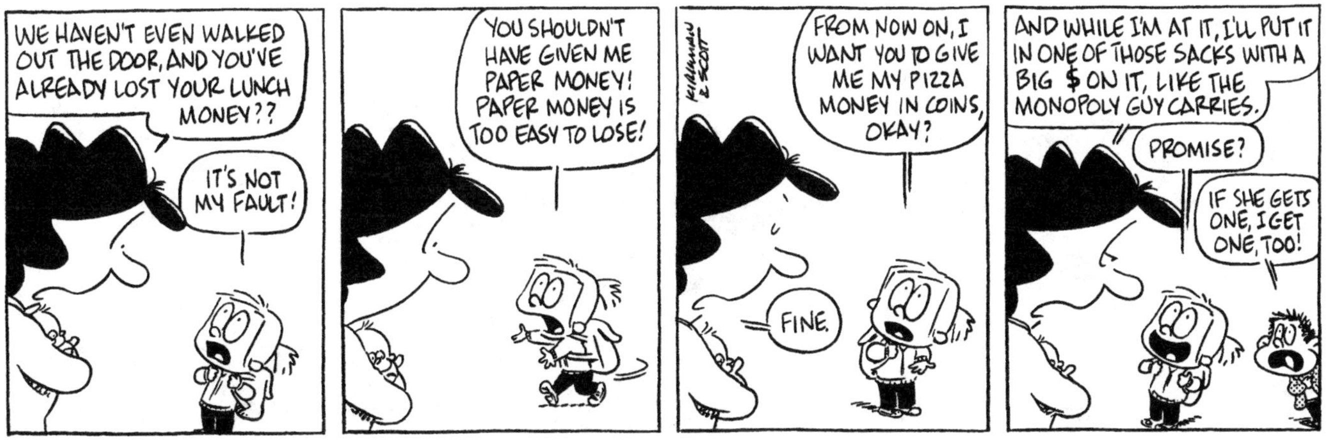
WE HAVEN'T EVEN WALKED OUT THE DOOR, AND YOU'VE ALREADY LOST YOUR LUNCH MONEY??
IT'S NOT MY FAULT!
YOU SHOULDN'T HAVE GIVEN ME PAPER MONEY! PAPER MONEY IS TOO EASY TO LOSE!
KIRKMAN & SCOTT
FROM NOW ON, I WANT YOU TO GIVE ME MY PIZZA MONEY IN COINS, OKAY?
FINE.
AND WHILE I'M AT IT, I'LL PUT IT IN ONE OF THOSE SACKS WITH A BIG $ ON IT, LIKE THE MONOPOLY GUY CARRIES.
PROMISE?
IF SHE GETS ONE, I GET ONE, TOO!

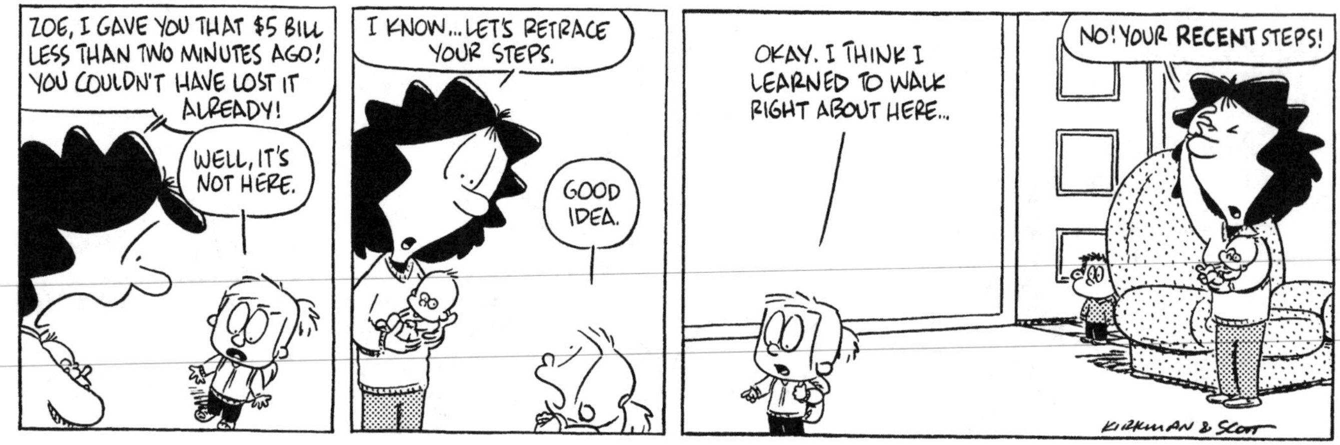
ZOE, I GAVE YOU THAT $5 BILL LESS THAN TWO MINUTES AGO! YOU COULDN'T HAVE LOST IT ALREADY!
WELL, IT'S NOT HERE.
I KNOW... LET'S RETRACE YOUR STEPS.
GOOD IDEA.
OKAY. I THINK I LEARNED TO WALK RIGHT ABOUT HERE...
NO! YOUR RECENT STEPS!
KIRKMAN & SCOTT

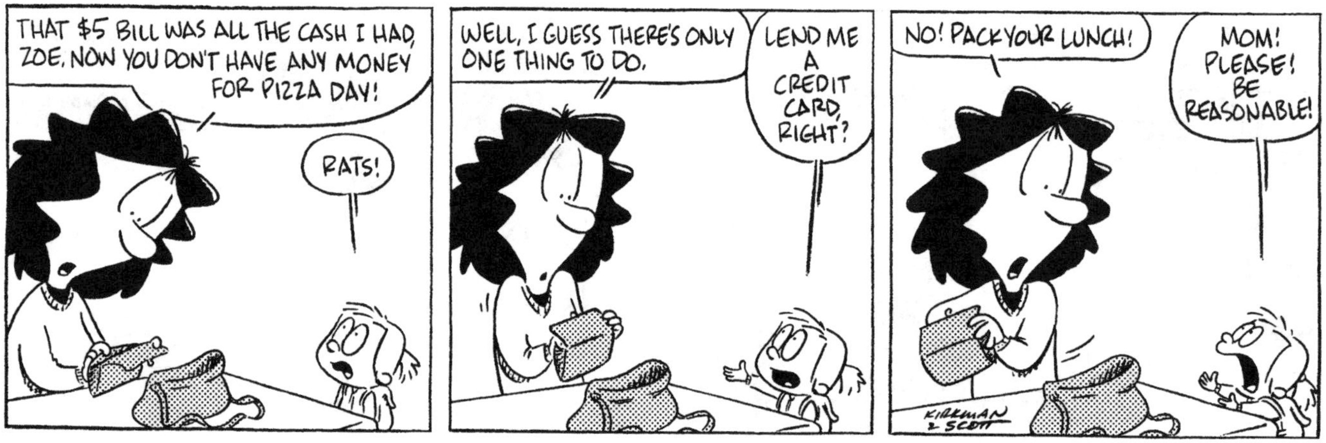
THAT $5 BILL WAS ALL THE CASH I HAD, ZOE. NOW YOU DON'T HAVE ANY MONEY FOR PIZZA DAY!
RATS!
WELL, I GUESS THERE'S ONLY ONE THING TO DO.
LEND ME A CREDIT CARD, RIGHT?
NO! PACK YOUR LUNCH!
MOM! PLEASE! BE REASONABLE!
KIRKMAN & SCOTT

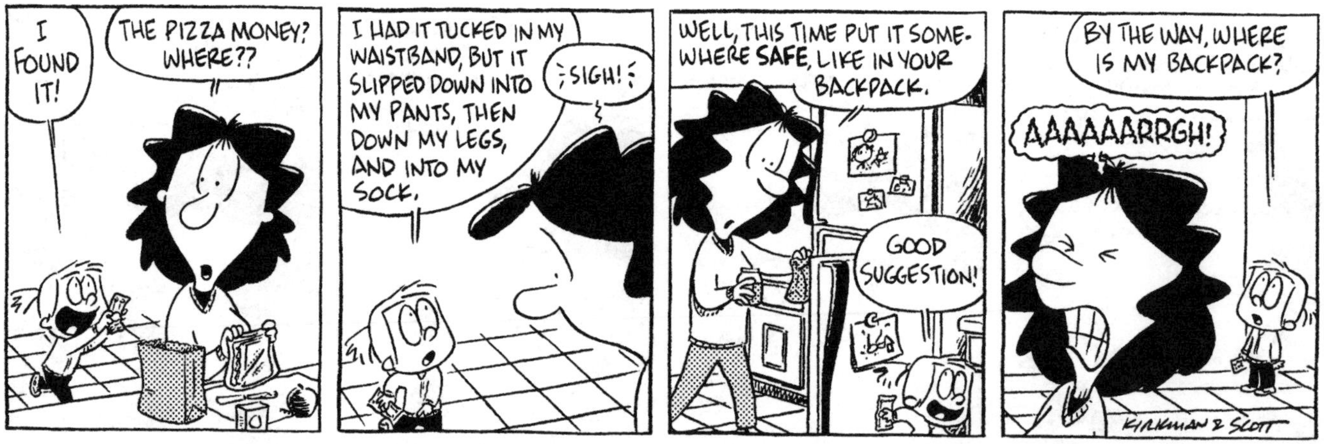
I FOUND IT!
THE PIZZA MONEY? WHERE??
I HAD IT TUCKED IN MY WAISTBAND, BUT IT SLIPPED DOWN INTO MY PANTS, THEN DOWN MY LEGS, AND INTO MY SOCK.
SIGH!
WELL, THIS TIME PUT IT SOMEWHERE SAFE, LIKE IN YOUR BACKPACK.
GOOD SUGGESTION!
BY THE WAY, WHERE IS MY BACKPACK?
AAAAAARRGH!
KIRKMAN & SCOTT

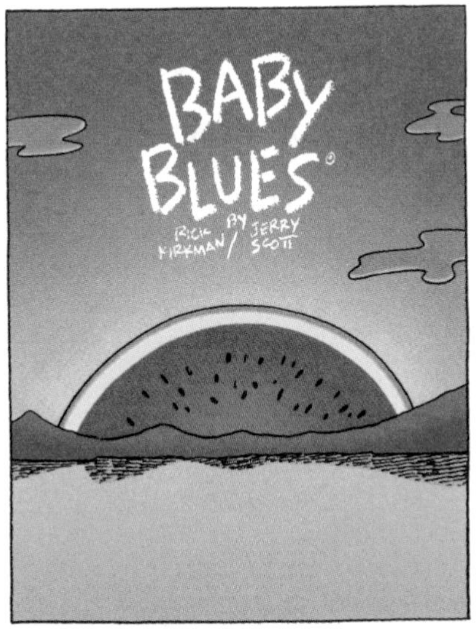
BABY BLUES®
RICK KIRKMAN / JERRY SCOTT

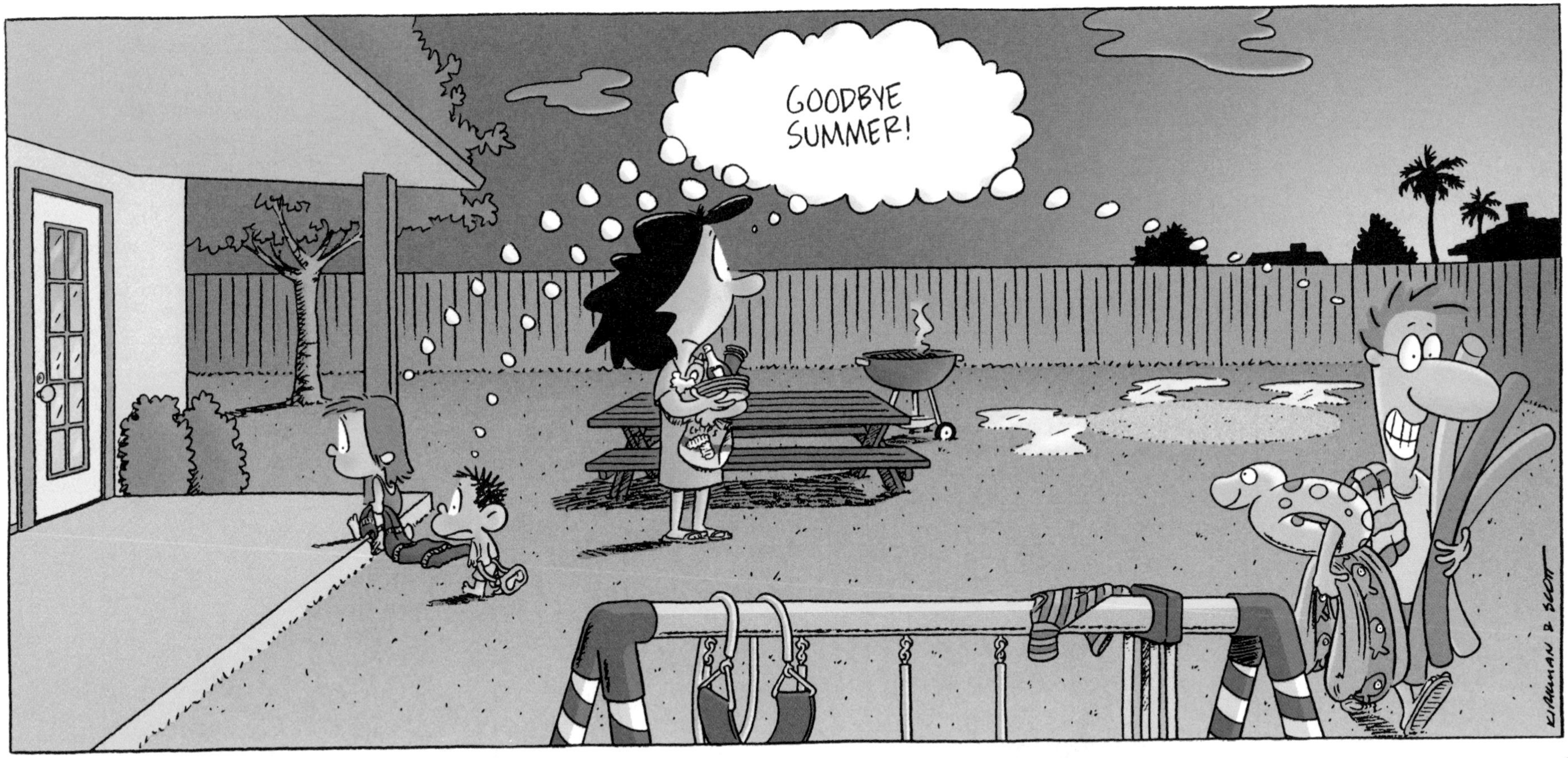
GOODBYE SUMMER!
KIRKMAN & SCOTT

PASSION DURING THE KIDYEARS

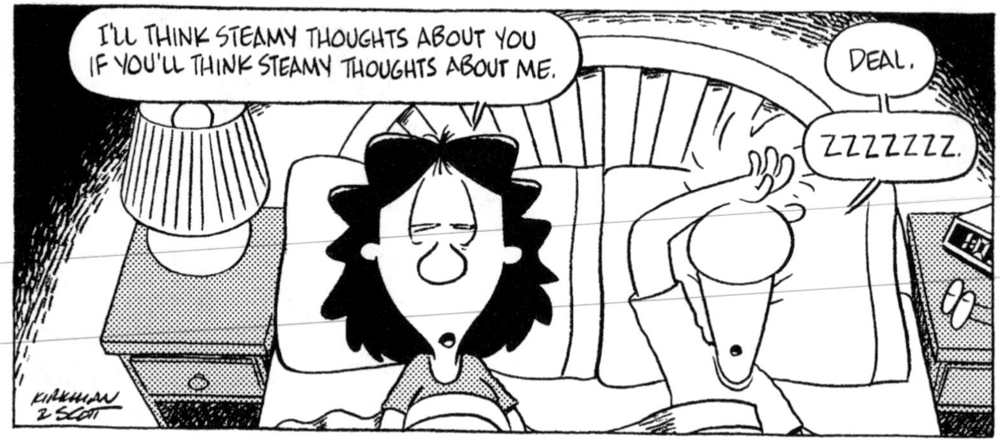

I'LL THINK STEAMY THOUGHTS ABOUT YOU IF YOU'LL THINK STEAMY THOUGHTS ABOUT ME.
DEAL.
ZZZZZZZ.
KIRKMAN & SCOTT

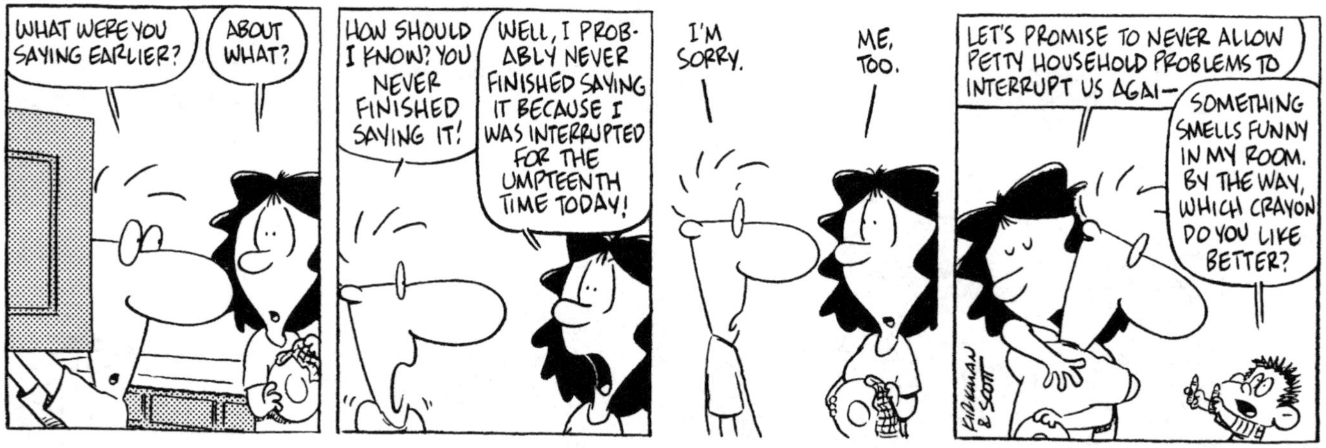

WHAT WERE YOU SAYING EARLIER?
ABOUT WHAT?
HOW SHOULD I KNOW? YOU NEVER FINISHED SAYING IT!
WELL, I PROBABLY NEVER FINISHED SAYING IT BECAUSE I WAS INTERRUPTED FOR THE UMPTEENTH TIME TODAY!
I'M SORRY.
ME, TOO.
LET'S PROMISE TO NEVER ALLOW PETTY HOUSEHOLD PROBLEMS TO INTERRUPT US AGAI—
SOMETHING SMELLS FUNNY IN MY ROOM. BY THE WAY, WHICH CRAYON DO YOU LIKE BETTER?
KIRKMAN & SCOTT

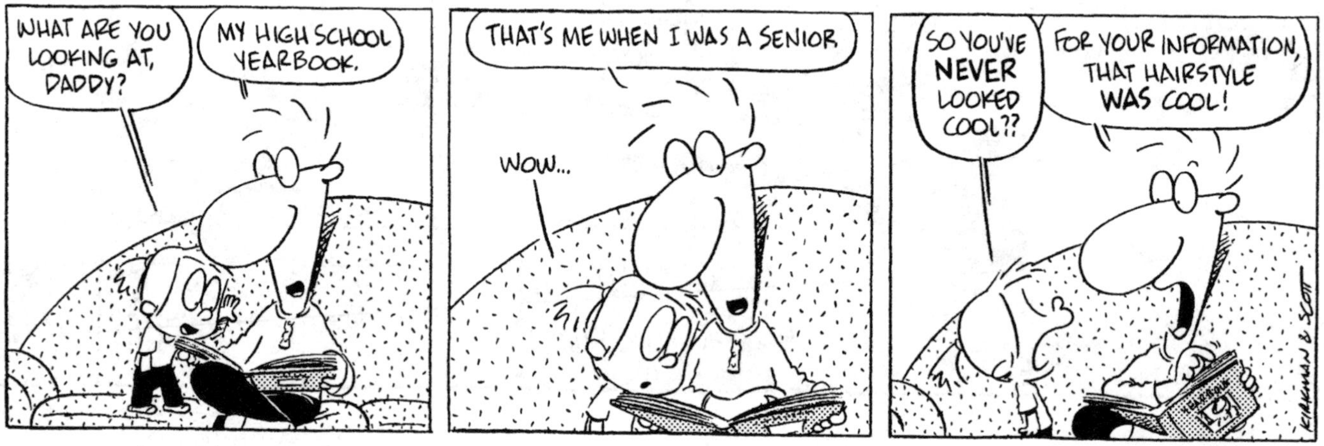

WHAT ARE YOU LOOKING AT, DADDY?
MY HIGH SCHOOL YEARBOOK.
THAT'S ME WHEN I WAS A SENIOR.
WOW...
SO YOU'VE **NEVER** LOOKED COOL??
FOR YOUR INFORMATION, THAT HAIRSTYLE **WAS** COOL!
KIRKMAN & SCOTT

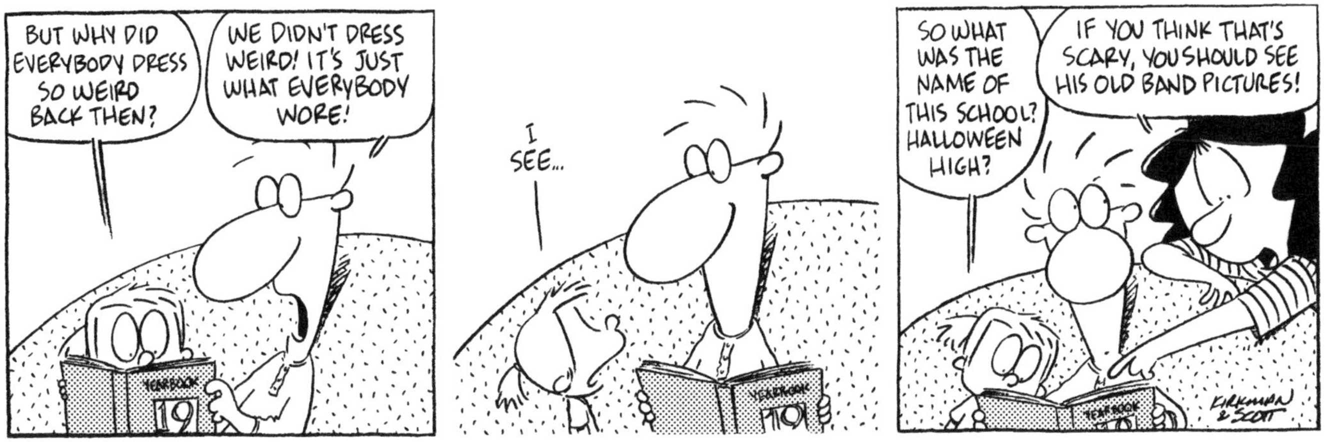
BUT WHY DID EVERYBODY DRESS SO WEIRD BACK THEN?
WE DIDN'T DRESS WEIRD! IT'S JUST WHAT EVERYBODY WORE!
I SEE...
SO WHAT WAS THE NAME OF THIS SCHOOL? HALLOWEEN HIGH?
IF YOU THINK THAT'S SCARY, YOU SHOULD SEE HIS OLD BAND PICTURES!
KIRKMAN & SCOTT

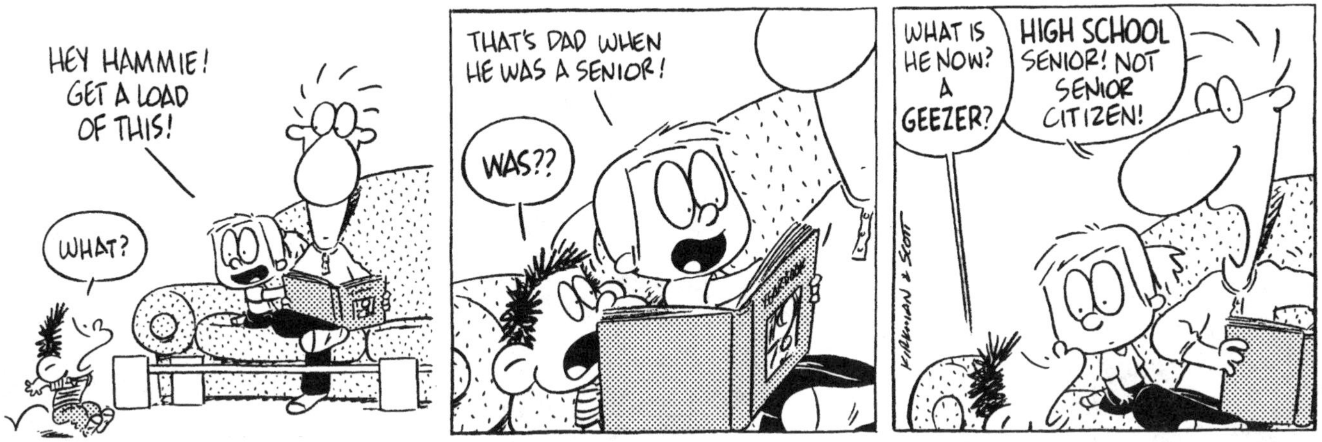
HEY HAMMIE! GET A LOAD OF THIS!
WHAT?
THAT'S DAD WHEN HE WAS A SENIOR!
WAS??
WHAT IS HE NOW? A GEEZER?
HIGH SCHOOL SENIOR! NOT SENIOR CITIZEN!
KIRKMAN & SCOTT

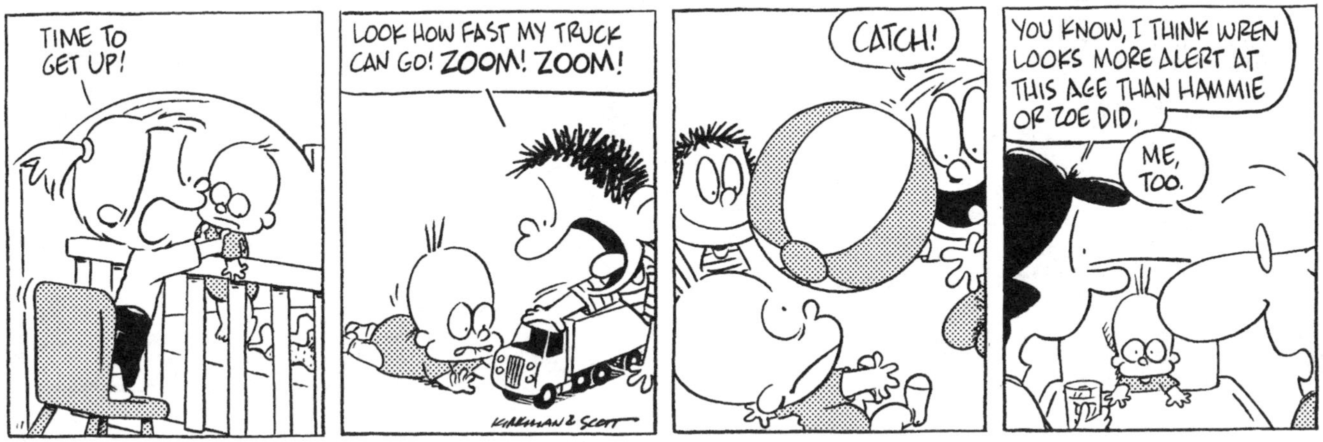
TIME TO GET UP!
LOOK HOW FAST MY TRUCK CAN GO! ZOOM! ZOOM!
KIRKMAN & SCOTT
CATCH!
YOU KNOW, I THINK WREN LOOKS MORE ALERT AT THIS AGE THAN HAMMIE OR ZOE DID.
ME, TOO.

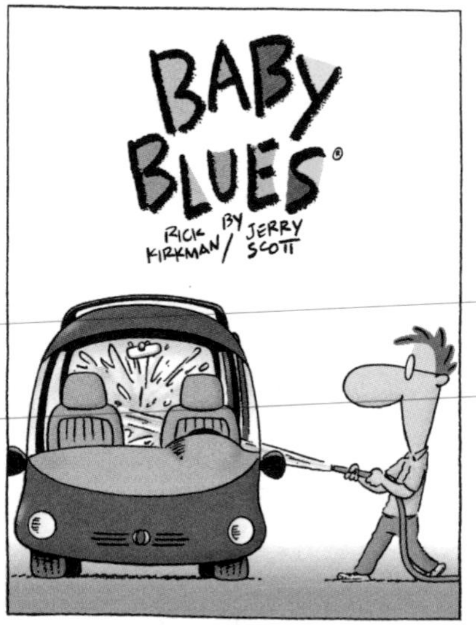
BABY BLUES®
RICK KIRKMAN / BY JERRY SCOTT

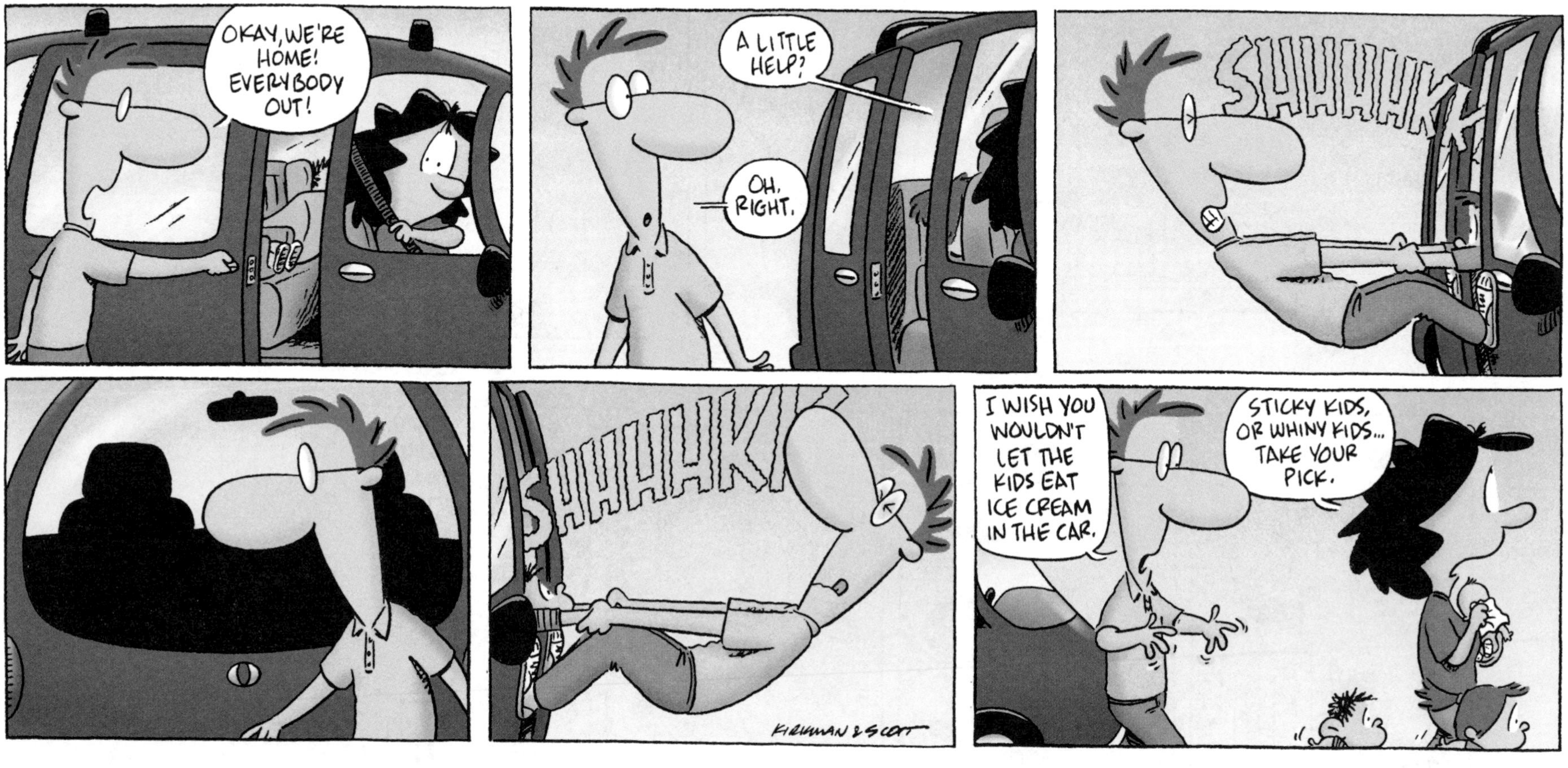
OKAY, WE'RE HOME! EVERYBODY OUT!
A LITTLE HELP?
OH, RIGHT.
SHHHHKK!
SHHHHKK!
KIRKMAN & SCOTT
I WISH YOU WOULDN'T LET THE KIDS EAT ICE CREAM IN THE CAR.
STICKY KIDS, OR WHINY KIDS... TAKE YOUR PICK.

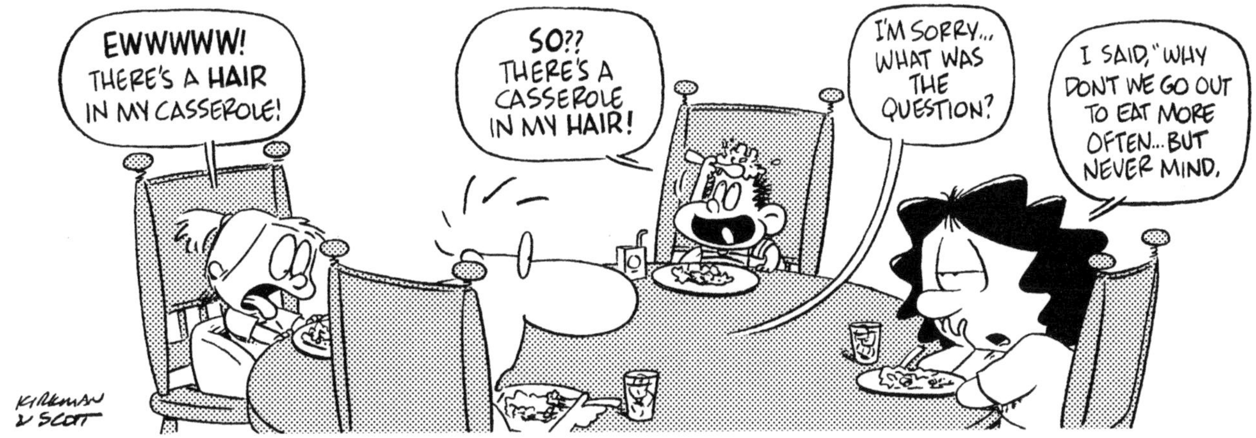
EWWWWW! THERE'S A HAIR IN MY CASSEROLE!
SO?? THERE'S A CASSEROLE IN MY HAIR!
I'M SORRY... WHAT WAS THE QUESTION?
I SAID, "WHY DON'T WE GO OUT TO EAT MORE OFTEN... BUT NEVER MIND.
KIRKMAN & SCOTT

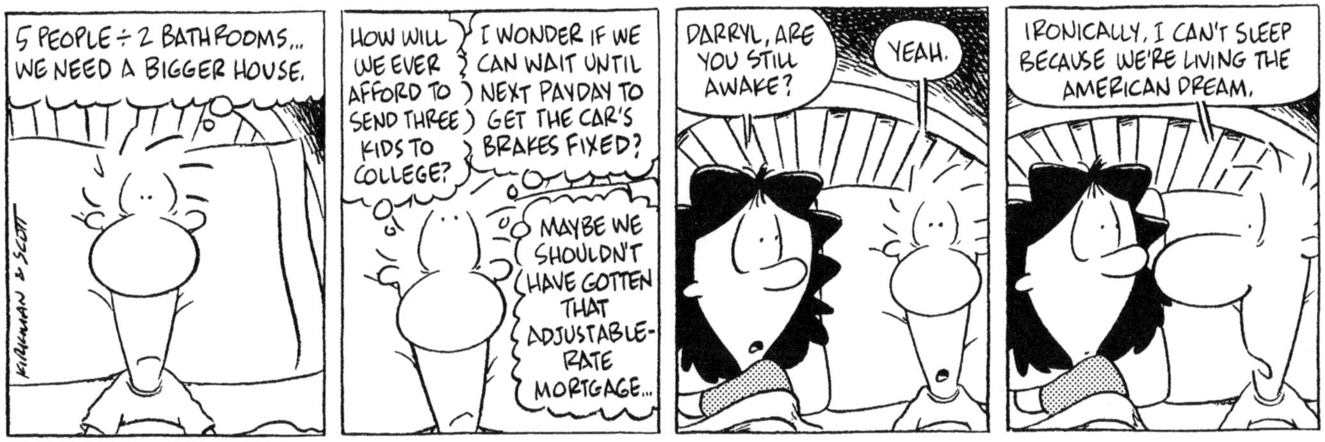
5 PEOPLE ÷ 2 BATHROOMS... WE NEED A BIGGER HOUSE.
KIRKMAN & SCOTT
HOW WILL WE EVER AFFORD TO SEND THREE KIDS TO COLLEGE?
I WONDER IF WE CAN WAIT UNTIL NEXT PAYDAY TO GET THE CAR'S BRAKES FIXED?
MAYBE WE SHOULDN'T HAVE GOTTEN THAT ADJUSTABLE-RATE MORTGAGE...
DARRYL, ARE YOU STILL AWAKE?
YEAH.
IRONICALLY, I CAN'T SLEEP BECAUSE WE'RE LIVING THE AMERICAN DREAM.

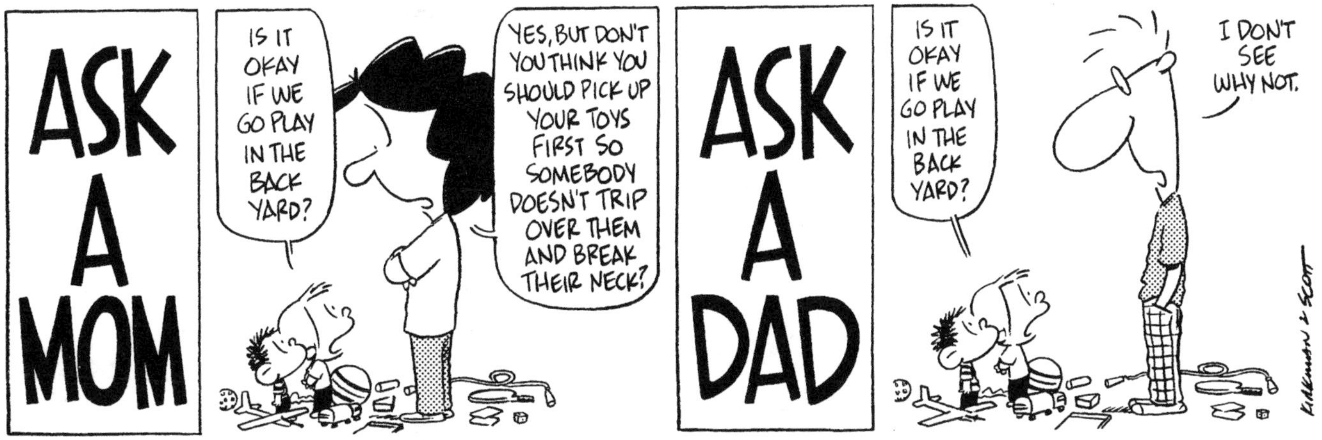
ASK A MOM
IS IT OKAY IF WE GO PLAY IN THE BACK YARD?
YES, BUT DON'T YOU THINK YOU SHOULD PICK UP YOUR TOYS FIRST SO SOMEBODY DOESN'T TRIP OVER THEM AND BREAK THEIR NECK?
ASK A DAD
IS IT OKAY IF WE GO PLAY IN THE BACK YARD?
I DON'T SEE WHY NOT.
KIRKMAN & SCOTT

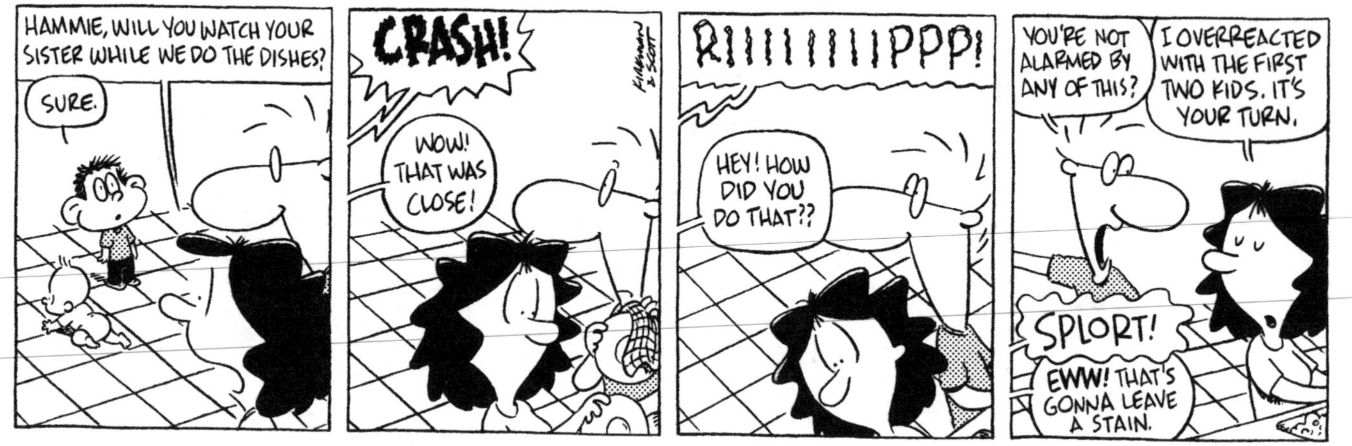
HAMMIE, WILL YOU WATCH YOUR SISTER WHILE WE DO THE DISHES?
SURE.
CRASH!
WOW! THAT WAS CLOSE!
KIRKMAN & SCOTT
RIIIIIIIIPPP!
HEY! HOW DID YOU DO THAT??
YOU'RE NOT ALARMED BY ANY OF THIS?
I OVERREACTED WITH THE FIRST TWO KIDS. IT'S YOUR TURN.
SPLORT!
EWW! THAT'S GONNA LEAVE A STAIN.

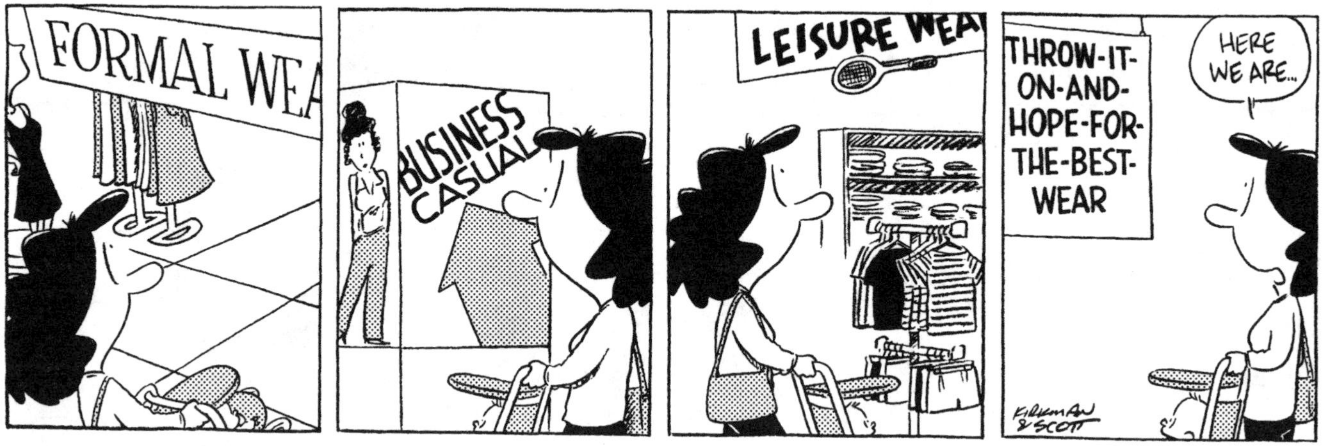
FORMAL WEA
BUSINESS CASUAL
LEISURE WEA
THROW-IT-ON-AND-HOPE-FOR-THE-BEST-WEAR
HERE WE ARE...
KIRKMAN & SCOTT

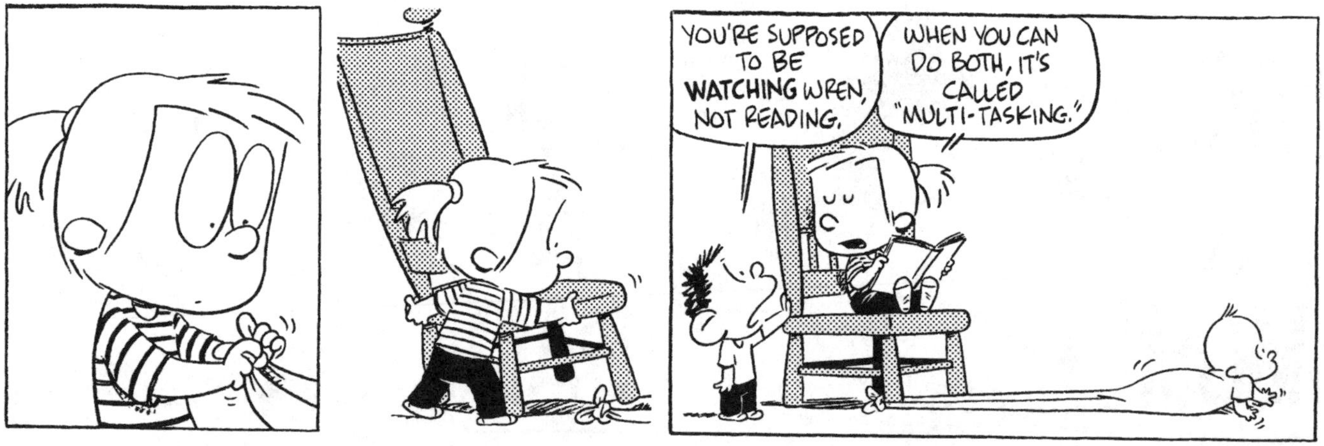
YOU'RE SUPPOSED TO BE WATCHING WREN, NOT READING.
WHEN YOU CAN DO BOTH, IT'S CALLED "MULTI-TASKING."

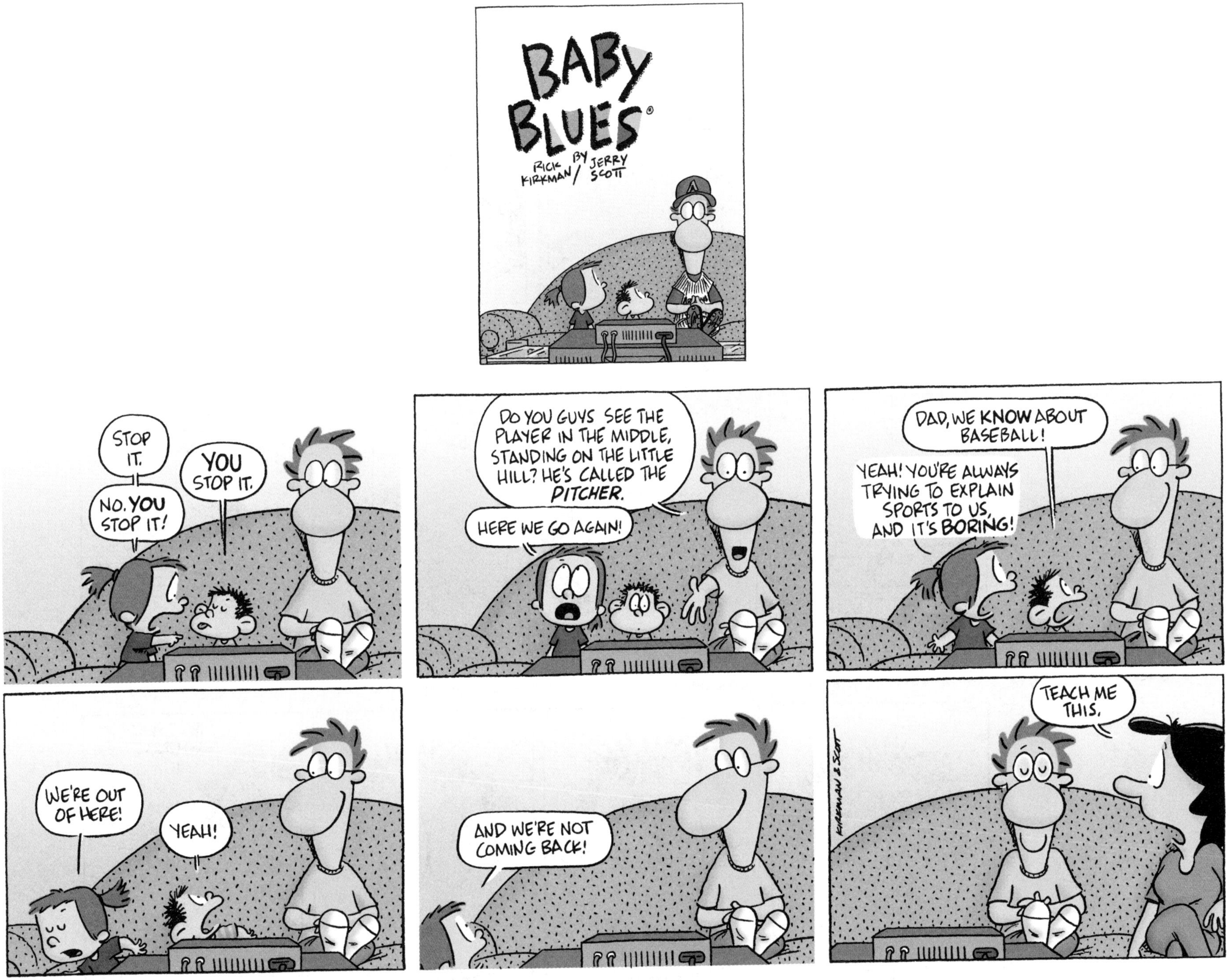
BABY BLUES®
BY RICK KIRKMAN / JERRY SCOTT
STOP IT.
NO. YOU STOP IT!
YOU STOP IT.
DO YOU GUYS SEE THE PLAYER IN THE MIDDLE, STANDING ON THE LITTLE HILL? HE'S CALLED THE PITCHER.
HERE WE GO AGAIN!
DAD, WE KNOW ABOUT BASEBALL!
YEAH! YOU'RE ALWAYS TRYING TO EXPLAIN SPORTS TO US, AND IT'S BORING!
WE'RE OUT OF HERE!
YEAH!
AND WE'RE NOT COMING BACK!
TEACH ME THIS.

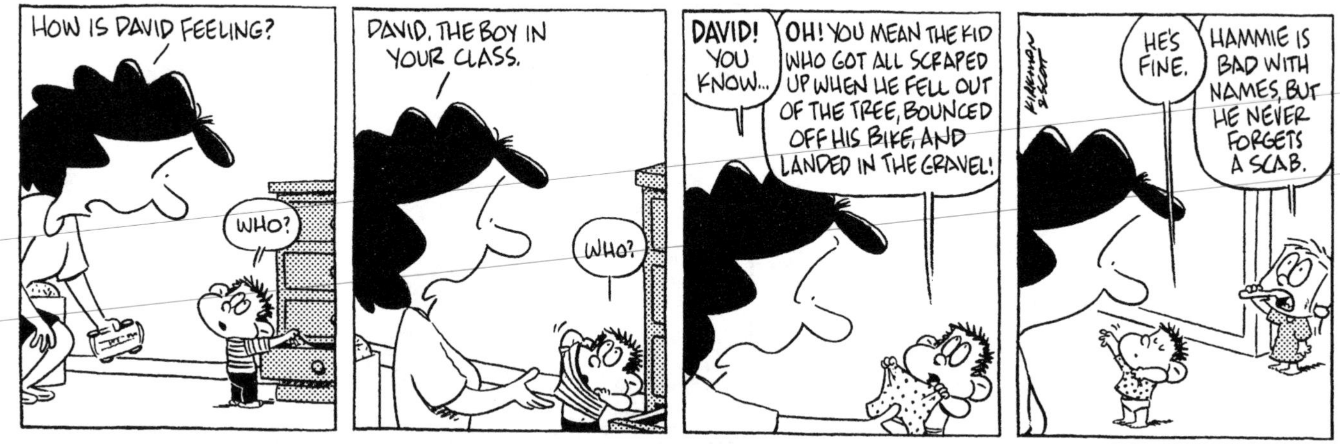
HOW IS DAVID FEELING?
WHO?
DAVID, THE BOY IN YOUR CLASS.
WHO?
DAVID! YOU KNOW...
OH! YOU MEAN THE KID WHO GOT ALL SCRAPED UP WHEN HE FELL OUT OF THE TREE, BOUNCED OFF HIS BIKE, AND LANDED IN THE GRAVEL!
HE'S FINE.
HAMMIE IS BAD WITH NAMES, BUT HE NEVER FORGETS A SCAB.

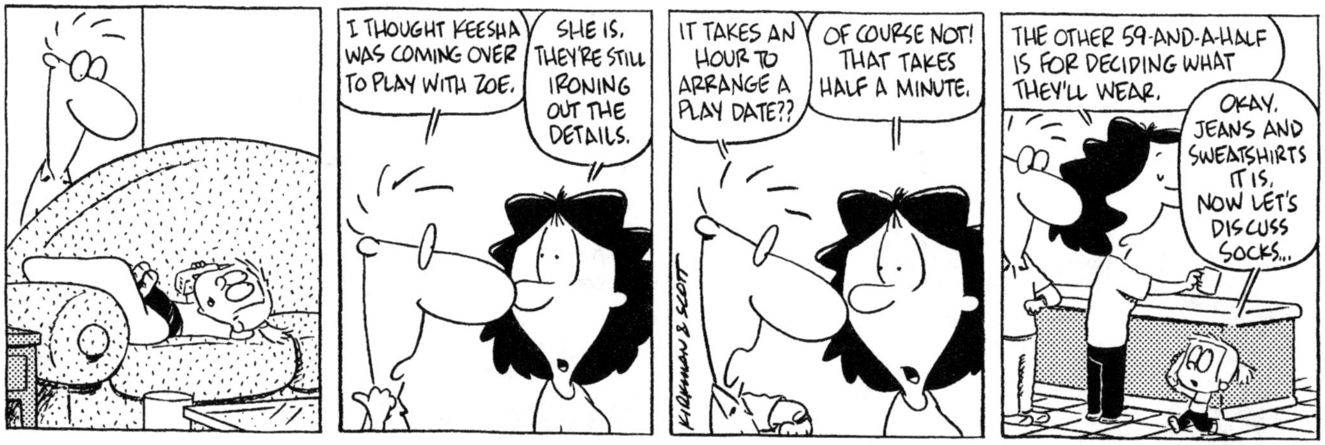
I THOUGHT KEESHA WAS COMING OVER TO PLAY WITH ZOE.
SHE IS. THEY'RE STILL IRONING OUT THE DETAILS.
IT TAKES AN HOUR TO ARRANGE A PLAY DATE??
OF COURSE NOT! THAT TAKES HALF A MINUTE.
THE OTHER 59-AND-A-HALF IS FOR DECIDING WHAT THEY'LL WEAR.
OKAY. JEANS AND SWEATSHIRTS IT IS. NOW LET'S DISCUSS SOCKS...

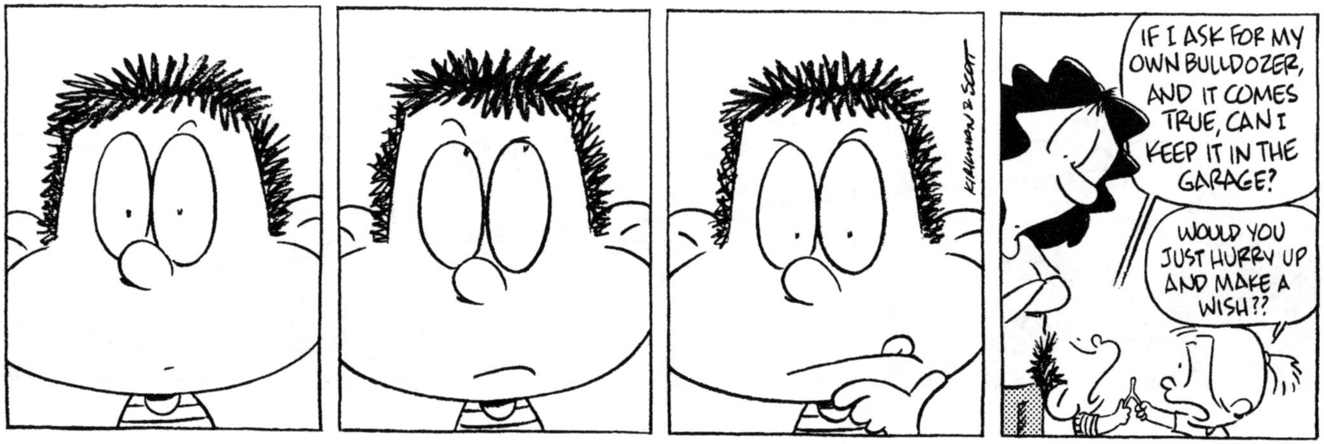
IF I ASK FOR MY OWN BULLDOZER, AND IT COMES TRUE, CAN I KEEP IT IN THE GARAGE?
WOULD YOU JUST HURRY UP AND MAKE A WISH??

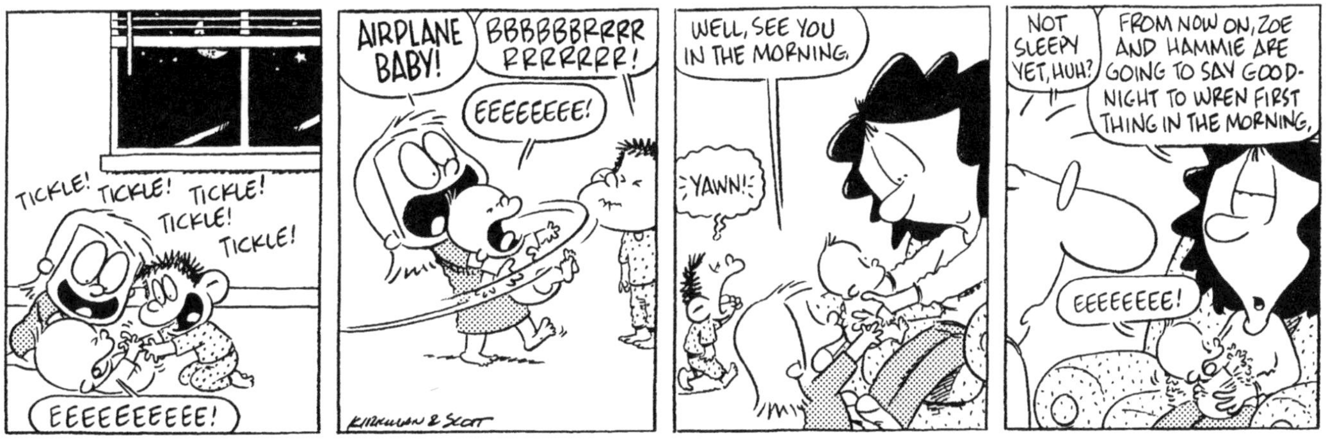
TICKLE! TICKLE! TICKLE! TICKLE! TICKLE!
EEEEEEEEEE!
AIRPLANE BABY!
BBBBBBBRRRR RRRRRRR!
EEEEEEEE!
KIRKMAN & SCOTT
WELL, SEE YOU IN THE MORNING.
YAWN!
NOT SLEEPY YET, HUH?
FROM NOW ON, ZOE AND HAMMIE ARE GOING TO SAY GOOD-NIGHT TO WREN FIRST THING IN THE MORNING.
EEEEEEEE!

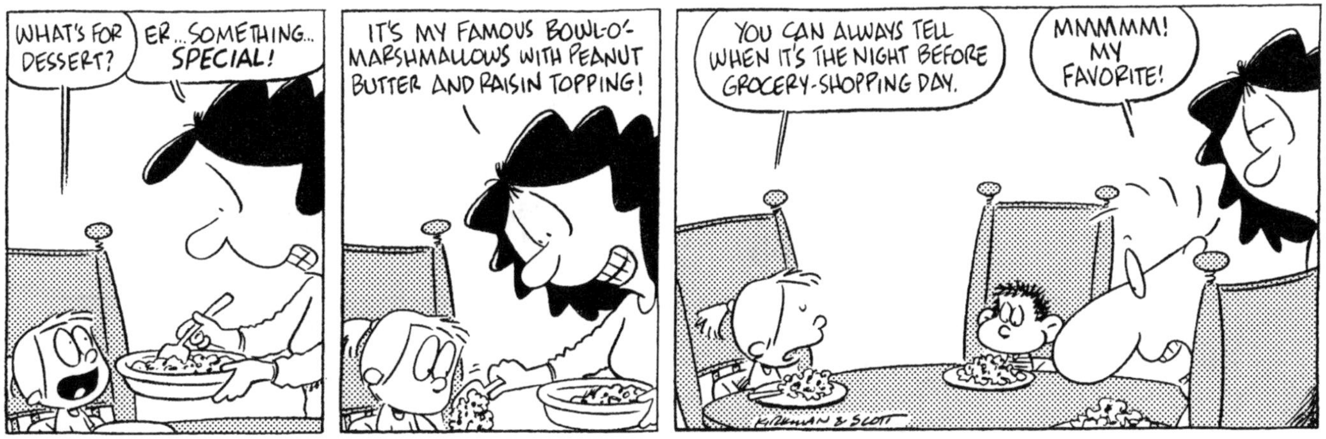
WHAT'S FOR DESSERT?
ER... SOMETHING... SPECIAL!
IT'S MY FAMOUS BOWL-O'-MARSHMALLOWS WITH PEANUT BUTTER AND RAISIN TOPPING!
YOU CAN ALWAYS TELL WHEN IT'S THE NIGHT BEFORE GROCERY-SHOPPING DAY.
MMMMMM! MY FAVORITE!
KIRKMAN & SCOTT

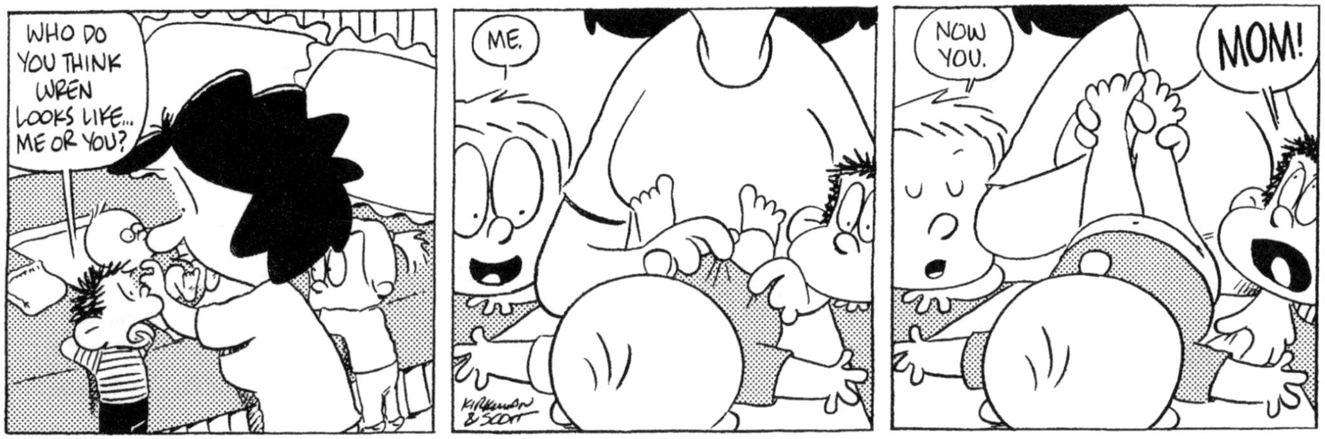
WHO DO YOU THINK WREN LOOKS LIKE... ME OR YOU?
ME.
KIRKMAN & SCOTT
NOW YOU.
MOM!

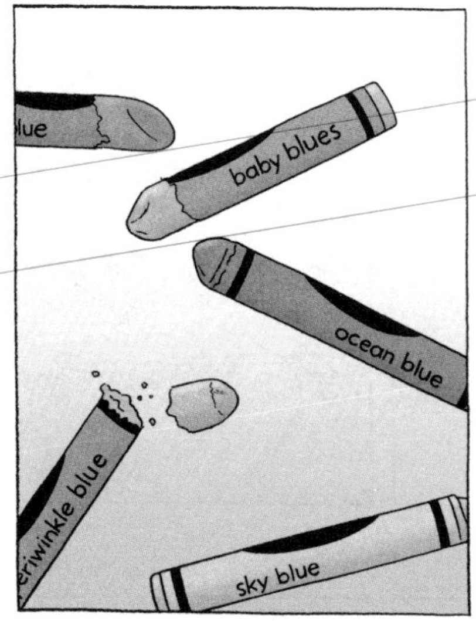

blue
baby blues
ocean blue
eriwinkle blue
sky blue

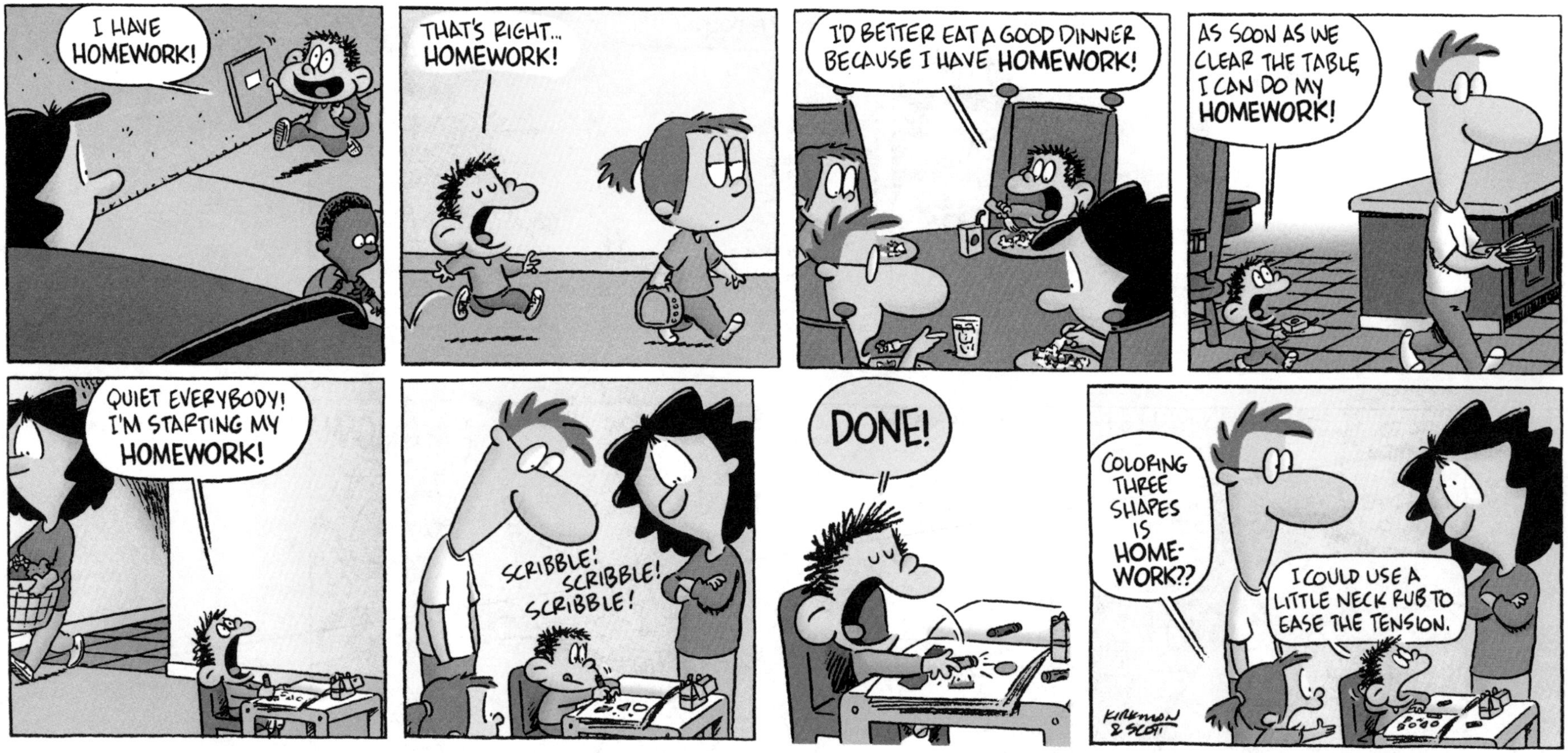

I HAVE HOMEWORK!
THAT'S RIGHT... HOMEWORK!
I'D BETTER EAT A GOOD DINNER BECAUSE I HAVE HOMEWORK!
AS SOON AS WE CLEAR THE TABLE, I CAN DO MY HOMEWORK!
QUIET EVERYBODY! I'M STARTING MY HOMEWORK!
SCRIBBLE! SCRIBBLE! SCRIBBLE!
DONE!
COLORING THREE SHAPES IS HOME-WORK??
I COULD USE A LITTLE NECK RUB TO EASE THE TENSION.
KIRKMAN & SCOTT

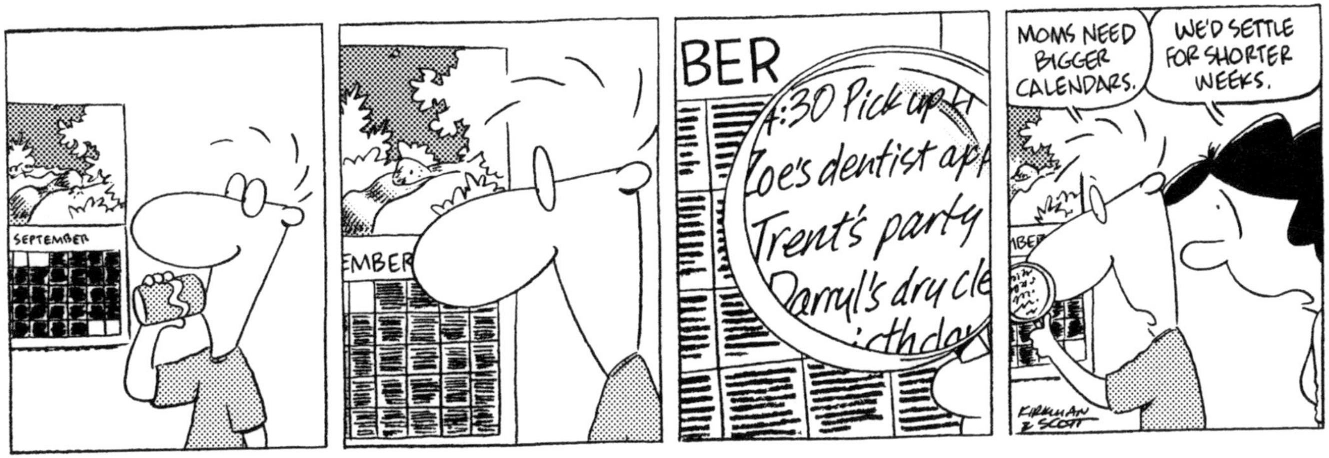
SEPTEMBER
EMBER
BER
4:30 Pick up H
Zoe's dentist app
Trent's party
Darryl's dry cle
MOMS NEED BIGGER CALENDARS.
WE'D SETTLE FOR SHORTER WEEKS.
KIRKMAN & SCOTT

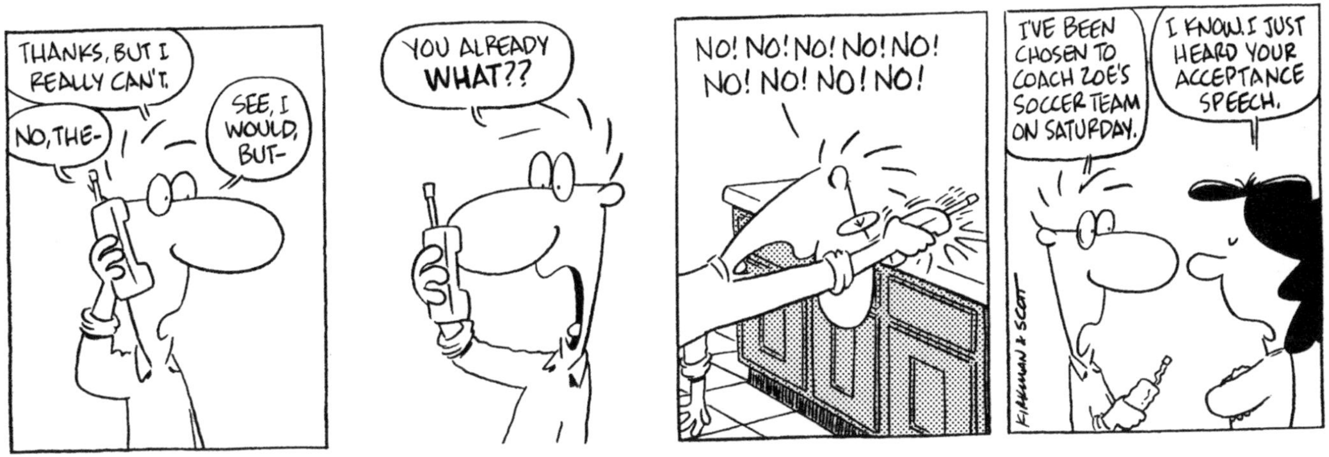
THANKS, BUT I REALLY CAN'T.
NO, THE-
SEE, I WOULD, BUT-
YOU ALREADY **WHAT**??
NO! NO! NO! NO! NO! NO! NO! NO! NO!
KIRKMAN & SCOTT
I'VE BEEN CHOSEN TO COACH ZOE'S SOCCER TEAM ON SATURDAY.
I KNOW. I JUST HEARD YOUR ACCEPTANCE SPEECH.

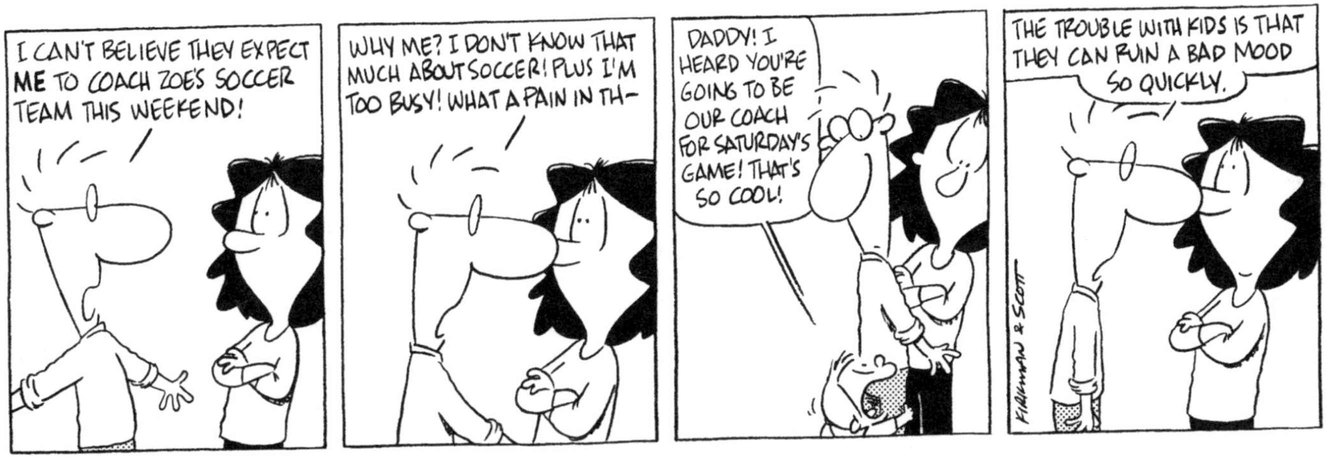
I CAN'T BELIEVE THEY EXPECT **ME** TO COACH ZOE'S SOCCER TEAM THIS WEEKEND!
WHY ME? I DON'T KNOW THAT MUCH ABOUT SOCCER! PLUS I'M TOO BUSY! WHAT A PAIN IN TH-
DADDY! I HEARD YOU'RE GOING TO BE OUR COACH FOR SATURDAY'S GAME! THAT'S SO COOL!
KIRKMAN & SCOTT
THE TROUBLE WITH KIDS IS THAT THEY CAN RUIN A BAD MOOD SO QUICKLY.

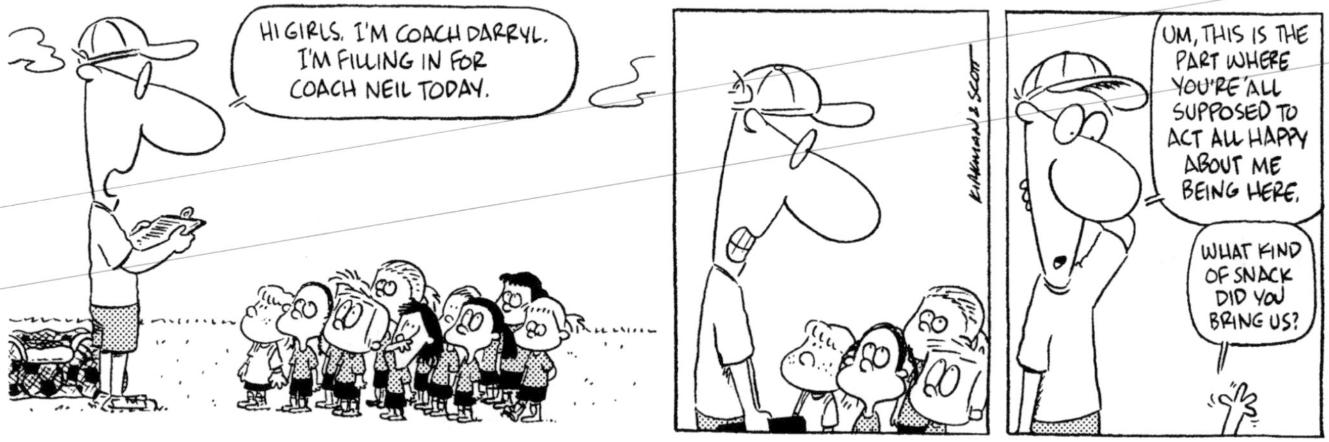
HI GIRLS. I'M COACH DARRYL. I'M FILLING IN FOR COACH NEIL TODAY.
KIRKMAN & SCOTT
UM, THIS IS THE PART WHERE YOU'RE ALL SUPPOSED TO ACT ALL HAPPY ABOUT ME BEING HERE.
WHAT KIND OF SNACK DID YOU BRING US?

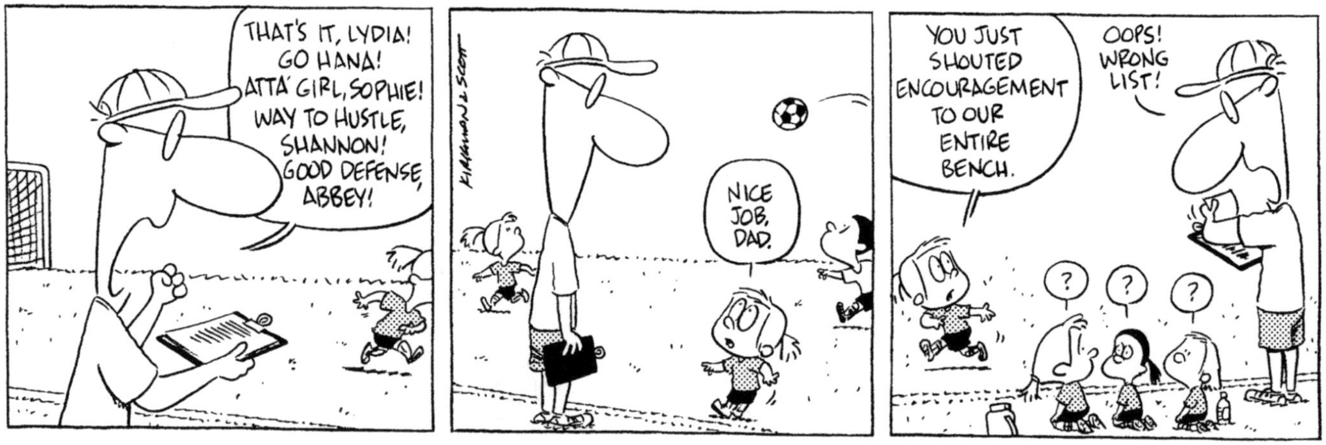
THAT'S IT, LYDIA! GO HANA! ATTA' GIRL, SOPHIE! WAY TO HUSTLE, SHANNON! GOOD DEFENSE, ABBEY!
KIRKMAN & SCOTT
NICE JOB, DAD.
YOU JUST SHOUTED ENCOURAGEMENT TO OUR ENTIRE BENCH.
OOPS! WRONG LIST!
?
?
?

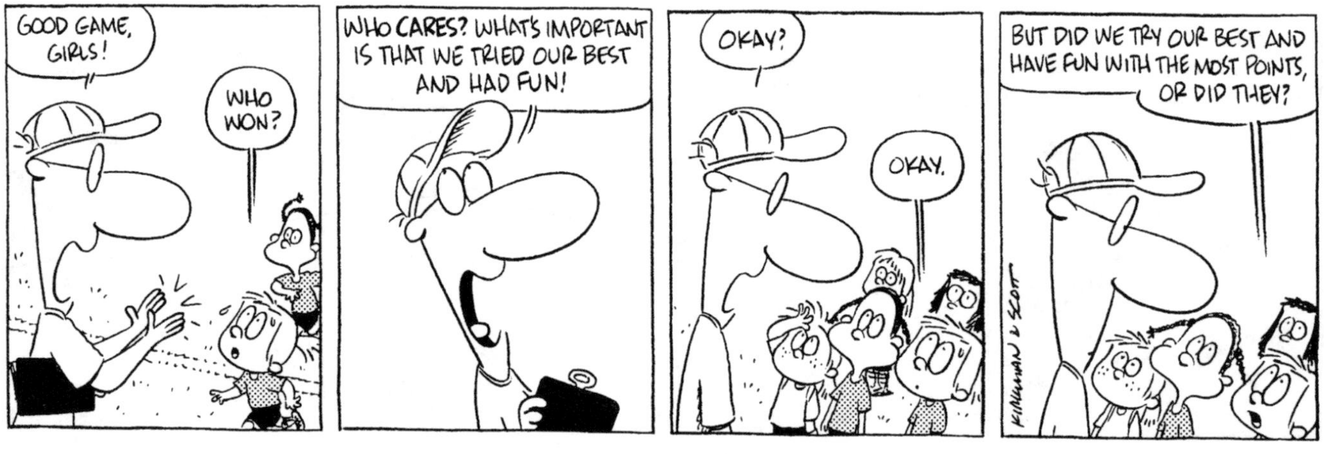
GOOD GAME, GIRLS!
WHO WON?
WHO CARES? WHAT'S IMPORTANT IS THAT WE TRIED OUR BEST AND HAD FUN!
OKAY?
OKAY.
KIRKMAN & SCOTT
BUT DID WE TRY OUR BEST AND HAVE FUN WITH THE MOST POINTS, OR DID THEY?

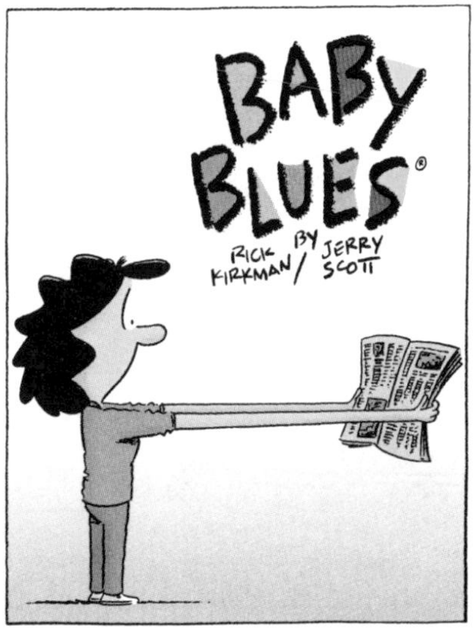
BABY BLUES®
BY RICK KIRKMAN / JERRY SCOTT

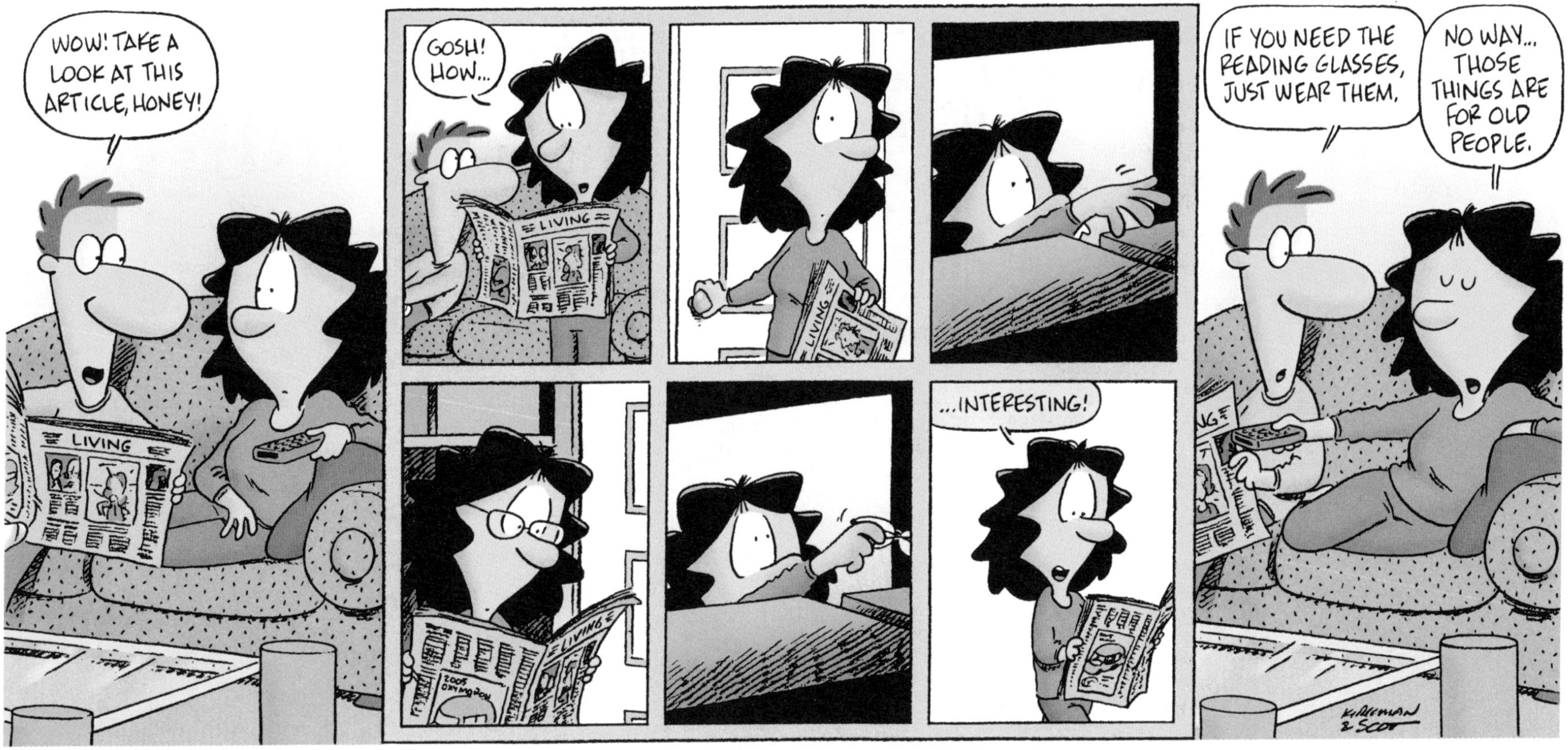
WOW! TAKE A LOOK AT THIS ARTICLE, HONEY!
GOSH! HOW...
...INTERESTING!
IF YOU NEED THE READING GLASSES, JUST WEAR THEM.
NO WAY... THOSE THINGS ARE FOR OLD PEOPLE.

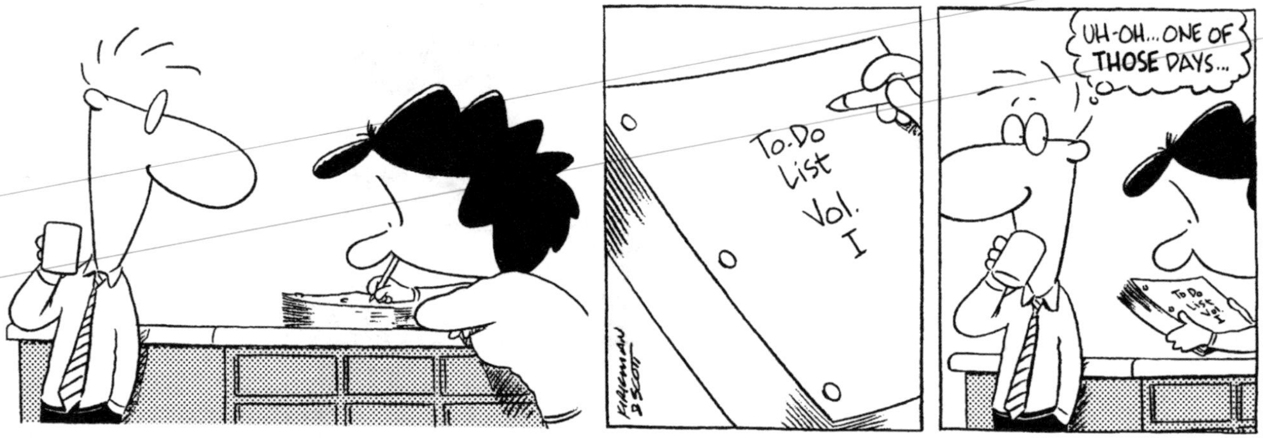
To-Do List Vol. I
UH-OH...ONE OF THOSE DAYS...
To Do List Vol. I

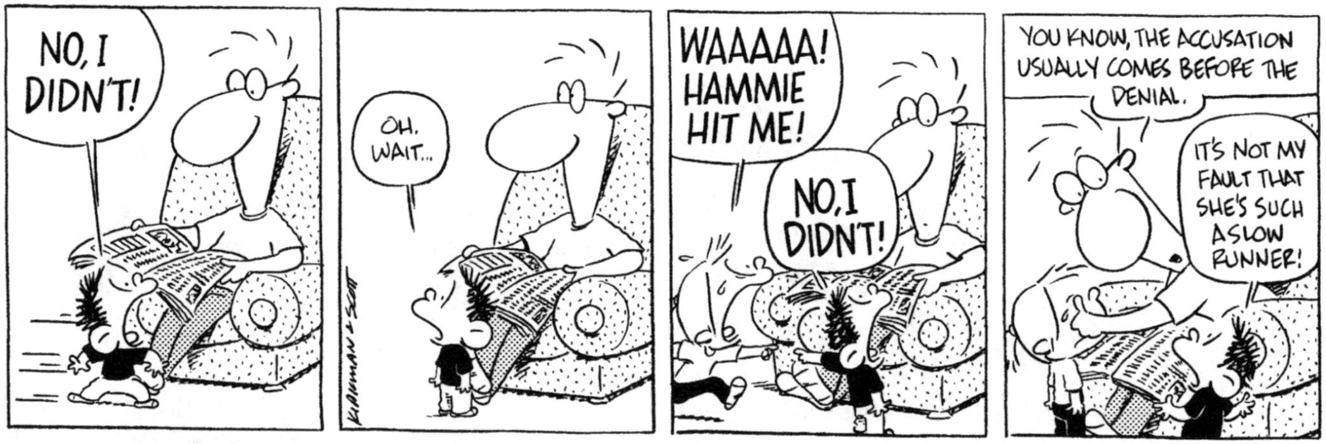
NO, I DIDN'T!
OH. WAIT...
WAAAAA! HAMMIE HIT ME!
NO, I DIDN'T!
YOU KNOW, THE ACCUSATION USUALLY COMES BEFORE THE DENIAL.
IT'S NOT MY FAULT THAT SHE'S SUCH A SLOW RUNNER!

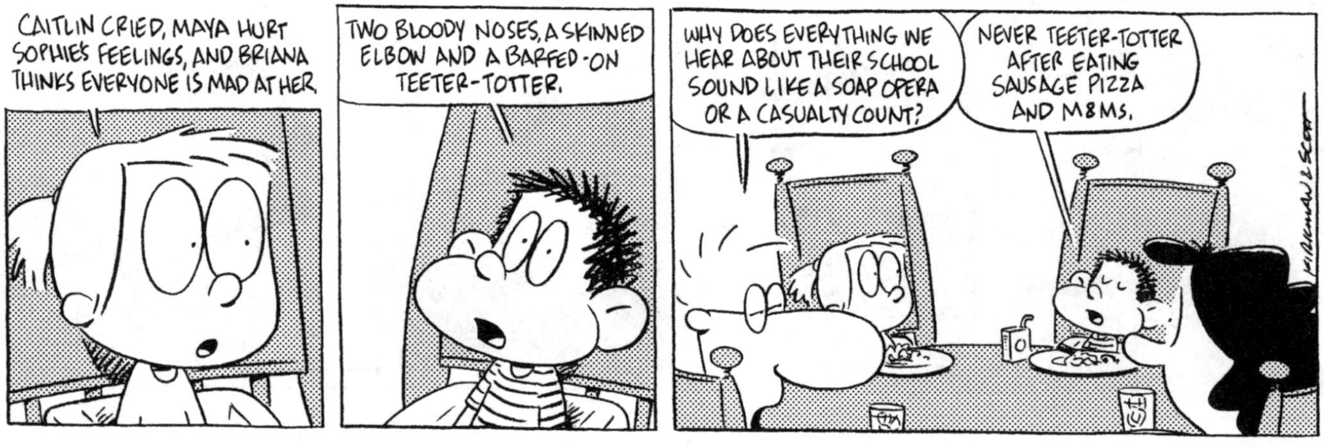
CAITLIN CRIED, MAYA HURT SOPHIE'S FEELINGS, AND BRIANA THINKS EVERYONE IS MAD AT HER.
TWO BLOODY NOSES, A SKINNED ELBOW AND A BARFED-ON TEETER-TOTTER.
WHY DOES EVERYTHING WE HEAR ABOUT THEIR SCHOOL SOUND LIKE A SOAP OPERA OR A CASUALTY COUNT?
NEVER TEETER-TOTTER AFTER EATING SAUSAGE PIZZA AND M&MS.

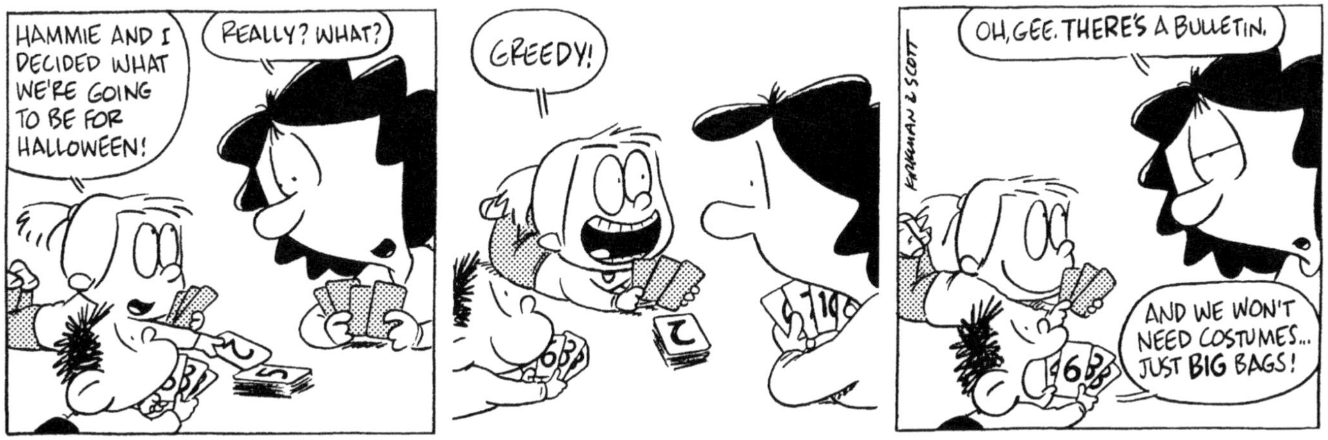
HAMMIE AND I DECIDED WHAT WE'RE GOING TO BE FOR HALLOWEEN!
REALLY? WHAT?
GREEDY!
KIRKMAN & SCOTT
OH, GEE. THERE'S A BULLETIN.
AND WE WON'T NEED COSTUMES... JUST BIG BAGS!

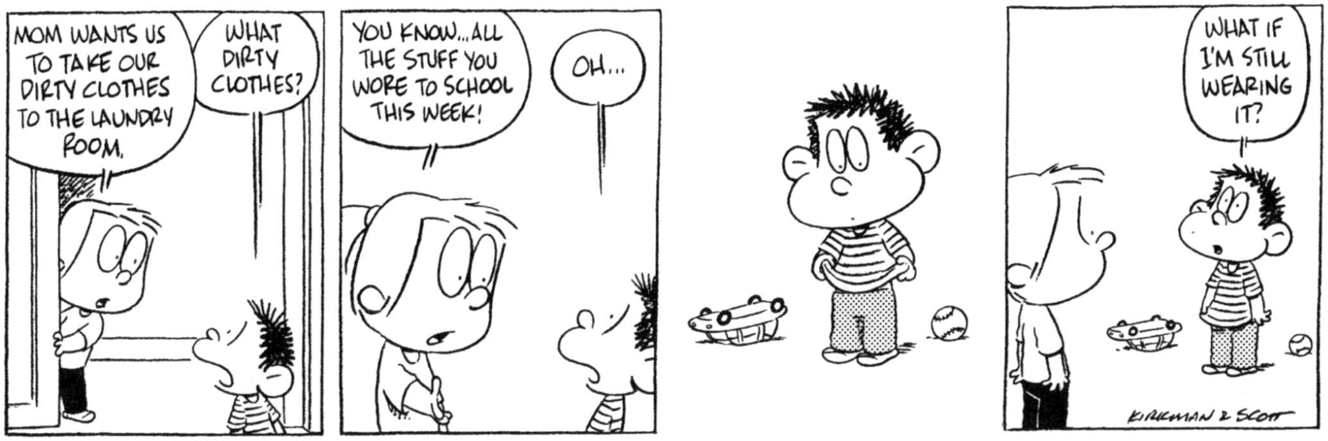
MOM WANTS US TO TAKE OUR DIRTY CLOTHES TO THE LAUNDRY ROOM.
WHAT DIRTY CLOTHES?
YOU KNOW... ALL THE STUFF YOU WORE TO SCHOOL THIS WEEK!
OH...
WHAT IF I'M STILL WEARING IT?
KIRKMAN & SCOTT

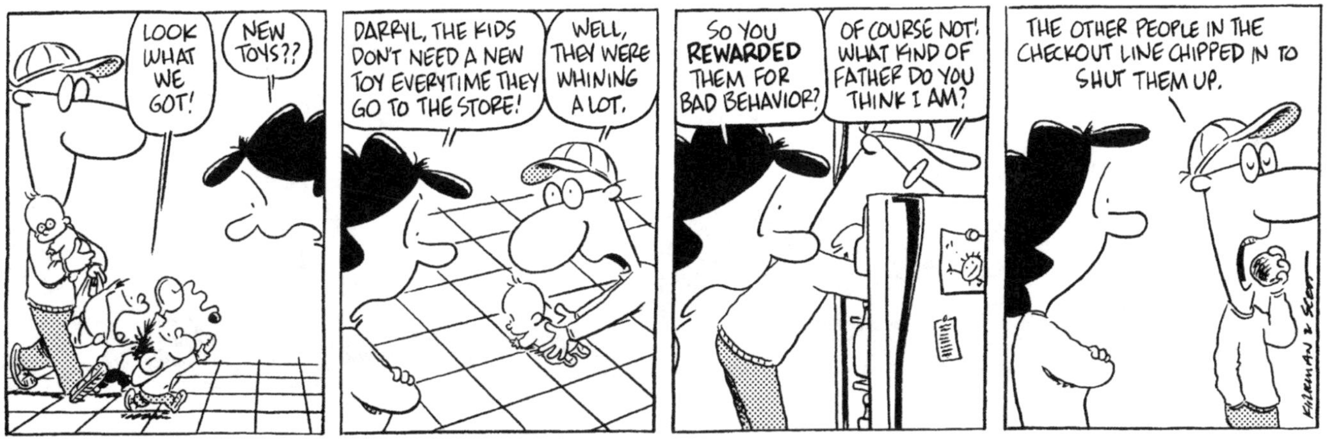
LOOK WHAT WE GOT!
NEW TOYS??
DARRYL, THE KIDS DON'T NEED A NEW TOY EVERYTIME THEY GO TO THE STORE!
WELL, THEY WERE WHINING A LOT.
SO YOU REWARDED THEM FOR BAD BEHAVIOR?
OF COURSE NOT! WHAT KIND OF FATHER DO YOU THINK I AM?
THE OTHER PEOPLE IN THE CHECKOUT LINE CHIPPED IN TO SHUT THEM UP.
KIRKMAN & SCOTT

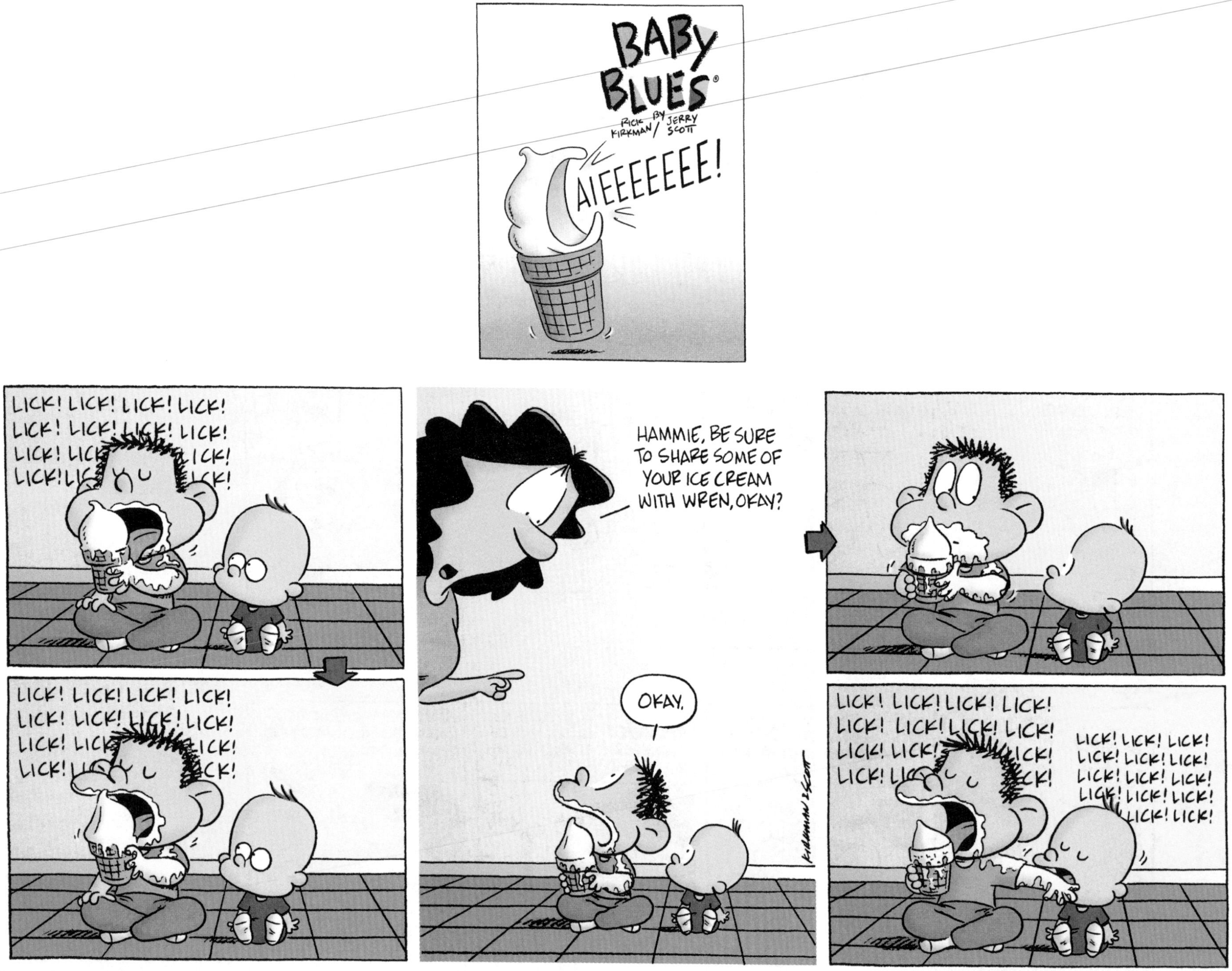
BABY BLUES®
BY RICK KIRKMAN / JERRY SCOTT
AIEEEEEEE!
LICK! LICK! LICK! LICK! LICK! LICK! LICK! LICK! LICK! LICK! LICK! LICK! LICK! LICK! LICK! LICK!
LICK! LICK! LICK! LICK! LICK! LICK! LICK! LICK! LICK! LICK! LICK! LICK! LICK! LICK! LICK! LICK!
HAMMIE, BE SURE TO SHARE SOME OF YOUR ICE CREAM WITH WREN, OKAY?
OKAY.
KIRKMAN & SCOTT
LICK! LICK! LICK! LICK! LICK! LICK! LICK! LICK! LICK! LICK! LICK! LICK! LICK! LICK! LICK! LICK!
LICK! LICK! LICK! LICK! LICK! LICK! LICK! LICK! LICK! LICK! LICK! LICK! LICK! LICK! LICK!

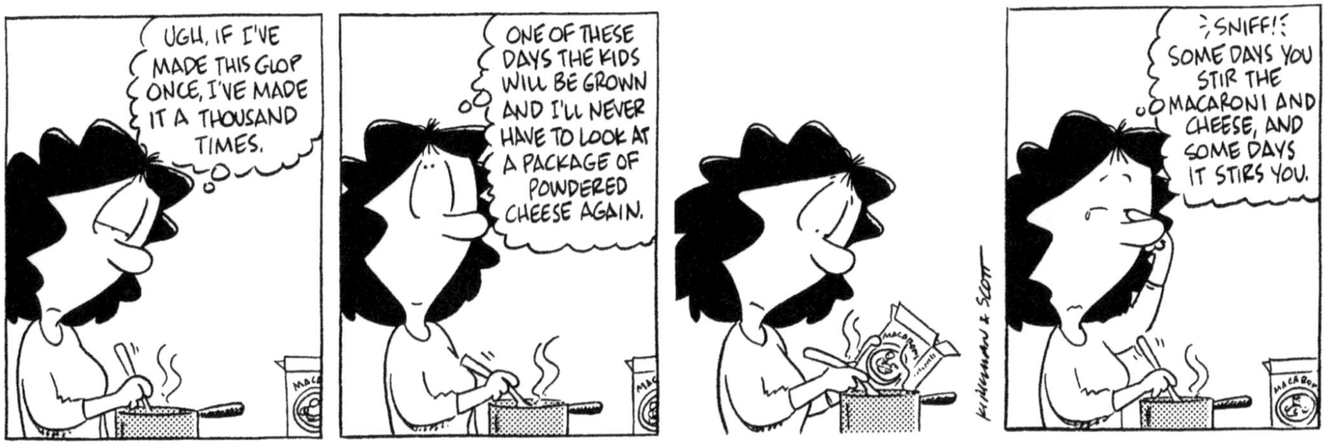
UGH, IF I'VE MADE THIS GLOP ONCE, I'VE MADE IT A THOUSAND TIMES.
ONE OF THESE DAYS THE KIDS WILL BE GROWN AND I'LL NEVER HAVE TO LOOK AT A PACKAGE OF POWDERED CHEESE AGAIN.
KIRKMAN & SCOTT
SNIFF!
SOME DAYS YOU STIR THE MACARONI AND CHEESE, AND SOME DAYS IT STIRS YOU.

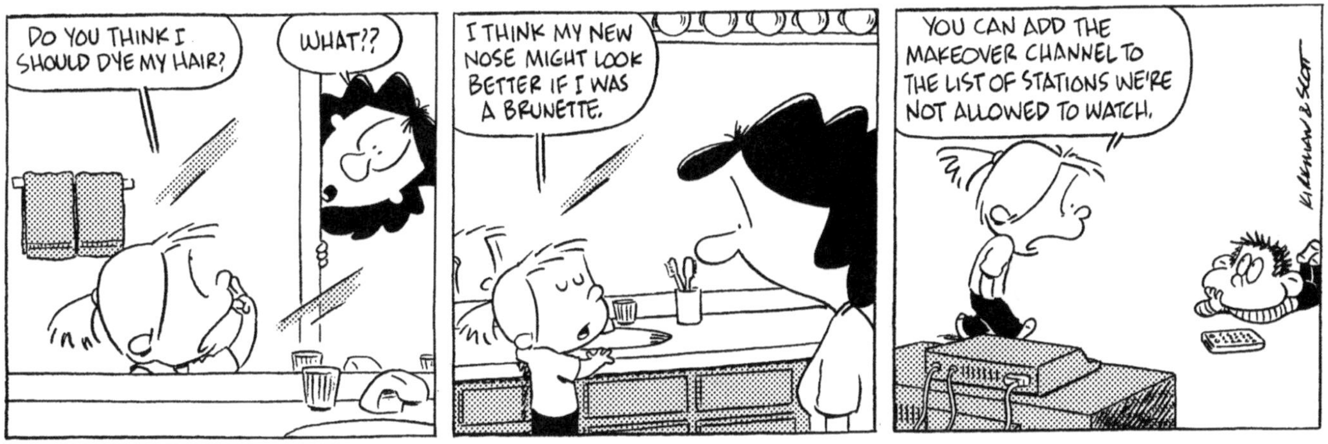
DO YOU THINK I SHOULD DYE MY HAIR?
WHAT??
I THINK MY NEW NOSE MIGHT LOOK BETTER IF I WAS A BRUNETTE.
YOU CAN ADD THE MAKEOVER CHANNEL TO THE LIST OF STATIONS WE'RE NOT ALLOWED TO WATCH.
KIRKMAN & SCOTT

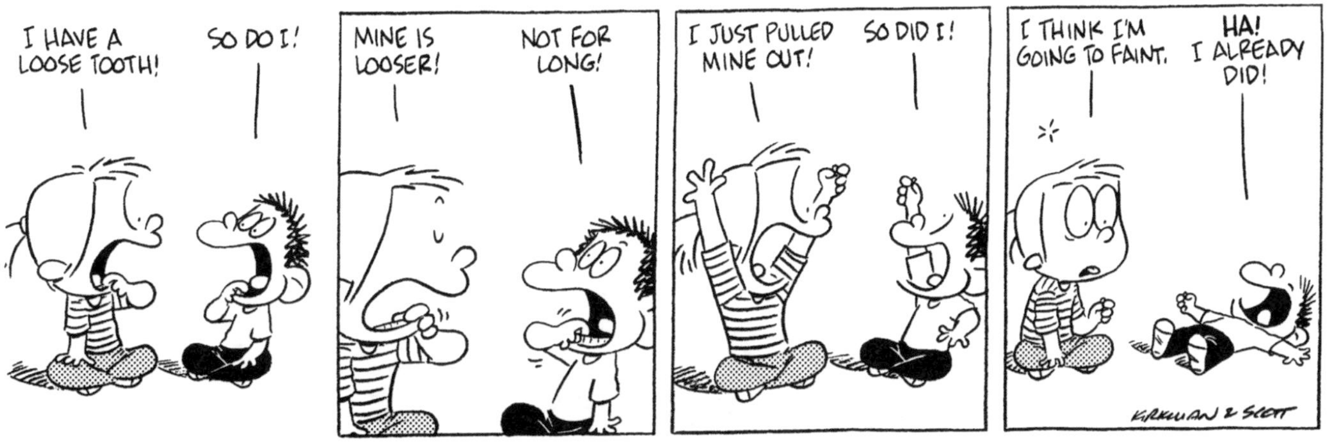
I HAVE A LOOSE TOOTH!
SO DO I!
MINE IS LOOSER!
NOT FOR LONG!
I JUST PULLED MINE OUT!
SO DID I!
I THINK I'M GOING TO FAINT.
HA! I ALREADY DID!
KIRKMAN & SCOTT

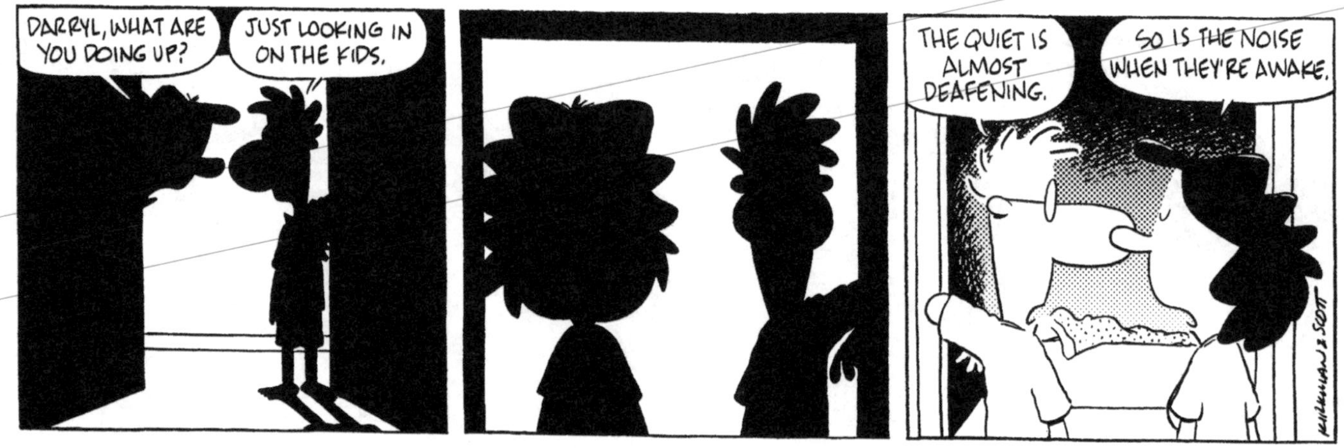
DARRYL, WHAT ARE YOU DOING UP?
JUST LOOKING IN ON THE KIDS.
THE QUIET IS ALMOST DEAFENING.
SO IS THE NOISE WHEN THEY'RE AWAKE.
KIRKMAN & SCOTT

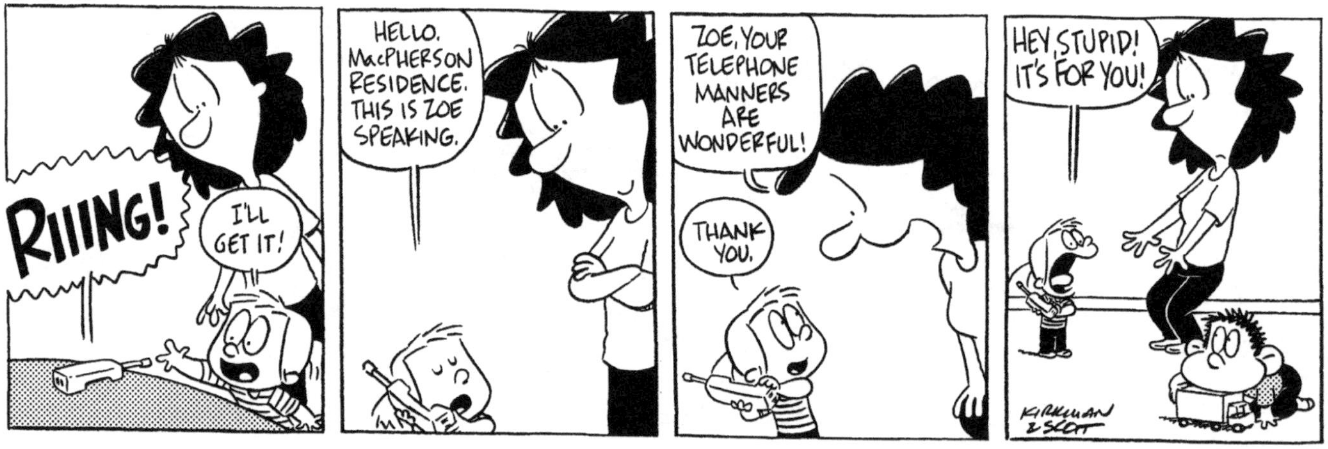
RIIING!
I'LL GET IT!
HELLO. MacPHERSON RESIDENCE. THIS IS ZOE SPEAKING.
ZOE, YOUR TELEPHONE MANNERS ARE WONDERFUL!
THANK YOU.
HEY, STUPID! IT'S FOR YOU!
KIRKMAN & SCOTT

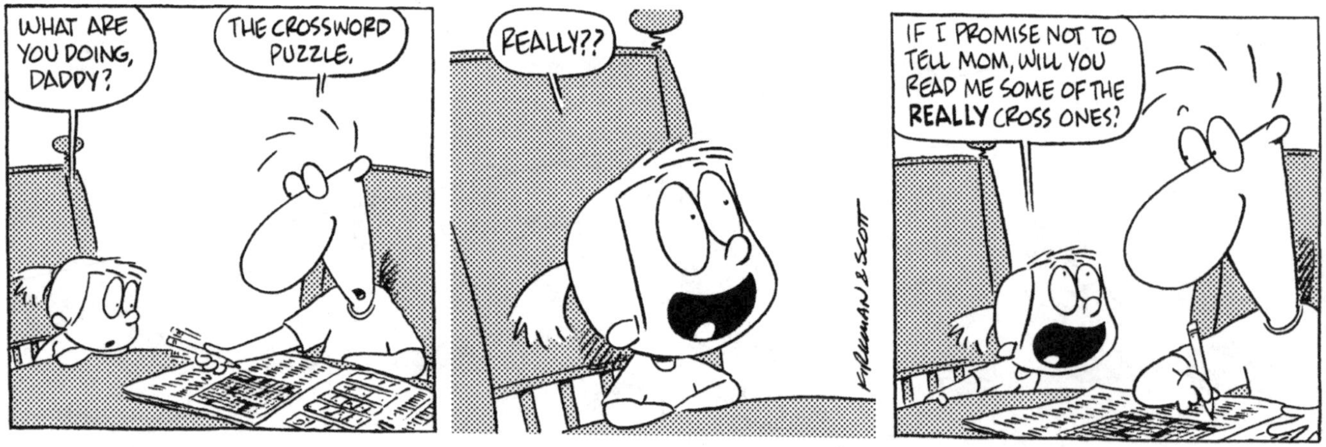
WHAT ARE YOU DOING, DADDY?
THE CROSSWORD PUZZLE.
REALLY??
KIRKMAN & SCOTT
IF I PROMISE NOT TO TELL MOM, WILL YOU READ ME SOME OF THE **REALLY** CROSS ONES?

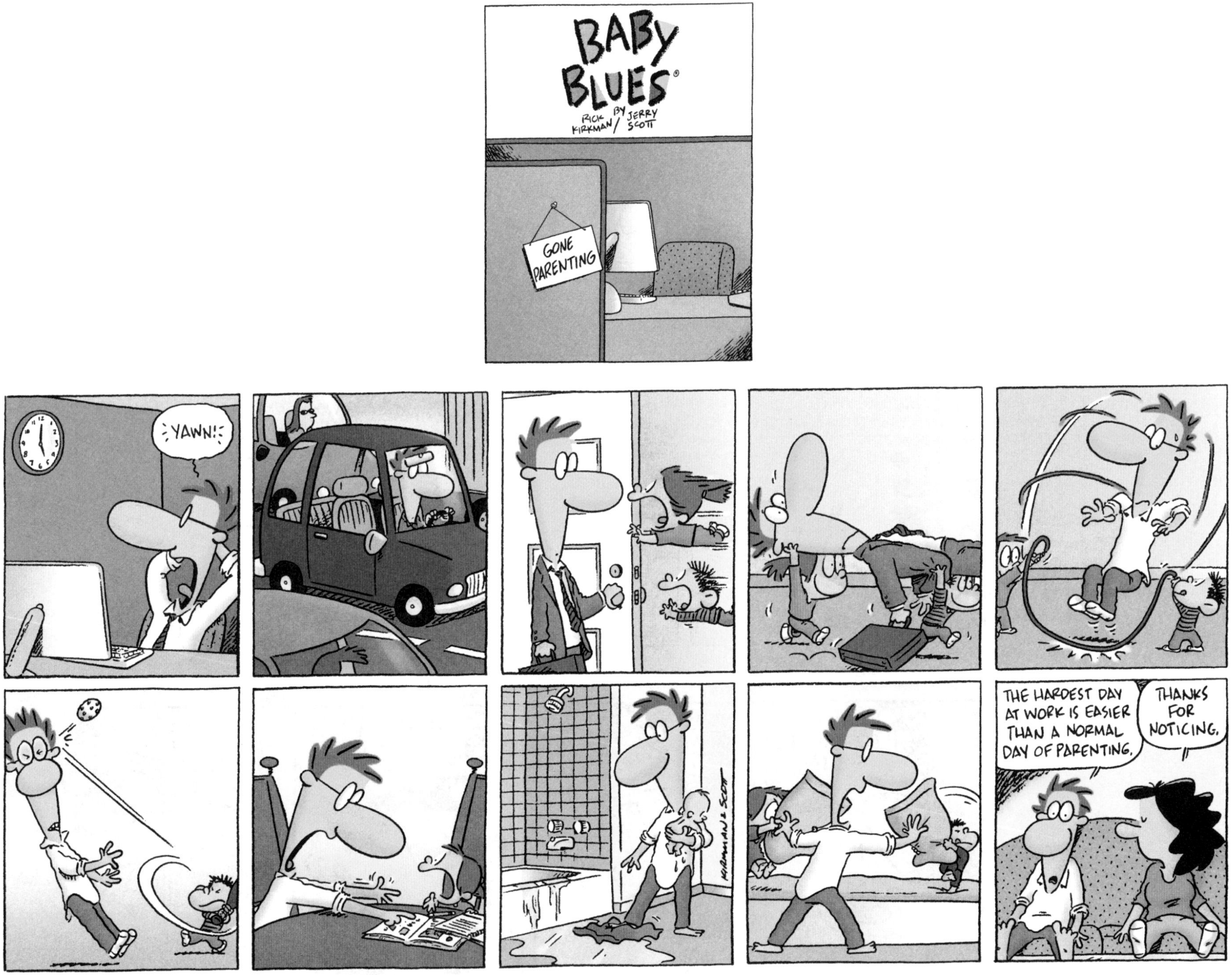
BABY BLUES®
RICK KIRKMAN / BY JERRY SCOTT
GONE PARENTING
YAWN!
KIRKMAN & SCOTT
THE HARDEST DAY AT WORK IS EASIER THAN A NORMAL DAY OF PARENTING.
THANKS FOR NOTICING.

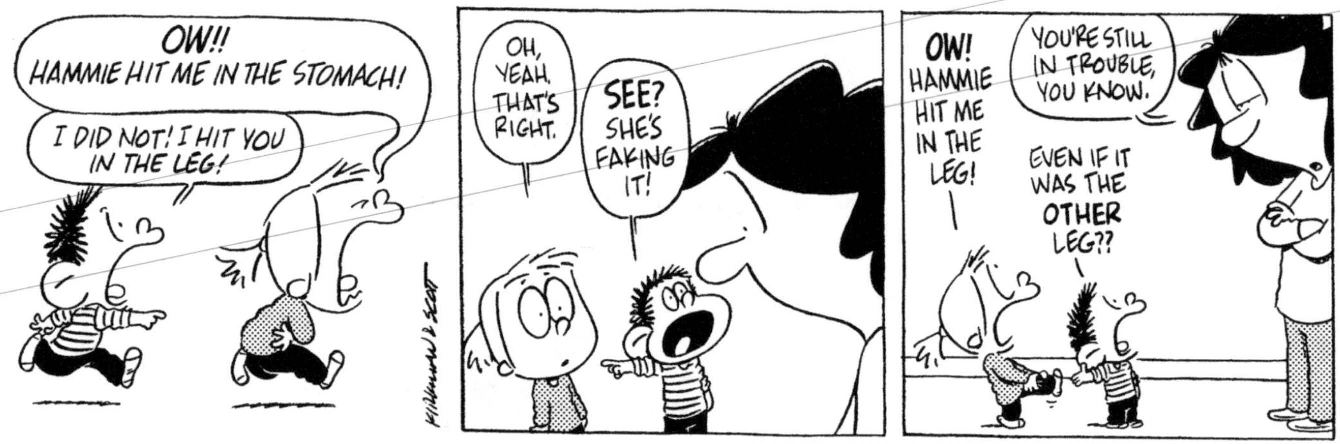
OW!!
HAMMIE HIT ME IN THE STOMACH!
I DID NOT! I HIT YOU IN THE LEG!
OH, YEAH. THAT'S RIGHT.
SEE? SHE'S FAKING IT!
OW! HAMMIE HIT ME IN THE LEG!
YOU'RE STILL IN TROUBLE, YOU KNOW.
EVEN IF IT WAS THE OTHER LEG??
KIRKMAN & SCOTT

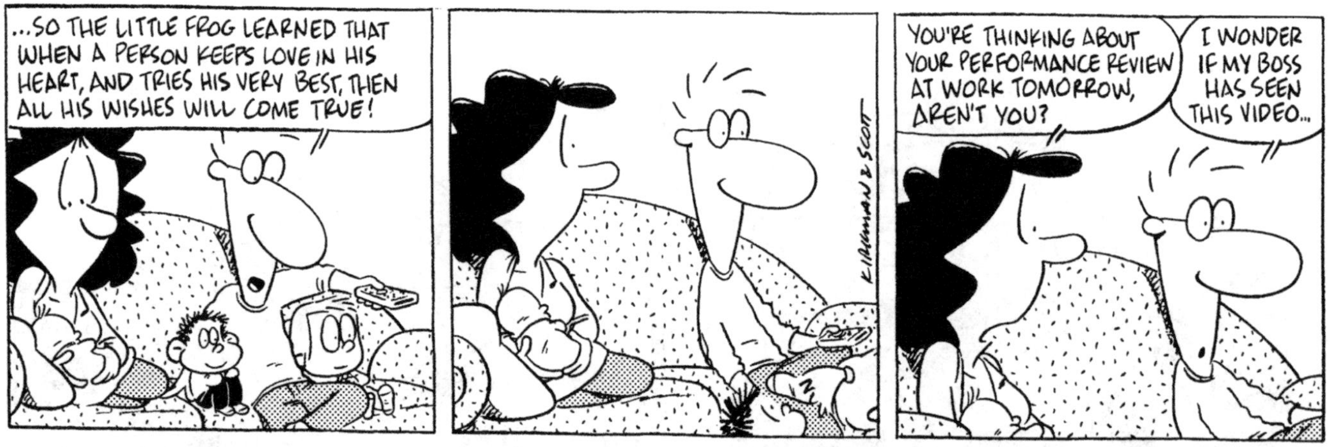
...SO THE LITTLE FROG LEARNED THAT WHEN A PERSON KEEPS LOVE IN HIS HEART, AND TRIES HIS VERY BEST, THEN ALL HIS WISHES WILL COME TRUE!
KIRKMAN & SCOTT
YOU'RE THINKING ABOUT YOUR PERFORMANCE REVIEW AT WORK TOMORROW, AREN'T YOU?
I WONDER IF MY BOSS HAS SEEN THIS VIDEO...

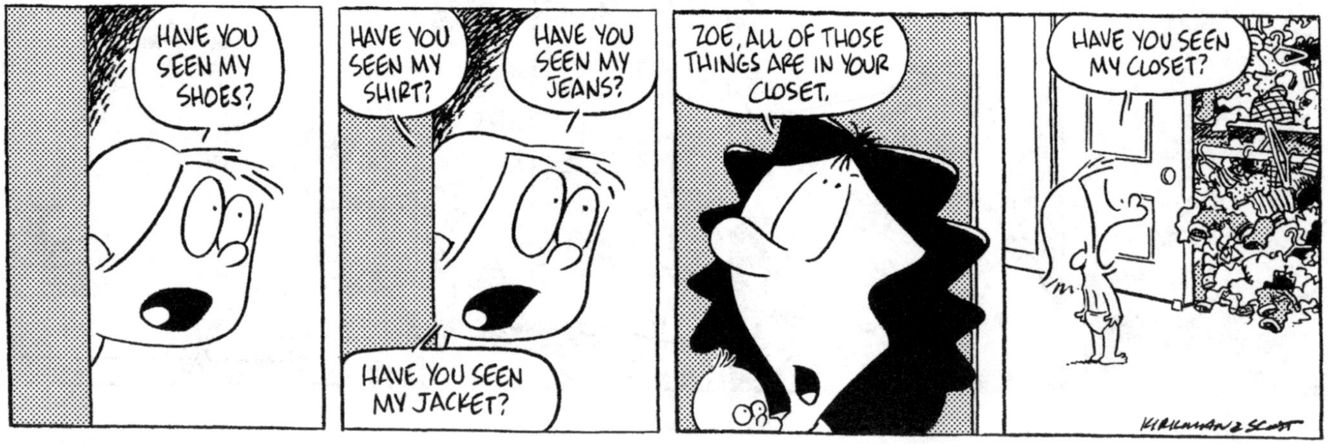
HAVE YOU SEEN MY SHOES?
HAVE YOU SEEN MY SHIRT?
HAVE YOU SEEN MY JEANS?
HAVE YOU SEEN MY JACKET?
ZOE, ALL OF THOSE THINGS ARE IN YOUR CLOSET.
HAVE YOU SEEN MY CLOSET?
KIRKMAN & SCOTT

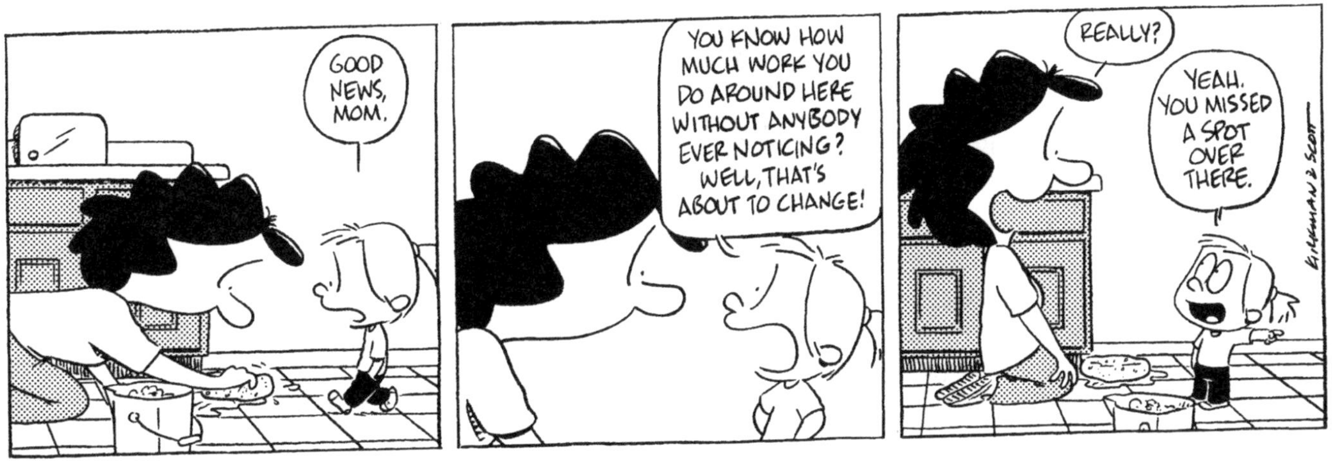
GOOD NEWS, MOM.
YOU KNOW HOW MUCH WORK YOU DO AROUND HERE WITHOUT ANYBODY EVER NOTICING? WELL, THAT'S ABOUT TO CHANGE!
REALLY?
YEAH. YOU MISSED A SPOT OVER THERE.

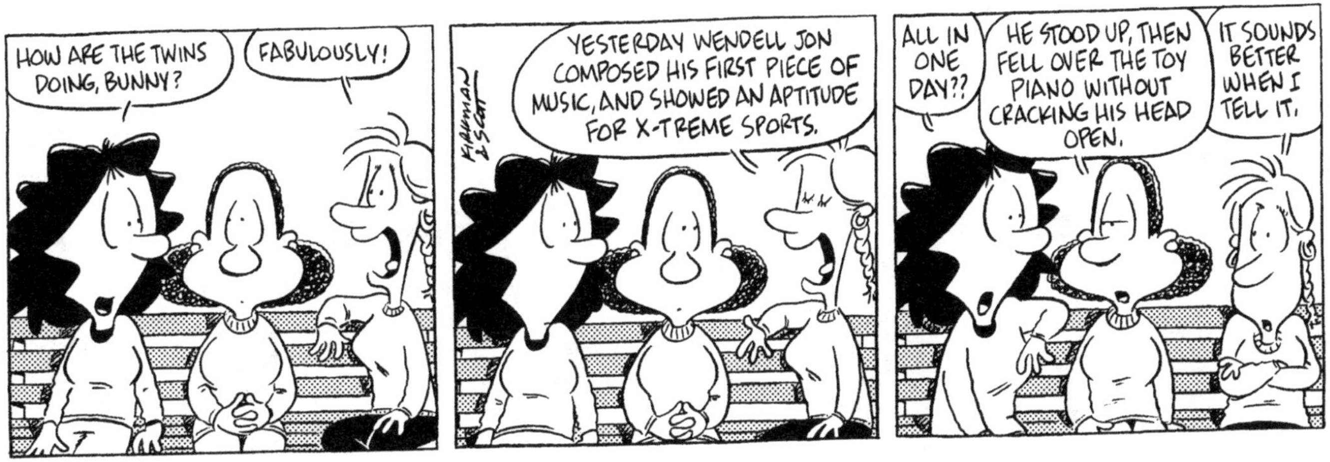
HOW ARE THE TWINS DOING, BUNNY?
FABULOUSLY!
YESTERDAY WENDELL JON COMPOSED HIS FIRST PIECE OF MUSIC, AND SHOWED AN APTITUDE FOR X-TREME SPORTS.
ALL IN ONE DAY??
HE STOOD UP, THEN FELL OVER THE TOY PIANO WITHOUT CRACKING HIS HEAD OPEN.
IT SOUNDS BETTER WHEN I TELL IT.

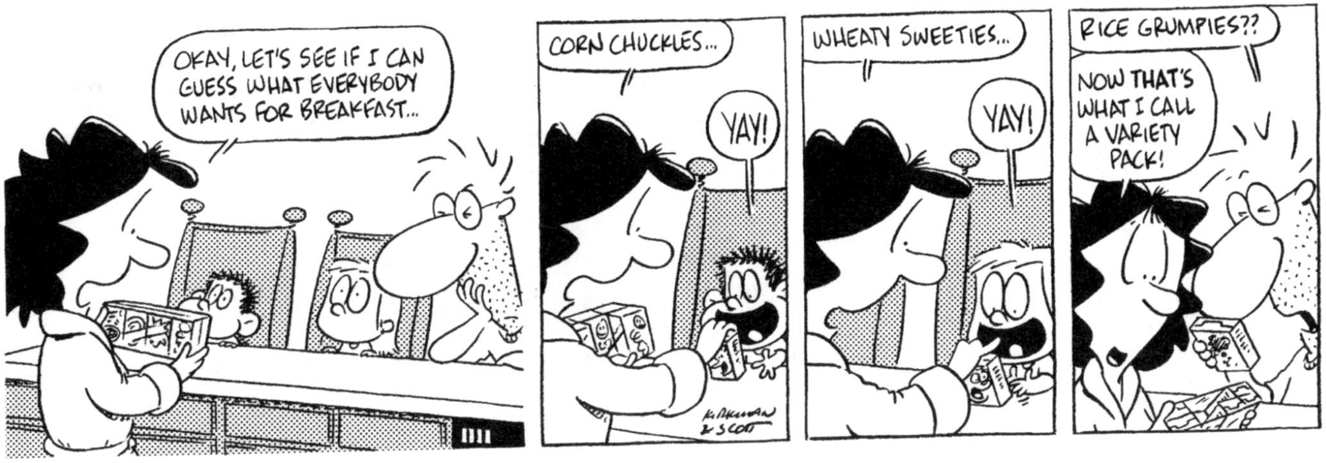
OKAY, LET'S SEE IF I CAN GUESS WHAT EVERYBODY WANTS FOR BREAKFAST...
CORN CHUCKLES...
YAY!
WHEATY SWEETIES...
YAY!
RICE GRUMPIES??
NOW THAT'S WHAT I CALL A VARIETY PACK!

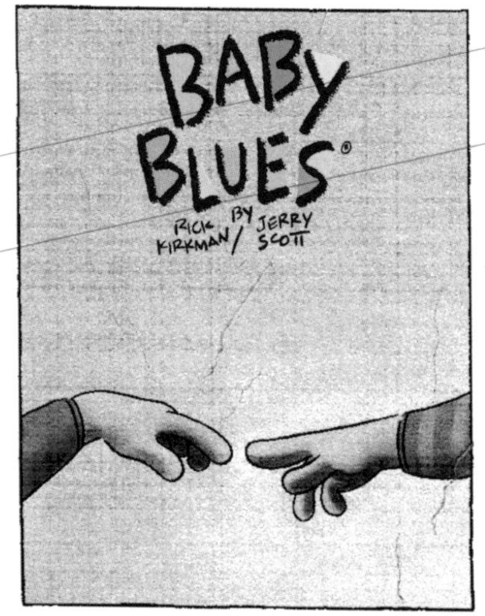
BABY BLUES®
BY RICK KIRKMAN / JERRY SCOTT

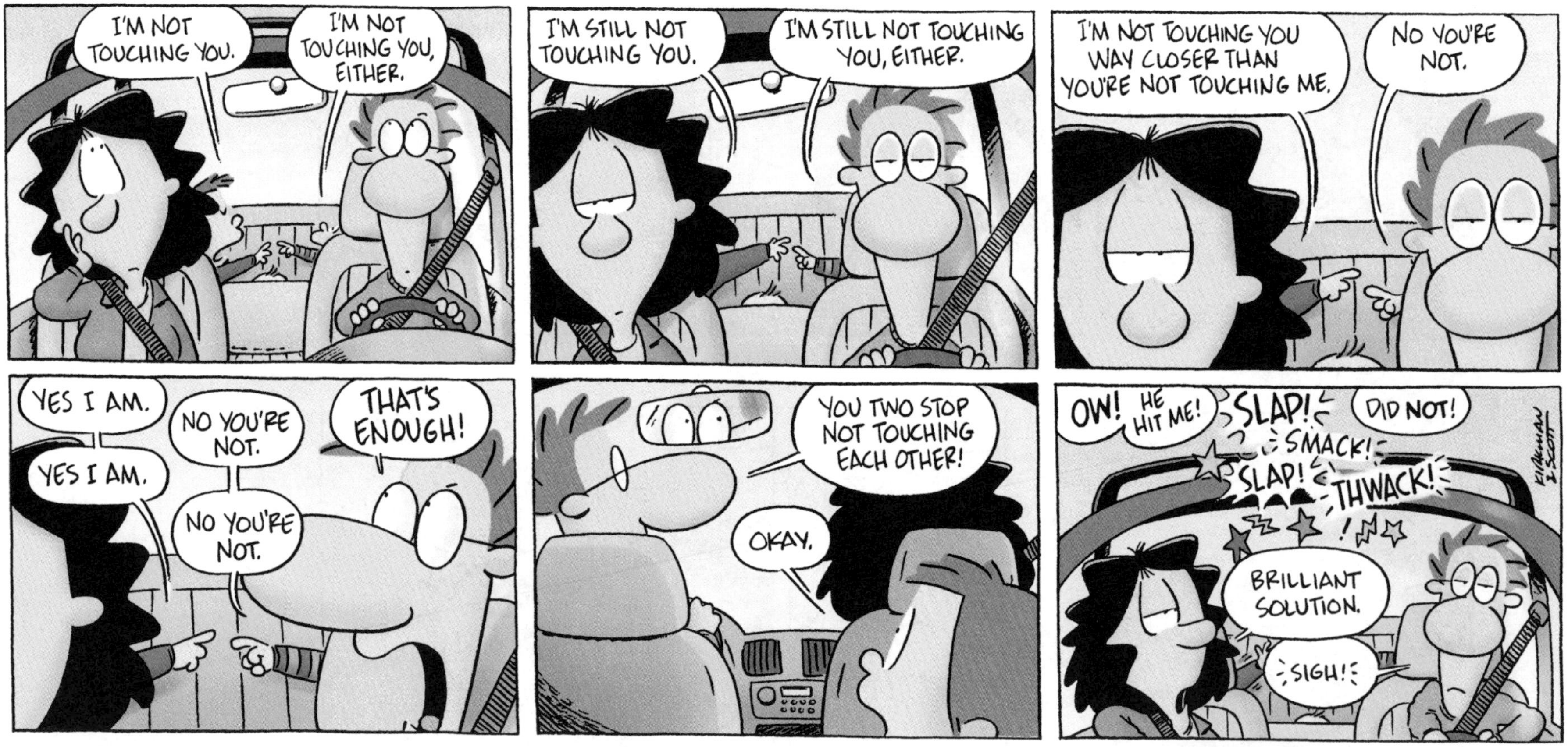
I'M NOT TOUCHING YOU.
I'M NOT TOUCHING YOU, EITHER.
I'M STILL NOT TOUCHING YOU.
I'M STILL NOT TOUCHING YOU, EITHER.
I'M NOT TOUCHING YOU WAY CLOSER THAN YOU'RE NOT TOUCHING ME.
NO YOU'RE NOT.
YES I AM.
NO YOU'RE NOT.
YES I AM.
NO YOU'RE NOT.
THAT'S ENOUGH!
YOU TWO STOP NOT TOUCHING EACH OTHER!
OKAY.
OW!
HE HIT ME!
SLAP!
DID NOT!
SMACK!
SLAP!
THWACK!
BRILLIANT SOLUTION.
SIGH!
KIRKMAN & SCOTT

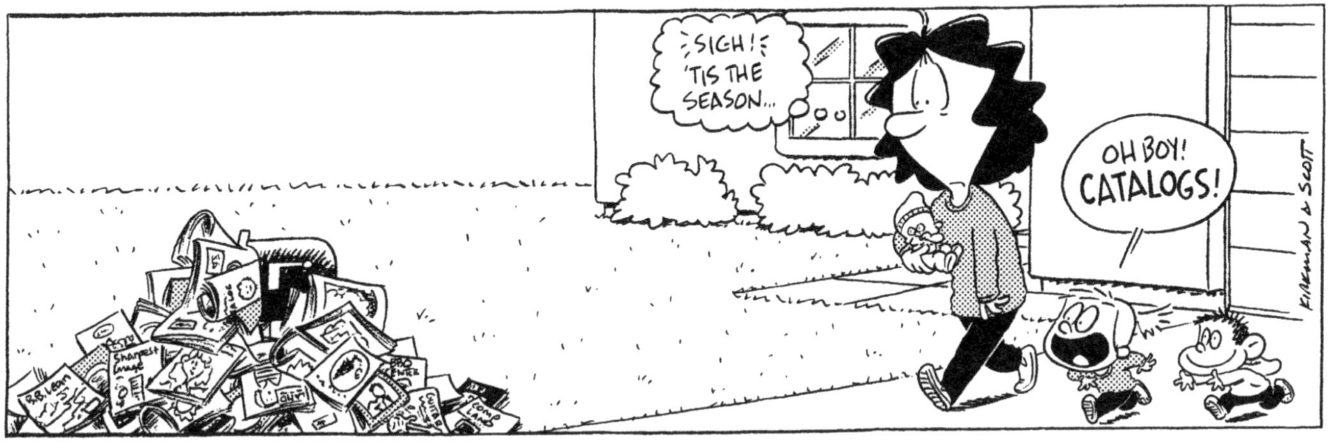
SIGH! 'TIS THE SEASON...
OH BOY! CATALOGS!
KIRKMAN & SCOTT

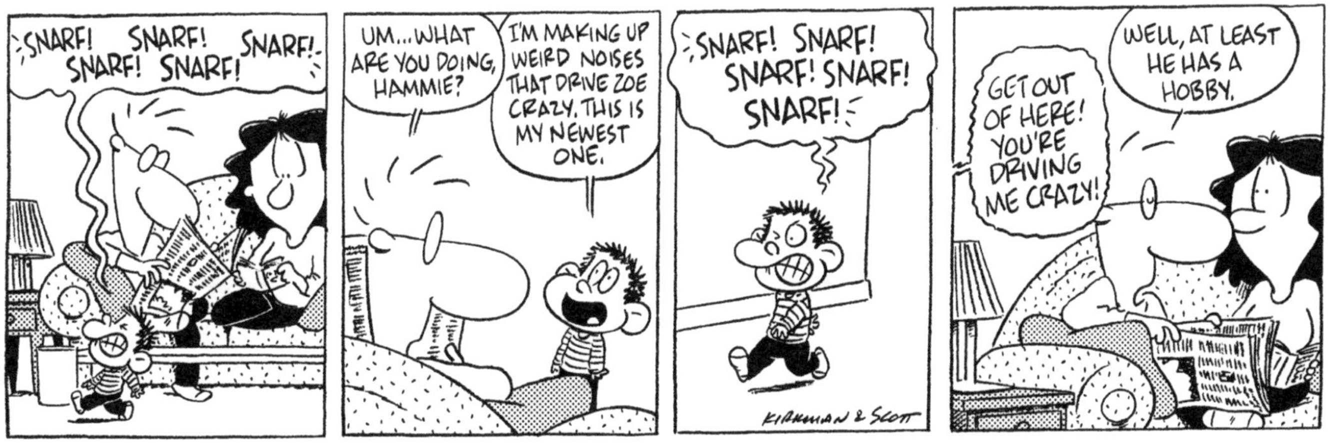
SNARF! SNARF! SNARF! SNARF! SNARF!
UM...WHAT ARE YOU DOING, HAMMIE?
I'M MAKING UP WEIRD NOISES THAT DRIVE ZOE CRAZY. THIS IS MY NEWEST ONE.
SNARF! SNARF! SNARF! SNARF! SNARF!
KIRKMAN & SCOTT
GET OUT OF HERE! YOU'RE DRIVING ME CRAZY!
WELL, AT LEAST HE HAS A HOBBY.

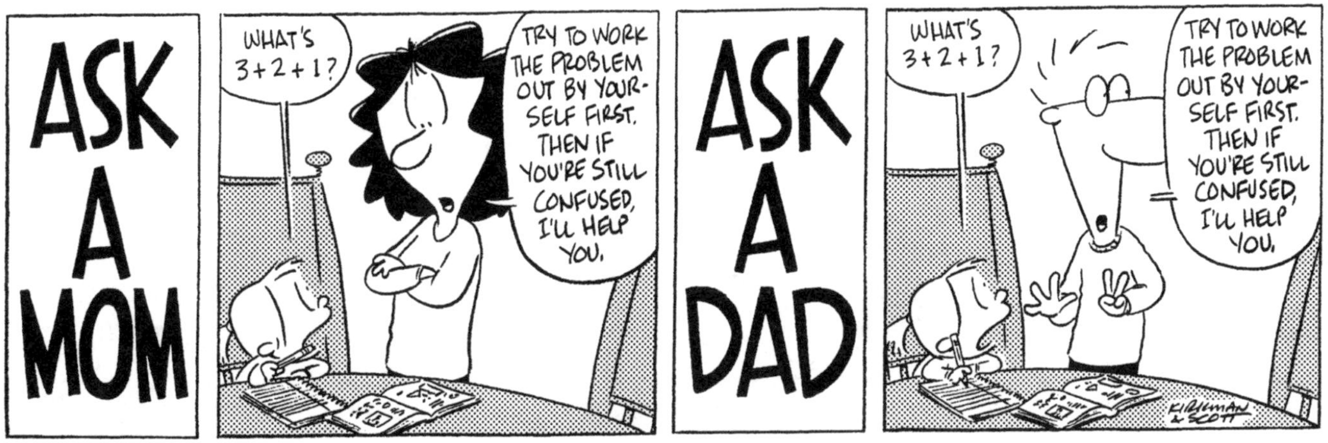
ASK A MOM
WHAT'S 3+2+1?
TRY TO WORK THE PROBLEM OUT BY YOURSELF FIRST. THEN IF YOU'RE STILL CONFUSED, I'LL HELP YOU.
ASK A DAD
WHAT'S 3+2+1?
TRY TO WORK THE PROBLEM OUT BY YOURSELF FIRST. THEN IF YOU'RE STILL CONFUSED, I'LL HELP YOU.
KIRKMAN & SCOTT

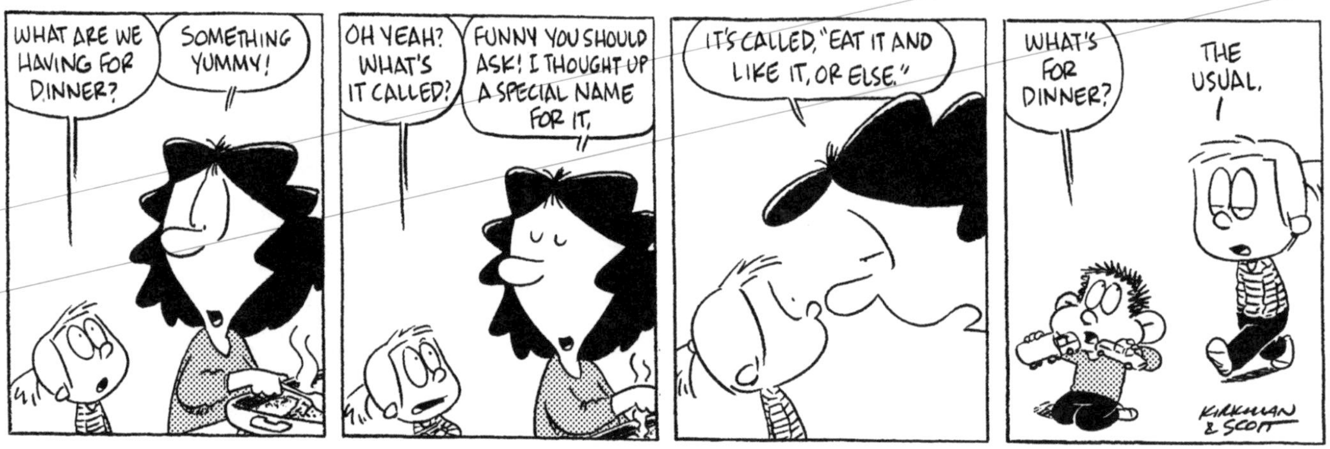
WHAT ARE WE HAVING FOR DINNER?
SOMETHING YUMMY!
OH YEAH? WHAT'S IT CALLED?
FUNNY YOU SHOULD ASK! I THOUGHT UP A SPECIAL NAME FOR IT.
IT'S CALLED, "EAT IT AND LIKE IT, OR ELSE."
WHAT'S FOR DINNER?
THE USUAL.
KIRKMAN & SCOTT

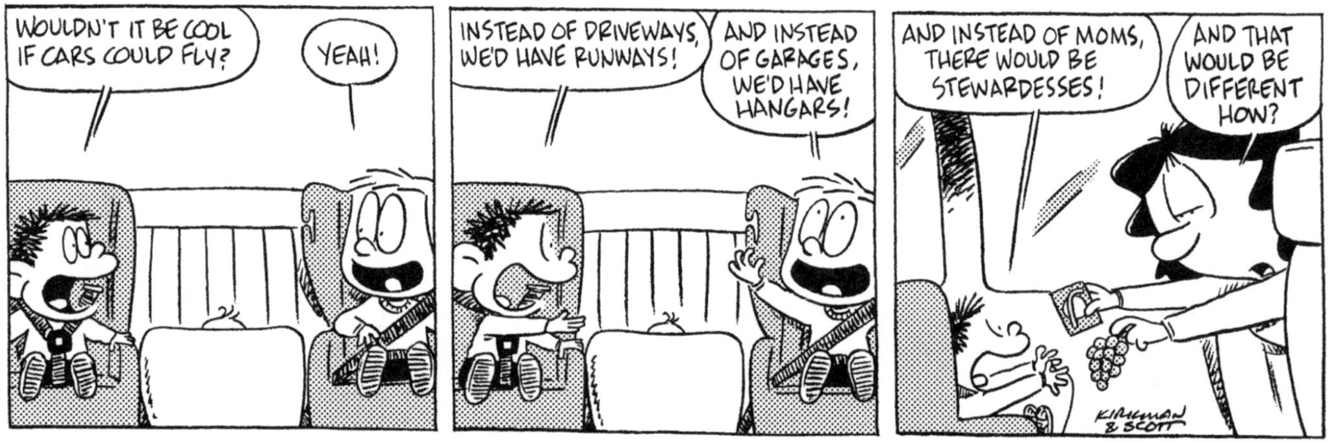
WOULDN'T IT BE COOL IF CARS COULD FLY?
YEAH!
INSTEAD OF DRIVEWAYS, WE'D HAVE RUNWAYS!
AND INSTEAD OF GARAGES, WE'D HAVE HANGARS!
AND INSTEAD OF MOMS, THERE WOULD BE STEWARDESSES!
AND THAT WOULD BE DIFFERENT HOW?
KIRKMAN & SCOTT

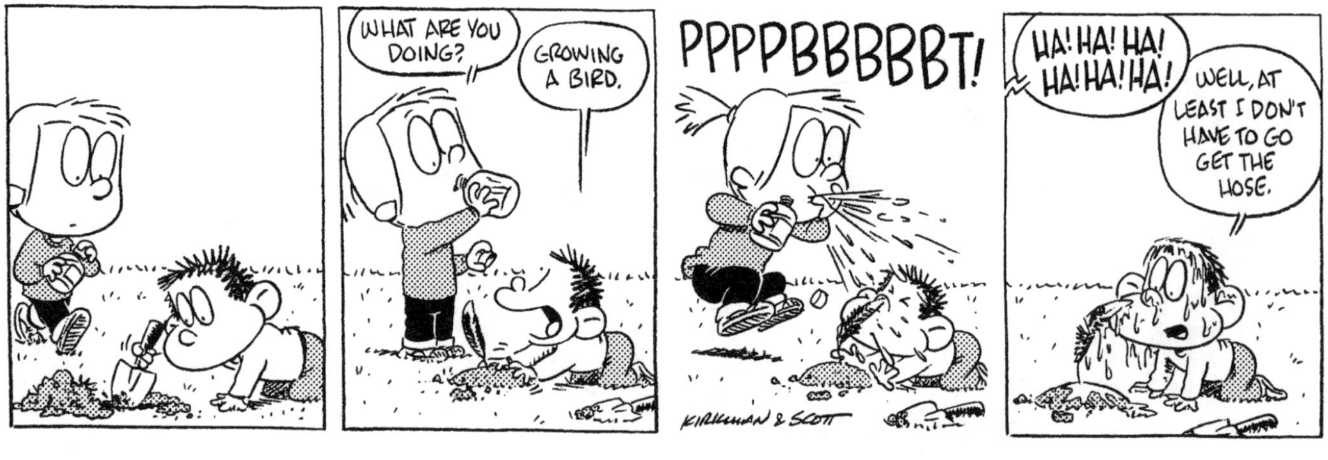
WHAT ARE YOU DOING?
GROWING A BIRD.
PPPPBBBBBT!
KIRKMAN & SCOTT
HA! HA! HA! HA! HA! HA!
WELL, AT LEAST I DON'T HAVE TO GO GET THE HOSE.

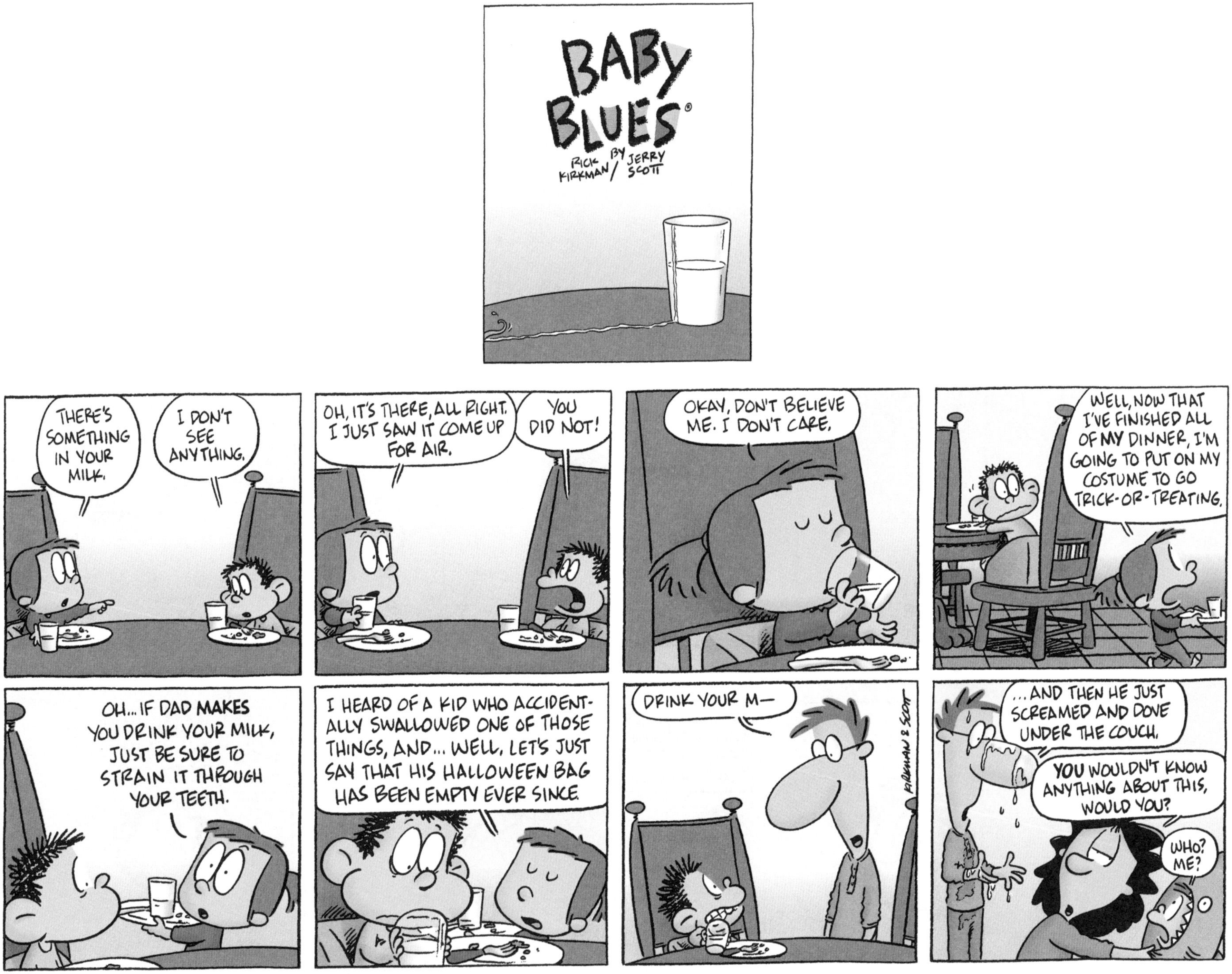
BABY BLUES®
BY RICK KIRKMAN / JERRY SCOTT
THERE'S SOMETHING IN YOUR MILK.
I DON'T SEE ANYTHING.
OH, IT'S THERE, ALL RIGHT. I JUST SAW IT COME UP FOR AIR.
YOU DID NOT!
OKAY, DON'T BELIEVE ME. I DON'T CARE.
WELL, NOW THAT I'VE FINISHED ALL OF MY DINNER, I'M GOING TO PUT ON MY COSTUME TO GO TRICK-OR-TREATING.
OH... IF DAD MAKES YOU DRINK YOUR MILK, JUST BE SURE TO STRAIN IT THROUGH YOUR TEETH.
I HEARD OF A KID WHO ACCIDENTALLY SWALLOWED ONE OF THOSE THINGS, AND... WELL, LET'S JUST SAY THAT HIS HALLOWEEN BAG HAS BEEN EMPTY EVER SINCE.
DRINK YOUR M—
KIRKMAN & SCOTT
...AND THEN HE JUST SCREAMED AND DOVE UNDER THE COUCH.
YOU WOULDN'T KNOW ANYTHING ABOUT THIS, WOULD YOU?
WHO? ME?

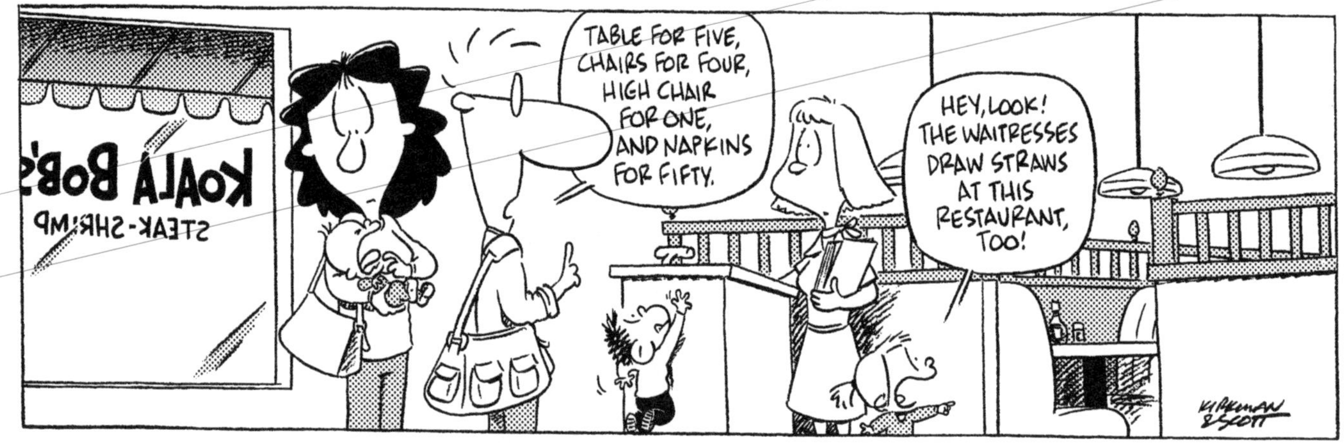
KOALA BOB'S
STEAK-SHRIMP
TABLE FOR FIVE, CHAIRS FOR FOUR, HIGH CHAIR FOR ONE, AND NAPKINS FOR FIFTY.
HEY, LOOK! THE WAITRESSES DRAW STRAWS AT THIS RESTAURANT, TOO!
KIRKMAN & SCOTT

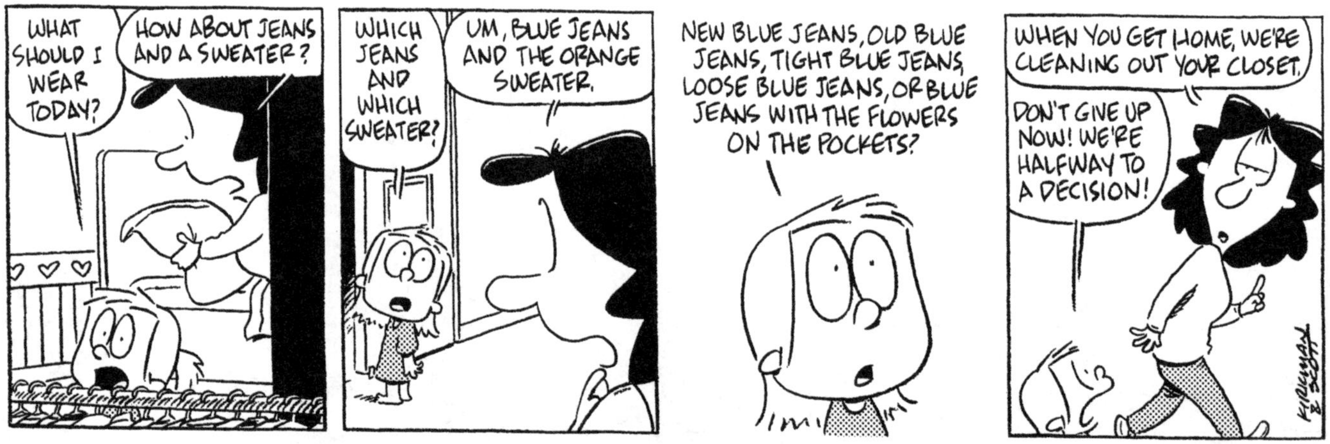
WHAT SHOULD I WEAR TODAY?
HOW ABOUT JEANS AND A SWEATER?
WHICH JEANS AND WHICH SWEATER?
UM, BLUE JEANS AND THE ORANGE SWEATER.
NEW BLUE JEANS, OLD BLUE JEANS, TIGHT BLUE JEANS, LOOSE BLUE JEANS, OR BLUE JEANS WITH THE FLOWERS ON THE POCKETS?
WHEN YOU GET HOME, WE'RE CLEANING OUT YOUR CLOSET.
DON'T GIVE UP NOW! WE'RE HALFWAY TO A DECISION!
KIRKMAN & SCOTT

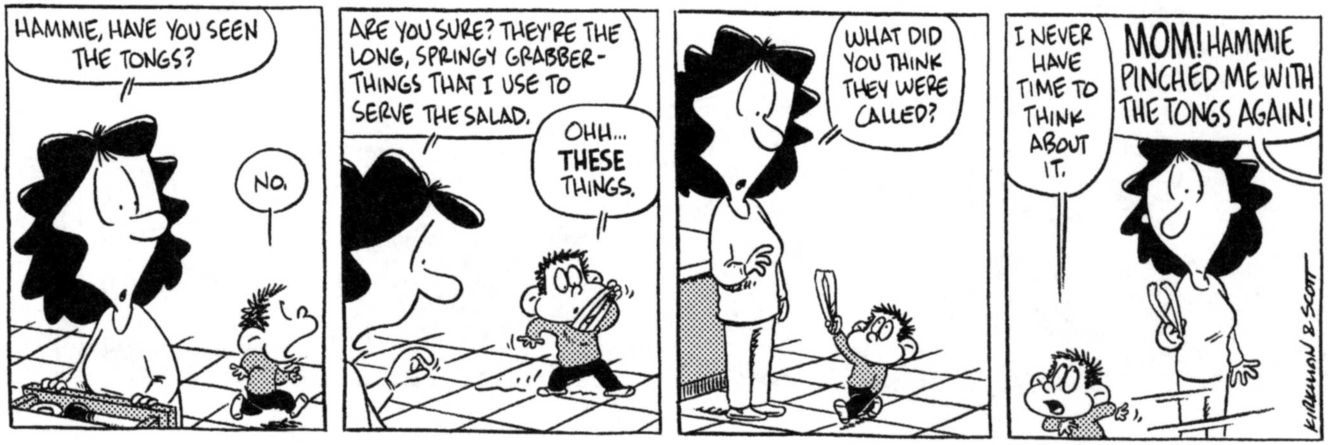
HAMMIE, HAVE YOU SEEN THE TONGS?
NO.
ARE YOU SURE? THEY'RE THE LONG, SPRINGY GRABBER-THINGS THAT I USE TO SERVE THE SALAD.
OHH... THESE THINGS.
WHAT DID YOU THINK THEY WERE CALLED?
I NEVER HAVE TIME TO THINK ABOUT IT.
MOM! HAMMIE PINCHED ME WITH THE TONGS AGAIN!
KIRKMAN & SCOTT

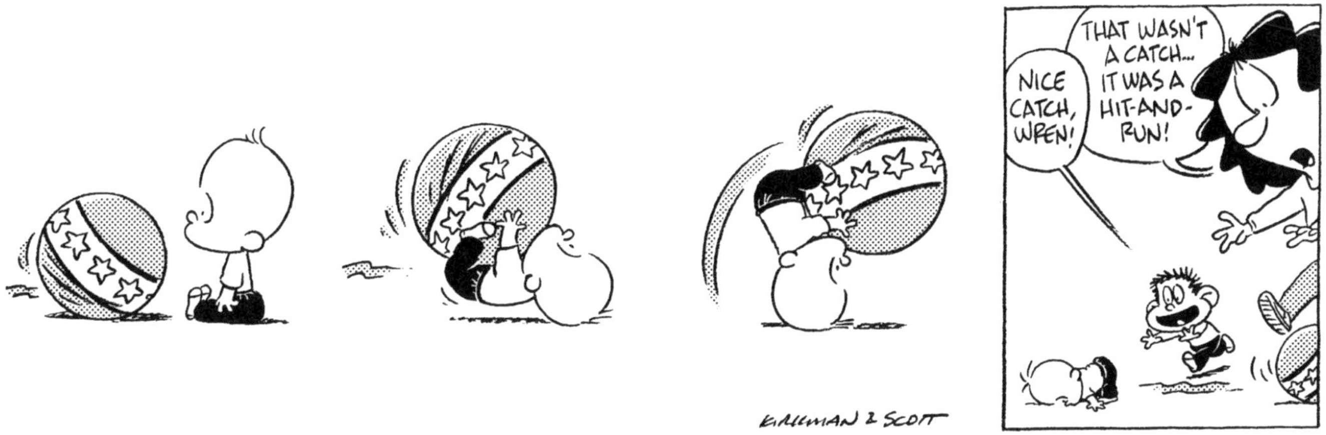
KIRKMAN & SCOTT
NICE CATCH, WREN!
THAT WASN'T A CATCH... IT WAS A HIT-AND-RUN!

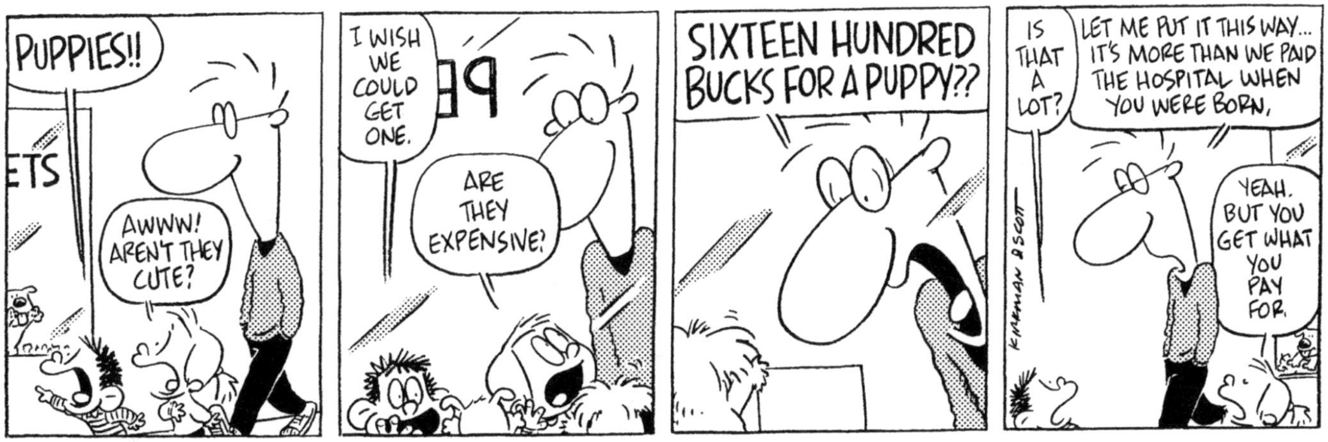
PUPPIES!!
ETS
AWWW! AREN'T THEY CUTE?
I WISH WE COULD GET ONE.
PE
ARE THEY EXPENSIVE?
SIXTEEN HUNDRED BUCKS FOR A PUPPY??
KIRKMAN & SCOTT
IS THAT A LOT?
LET ME PUT IT THIS WAY... IT'S MORE THAN WE PAID THE HOSPITAL WHEN YOU WERE BORN.
YEAH. BUT YOU GET WHAT YOU PAY FOR.

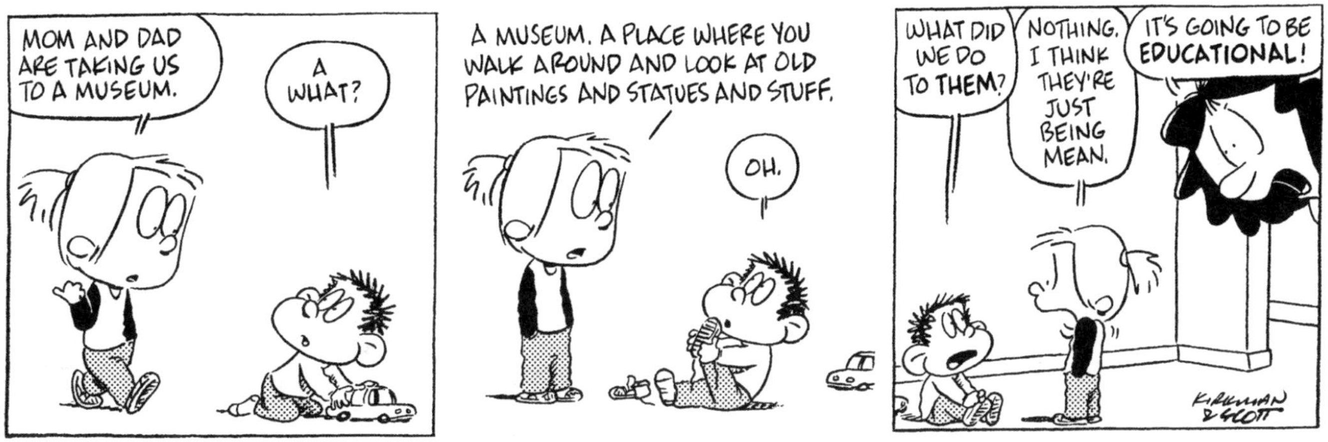
MOM AND DAD ARE TAKING US TO A MUSEUM.
A WHAT?
A MUSEUM. A PLACE WHERE YOU WALK AROUND AND LOOK AT OLD PAINTINGS AND STATUES AND STUFF.
OH.
WHAT DID WE DO TO THEM?
NOTHING. I THINK THEY'RE JUST BEING MEAN.
IT'S GOING TO BE EDUCATIONAL!
KIRKMAN & SCOTT

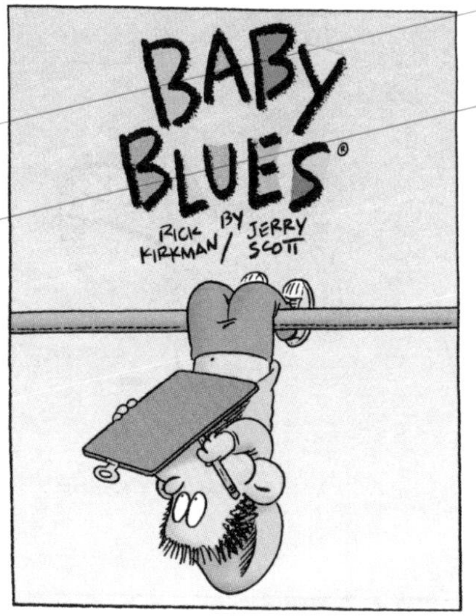
BABY BLUES®
BY
RICK KIRKMAN / JERRY SCOTT

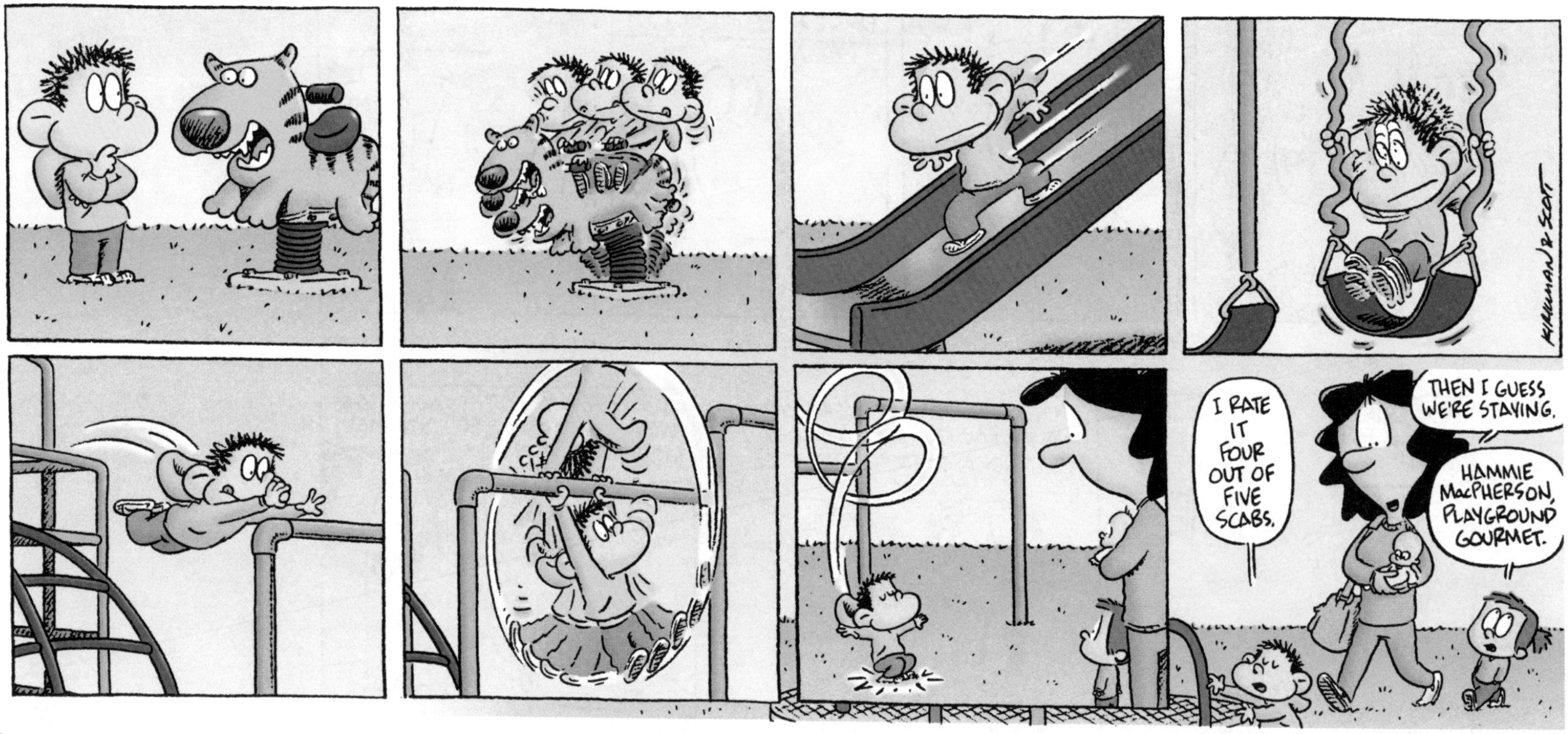
KIRKMAN & SCOTT
I RATE IT FOUR OUT OF FIVE SCABS.
THEN I GUESS WE'RE STAYING.
HAMMIE MacPHERSON, PLAYGROUND GOURMET.

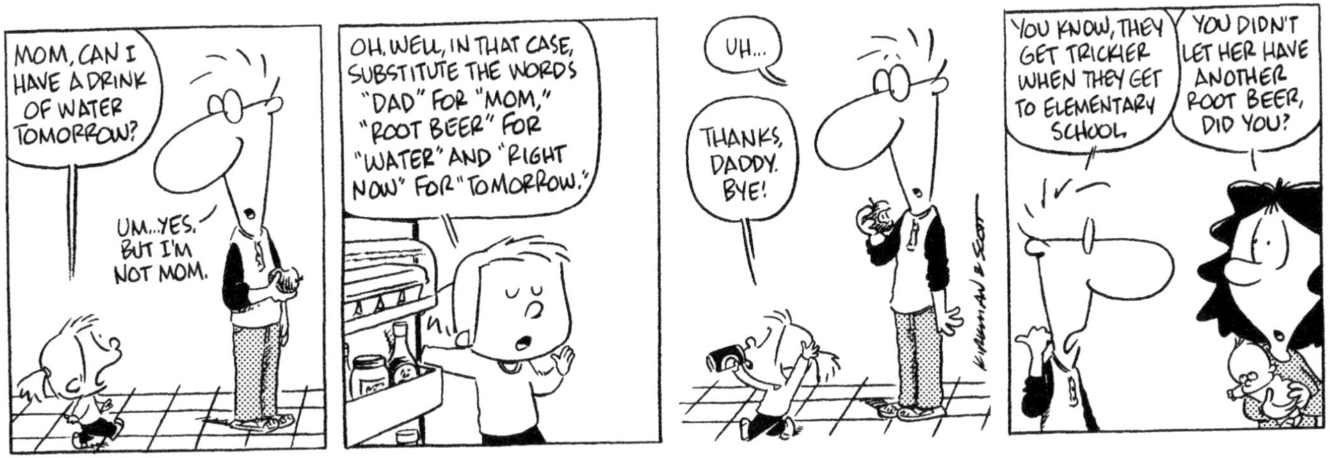
MOM, CAN I HAVE A DRINK OF WATER TOMORROW?
UM...YES. BUT I'M NOT MOM.
OH, WELL, IN THAT CASE, SUBSTITUTE THE WORDS "DAD" FOR "MOM," "ROOT BEER" FOR "WATER" AND "RIGHT NOW" FOR "TOMORROW."
UH...
THANKS, DADDY. BYE!
YOU KNOW, THEY GET TRICKIER WHEN THEY GET TO ELEMENTARY SCHOOL.
YOU DIDN'T LET HER HAVE ANOTHER ROOT BEER, DID YOU?

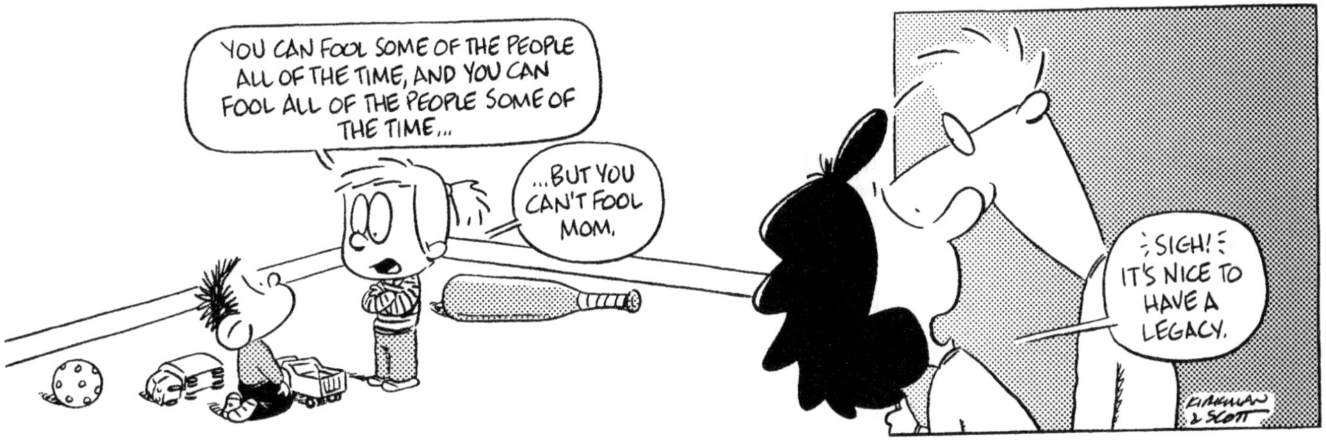
YOU CAN FOOL SOME OF THE PEOPLE ALL OF THE TIME, AND YOU CAN FOOL ALL OF THE PEOPLE SOME OF THE TIME...
...BUT YOU CAN'T FOOL MOM.
SIGH! IT'S NICE TO HAVE A LEGACY.

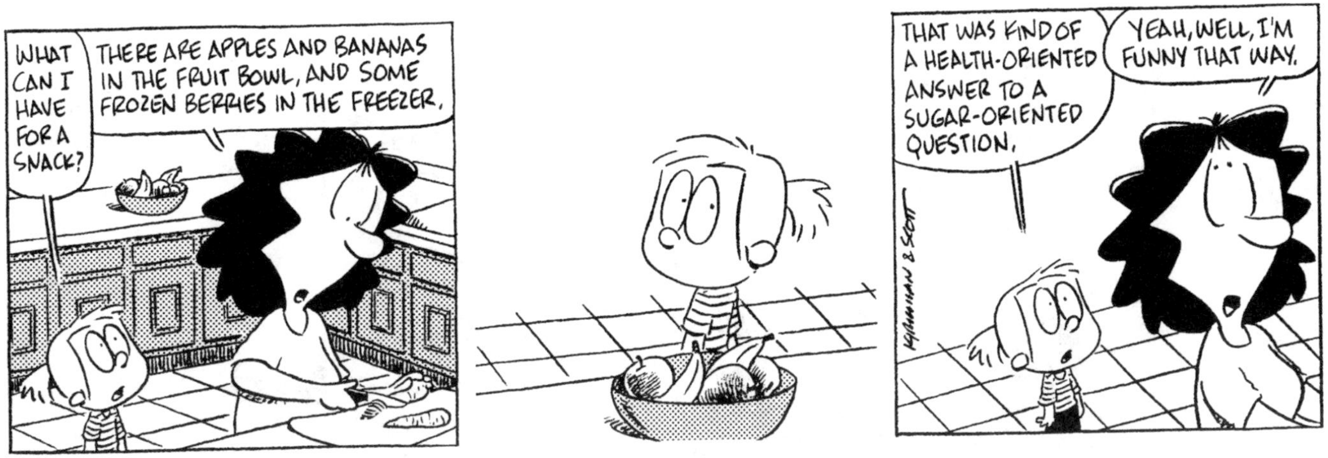
WHAT CAN I HAVE FOR A SNACK?
THERE ARE APPLES AND BANANAS IN THE FRUIT BOWL, AND SOME FROZEN BERRIES IN THE FREEZER.
THAT WAS KIND OF A HEALTH-ORIENTED ANSWER TO A SUGAR-ORIENTED QUESTION.
YEAH, WELL, I'M FUNNY THAT WAY.

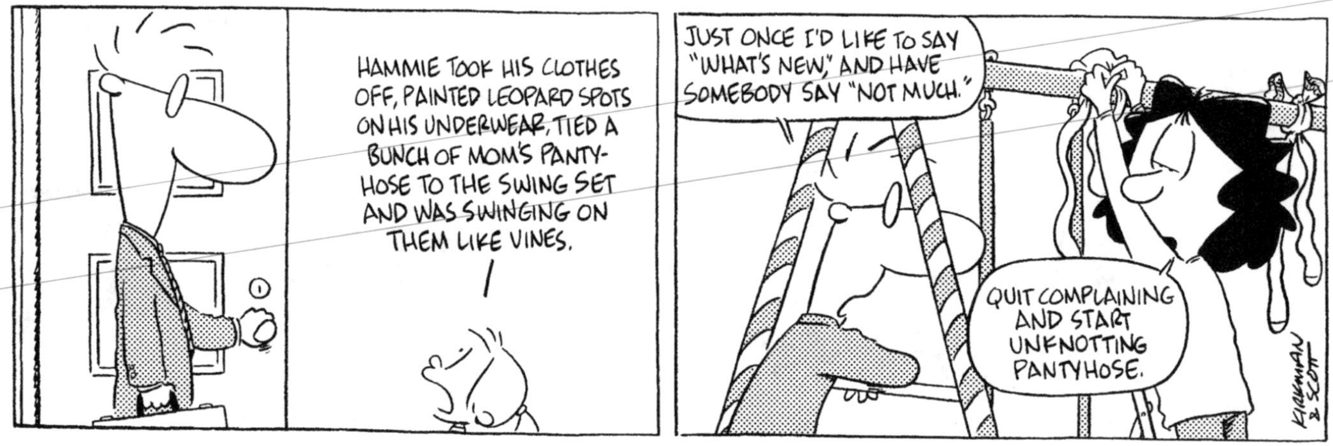
HAMMIE TOOK HIS CLOTHES OFF, PAINTED LEOPARD SPOTS ON HIS UNDERWEAR, TIED A BUNCH OF MOM'S PANTY-HOSE TO THE SWING SET AND WAS SWINGING ON THEM LIKE VINES.
JUST ONCE I'D LIKE TO SAY "WHAT'S NEW," AND HAVE SOMEBODY SAY "NOT MUCH."
QUIT COMPLAINING AND START UNKNOTTING PANTYHOSE.
KIRKMAN & SCOTT

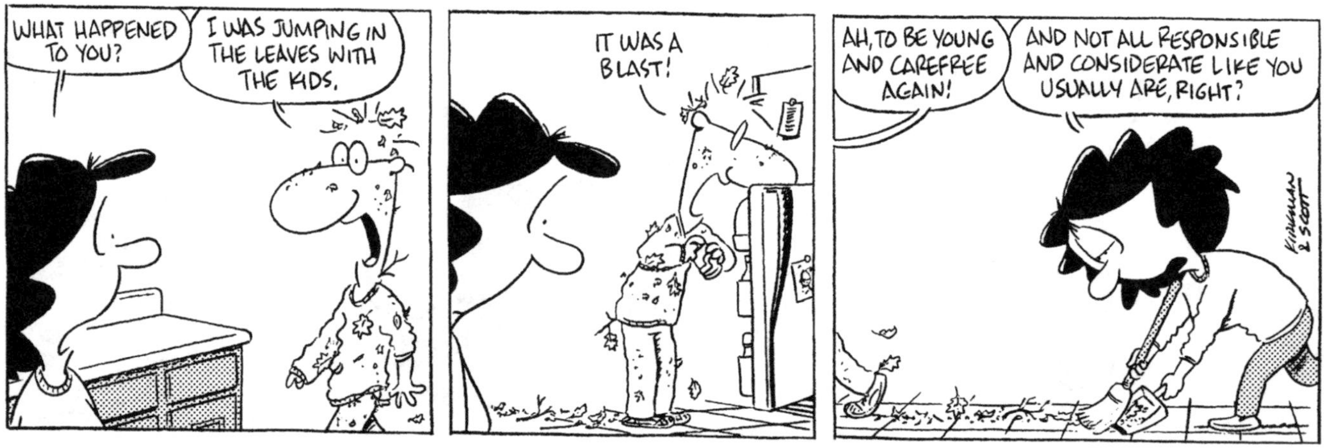
WHAT HAPPENED TO YOU?
I WAS JUMPING IN THE LEAVES WITH THE KIDS.
IT WAS A BLAST!
AH, TO BE YOUNG AND CAREFREE AGAIN!
AND NOT ALL RESPONSIBLE AND CONSIDERATE LIKE YOU USUALLY ARE, RIGHT?
KIRKMAN & SCOTT

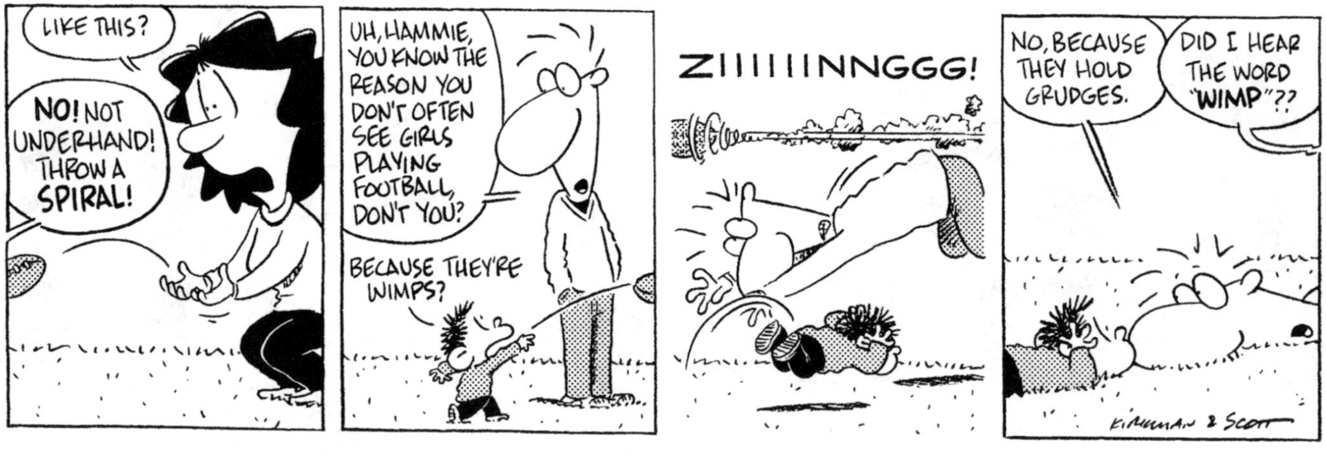
LIKE THIS?
NO! NOT UNDERHAND! THROW A SPIRAL!
UH, HAMMIE, YOU KNOW THE REASON YOU DON'T OFTEN SEE GIRLS PLAYING FOOTBALL, DON'T YOU?
BECAUSE THEY'RE WIMPS?
ZIIIIIINNGGG!
NO, BECAUSE THEY HOLD GRUDGES.
DID I HEAR THE WORD "WIMP"??
KIRKMAN & SCOTT

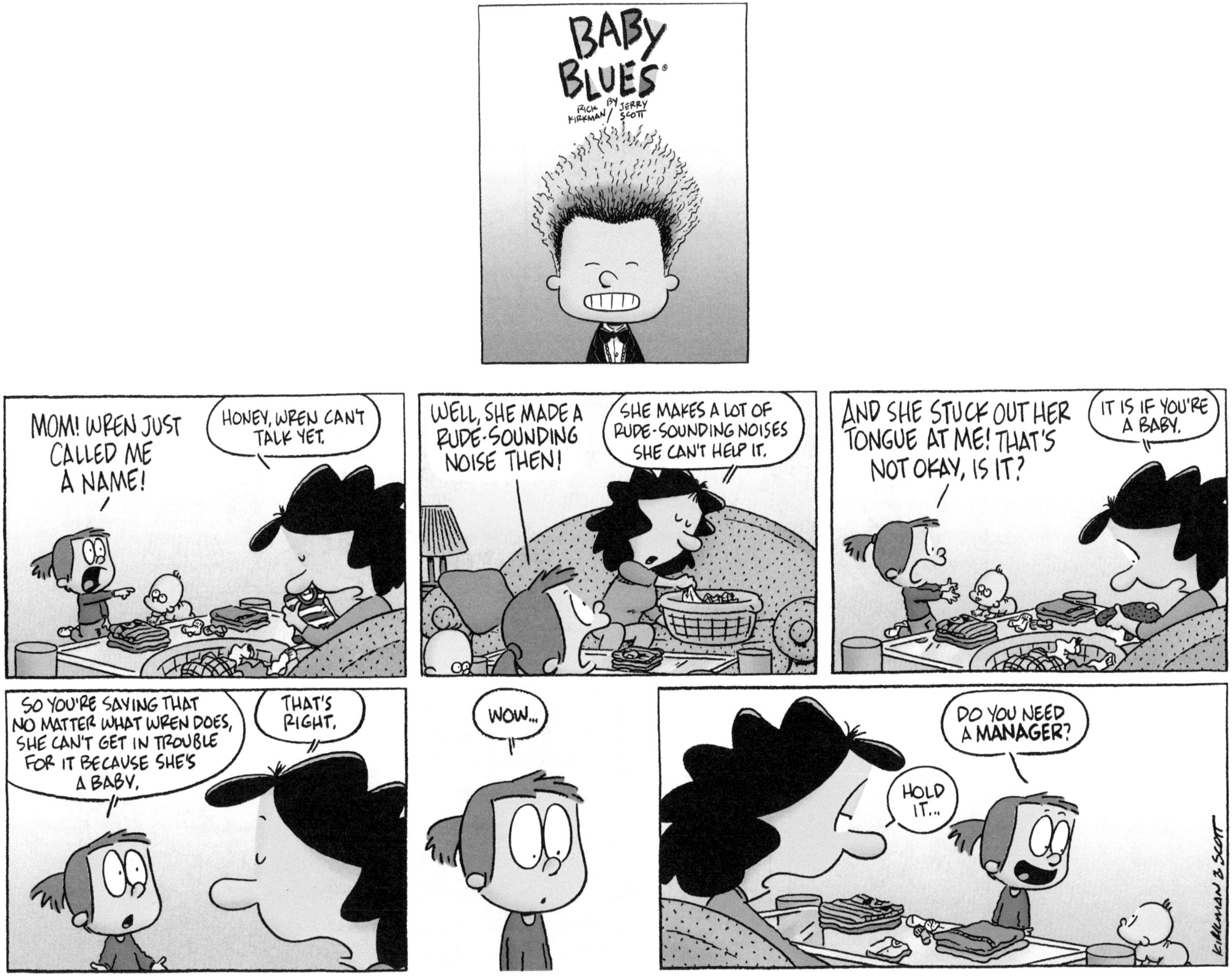
BABY BLUES®
BY RICK KIRKMAN / JERRY SCOTT
MOM! WREN JUST CALLED ME A NAME!
HONEY, WREN CAN'T TALK YET.
WELL, SHE MADE A RUDE-SOUNDING NOISE THEN!
SHE MAKES A LOT OF RUDE-SOUNDING NOISES SHE CAN'T HELP IT.
AND SHE STUCK OUT HER TONGUE AT ME! THAT'S NOT OKAY, IS IT?
IT IS IF YOU'RE A BABY.
SO YOU'RE SAYING THAT NO MATTER WHAT WREN DOES, SHE CAN'T GET IN TROUBLE FOR IT BECAUSE SHE'S A BABY.
THAT'S RIGHT.
WOW...
DO YOU NEED A MANAGER?
HOLD IT...
KIRKMAN & SCOTT

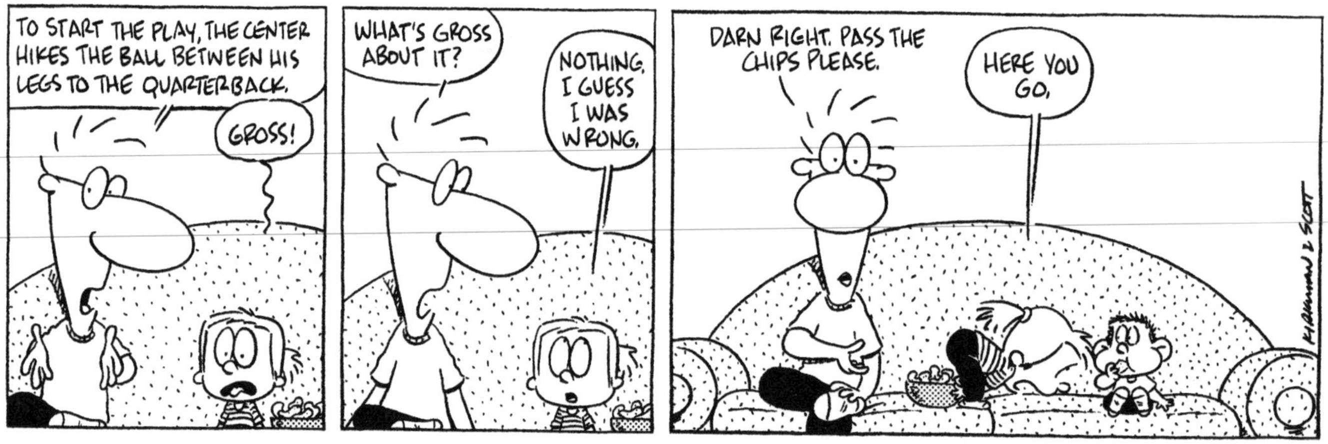
TO START THE PLAY, THE CENTER HIKES THE BALL BETWEEN HIS LEGS TO THE QUARTERBACK.
GROSS!
WHAT'S GROSS ABOUT IT?
NOTHING. I GUESS I WAS WRONG.
DARN RIGHT. PASS THE CHIPS PLEASE.
HERE YOU GO.
KIRKMAN & SCOTT

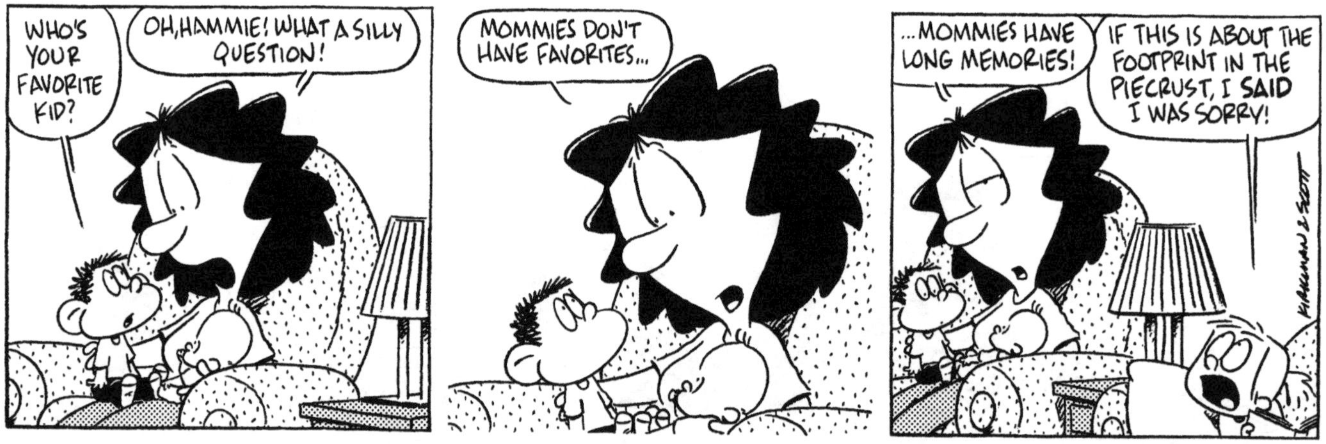
WHO'S YOUR FAVORITE KID?
OH, HAMMIE! WHAT A SILLY QUESTION!
MOMMIES DON'T HAVE FAVORITES...
...MOMMIES HAVE LONG MEMORIES!
IF THIS IS ABOUT THE FOOTPRINT IN THE PIECRUST, I SAID I WAS SORRY!
KIRKMAN & SCOTT

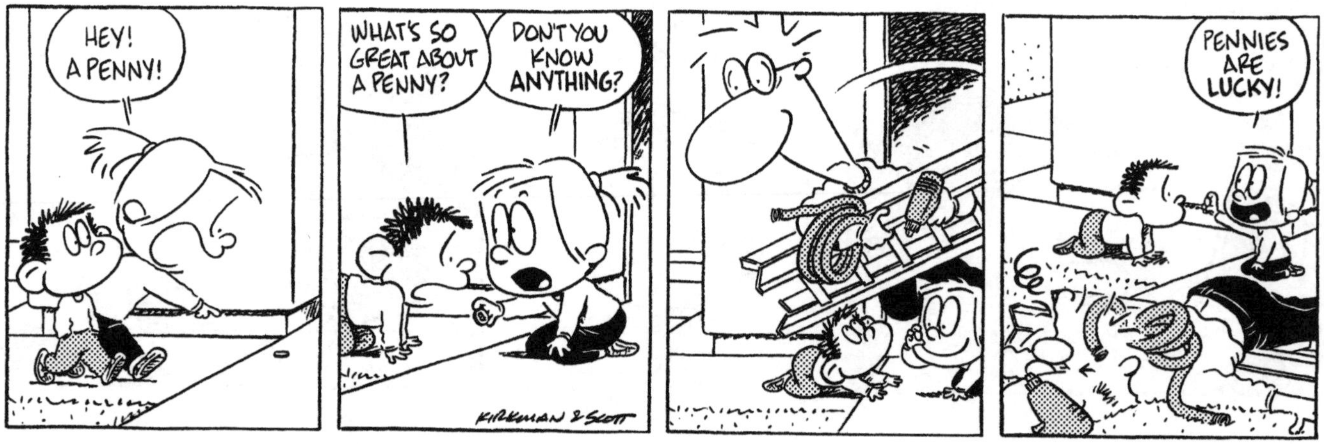
HEY! A PENNY!
WHAT'S SO GREAT ABOUT A PENNY?
DON'T YOU KNOW ANYTHING?
PENNIES ARE LUCKY!
KIRKMAN & SCOTT

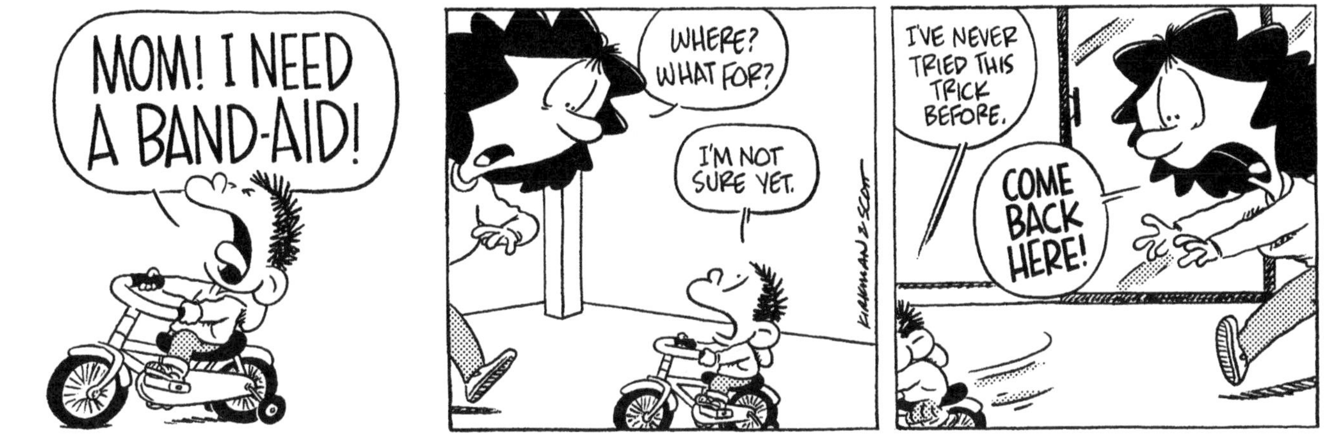
MOM! I NEED A BAND-AID!
WHERE? WHAT FOR?
I'M NOT SURE YET.
KIRKMAN & SCOTT
I'VE NEVER TRIED THIS TRICK BEFORE.
COME BACK HERE!

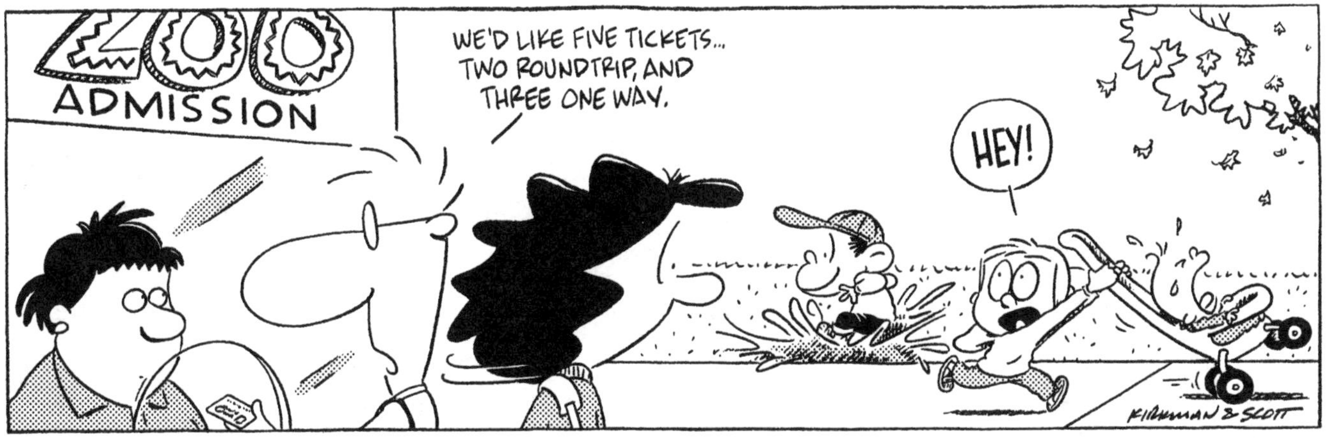
ZOO ADMISSION
WE'D LIKE FIVE TICKETS... TWO ROUNDTRIP, AND THREE ONE WAY.
HEY!
KIRKMAN & SCOTT

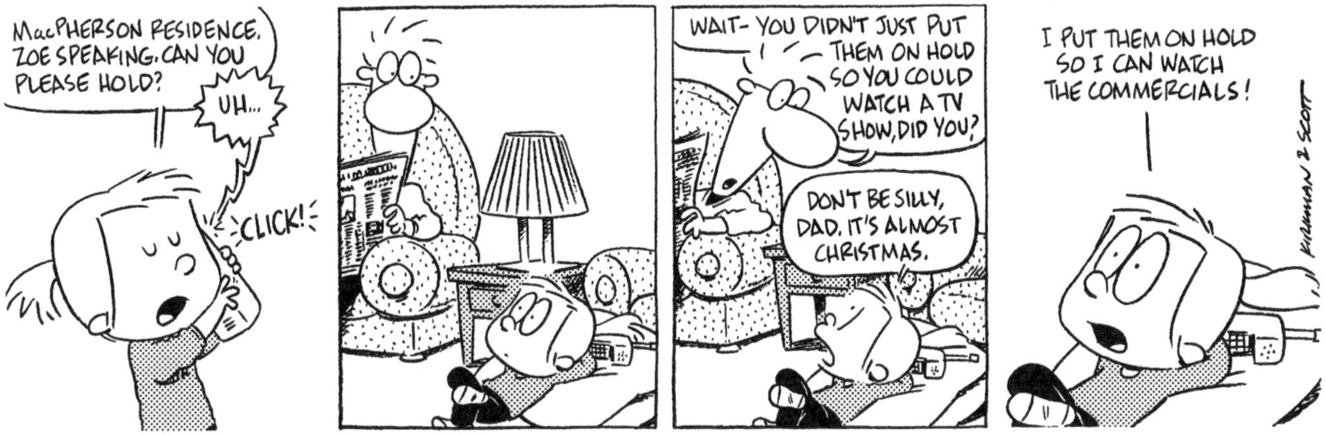
MacPHERSON RESIDENCE. ZOE SPEAKING. CAN YOU PLEASE HOLD?
UH...
CLICK!
WAIT- YOU DIDN'T JUST PUT THEM ON HOLD SO YOU COULD WATCH A TV SHOW, DID YOU?
DON'T BE SILLY, DAD. IT'S ALMOST CHRISTMAS.
I PUT THEM ON HOLD SO I CAN WATCH THE COMMERCIALS!
KIRKMAN & SCOTT

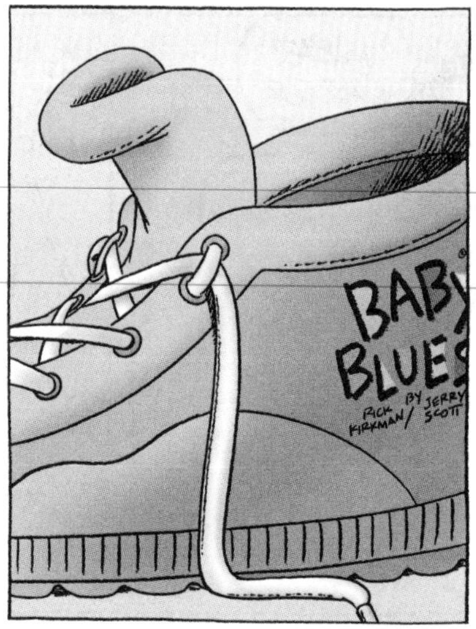
BABY BLUES
RICK KIRKMAN / BY JERRY SCOTT

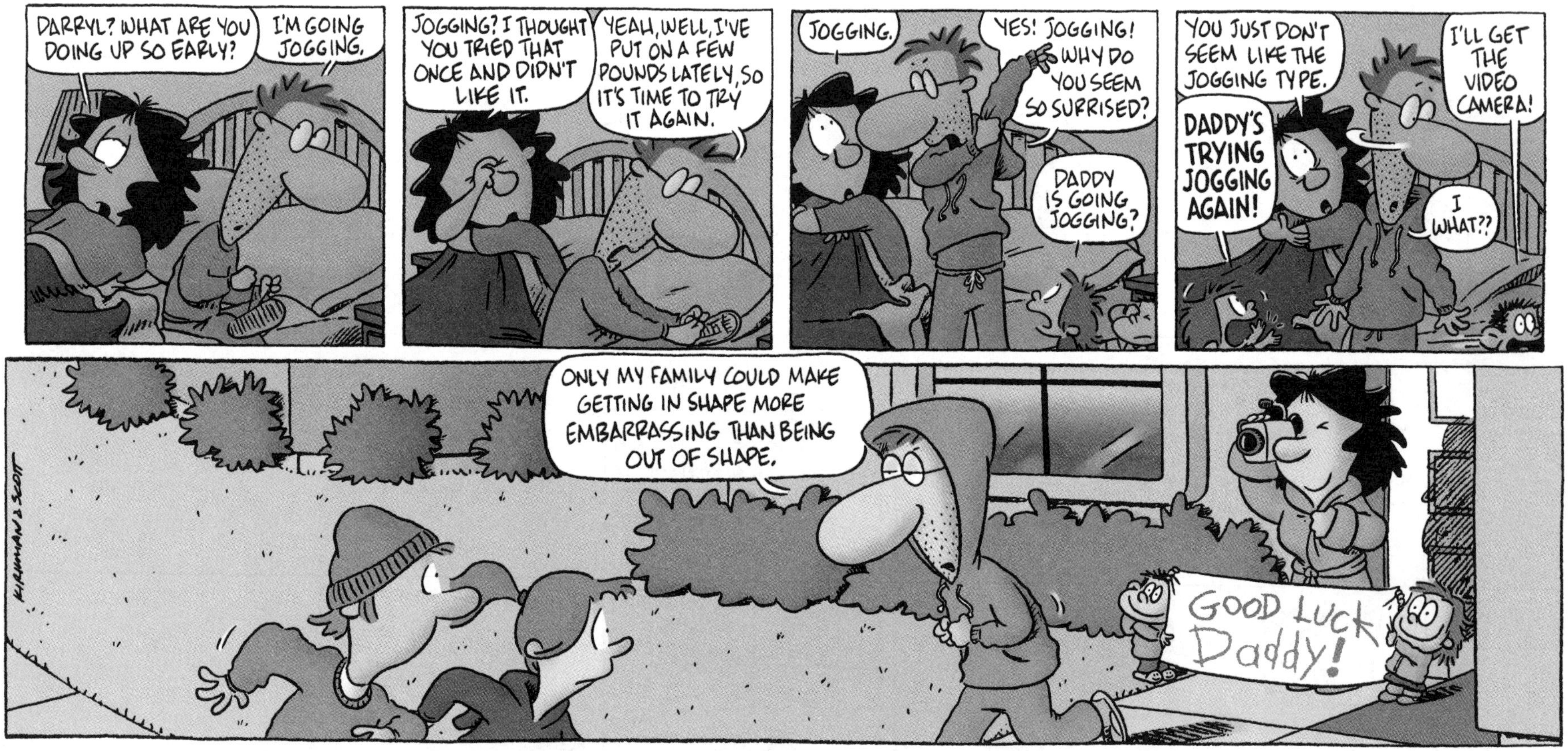
DARRYL? WHAT ARE YOU DOING UP SO EARLY?
I'M GOING JOGGING.
JOGGING? I THOUGHT YOU TRIED THAT ONCE AND DIDN'T LIKE IT.
YEAH, WELL, I'VE PUT ON A FEW POUNDS LATELY, SO IT'S TIME TO TRY IT AGAIN.
JOGGING.
YES! JOGGING! WHY DO YOU SEEM SO SURPRISED?
DADDY IS GOING JOGGING?
YOU JUST DON'T SEEM LIKE THE JOGGING TYPE.
DADDY'S TRYING JOGGING AGAIN!
I'LL GET THE VIDEO CAMERA!
I WHAT??
KIRKMAN & SCOTT
ONLY MY FAMILY COULD MAKE GETTING IN SHAPE MORE EMBARRASSING THAN BEING OUT OF SHAPE.
GOOD LUCK Daddy!

A Really, Really, Really Bad Answer:

DON'T YOU JUST HATE ALL THE STRESS OF THE HOLIDAYS?
WHAT STRESS?

OKAY, I HAVE THE PIES MADE, BUT I STILL HAVE TO BUY THE BREADCR–
WANDA, WHY DO YOU ALWAYS MAKE SUCH A BIG DEAL OUT OF THANKSGIVING DINNER?
JUST TOSS THE TURKEY IN THE OVEN AND BE DONE WITH IT!
SO THAT'S BREADCRUMBS, LETTUCE, CRANBERRIES...
LET ME CLARIFY...

YOUR PINECONE TURKEYS AND MARSH-MALLOW PILGRIMS MAKE A REALLY CUTE THANKSGIVING CENTERPIECE.
THANKS!
WHAT ABOUT WREN? SHE NEEDS TO HAVE SOMETHING ON THERE, TOO.
SHE'S JUST A BABY! WHAT CAN SHE ADD?
WHAT'S THIS WET SPOT IN THE MIDDLE OF THE TABLECLOTH?
DROOL.

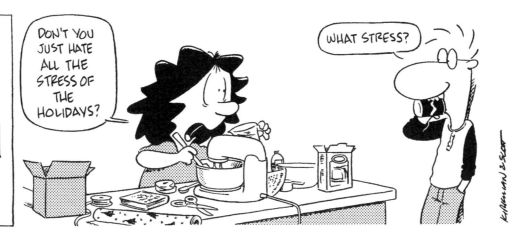

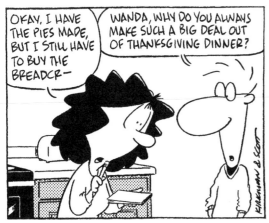

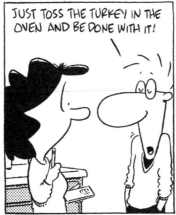

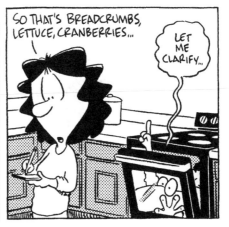

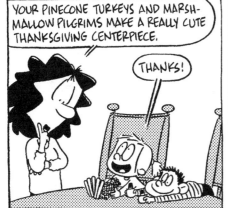

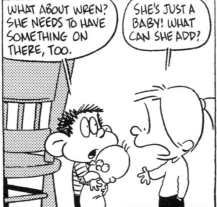

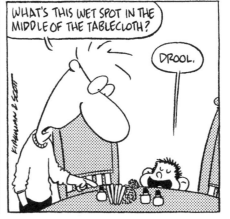

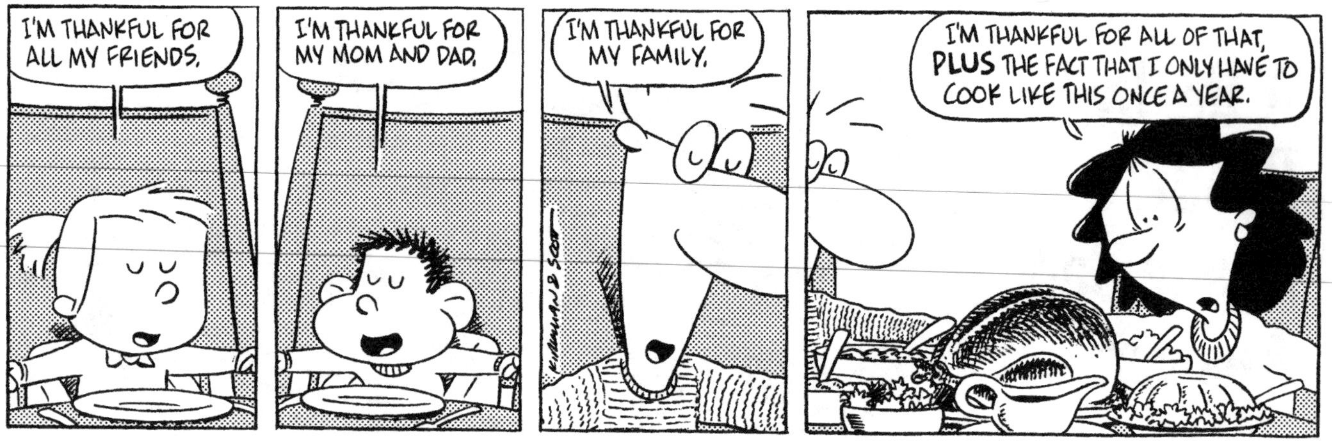
I'M THANKFUL FOR ALL MY FRIENDS.
I'M THANKFUL FOR MY MOM AND DAD.
I'M THANKFUL FOR MY FAMILY.
I'M THANKFUL FOR ALL OF THAT, **PLUS** THE FACT THAT I ONLY HAVE TO COOK LIKE THIS ONCE A YEAR.

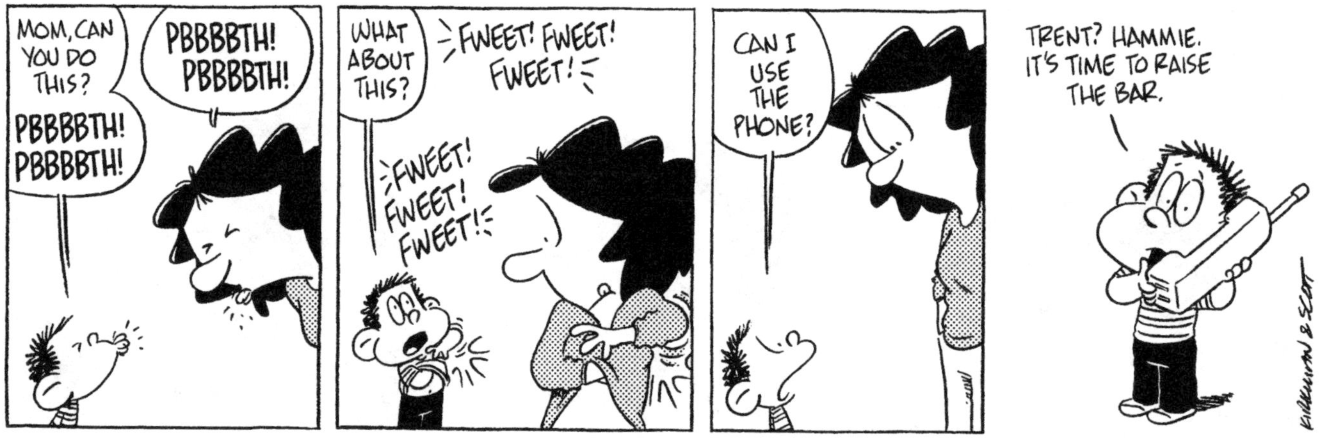
MOM, CAN YOU DO THIS?
PBBBBTH! PBBBBTH!
PBBBBTH! PBBBBTH!
WHAT ABOUT THIS?
FWEET! FWEET! FWEET!
FWEET! FWEET! FWEET!
CAN I USE THE PHONE?
TRENT? HAMMIE. IT'S TIME TO RAISE THE BAR.

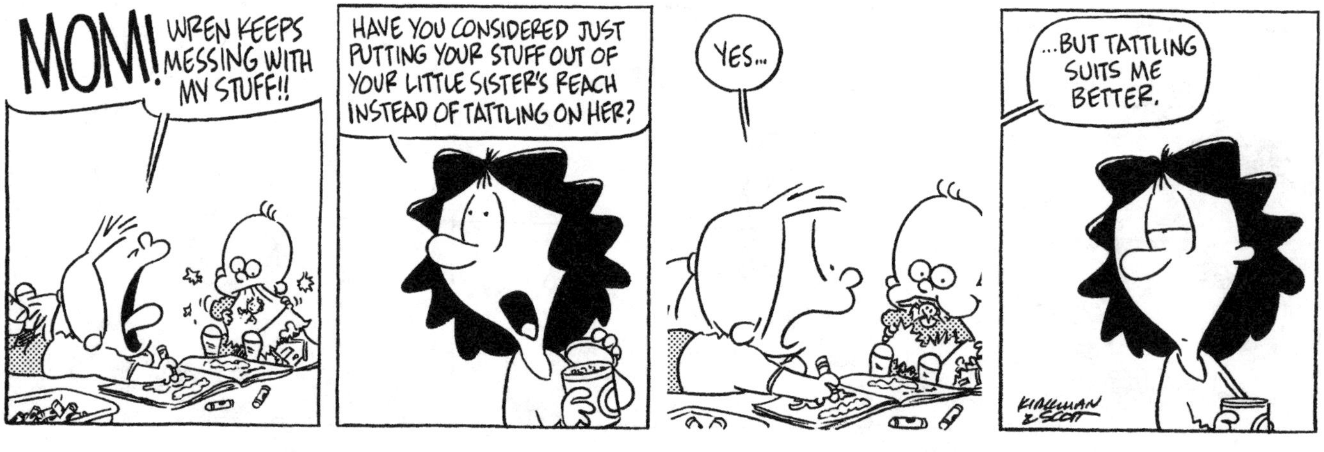
MOM! WREN KEEPS MESSING WITH MY STUFF!!
HAVE YOU CONSIDERED JUST PUTTING YOUR STUFF OUT OF YOUR LITTLE SISTER'S REACH INSTEAD OF TATTLING ON HER?
YES...
...BUT TATTLING SUITS ME BETTER.

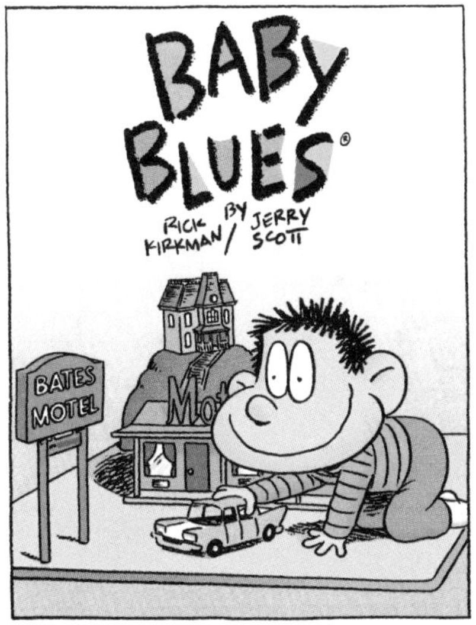
BABY BLUES®
BY RICK KIRKMAN / JERRY SCOTT
BATES MOTEL
MOT

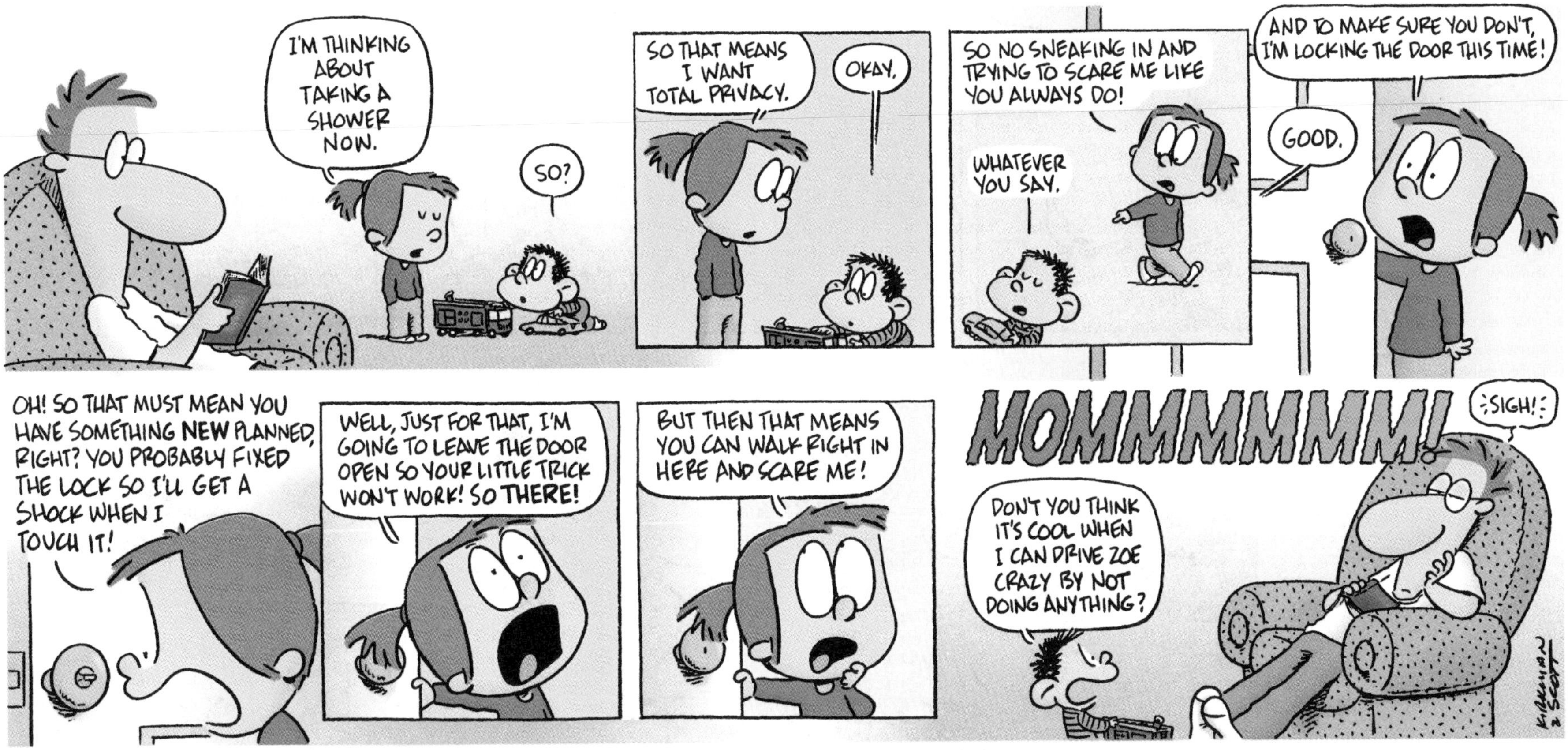
I'M THINKING ABOUT TAKING A SHOWER NOW.
SO?
SO THAT MEANS I WANT TOTAL PRIVACY.
OKAY.
SO NO SNEAKING IN AND TRYING TO SCARE ME LIKE YOU ALWAYS DO!
WHATEVER YOU SAY.
AND TO MAKE SURE YOU DON'T, I'M LOCKING THE DOOR THIS TIME!
GOOD.
OH! SO THAT MUST MEAN YOU HAVE SOMETHING NEW PLANNED, RIGHT? YOU PROBABLY FIXED THE LOCK SO I'LL GET A SHOCK WHEN I TOUCH IT!
WELL, JUST FOR THAT, I'M GOING TO LEAVE THE DOOR OPEN SO YOUR LITTLE TRICK WON'T WORK! SO THERE!
BUT THEN THAT MEANS YOU CAN WALK RIGHT IN HERE AND SCARE ME!
MOMMMMMMM!
SIGH!
DON'T YOU THINK IT'S COOL WHEN I CAN DRIVE ZOE CRAZY BY NOT DOING ANYTHING?
KIRKMAN & SCOTT

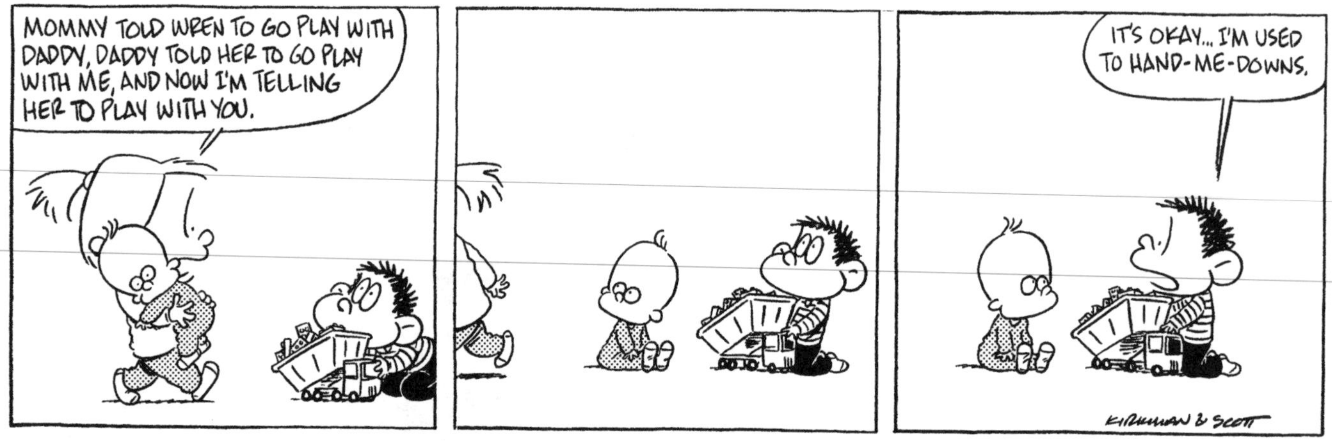
MOMMY TOLD WREN TO GO PLAY WITH DADDY, DADDY TOLD HER TO GO PLAY WITH ME, AND NOW I'M TELLING HER TO PLAY WITH YOU.
IT'S OKAY... I'M USED TO HAND-ME-DOWNS.
KIRKMAN & SCOTT

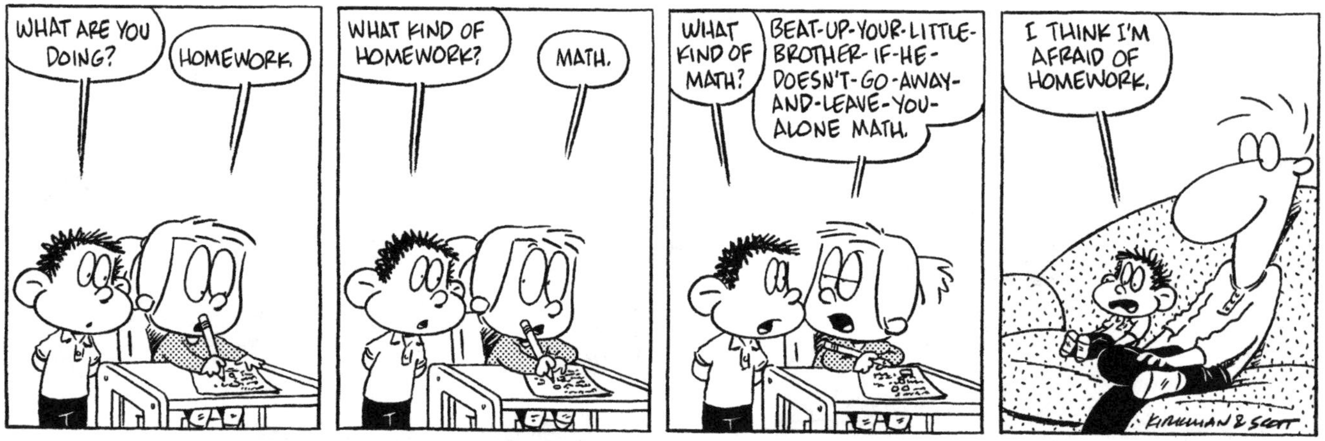
WHAT ARE YOU DOING?
HOMEWORK.
WHAT KIND OF HOMEWORK?
MATH.
WHAT KIND OF MATH?
BEAT-UP-YOUR-LITTLE-BROTHER-IF-HE-DOESN'T-GO-AWAY-AND-LEAVE-YOU-ALONE MATH.
I THINK I'M AFRAID OF HOMEWORK.
KIRKMAN & SCOTT

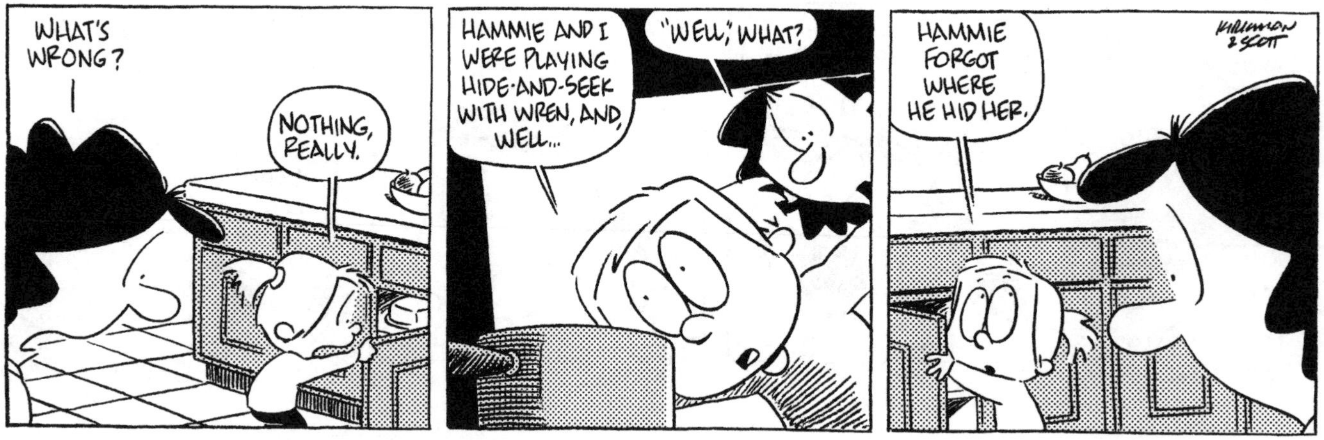
WHAT'S WRONG?
NOTHING, REALLY.
HAMMIE AND I WERE PLAYING HIDE-AND-SEEK WITH WREN, AND, WELL...
"WELL," WHAT?
HAMMIE FORGOT WHERE HE HID HER.
KIRKMAN & SCOTT

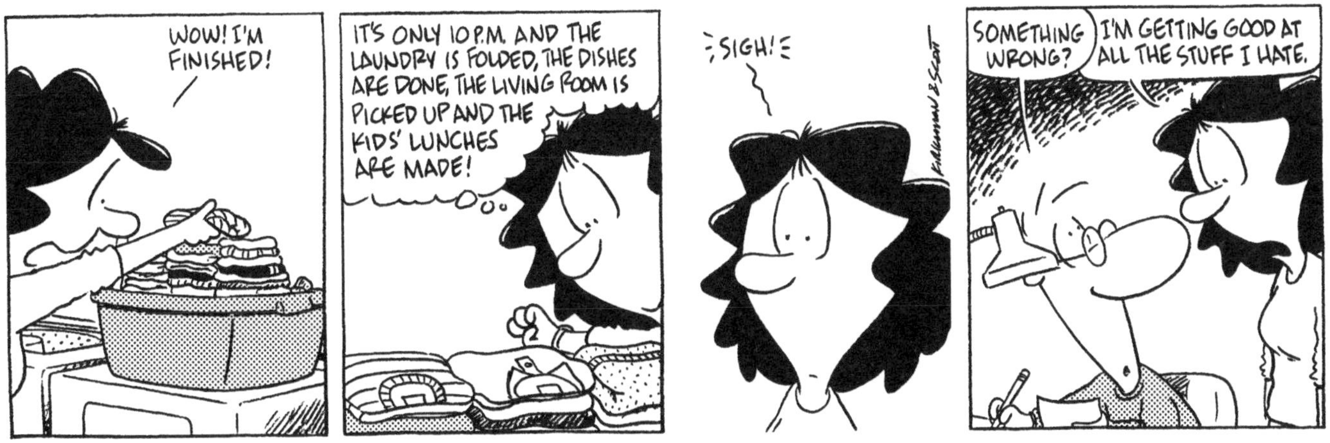
WOW! I'M FINISHED!
IT'S ONLY 10 P.M. AND THE LAUNDRY IS FOLDED, THE DISHES ARE DONE, THE LIVING ROOM IS PICKED UP AND THE KIDS' LUNCHES ARE MADE!
SIGH!
SOMETHING WRONG?
I'M GETTING GOOD AT ALL THE STUFF I HATE.

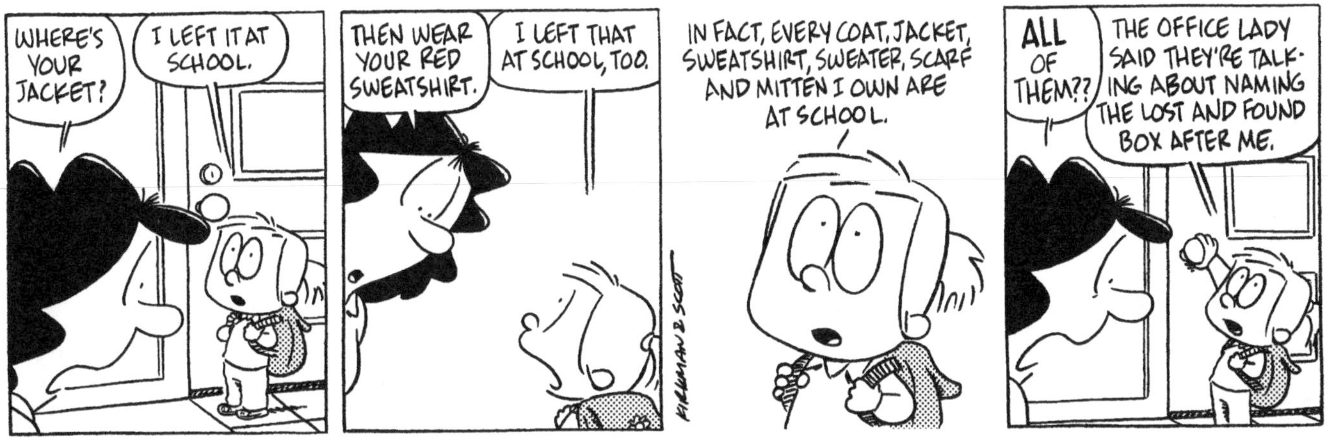
WHERE'S YOUR JACKET?
I LEFT IT AT SCHOOL.
THEN WEAR YOUR RED SWEATSHIRT.
I LEFT THAT AT SCHOOL, TOO.
IN FACT, EVERY COAT, JACKET, SWEATSHIRT, SWEATER, SCARF AND MITTEN I OWN ARE AT SCHOOL.
ALL OF THEM??
THE OFFICE LADY SAID THEY'RE TALKING ABOUT NAMING THE LOST AND FOUND BOX AFTER ME.

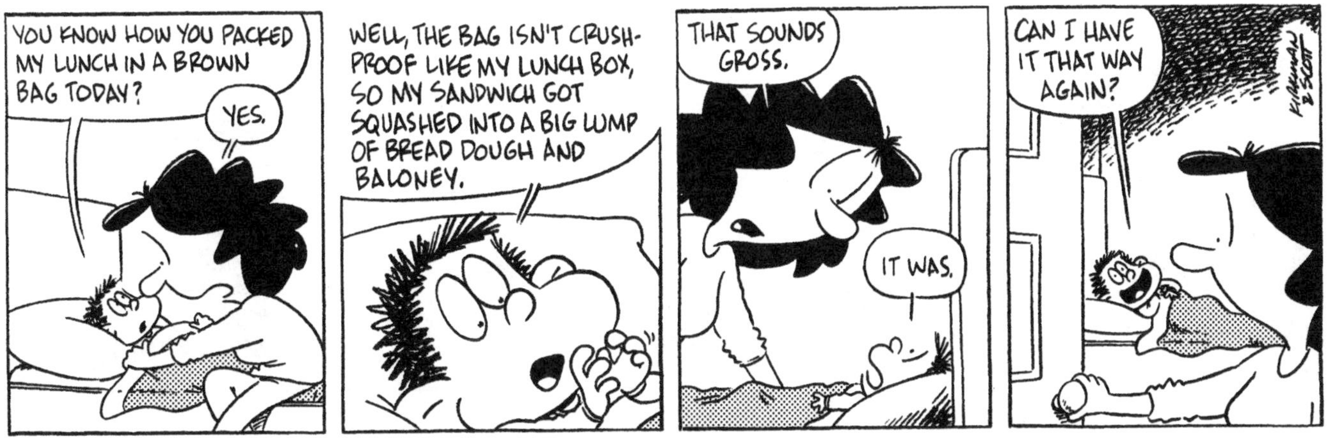
YOU KNOW HOW YOU PACKED MY LUNCH IN A BROWN BAG TODAY?
YES.
WELL, THE BAG ISN'T CRUSH-PROOF LIKE MY LUNCH BOX, SO MY SANDWICH GOT SQUASHED INTO A BIG LUMP OF BREAD DOUGH AND BALONEY.
THAT SOUNDS GROSS.
IT WAS.
CAN I HAVE IT THAT WAY AGAIN?

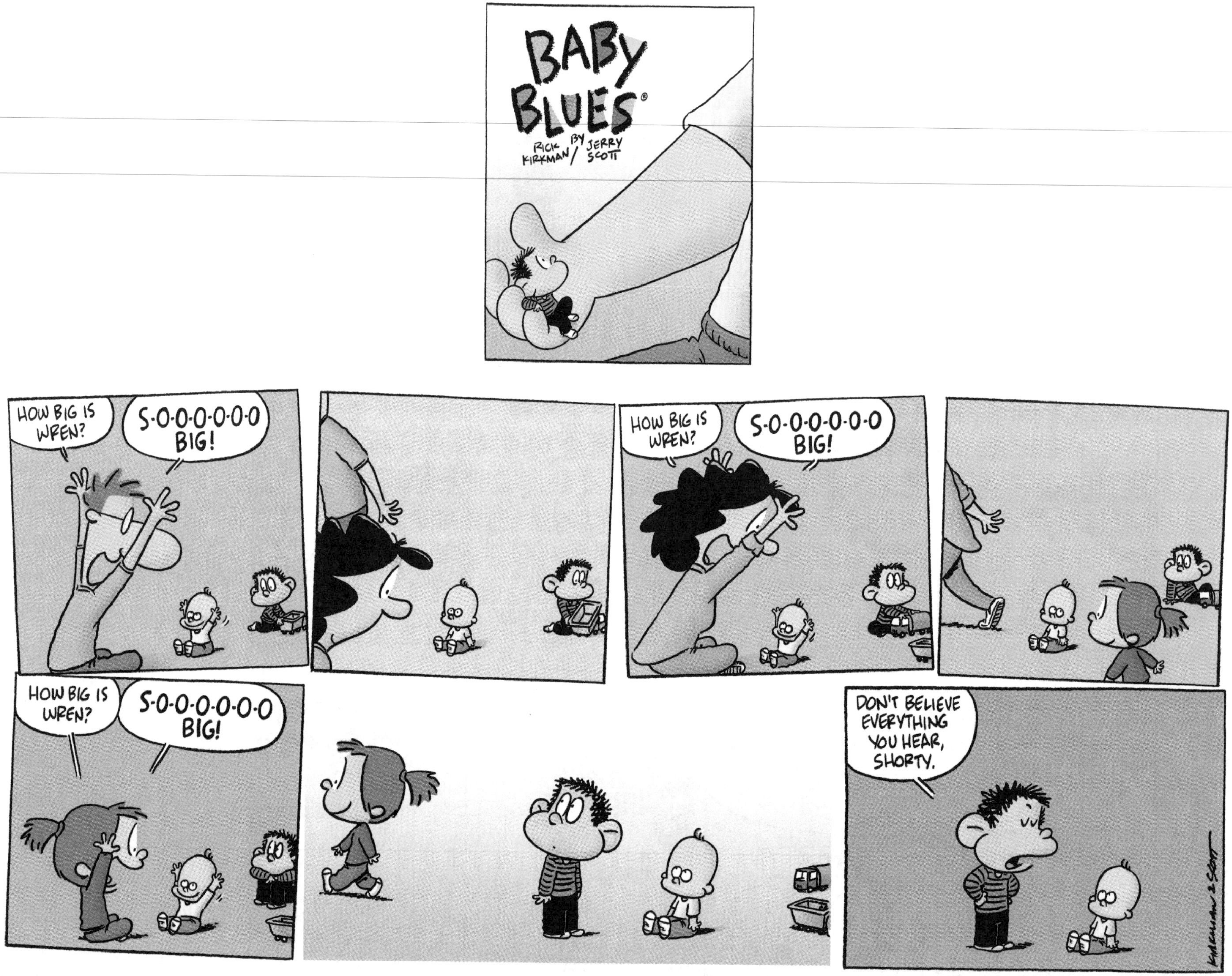
BABY BLUES®
BY RICK KIRKMAN / JERRY SCOTT
HOW BIG IS WREN?
S-O-O-O-O-O-O-O BIG!
HOW BIG IS WREN?
S-O-O-O-O-O-O-O BIG!
HOW BIG IS WREN?
S-O-O-O-O-O-O-O BIG!
DON'T BELIEVE EVERYTHING YOU HEAR, SHORTY.
KIRKMAN & SCOTT

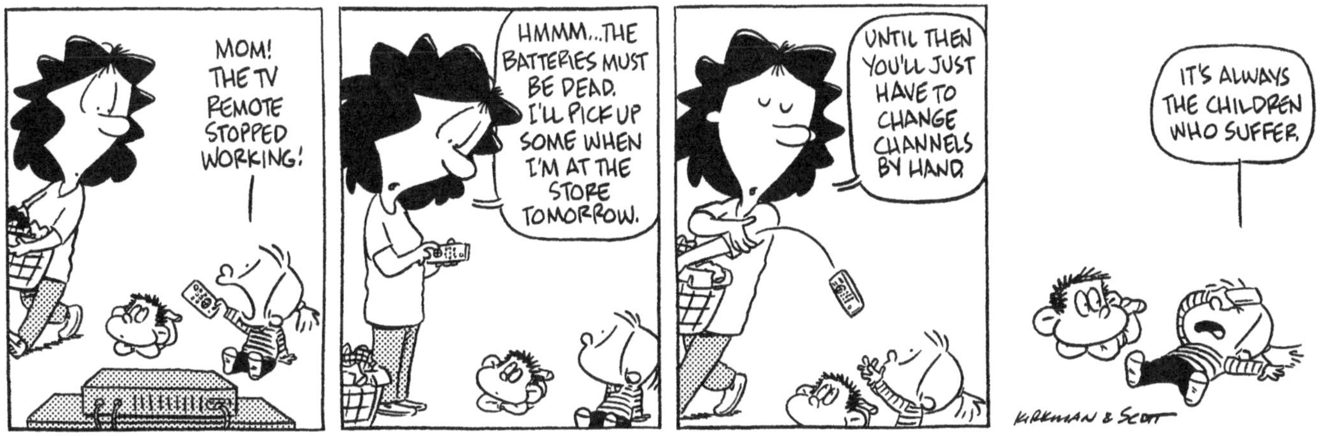
MOM! THE TV REMOTE STOPPED WORKING!
HMMM...THE BATTERIES MUST BE DEAD. I'LL PICK UP SOME WHEN I'M AT THE STORE TOMORROW.
UNTIL THEN YOU'LL JUST HAVE TO CHANGE CHANNELS BY HAND.
IT'S ALWAYS THE CHILDREN WHO SUFFER.
KIRKMAN & SCOTT

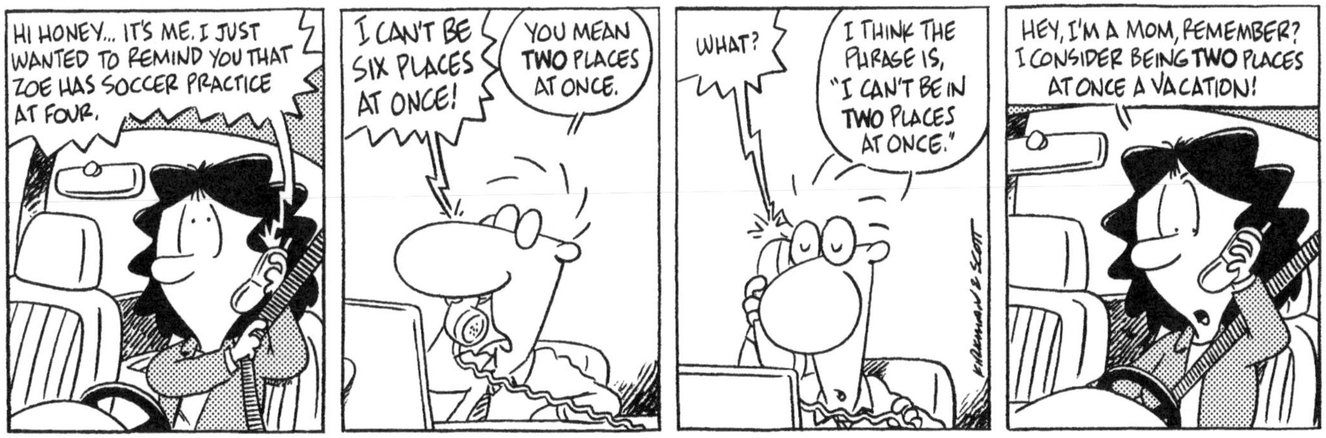
HI HONEY... IT'S ME. I JUST WANTED TO REMIND YOU THAT ZOE HAS SOCCER PRACTICE AT FOUR.
I CAN'T BE SIX PLACES AT ONCE!
YOU MEAN TWO PLACES AT ONCE.
WHAT?
I THINK THE PHRASE IS, "I CAN'T BE IN TWO PLACES AT ONCE."
KIRKMAN & SCOTT
HEY, I'M A MOM, REMEMBER? I CONSIDER BEING TWO PLACES AT ONCE A VACATION!

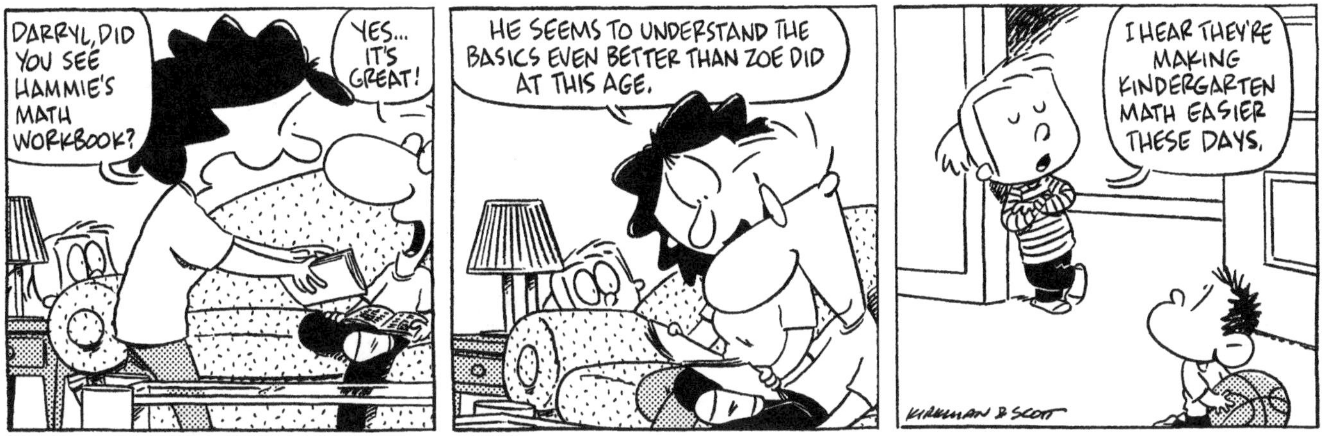
DARRYL, DID YOU SEE HAMMIE'S MATH WORKBOOK?
YES... IT'S GREAT!
HE SEEMS TO UNDERSTAND THE BASICS EVEN BETTER THAN ZOE DID AT THIS AGE.
I HEAR THEY'RE MAKING KINDERGARTEN MATH EASIER THESE DAYS.
KIRKMAN & SCOTT

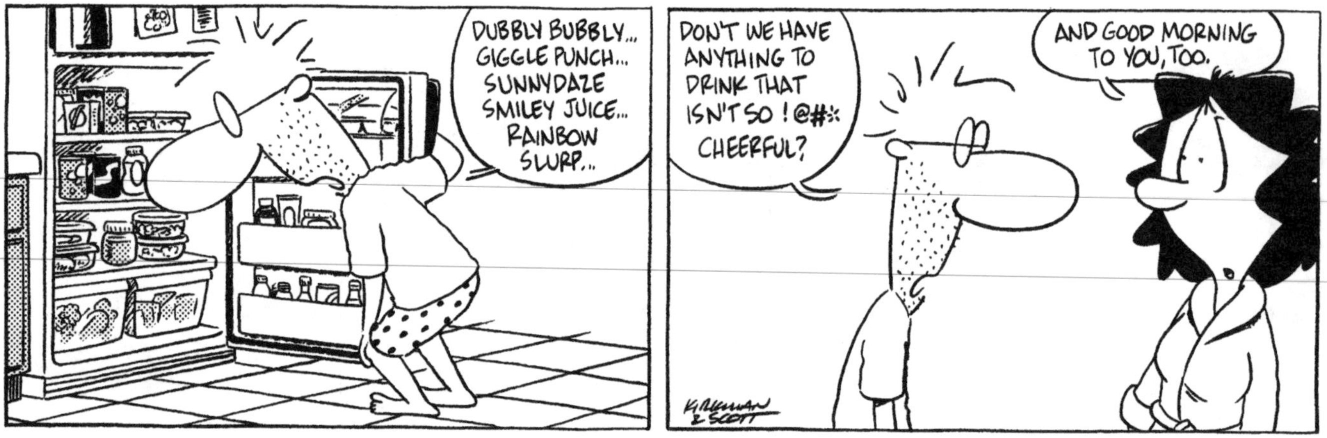
DUBBLY BUBBLY... GIGGLE PUNCH... SUNNYDAZE SMILEY JUICE... RAINBOW SLURP...
DON'T WE HAVE ANYTHING TO DRINK THAT ISN'T SO !@#* CHEERFUL?
AND GOOD MORNING TO YOU, TOO.
KIRKMAN & SCOTT

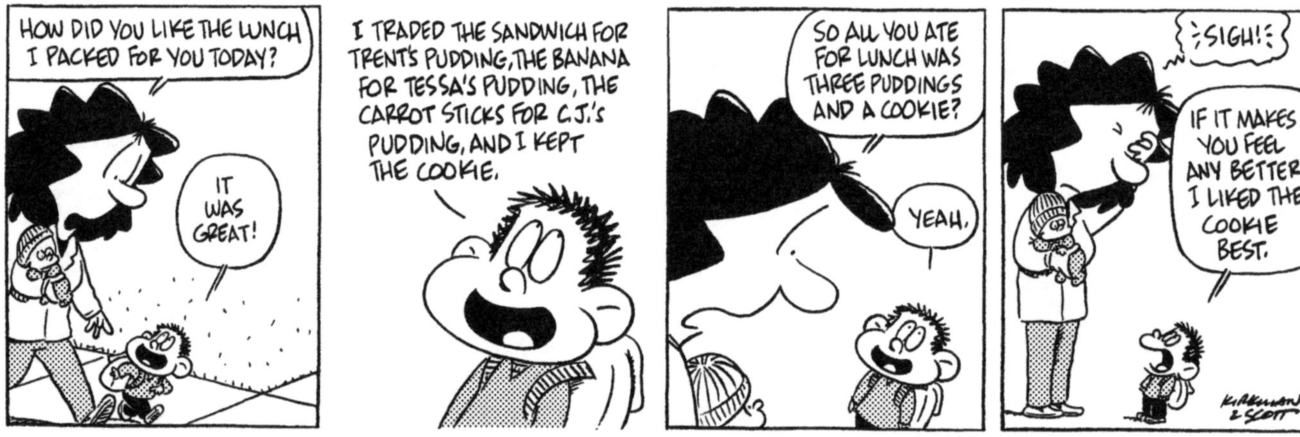
HOW DID YOU LIKE THE LUNCH I PACKED FOR YOU TODAY?
IT WAS GREAT!
I TRADED THE SANDWICH FOR TRENT'S PUDDING, THE BANANA FOR TESSA'S PUDDING, THE CARROT STICKS FOR C.J.'S PUDDING, AND I KEPT THE COOKIE.
SO ALL YOU ATE FOR LUNCH WAS THREE PUDDINGS AND A COOKIE?
YEAH.
SIGH!
IF IT MAKES YOU FEEL ANY BETTER, I LIKED THE COOKIE BEST.
KIRKMAN & SCOTT

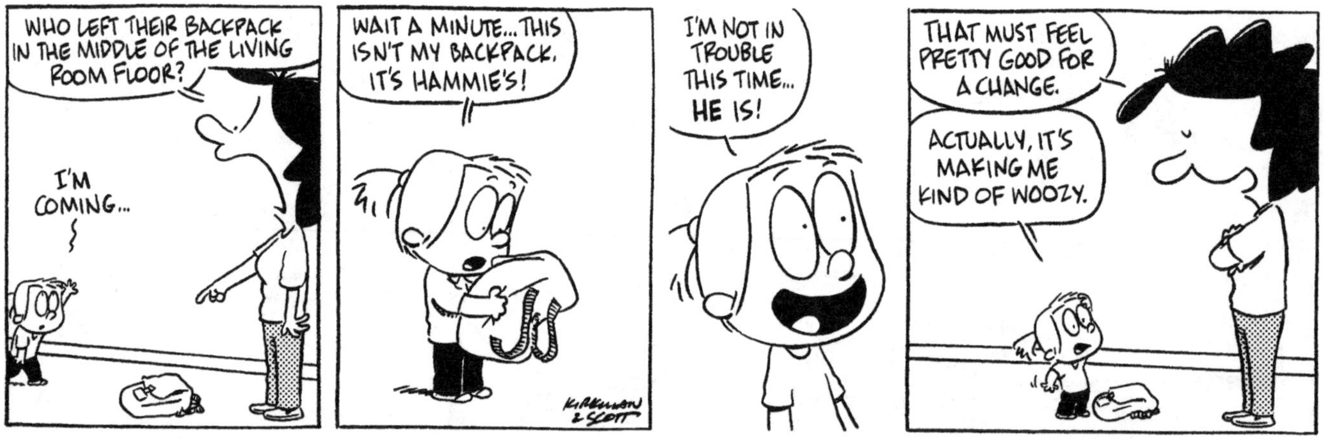
WHO LEFT THEIR BACKPACK IN THE MIDDLE OF THE LIVING ROOM FLOOR?
I'M COMING...
WAIT A MINUTE... THIS ISN'T MY BACKPACK. IT'S HAMMIE'S!
KIRKMAN & SCOTT
I'M NOT IN TROUBLE THIS TIME... HE IS!
THAT MUST FEEL PRETTY GOOD FOR A CHANGE.
ACTUALLY, IT'S MAKING ME KIND OF WOOZY.

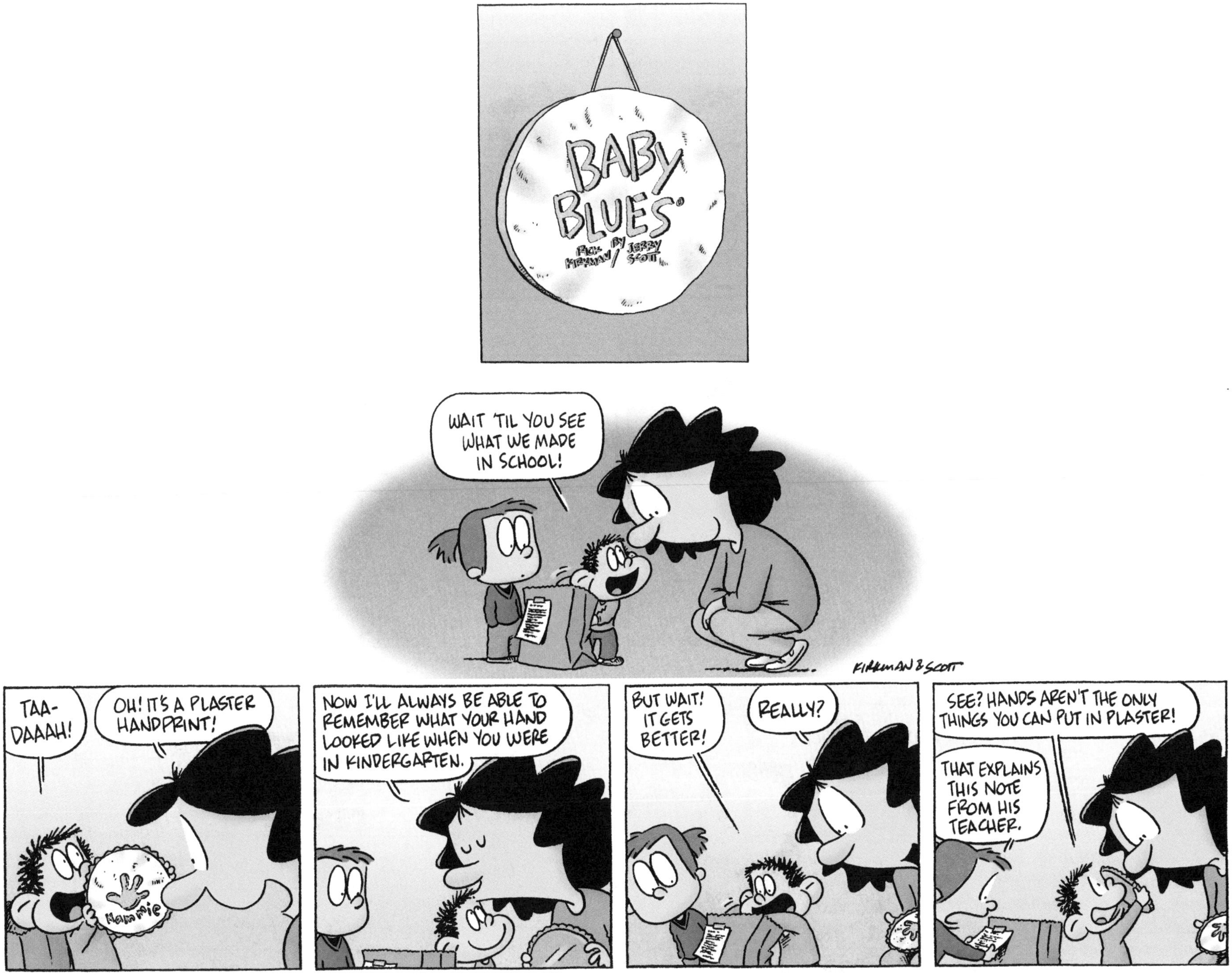
BABY BLUES®
RICK KIRKMAN / BY JERRY SCOTT
WAIT 'TIL YOU SEE WHAT WE MADE IN SCHOOL!
KIRKMAN & SCOTT
TAA-DAAAH!
OH! IT'S A PLASTER HANDPRINT!
Mammie
NOW I'LL ALWAYS BE ABLE TO REMEMBER WHAT YOUR HAND LOOKED LIKE WHEN YOU WERE IN KINDERGARTEN.
BUT WAIT! IT GETS BETTER!
REALLY?
SEE? HANDS AREN'T THE ONLY THINGS YOU CAN PUT IN PLASTER!
THAT EXPLAINS THIS NOTE FROM HIS TEACHER.

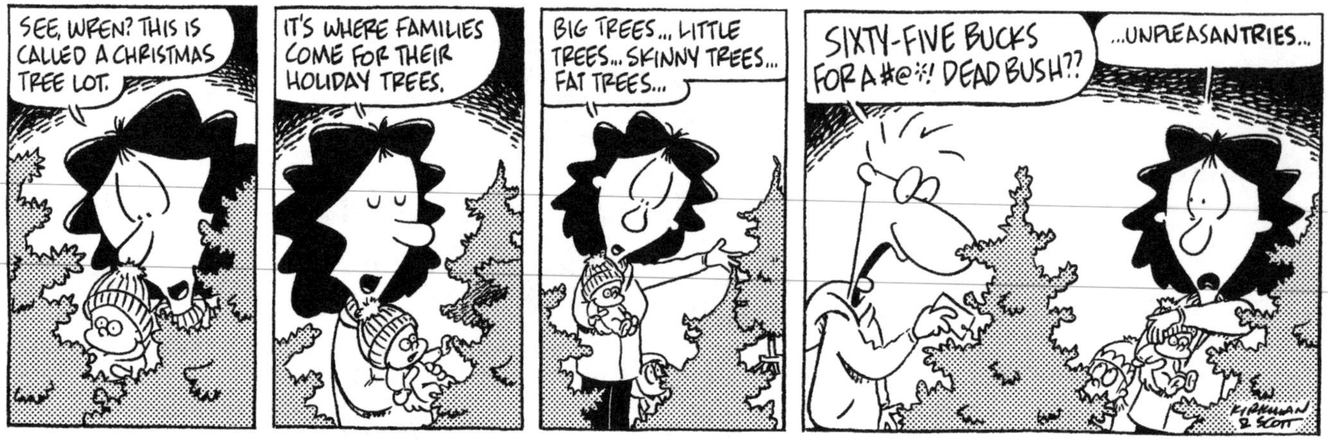
SEE, WREN? THIS IS CALLED A CHRISTMAS TREE LOT.
IT'S WHERE FAMILIES COME FOR THEIR HOLIDAY TREES.
BIG TREES... LITTLE TREES... SKINNY TREES... FAT TREES...
SIXTY-FIVE BUCKS FOR A #@*! DEAD BUSH??
...UNPLEASANTRIES...
KIRKMAN & SCOTT

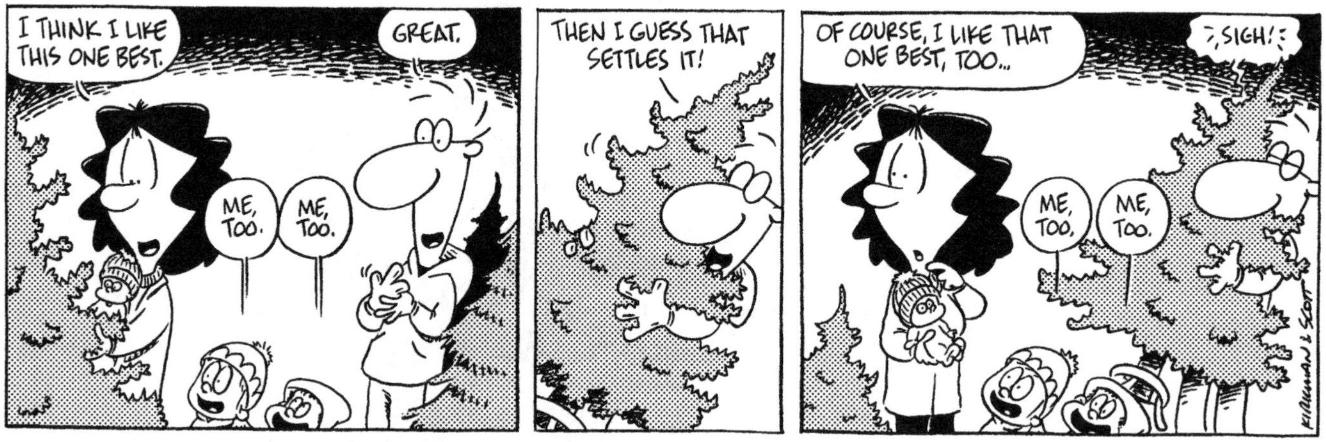
I THINK I LIKE THIS ONE BEST.
ME, TOO.
ME, TOO.
GREAT.
THEN I GUESS THAT SETTLES IT!
OF COURSE, I LIKE THAT ONE BEST, TOO...
ME, TOO.
ME, TOO.
SIGH!
KIRKMAN & SCOTT

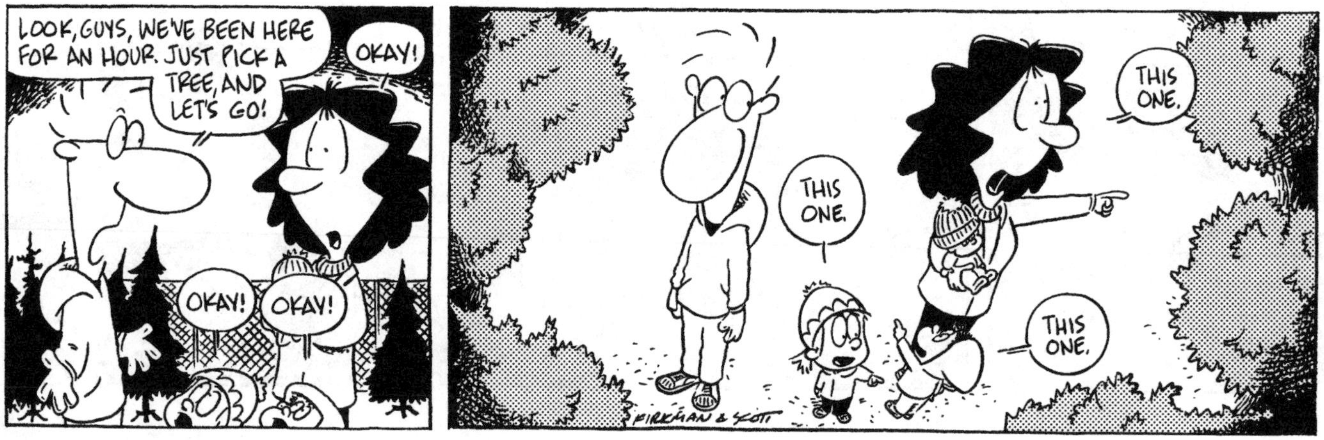
LOOK, GUYS, WE'VE BEEN HERE FOR AN HOUR. JUST PICK A TREE, AND LET'S GO!
OKAY!
OKAY!
OKAY!
THIS ONE.
THIS ONE.
THIS ONE.
KIRKMAN & SCOTT

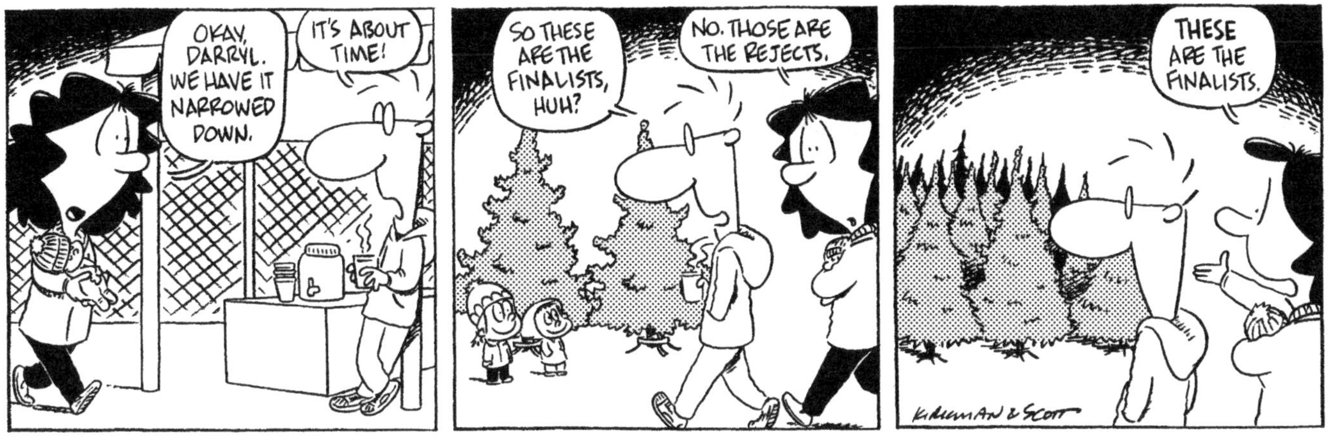
OKAY, DARRYL. WE HAVE IT NARROWED DOWN.
IT'S ABOUT TIME!
SO THESE ARE THE FINALISTS, HUH?
NO. THOSE ARE THE REJECTS.
THESE ARE THE FINALISTS.
KIRKMAN & SCOTT

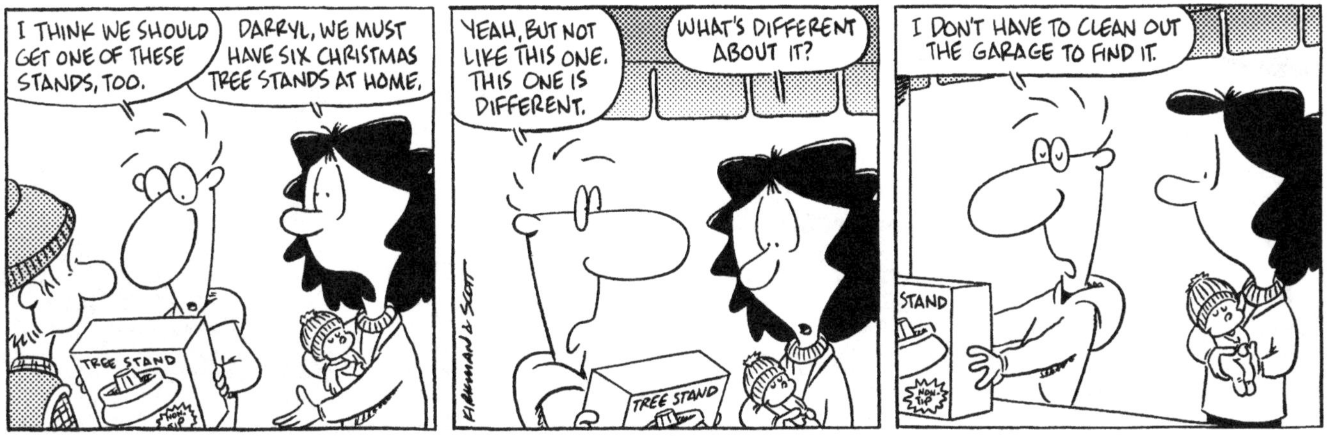
I THINK WE SHOULD GET ONE OF THESE STANDS, TOO.
DARRYL, WE MUST HAVE SIX CHRISTMAS TREE STANDS AT HOME.
TREE STAND
KIRKMAN & SCOTT
YEAH, BUT NOT LIKE THIS ONE. THIS ONE IS DIFFERENT.
WHAT'S DIFFERENT ABOUT IT?
TREE STAND
I DON'T HAVE TO CLEAN OUT THE GARAGE TO FIND IT.
STAND

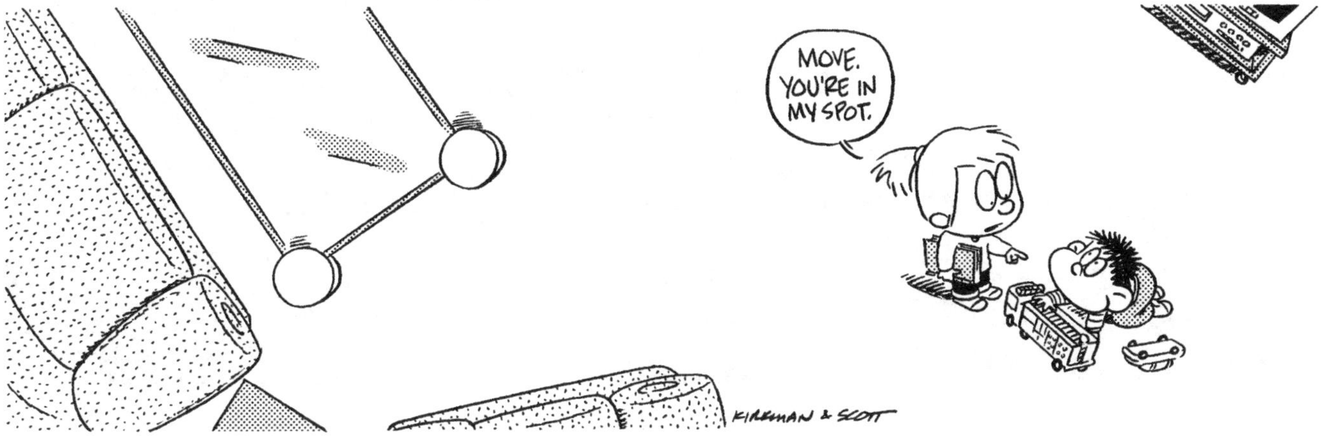
MOVE. YOU'RE IN MY SPOT.
KIRKMAN & SCOTT

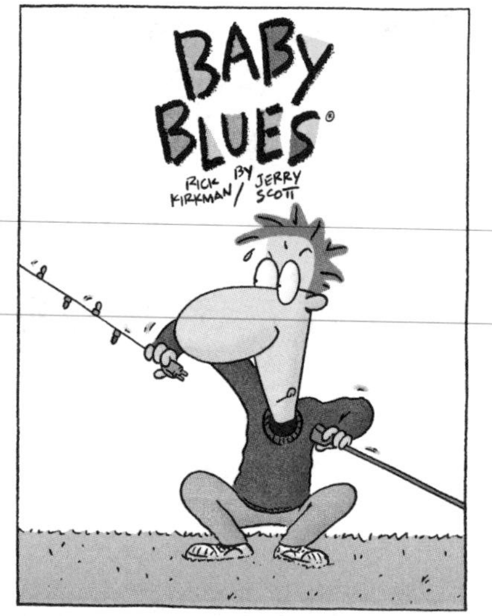
BABY BLUES®
BY RICK KIRKMAN / JERRY SCOTT

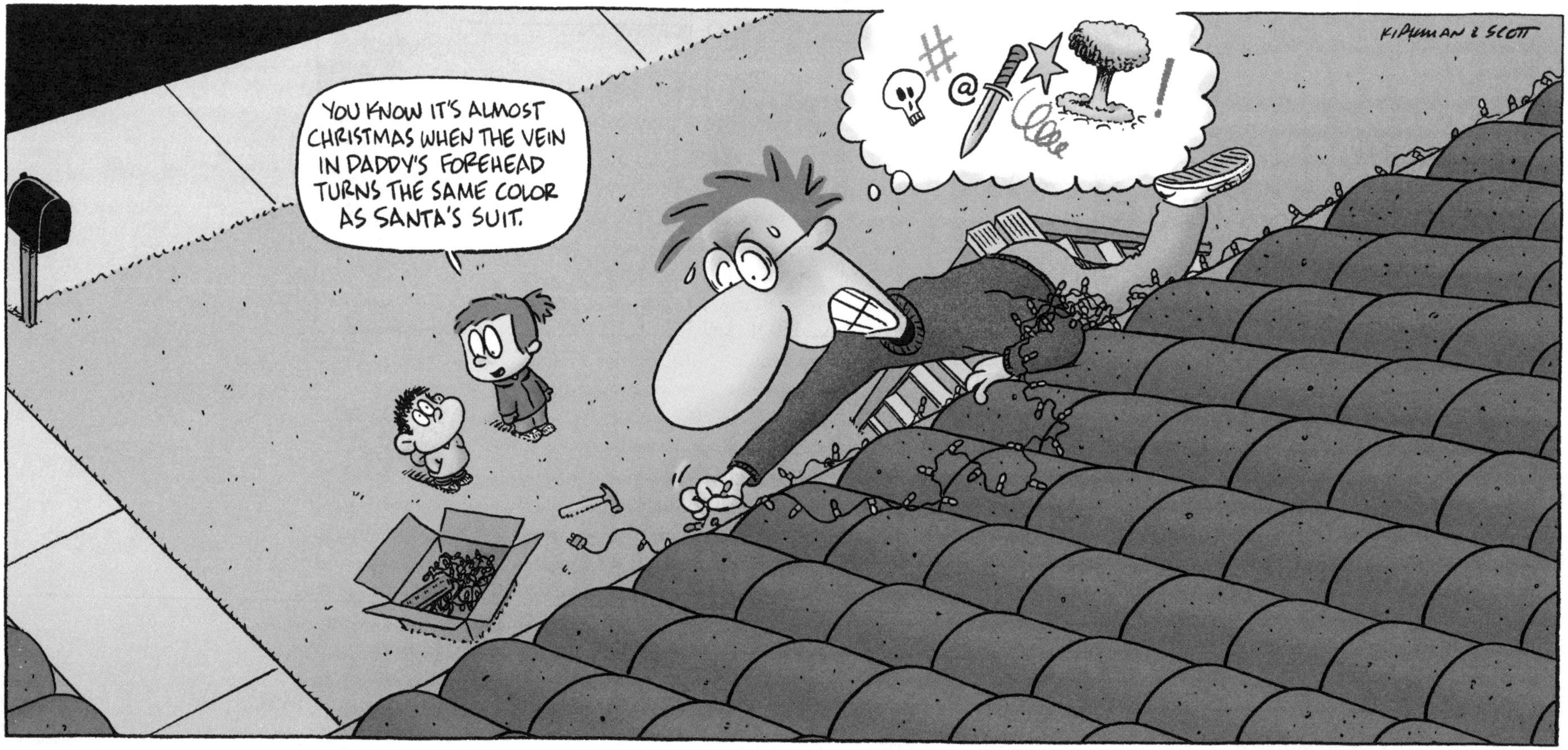
KIRKMAN & SCOTT
YOU KNOW IT'S ALMOST CHRISTMAS WHEN THE VEIN IN DADDY'S FOREHEAD TURNS THE SAME COLOR AS SANTA'S SUIT.
@ # !

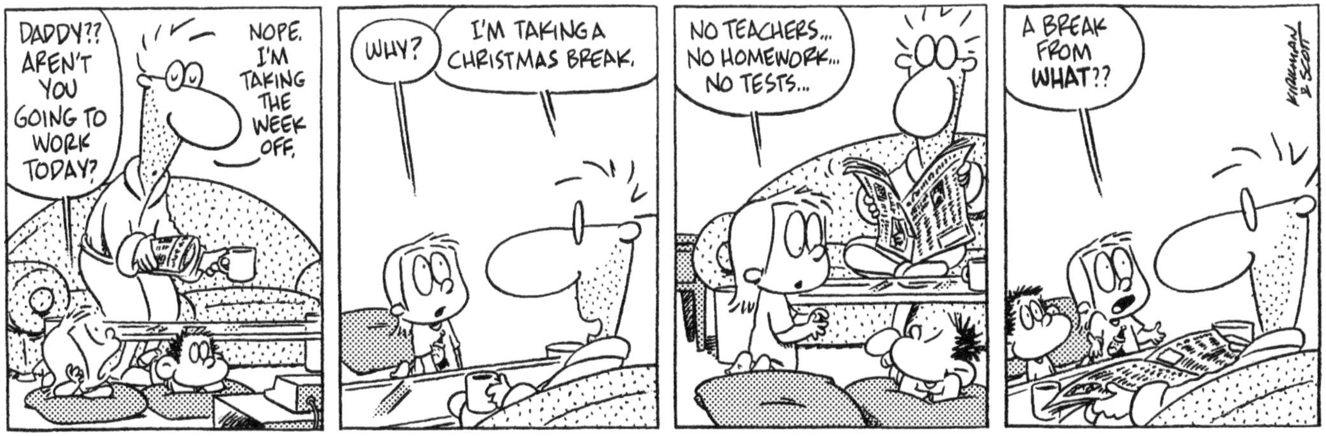
DADDY?? AREN'T YOU GOING TO WORK TODAY?
NOPE. I'M TAKING THE WEEK OFF.
WHY?
I'M TAKING A CHRISTMAS BREAK.
NO TEACHERS... NO HOMEWORK... NO TESTS...
A BREAK FROM WHAT??

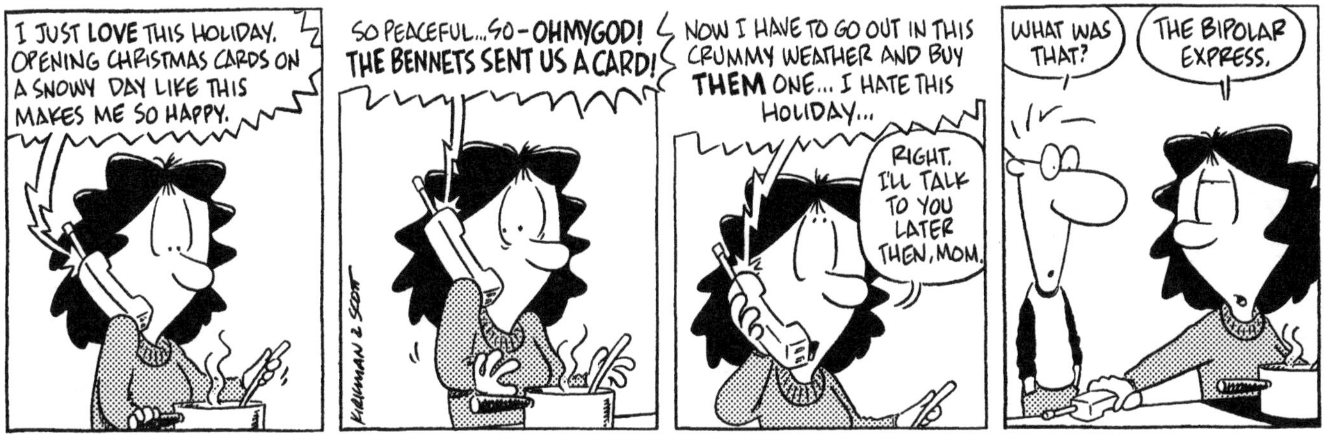
I JUST LOVE THIS HOLIDAY. OPENING CHRISTMAS CARDS ON A SNOWY DAY LIKE THIS MAKES ME SO HAPPY.
SO PEACEFUL... SO- OHMYGOD! THE BENNETS SENT US A CARD!
NOW I HAVE TO GO OUT IN THIS CRUMMY WEATHER AND BUY THEM ONE... I HATE THIS HOLIDAY...
RIGHT. I'LL TALK TO YOU LATER THEN, MOM.
WHAT WAS THAT?
THE BIPOLAR EXPRESS.

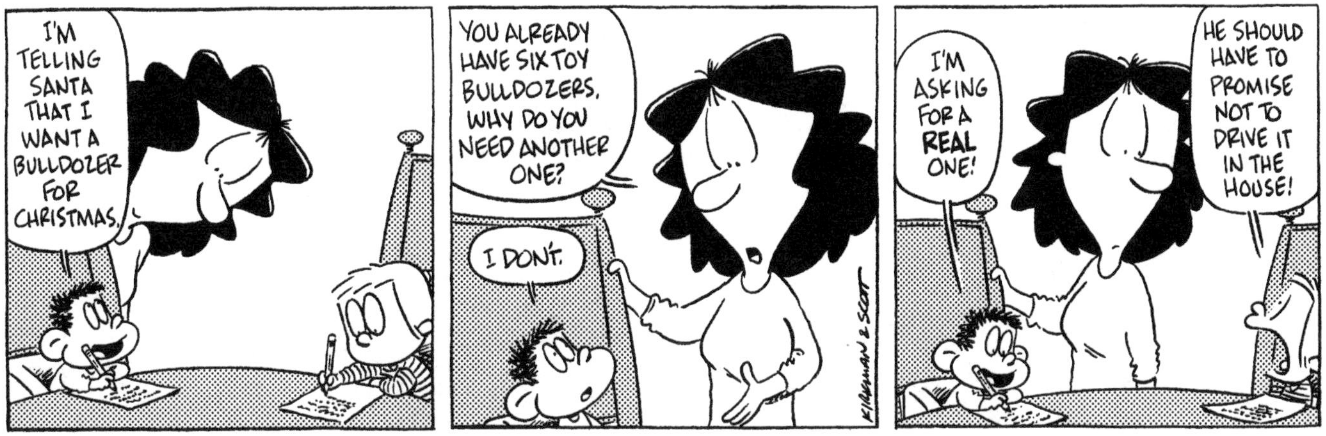
I'M TELLING SANTA THAT I WANT A BULLDOZER FOR CHRISTMAS.
YOU ALREADY HAVE SIX TOY BULLDOZERS. WHY DO YOU NEED ANOTHER ONE?
I DON'T.
I'M ASKING FOR A REAL ONE!
HE SHOULD HAVE TO PROMISE NOT TO DRIVE IT IN THE HOUSE!

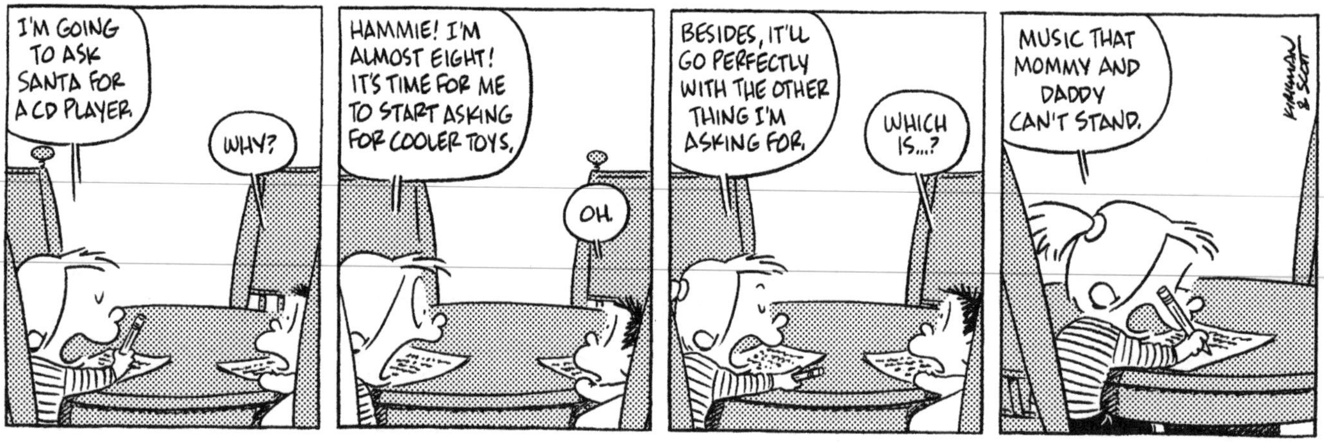
I'M GOING TO ASK SANTA FOR A CD PLAYER.
WHY?
HAMMIE! I'M ALMOST EIGHT! IT'S TIME FOR ME TO START ASKING FOR COOLER TOYS.
OH.
BESIDES, IT'LL GO PERFECTLY WITH THE OTHER THING I'M ASKING FOR.
WHICH IS...?
MUSIC THAT MOMMY AND DADDY CAN'T STAND.
KIRKMAN & SCOTT

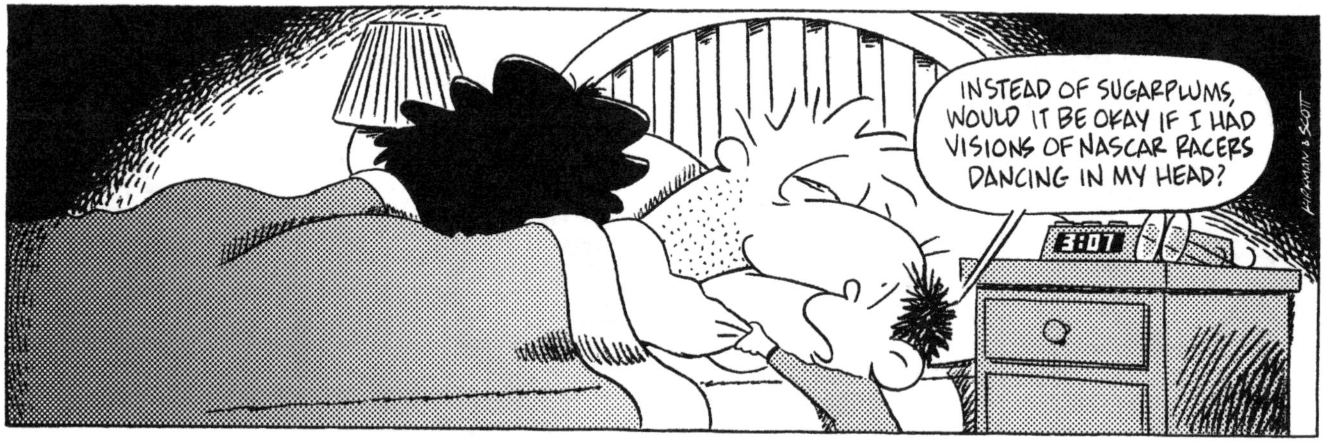
INSTEAD OF SUGARPLUMS, WOULD IT BE OKAY IF I HAD VISIONS OF NASCAR RACERS DANCING IN MY HEAD?
3:07
KIRKMAN & SCOTT

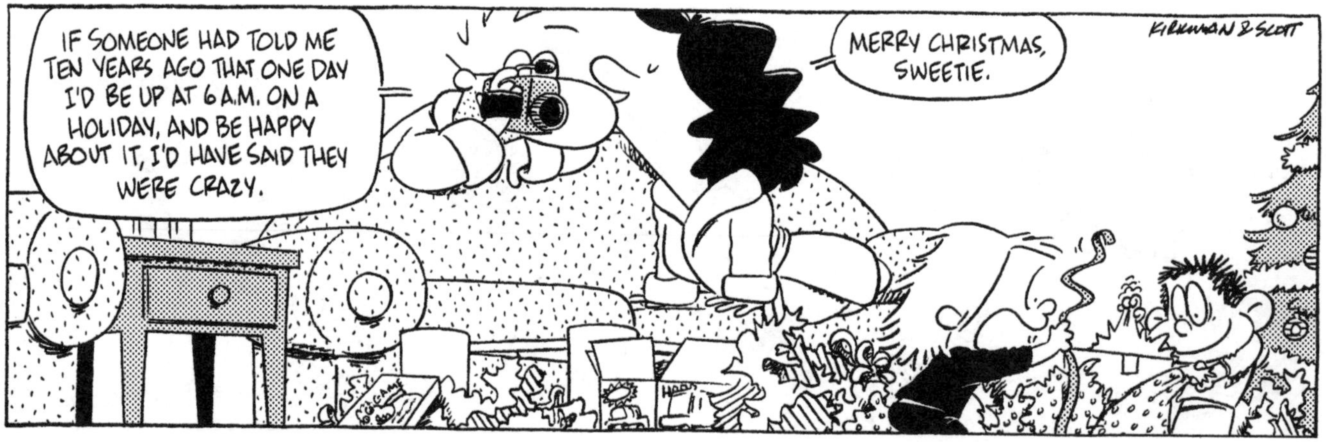
IF SOMEONE HAD TOLD ME TEN YEARS AGO THAT ONE DAY I'D BE UP AT 6 A.M. ON A HOLIDAY, AND BE HAPPY ABOUT IT, I'D HAVE SAID THEY WERE CRAZY.
MERRY CHRISTMAS, SWEETIE.
KIRKMAN & SCOTT

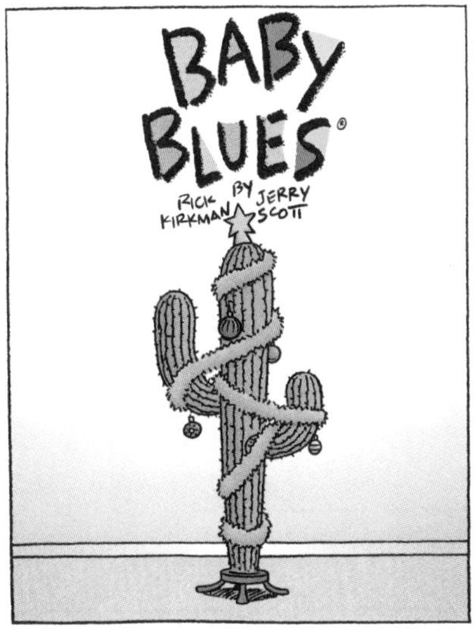
BABY BLUES®
BY RICK KIRKMAN JERRY SCOTT

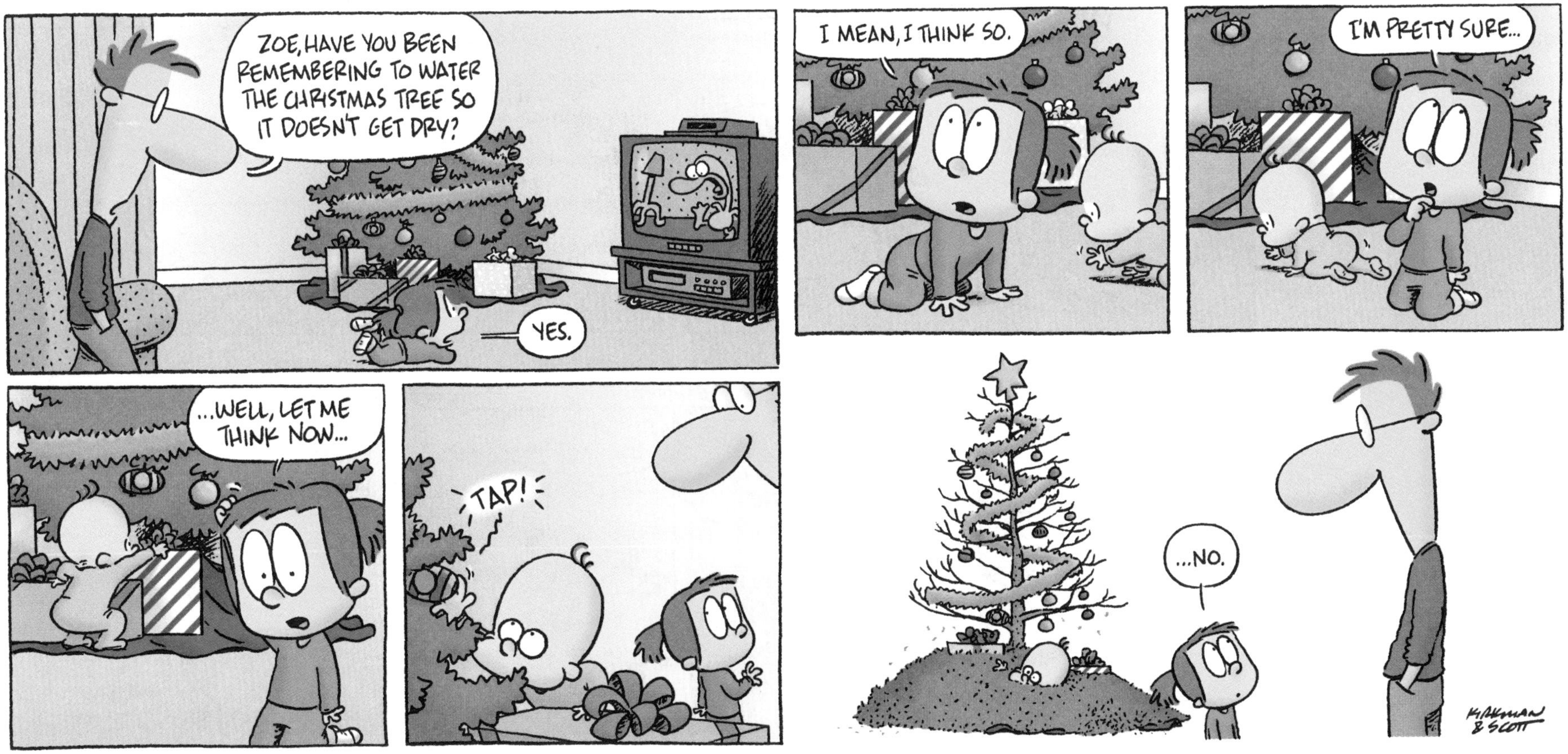
ZOE, HAVE YOU BEEN REMEMBERING TO WATER THE CHRISTMAS TREE SO IT DOESN'T GET DRY?
YES.
I MEAN, I THINK SO.
I'M PRETTY SURE...
...WELL, LET ME THINK NOW...
TAP!
...NO.
KIRKMAN & SCOTT

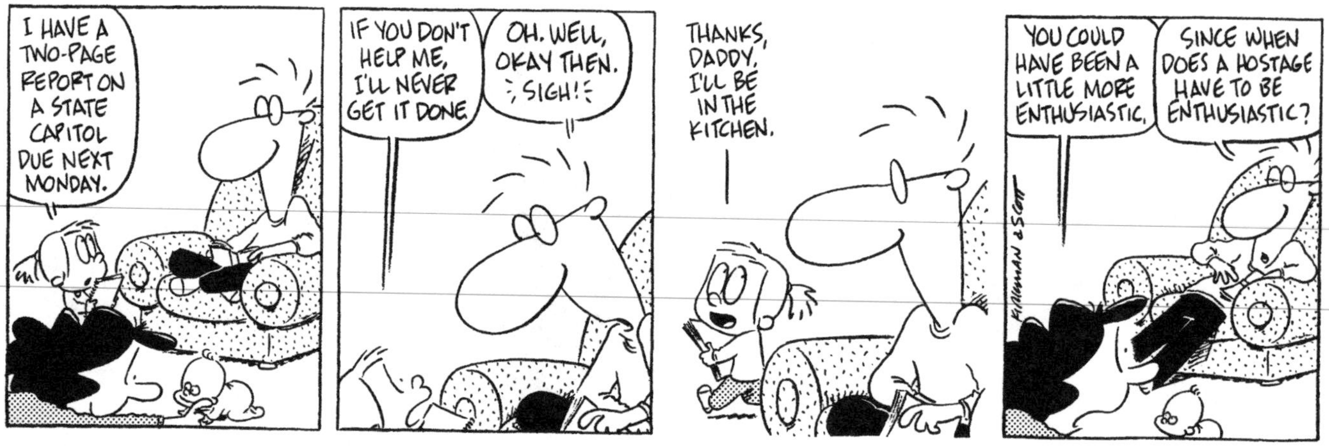
I HAVE A TWO-PAGE REPORT ON A STATE CAPITOL DUE NEXT MONDAY.
IF YOU DON'T HELP ME, I'LL NEVER GET IT DONE.
OH. WELL, OKAY THEN. SIGH!
THANKS, DADDY. I'LL BE IN THE KITCHEN.
YOU COULD HAVE BEEN A LITTLE MORE ENTHUSIASTIC.
SINCE WHEN DOES A HOSTAGE HAVE TO BE ENTHUSIASTIC?
KIRKMAN & SCOTT

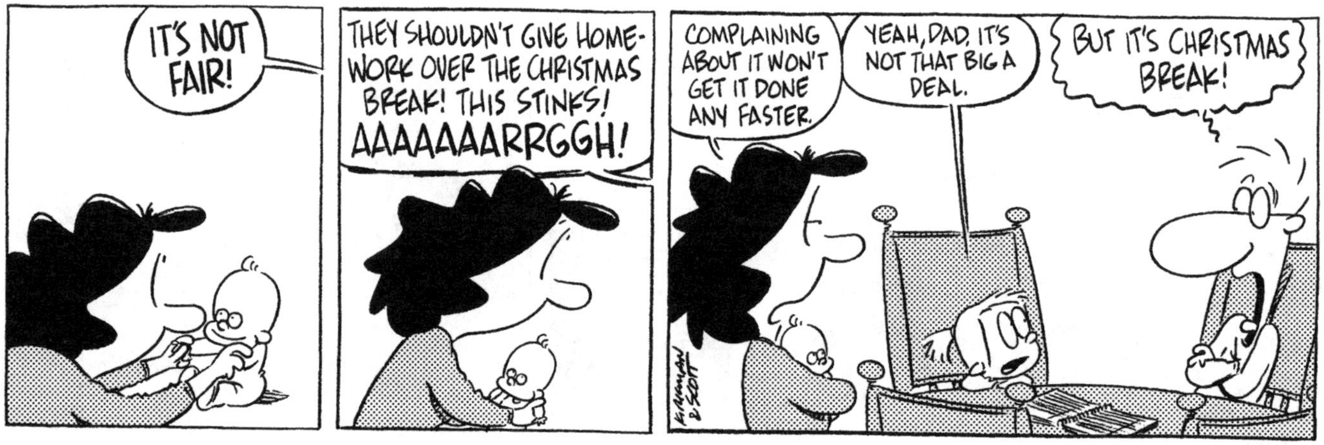
IT'S NOT FAIR!
THEY SHOULDN'T GIVE HOMEWORK OVER THE CHRISTMAS BREAK! THIS STINKS! AAAAAAARRGGH!
COMPLAINING ABOUT IT WON'T GET IT DONE ANY FASTER.
YEAH, DAD, IT'S NOT THAT BIG A DEAL.
BUT IT'S CHRISTMAS BREAK!
KIRKMAN & SCOTT

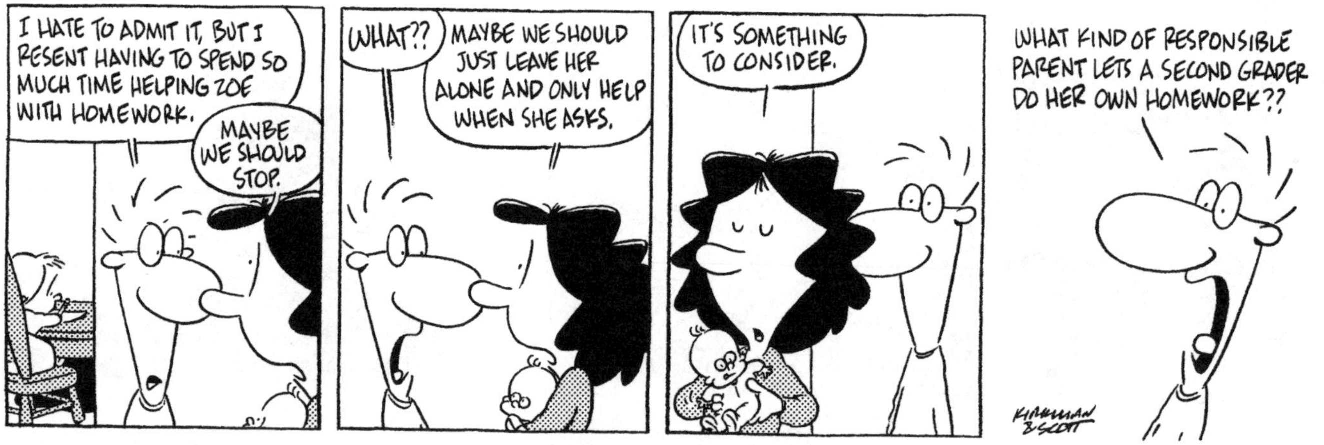
I HATE TO ADMIT IT, BUT I RESENT HAVING TO SPEND SO MUCH TIME HELPING ZOE WITH HOMEWORK.
MAYBE WE SHOULD STOP.
WHAT??
MAYBE WE SHOULD JUST LEAVE HER ALONE AND ONLY HELP WHEN SHE ASKS.
IT'S SOMETHING TO CONSIDER.
WHAT KIND OF RESPONSIBLE PARENT LETS A SECOND GRADER DO HER OWN HOMEWORK??
KIRKMAN & SCOTT

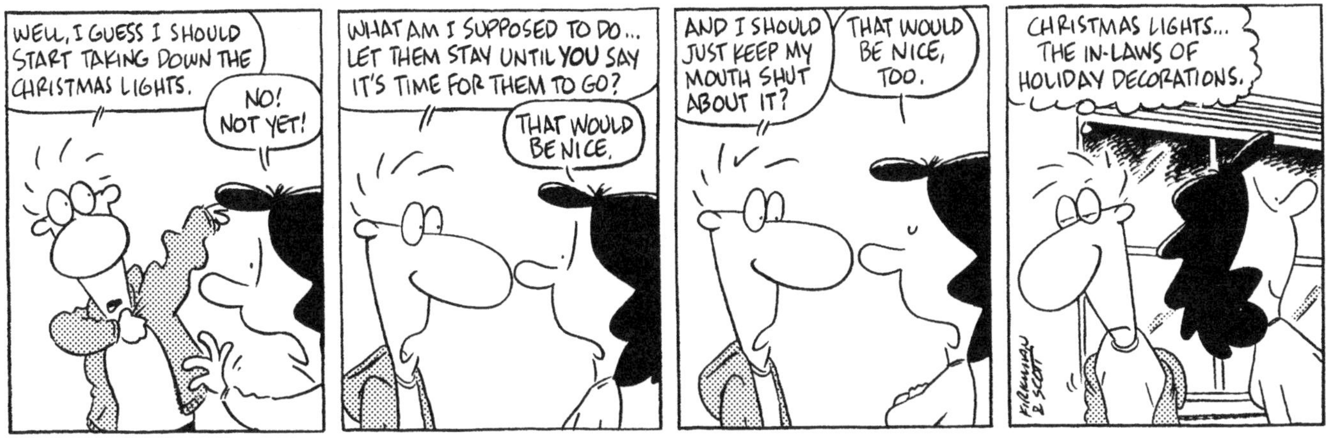
WELL, I GUESS I SHOULD START TAKING DOWN THE CHRISTMAS LIGHTS.
NO! NOT YET!
WHAT AM I SUPPOSED TO DO... LET THEM STAY UNTIL YOU SAY IT'S TIME FOR THEM TO GO?
THAT WOULD BE NICE.
AND I SHOULD JUST KEEP MY MOUTH SHUT ABOUT IT?
THAT WOULD BE NICE, TOO.
CHRISTMAS LIGHTS... THE IN-LAWS OF HOLIDAY DECORATIONS.
KIRKMAN & SCOTT

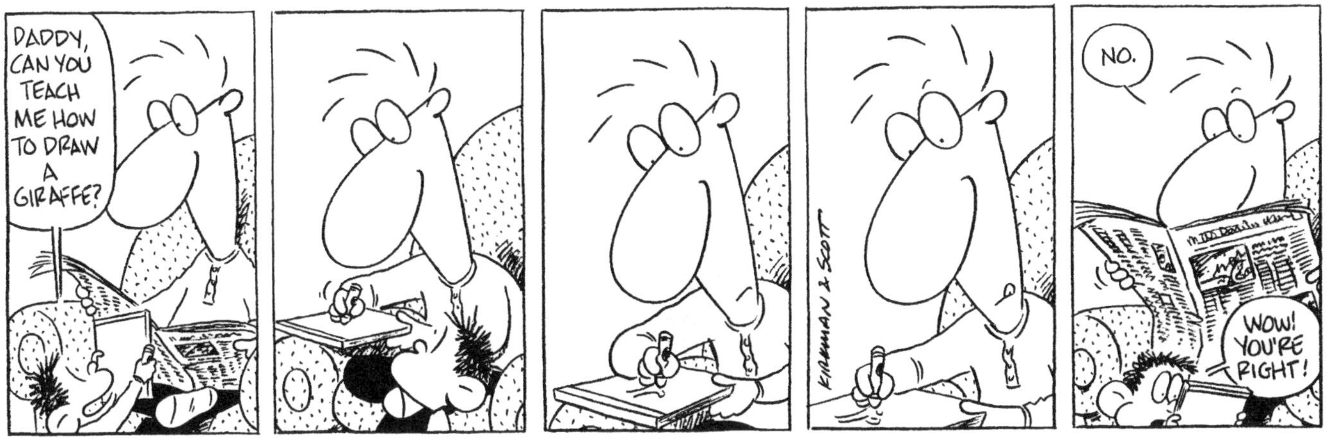
DADDY, CAN YOU TEACH ME HOW TO DRAW A GIRAFFE?
KIRKMAN & SCOTT
NO.
WOW! YOU'RE RIGHT!

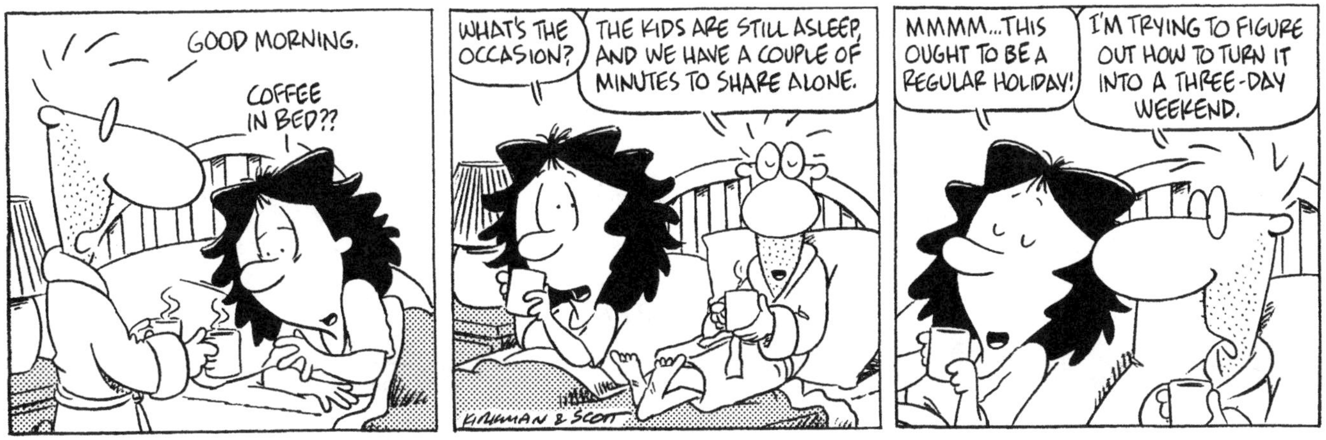
GOOD MORNING.
COFFEE IN BED??
WHAT'S THE OCCASION?
THE KIDS ARE STILL ASLEEP, AND WE HAVE A COUPLE OF MINUTES TO SHARE ALONE.
KIRKMAN & SCOTT
MMMM...THIS OUGHT TO BE A REGULAR HOLIDAY!
I'M TRYING TO FIGURE OUT HOW TO TURN IT INTO A THREE-DAY WEEKEND.

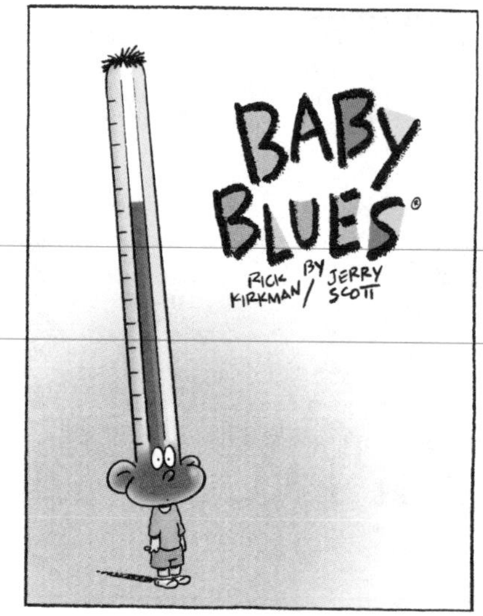
BABY BLUES®
BY RICK KIRKMAN / JERRY SCOTT

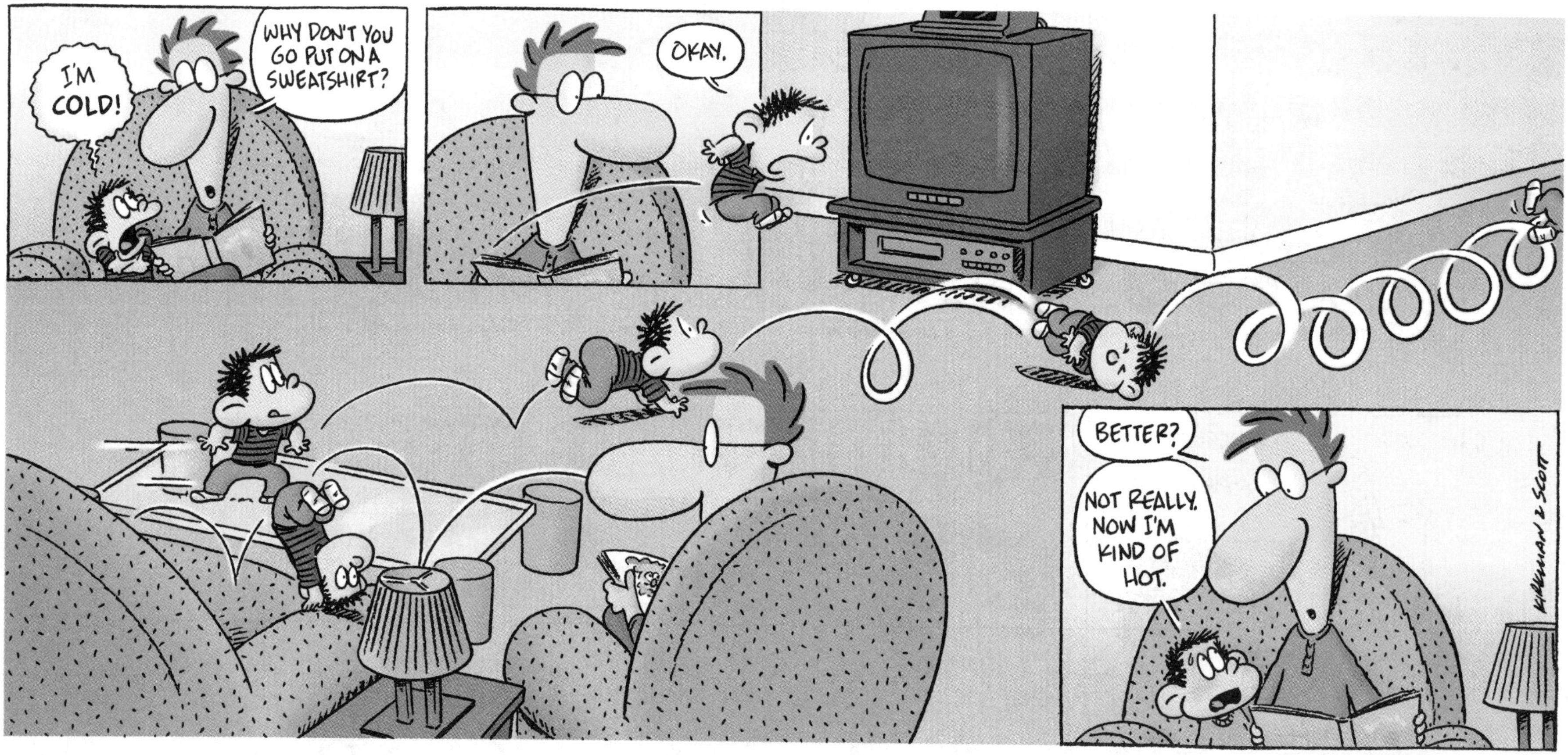
I'M COLD!
WHY DON'T YOU GO PUT ON A SWEATSHIRT?
OKAY.
BETTER?
NOT REALLY. NOW I'M KIND OF HOT.
KIRKMAN & SCOTT

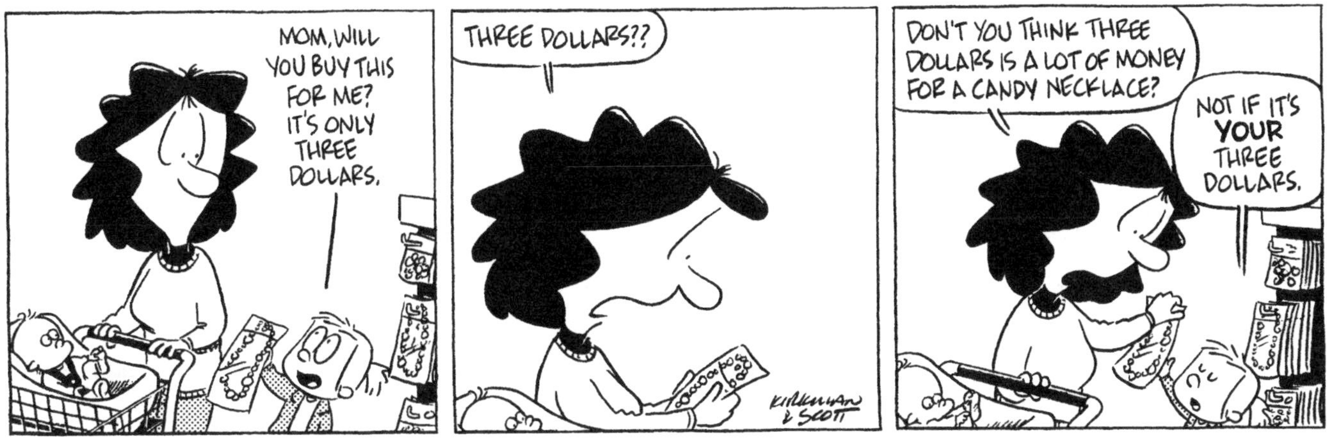
MOM, WILL YOU BUY THIS FOR ME? IT'S ONLY THREE DOLLARS.
THREE DOLLARS??
KIRKMAN & SCOTT
DON'T YOU THINK THREE DOLLARS IS A LOT OF MONEY FOR A CANDY NECKLACE?
NOT IF IT'S **YOUR** THREE DOLLARS.

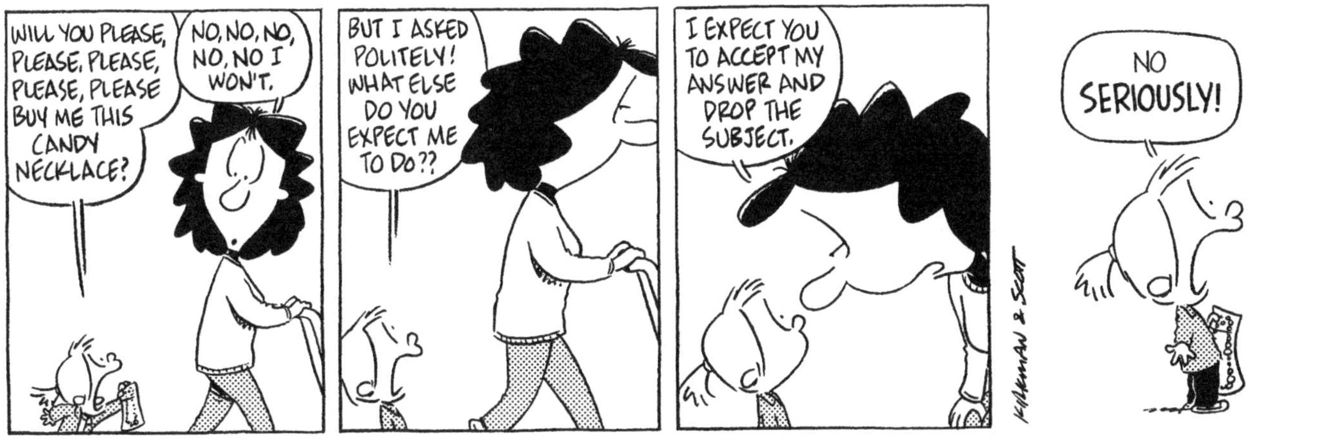
WILL YOU PLEASE, PLEASE, PLEASE, PLEASE, PLEASE BUY ME THIS CANDY NECKLACE?
NO, NO, NO, NO, NO I WON'T.
BUT I ASKED POLITELY! WHAT ELSE DO YOU EXPECT ME TO DO??
I EXPECT YOU TO ACCEPT MY ANSWER AND DROP THE SUBJECT.
KIRKMAN & SCOTT
NO **SERIOUSLY!**

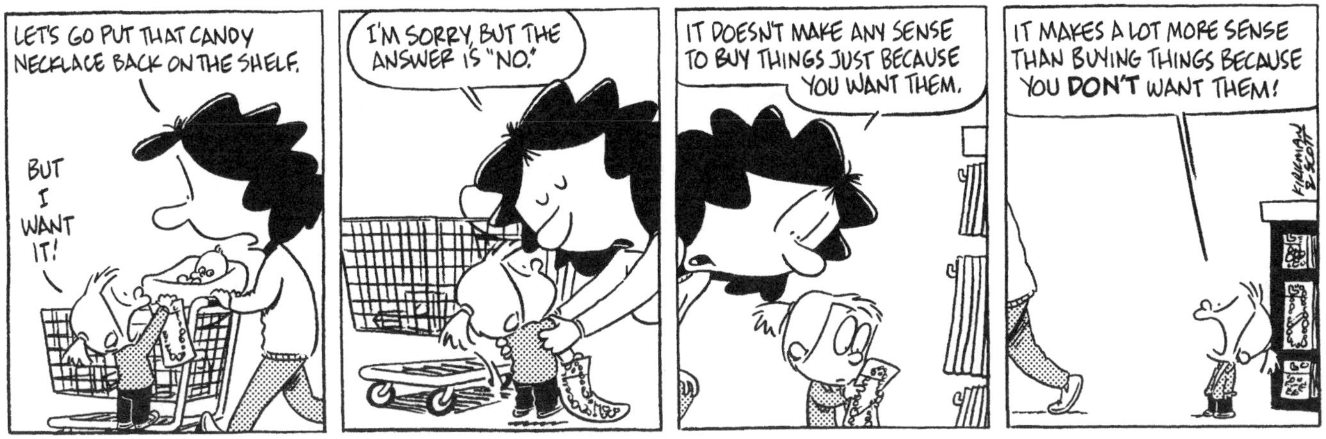
LET'S GO PUT THAT CANDY NECKLACE BACK ON THE SHELF.
BUT I WANT IT!
I'M SORRY, BUT THE ANSWER IS "NO."
IT DOESN'T MAKE ANY SENSE TO BUY THINGS JUST BECAUSE YOU WANT THEM.
IT MAKES A LOT MORE SENSE THAN BUYING THINGS BECAUSE YOU **DON'T** WANT THEM!
KIRKMAN & SCOTT

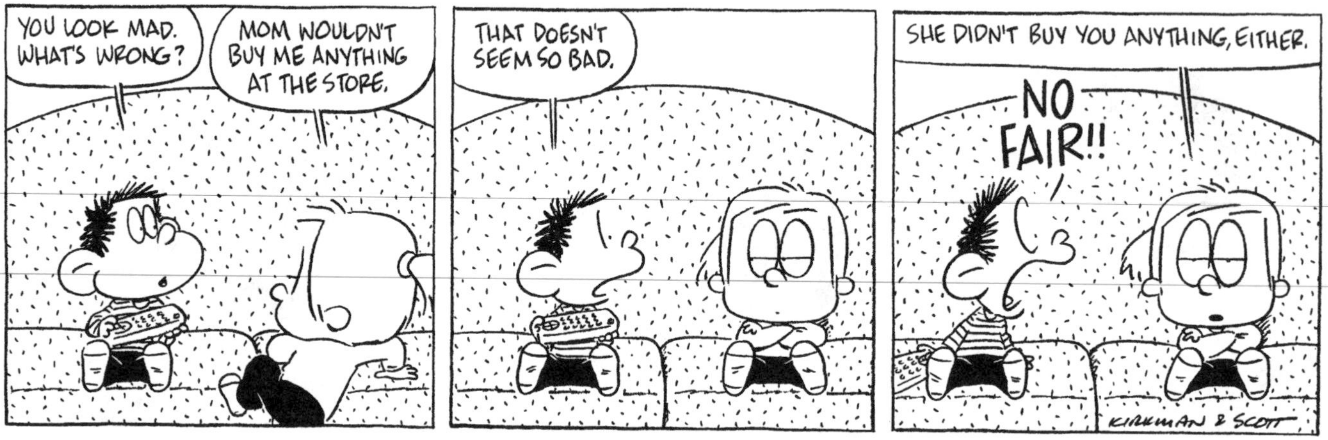
YOU LOOK MAD. WHAT'S WRONG?
MOM WOULDN'T BUY ME ANYTHING AT THE STORE.
THAT DOESN'T SEEM SO BAD.
SHE DIDN'T BUY YOU ANYTHING, EITHER.
NO FAIR!!
KIRKMAN & SCOTT

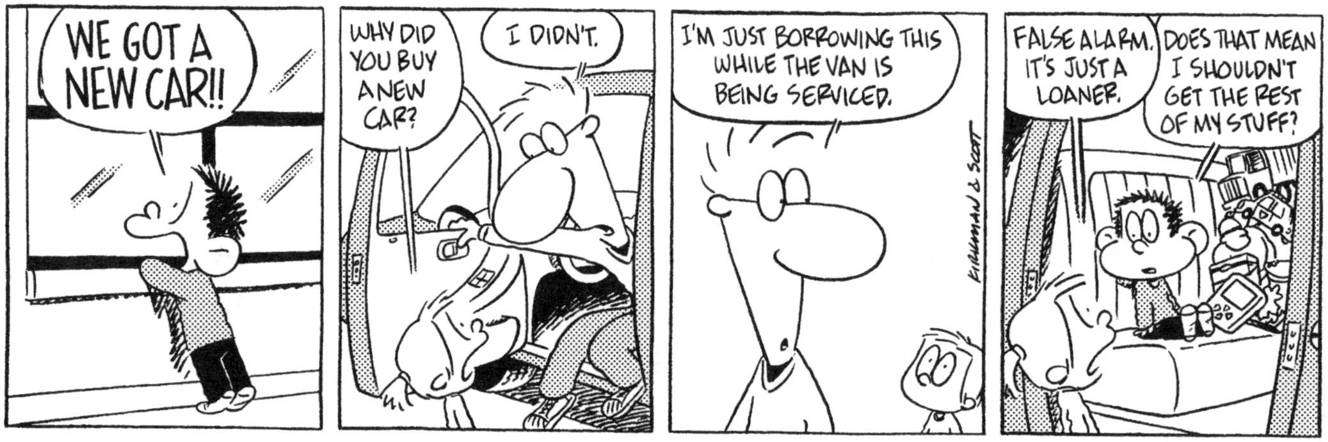
WE GOT A NEW CAR!!
WHY DID YOU BUY A NEW CAR?
I DIDN'T.
I'M JUST BORROWING THIS WHILE THE VAN IS BEING SERVICED.
KIRKMAN & SCOTT
FALSE ALARM. IT'S JUST A LOANER.
DOES THAT MEAN I SHOULDN'T GET THE REST OF MY STUFF?

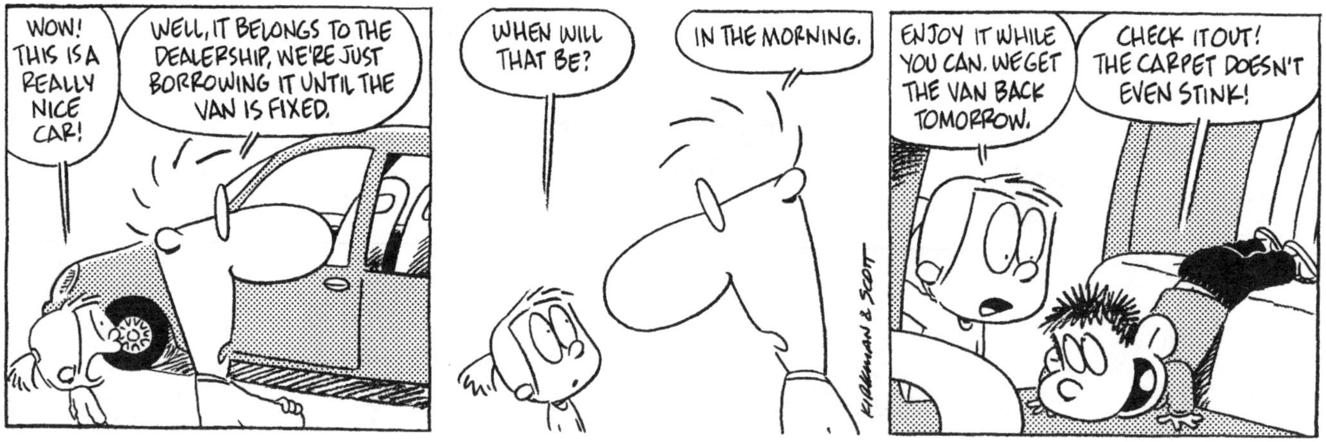
WOW! THIS IS A REALLY NICE CAR!
WELL, IT BELONGS TO THE DEALERSHIP, WE'RE JUST BORROWING IT UNTIL THE VAN IS FIXED.
WHEN WILL THAT BE?
IN THE MORNING.
KIRKMAN & SCOTT
ENJOY IT WHILE YOU CAN. WE GET THE VAN BACK TOMORROW.
CHECK IT OUT! THE CARPET DOESN'T EVEN STINK!

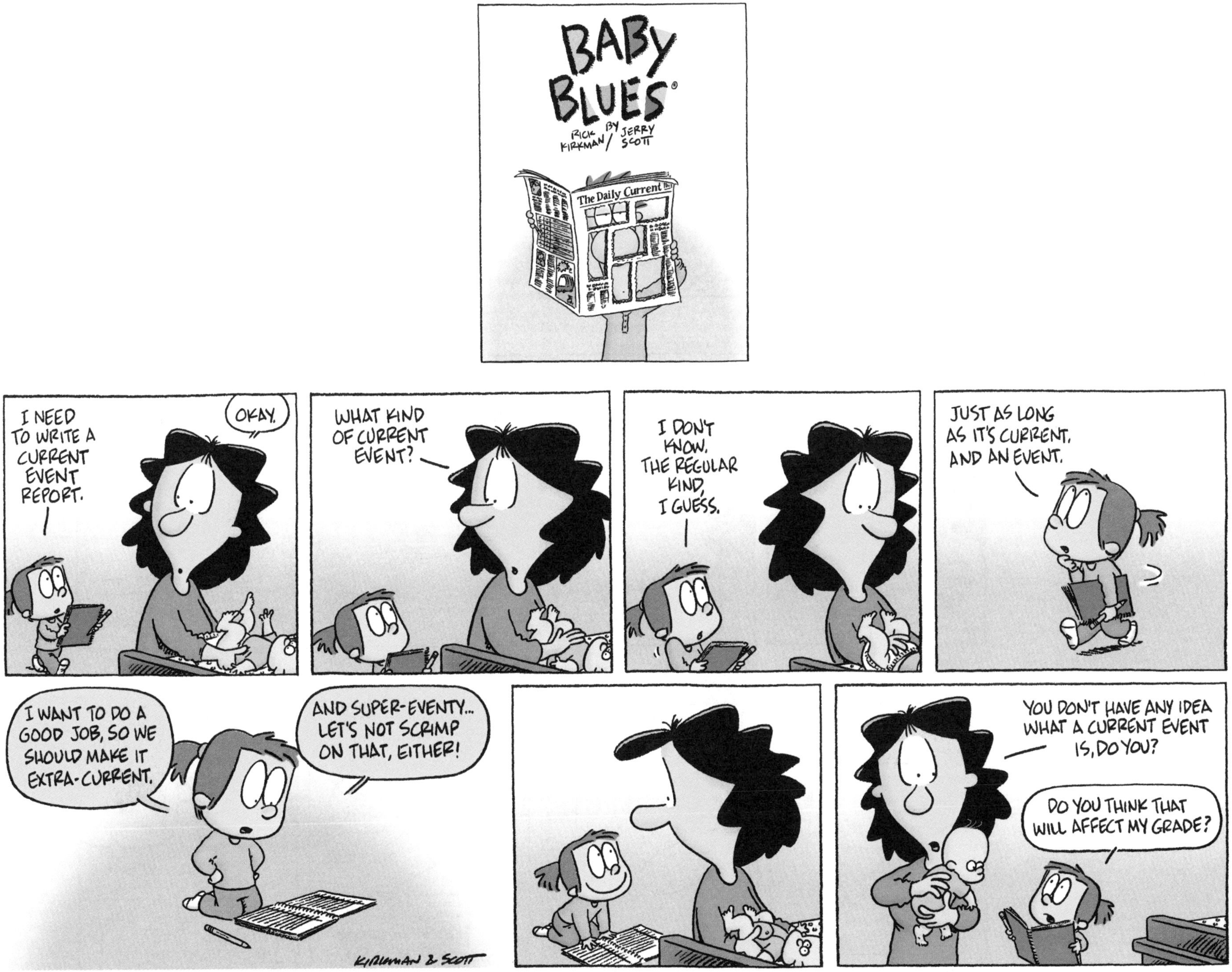
BABY BLUES®
RICK KIRKMAN / BY / JERRY SCOTT
The Daily Current
I NEED TO WRITE A CURRENT EVENT REPORT.
OKAY.
WHAT KIND OF CURRENT EVENT?
I DON'T KNOW. THE REGULAR KIND, I GUESS.
JUST AS LONG AS IT'S CURRENT, AND AN EVENT.
I WANT TO DO A GOOD JOB, SO WE SHOULD MAKE IT EXTRA-CURRENT.
AND SUPER-EVENTY... LET'S NOT SCRIMP ON THAT, EITHER!
KIRKMAN & SCOTT
YOU DON'T HAVE ANY IDEA WHAT A CURRENT EVENT IS, DO YOU?
DO YOU THINK THAT WILL AFFECT MY GRADE?

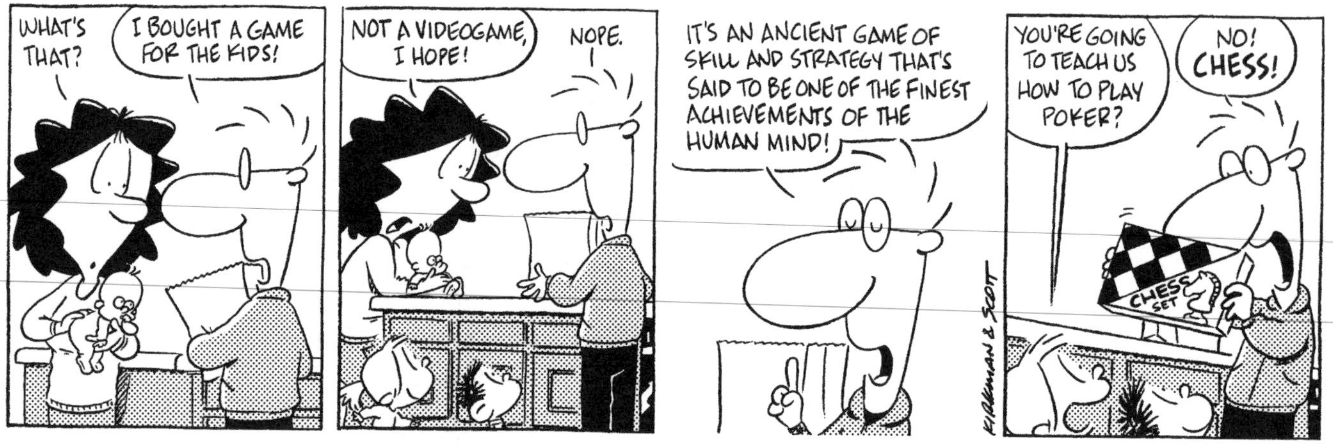
WHAT'S THAT?
I BOUGHT A GAME FOR THE KIDS!
NOT A VIDEOGAME, I HOPE!
NOPE.
IT'S AN ANCIENT GAME OF SKILL AND STRATEGY THAT'S SAID TO BE ONE OF THE FINEST ACHIEVEMENTS OF THE HUMAN MIND!
KIRKMAN & SCOTT
YOU'RE GOING TO TEACH US HOW TO PLAY POKER?
NO! CHESS!
CHESS SET

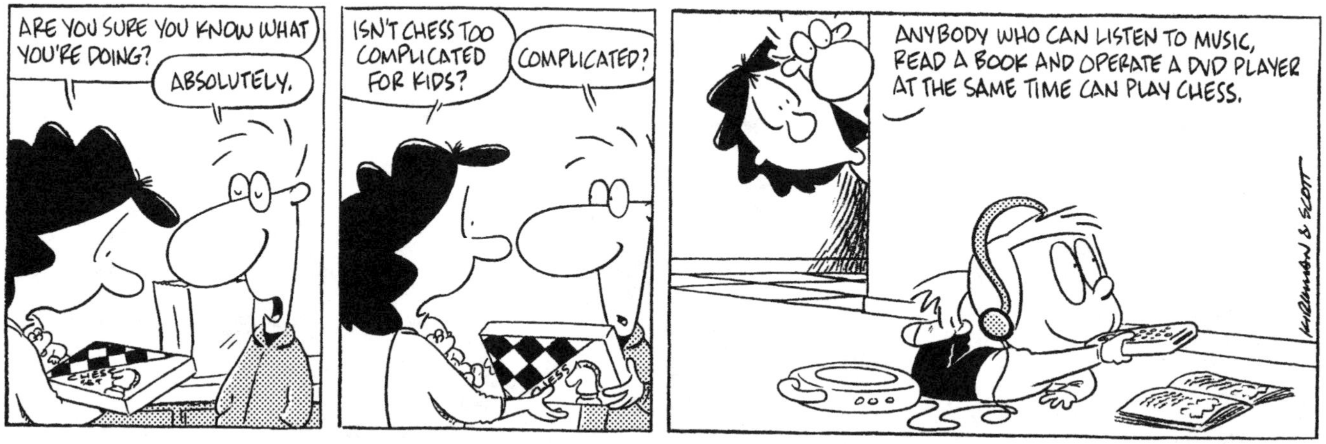
ARE YOU SURE YOU KNOW WHAT YOU'RE DOING?
ABSOLUTELY.
ISN'T CHESS TOO COMPLICATED FOR KIDS?
COMPLICATED?
ANYBODY WHO CAN LISTEN TO MUSIC, READ A BOOK AND OPERATE A DVD PLAYER AT THE SAME TIME CAN PLAY CHESS.
KIRKMAN & SCOTT

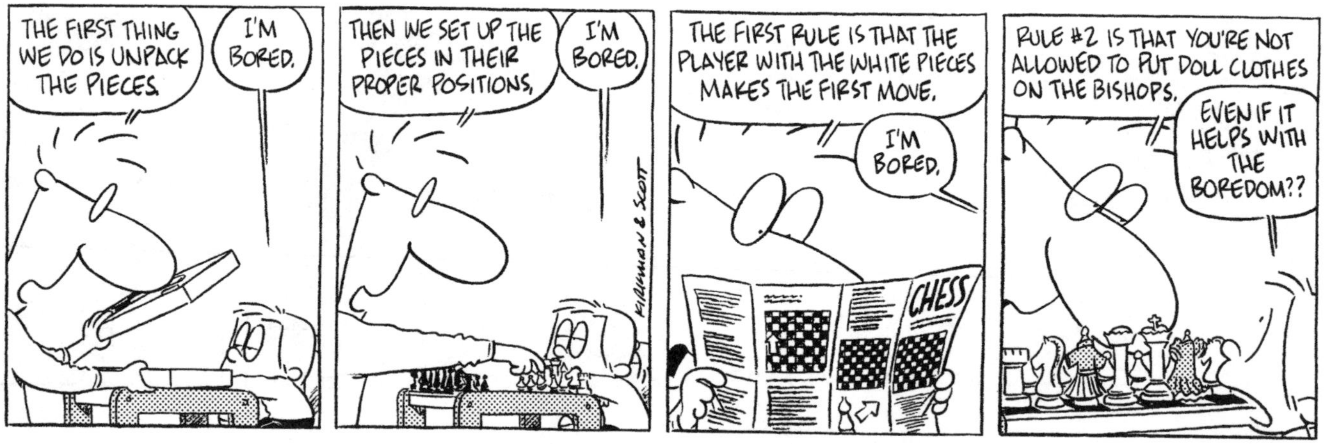
THE FIRST THING WE DO IS UNPACK THE PIECES.
I'M BORED.
THEN WE SET UP THE PIECES IN THEIR PROPER POSITIONS,
I'M BORED.
KIRKMAN & SCOTT
THE FIRST RULE IS THAT THE PLAYER WITH THE WHITE PIECES MAKES THE FIRST MOVE.
I'M BORED.
CHESS
RULE #2 IS THAT YOU'RE NOT ALLOWED TO PUT DOLL CLOTHES ON THE BISHOPS.
EVEN IF IT HELPS WITH THE BOREDOM??

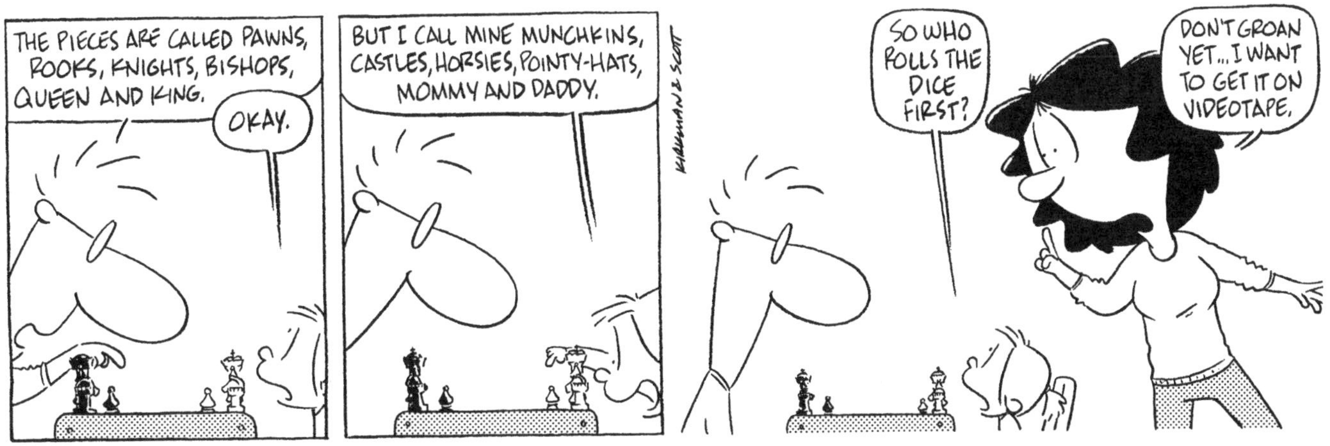
THE PIECES ARE CALLED PAWNS, ROOKS, KNIGHTS, BISHOPS, QUEEN AND KING.
OKAY.
BUT I CALL MINE MUNCHKINS, CASTLES, HORSIES, POINTY-HATS, MOMMY AND DADDY.
KIRKMAN & SCOTT
SO WHO ROLLS THE DICE FIRST?
DON'T GROAN YET... I WANT TO GET IT ON VIDEOTAPE.

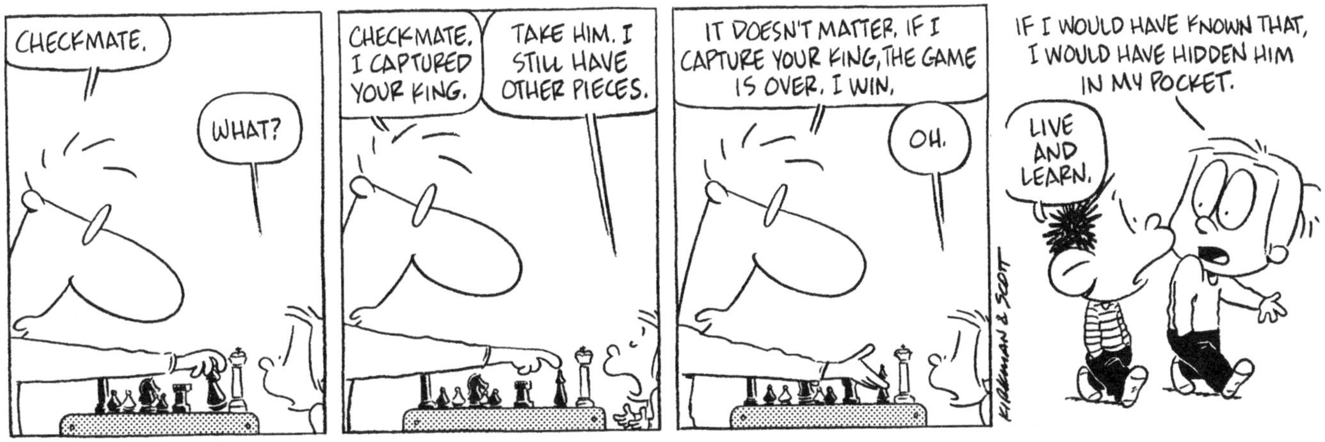
CHECKMATE.
WHAT?
CHECKMATE. I CAPTURED YOUR KING.
TAKE HIM. I STILL HAVE OTHER PIECES.
IT DOESN'T MATTER. IF I CAPTURE YOUR KING, THE GAME IS OVER. I WIN.
OH.
KIRKMAN & SCOTT
IF I WOULD HAVE KNOWN THAT, I WOULD HAVE HIDDEN HIM IN MY POCKET.
LIVE AND LEARN.

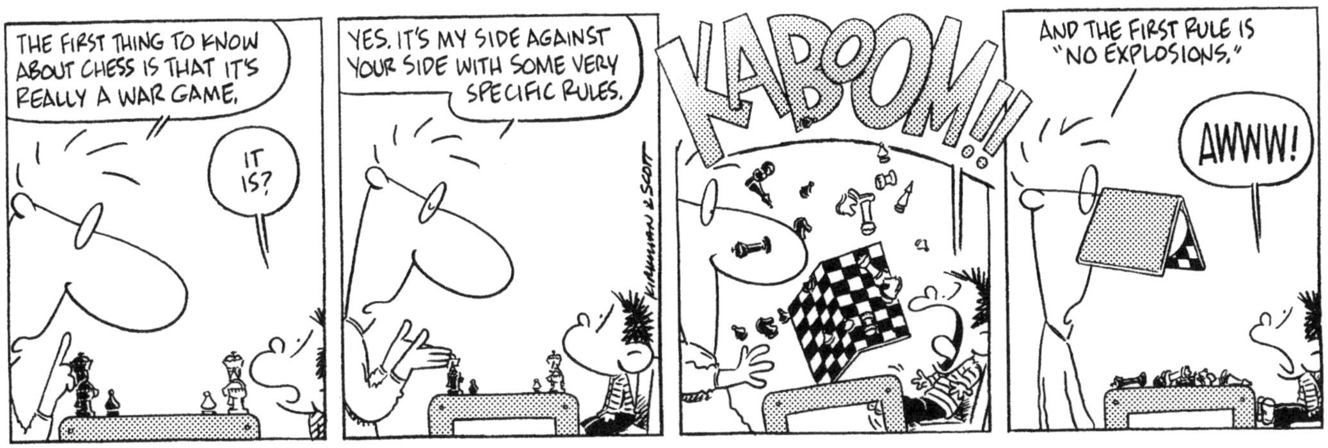
THE FIRST THING TO KNOW ABOUT CHESS IS THAT IT'S REALLY A WAR GAME.
IT IS?
YES. IT'S MY SIDE AGAINST YOUR SIDE WITH SOME VERY SPECIFIC RULES.
KIRKMAN & SCOTT
KABOOM!!
AND THE FIRST RULE IS "NO EXPLOSIONS."
AWWW!

BABY BLUES ®
BY RICK KIRKMAN & JERRY SCOTT

TO DO

WANT TO HEAR MY PLAN FOR THE DAY?

:GROAN!:

WHAT?? WHAT IS IT WITH YOU AND PLANS?

CAN'T WE JUST HAVE ONE SUNDAY THAT'S NOT ONE BIG TO-DO LIST?

SURE.

REALLY??

YOU MEAN THERE WOULD BE NO CHORES, NO ERRANDS, NO TRIPS TO THE ZOO OR THE MALL, OR ANYTHING?

NOPE.

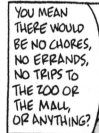

JUST A TOTALLY FREE DAY WITH NO OBLIGATIONS.

UH-HUH.

ALL RIGHT!!

SO WHAT SHOULD WE DO?

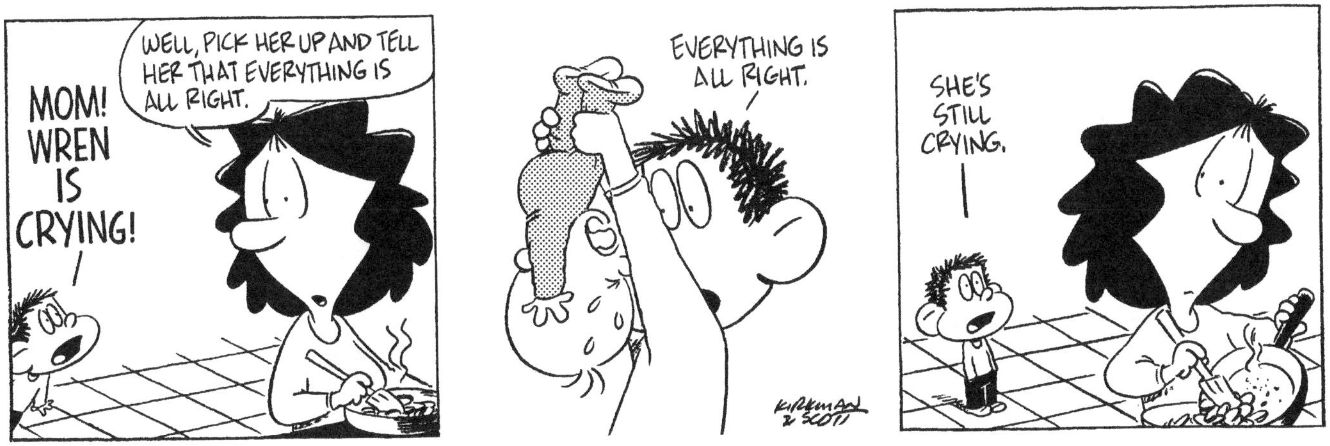
MOM! WREN IS CRYING!
WELL, PICK HER UP AND TELL HER THAT EVERYTHING IS ALL RIGHT.
EVERYTHING IS ALL RIGHT.
SHE'S STILL CRYING.
KIRKMAN & SCOTT

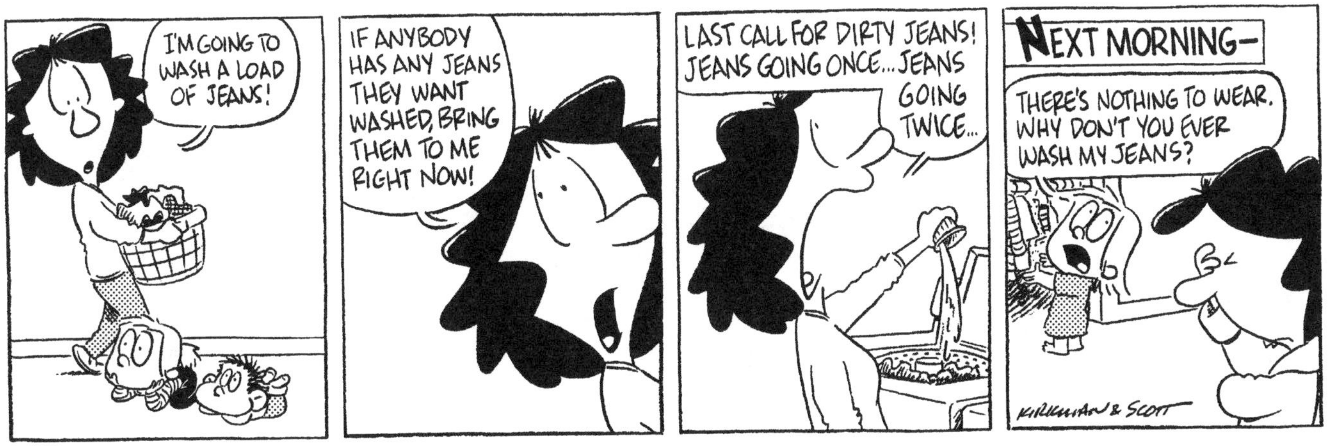
I'M GOING TO WASH A LOAD OF JEANS!
IF ANYBODY HAS ANY JEANS THEY WANT WASHED, BRING THEM TO ME RIGHT NOW!
LAST CALL FOR DIRTY JEANS! JEANS GOING ONCE... JEANS GOING TWICE...
NEXT MORNING—
THERE'S NOTHING TO WEAR. WHY DON'T YOU EVER WASH MY JEANS?
KIRKMAN & SCOTT

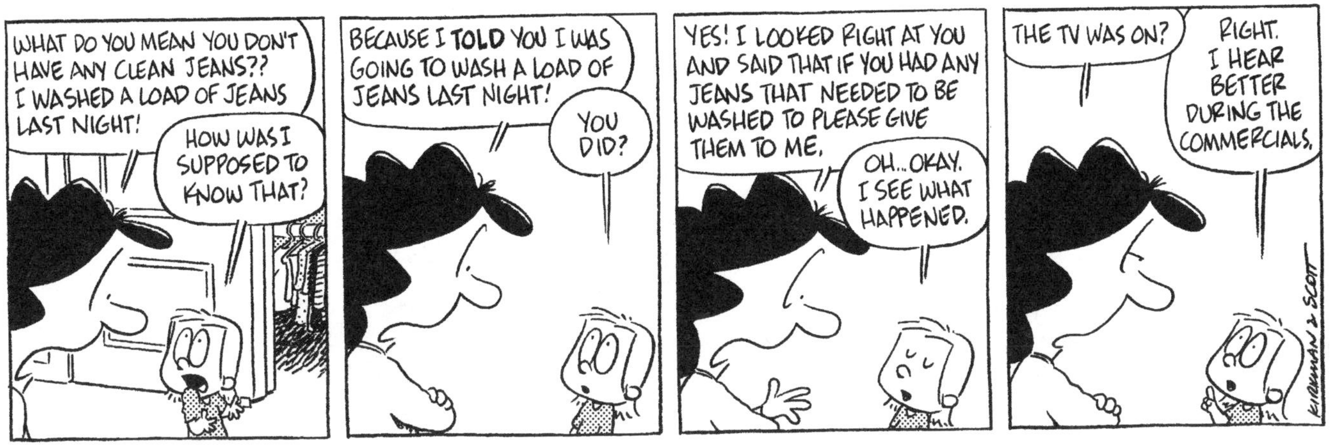
WHAT DO YOU MEAN YOU DON'T HAVE ANY CLEAN JEANS?? I WASHED A LOAD OF JEANS LAST NIGHT!
HOW WAS I SUPPOSED TO KNOW THAT?
BECAUSE I TOLD YOU I WAS GOING TO WASH A LOAD OF JEANS LAST NIGHT!
YOU DID?
YES! I LOOKED RIGHT AT YOU AND SAID THAT IF YOU HAD ANY JEANS THAT NEEDED TO BE WASHED TO PLEASE GIVE THEM TO ME.
OH... OKAY. I SEE WHAT HAPPENED.
THE TV WAS ON?
RIGHT. I HEAR BETTER DURING THE COMMERCIALS.
KIRKMAN & SCOTT

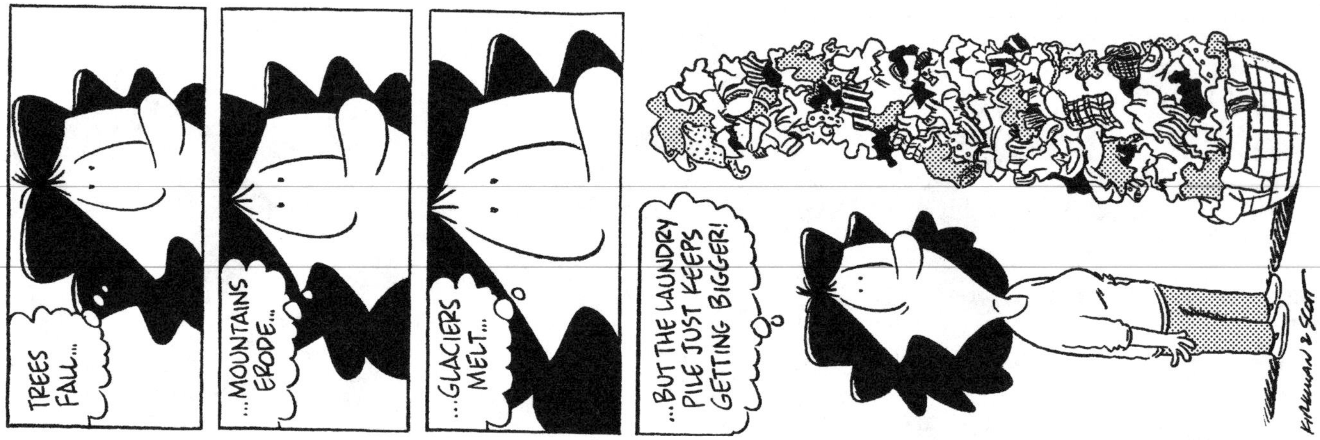
TREES FALL...
...MOUNTAINS ERODE...
...GLACIERS MELT...
...BUT THE LAUNDRY PILE JUST KEEPS GETTING BIGGER!

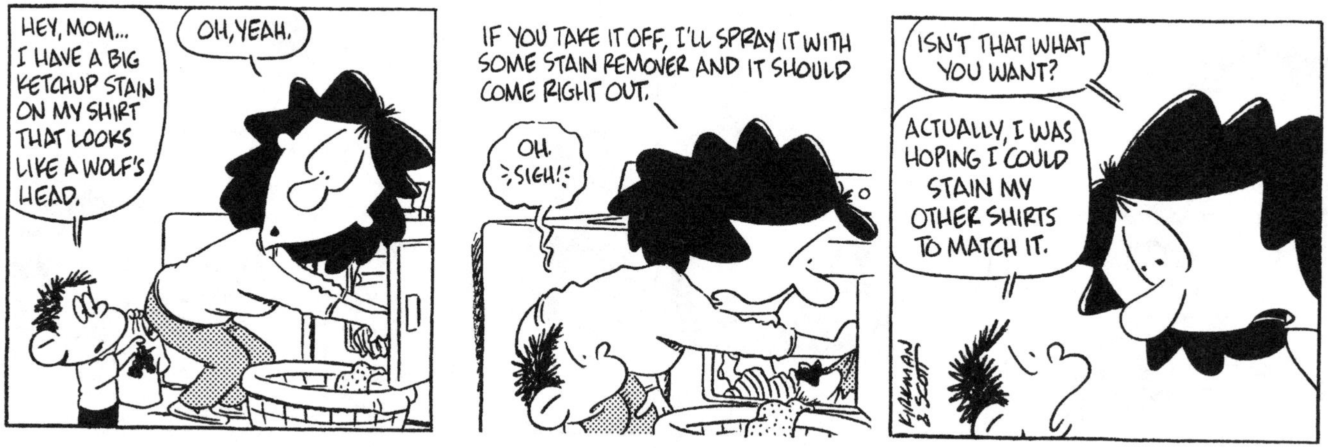
HEY, MOM... I HAVE A BIG KETCHUP STAIN ON MY SHIRT THAT LOOKS LIKE A WOLF'S HEAD.
OH, YEAH.
IF YOU TAKE IT OFF, I'LL SPRAY IT WITH SOME STAIN REMOVER AND IT SHOULD COME RIGHT OUT.
OH. SIGH!
ISN'T THAT WHAT YOU WANT?
ACTUALLY, I WAS HOPING I COULD STAIN MY OTHER SHIRTS TO MATCH IT.

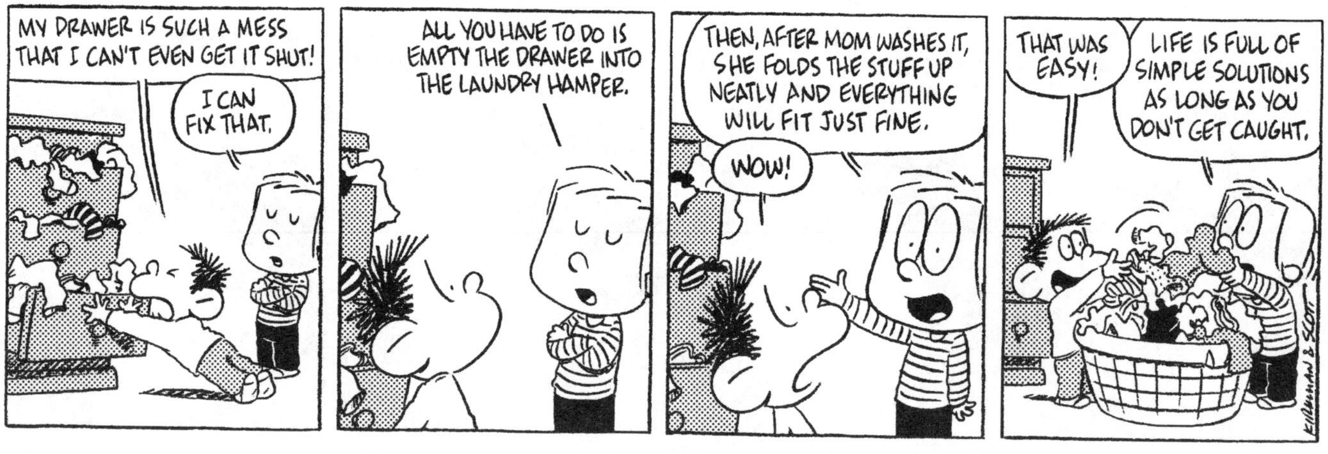
MY DRAWER IS SUCH A MESS THAT I CAN'T EVEN GET IT SHUT!
I CAN FIX THAT.
ALL YOU HAVE TO DO IS EMPTY THE DRAWER INTO THE LAUNDRY HAMPER.
THEN, AFTER MOM WASHES IT, SHE FOLDS THE STUFF UP NEATLY AND EVERYTHING WILL FIT JUST FINE.
WOW!
THAT WAS EASY!
LIFE IS FULL OF SIMPLE SOLUTIONS AS LONG AS YOU DON'T GET CAUGHT.

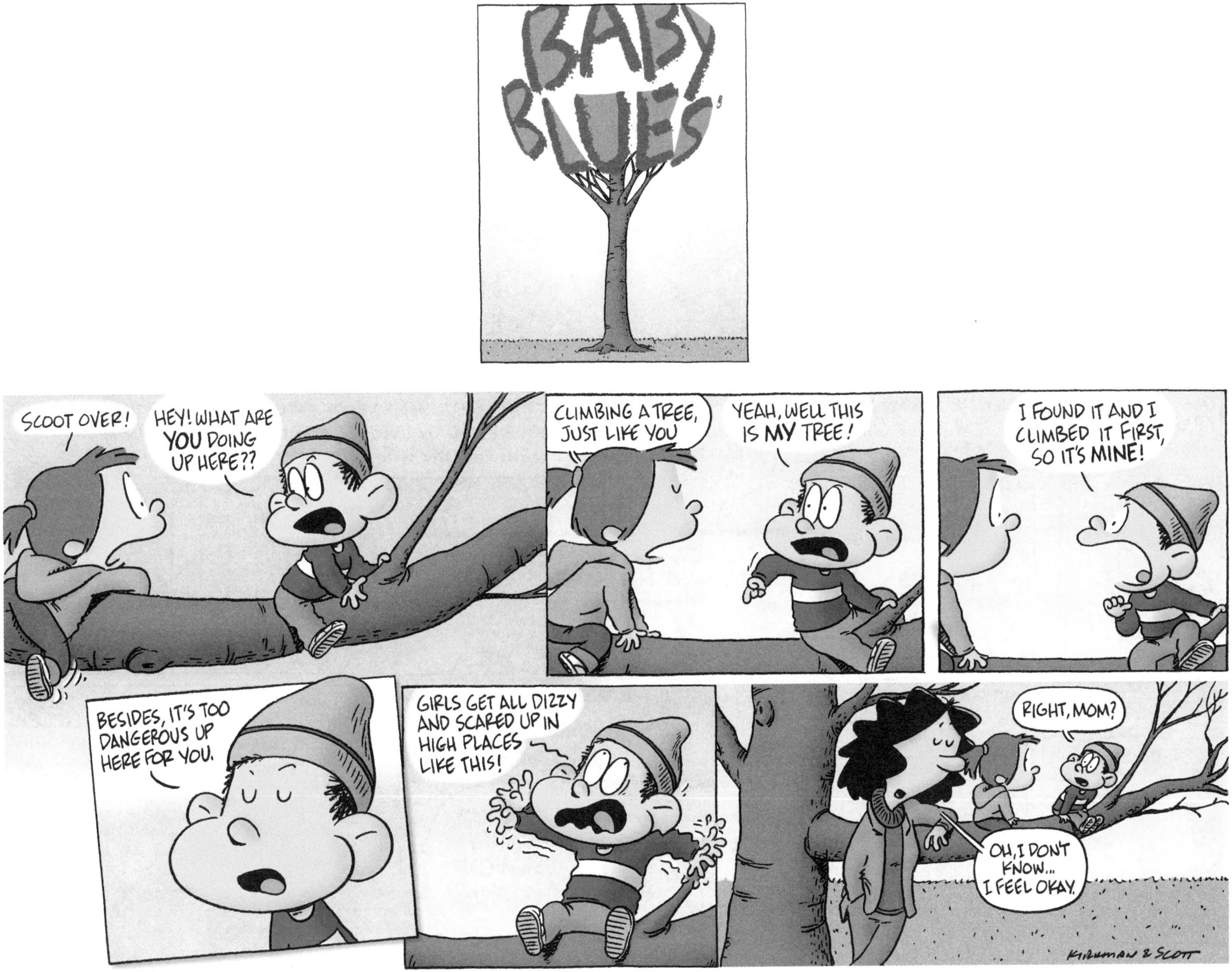
BABY BLUES
SCOOT OVER!
HEY! WHAT ARE YOU DOING UP HERE??
CLIMBING A TREE, JUST LIKE YOU
YEAH, WELL THIS IS MY TREE!
I FOUND IT AND I CLIMBED IT FIRST, SO IT'S MINE!
BESIDES, IT'S TOO DANGEROUS UP HERE FOR YOU.
GIRLS GET ALL DIZZY AND SCARED UP IN HIGH PLACES LIKE THIS!
RIGHT, MOM?
OH, I DON'T KNOW... I FEEL OKAY.
KIRKMAN & SCOTT

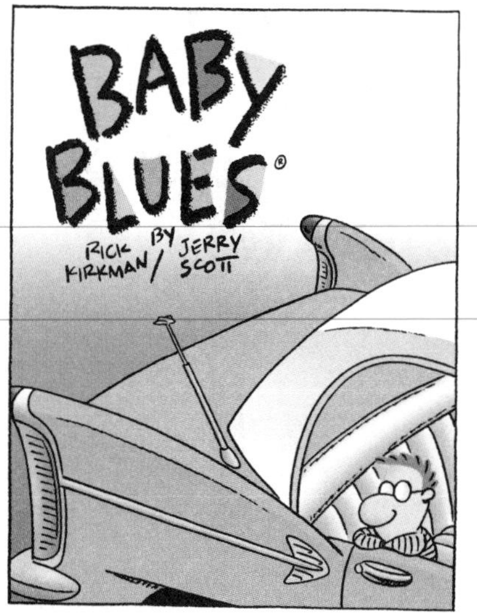
BABY BLUES®
RICK KIRKMAN / BY JERRY SCOTT

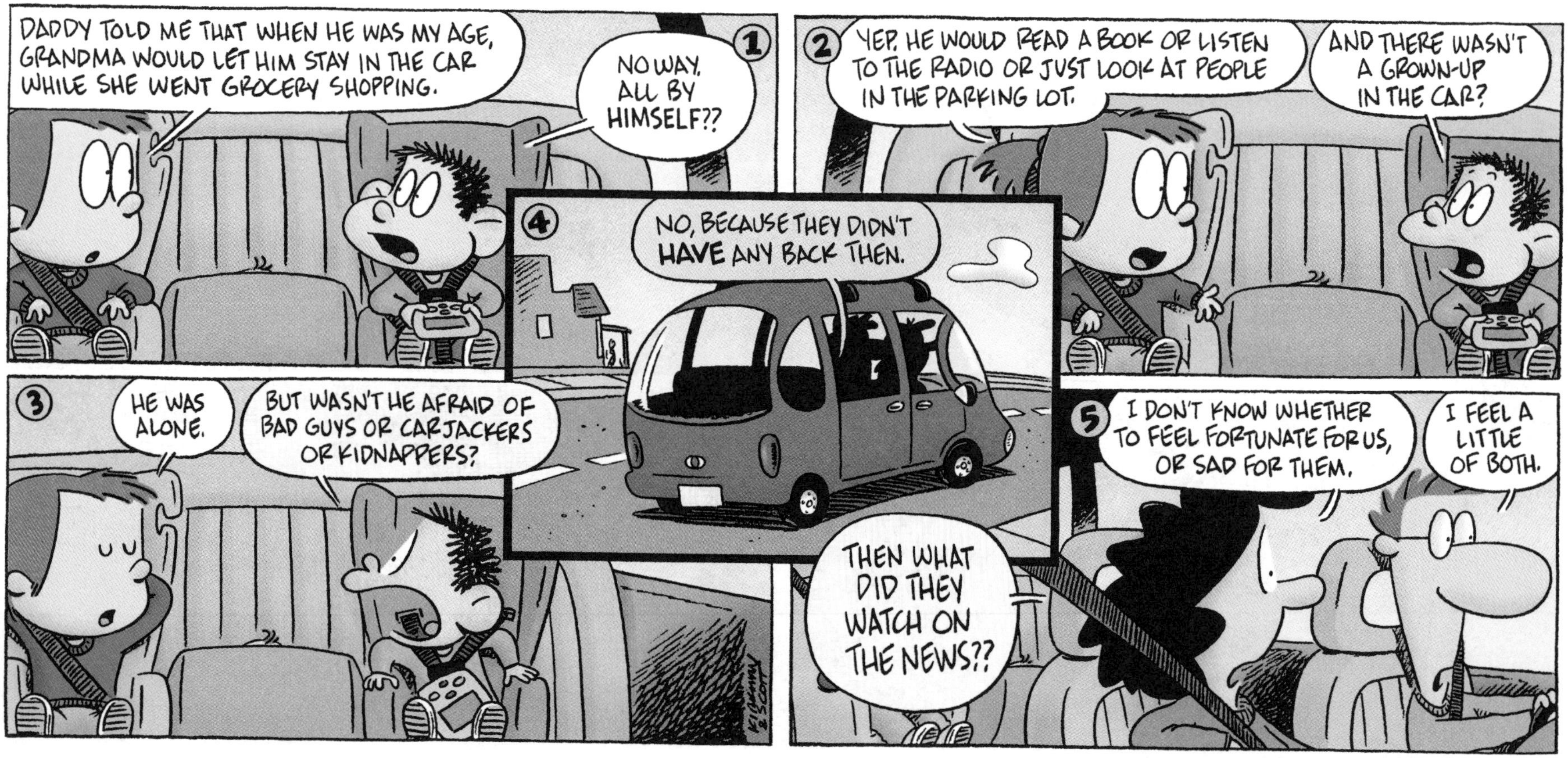
DADDY TOLD ME THAT WHEN HE WAS MY AGE, GRANDMA WOULD LET HIM STAY IN THE CAR WHILE SHE WENT GROCERY SHOPPING.
NO WAY. ALL BY HIMSELF??
YEP. HE WOULD READ A BOOK OR LISTEN TO THE RADIO OR JUST LOOK AT PEOPLE IN THE PARKING LOT.
AND THERE WASN'T A GROWN-UP IN THE CAR?
HE WAS ALONE.
BUT WASN'T HE AFRAID OF BAD GUYS OR CARJACKERS OR KIDNAPPERS?
NO, BECAUSE THEY DIDN'T HAVE ANY BACK THEN.
THEN WHAT DID THEY WATCH ON THE NEWS??
I DON'T KNOW WHETHER TO FEEL FORTUNATE FOR US, OR SAD FOR THEM.
I FEEL A LITTLE OF BOTH.

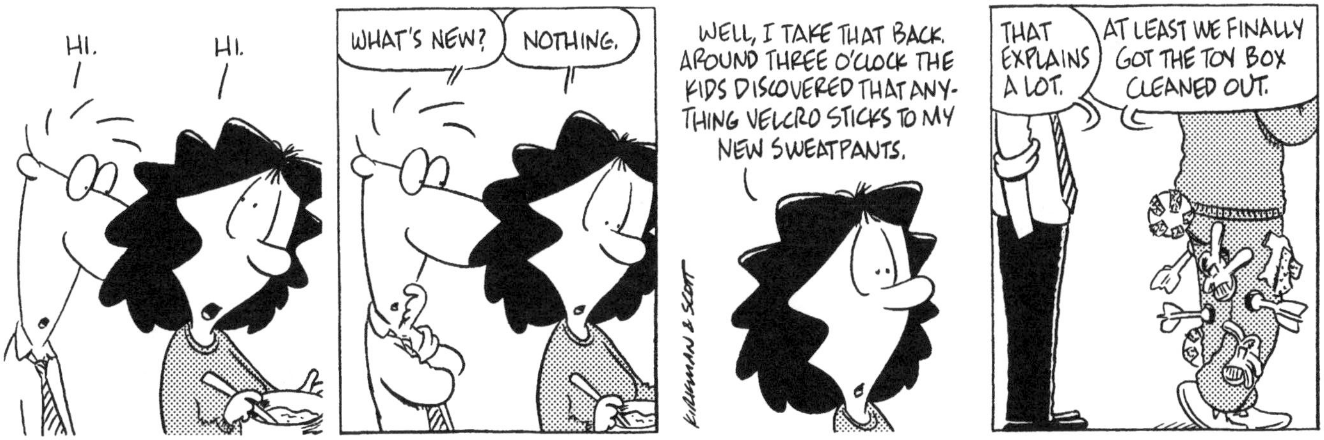
HI.
HI.
WHAT'S NEW?
NOTHING.
KIRKMAN & SCOTT
WELL, I TAKE THAT BACK. AROUND THREE O'CLOCK THE KIDS DISCOVERED THAT ANYTHING VELCRO STICKS TO MY NEW SWEATPANTS.
THAT EXPLAINS A LOT.
AT LEAST WE FINALLY GOT THE TOY BOX CLEANED OUT.

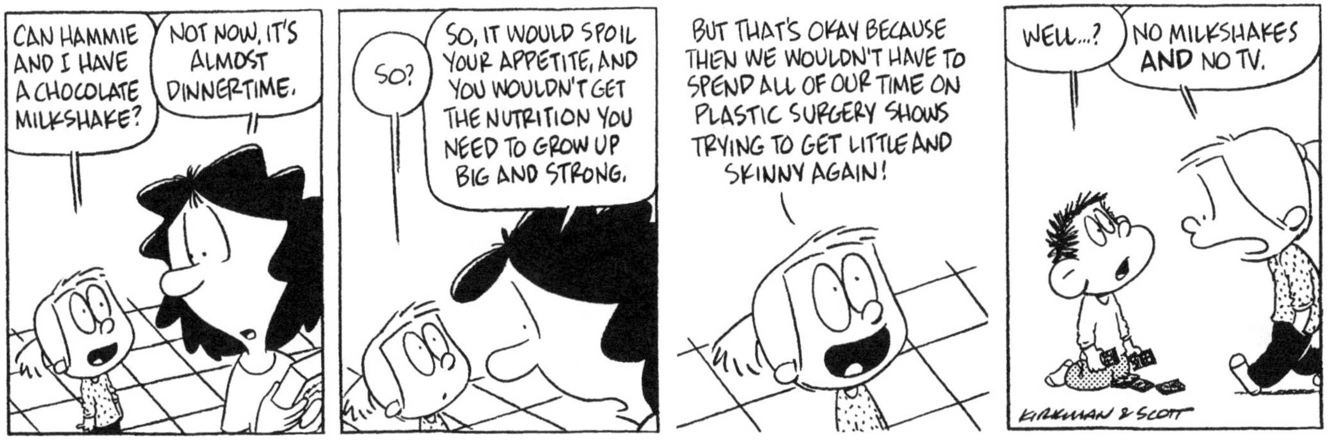
CAN HAMMIE AND I HAVE A CHOCOLATE MILKSHAKE?
NOT NOW, IT'S ALMOST DINNERTIME.
SO?
SO, IT WOULD SPOIL YOUR APPETITE, AND YOU WOULDN'T GET THE NUTRITION YOU NEED TO GROW UP BIG AND STRONG.
BUT THAT'S OKAY BECAUSE THEN WE WOULDN'T HAVE TO SPEND ALL OF OUR TIME ON PLASTIC SURGERY SHOWS TRYING TO GET LITTLE AND SKINNY AGAIN!
WELL...?
NO MILKSHAKES AND NO TV.
KIRKMAN & SCOTT

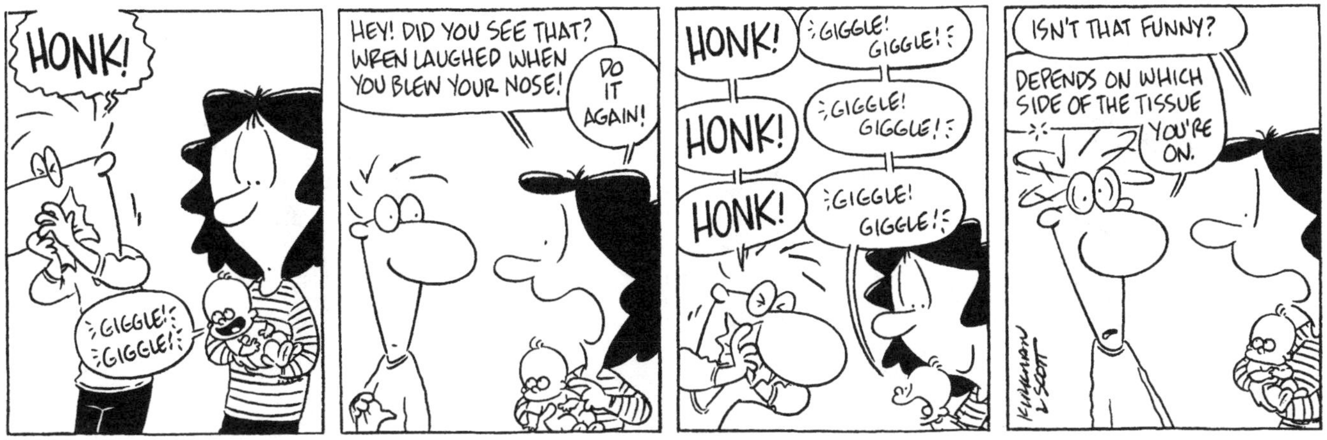
HONK!
GIGGLE! GIGGLE!
HEY! DID YOU SEE THAT? WREN LAUGHED WHEN YOU BLEW YOUR NOSE!
DO IT AGAIN!
HONK!
GIGGLE! GIGGLE!
HONK!
GIGGLE! GIGGLE!
HONK!
GIGGLE! GIGGLE!
KIRKMAN & SCOTT
ISN'T THAT FUNNY?
DEPENDS ON WHICH SIDE OF THE TISSUE YOU'RE ON.

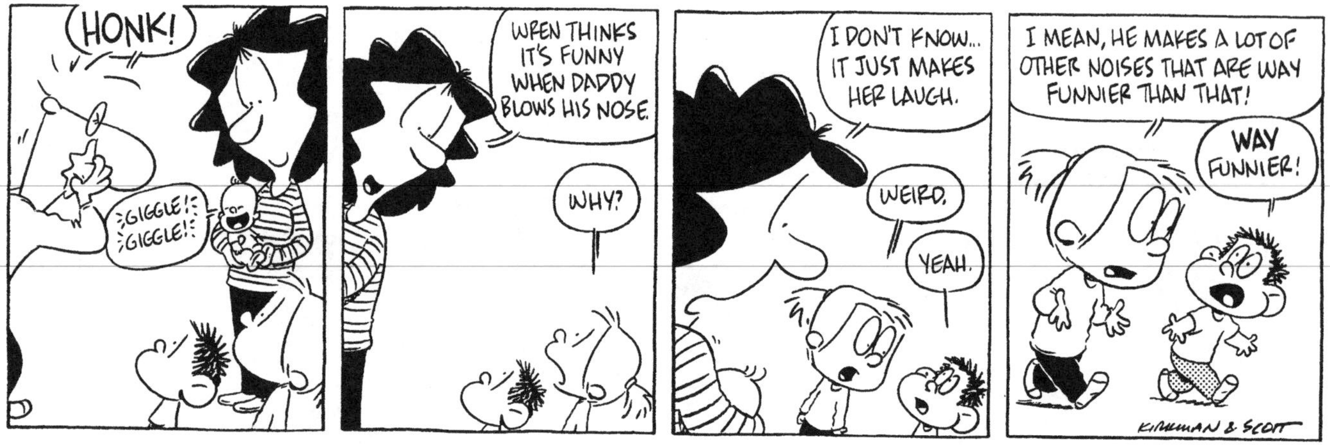
HONK!
GIGGLE! GIGGLE!
WREN THINKS IT'S FUNNY WHEN DADDY BLOWS HIS NOSE.
WHY?
I DON'T KNOW... IT JUST MAKES HER LAUGH.
WEIRD.
YEAH.
I MEAN, HE MAKES A LOT OF OTHER NOISES THAT ARE WAY FUNNIER THAN THAT!
WAY FUNNIER!
KIRKMAN & SCOTT

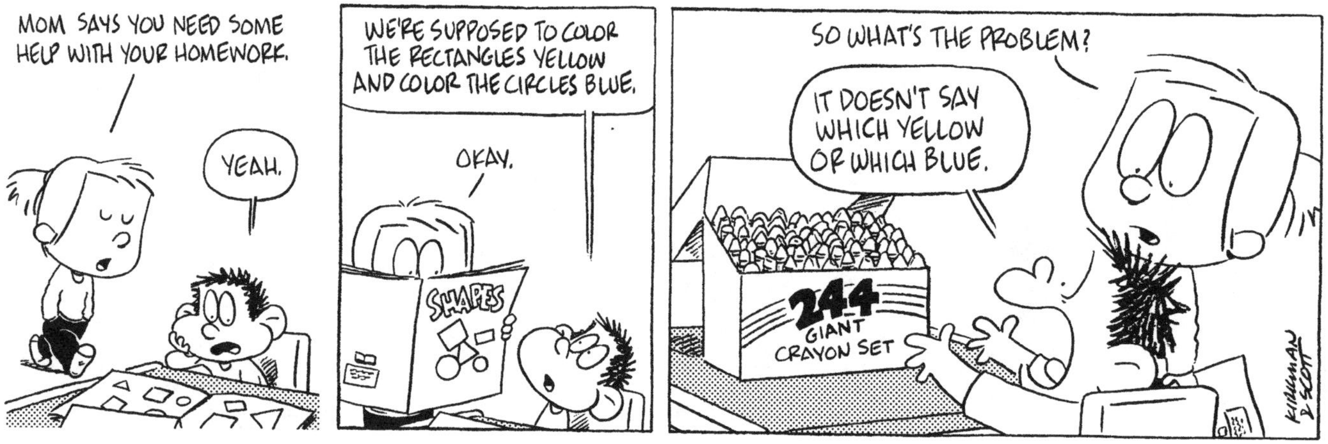
MOM SAYS YOU NEED SOME HELP WITH YOUR HOMEWORK.
YEAH.
WE'RE SUPPOSED TO COLOR THE RECTANGLES YELLOW AND COLOR THE CIRCLES BLUE.
OKAY.
SHAPES
SO WHAT'S THE PROBLEM?
IT DOESN'T SAY WHICH YELLOW OR WHICH BLUE.
244 GIANT CRAYON SET
KIRKMAN & SCOTT

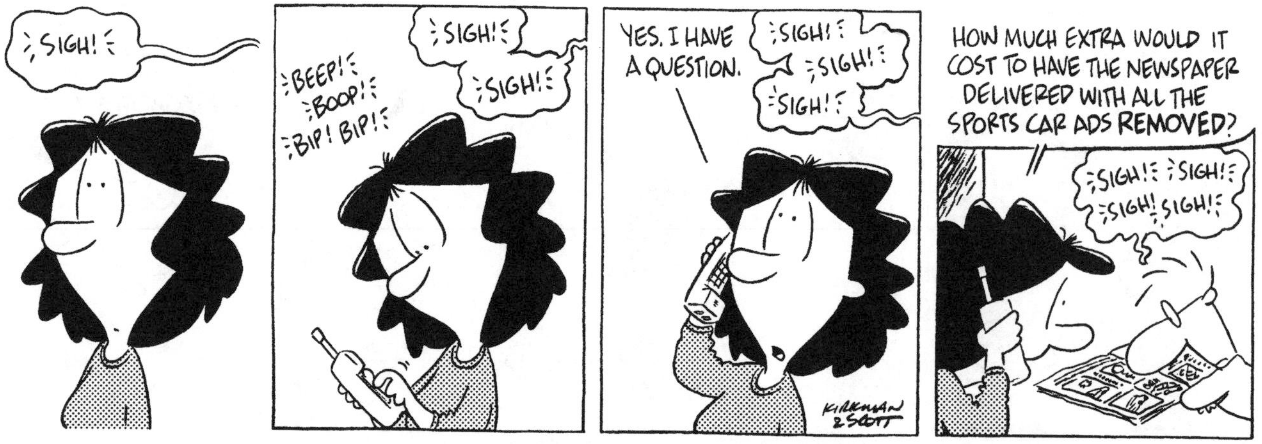
SIGH!
SIGH!
SIGH!
BEEP! BOOP! BIP! BIP!
YES. I HAVE A QUESTION.
SIGH! SIGH! SIGH!
KIRKMAN & SCOTT
HOW MUCH EXTRA WOULD IT COST TO HAVE THE NEWSPAPER DELIVERED WITH ALL THE SPORTS CAR ADS REMOVED?
SIGH! SIGH! SIGH! SIGH!

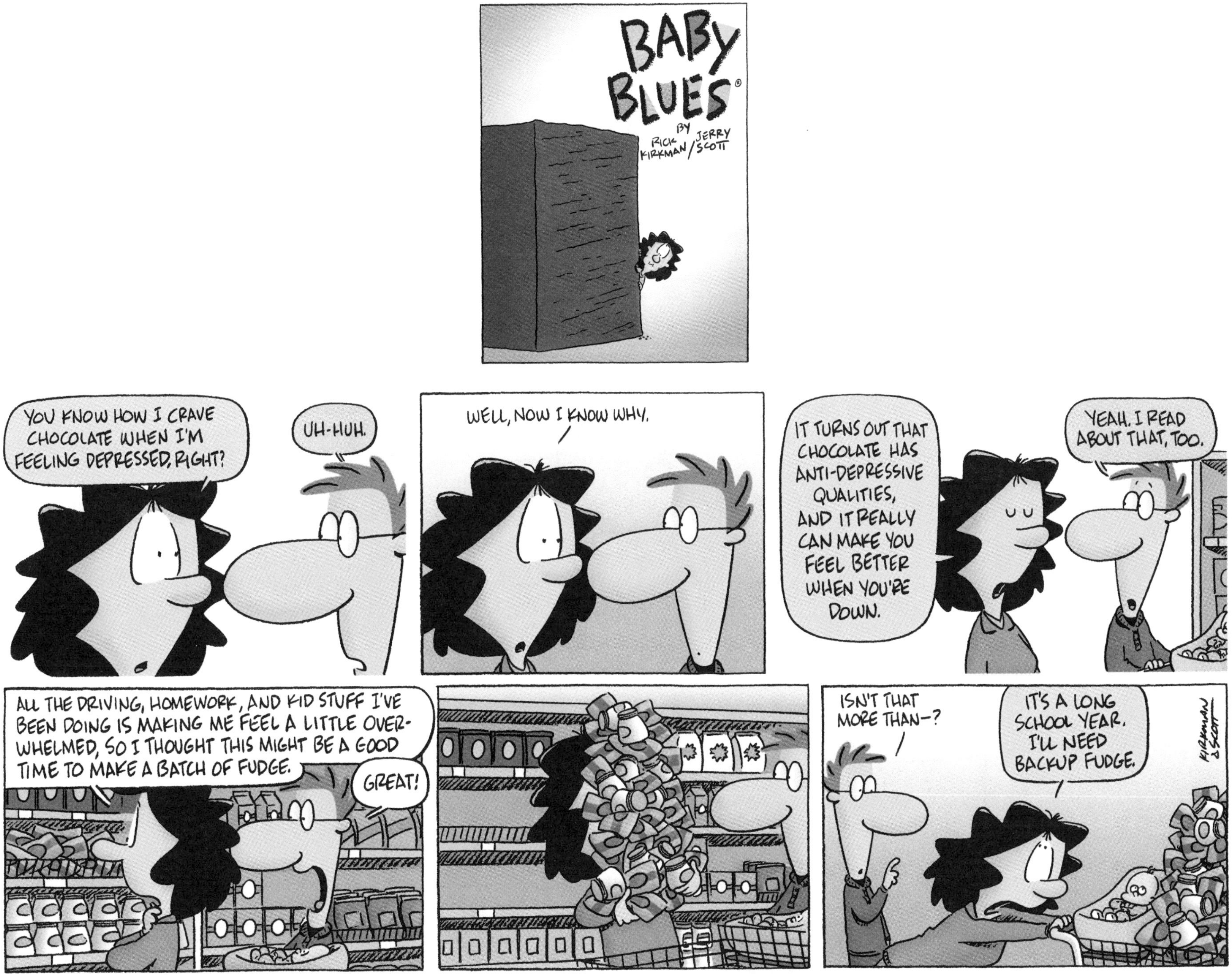
BABY BLUES®
BY RICK KIRKMAN / JERRY SCOTT
YOU KNOW HOW I CRAVE CHOCOLATE WHEN I'M FEELING DEPRESSED, RIGHT?
UH-HUH.
WELL, NOW I KNOW WHY.
IT TURNS OUT THAT CHOCOLATE HAS ANTI-DEPRESSIVE QUALITIES, AND IT REALLY CAN MAKE YOU FEEL BETTER WHEN YOU'RE DOWN.
YEAH. I READ ABOUT THAT, TOO.
ALL THE DRIVING, HOMEWORK, AND KID STUFF I'VE BEEN DOING IS MAKING ME FEEL A LITTLE OVER-WHELMED, SO I THOUGHT THIS MIGHT BE A GOOD TIME TO MAKE A BATCH OF FUDGE.
GREAT!
ISN'T THAT MORE THAN—?
IT'S A LONG SCHOOL YEAR. I'LL NEED BACKUP FUDGE.
KIRKMAN & SCOTT

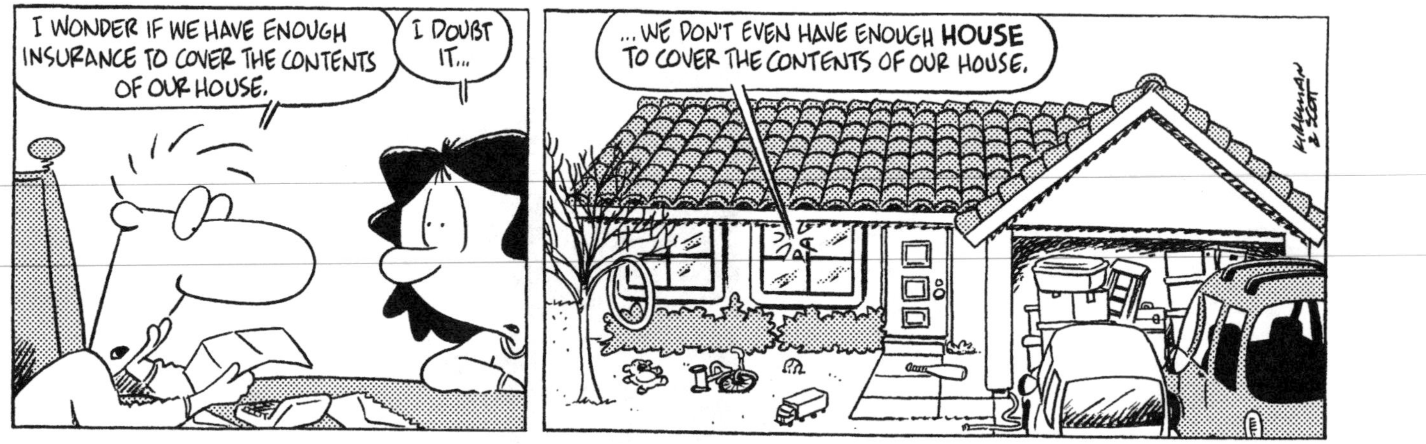
I WONDER IF WE HAVE ENOUGH INSURANCE TO COVER THE CONTENTS OF OUR HOUSE.
I DOUBT IT...
...WE DON'T EVEN HAVE ENOUGH **HOUSE** TO COVER THE CONTENTS OF OUR HOUSE.

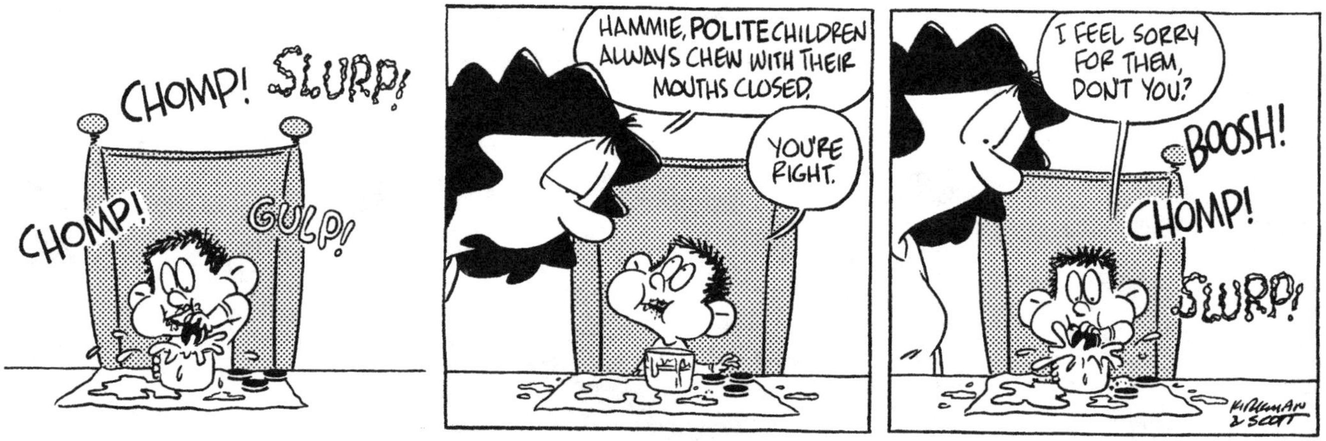
CHOMP! SLURP!
CHOMP! GULP!
HAMMIE, **POLITE** CHILDREN ALWAYS CHEW WITH THEIR MOUTHS CLOSED.
YOU'RE RIGHT.
I FEEL SORRY FOR THEM, DON'T YOU?
BOOSH!
CHOMP!
SLURP!

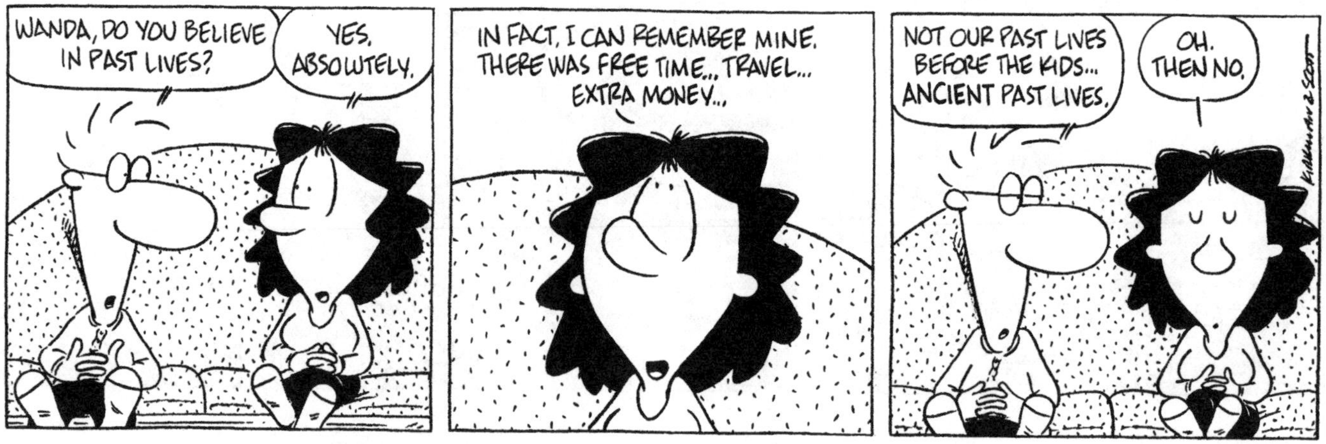
WANDA, DO YOU BELIEVE IN PAST LIVES?
YES. ABSOLUTELY.
IN FACT, I CAN REMEMBER MINE. THERE WAS FREE TIME... TRAVEL... EXTRA MONEY...
NOT OUR PAST LIVES BEFORE THE KIDS... **ANCIENT** PAST LIVES.
OH. THEN NO.

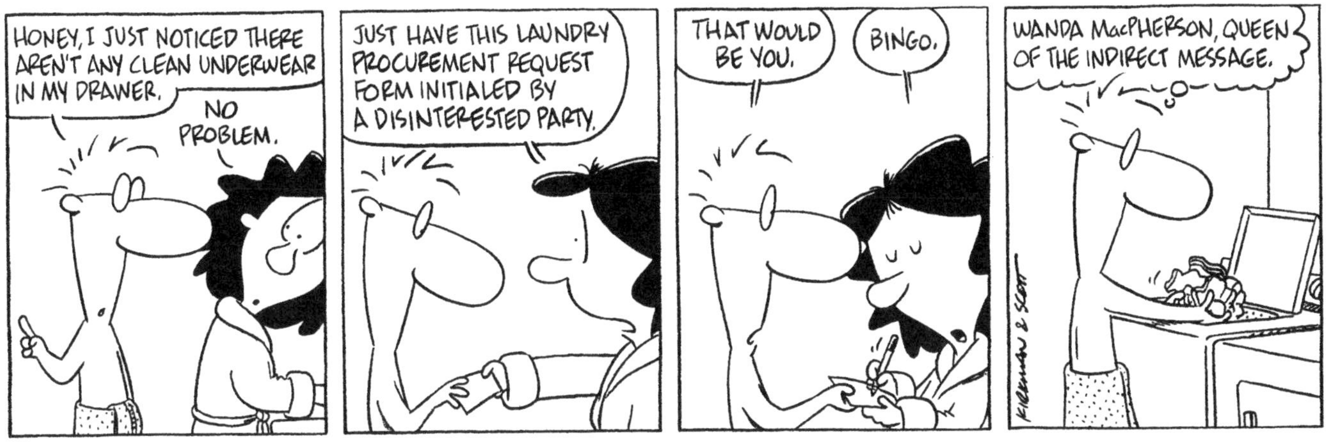
HONEY, I JUST NOTICED THERE AREN'T ANY CLEAN UNDERWEAR IN MY DRAWER.
NO PROBLEM.
JUST HAVE THIS LAUNDRY PROCUREMENT REQUEST FORM INITIALED BY A DISINTERESTED PARTY.
THAT WOULD BE YOU.
BINGO.
WANDA MacPHERSON, QUEEN OF THE INDIRECT MESSAGE.
KIRKMAN & SCOTT

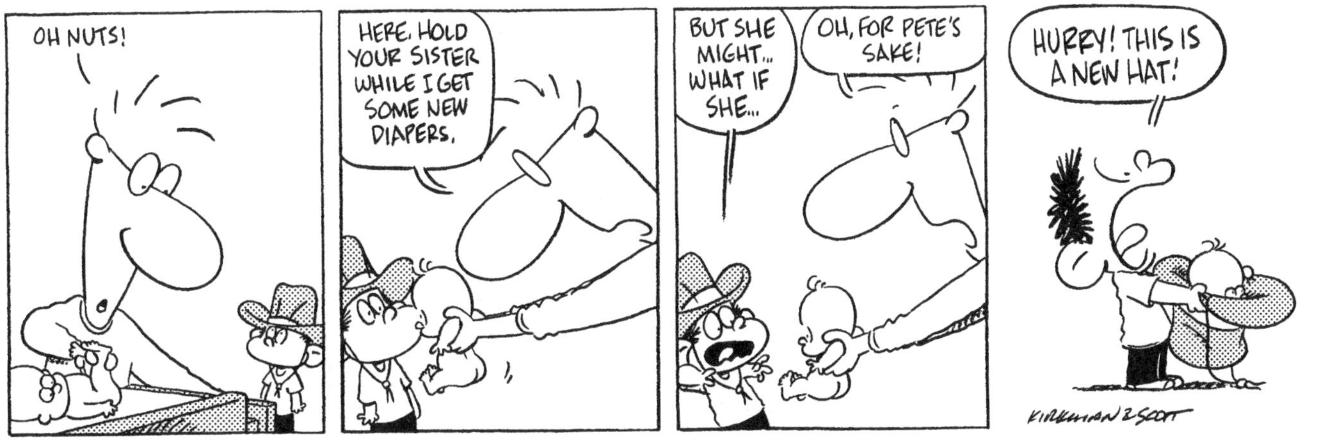
OH NUTS!
HERE. HOLD YOUR SISTER WHILE I GET SOME NEW DIAPERS.
BUT SHE MIGHT... WHAT IF SHE...
OH, FOR PETE'S SAKE!
HURRY! THIS IS A NEW HAT!
KIRKMAN & SCOTT

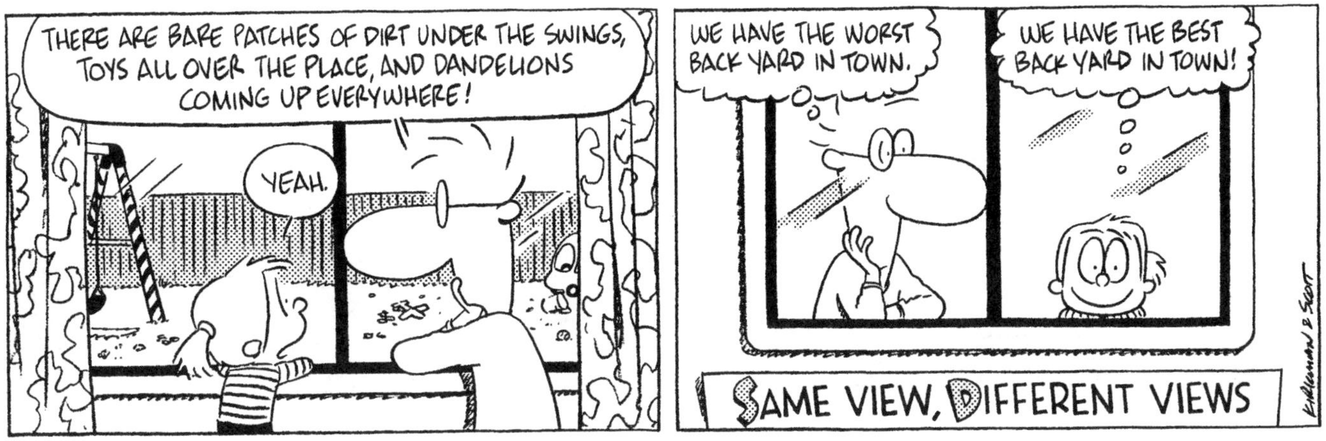
THERE ARE BARE PATCHES OF DIRT UNDER THE SWINGS, TOYS ALL OVER THE PLACE, AND DANDELIONS COMING UP EVERYWHERE!
YEAH.
WE HAVE THE WORST BACK YARD IN TOWN.
WE HAVE THE BEST BACK YARD IN TOWN!
SAME VIEW, DIFFERENT VIEWS
KIRKMAN & SCOTT

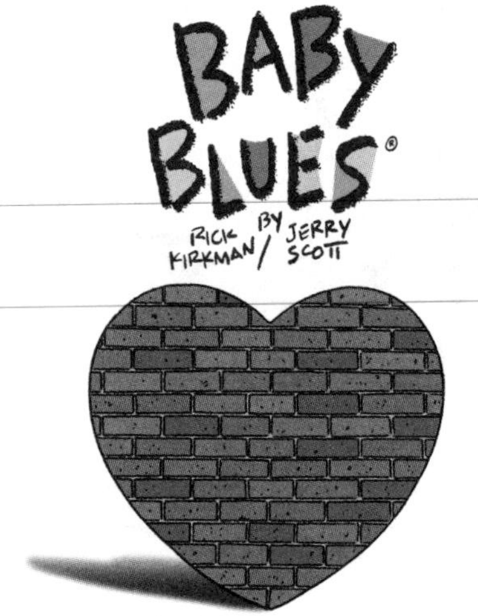
BABY BLUES®
BY RICK KIRKMAN / JERRY SCOTT

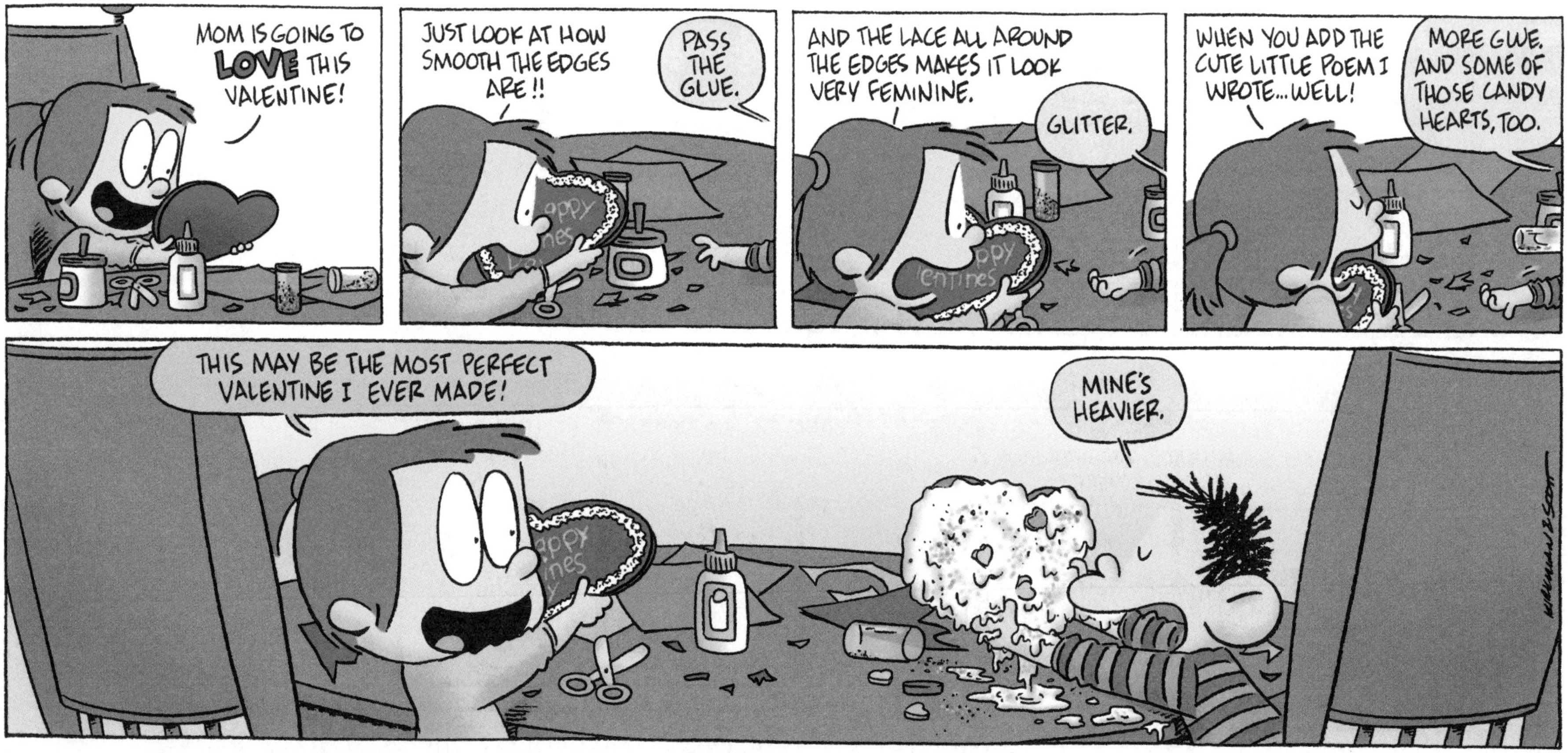
MOM IS GOING TO LOVE THIS VALENTINE!
JUST LOOK AT HOW SMOOTH THE EDGES ARE!!
PASS THE GLUE.
AND THE LACE ALL AROUND THE EDGES MAKES IT LOOK VERY FEMININE.
GLITTER.
WHEN YOU ADD THE CUTE LITTLE POEM I WROTE... WELL!
MORE GLUE. AND SOME OF THOSE CANDY HEARTS, TOO.
THIS MAY BE THE MOST PERFECT VALENTINE I EVER MADE!
MINE'S HEAVIER.

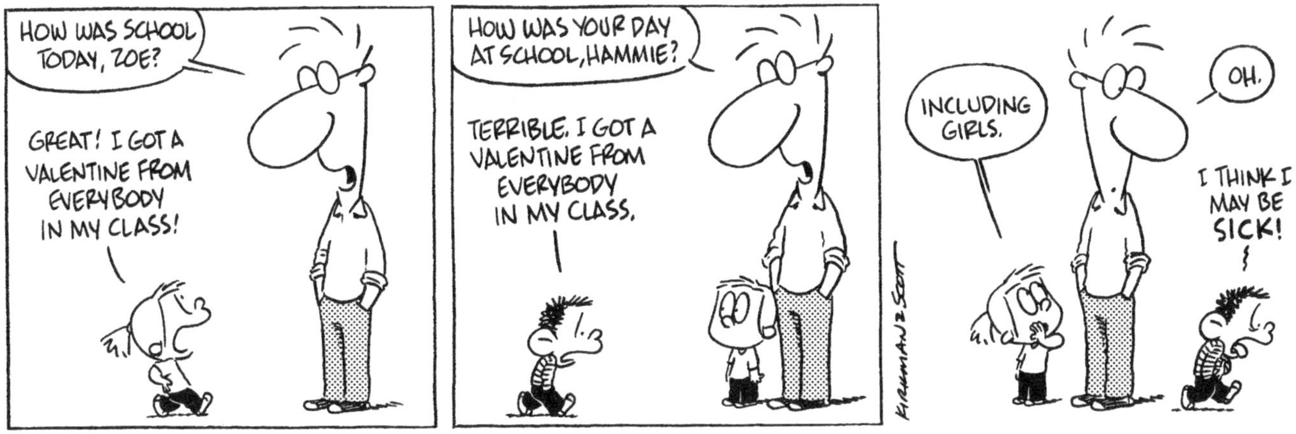
HOW WAS SCHOOL TODAY, ZOE?
GREAT! I GOT A VALENTINE FROM EVERYBODY IN MY CLASS!
HOW WAS YOUR DAY AT SCHOOL, HAMMIE?
TERRIBLE. I GOT A VALENTINE FROM EVERYBODY IN MY CLASS.
INCLUDING GIRLS.
OH.
I THINK I MAY BE SICK!

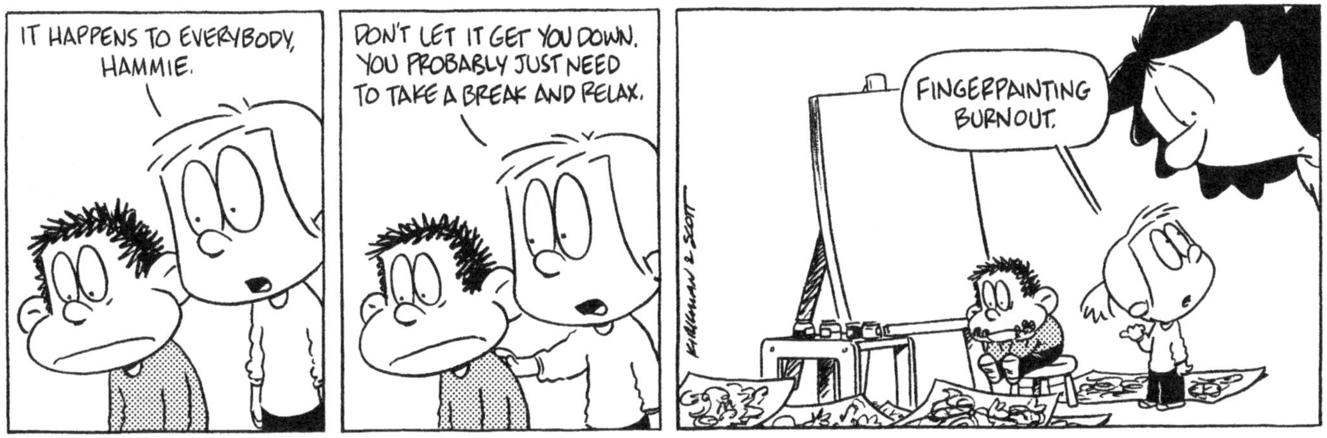
IT HAPPENS TO EVERYBODY, HAMMIE.
DON'T LET IT GET YOU DOWN. YOU PROBABLY JUST NEED TO TAKE A BREAK AND RELAX.
FINGERPAINTING BURNOUT.

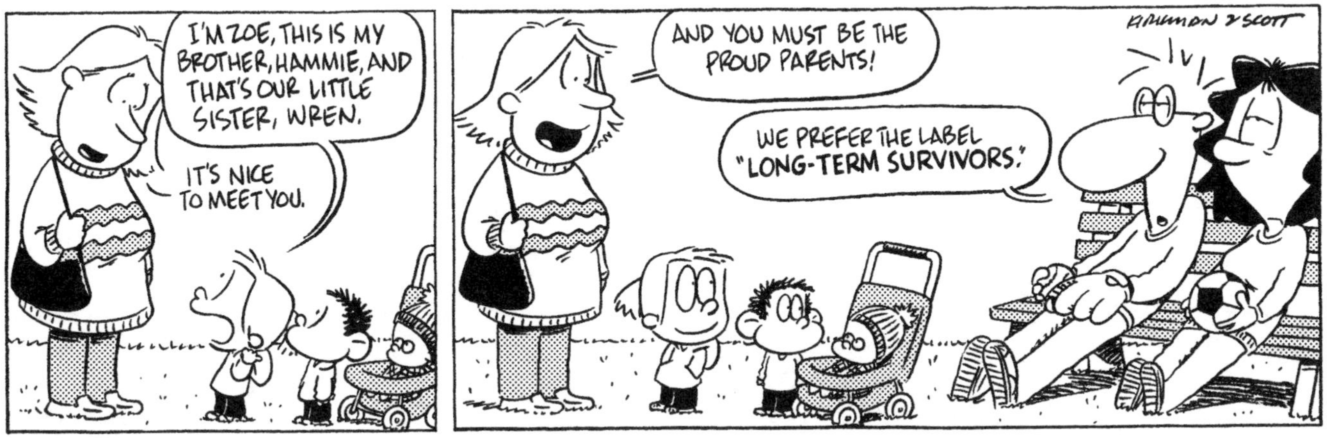
I'M ZOE, THIS IS MY BROTHER, HAMMIE, AND THAT'S OUR LITTLE SISTER, WREN.
IT'S NICE TO MEET YOU.
AND YOU MUST BE THE PROUD PARENTS!
WE PREFER THE LABEL "LONG-TERM SURVIVORS."

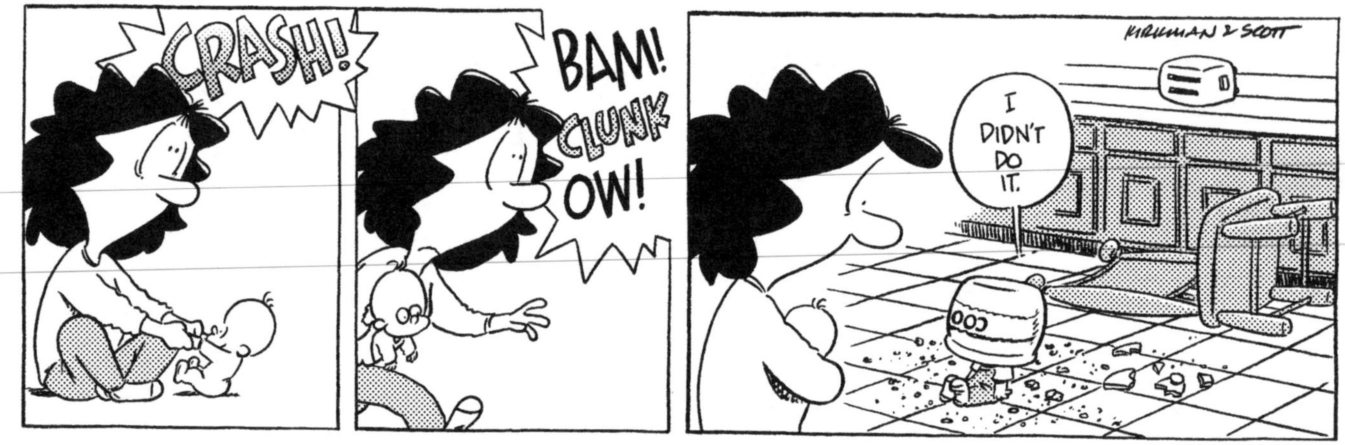
CRASH!
BAM!
CLUNK
OW!
KIRKMAN & SCOTT
I DIDN'T DO IT.

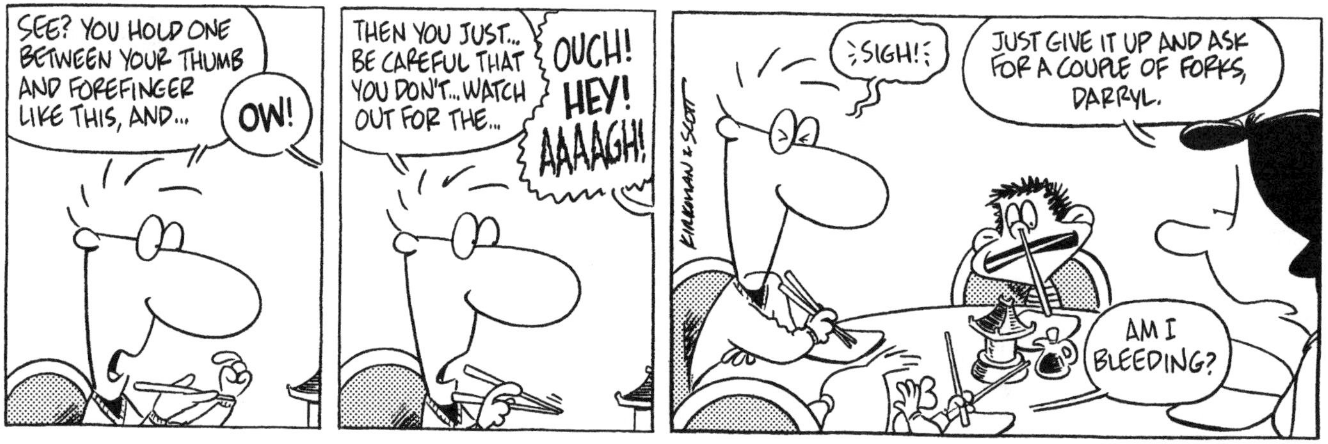
SEE? YOU HOLD ONE BETWEEN YOUR THUMB AND FOREFINGER LIKE THIS, AND...
OW!
THEN YOU JUST... BE CAREFUL THAT YOU DON'T... WATCH OUT FOR THE...
OUCH! HEY! AAAAGH!
KIRKMAN & SCOTT
SIGH!
JUST GIVE IT UP AND ASK FOR A COUPLE OF FORKS, DARRYL.
AM I BLEEDING?

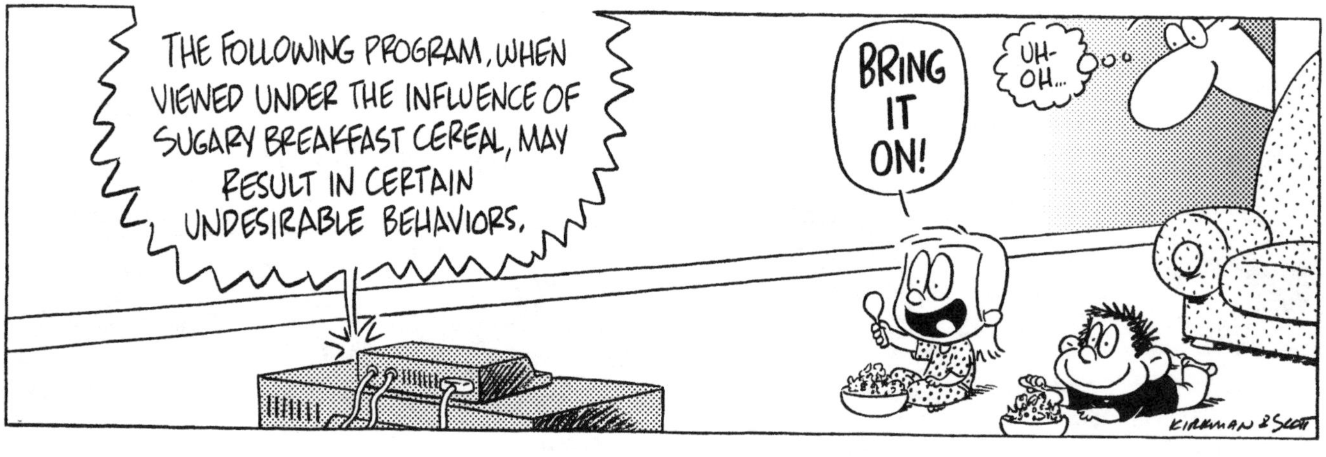
THE FOLLOWING PROGRAM, WHEN VIEWED UNDER THE INFLUENCE OF SUGARY BREAKFAST CEREAL, MAY RESULT IN CERTAIN UNDESIRABLE BEHAVIORS.
BRING IT ON!
UH-OH...
KIRKMAN & SCOTT

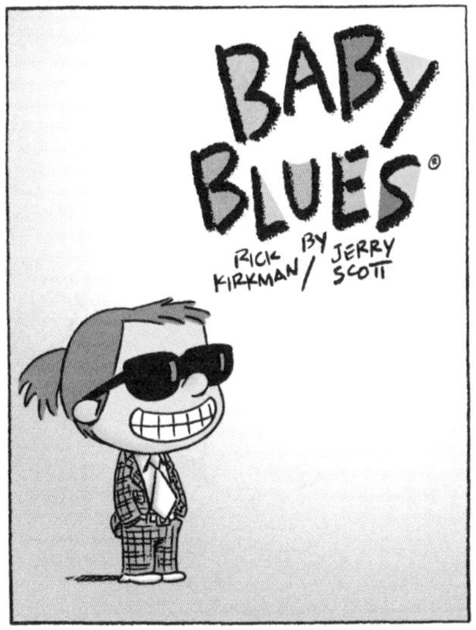
BABY BLUES®
BY RICK KIRKMAN / JERRY SCOTT

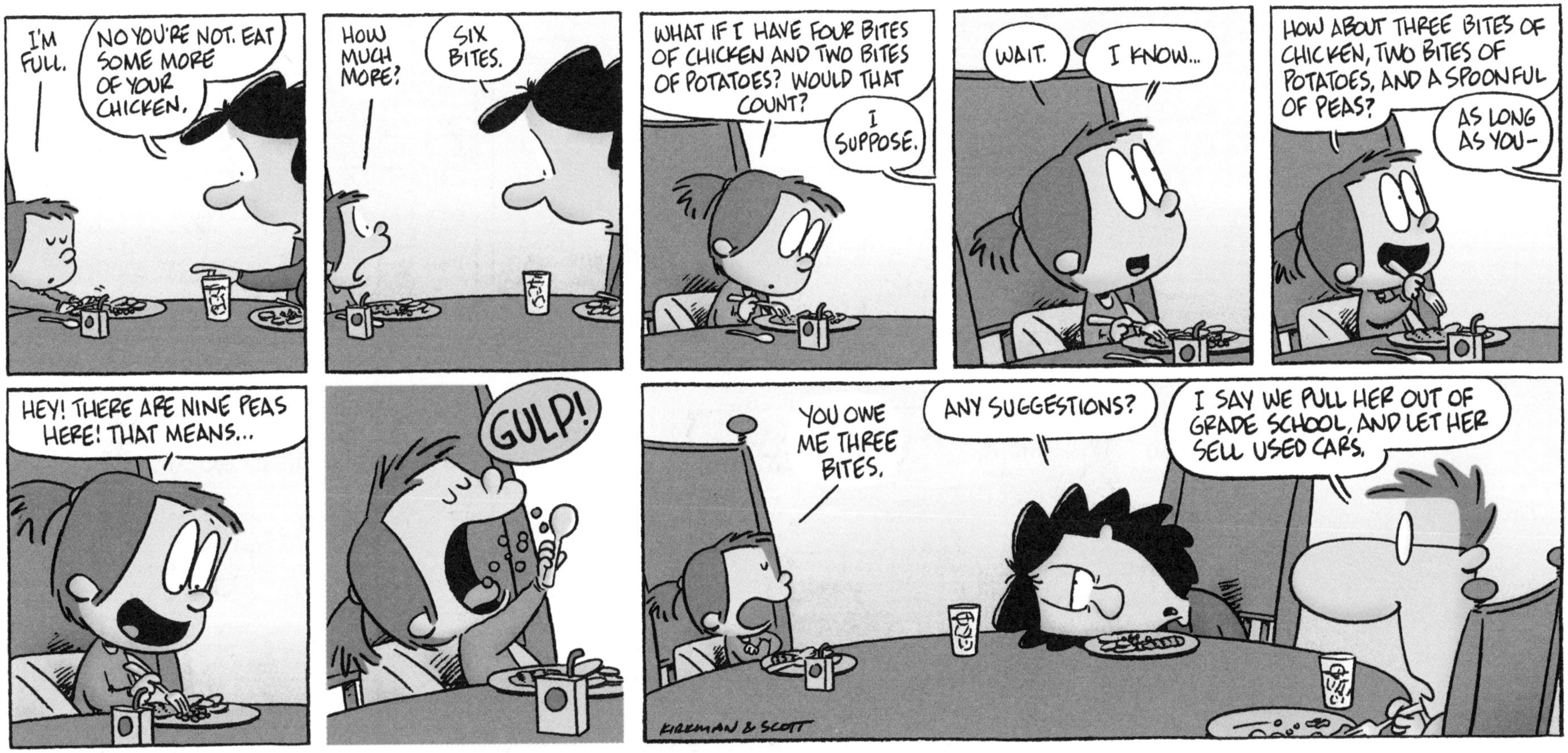
I'M FULL.
NO YOU'RE NOT. EAT SOME MORE OF YOUR CHICKEN.
HOW MUCH MORE?
SIX BITES.
WHAT IF I HAVE FOUR BITES OF CHICKEN AND TWO BITES OF POTATOES? WOULD THAT COUNT?
I SUPPOSE.
WAIT.
I KNOW...
HOW ABOUT THREE BITES OF CHICKEN, TWO BITES OF POTATOES, AND A SPOONFUL OF PEAS?
AS LONG AS YOU-
HEY! THERE ARE NINE PEAS HERE! THAT MEANS...
GULP!
YOU OWE ME THREE BITES.
ANY SUGGESTIONS?
I SAY WE PULL HER OUT OF GRADE SCHOOL, AND LET HER SELL USED CARS.
KIRKMAN & SCOTT

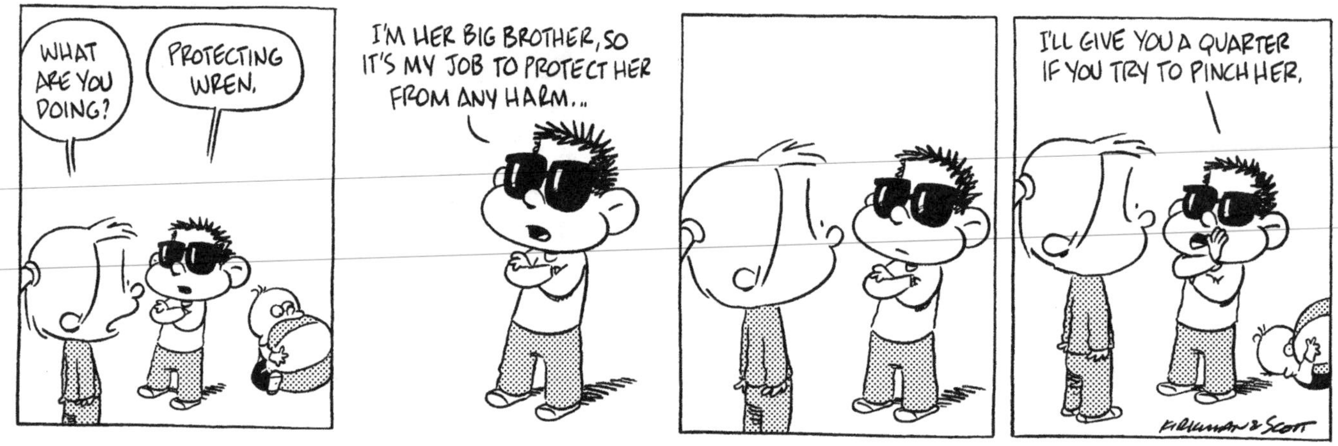
WHAT ARE YOU DOING?
PROTECTING WREN.
I'M HER BIG BROTHER, SO IT'S MY JOB TO PROTECT HER FROM ANY HARM...
I'LL GIVE YOU A QUARTER IF YOU TRY TO PINCH HER.
KIRKMAN & SCOTT

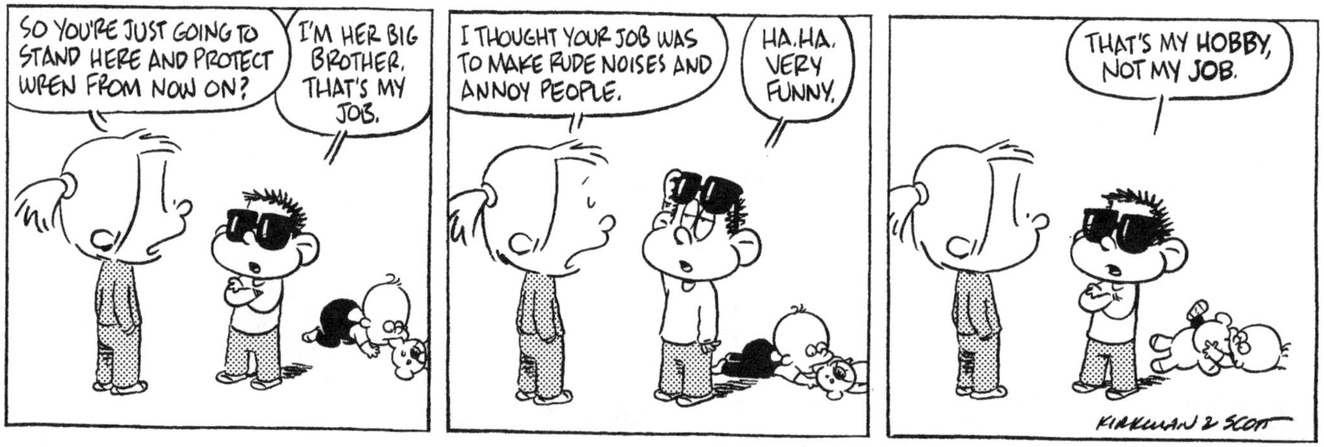
SO YOU'RE JUST GOING TO STAND HERE AND PROTECT WREN FROM NOW ON?
I'M HER BIG BROTHER. THAT'S MY JOB.
I THOUGHT YOUR JOB WAS TO MAKE RUDE NOISES AND ANNOY PEOPLE.
HA.HA. VERY FUNNY.
THAT'S MY HOBBY, NOT MY JOB.
KIRKMAN & SCOTT

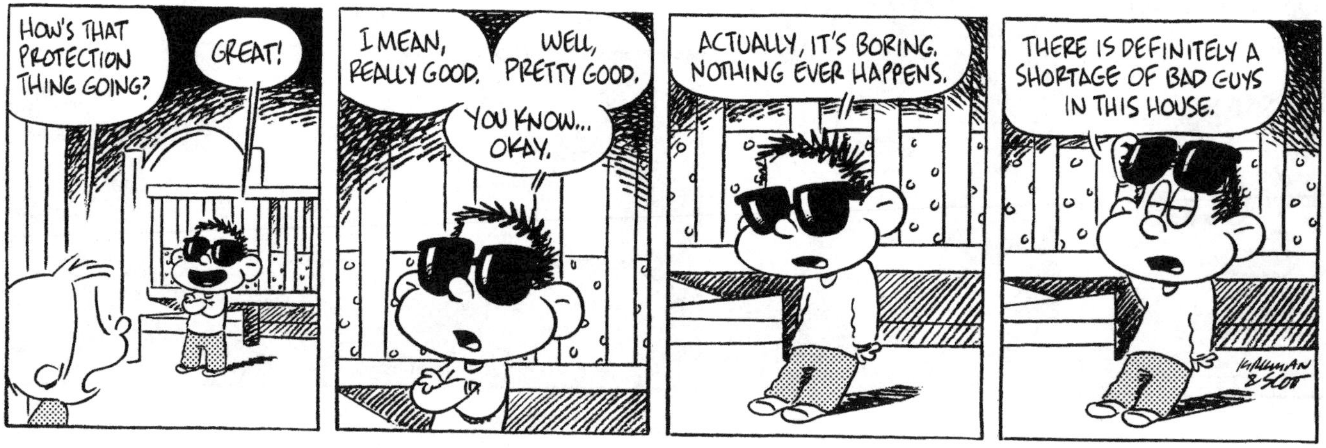
HOW'S THAT PROTECTION THING GOING?
GREAT!
I MEAN, REALLY GOOD.
WELL, PRETTY GOOD.
YOU KNOW... OKAY.
ACTUALLY, IT'S BORING. NOTHING EVER HAPPENS.
THERE IS DEFINITELY A SHORTAGE OF BAD GUYS IN THIS HOUSE.
KIRKMAN & SCOTT

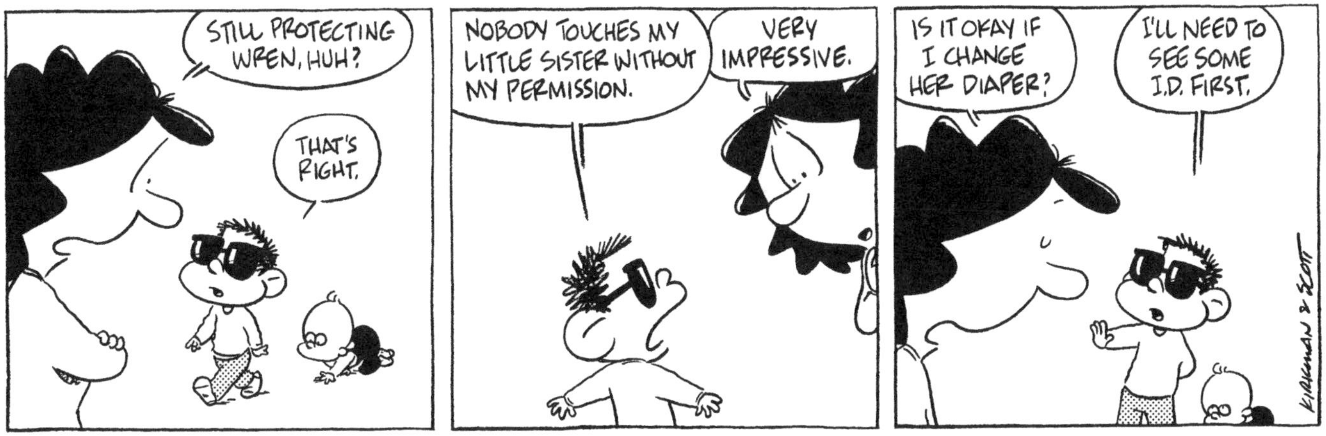
STILL PROTECTING WREN, HUH?
THAT'S RIGHT.
NOBODY TOUCHES MY LITTLE SISTER WITHOUT MY PERMISSION.
VERY IMPRESSIVE.
IS IT OKAY IF I CHANGE HER DIAPER?
I'LL NEED TO SEE SOME I.D. FIRST.
KIRKMAN & SCOTT

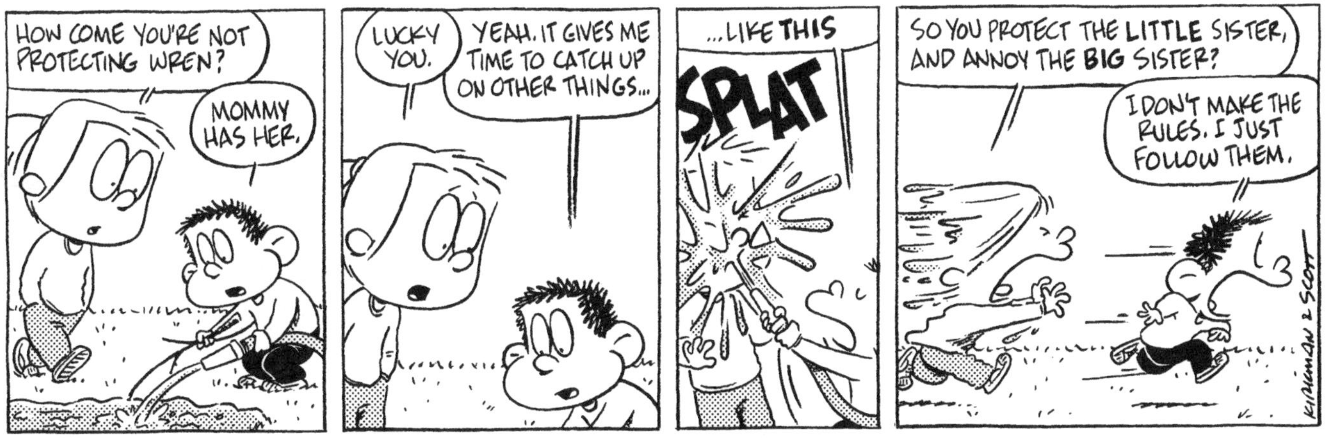
HOW COME YOU'RE NOT PROTECTING WREN?
MOMMY HAS HER.
LUCKY YOU.
YEAH. IT GIVES ME TIME TO CATCH UP ON OTHER THINGS...
...LIKE THIS
SPLAT
SO YOU PROTECT THE LITTLE SISTER, AND ANNOY THE BIG SISTER?
I DON'T MAKE THE RULES. I JUST FOLLOW THEM.
KIRKMAN & SCOTT

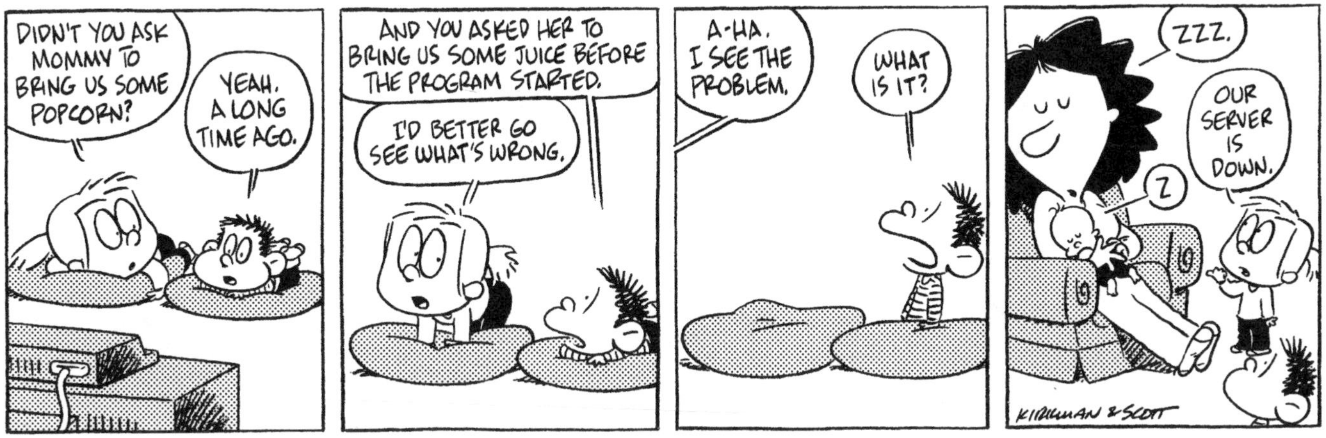
DIDN'T YOU ASK MOMMY TO BRING US SOME POPCORN?
YEAH. A LONG TIME AGO.
AND YOU ASKED HER TO BRING US SOME JUICE BEFORE THE PROGRAM STARTED.
I'D BETTER GO SEE WHAT'S WRONG.
A-HA. I SEE THE PROBLEM.
WHAT IS IT?
ZZZ.
Z
OUR SERVER IS DOWN.
KIRKMAN & SCOTT

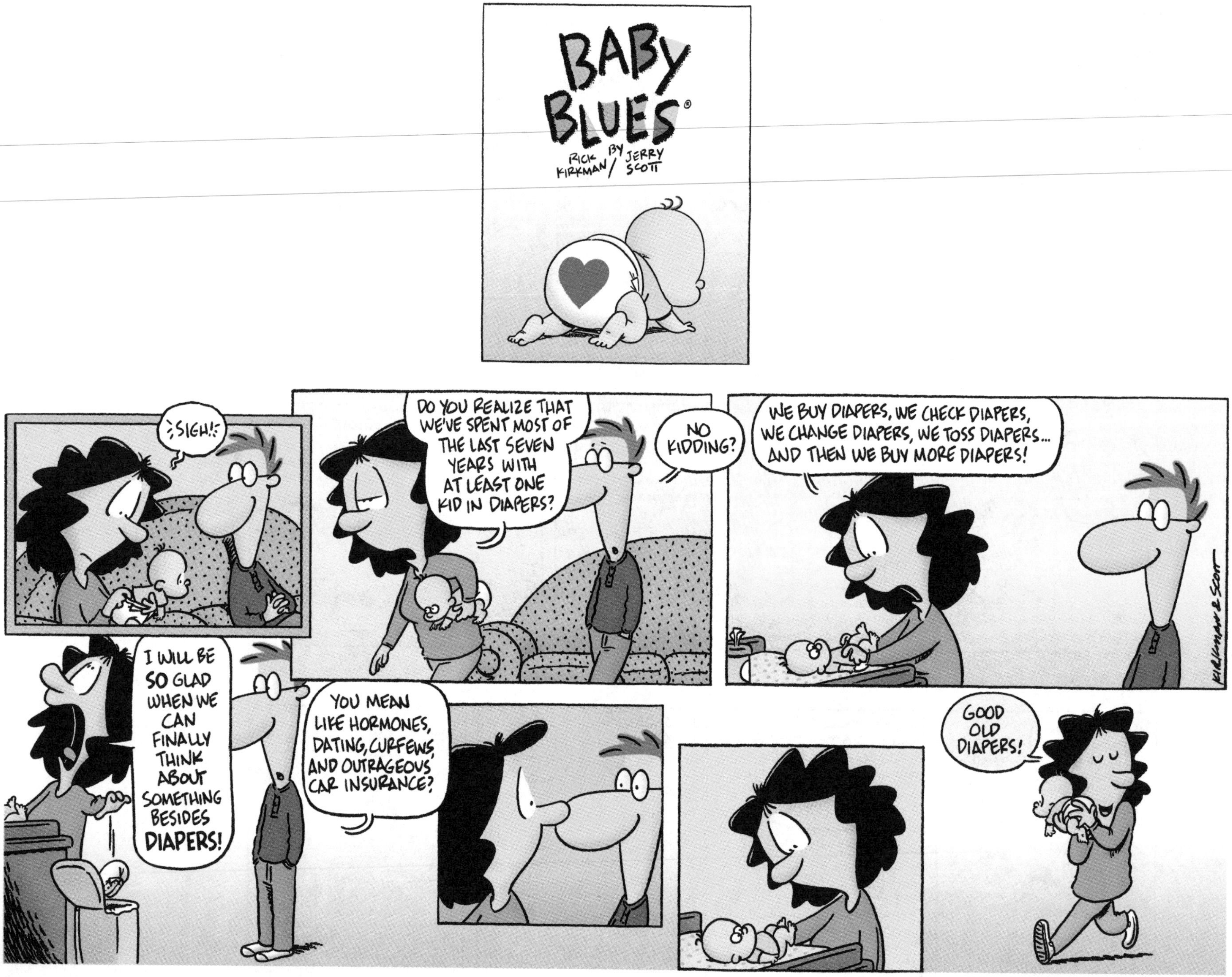
BABY BLUES®
RICK KIRKMAN / BY JERRY SCOTT
SIGH!
DO YOU REALIZE THAT WE'VE SPENT MOST OF THE LAST SEVEN YEARS WITH AT LEAST ONE KID IN DIAPERS?
NO KIDDING?
WE BUY DIAPERS, WE CHECK DIAPERS, WE CHANGE DIAPERS, WE TOSS DIAPERS... AND THEN WE BUY MORE DIAPERS!
KIRKMAN & SCOTT
I WILL BE SO GLAD WHEN WE CAN FINALLY THINK ABOUT SOMETHING BESIDES DIAPERS!
YOU MEAN LIKE HORMONES, DATING, CURFEWS, AND OUTRAGEOUS CAR INSURANCE?
GOOD OLD DIAPERS!

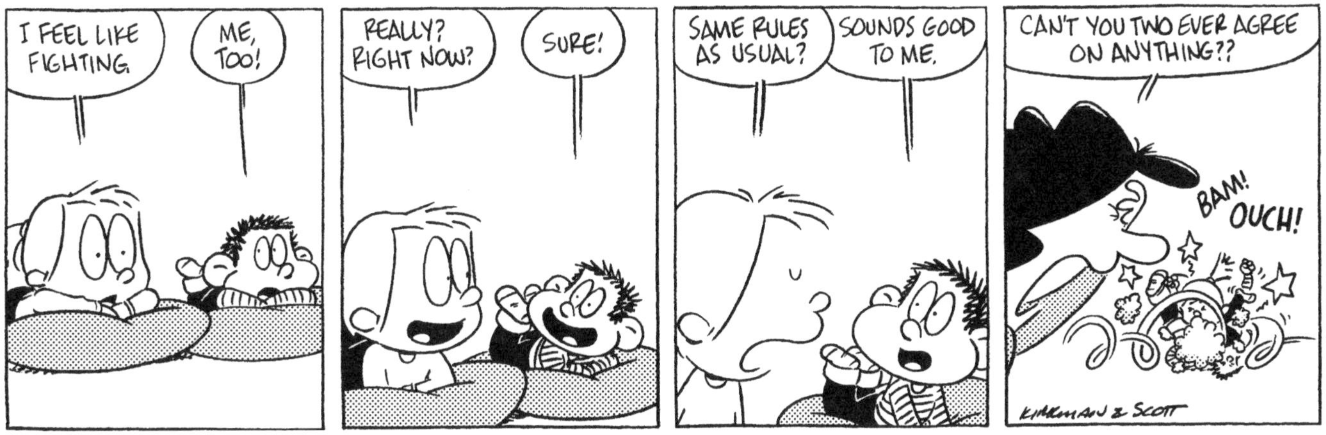
I FEEL LIKE FIGHTING.
ME, TOO!
REALLY? RIGHT NOW?
SURE!
SAME RULES AS USUAL?
SOUNDS GOOD TO ME.
CAN'T YOU TWO EVER AGREE ON ANYTHING??
BAM!
OUCH!

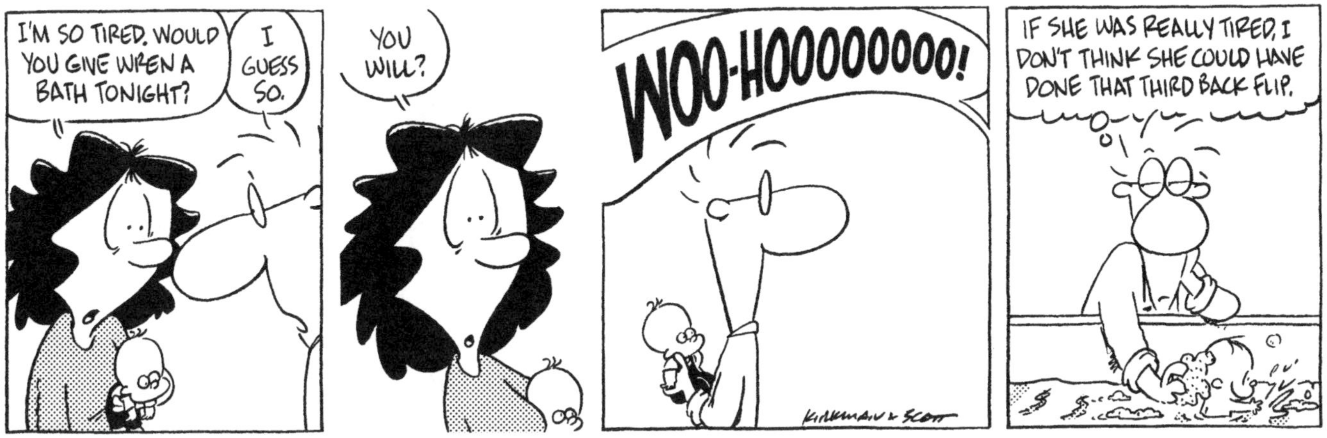
I'M SO TIRED. WOULD YOU GIVE WREN A BATH TONIGHT?
I GUESS SO.
YOU WILL?
WOO-HOOOOOOOO!
IF SHE WAS REALLY TIRED, I DON'T THINK SHE COULD HAVE DONE THAT THIRD BACK FLIP.

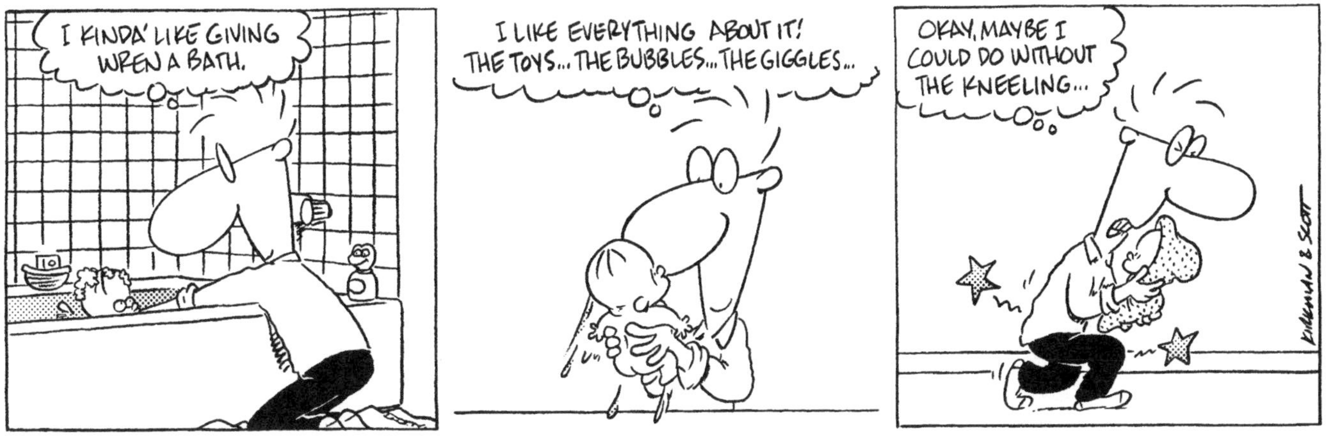
I KINDA' LIKE GIVING WREN A BATH.
I LIKE EVERYTHING ABOUT IT! THE TOYS... THE BUBBLES... THE GIGGLES...
OKAY, MAYBE I COULD DO WITHOUT THE KNEELING...

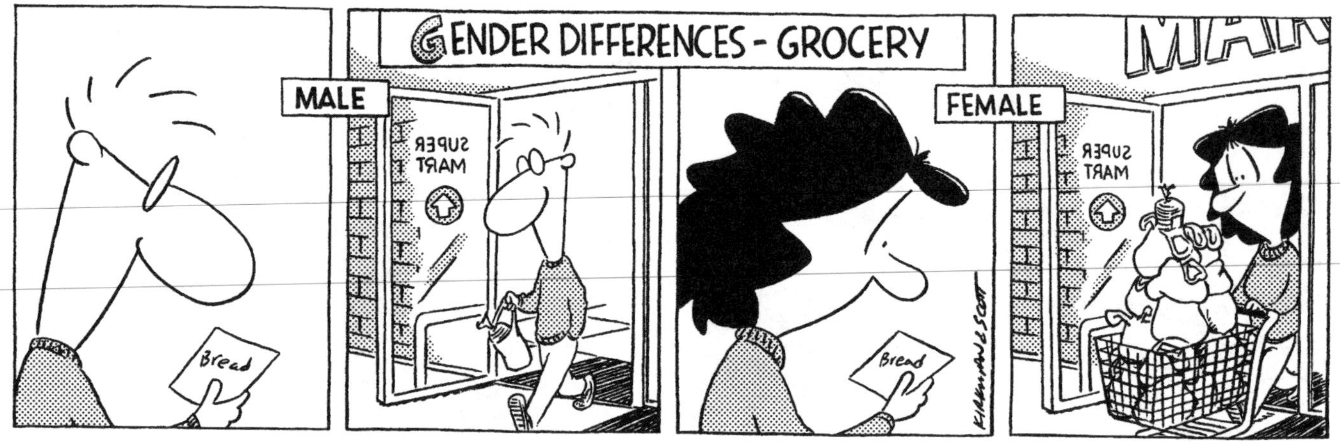
GENDER DIFFERENCES - GROCERY
MALE
Bread
SUPER MART
FEMALE
Bread
KIRKMAN & SCOTT

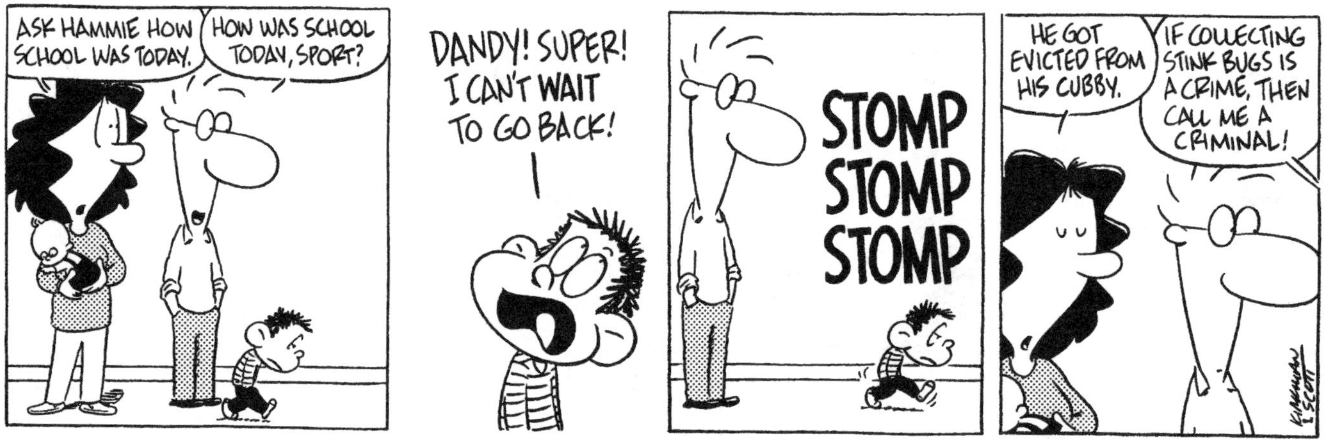
ASK HAMMIE HOW SCHOOL WAS TODAY.
HOW WAS SCHOOL TODAY, SPORT?
DANDY! SUPER! I CAN'T WAIT TO GO BACK!
STOMP STOMP STOMP
HE GOT EVICTED FROM HIS CUBBY.
IF COLLECTING STINK BUGS IS A CRIME, THEN CALL ME A CRIMINAL!
KIRKMAN & SCOTT

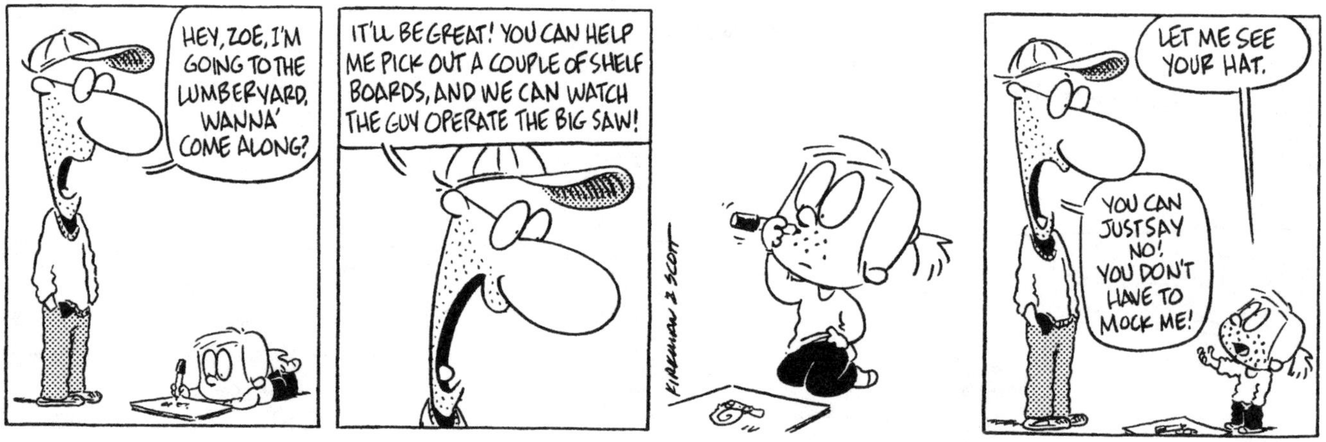
HEY, ZOE, I'M GOING TO THE LUMBERYARD. WANNA' COME ALONG?
IT'LL BE GREAT! YOU CAN HELP ME PICK OUT A COUPLE OF SHELF BOARDS, AND WE CAN WATCH THE GUY OPERATE THE BIG SAW!
KIRKMAN & SCOTT
LET ME SEE YOUR HAT.
YOU CAN JUST SAY NO! YOU DON'T HAVE TO MOCK ME!

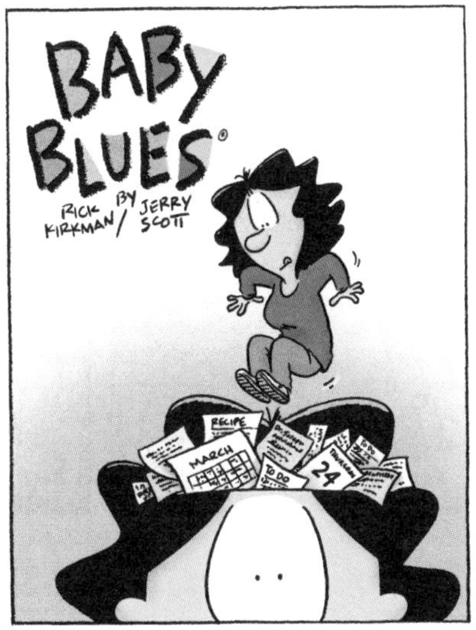
BABY BLUES®
BY RICK KIRKMAN / JERRY SCOTT
RECIPE
MARCH
TO DO
24

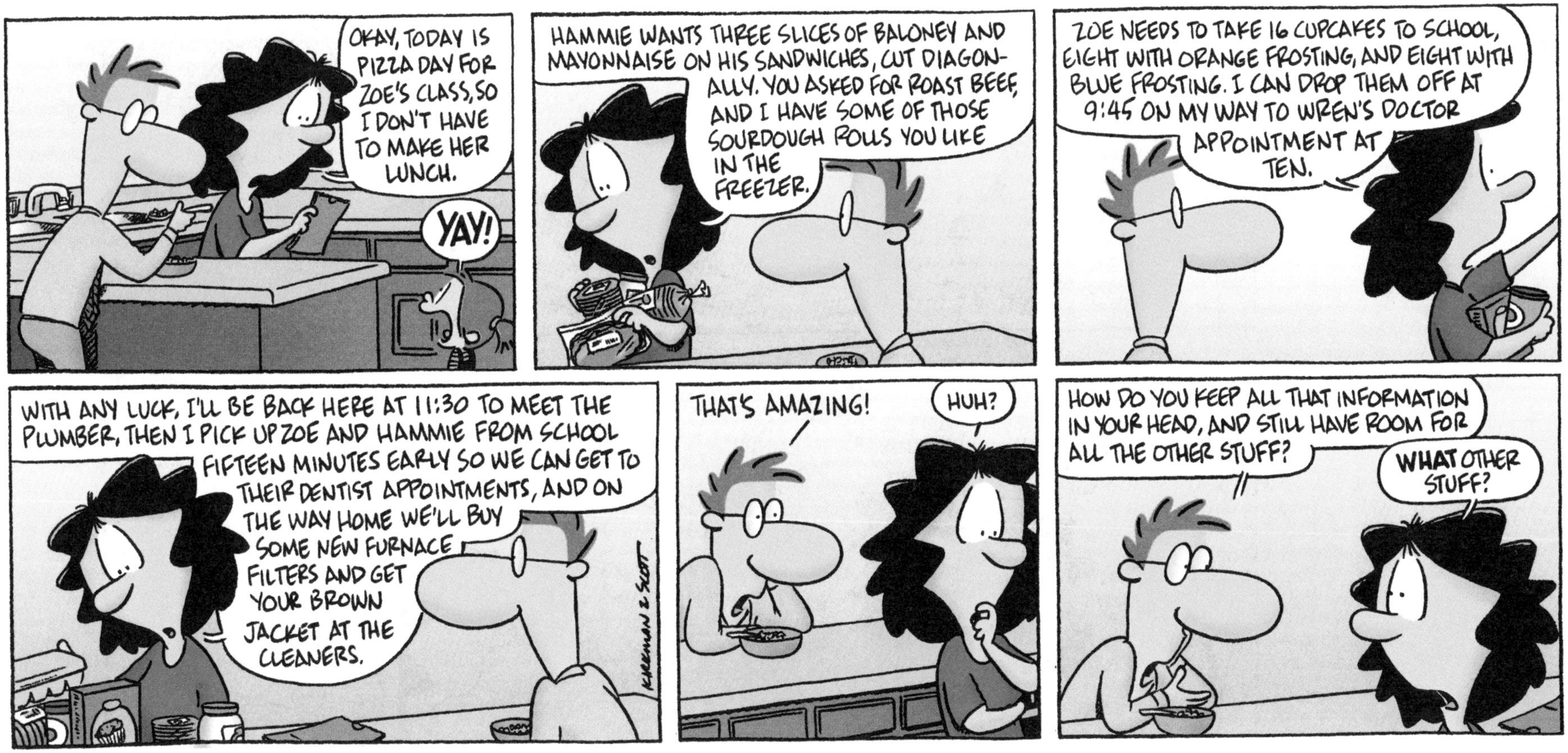
OKAY, TODAY IS PIZZA DAY FOR ZOE'S CLASS, SO I DON'T HAVE TO MAKE HER LUNCH.
YAY!
HAMMIE WANTS THREE SLICES OF BALONEY AND MAYONNAISE ON HIS SANDWICHES, CUT DIAGONALLY. YOU ASKED FOR ROAST BEEF, AND I HAVE SOME OF THOSE SOURDOUGH ROLLS YOU LIKE IN THE FREEZER.
ZOE NEEDS TO TAKE 16 CUPCAKES TO SCHOOL, EIGHT WITH ORANGE FROSTING, AND EIGHT WITH BLUE FROSTING. I CAN DROP THEM OFF AT 9:45 ON MY WAY TO WREN'S DOCTOR APPOINTMENT AT TEN.
WITH ANY LUCK, I'LL BE BACK HERE AT 11:30 TO MEET THE PLUMBER, THEN I PICK UP ZOE AND HAMMIE FROM SCHOOL FIFTEEN MINUTES EARLY SO WE CAN GET TO THEIR DENTIST APPOINTMENTS, AND ON THE WAY HOME WE'LL BUY SOME NEW FURNACE FILTERS AND GET YOUR BROWN JACKET AT THE CLEANERS.
KIRKMAN & SCOTT
THAT'S AMAZING!
HUH?
HOW DO YOU KEEP ALL THAT INFORMATION IN YOUR HEAD, AND STILL HAVE ROOM FOR ALL THE OTHER STUFF?
WHAT OTHER STUFF?

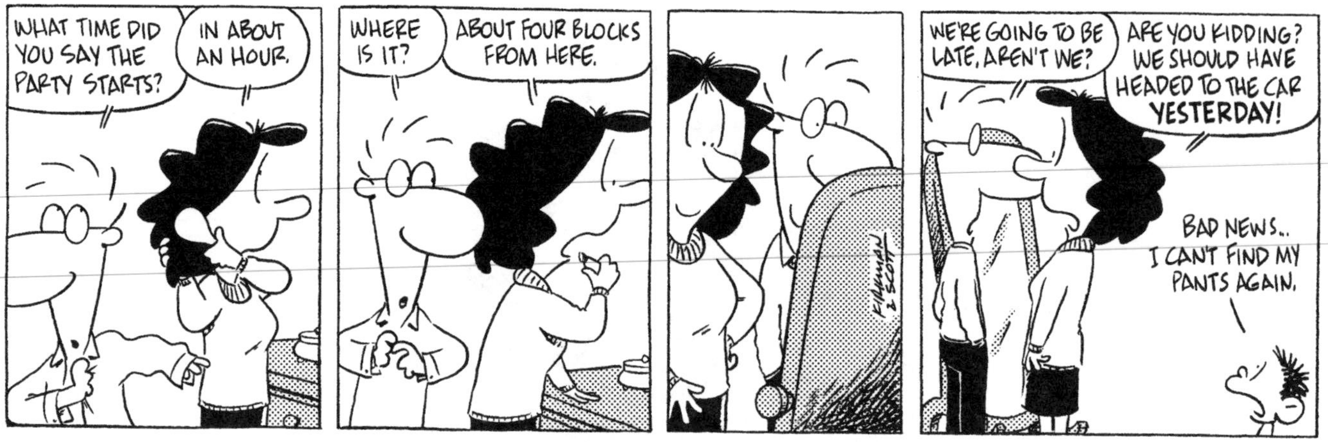
WHAT TIME DID YOU SAY THE PARTY STARTS?
IN ABOUT AN HOUR.
WHERE IS IT?
ABOUT FOUR BLOCKS FROM HERE.
WE'RE GOING TO BE LATE, AREN'T WE?
ARE YOU KIDDING? WE SHOULD HAVE HEADED TO THE CAR YESTERDAY!
BAD NEWS.. I CAN'T FIND MY PANTS AGAIN.

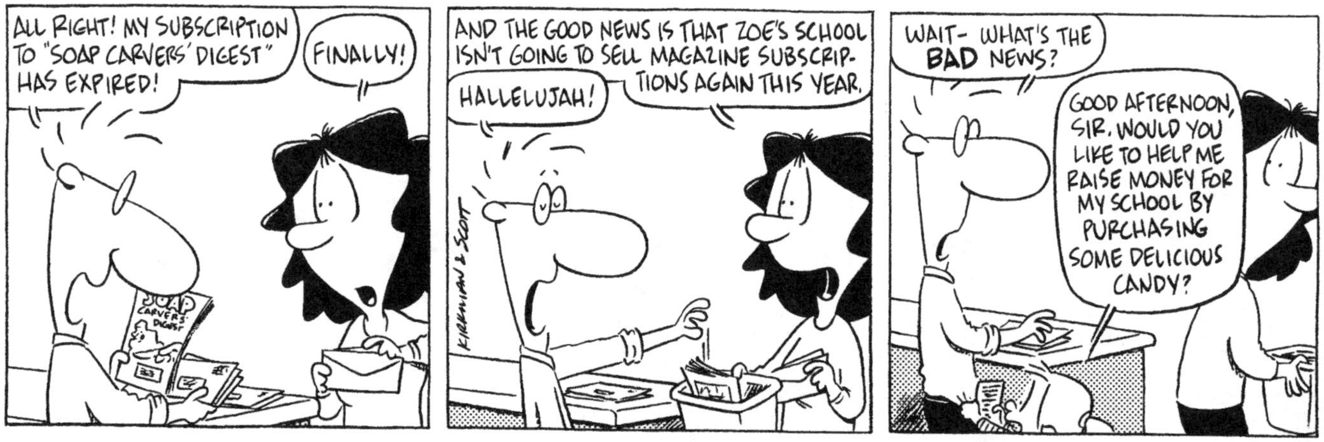
ALL RIGHT! MY SUBSCRIPTION TO "SOAP CARVERS' DIGEST" HAS EXPIRED!
FINALLY!
AND THE GOOD NEWS IS THAT ZOE'S SCHOOL ISN'T GOING TO SELL MAGAZINE SUBSCRIPTIONS AGAIN THIS YEAR.
HALLELUJAH!
WAIT- WHAT'S THE BAD NEWS?
GOOD AFTERNOON, SIR. WOULD YOU LIKE TO HELP ME RAISE MONEY FOR MY SCHOOL BY PURCHASING SOME DELICIOUS CANDY?

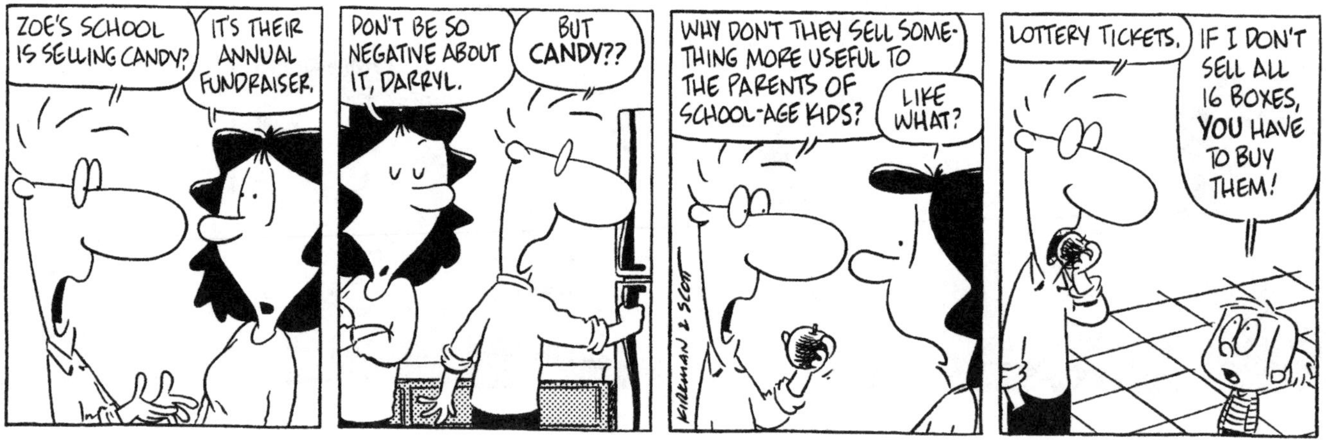
ZOE'S SCHOOL IS SELLING CANDY?
IT'S THEIR ANNUAL FUNDRAISER.
DON'T BE SO NEGATIVE ABOUT IT, DARRYL.
BUT CANDY??
WHY DON'T THEY SELL SOMETHING MORE USEFUL TO THE PARENTS OF SCHOOL-AGE KIDS?
LIKE WHAT?
LOTTERY TICKETS.
IF I DON'T SELL ALL 16 BOXES, YOU HAVE TO BUY THEM!

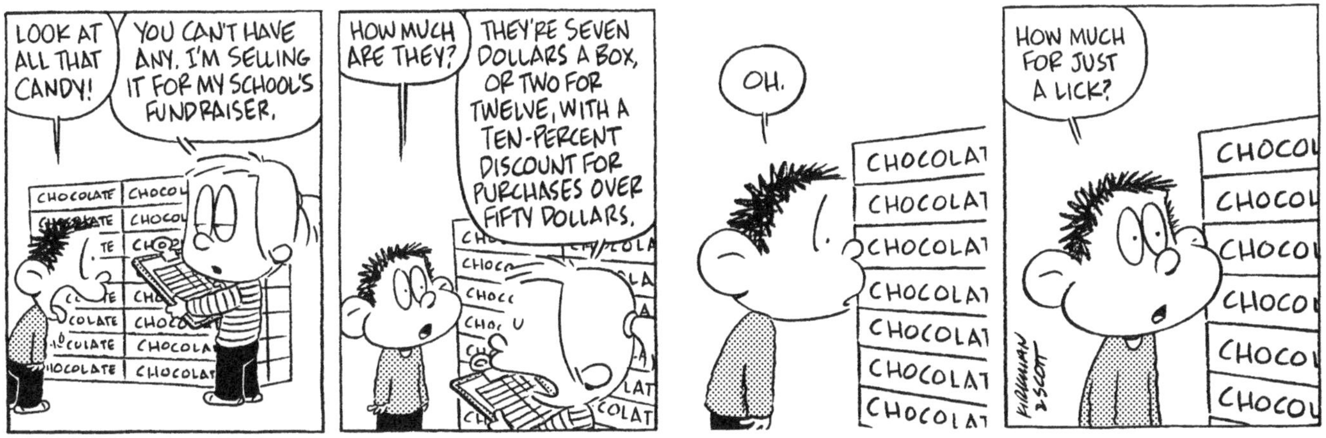
LOOK AT ALL THAT CANDY!
YOU CAN'T HAVE ANY. I'M SELLING IT FOR MY SCHOOL'S FUNDRAISER.
HOW MUCH ARE THEY?
THEY'RE SEVEN DOLLARS A BOX, OR TWO FOR TWELVE, WITH A TEN-PERCENT DISCOUNT FOR PURCHASES OVER FIFTY DOLLARS.
OH.
HOW MUCH FOR JUST A LICK?
KIRKMAN & SCOTT

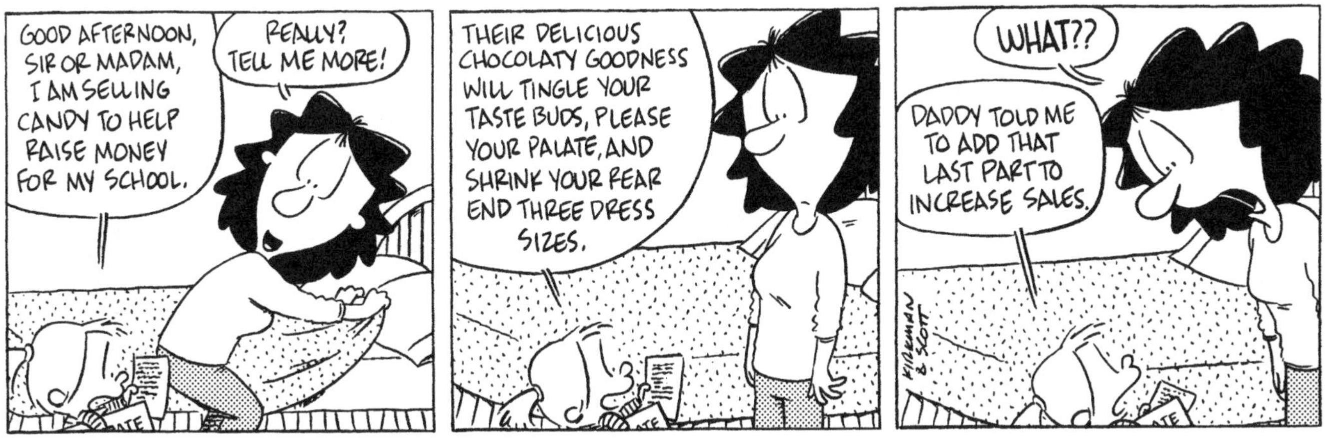
GOOD AFTERNOON, SIR OR MADAM, I AM SELLING CANDY TO HELP RAISE MONEY FOR MY SCHOOL.
REALLY? TELL ME MORE!
THEIR DELICIOUS CHOCOLATY GOODNESS WILL TINGLE YOUR TASTE BUDS, PLEASE YOUR PALATE, AND SHRINK YOUR REAR END THREE DRESS SIZES.
WHAT??
DADDY TOLD ME TO ADD THAT LAST PART TO INCREASE SALES.
KIRKMAN & SCOTT

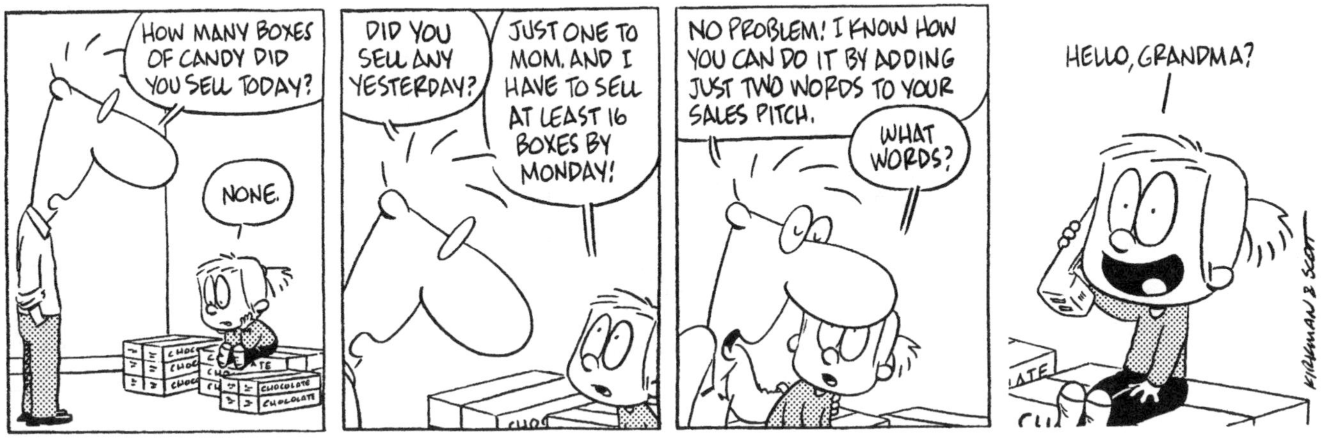
HOW MANY BOXES OF CANDY DID YOU SELL TODAY?
NONE.
DID YOU SELL ANY YESTERDAY?
JUST ONE TO MOM. AND I HAVE TO SELL AT LEAST 16 BOXES BY MONDAY!
NO PROBLEM! I KNOW HOW YOU CAN DO IT BY ADDING JUST TWO WORDS TO YOUR SALES PITCH.
WHAT WORDS?
HELLO, GRANDMA?
KIRKMAN & SCOTT

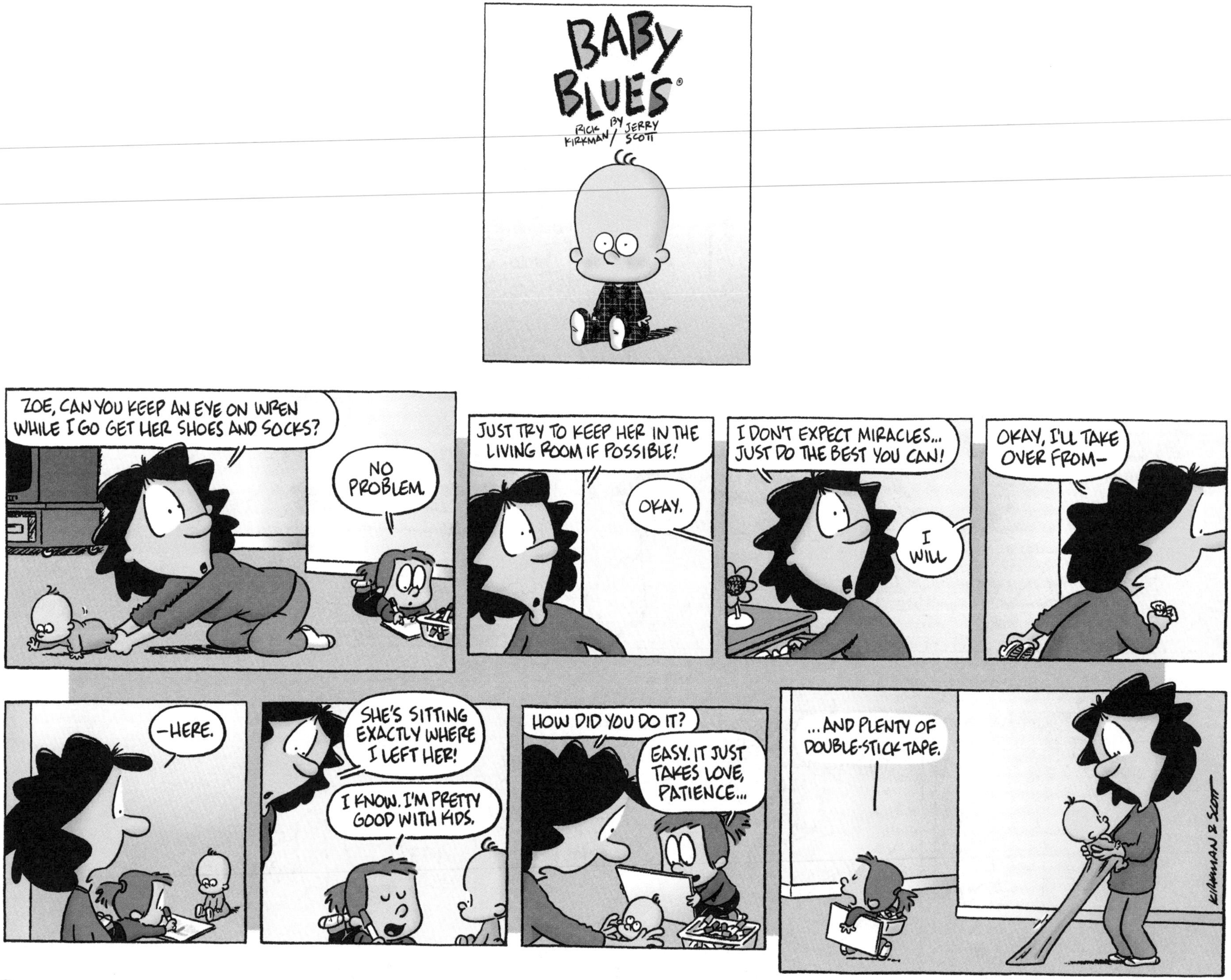
BABY BLUES®
BY RICK KIRKMAN / JERRY SCOTT
ZOE, CAN YOU KEEP AN EYE ON WREN WHILE I GO GET HER SHOES AND SOCKS?
NO PROBLEM.
JUST TRY TO KEEP HER IN THE LIVING ROOM IF POSSIBLE!
OKAY.
I DON'T EXPECT MIRACLES... JUST DO THE BEST YOU CAN!
I WILL
OKAY, I'LL TAKE OVER FROM—
—HERE.
SHE'S SITTING EXACTLY WHERE I LEFT HER!
I KNOW. I'M PRETTY GOOD WITH KIDS.
HOW DID YOU DO IT?
EASY. IT JUST TAKES LOVE, PATIENCE...
...AND PLENTY OF DOUBLE-STICK TAPE.
KIRKMAN & SCOTT

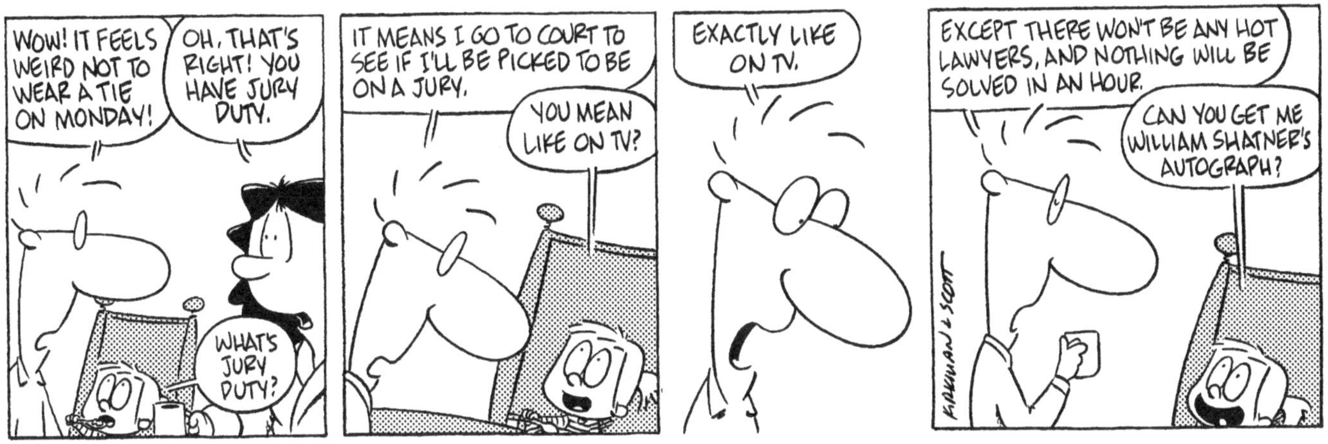
WOW! IT FEELS WEIRD NOT TO WEAR A TIE ON MONDAY!
OH, THAT'S RIGHT! YOU HAVE JURY DUTY.
WHAT'S JURY DUTY?
IT MEANS I GO TO COURT TO SEE IF I'LL BE PICKED TO BE ON A JURY.
YOU MEAN LIKE ON TV?
EXACTLY LIKE ON TV.
EXCEPT THERE WON'T BE ANY HOT LAWYERS, AND NOTHING WILL BE SOLVED IN AN HOUR.
CAN YOU GET ME WILLIAM SHATNER'S AUTOGRAPH?

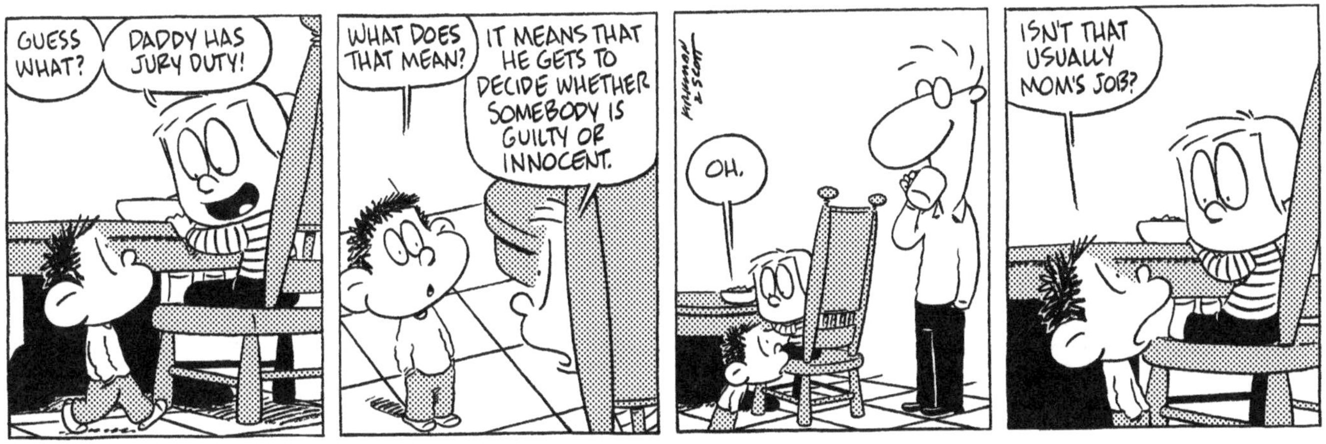
GUESS WHAT?
DADDY HAS JURY DUTY!
WHAT DOES THAT MEAN?
IT MEANS THAT HE GETS TO DECIDE WHETHER SOMEBODY IS GUILTY OR INNOCENT.
OH.
ISN'T THAT USUALLY MOM'S JOB?

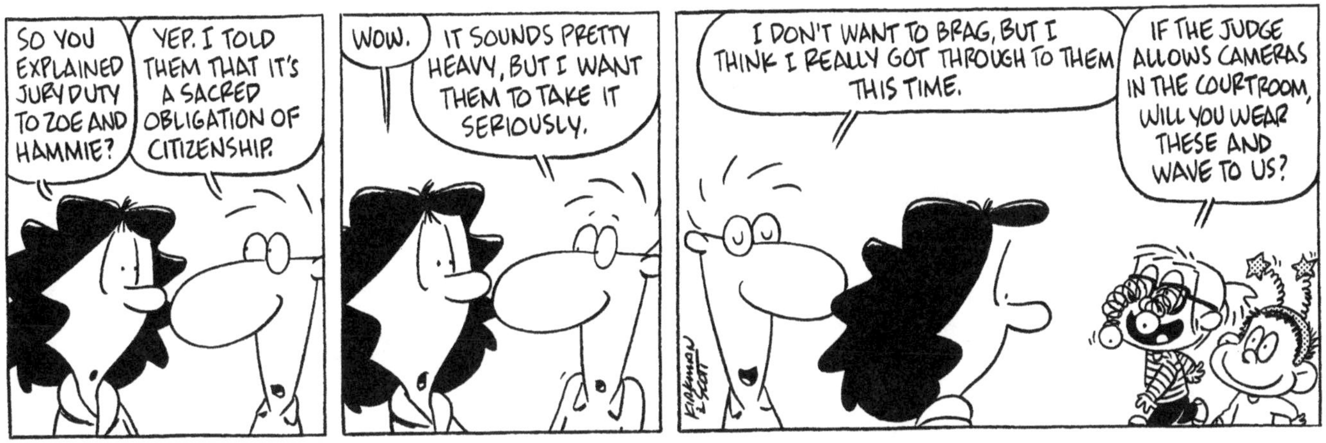
SO YOU EXPLAINED JURY DUTY TO ZOE AND HAMMIE?
YEP. I TOLD THEM THAT IT'S A SACRED OBLIGATION OF CITIZENSHIP.
WOW.
IT SOUNDS PRETTY HEAVY, BUT I WANT THEM TO TAKE IT SERIOUSLY.
I DON'T WANT TO BRAG, BUT I THINK I REALLY GOT THROUGH TO THEM THIS TIME.
IF THE JUDGE ALLOWS CAMERAS IN THE COURTROOM, WILL YOU WEAR THESE AND WAVE TO US?

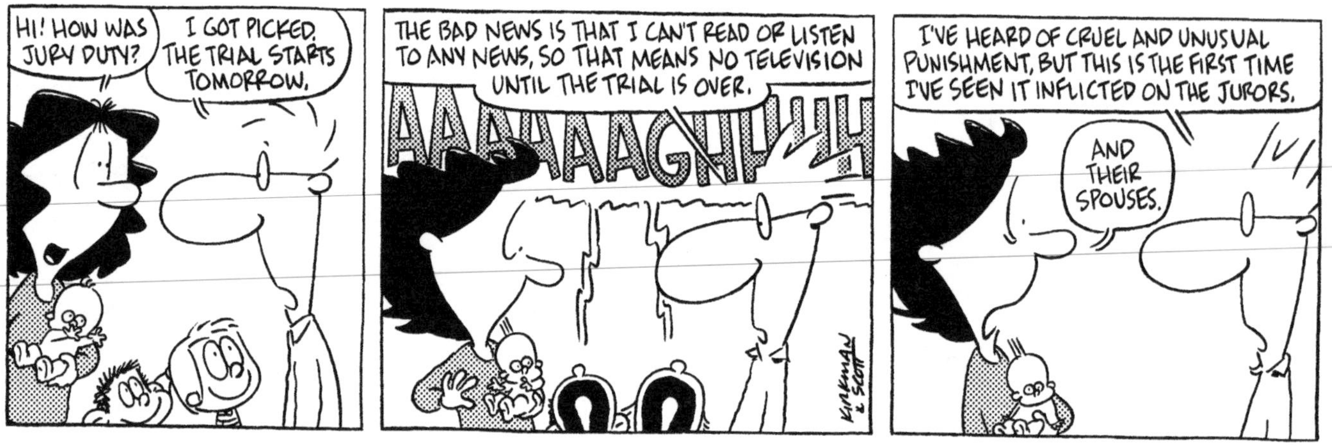
HI! HOW WAS JURY DUTY?
I GOT PICKED. THE TRIAL STARTS TOMORROW.
THE BAD NEWS IS THAT I CAN'T READ OR LISTEN TO ANY NEWS, SO THAT MEANS NO TELEVISION UNTIL THE TRIAL IS OVER.
AAAAAAAGHHHH
I'VE HEARD OF CRUEL AND UNUSUAL PUNISHMENT, BUT THIS IS THE FIRST TIME I'VE SEEN IT INFLICTED ON THE JURORS.
AND THEIR SPOUSES.
KIRKMAN & SCOTT

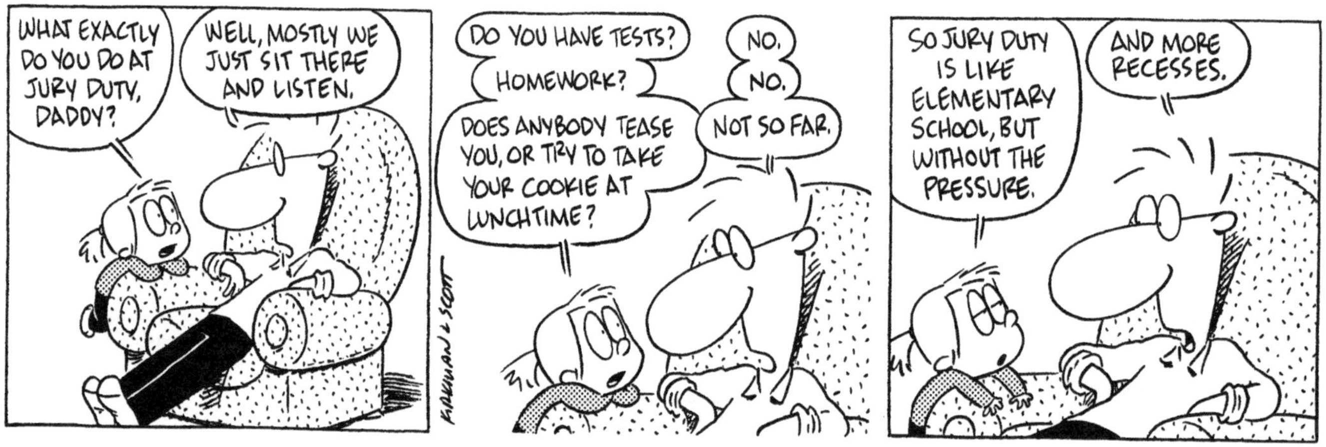
WHAT EXACTLY DO YOU DO AT JURY DUTY, DADDY?
WELL, MOSTLY WE JUST SIT THERE AND LISTEN.
DO YOU HAVE TESTS?
NO.
HOMEWORK?
NO.
DOES ANYBODY TEASE YOU, OR TRY TO TAKE YOUR COOKIE AT LUNCHTIME?
NOT SO FAR.
SO JURY DUTY IS LIKE ELEMENTARY SCHOOL, BUT WITHOUT THE PRESSURE.
AND MORE RECESSES.
KIRKMAN & SCOTT

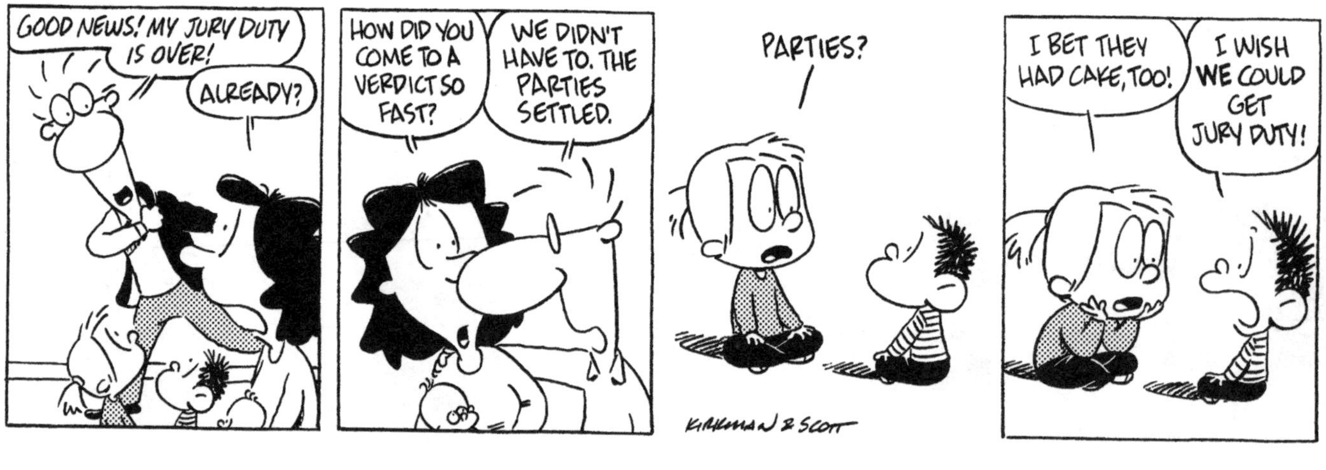
GOOD NEWS! MY JURY DUTY IS OVER!
ALREADY?
HOW DID YOU COME TO A VERDICT SO FAST?
WE DIDN'T HAVE TO. THE PARTIES SETTLED.
PARTIES?
I BET THEY HAD CAKE, TOO!
I WISH WE COULD GET JURY DUTY!
KIRKMAN & SCOTT

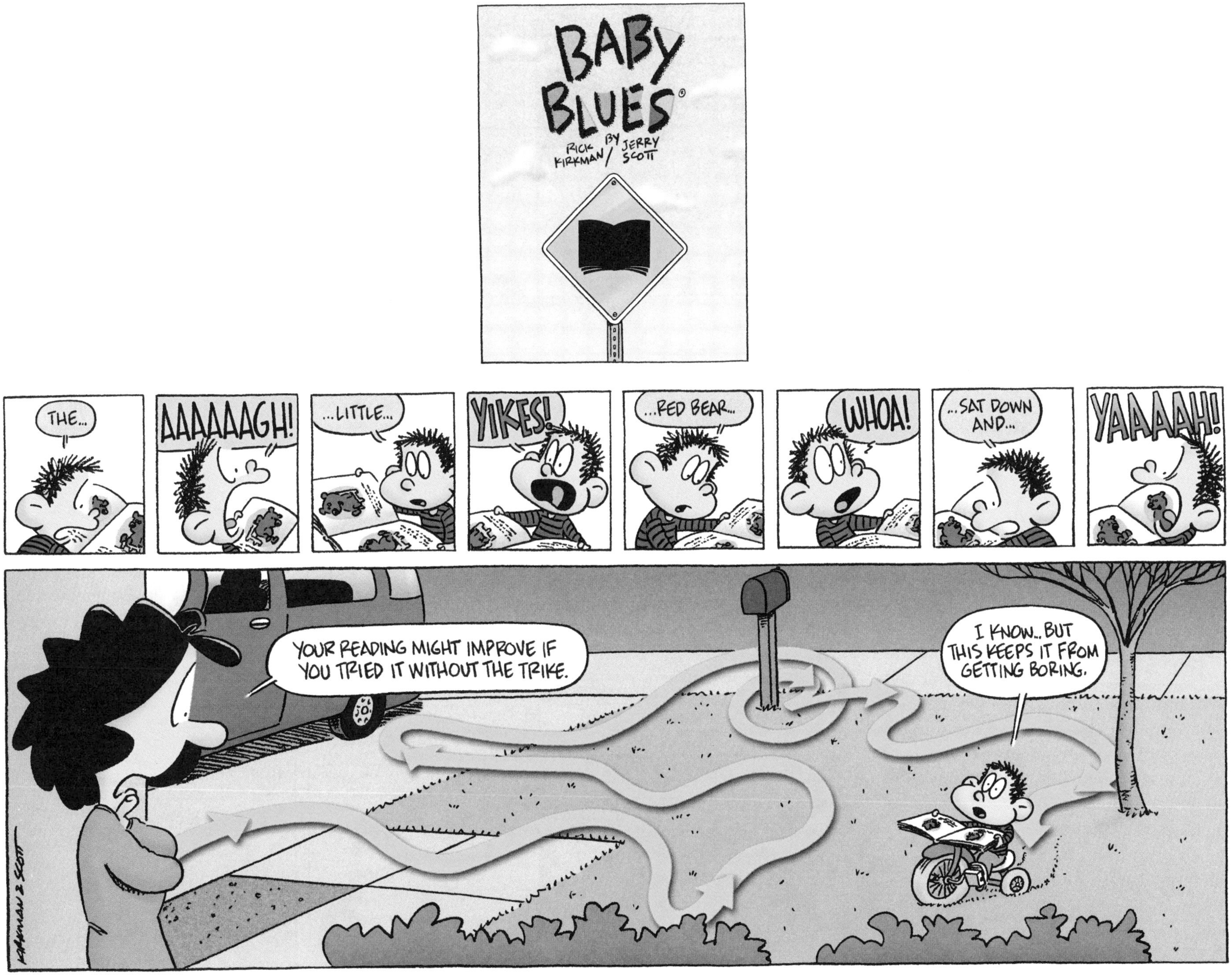
BABY BLUES®
BY RICK KIRKMAN / JERRY SCOTT
THE...
AAAAAAGH!
...LITTLE...
YIKES!
...RED BEAR...
WHOA!
...SAT DOWN AND...
YAAAAH!
YOUR READING MIGHT IMPROVE IF YOU TRIED IT WITHOUT THE TRIKE.
I KNOW... BUT THIS KEEPS IT FROM GETTING BORING.
KIRKMAN & SCOTT

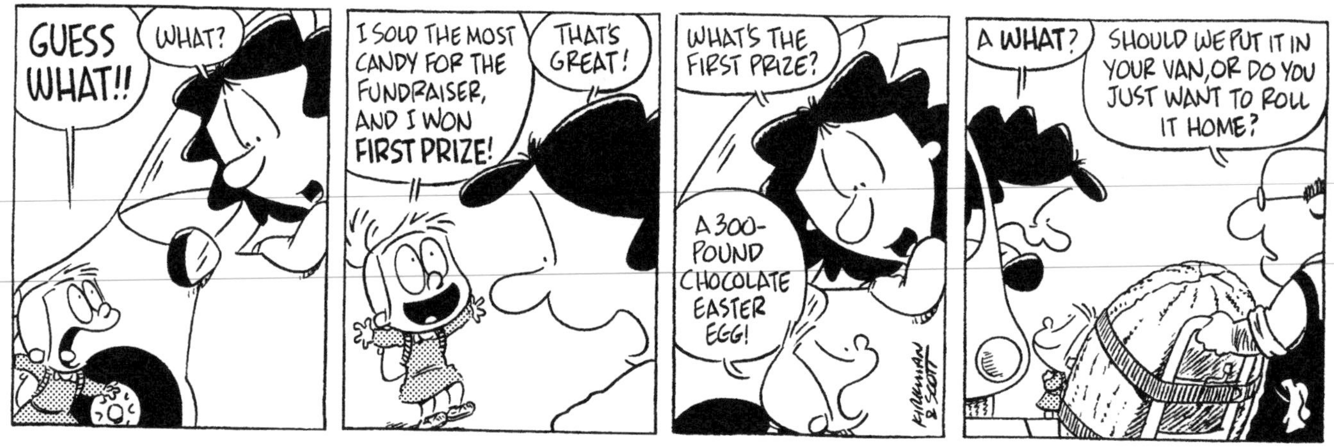
GUESS WHAT!!
WHAT?
I SOLD THE MOST CANDY FOR THE FUNDRAISER, AND I WON **FIRST PRIZE**!
THAT'S GREAT!
WHAT'S THE FIRST PRIZE?
A 300-POUND CHOCOLATE EASTER EGG!
KIRKMAN & SCOTT
A **WHAT**?
SHOULD WE PUT IT IN YOUR VAN, OR DO YOU JUST WANT TO ROLL IT HOME?

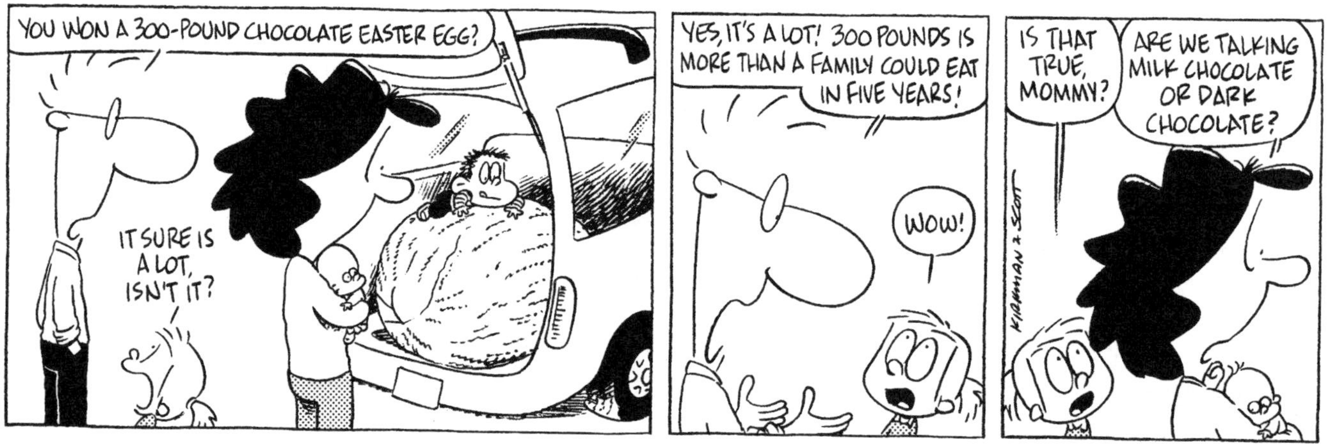
YOU WON A 300-POUND CHOCOLATE EASTER EGG?
IT SURE IS A LOT, ISN'T IT?
YES, IT'S A LOT! 300 POUNDS IS MORE THAN A FAMILY COULD EAT IN FIVE YEARS!
WOW!
KIRKMAN & SCOTT
IS THAT TRUE, MOMMY?
ARE WE TALKING MILK CHOCOLATE OR DARK CHOCOLATE?

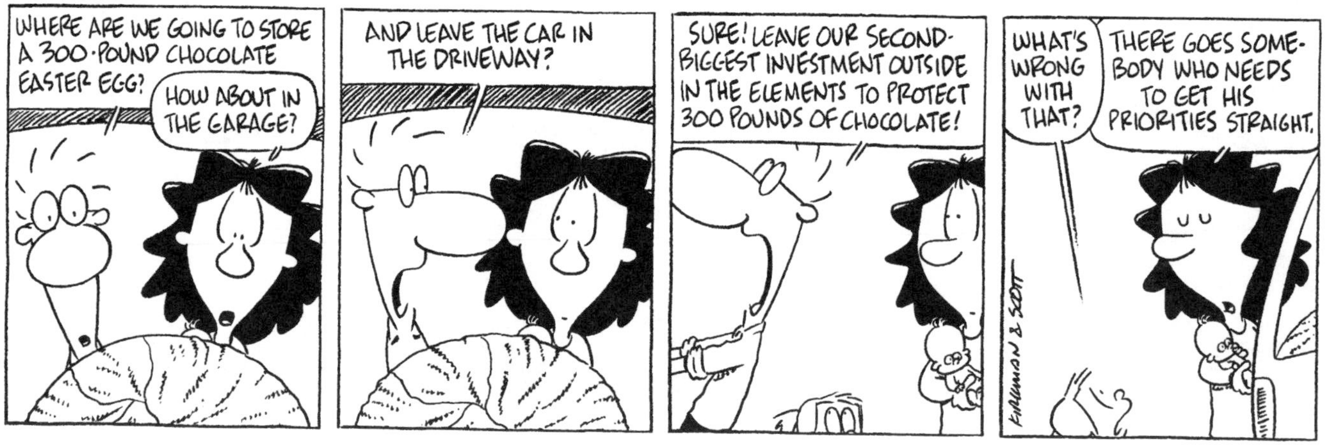
WHERE ARE WE GOING TO STORE A 300-POUND CHOCOLATE EASTER EGG?
HOW ABOUT IN THE GARAGE?
AND LEAVE THE CAR IN THE DRIVEWAY?
SURE! LEAVE OUR SECOND-BIGGEST INVESTMENT OUTSIDE IN THE ELEMENTS TO PROTECT 300 POUNDS OF CHOCOLATE!
KIRKMAN & SCOTT
WHAT'S WRONG WITH THAT?
THERE GOES SOMEBODY WHO NEEDS TO GET HIS PRIORITIES STRAIGHT.

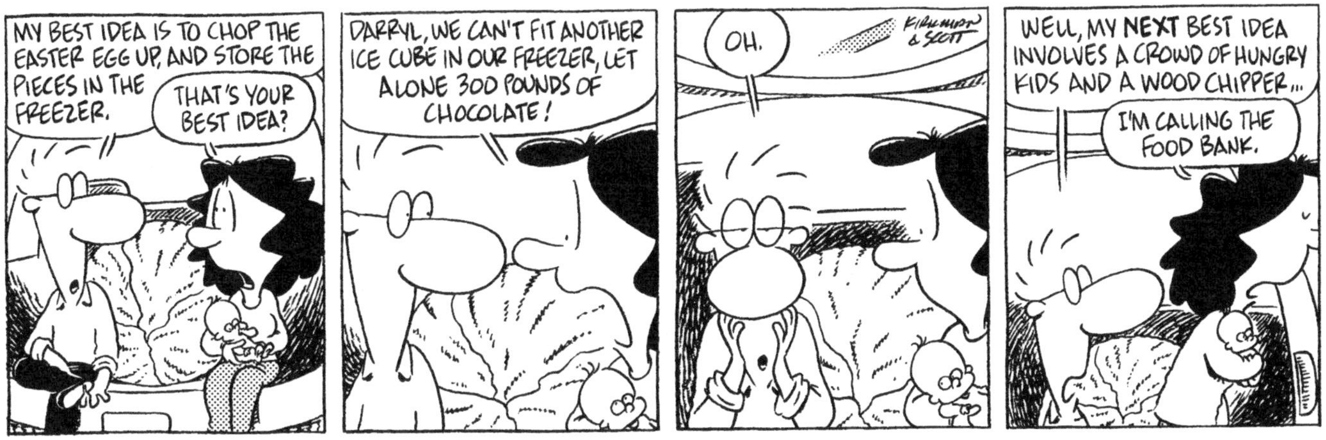
MY BEST IDEA IS TO CHOP THE EASTER EGG UP, AND STORE THE PIECES IN THE FREEZER.
THAT'S YOUR BEST IDEA?
DARRYL, WE CAN'T FIT ANOTHER ICE CUBE IN OUR FREEZER, LET ALONE 300 POUNDS OF CHOCOLATE!
OH.
KIRKMAN & SCOTT
WELL, MY **NEXT** BEST IDEA INVOLVES A CROWD OF HUNGRY KIDS AND A WOOD CHIPPER...
I'M CALLING THE FOOD BANK.

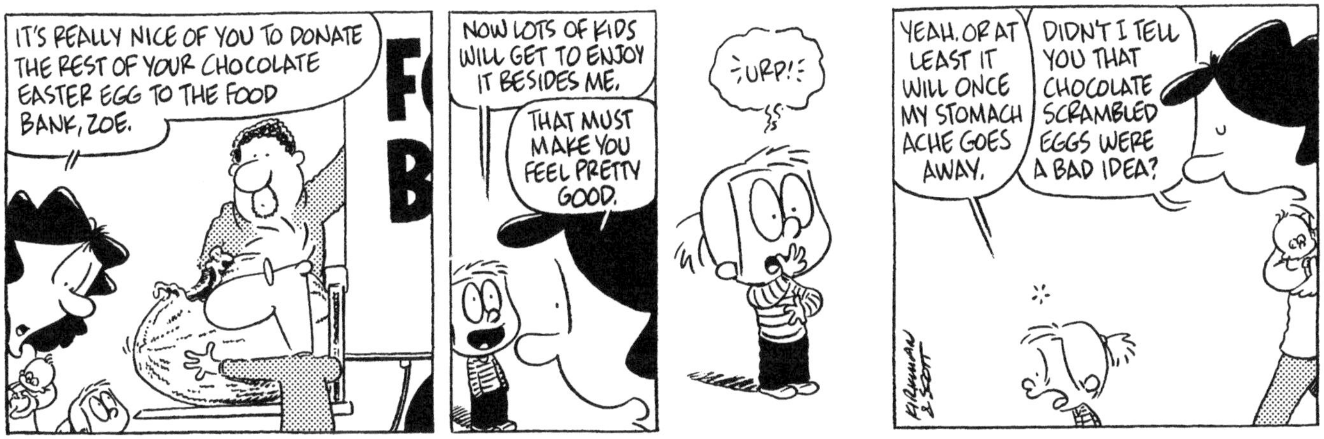
IT'S REALLY NICE OF YOU TO DONATE THE REST OF YOUR CHOCOLATE EASTER EGG TO THE FOOD BANK, ZOE.
NOW LOTS OF KIDS WILL GET TO ENJOY IT BESIDES ME.
THAT MUST MAKE YOU FEEL PRETTY GOOD.
URP!
KIRKMAN & SCOTT
YEAH. OR AT LEAST IT WILL ONCE MY STOMACH ACHE GOES AWAY.
DIDN'T I TELL YOU THAT CHOCOLATE SCRAMBLED EGGS WERE A BAD IDEA?

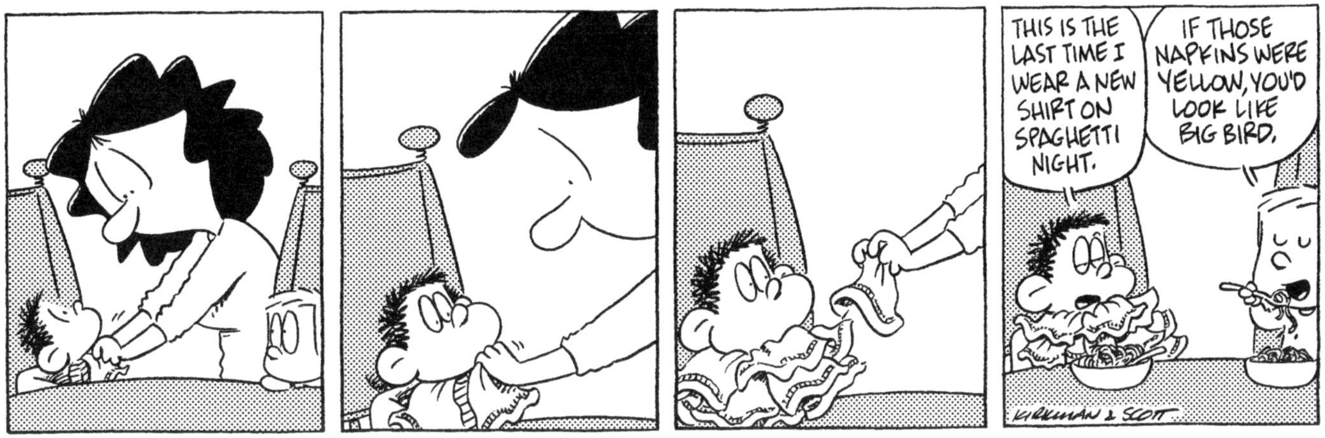
THIS IS THE LAST TIME I WEAR A NEW SHIRT ON SPAGHETTI NIGHT.
IF THOSE NAPKINS WERE YELLOW, YOU'D LOOK LIKE BIG BIRD.
KIRKMAN & SCOTT

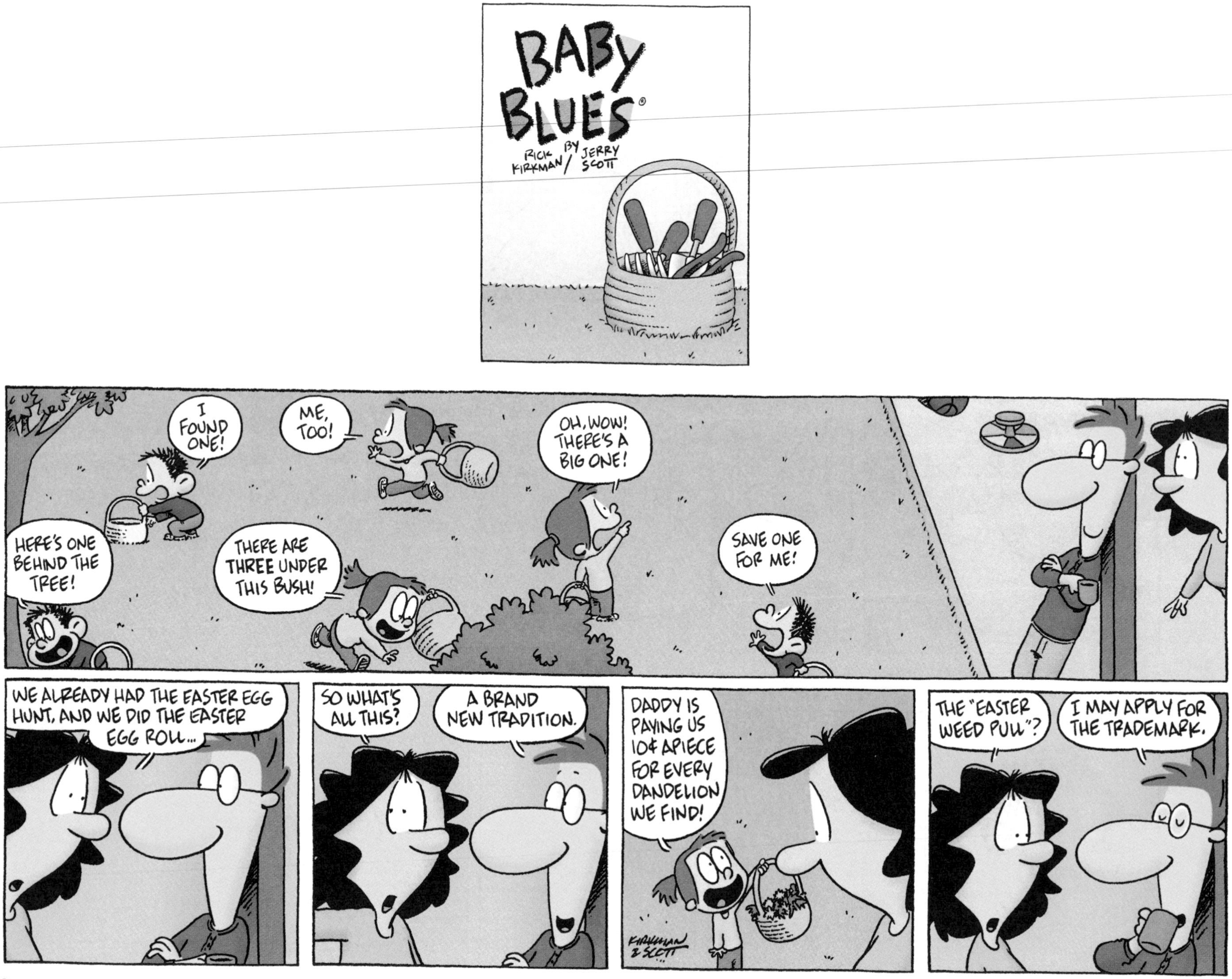
BABY BLUES®
RICK KIRKMAN / BY JERRY SCOTT
I FOUND ONE!
ME, TOO!
OH, WOW! THERE'S A BIG ONE!
HERE'S ONE BEHIND THE TREE!
THERE ARE THREE UNDER THIS BUSH!
SAVE ONE FOR ME!
WE ALREADY HAD THE EASTER EGG HUNT, AND WE DID THE EASTER EGG ROLL...
SO WHAT'S ALL THIS?
A BRAND NEW TRADITION.
DADDY IS PAYING US 10¢ APIECE FOR EVERY DANDELION WE FIND!
THE "EASTER WEED PULL"?
I MAY APPLY FOR THE TRADEMARK.
KIRKMAN & SCOTT

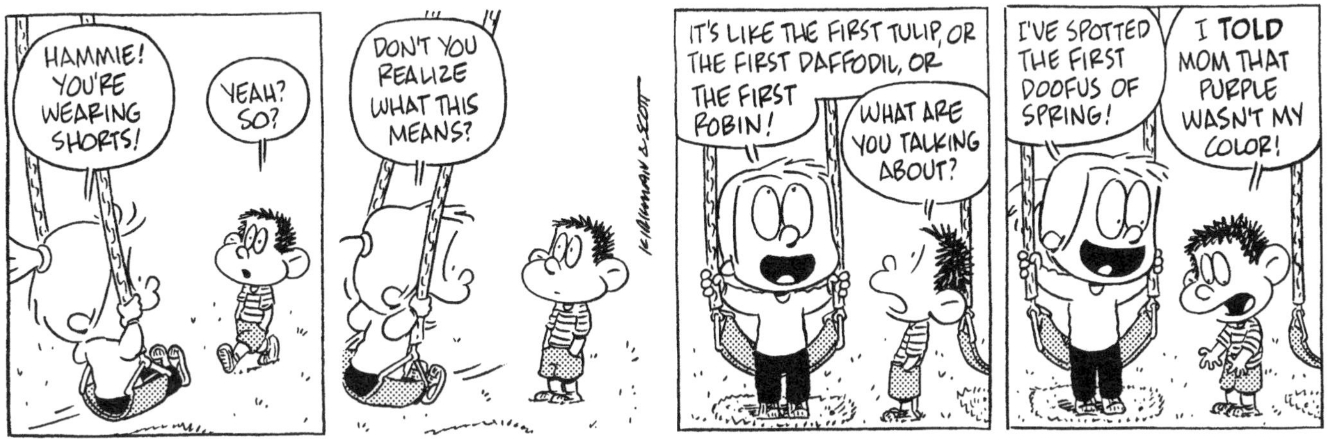
HAMMIE! YOU'RE WEARING SHORTS!
YEAH? SO?
DON'T YOU REALIZE WHAT THIS MEANS?
KIRKMAN & SCOTT
IT'S LIKE THE FIRST TULIP, OR THE FIRST DAFFODIL, OR THE FIRST ROBIN!
WHAT ARE YOU TALKING ABOUT?
I'VE SPOTTED THE FIRST DOOFUS OF SPRING!
I **TOLD** MOM THAT PURPLE WASN'T MY COLOR!

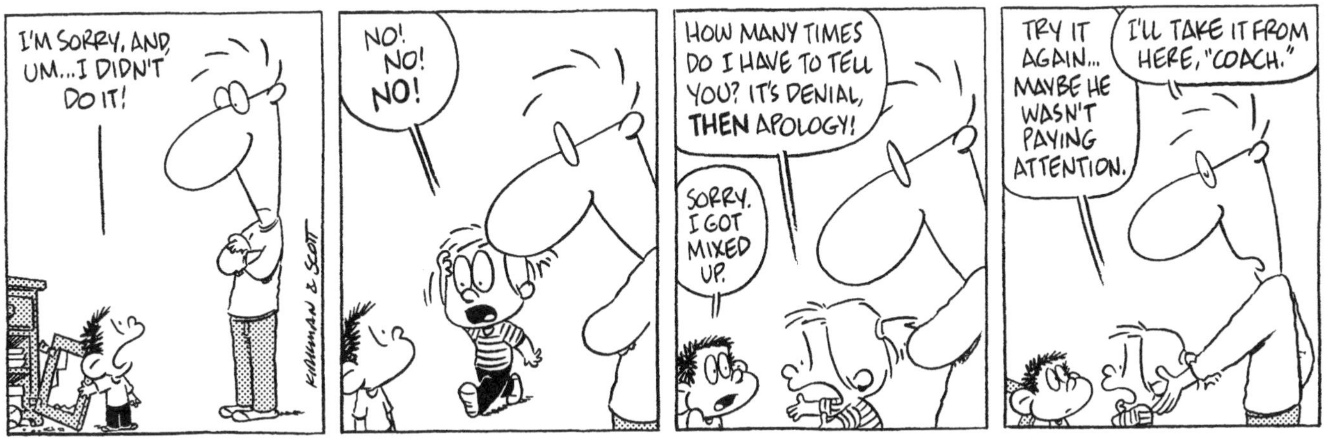
I'M SORRY, AND, UM...I DIDN'T DO IT!
KIRKMAN & SCOTT
NO! NO! **NO!**
HOW MANY TIMES DO I HAVE TO TELL YOU? IT'S DENIAL, **THEN** APOLOGY!
SORRY. I GOT MIXED UP.
TRY IT AGAIN... MAYBE HE WASN'T PAYING ATTENTION.
I'LL TAKE IT FROM HERE, "COACH."

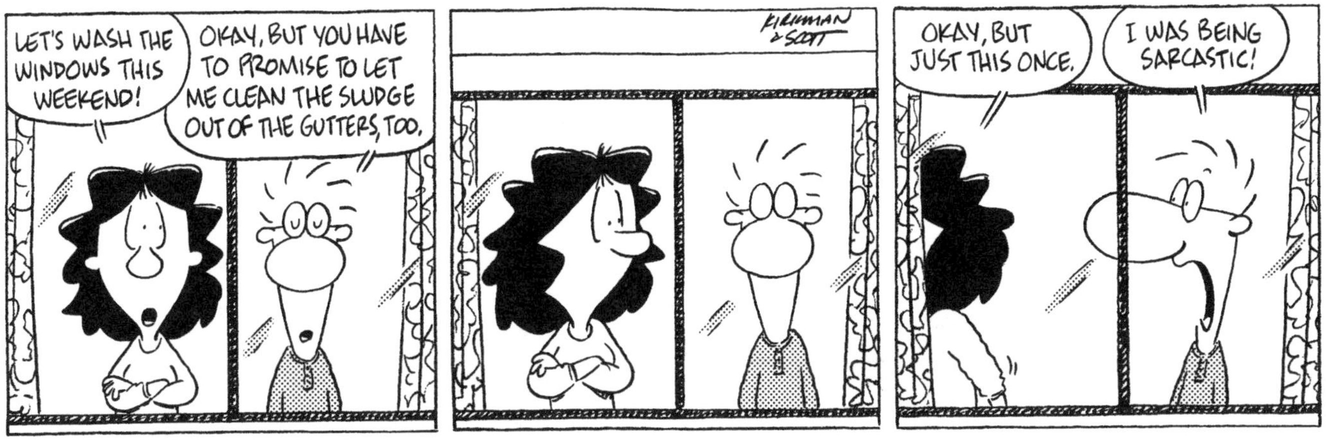
LET'S WASH THE WINDOWS THIS WEEKEND!
OKAY, BUT YOU HAVE TO PROMISE TO LET ME CLEAN THE SLUDGE OUT OF THE GUTTERS, TOO.
KIRKMAN & SCOTT
OKAY, BUT JUST THIS ONCE.
I WAS BEING SARCASTIC!

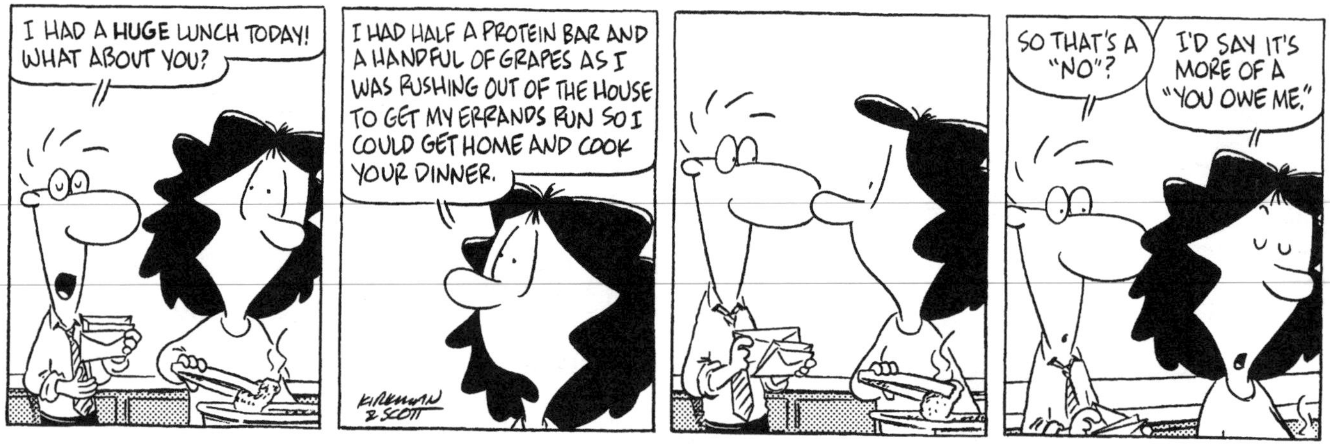

I HAD A **HUGE** LUNCH TODAY! WHAT ABOUT YOU?
I HAD HALF A PROTEIN BAR AND A HANDFUL OF GRAPES AS I WAS RUSHING OUT OF THE HOUSE TO GET MY ERRANDS RUN SO I COULD GET HOME AND COOK YOUR DINNER.
KIRKMAN & SCOTT
SO THAT'S A "NO"?
I'D SAY IT'S MORE OF A "YOU OWE ME."

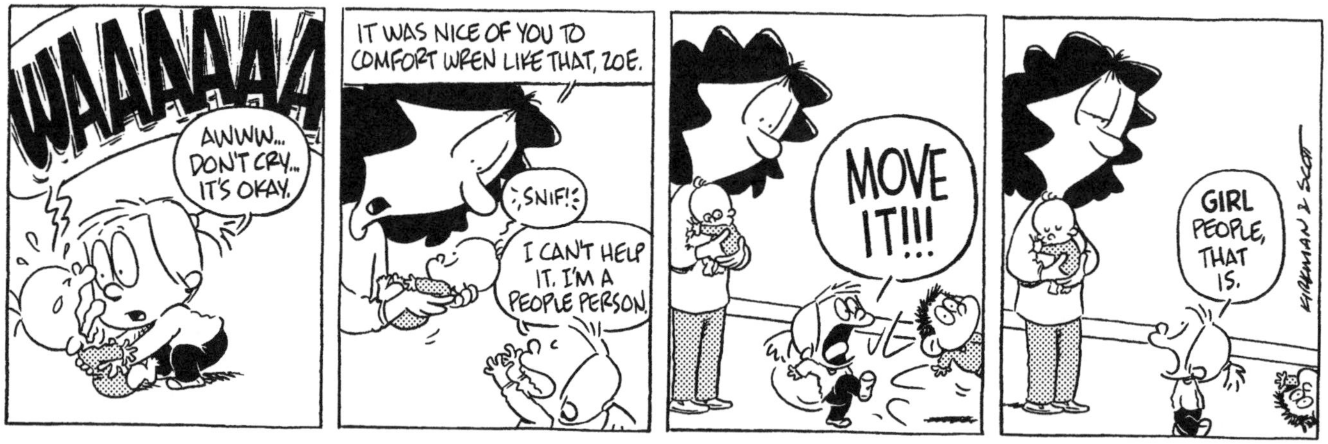

WAAAAAA
AWWW... DON'T CRY... IT'S OKAY.
IT WAS NICE OF YOU TO COMFORT WREN LIKE THAT, ZOE.
SNIF!
I CAN'T HELP IT. I'M A PEOPLE PERSON.
MOVE IT!!!
GIRL PEOPLE, THAT IS.
KIRKMAN & SCOTT

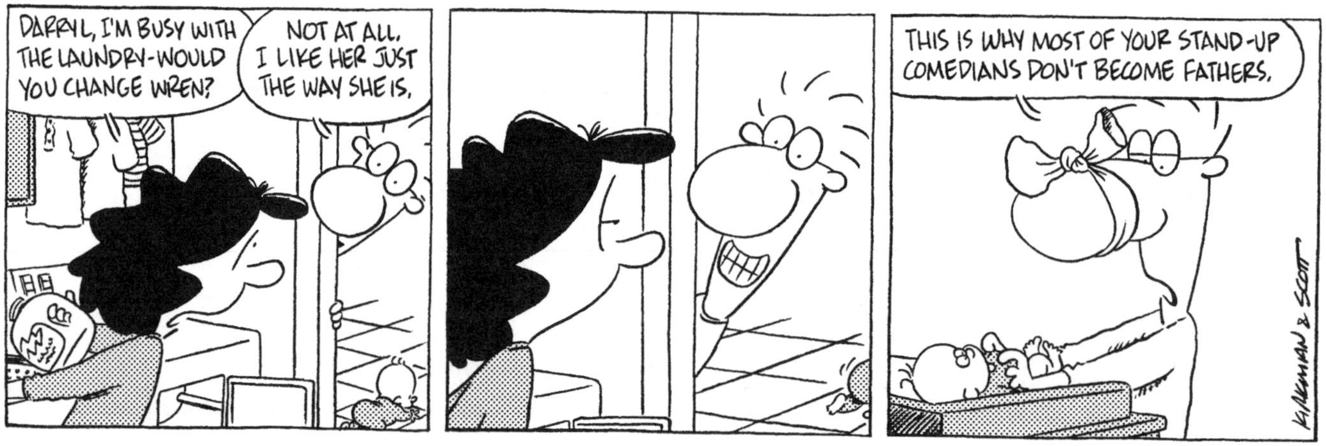

DARRYL, I'M BUSY WITH THE LAUNDRY-WOULD YOU CHANGE WREN?
NOT AT ALL. I LIKE HER JUST THE WAY SHE IS.
THIS IS WHY MOST OF YOUR STAND-UP COMEDIANS DON'T BECOME FATHERS.
KIRKMAN & SCOTT

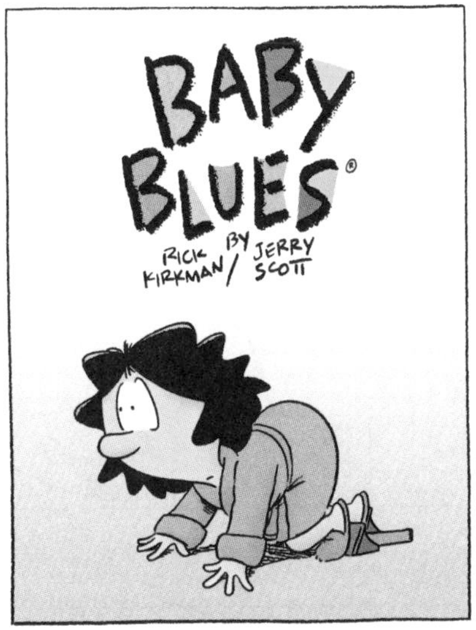
BABY BLUES®
BY RICK KIRKMAN/ JERRY SCOTT

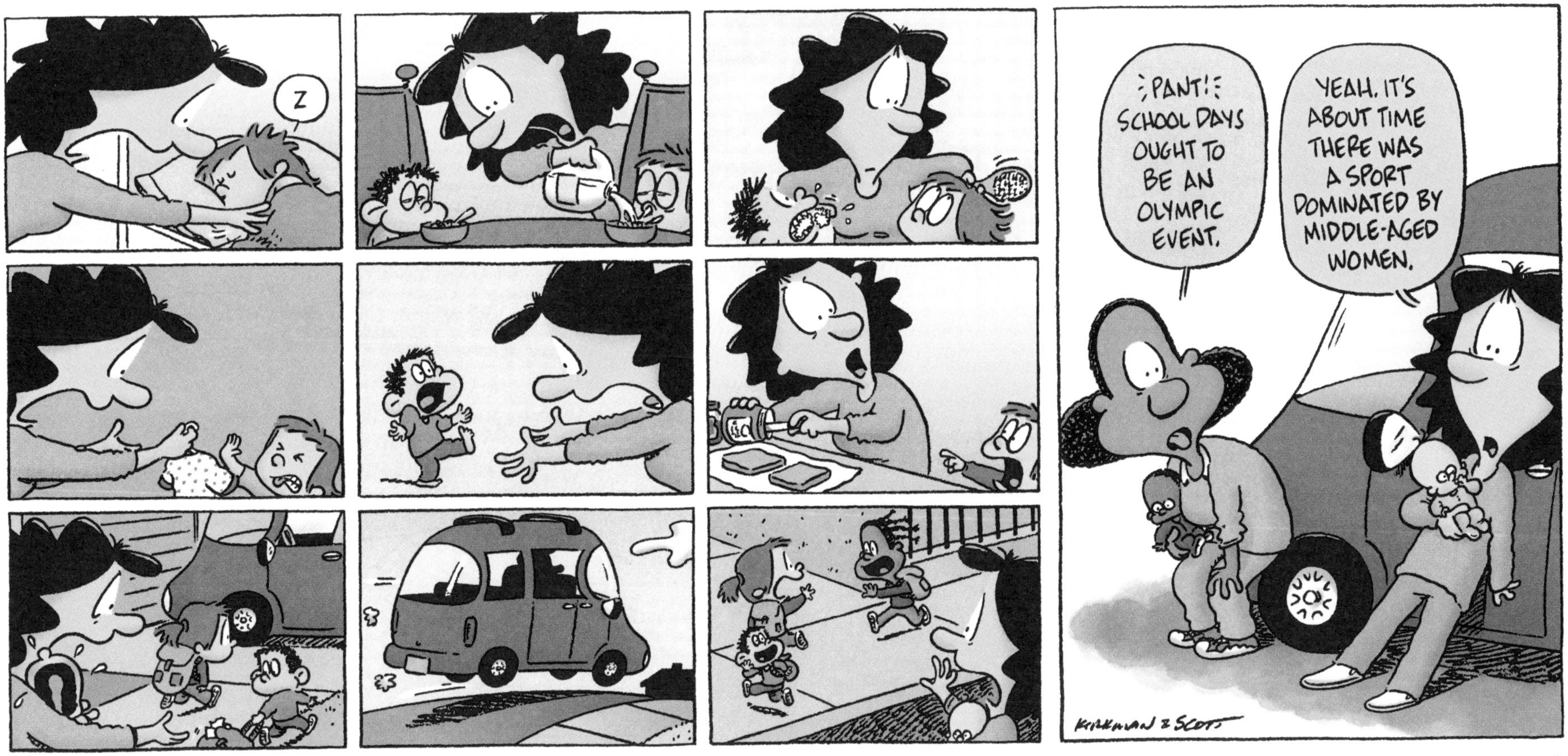
Z
PANT! SCHOOL DAYS OUGHT TO BE AN OLYMPIC EVENT.
YEAH. IT'S ABOUT TIME THERE WAS A SPORT DOMINATED BY MIDDLE-AGED WOMEN.
KIRKMAN & SCOTT

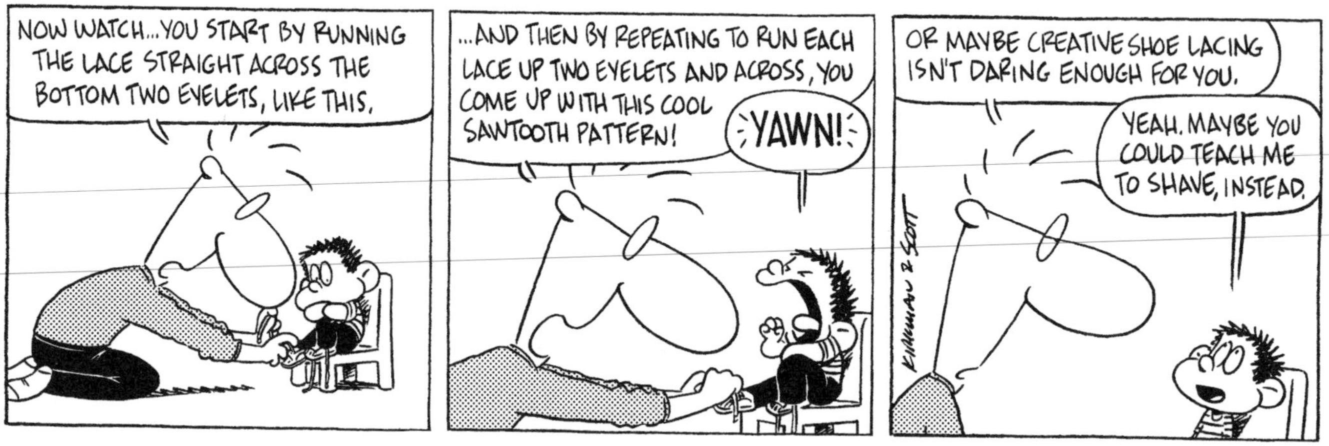
NOW WATCH...YOU START BY RUNNING THE LACE STRAIGHT ACROSS THE BOTTOM TWO EYELETS, LIKE THIS.
...AND THEN BY REPEATING TO RUN EACH LACE UP TWO EYELETS AND ACROSS, YOU COME UP WITH THIS COOL SAWTOOTH PATTERN!
YAWN!
OR MAYBE CREATIVE SHOE LACING ISN'T DARING ENOUGH FOR YOU.
YEAH. MAYBE YOU COULD TEACH ME TO SHAVE, INSTEAD.
KIRKMAN & SCOTT

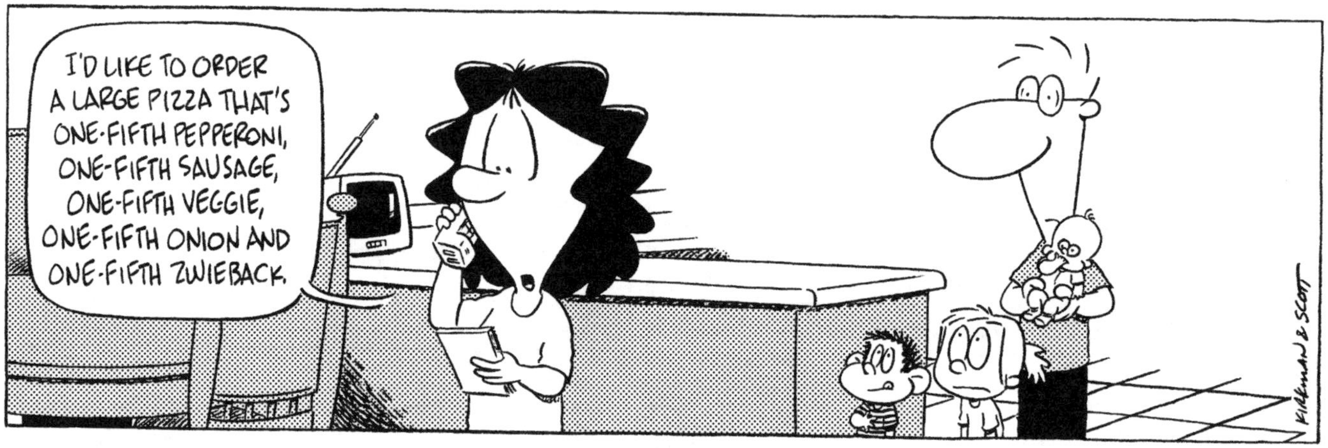
I'D LIKE TO ORDER A LARGE PIZZA THAT'S ONE-FIFTH PEPPERONI, ONE-FIFTH SAUSAGE, ONE-FIFTH VEGGIE, ONE-FIFTH ONION AND ONE-FIFTH ZWIEBACK.
KIRKMAN & SCOTT

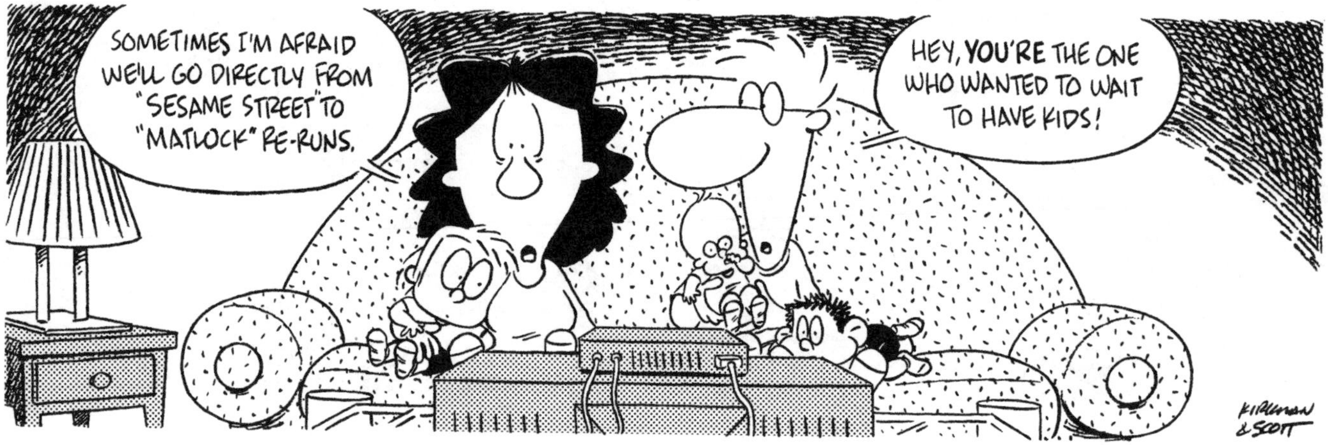
SOMETIMES I'M AFRAID WE'LL GO DIRECTLY FROM "SESAME STREET" TO "MATLOCK" RE-RUNS.
HEY, **YOU'RE** THE ONE WHO WANTED TO WAIT TO HAVE KIDS!
KIRKMAN & SCOTT

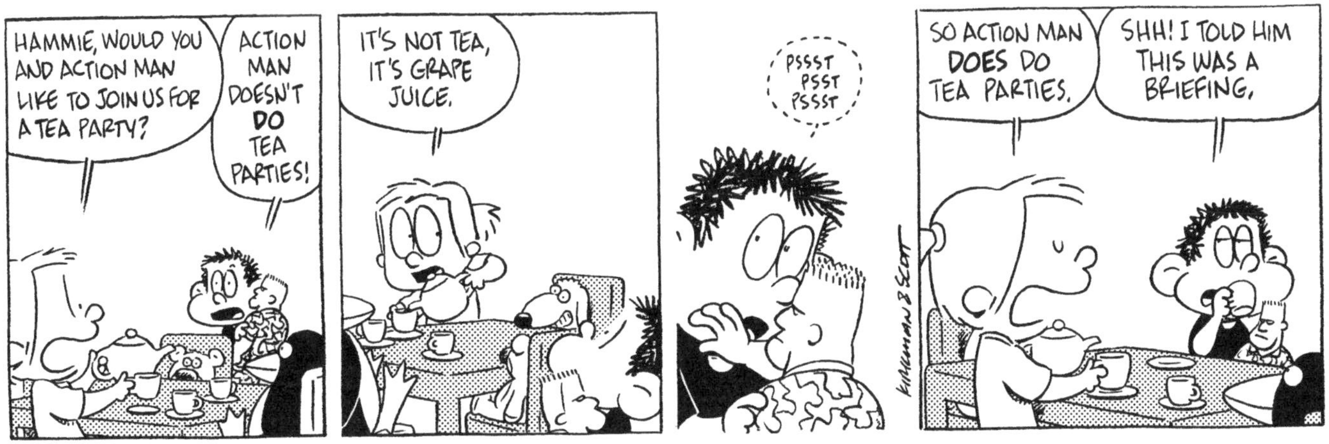
HAMMIE, WOULD YOU AND ACTION MAN LIKE TO JOIN US FOR A TEA PARTY?
ACTION MAN DOESN'T **DO** TEA PARTIES!
IT'S NOT TEA, IT'S GRAPE JUICE.
PSSST PSSST PSSST
KIRKMAN & SCOTT
SO ACTION MAN **DOES** DO TEA PARTIES.
SHH! I TOLD HIM THIS WAS A BRIEFING.

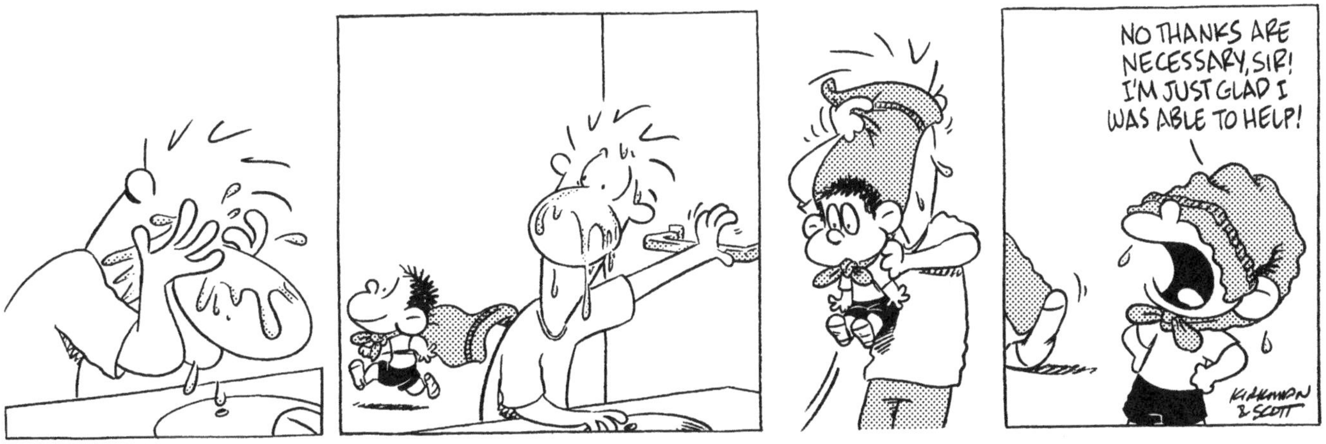
NO THANKS ARE NECESSARY, SIR! I'M JUST GLAD I WAS ABLE TO HELP!
KIRKMAN & SCOTT

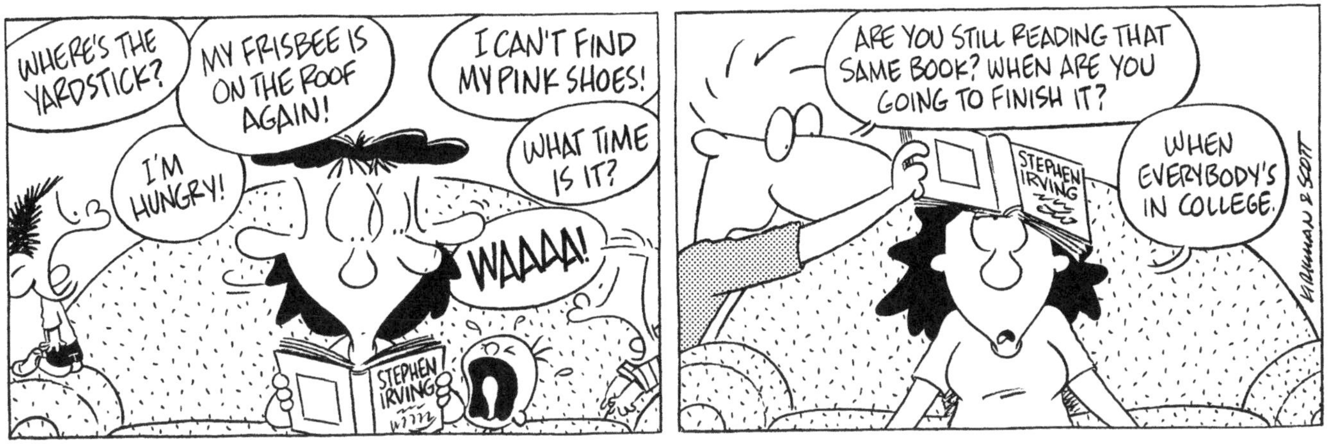
WHERE'S THE YARDSTICK?
MY FRISBEE IS ON THE ROOF AGAIN!
I CAN'T FIND MY PINK SHOES!
I'M HUNGRY!
WHAT TIME IS IT?
WAAAA!
STEPHEN IRVING
ARE YOU STILL READING THAT SAME BOOK? WHEN ARE YOU GOING TO FINISH IT?
STEPHEN IRVING
WHEN EVERYBODY'S IN COLLEGE.
KIRKMAN & SCOTT

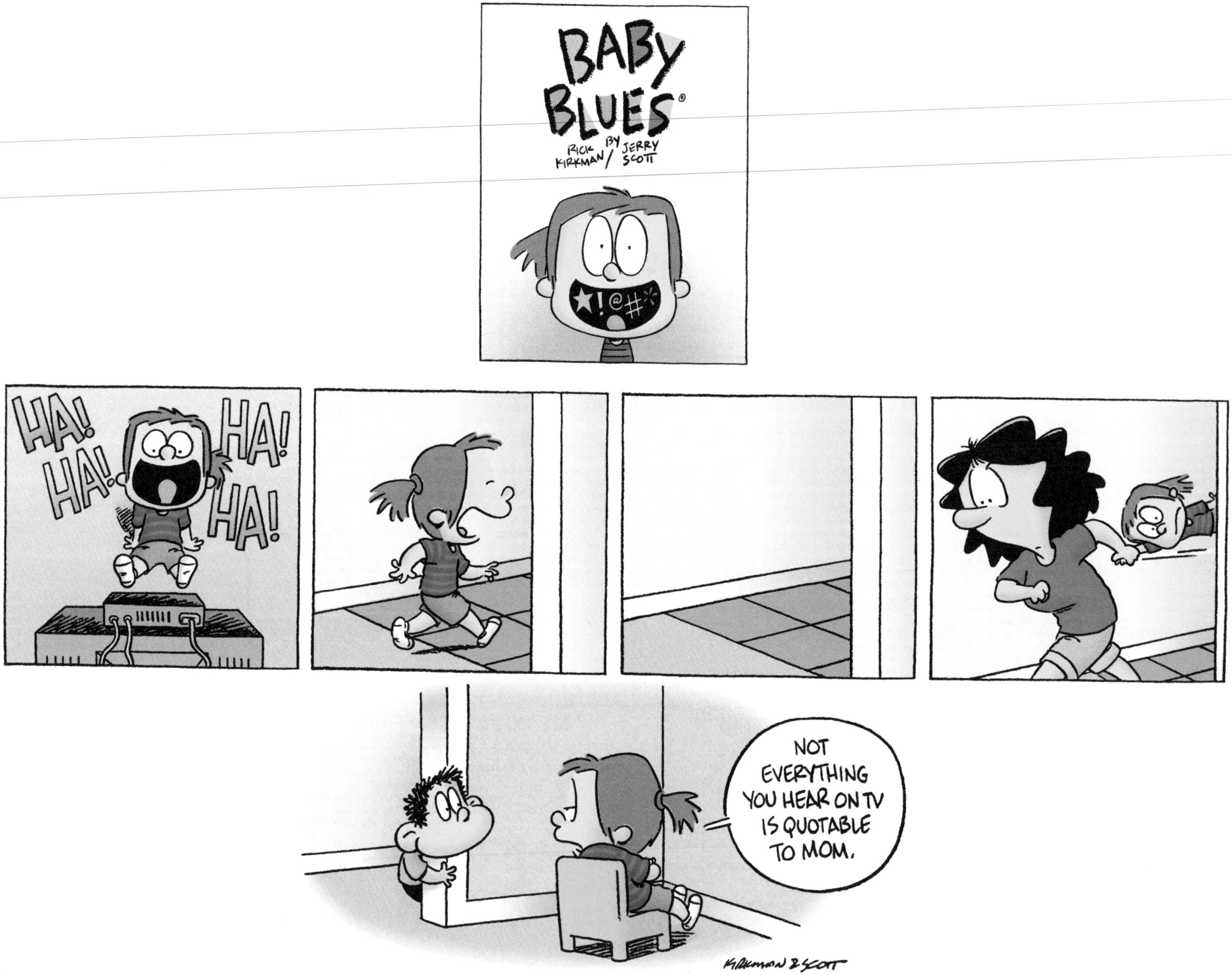
BABY BLUES®
RICK KIRKMAN / BY JERRY SCOTT
★!@#*
HA! HA! HA! HA!
NOT EVERYTHING YOU HEAR ON TV IS QUOTABLE TO MOM.
KIRKMAN & SCOTT

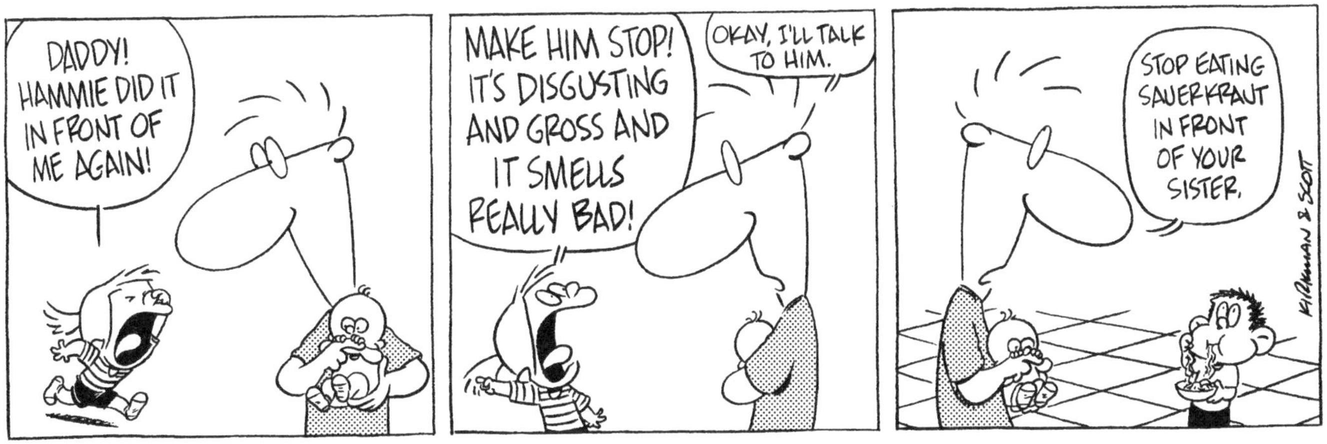
DADDY! HAMMIE DID IT IN FRONT OF ME AGAIN!
MAKE HIM STOP! IT'S DISGUSTING AND GROSS AND IT SMELLS REALLY BAD!
OKAY, I'LL TALK TO HIM.
STOP EATING SAUERKRAUT IN FRONT OF YOUR SISTER.
KIRKMAN & SCOTT

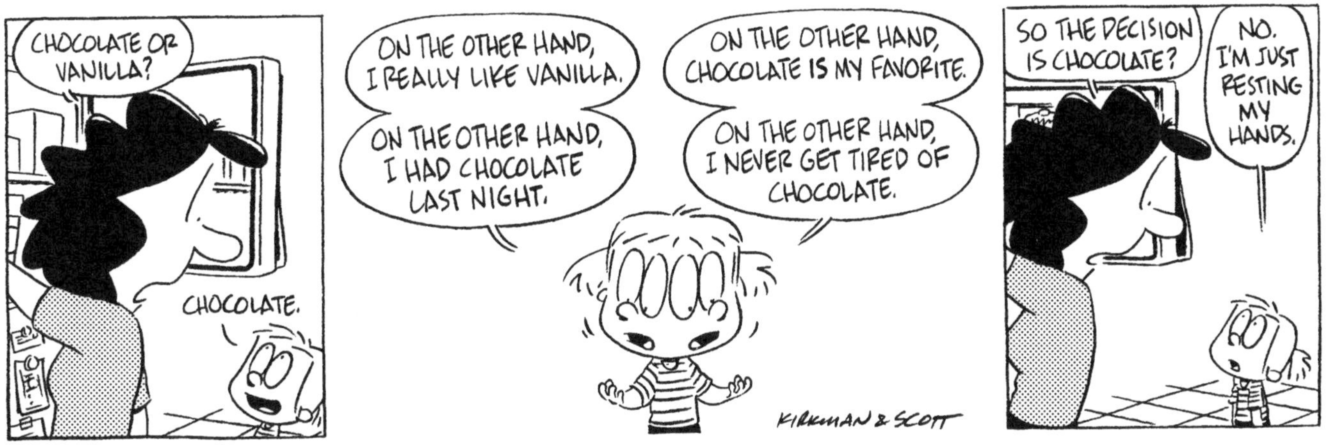
CHOCOLATE OR VANILLA?
CHOCOLATE.
ON THE OTHER HAND, I REALLY LIKE VANILLA.
ON THE OTHER HAND, I HAD CHOCOLATE LAST NIGHT.
ON THE OTHER HAND, CHOCOLATE IS MY FAVORITE.
ON THE OTHER HAND, I NEVER GET TIRED OF CHOCOLATE.
KIRKMAN & SCOTT
SO THE DECISION IS CHOCOLATE?
NO. I'M JUST RESTING MY HANDS.

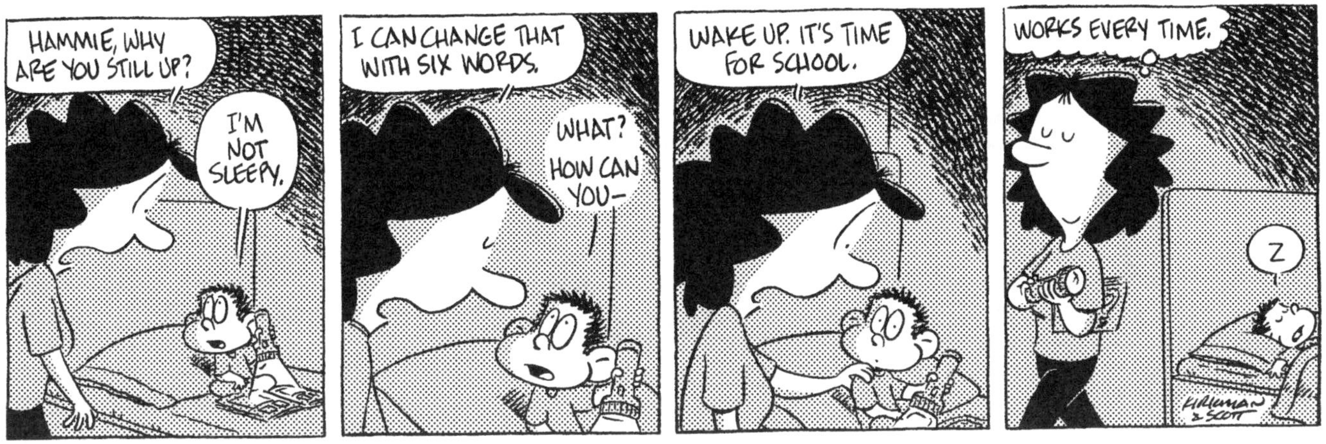
HAMMIE, WHY ARE YOU STILL UP?
I'M NOT SLEEPY.
I CAN CHANGE THAT WITH SIX WORDS.
WHAT? HOW CAN YOU–
WAKE UP. IT'S TIME FOR SCHOOL.
WORKS EVERY TIME.
Z
KIRKMAN & SCOTT

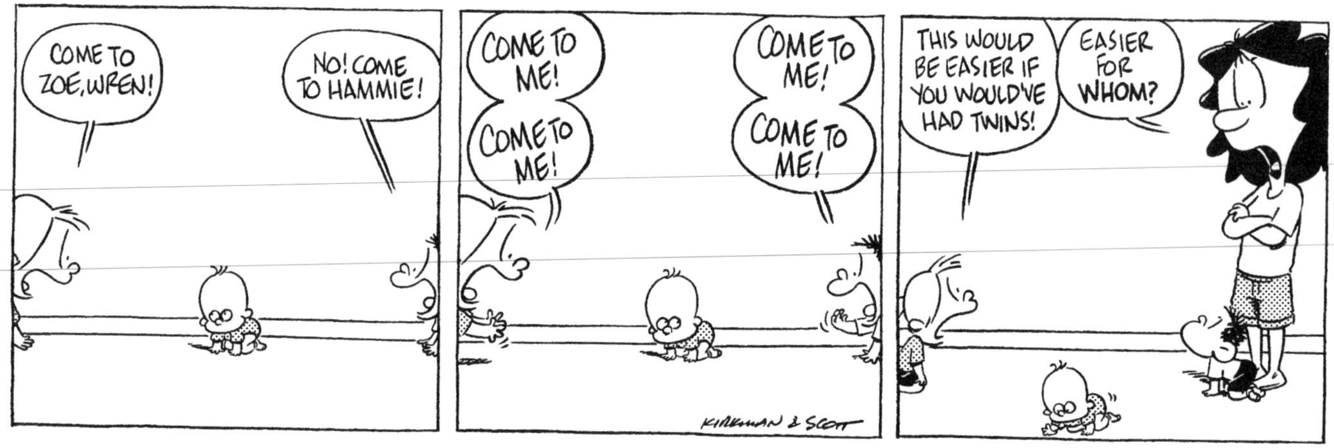
COME TO ZOE, WREN!
NO! COME TO HAMMIE!
COME TO ME!
COME TO ME!
COME TO ME!
COME TO ME!
KIRKMAN & SCOTT
THIS WOULD BE EASIER IF YOU WOULD'VE HAD TWINS!
EASIER FOR WHOM?

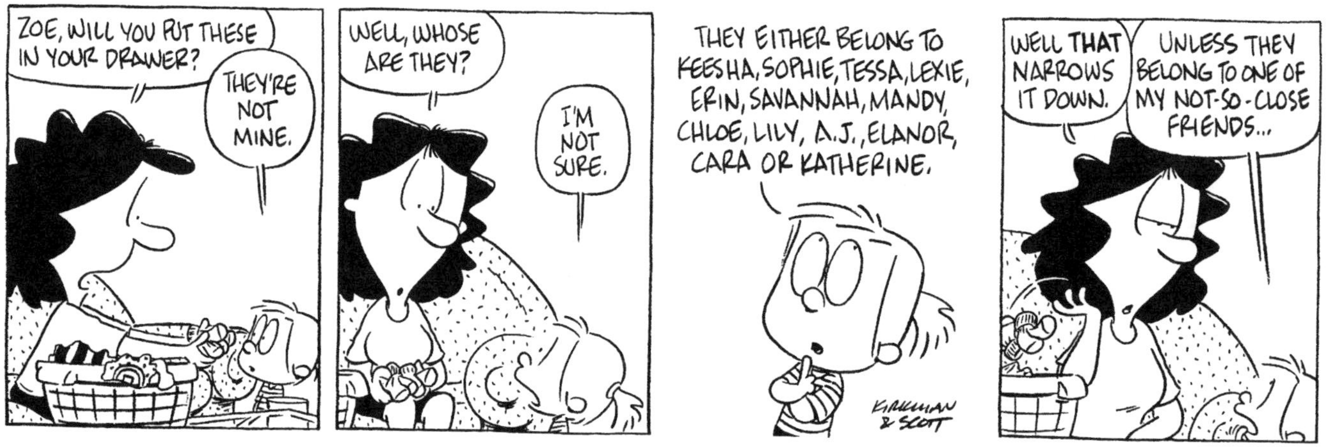
ZOE, WILL YOU PUT THESE IN YOUR DRAWER?
THEY'RE NOT MINE.
WELL, WHOSE ARE THEY?
I'M NOT SURE.
THEY EITHER BELONG TO KEESHA, SOPHIE, TESSA, LEXIE, ERIN, SAVANNAH, MANDY, CHLOE, LILY, A.J., ELANOR, CARA OR KATHERINE.
KIRKMAN & SCOTT
WELL THAT NARROWS IT DOWN.
UNLESS THEY BELONG TO ONE OF MY NOT-SO-CLOSE FRIENDS...

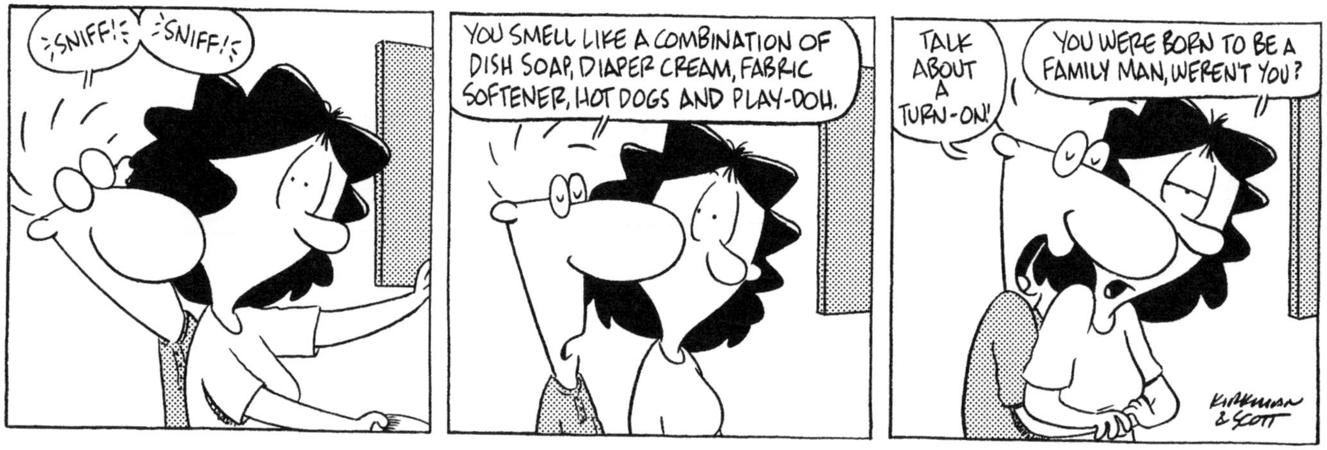
SNIFF!
SNIFF!
YOU SMELL LIKE A COMBINATION OF DISH SOAP, DIAPER CREAM, FABRIC SOFTENER, HOT DOGS AND PLAY-DOH.
TALK ABOUT A TURN-ON!
YOU WERE BORN TO BE A FAMILY MAN, WEREN'T YOU?
KIRKMAN & SCOTT

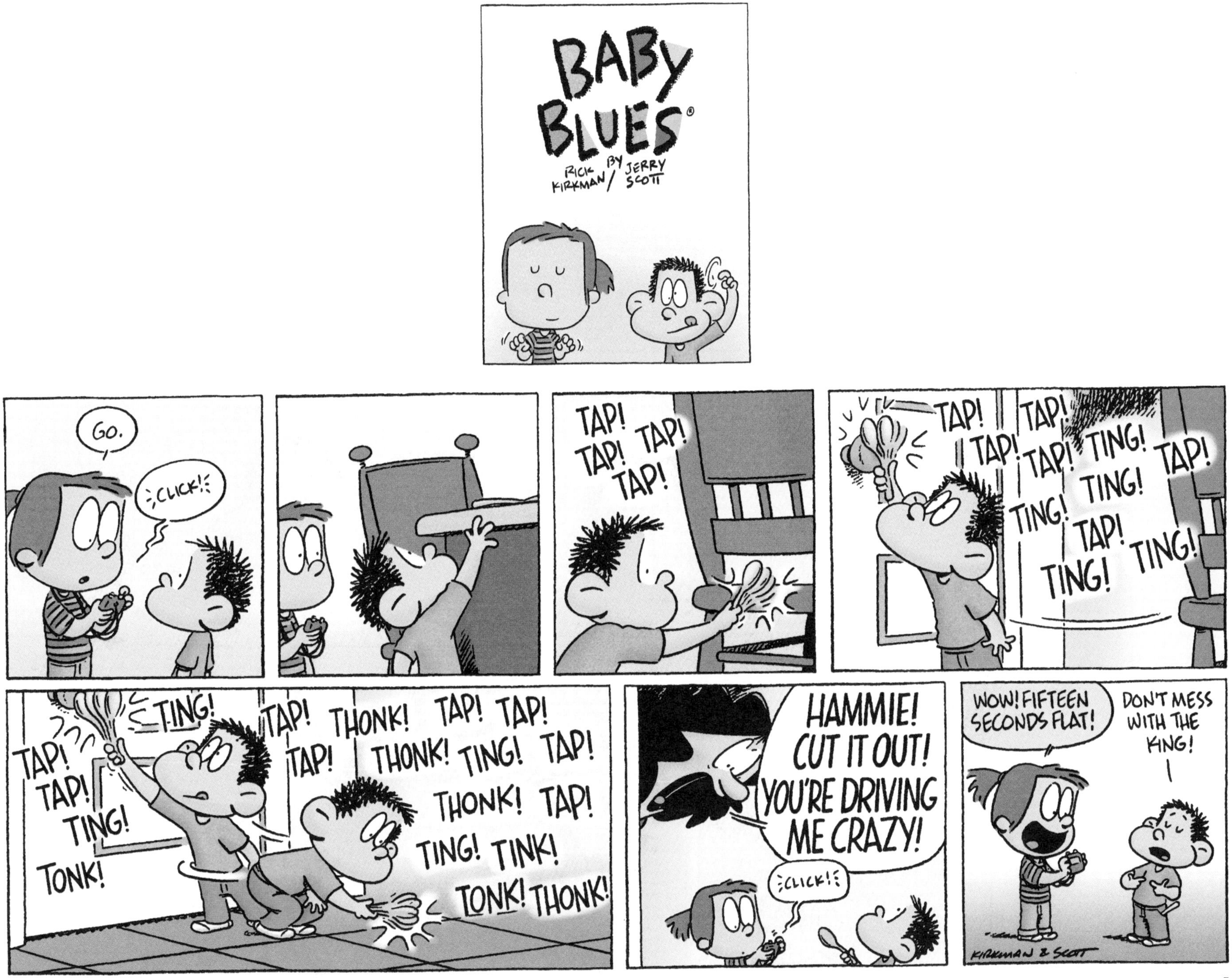

BABY BLUES®
BY RICK KIRKMAN / JERRY SCOTT
GO.
CLICK!
TAP! TAP! TAP! TAP!
TAP! TAP! TAP! TAP! TING! TING! TAP! TING! TAP! TING! TING!
TAP! TAP! TING! TONK! TING! TAP! THONK! TAP! TAP! TAP! THONK! TING! TAP! THONK! TAP! TING! TINK! TONK! THONK!
HAMMIE! CUT IT OUT! YOU'RE DRIVING ME CRAZY!
CLICK!
WOW! FIFTEEN SECONDS FLAT!
DON'T MESS WITH THE KING!
KIRKMAN & SCOTT

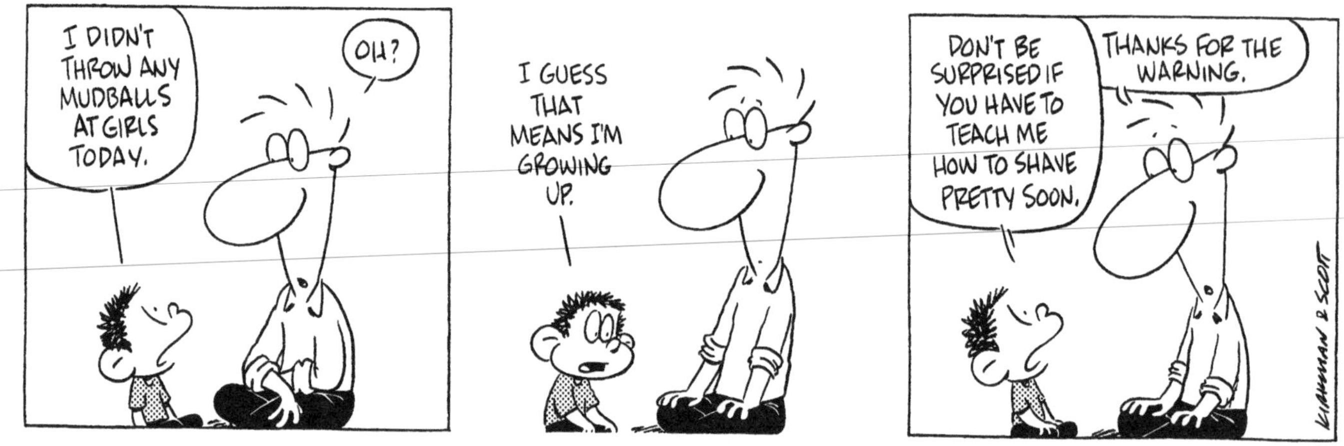
I DIDN'T THROW ANY MUDBALLS AT GIRLS TODAY.
OH?
I GUESS THAT MEANS I'M GROWING UP.
DON'T BE SURPRISED IF YOU HAVE TO TEACH ME HOW TO SHAVE PRETTY SOON.
THANKS FOR THE WARNING.
KIRKMAN & SCOTT

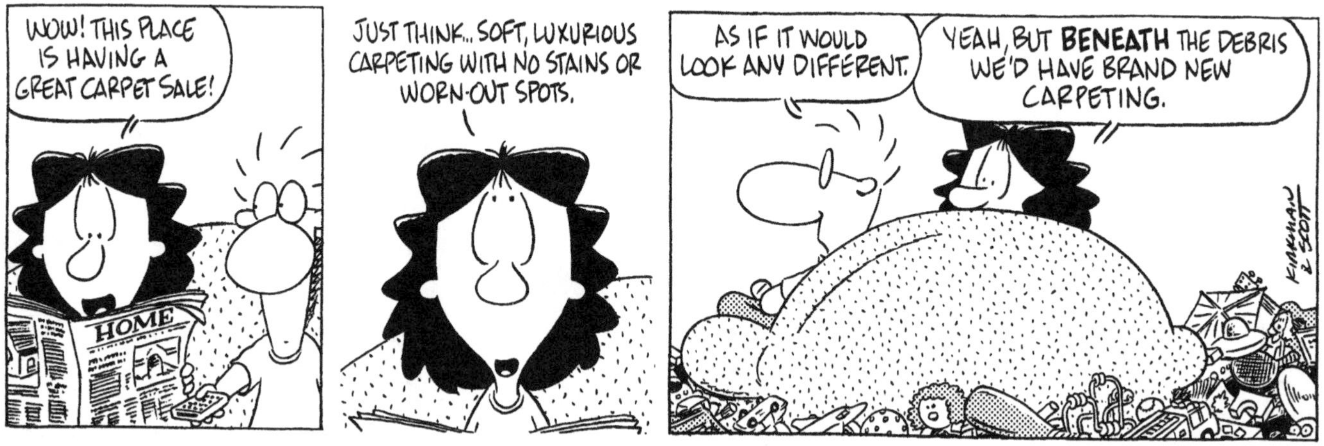
WOW! THIS PLACE IS HAVING A GREAT CARPET SALE!
HOME
JUST THINK... SOFT, LUXURIOUS CARPETING WITH NO STAINS OR WORN-OUT SPOTS.
AS IF IT WOULD LOOK ANY DIFFERENT.
YEAH, BUT **BENEATH** THE DEBRIS WE'D HAVE BRAND NEW CARPETING.
KIRKMAN & SCOTT

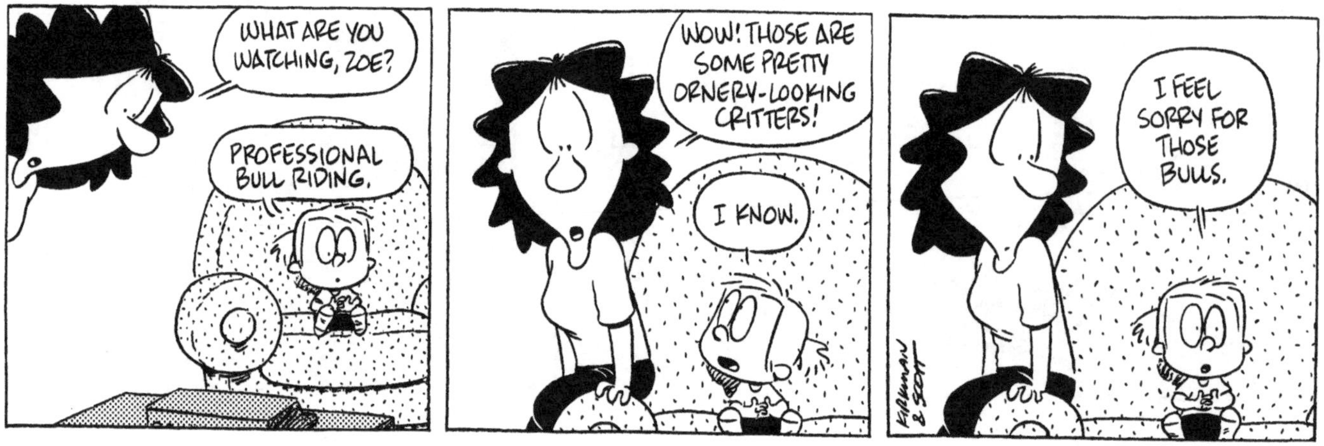
WHAT ARE YOU WATCHING, ZOE?
PROFESSIONAL BULL RIDING.
WOW! THOSE ARE SOME PRETTY ORNERY-LOOKING CRITTERS!
I KNOW.
I FEEL SORRY FOR THOSE BULLS.
KIRKMAN & SCOTT

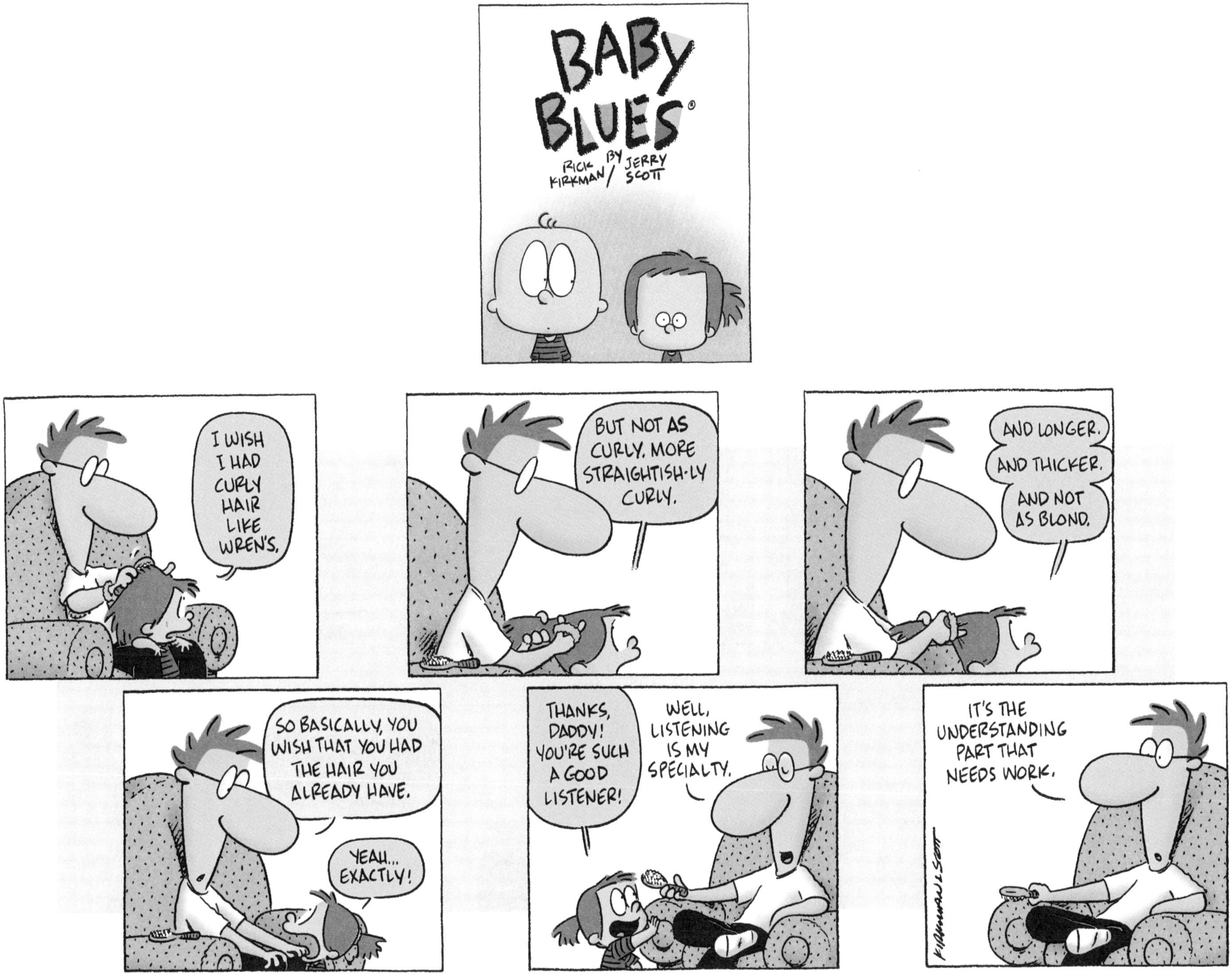
BABY BLUES®
BY RICK KIRKMAN / JERRY SCOTT
I WISH I HAD CURLY HAIR LIKE WREN'S.
BUT NOT AS CURLY. MORE STRAIGHTISH-LY CURLY.
AND LONGER.
AND THICKER.
AND NOT AS BLOND.
SO BASICALLY, YOU WISH THAT YOU HAD THE HAIR YOU ALREADY HAVE.
YEAH... EXACTLY!
THANKS, DADDY! YOU'RE SUCH A GOOD LISTENER!
WELL, LISTENING IS MY SPECIALTY.
IT'S THE UNDERSTANDING PART THAT NEEDS WORK.
KIRKMAN & SCOTT

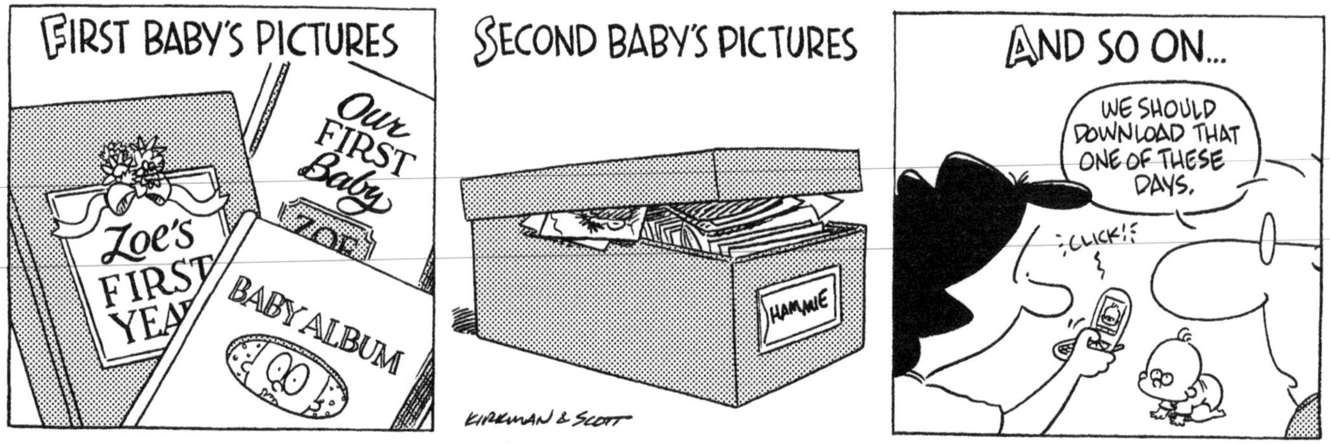
FIRST BABY'S PICTURES
Our FIRST Baby
Zoe's FIRST YEAR
BABY ALBUM
SECOND BABY'S PICTURES
HAMMIE
AND SO ON...
WE SHOULD DOWNLOAD THAT ONE OF THESE DAYS.
CLICK
KIRKMAN & SCOTT

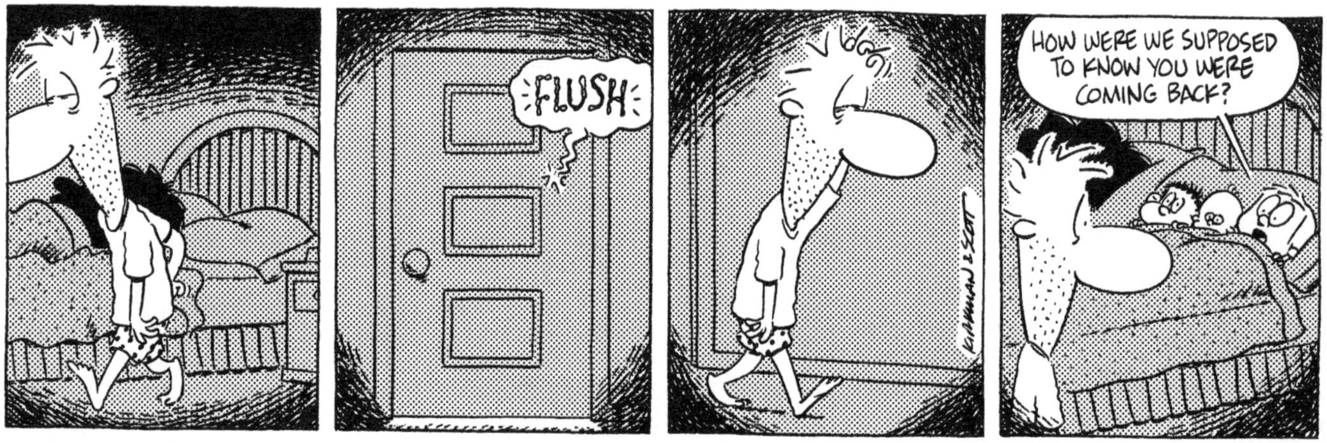
FLUSH
KIRKMAN & SCOTT
HOW WERE WE SUPPOSED TO KNOW YOU WERE COMING BACK?

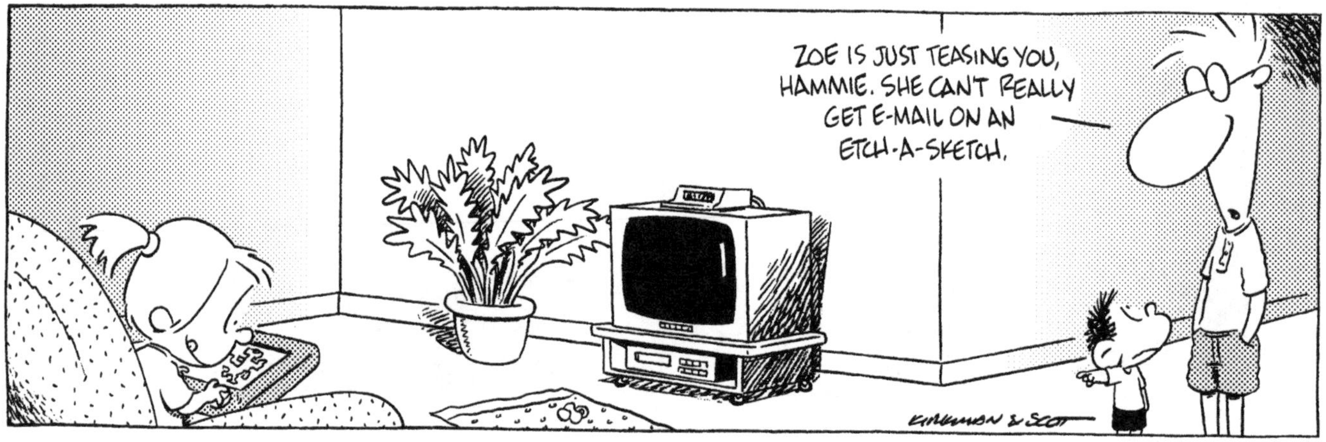
ZOE IS JUST TEASING YOU, HAMMIE. SHE CAN'T REALLY GET E-MAIL ON AN ETCH-A-SKETCH.
KIRKMAN & SCOTT

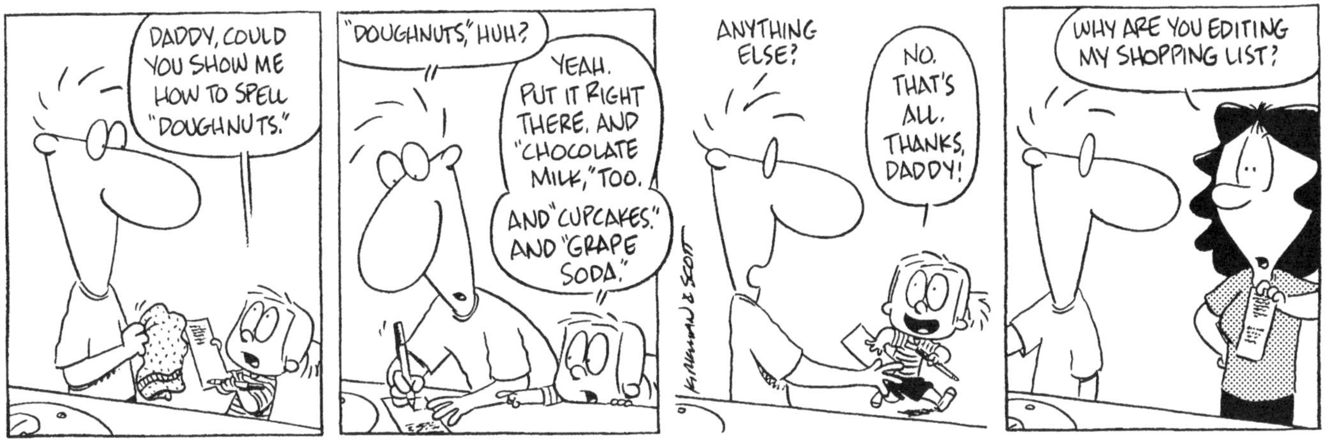
DADDY, COULD YOU SHOW ME HOW TO SPELL "DOUGHNUTS."
"DOUGHNUTS," HUH?
YEAH. PUT IT RIGHT THERE. AND "CHOCOLATE MILK," TOO.
AND "CUPCAKES." AND "GRAPE SODA."
ANYTHING ELSE?
NO. THAT'S ALL. THANKS, DADDY!
WHY ARE YOU EDITING MY SHOPPING LIST?

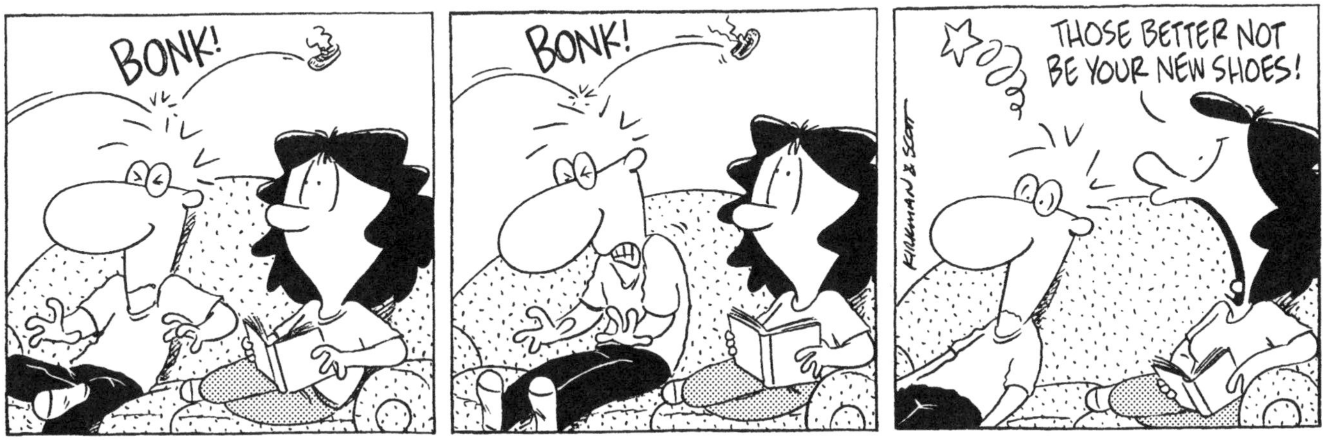
BONK!
BONK!
THOSE BETTER NOT BE YOUR NEW SHOES!

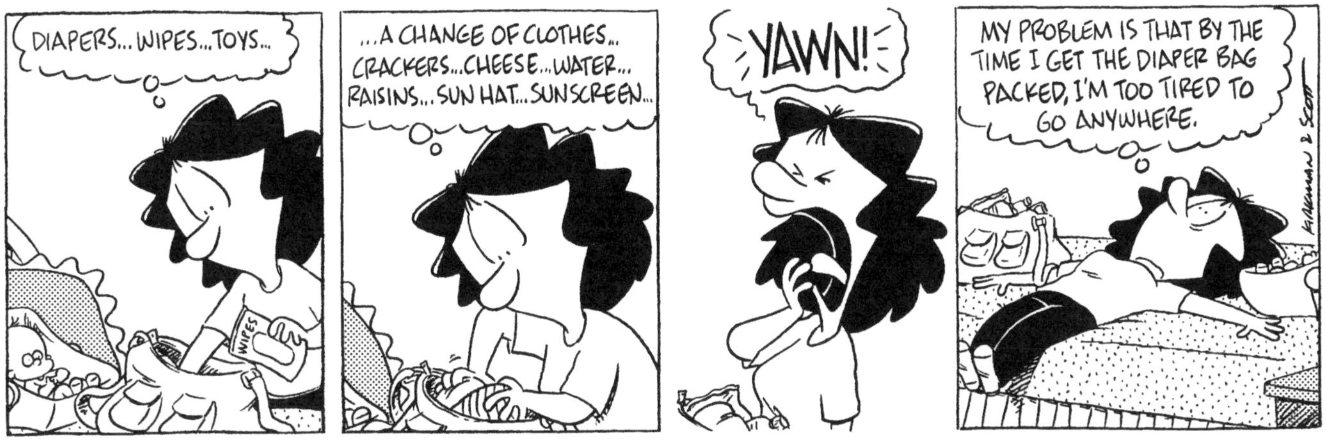
DIAPERS... WIPES... TOYS...
WIPES
... A CHANGE OF CLOTHES... CRACKERS... CHEESE... WATER... RAISINS... SUN HAT... SUNSCREEN...
YAWN!
MY PROBLEM IS THAT BY THE TIME I GET THE DIAPER BAG PACKED, I'M TOO TIRED TO GO ANYWHERE.

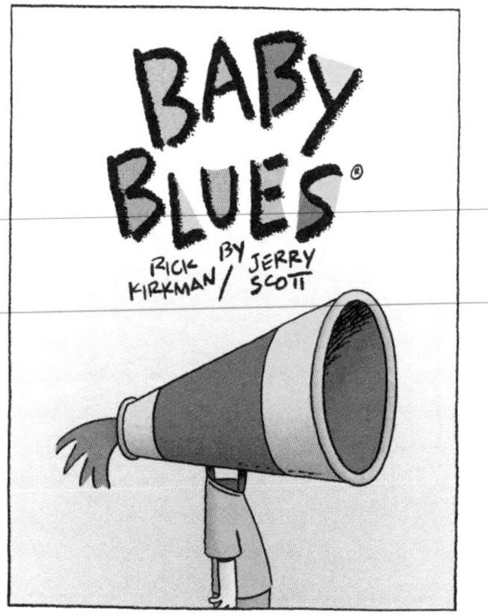
BABY BLUES®
BY RICK KIRKMAN / JERRY SCOTT

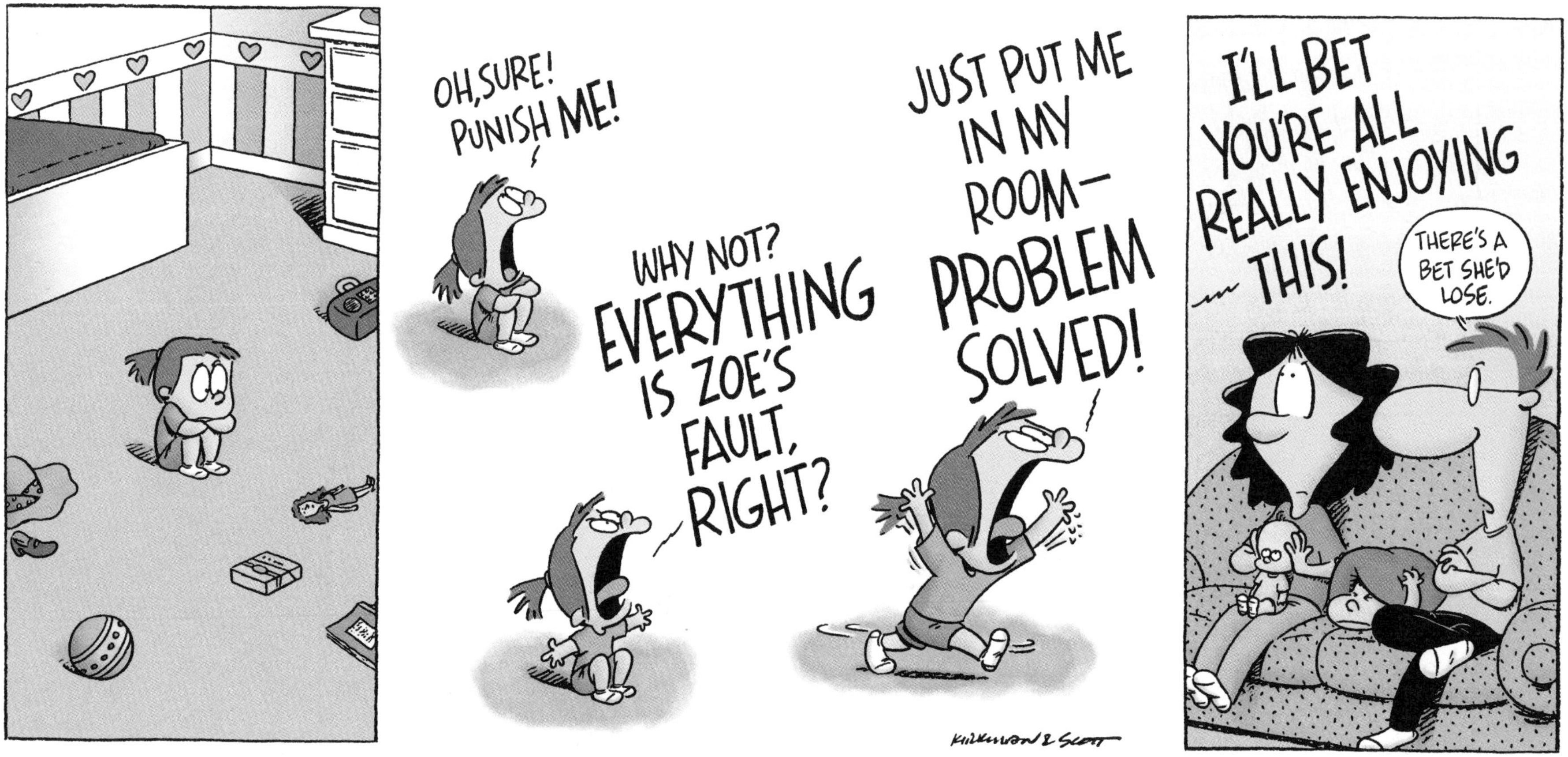
OH, SURE! PUNISH ME!
WHY NOT? EVERYTHING IS ZOE'S FAULT, RIGHT?
JUST PUT ME IN MY ROOM— PROBLEM SOLVED!
I'LL BET YOU'RE ALL REALLY ENJOYING THIS!
THERE'S A BET SHE'D LOSE.

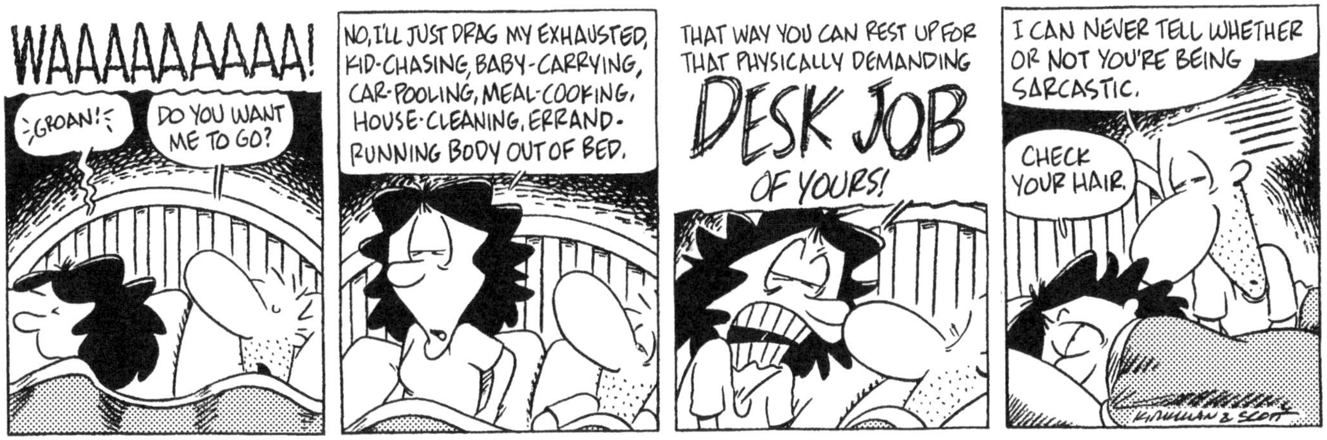
WAAAAAAAAA!
GROAN!
DO YOU WANT ME TO GO?
NO, I'LL JUST DRAG MY EXHAUSTED, KID-CHASING, BABY-CARRYING, CAR-POOLING, MEAL-COOKING, HOUSE-CLEANING, ERRAND-RUNNING BODY OUT OF BED.
THAT WAY YOU CAN REST UP FOR THAT PHYSICALLY DEMANDING
DESK JOB
OF YOURS!
I CAN NEVER TELL WHETHER OR NOT YOU'RE BEING SARCASTIC.
CHECK YOUR HAIR.

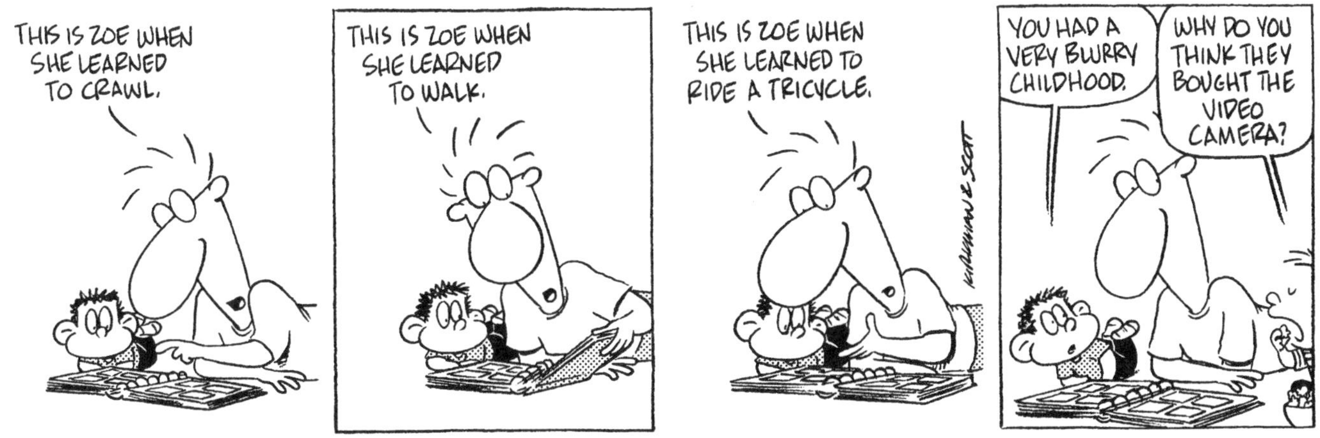
THIS IS ZOE WHEN SHE LEARNED TO CRAWL.
THIS IS ZOE WHEN SHE LEARNED TO WALK.
THIS IS ZOE WHEN SHE LEARNED TO RIDE A TRICYCLE.
YOU HAD A VERY BLURRY CHILDHOOD.
WHY DO YOU THINK THEY BOUGHT THE VIDEO CAMERA?

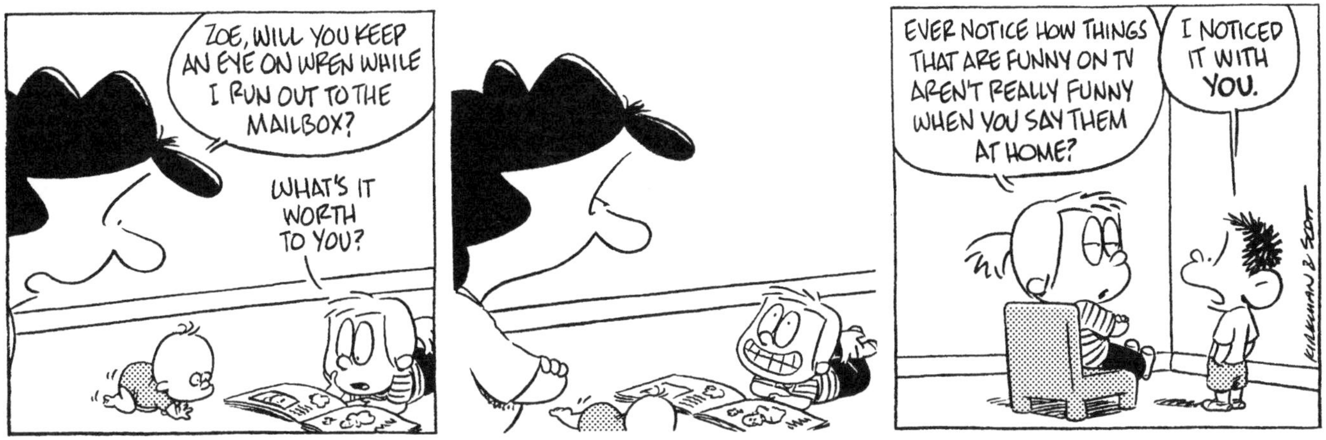
ZOE, WILL YOU KEEP AN EYE ON WREN WHILE I RUN OUT TO THE MAILBOX?
WHAT'S IT WORTH TO YOU?
EVER NOTICE HOW THINGS THAT ARE FUNNY ON TV AREN'T REALLY FUNNY WHEN YOU SAY THEM AT HOME?
I NOTICED IT WITH YOU.

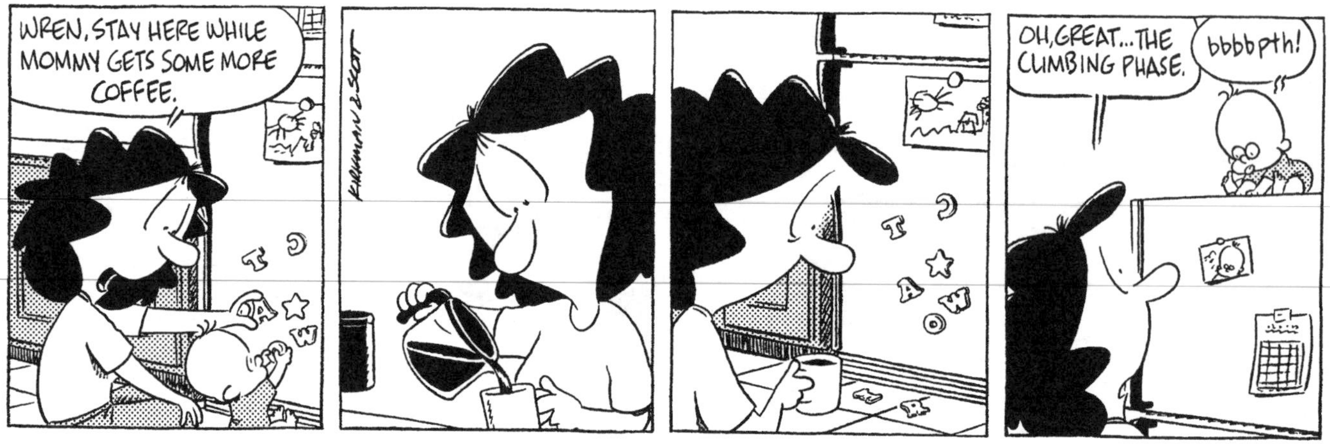
WREN, STAY HERE WHILE MOMMY GETS SOME MORE COFFEE.
OH, GREAT... THE CLIMBING PHASE.
bbbbpth!

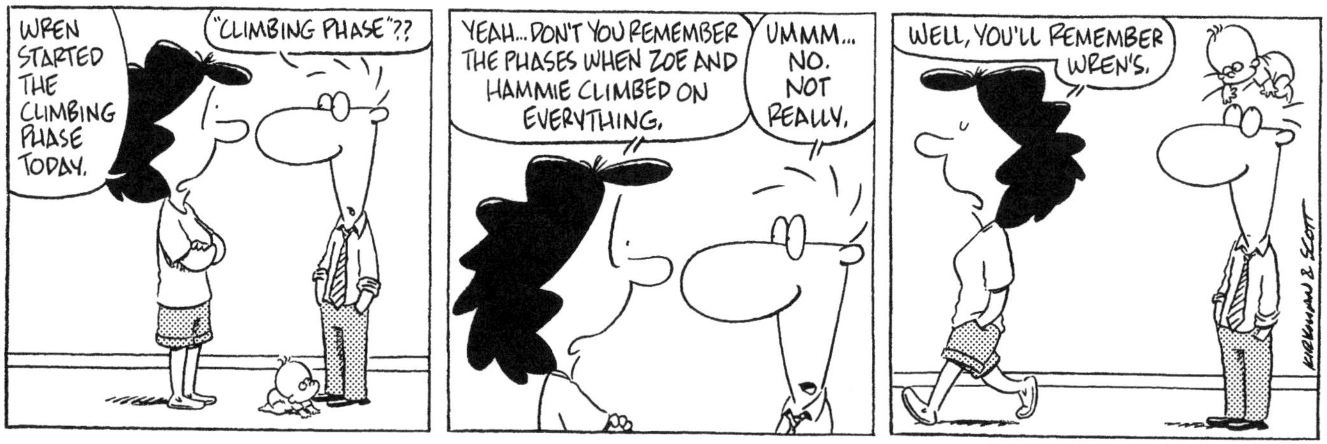
WREN STARTED THE CLIMBING PHASE TODAY.
"CLIMBING PHASE"??
YEAH... DON'T YOU REMEMBER THE PHASES WHEN ZOE AND HAMMIE CLIMBED ON EVERYTHING.
UMMM... NO. NOT REALLY.
WELL, YOU'LL REMEMBER WREN'S.

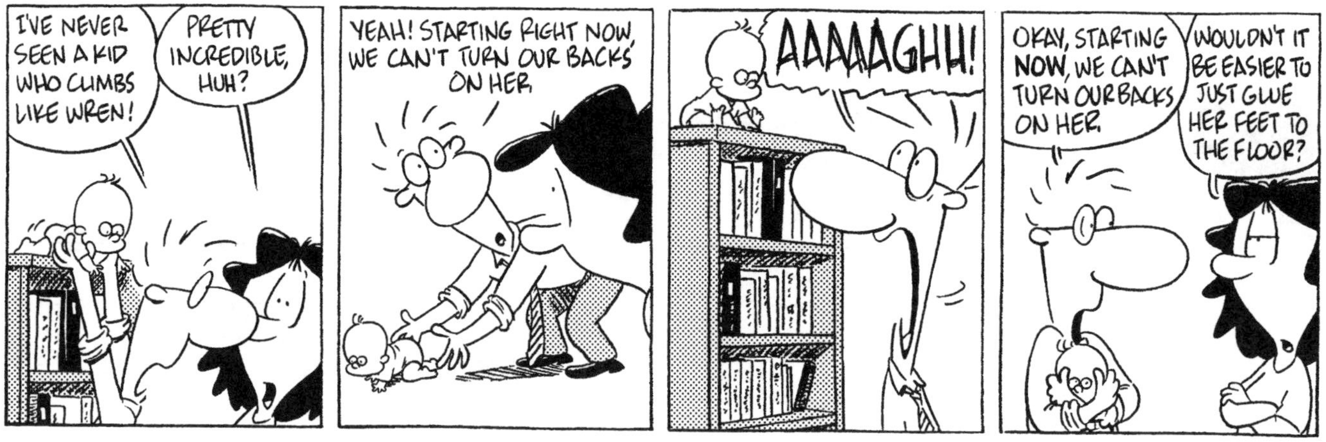
I'VE NEVER SEEN A KID WHO CLIMBS LIKE WREN!
PRETTY INCREDIBLE, HUH?
YEAH! STARTING RIGHT NOW, WE CAN'T TURN OUR BACKS ON HER.
AAAAAGHH!
OKAY, STARTING NOW, WE CAN'T TURN OUR BACKS ON HER.
WOULDN'T IT BE EASIER TO JUST GLUE HER FEET TO THE FLOOR?

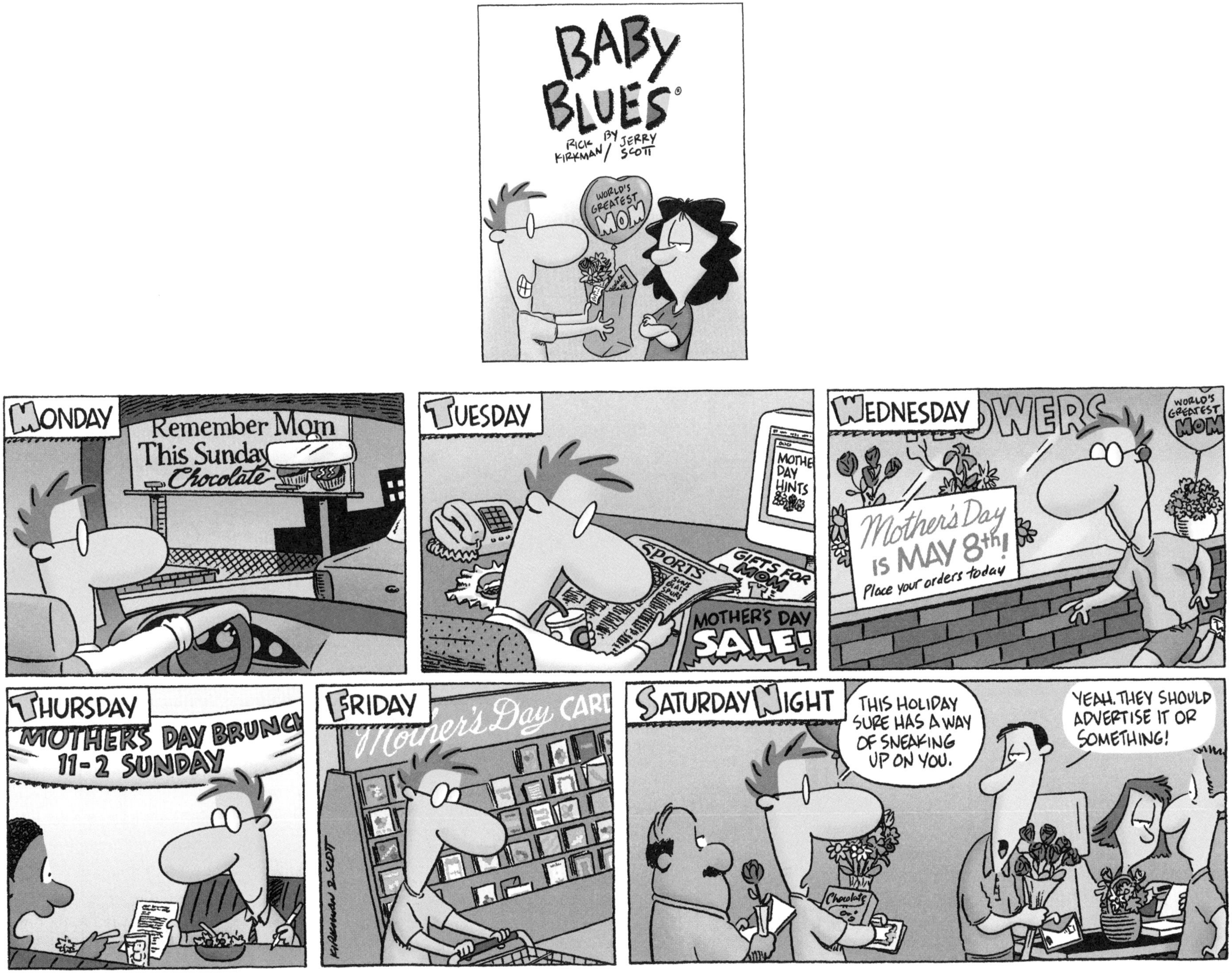
BABY BLUES®
RICK KIRKMAN / BY JERRY SCOTT
WORLD'S GREATEST MOM
MONDAY
Remember Mom This Sunday Chocolate
TUESDAY
MOTHER DAY HINTS
SPORTS
GIFTS FOR MOM
MOTHER'S DAY SALE!
WEDNESDAY
Mother's Day IS MAY 8th! Place your orders today
WORLD'S GREATEST MOM
THURSDAY
MOTHERS DAY BRUNCH 11-2 SUNDAY
FRIDAY
Mother's Day CARD
SATURDAY NIGHT
THIS HOLIDAY SURE HAS A WAY OF SNEAKING UP ON YOU.
YEAH. THEY SHOULD ADVERTISE IT OR SOMETHING!
Chocolate

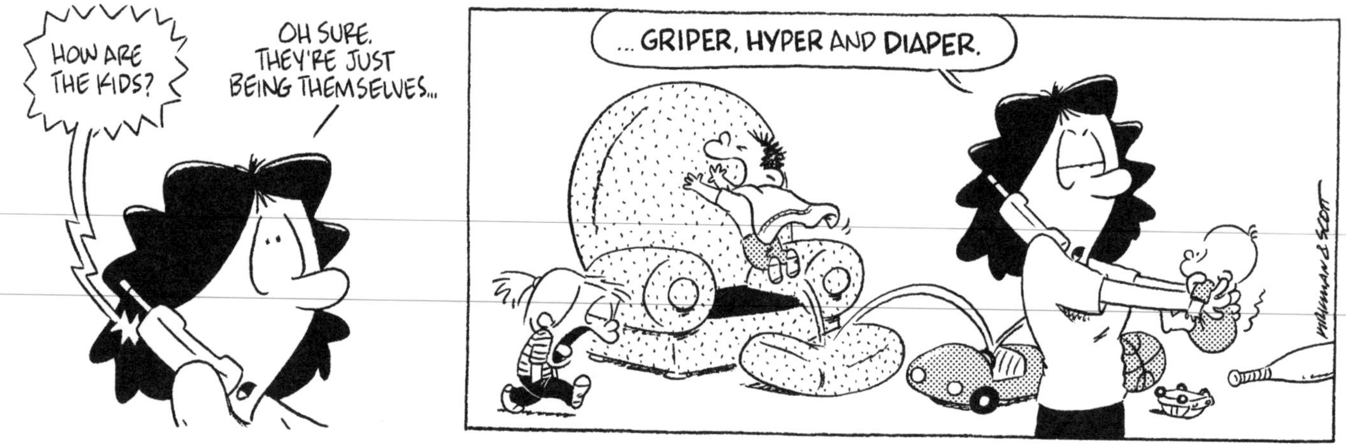
HOW ARE THE KIDS?
OH SURE. THEY'RE JUST BEING THEMSELVES...
... GRIPER, HYPER AND DIAPER.
KIRKMAN & SCOTT

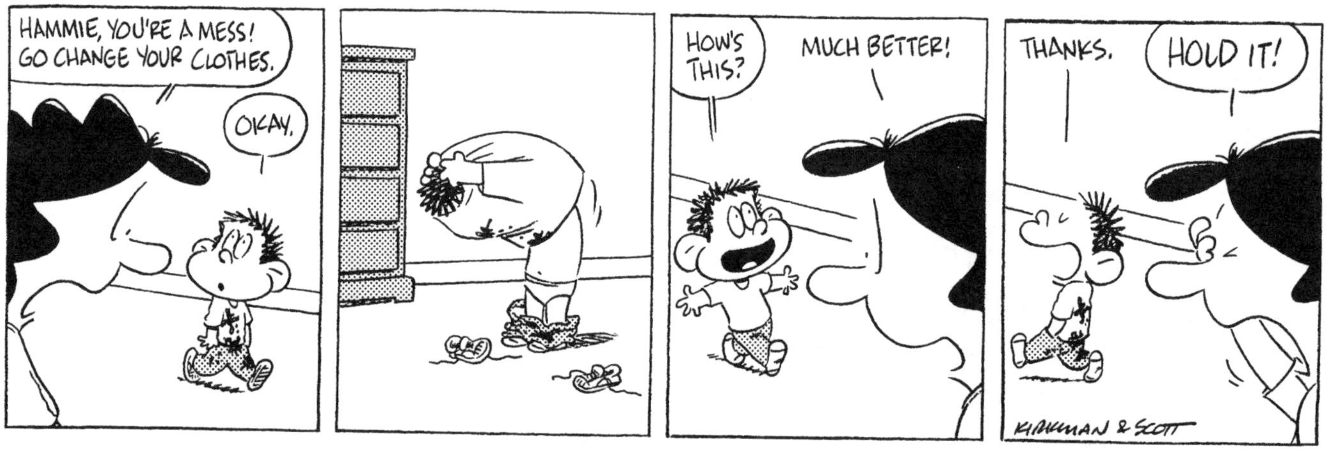
HAMMIE, YOU'RE A MESS! GO CHANGE YOUR CLOTHES.
OKAY.
HOW'S THIS?
MUCH BETTER!
THANKS.
HOLD IT!
KIRKMAN & SCOTT

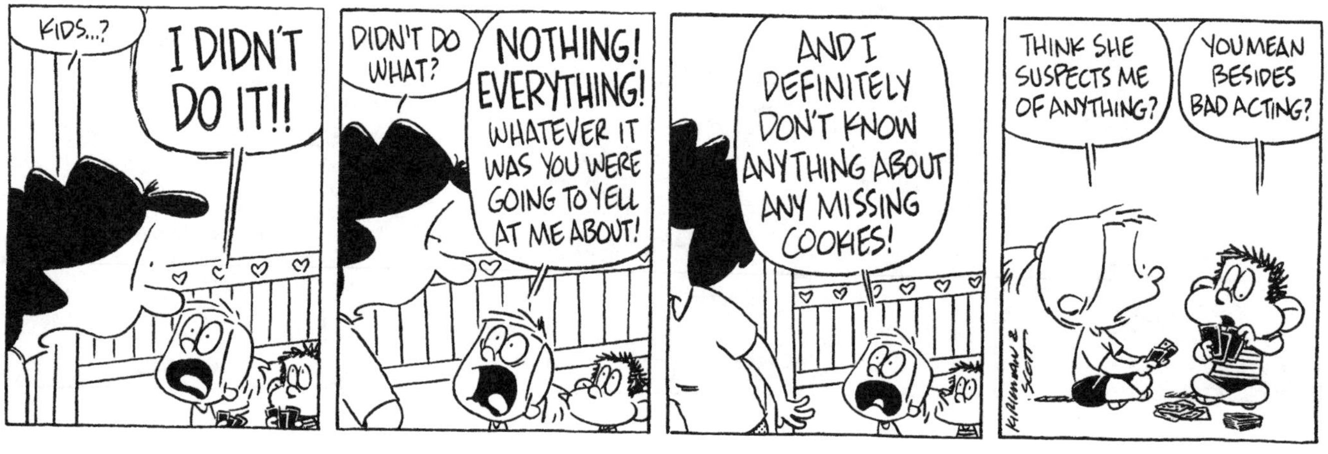
KIDS...?
I DIDN'T DO IT!!
DIDN'T DO WHAT?
NOTHING! EVERYTHING! WHATEVER IT WAS YOU WERE GOING TO YELL AT ME ABOUT!
AND I DEFINITELY DON'T KNOW ANYTHING ABOUT ANY MISSING COOKIES!
THINK SHE SUSPECTS ME OF ANYTHING?
YOU MEAN BESIDES BAD ACTING?
KIRKMAN & SCOTT

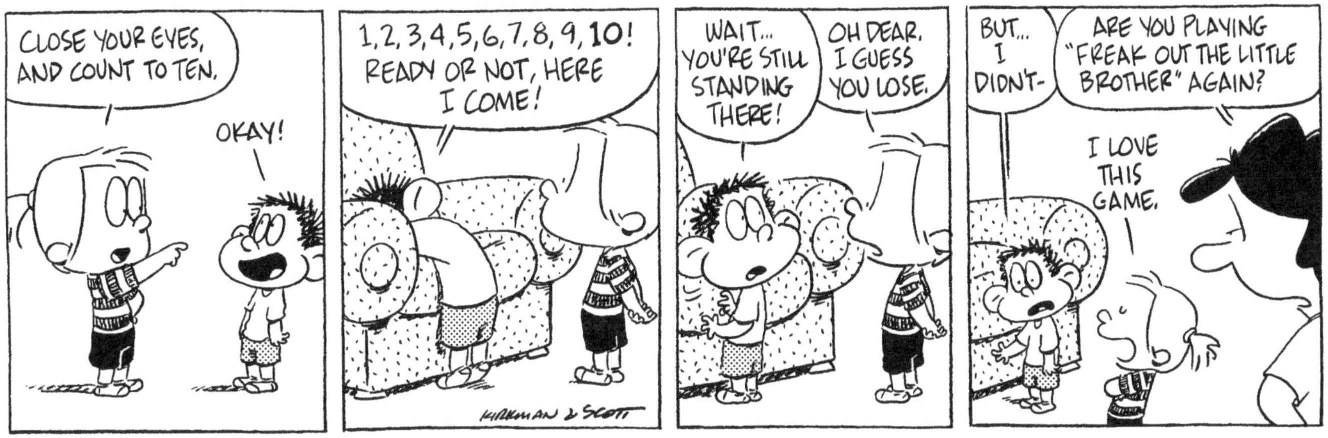
CLOSE YOUR EYES, AND COUNT TO TEN.
OKAY!
1, 2, 3, 4, 5, 6, 7, 8, 9, 10! READY OR NOT, HERE I COME!
KIRKMAN & SCOTT
WAIT... YOU'RE STILL STANDING THERE!
OH DEAR. I GUESS YOU LOSE.
BUT... I DIDN'T-
ARE YOU PLAYING "FREAK OUT THE LITTLE BROTHER" AGAIN?
I LOVE THIS GAME.

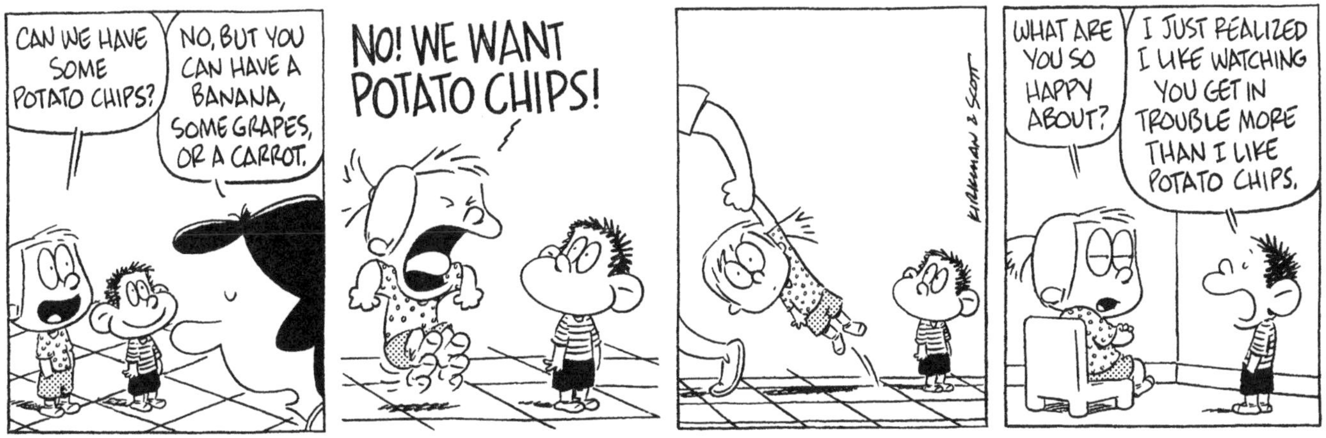
CAN WE HAVE SOME POTATO CHIPS?
NO, BUT YOU CAN HAVE A BANANA, SOME GRAPES, OR A CARROT.
NO! WE WANT POTATO CHIPS!
KIRKMAN & SCOTT
WHAT ARE YOU SO HAPPY ABOUT?
I JUST REALIZED I LIKE WATCHING YOU GET IN TROUBLE MORE THAN I LIKE POTATO CHIPS.

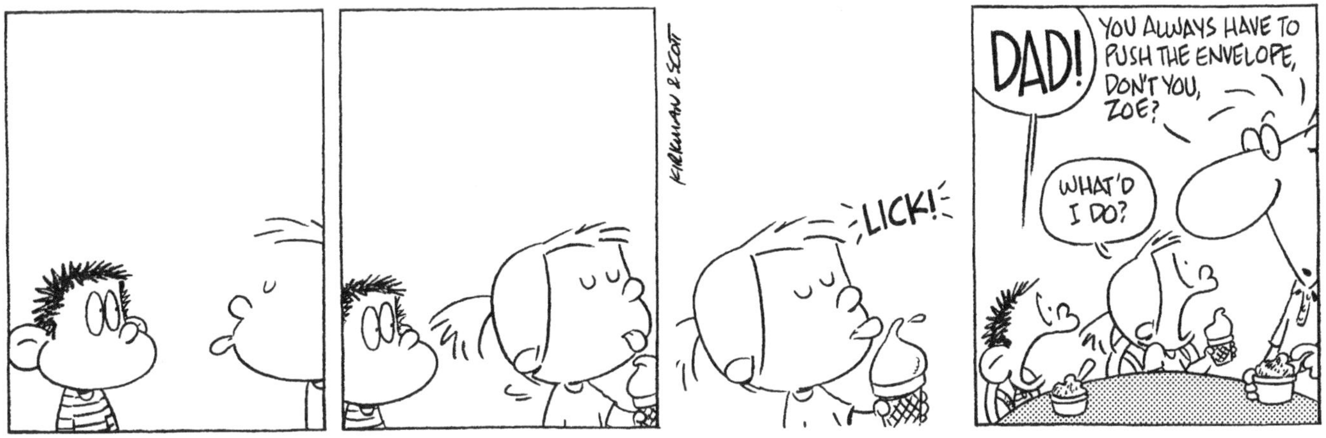
KIRKMAN & SCOTT
LICK!
DAD!
YOU ALWAYS HAVE TO PUSH THE ENVELOPE, DON'T YOU, ZOE?
WHAT'D I DO?

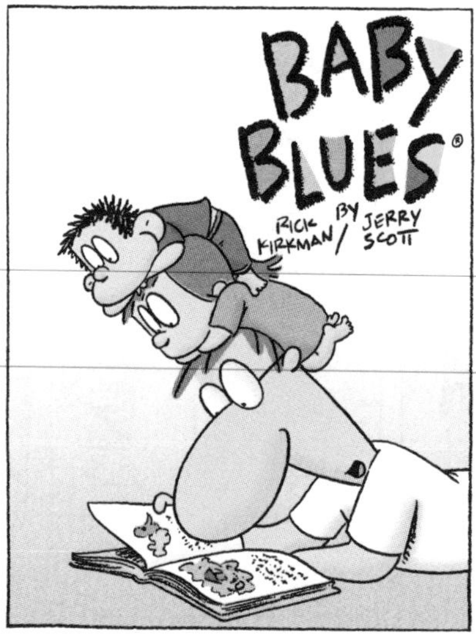
BABY BLUES®
BY RICK KIRKMAN / JERRY SCOTT

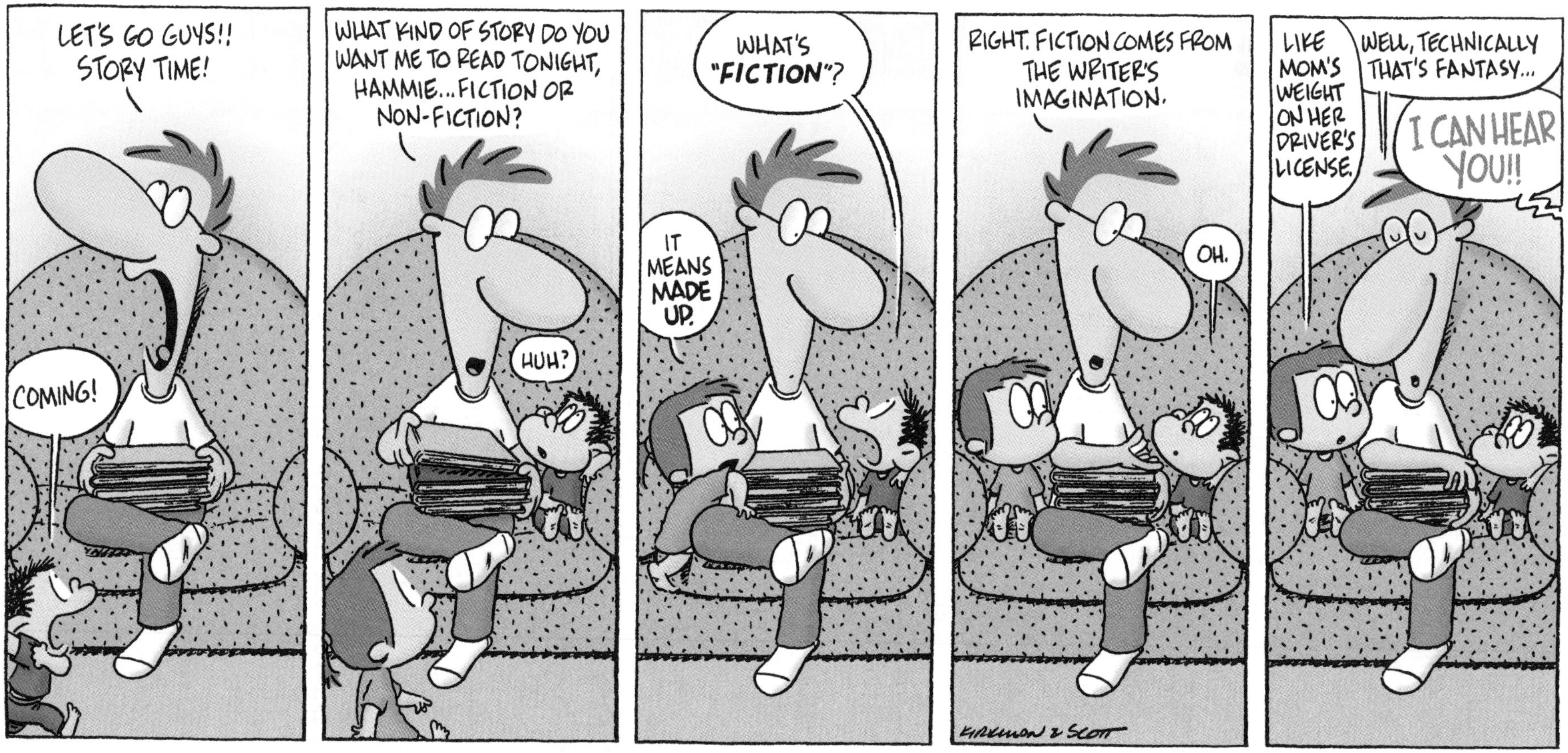
LET'S GO GUYS!! STORY TIME!
COMING!
WHAT KIND OF STORY DO YOU WANT ME TO READ TONIGHT, HAMMIE...FICTION OR NON-FICTION?
HUH?
WHAT'S "FICTION"?
IT MEANS MADE UP.
RIGHT. FICTION COMES FROM THE WRITER'S IMAGINATION.
OH.
LIKE MOM'S WEIGHT ON HER DRIVER'S LICENSE.
WELL, TECHNICALLY THAT'S FANTASY...
I CAN HEAR YOU!!
KIRKMAN & SCOTT

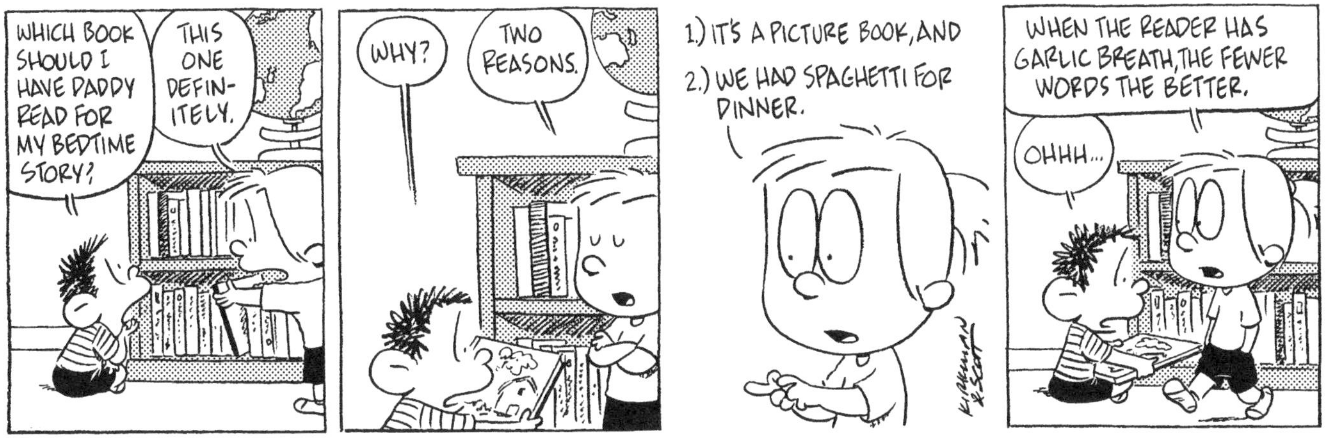
WHICH BOOK SHOULD I HAVE DADDY READ FOR MY BEDTIME STORY?
THIS ONE DEFIN-ITELY.
WHY?
TWO REASONS.
1.) IT'S A PICTURE BOOK, AND
2.) WE HAD SPAGHETTI FOR DINNER.
WHEN THE READER HAS GARLIC BREATH, THE FEWER WORDS THE BETTER.
OHHH...

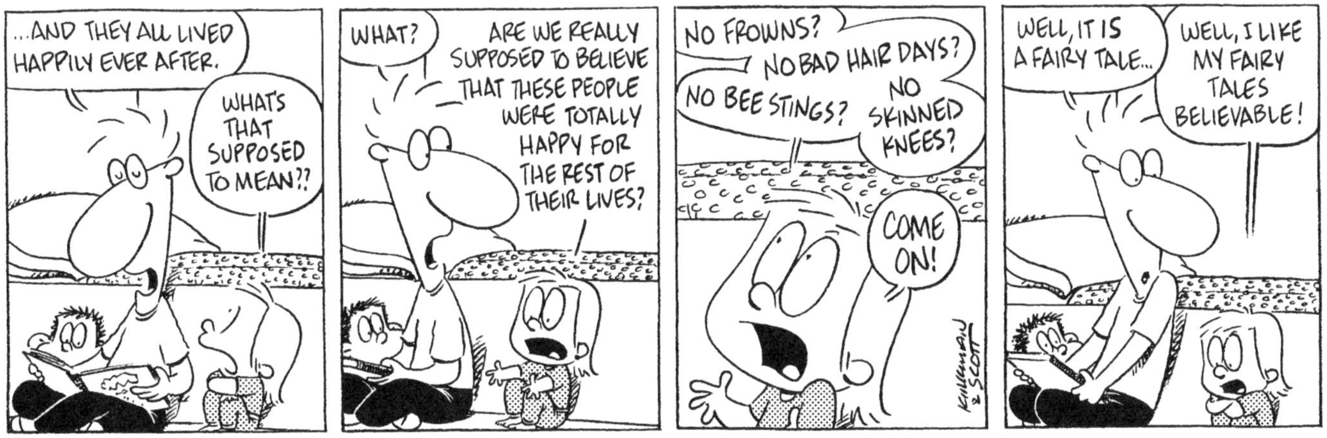
...AND THEY ALL LIVED HAPPILY EVER AFTER.
WHAT'S THAT SUPPOSED TO MEAN??
WHAT?
ARE WE REALLY SUPPOSED TO BELIEVE THAT THESE PEOPLE WERE TOTALLY HAPPY FOR THE REST OF THEIR LIVES?
NO FROWNS?
NO BAD HAIR DAYS?
NO BEE STINGS?
NO SKINNED KNEES?
COME ON!
WELL, IT IS A FAIRY TALE...
WELL, I LIKE MY FAIRY TALES BELIEVABLE!

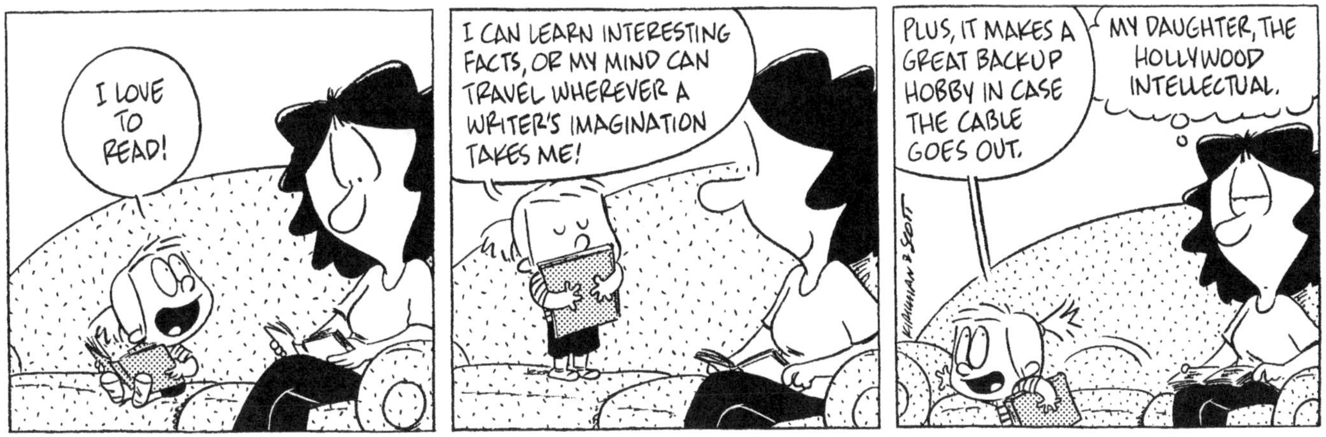
I LOVE TO READ!
I CAN LEARN INTERESTING FACTS, OR MY MIND CAN TRAVEL WHEREVER A WRITER'S IMAGINATION TAKES ME!
PLUS, IT MAKES A GREAT BACKUP HOBBY IN CASE THE CABLE GOES OUT.
MY DAUGHTER, THE HOLLYWOOD INTELLECTUAL.

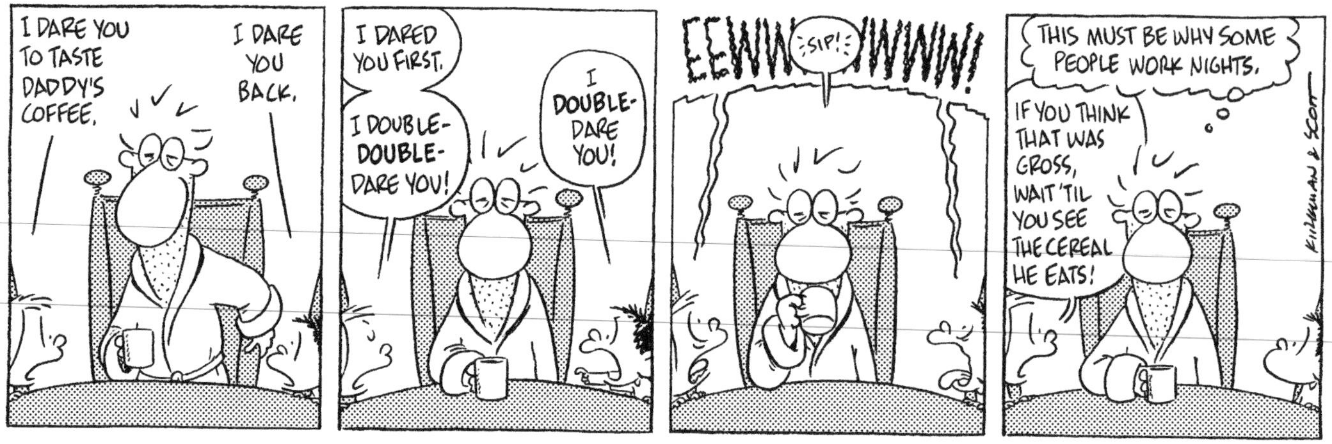
I DARE YOU TO TASTE DADDY'S COFFEE.
I DARE YOU BACK.
I DARED YOU FIRST.
I DOUBLE-DOUBLE-DOUBLE-DARE YOU!
I DOUBLE-DARE YOU!
EEWWWWWW!
SIP!
THIS MUST BE WHY SOME PEOPLE WORK NIGHTS.
IF YOU THINK THAT WAS GROSS, WAIT 'TIL YOU SEE THE CEREAL HE EATS!
KIRKMAN & SCOTT

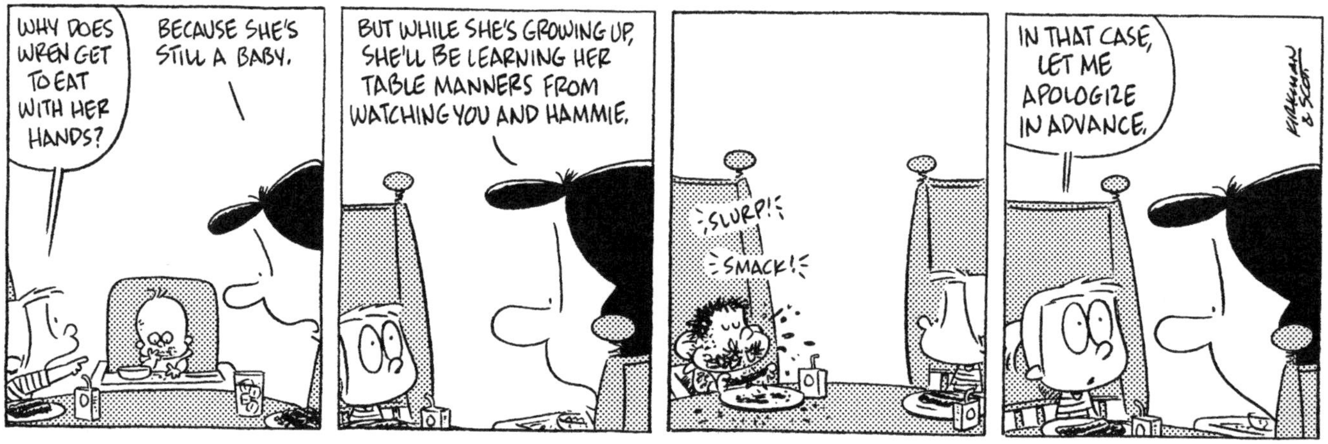
WHY DOES WREN GET TO EAT WITH HER HANDS?
BECAUSE SHE'S STILL A BABY.
BUT WHILE SHE'S GROWING UP, SHE'LL BE LEARNING HER TABLE MANNERS FROM WATCHING YOU AND HAMMIE.
SLURP!
SMACK!
IN THAT CASE, LET ME APOLOGIZE IN ADVANCE.
KIRKMAN & SCOTT

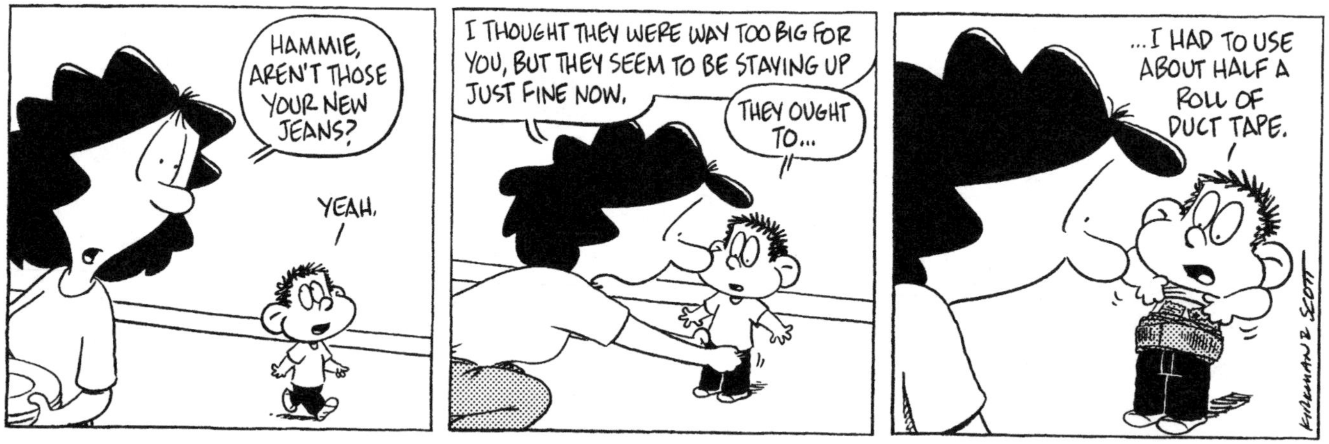
HAMMIE, AREN'T THOSE YOUR NEW JEANS?
YEAH.
I THOUGHT THEY WERE WAY TOO BIG FOR YOU, BUT THEY SEEM TO BE STAYING UP JUST FINE NOW.
THEY OUGHT TO...
...I HAD TO USE ABOUT HALF A ROLL OF DUCT TAPE.
KIRKMAN & SCOTT

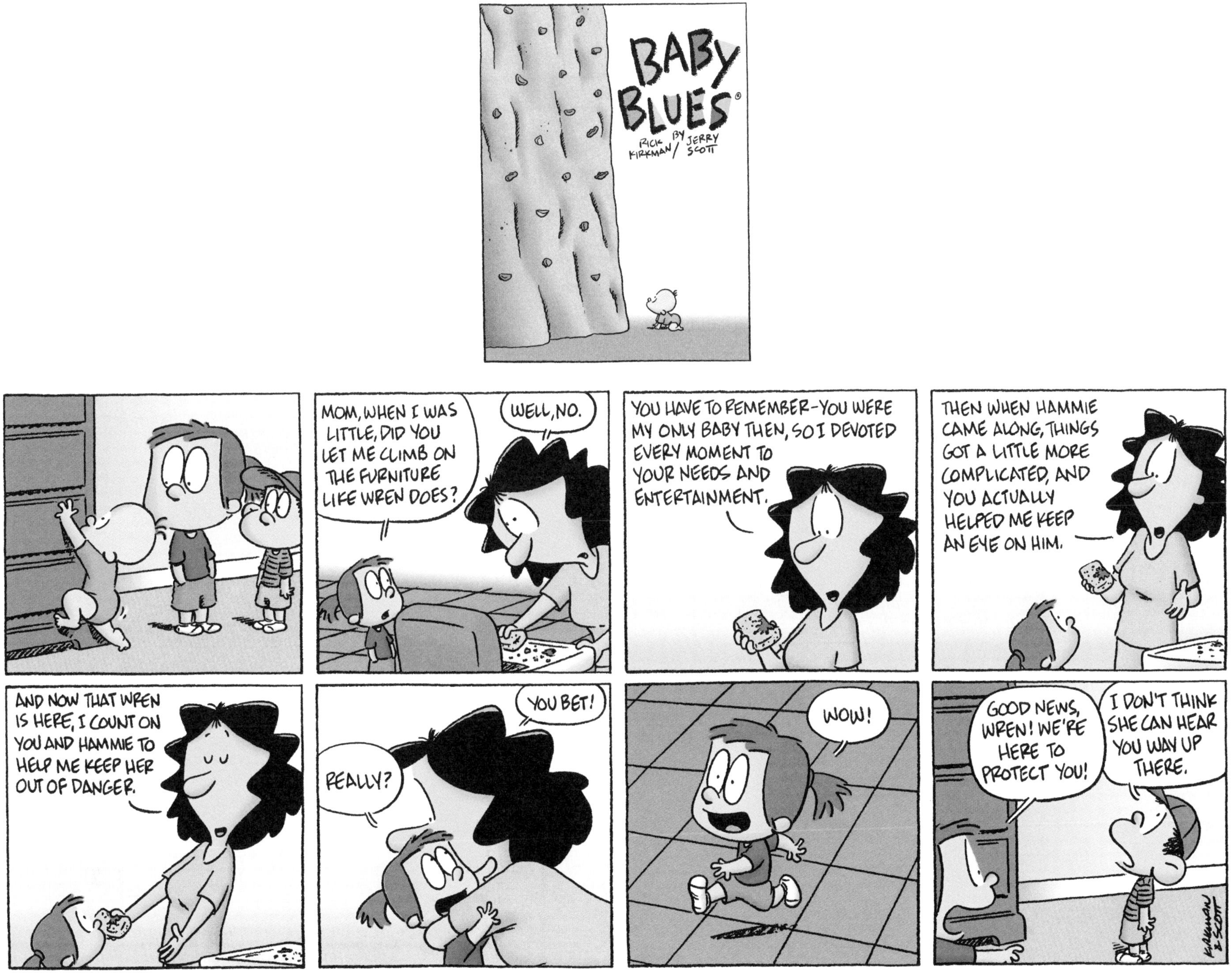
BABY BLUES®
BY RICK KIRKMAN/JERRY SCOTT
MOM, WHEN I WAS LITTLE, DID YOU LET ME CLIMB ON THE FURNITURE LIKE WREN DOES?
WELL, NO.
YOU HAVE TO REMEMBER–YOU WERE MY ONLY BABY THEN, SO I DEVOTED EVERY MOMENT TO YOUR NEEDS AND ENTERTAINMENT.
THEN WHEN HAMMIE CAME ALONG, THINGS GOT A LITTLE MORE COMPLICATED, AND YOU ACTUALLY HELPED ME KEEP AN EYE ON HIM.
AND NOW THAT WREN IS HERE, I COUNT ON YOU AND HAMMIE TO HELP ME KEEP HER OUT OF DANGER.
REALLY?
YOU BET!
WOW!
GOOD NEWS, WREN! WE'RE HERE TO PROTECT YOU!
I DON'T THINK SHE CAN HEAR YOU WAY UP THERE.
KIRKMAN & SCOTT

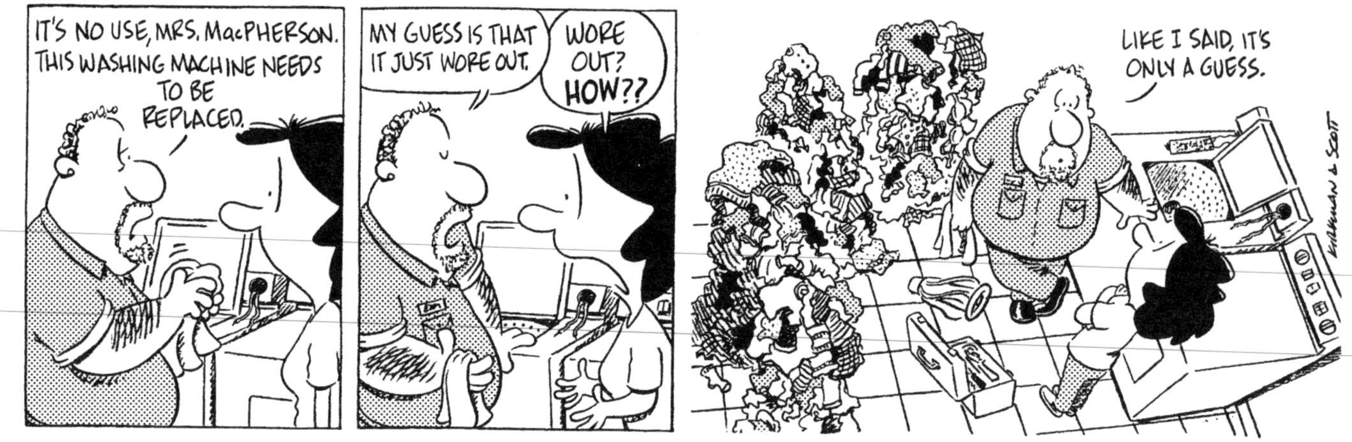
IT'S NO USE, MRS. MacPHERSON. THIS WASHING MACHINE NEEDS TO BE REPLACED.
MY GUESS IS THAT IT JUST WORE OUT.
WORE OUT? HOW??
LIKE I SAID, IT'S ONLY A GUESS.
KIRKMAN & SCOTT

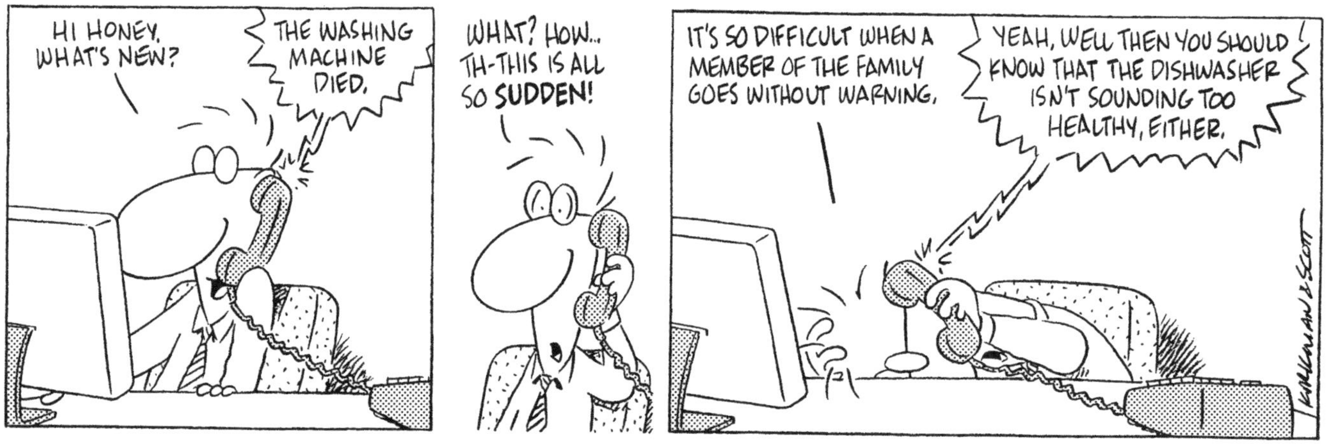
HI HONEY. WHAT'S NEW?
THE WASHING MACHINE DIED.
WHAT? HOW... TH-THIS IS ALL SO SUDDEN!
IT'S SO DIFFICULT WHEN A MEMBER OF THE FAMILY GOES WITHOUT WARNING.
YEAH, WELL THEN YOU SHOULD KNOW THAT THE DISHWASHER ISN'T SOUNDING TOO HEALTHY, EITHER.
KIRKMAN & SCOTT

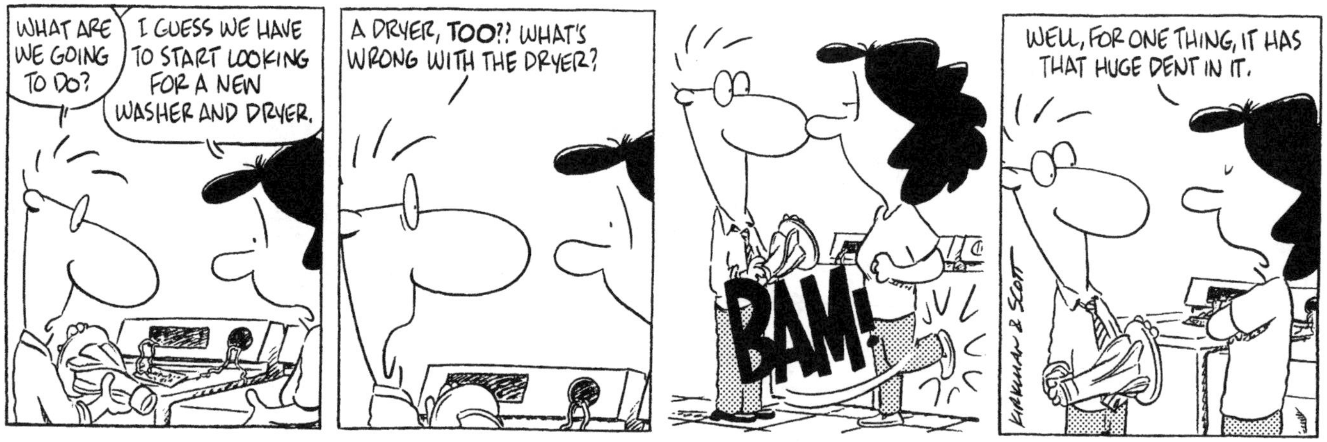
WHAT ARE WE GOING TO DO?
I GUESS WE HAVE TO START LOOKING FOR A NEW WASHER AND DRYER.
A DRYER, TOO?? WHAT'S WRONG WITH THE DRYER?
BAM!
KIRKMAN & SCOTT
WELL, FOR ONE THING, IT HAS THAT HUGE DENT IN IT.

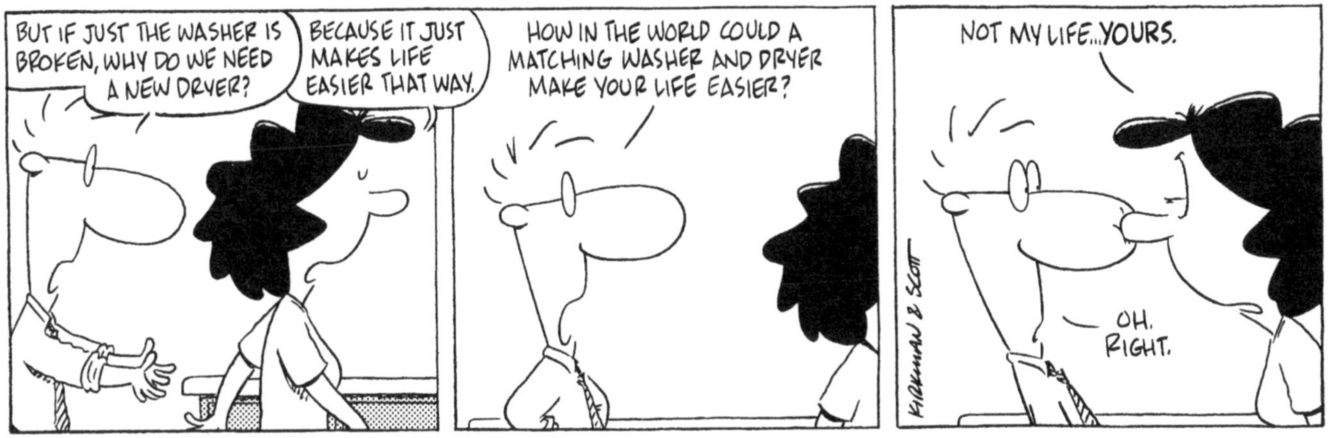
BUT IF JUST THE WASHER IS BROKEN, WHY DO WE NEED A NEW DRYER?
BECAUSE IT JUST MAKES LIFE EASIER THAT WAY.
HOW IN THE WORLD COULD A MATCHING WASHER AND DRYER MAKE YOUR LIFE EASIER?
KIRKMAN & SCOTT
NOT MY LIFE... YOURS.
OH. RIGHT.

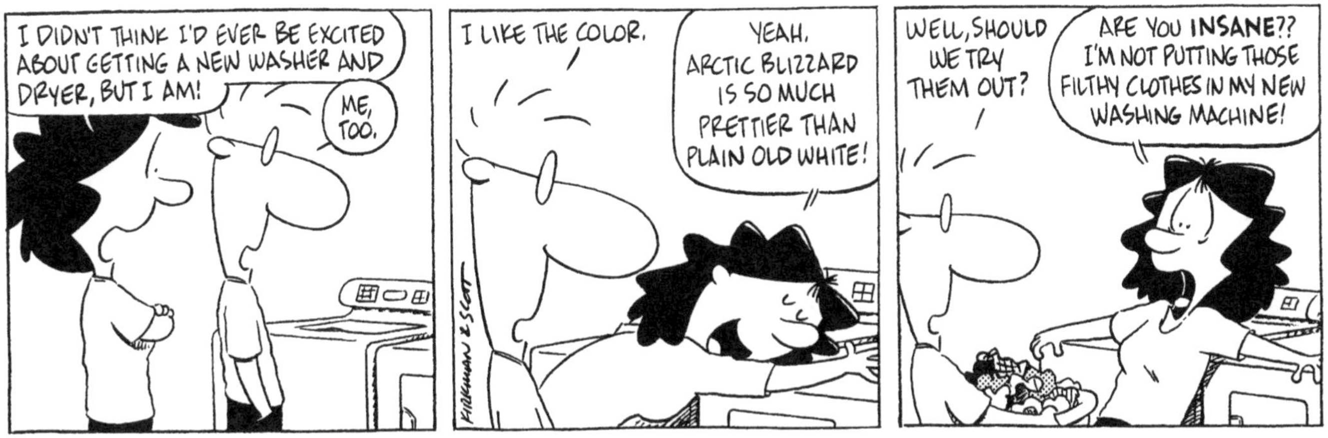
I DIDN'T THINK I'D EVER BE EXCITED ABOUT GETTING A NEW WASHER AND DRYER, BUT I AM!
ME, TOO.
KIRKMAN & SCOTT
I LIKE THE COLOR.
YEAH. ARCTIC BLIZZARD IS SO MUCH PRETTIER THAN PLAIN OLD WHITE!
WELL, SHOULD WE TRY THEM OUT?
ARE YOU INSANE?? I'M NOT PUTTING THOSE FILTHY CLOTHES IN MY NEW WASHING MACHINE!

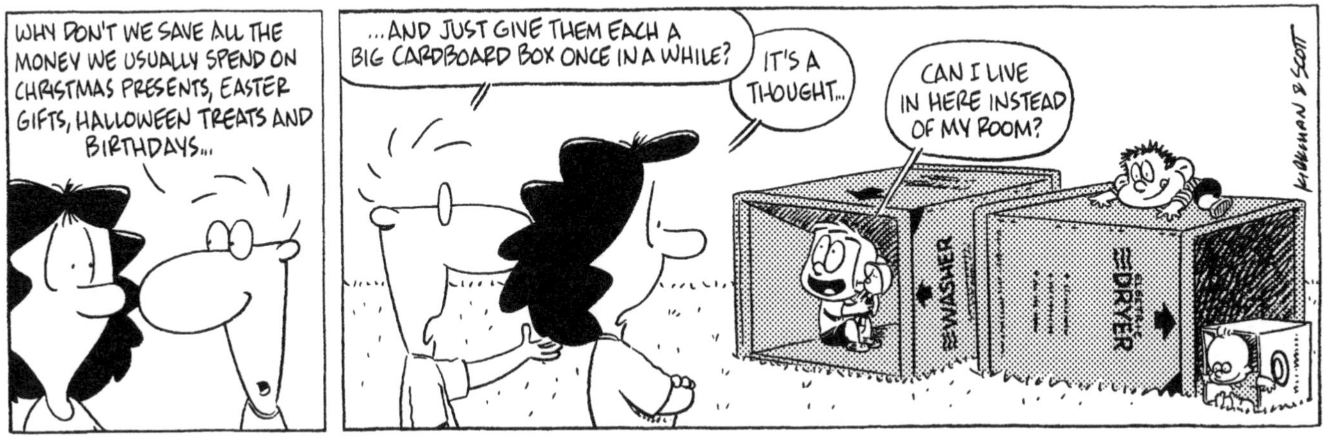
WHY DON'T WE SAVE ALL THE MONEY WE USUALLY SPEND ON CHRISTMAS PRESENTS, EASTER GIFTS, HALLOWEEN TREATS AND BIRTHDAYS...
...AND JUST GIVE THEM EACH A BIG CARDBOARD BOX ONCE IN A WHILE?
IT'S A THOUGHT...
CAN I LIVE IN HERE INSTEAD OF MY ROOM?
WASHER
DRYER
KIRKMAN & SCOTT

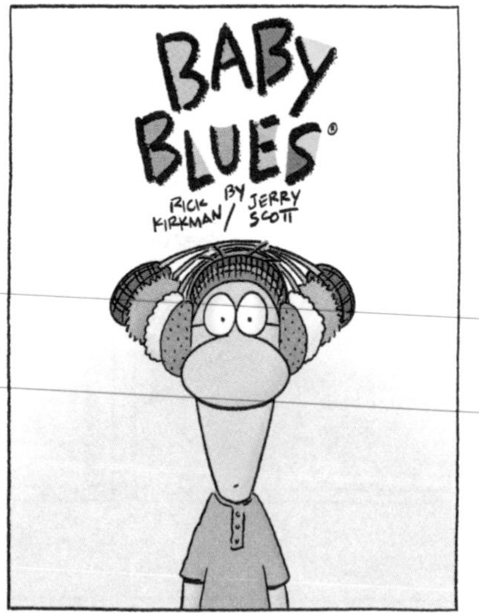
BABY BLUES®
RICK KIRKMAN / BY JERRY SCOTT

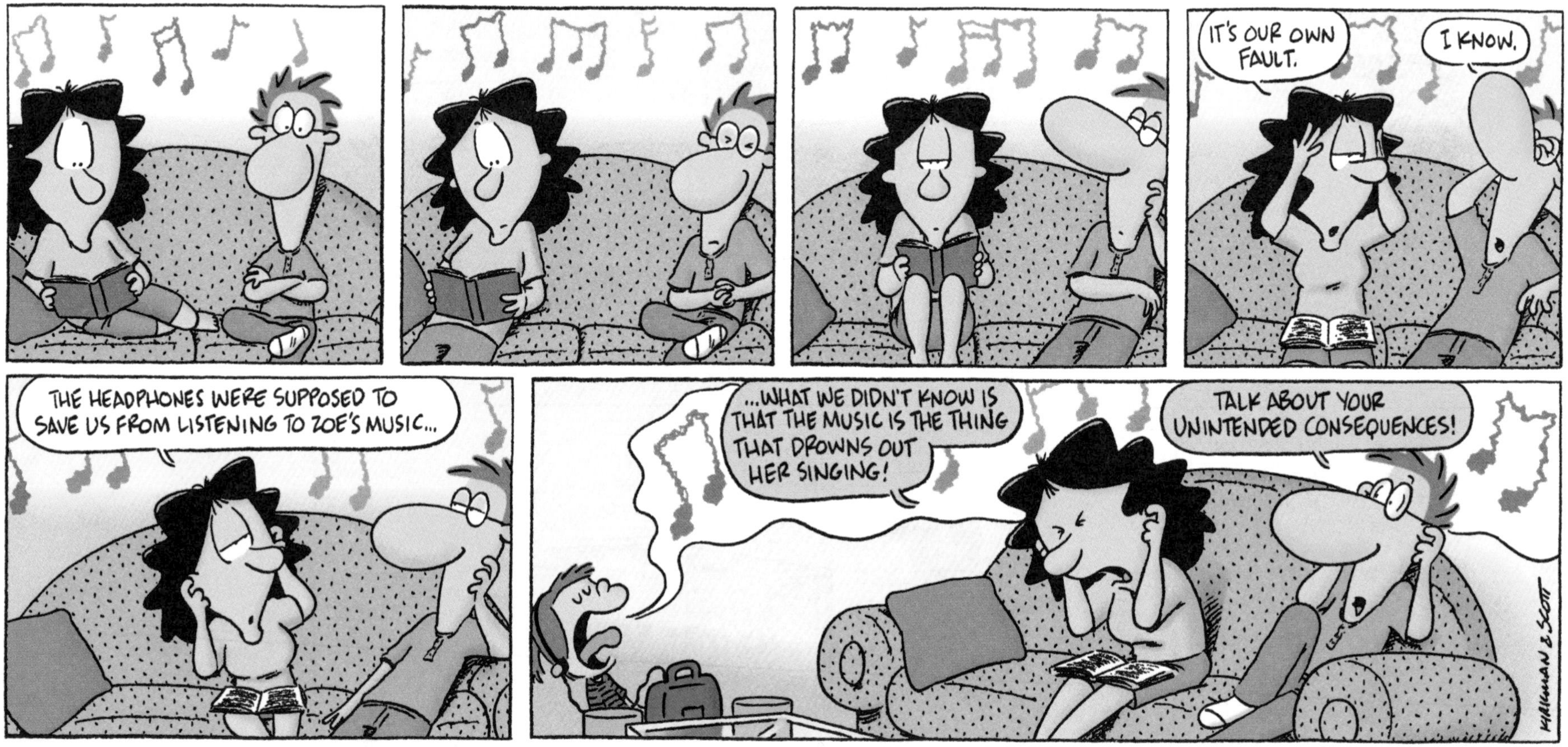
IT'S OUR OWN FAULT.
I KNOW.
THE HEADPHONES WERE SUPPOSED TO SAVE US FROM LISTENING TO ZOE'S MUSIC...
...WHAT WE DIDN'T KNOW IS THAT THE MUSIC IS THE THING THAT DROWNS OUT HER SINGING!
TALK ABOUT YOUR UNINTENDED CONSEQUENCES!
KIRKMAN & SCOTT

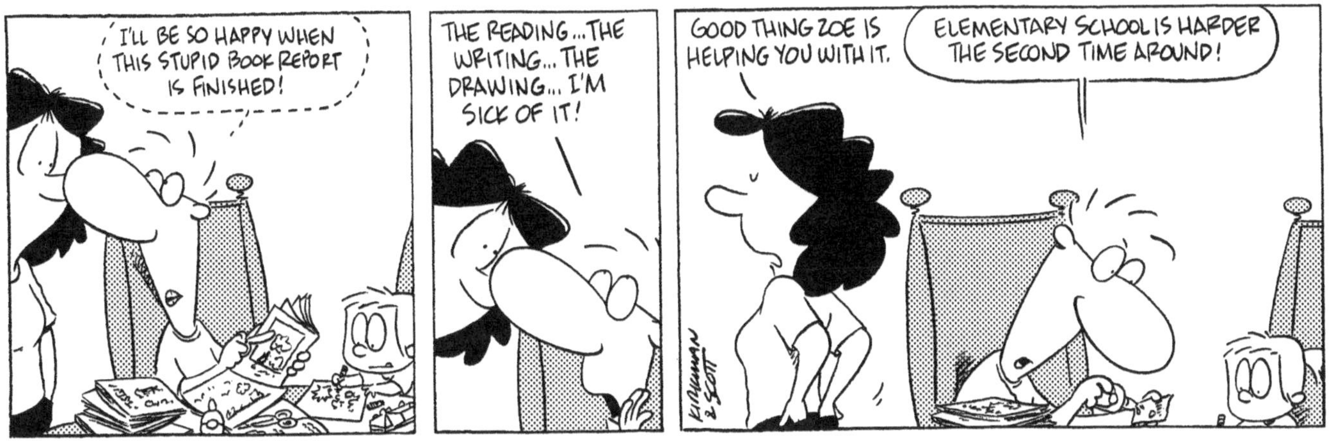
I'LL BE SO HAPPY WHEN THIS STUPID BOOK REPORT IS FINISHED!
THE READING... THE WRITING... THE DRAWING... I'M SICK OF IT!
GOOD THING ZOE IS HELPING YOU WITH IT.
ELEMENTARY SCHOOL IS HARDER THE SECOND TIME AROUND!
KIRKMAN & SCOTT

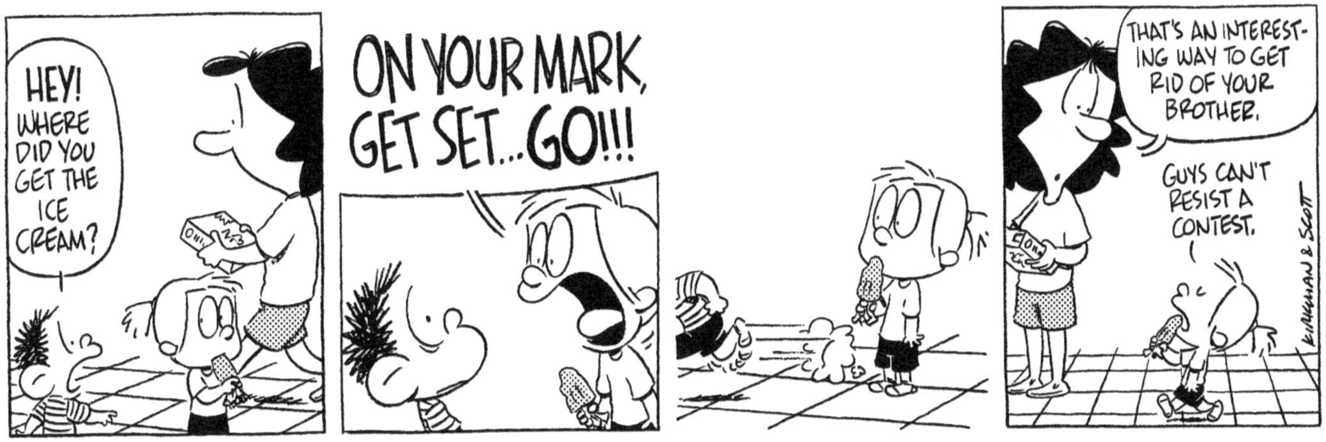
HEY! WHERE DID YOU GET THE ICE CREAM?
ON YOUR MARK, GET SET...GO!!!
THAT'S AN INTERESTING WAY TO GET RID OF YOUR BROTHER.
GUYS CAN'T RESIST A CONTEST.
KIRKMAN & SCOTT

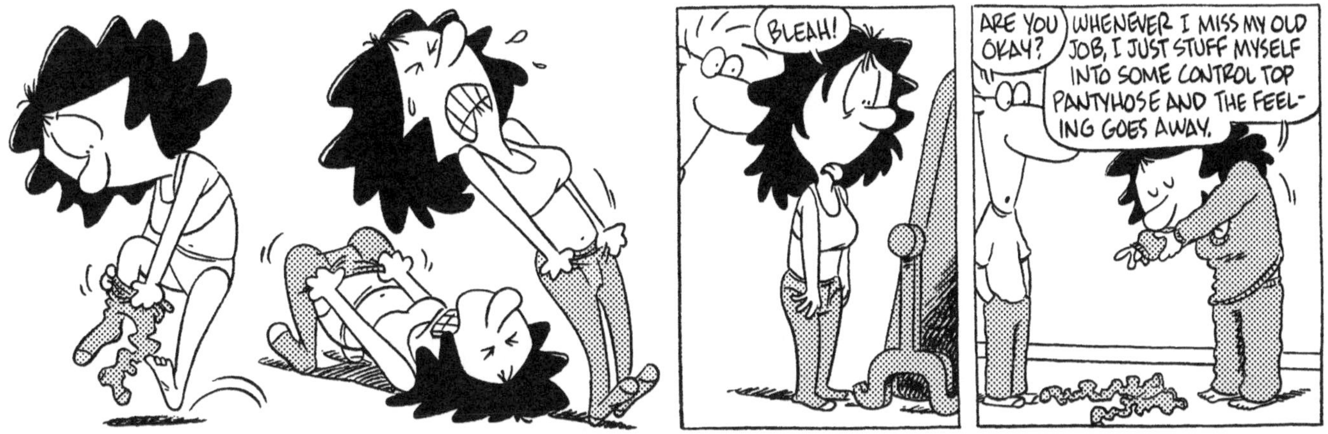
BLEAH!
ARE YOU OKAY?
WHENEVER I MISS MY OLD JOB, I JUST STUFF MYSELF INTO SOME CONTROL TOP PANTYHOSE AND THE FEELING GOES AWAY.

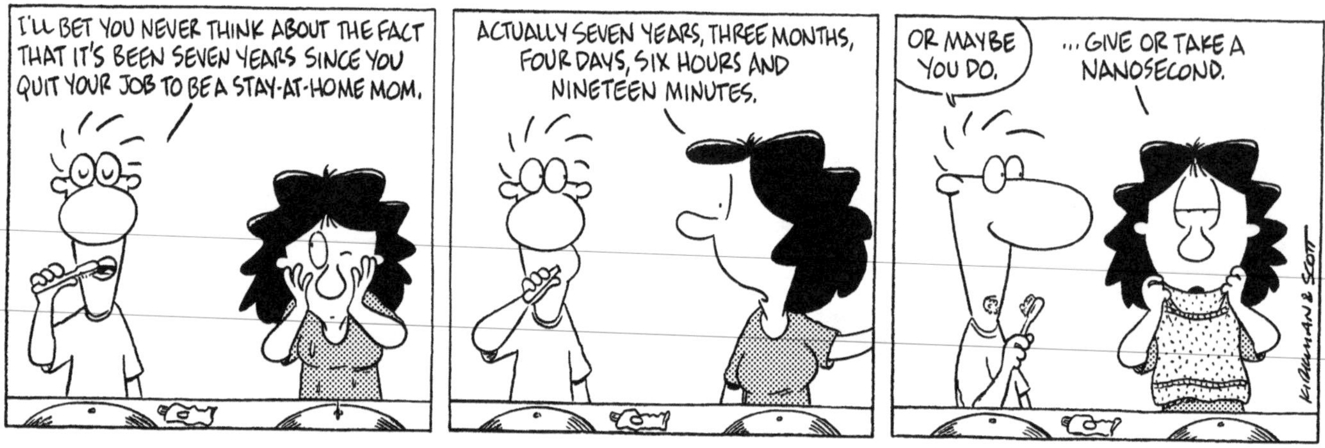
I'LL BET YOU NEVER THINK ABOUT THE FACT THAT IT'S BEEN SEVEN YEARS SINCE YOU QUIT YOUR JOB TO BE A STAY-AT-HOME MOM.
ACTUALLY SEVEN YEARS, THREE MONTHS, FOUR DAYS, SIX HOURS AND NINETEEN MINUTES.
OR MAYBE YOU DO.
...GIVE OR TAKE A NANOSECOND.
KIRKMAN & SCOTT

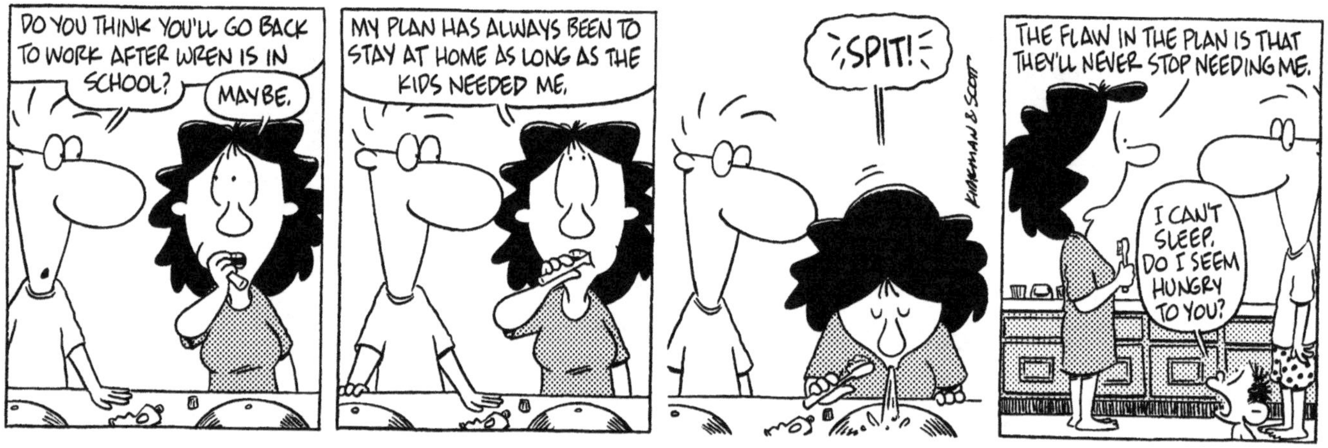
DO YOU THINK YOU'LL GO BACK TO WORK AFTER WREN IS IN SCHOOL?
MAYBE.
MY PLAN HAS ALWAYS BEEN TO STAY AT HOME AS LONG AS THE KIDS NEEDED ME.
SPIT!
KIRKMAN & SCOTT
THE FLAW IN THE PLAN IS THAT THEY'LL NEVER STOP NEEDING ME.
I CAN'T SLEEP. DO I SEEM HUNGRY TO YOU?

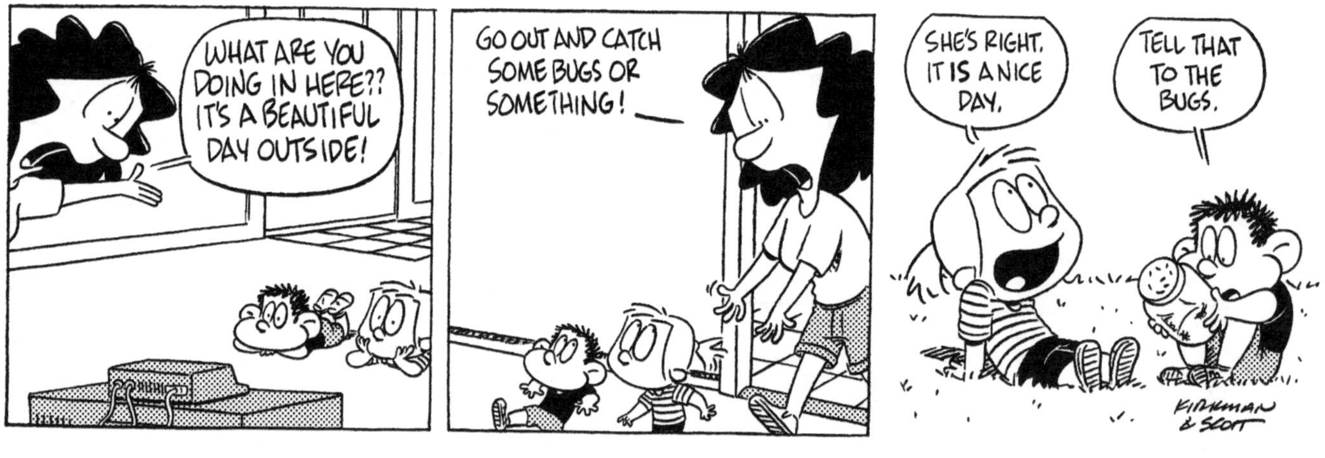
WHAT ARE YOU DOING IN HERE?? IT'S A BEAUTIFUL DAY OUTSIDE!
GO OUT AND CATCH SOME BUGS OR SOMETHING!
SHE'S RIGHT. IT IS A NICE DAY.
TELL THAT TO THE BUGS.
KIRKMAN & SCOTT

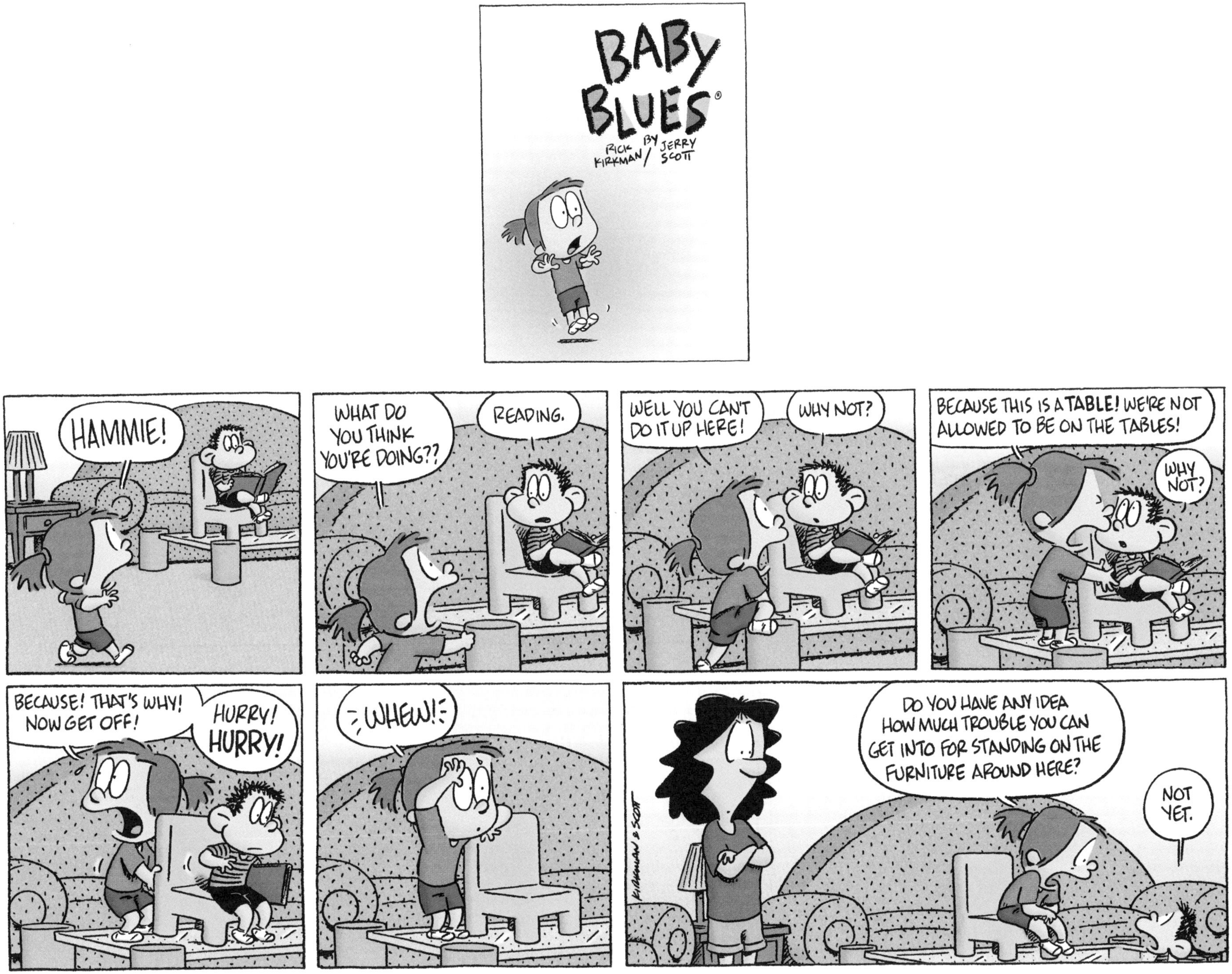
BABY BLUES®
BY RICK KIRKMAN / JERRY SCOTT
HAMMIE!
WHAT DO YOU THINK YOU'RE DOING??
READING.
WELL YOU CAN'T DO IT UP HERE!
WHY NOT?
BECAUSE THIS IS A **TABLE!** WE'RE NOT ALLOWED TO BE ON THE TABLES!
WHY NOT?
BECAUSE! THAT'S WHY! NOW GET OFF!
HURRY! HURRY!
WHEW!
KIRKMAN & SCOTT
DO YOU HAVE ANY IDEA HOW MUCH TROUBLE YOU CAN GET INTO FOR STANDING ON THE FURNITURE AROUND HERE?
NOT YET.

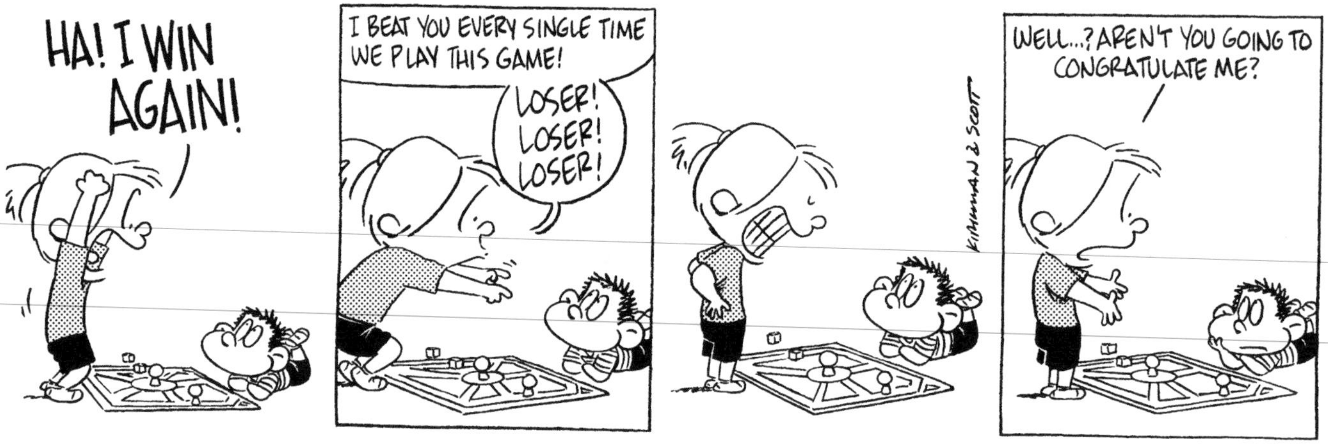
HA! I WIN AGAIN!
I BEAT YOU EVERY SINGLE TIME WE PLAY THIS GAME!
LOSER! LOSER! LOSER!
KIRKMAN & SCOTT
WELL...? AREN'T YOU GOING TO CONGRATULATE ME?

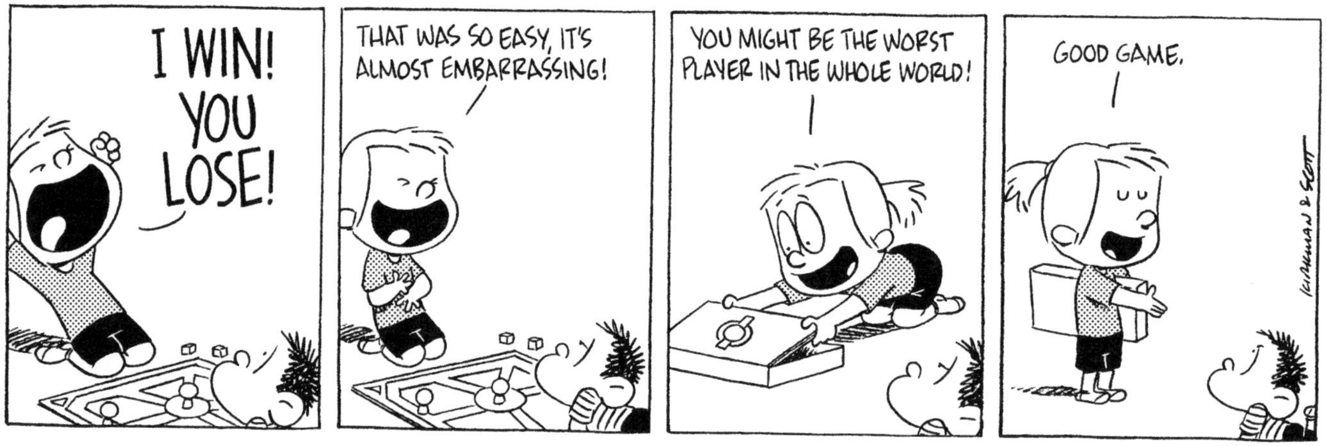
I WIN! YOU LOSE!
THAT WAS SO EASY, IT'S ALMOST EMBARRASSING!
YOU MIGHT BE THE WORST PLAYER IN THE WHOLE WORLD!
GOOD GAME.
KIRKMAN & SCOTT

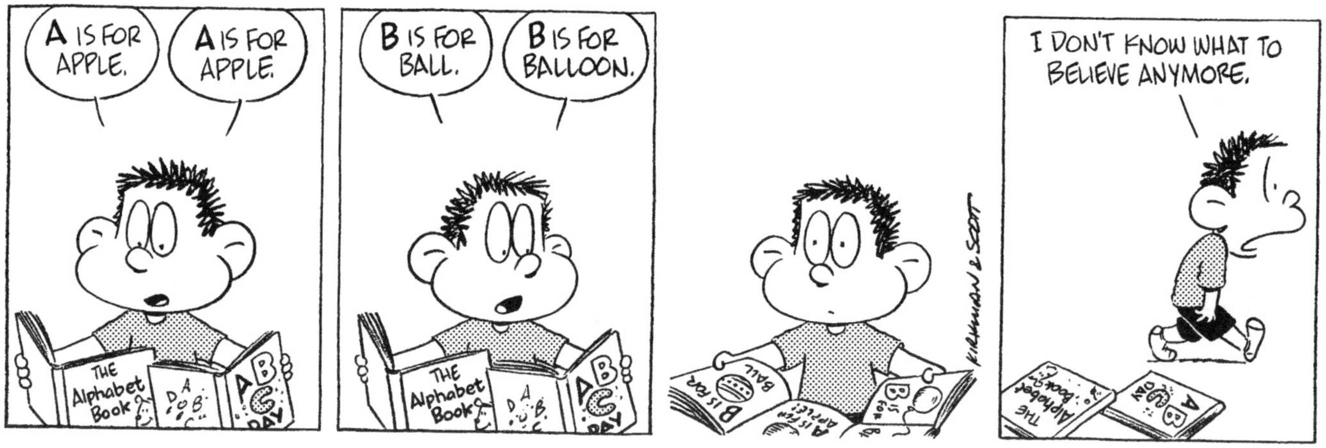
A IS FOR APPLE.
A IS FOR APPLE.
THE Alphabet Book
B IS FOR BALL.
B IS FOR BALLOON.
KIRKMAN & SCOTT
I DON'T KNOW WHAT TO BELIEVE ANYMORE.

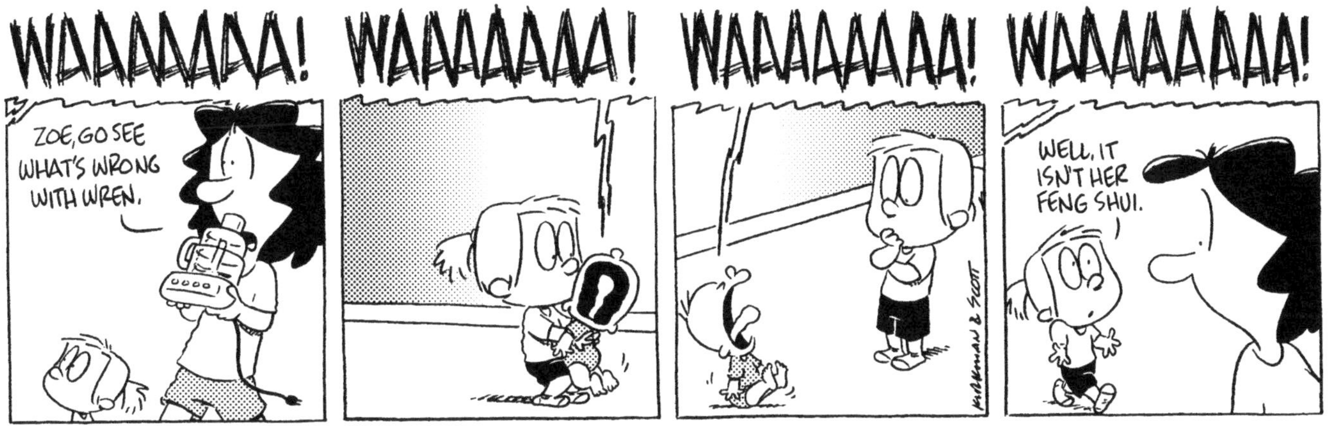
WAAAAAAA!
ZOE, GO SEE WHAT'S WRONG WITH WREN.
WAAAAAAAA!
WAAAAAAAAA!
KIRKMAN & SCOTT
WAAAAAAAAA!
WELL, IT ISN'T HER FENG SHUI.

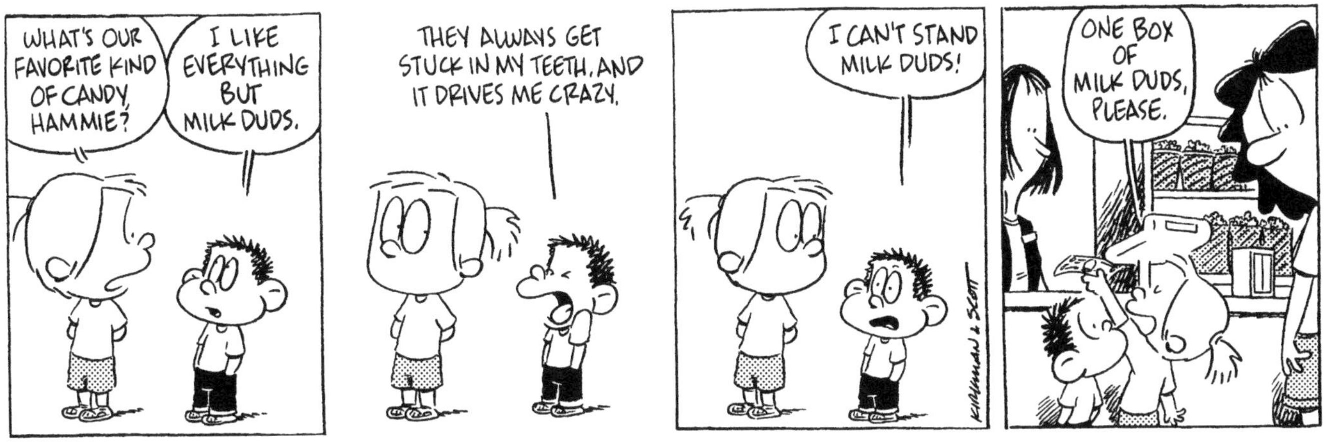
WHAT'S OUR FAVORITE KIND OF CANDY, HAMMIE?
I LIKE EVERYTHING BUT MILK DUDS.
THEY ALWAYS GET STUCK IN MY TEETH, AND IT DRIVES ME CRAZY.
I CAN'T STAND MILK DUDS!
KIRKMAN & SCOTT
ONE BOX OF MILK DUDS, PLEASE.

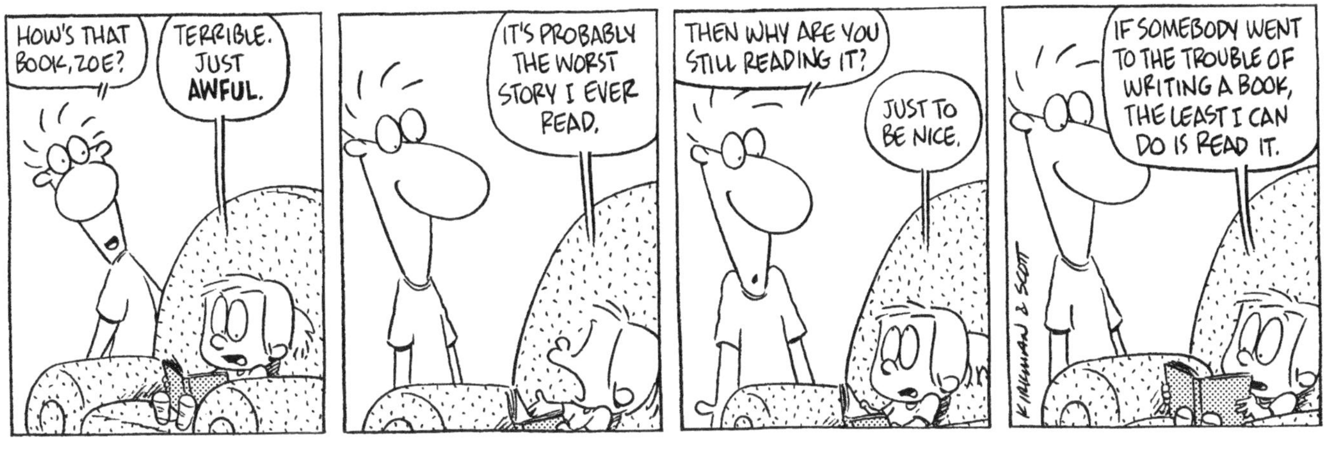
HOW'S THAT BOOK, ZOE?
TERRIBLE. JUST **AWFUL**.
IT'S PROBABLY THE WORST STORY I EVER READ.
THEN WHY ARE YOU STILL READING IT?
JUST TO BE NICE.
KIRKMAN & SCOTT
IF SOMEBODY WENT TO THE TROUBLE OF WRITING A BOOK, THE LEAST I CAN DO IS READ IT.

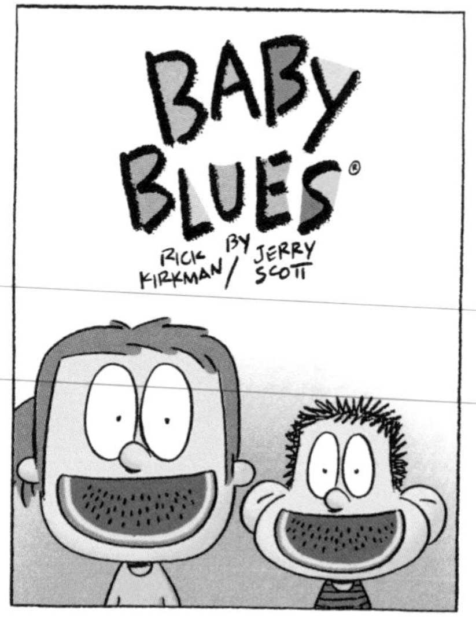
BABY BLUES®
BY RICK KIRKMAN / JERRY SCOTT

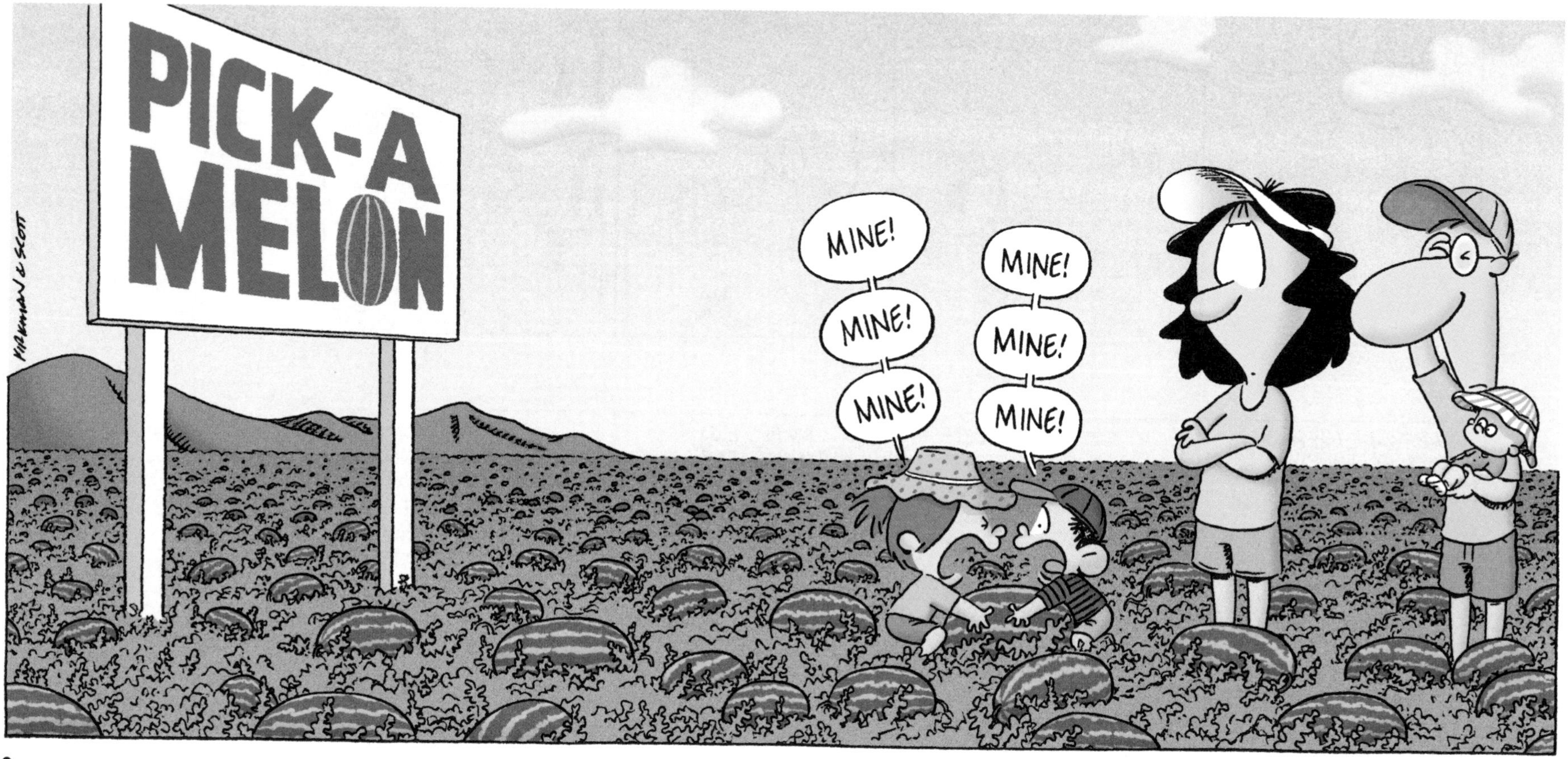
PICK-A MELON
KIRKMAN & SCOTT
MINE!
MINE!
MINE!
MINE!
MINE!
MINE!

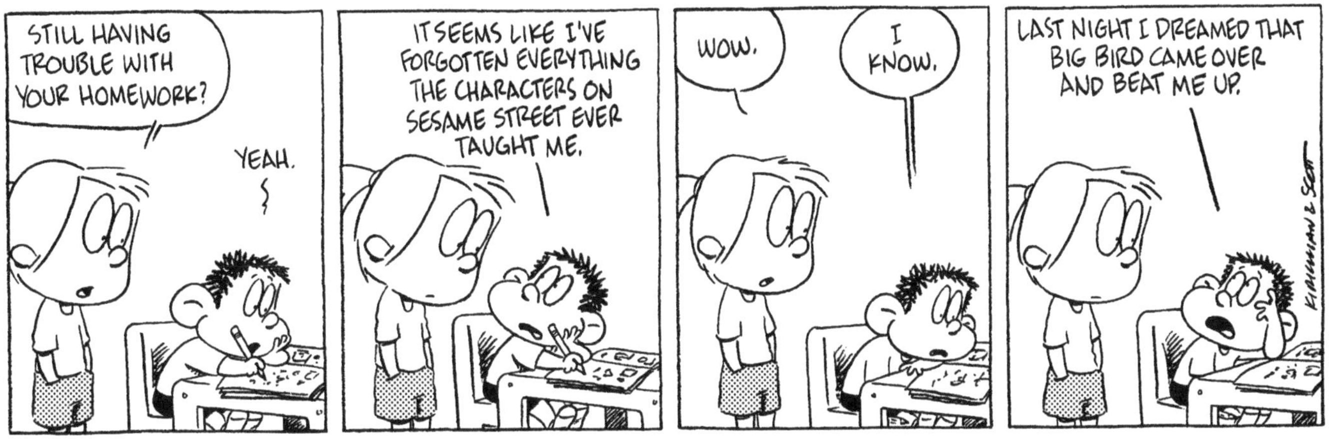
STILL HAVING TROUBLE WITH YOUR HOMEWORK?
YEAH.
IT SEEMS LIKE I'VE FORGOTTEN EVERYTHING THE CHARACTERS ON SESAME STREET EVER TAUGHT ME.
WOW.
I KNOW.
LAST NIGHT I DREAMED THAT BIG BIRD CAME OVER AND BEAT ME UP.
KIRKMAN & SCOTT

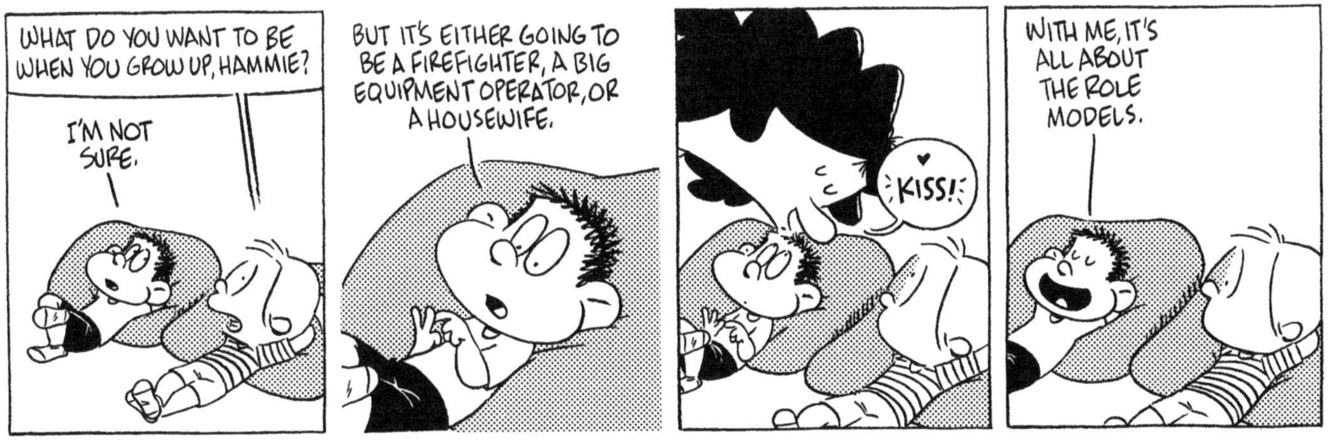
WHAT DO YOU WANT TO BE WHEN YOU GROW UP, HAMMIE?
I'M NOT SURE.
BUT IT'S EITHER GOING TO BE A FIREFIGHTER, A BIG EQUIPMENT OPERATOR, OR A HOUSEWIFE.
KISS!
WITH ME, IT'S ALL ABOUT THE ROLE MODELS.

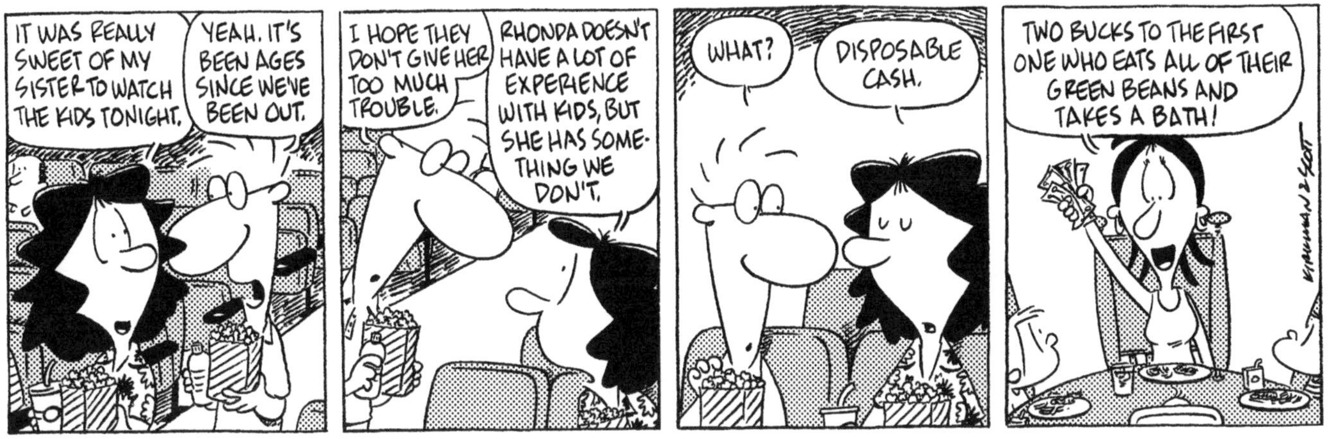
IT WAS REALLY SWEET OF MY SISTER TO WATCH THE KIDS TONIGHT.
YEAH. IT'S BEEN AGES SINCE WE'VE BEEN OUT.
I HOPE THEY DON'T GIVE HER TOO MUCH TROUBLE.
RHONDA DOESN'T HAVE A LOT OF EXPERIENCE WITH KIDS, BUT SHE HAS SOME-THING WE DON'T.
WHAT?
DISPOSABLE CASH.
TWO BUCKS TO THE FIRST ONE WHO EATS ALL OF THEIR GREEN BEANS AND TAKES A BATH!
KIRKMAN & SCOTT

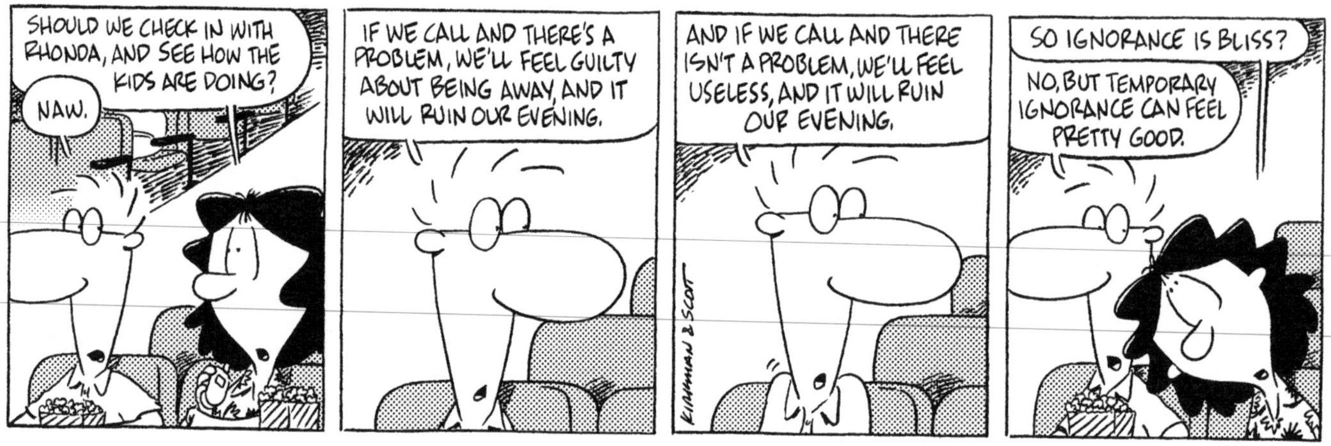
SHOULD WE CHECK IN WITH RHONDA, AND SEE HOW THE KIDS ARE DOING?
NAW.
IF WE CALL AND THERE'S A PROBLEM, WE'LL FEEL GUILTY ABOUT BEING AWAY, AND IT WILL RUIN OUR EVENING.
AND IF WE CALL AND THERE ISN'T A PROBLEM, WE'LL FEEL USELESS, AND IT WILL RUIN OUR EVENING.
KIRKMAN & SCOTT
SO IGNORANCE IS BLISS?
NO, BUT TEMPORARY IGNORANCE CAN FEEL PRETTY GOOD.

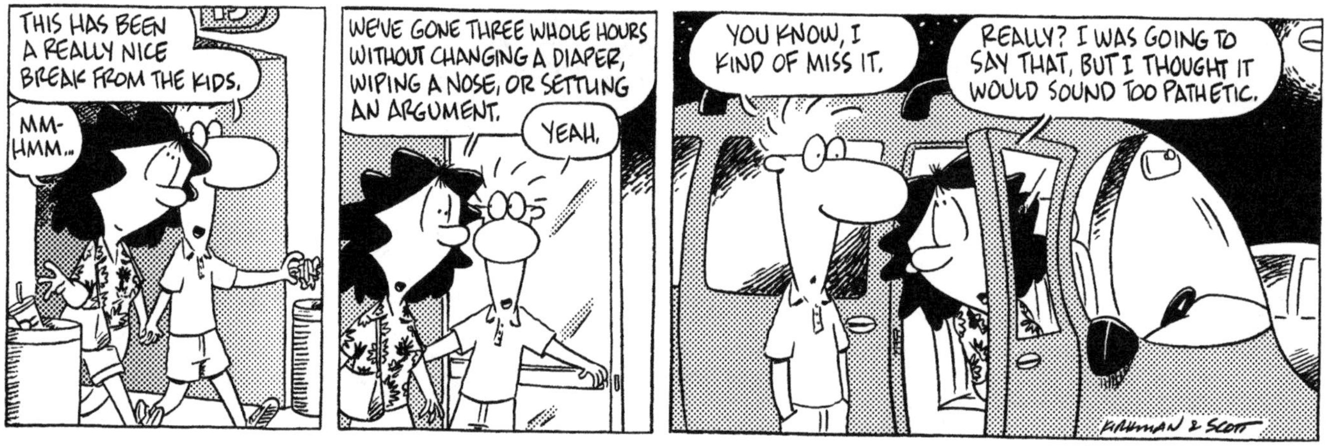
THIS HAS BEEN A REALLY NICE BREAK FROM THE KIDS.
MM-HMM...
WE'VE GONE THREE WHOLE HOURS WITHOUT CHANGING A DIAPER, WIPING A NOSE, OR SETTLING AN ARGUMENT.
YEAH.
YOU KNOW, I KIND OF MISS IT.
REALLY? I WAS GOING TO SAY THAT, BUT I THOUGHT IT WOULD SOUND TOO PATHETIC.
KIRKMAN & SCOTT

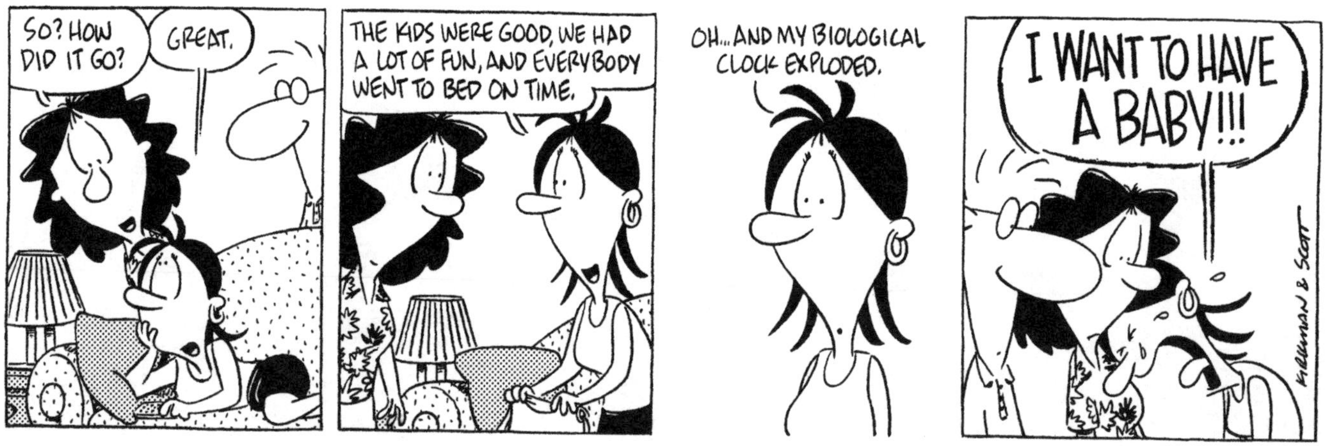
SO? HOW DID IT GO?
GREAT.
THE KIDS WERE GOOD, WE HAD A LOT OF FUN, AND EVERYBODY WENT TO BED ON TIME.
OH... AND MY BIOLOGICAL CLOCK EXPLODED.
I WANT TO HAVE A BABY!!!
KIRKMAN & SCOTT

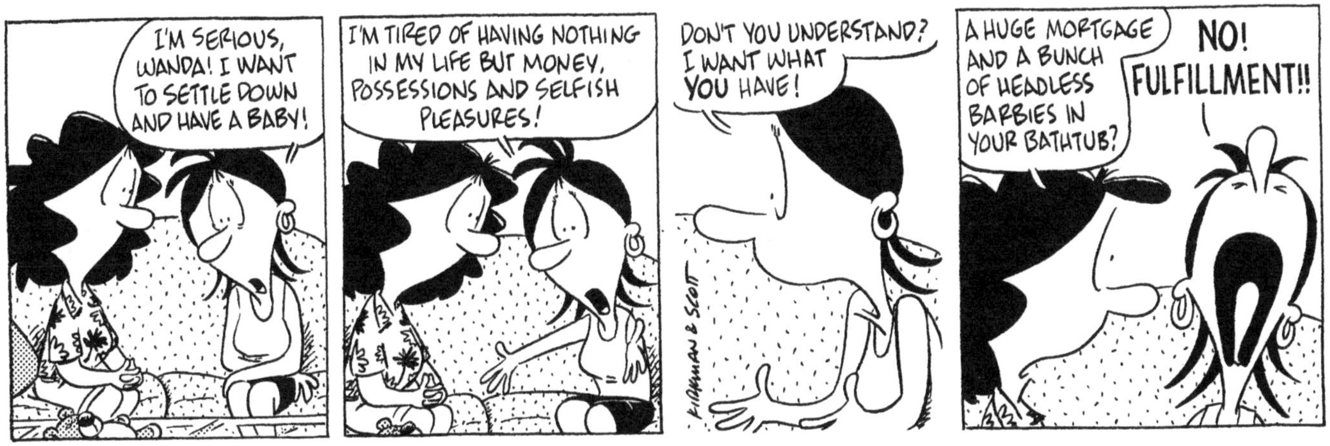
I'M SERIOUS, WANDA! I WANT TO SETTLE DOWN AND HAVE A BABY!
I'M TIRED OF HAVING NOTHING IN MY LIFE BUT MONEY, POSSESSIONS AND SELFISH PLEASURES!
DON'T YOU UNDERSTAND? I WANT WHAT YOU HAVE!
KIRKMAN & SCOTT
A HUGE MORTGAGE AND A BUNCH OF HEADLESS BARBIES IN YOUR BATHTUB?
NO! FULFILLMENT!!

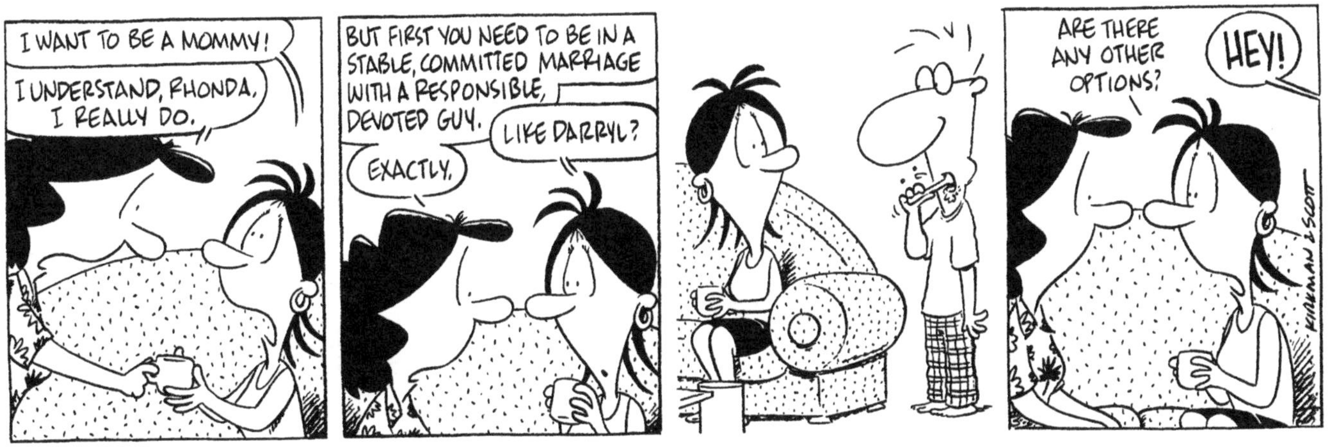
I WANT TO BE A MOMMY!
I UNDERSTAND, RHONDA. I REALLY DO.
BUT FIRST YOU NEED TO BE IN A STABLE, COMMITTED MARRIAGE WITH A RESPONSIBLE, DEVOTED GUY.
LIKE DARRYL?
EXACTLY.
ARE THERE ANY OTHER OPTIONS?
HEY!
KIRKMAN & SCOTT

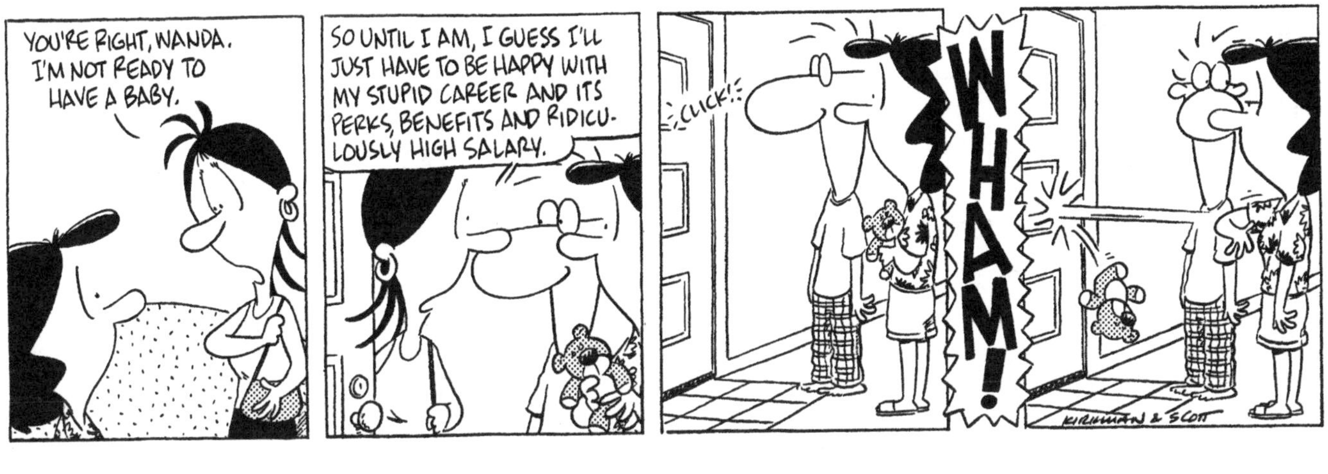
YOU'RE RIGHT, WANDA. I'M NOT READY TO HAVE A BABY.
SO UNTIL I AM, I GUESS I'LL JUST HAVE TO BE HAPPY WITH MY STUPID CAREER AND ITS PERKS, BENEFITS AND RIDICULOUSLY HIGH SALARY.
CLICK!
WHAM!
KIRKMAN & SCOTT

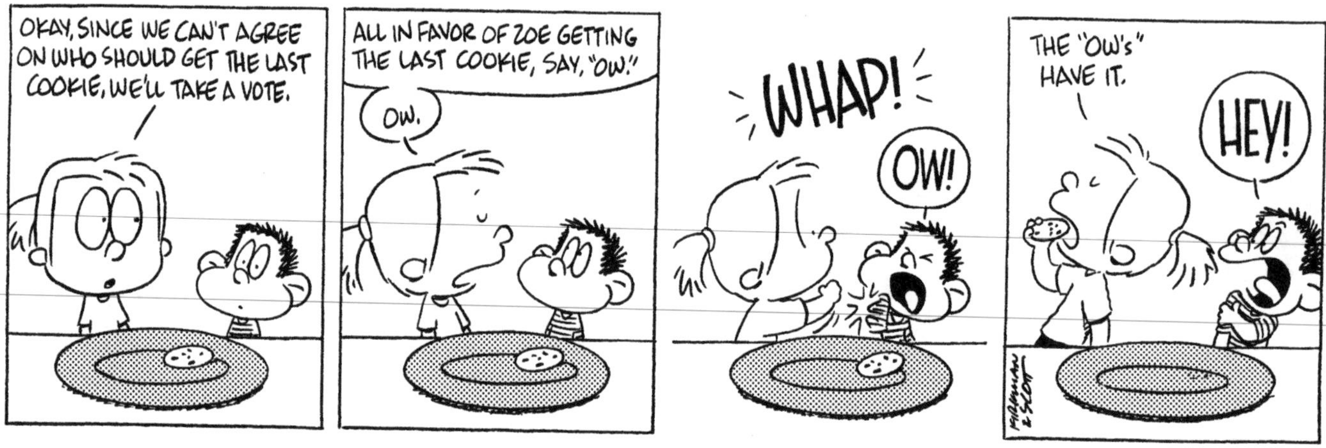
OKAY, SINCE WE CAN'T AGREE ON WHO SHOULD GET THE LAST COOKIE, WE'LL TAKE A VOTE.
ALL IN FAVOR OF ZOE GETTING THE LAST COOKIE, SAY, "OW."
OW.
WHAP!
OW!
THE "OW's" HAVE IT.
HEY!

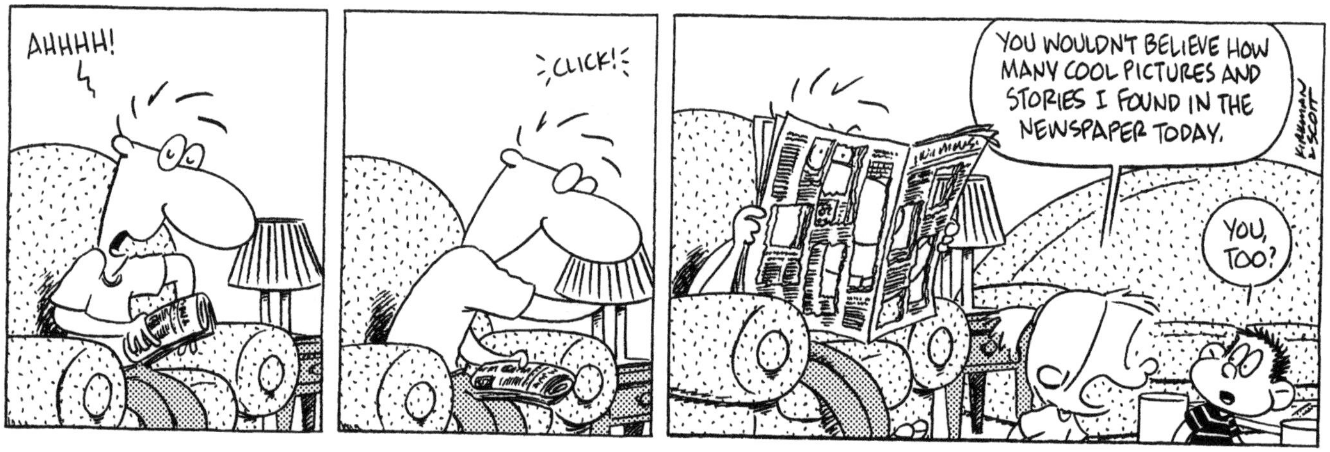
AHHHH!
CLICK!
YOU WOULDN'T BELIEVE HOW MANY COOL PICTURES AND STORIES I FOUND IN THE NEWSPAPER TODAY.
YOU, TOO?

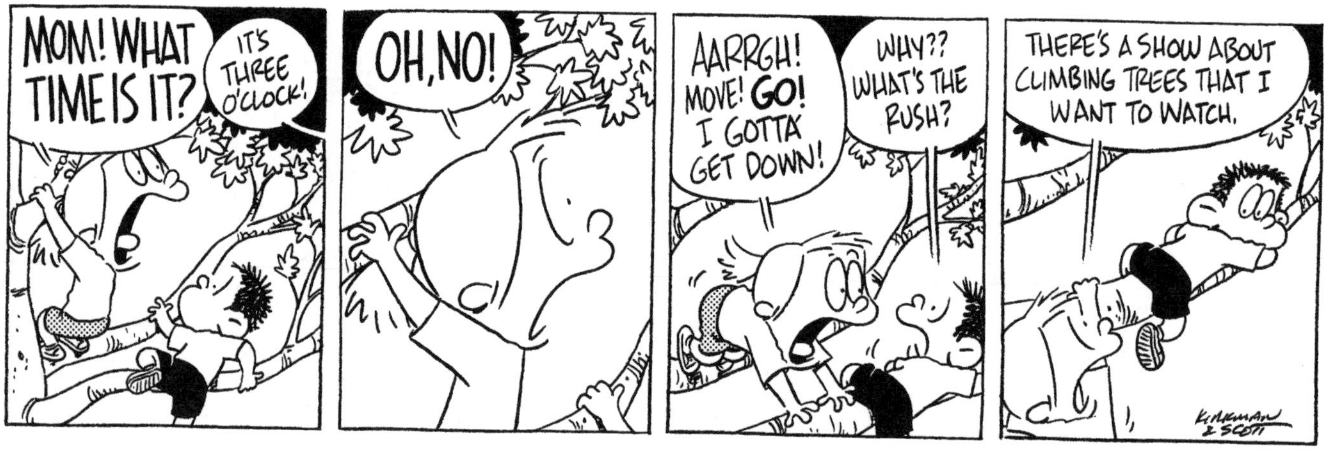
MOM! WHAT TIME IS IT?
IT'S THREE O'CLOCK!
OH, NO!
AARRGH! MOVE! GO! I GOTTA GET DOWN!
WHY?? WHAT'S THE RUSH?
THERE'S A SHOW ABOUT CLIMBING TREES THAT I WANT TO WATCH.

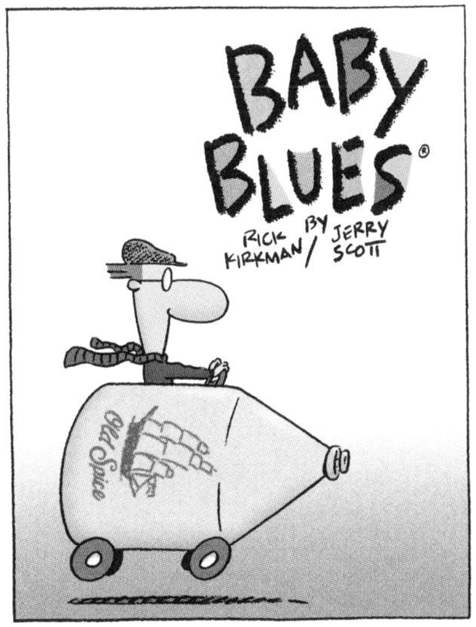
BABY BLUES®
BY RICK KIRKMAN / JERRY SCOTT
Old Spice

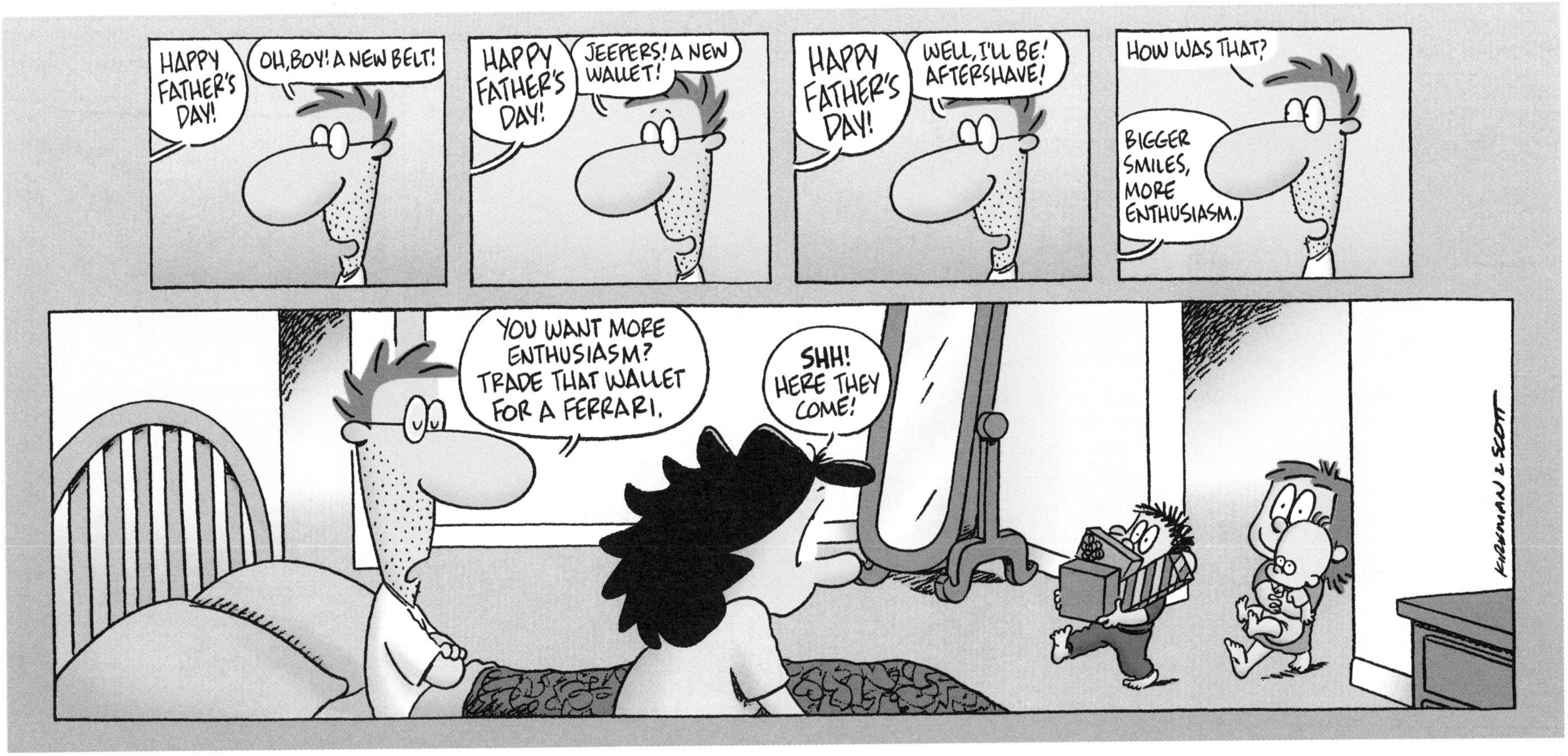
HAPPY FATHER'S DAY!
OH, BOY! A NEW BELT!
HAPPY FATHER'S DAY!
JEEPERS! A NEW WALLET!
HAPPY FATHER'S DAY!
WELL, I'LL BE! AFTERSHAVE!
HOW WAS THAT?
BIGGER SMILES, MORE ENTHUSIASM.
YOU WANT MORE ENTHUSIASM? TRADE THAT WALLET FOR A FERRARI.
SHH! HERE THEY COME!
KIRKMAN & SCOTT

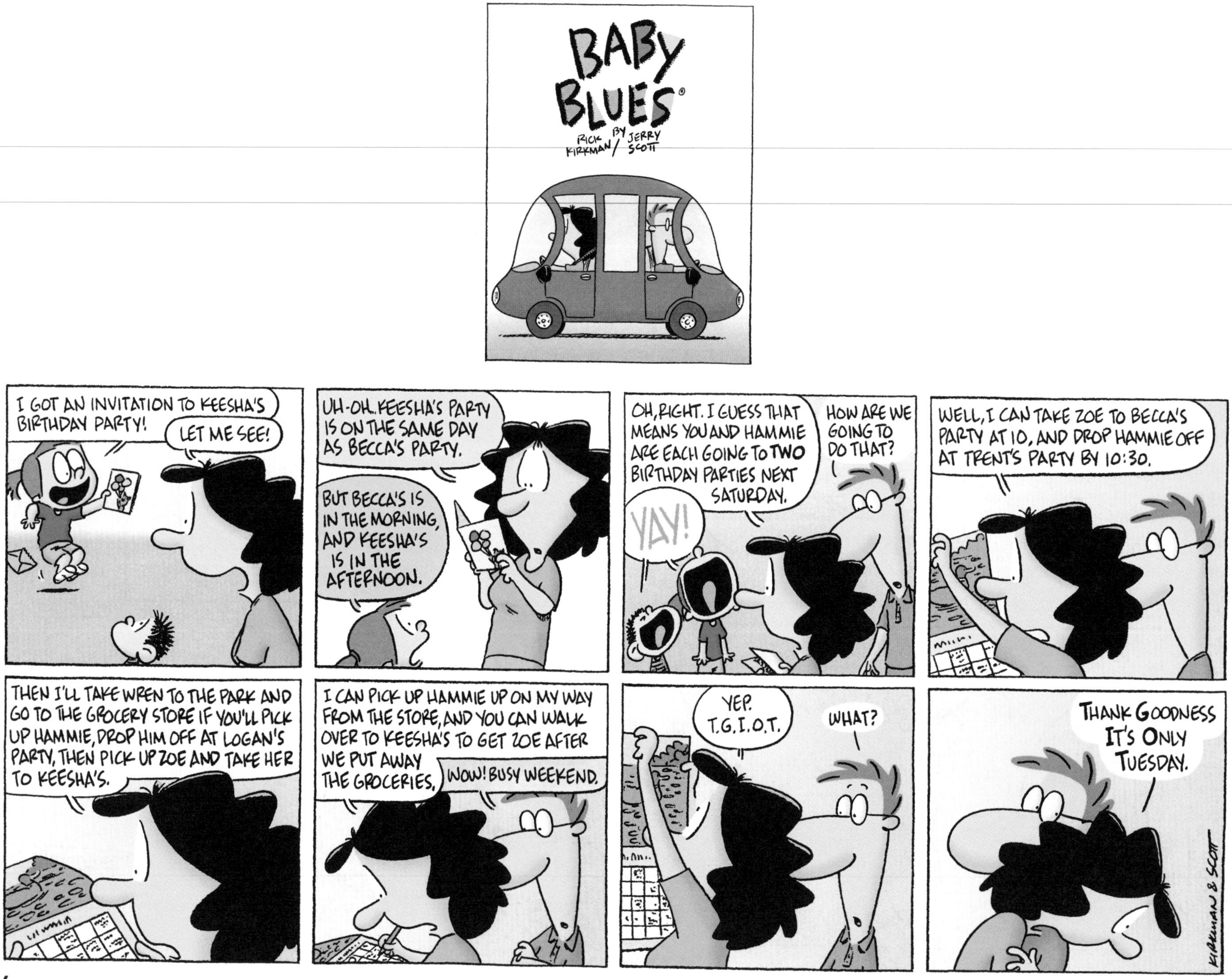
BABY BLUES®
RICK KIRKMAN / BY JERRY SCOTT
I GOT AN INVITATION TO KEESHA'S BIRTHDAY PARTY!
LET ME SEE!
UH-OH.. KEESHA'S PARTY IS ON THE SAME DAY AS BECCA'S PARTY.
BUT BECCA'S IS IN THE MORNING, AND KEESHA'S IS IN THE AFTERNOON.
OH, RIGHT. I GUESS THAT MEANS YOU AND HAMMIE ARE EACH GOING TO **TWO** BIRTHDAY PARTIES NEXT SATURDAY.
YAY!
HOW ARE WE GOING TO DO THAT?
WELL, I CAN TAKE ZOE TO BECCA'S PARTY AT 10, AND DROP HAMMIE OFF AT TRENT'S PARTY BY 10:30.
THEN I'LL TAKE WREN TO THE PARK AND GO TO THE GROCERY STORE IF YOU'LL PICK UP HAMMIE, DROP HIM OFF AT LOGAN'S PARTY, THEN PICK UP ZOE AND TAKE HER TO KEESHA'S.
I CAN PICK UP HAMMIE UP ON MY WAY FROM THE STORE, AND YOU CAN WALK OVER TO KEESHA'S TO GET ZOE AFTER WE PUT AWAY THE GROCERIES.
WOW! BUSY WEEKEND.
YEP. T.G.I.O.T.
WHAT?
THANK GOODNESS IT'S ONLY TUESDAY.
KIRKMAN & SCOTT

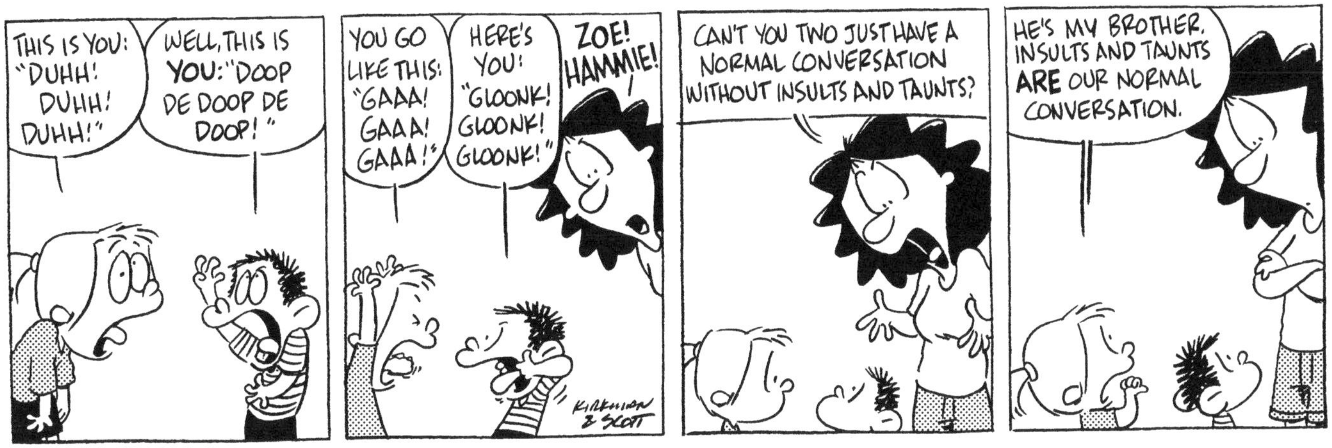
THIS IS YOU: "DUHH! DUHH! DUHH!"
WELL, THIS IS YOU: "DOOP DE DOOP DE DOOP!"
YOU GO LIKE THIS: "GAAA! GAAA! GAAA!"
HERE'S YOU: "GLOONK! GLOONK! GLOONK!"
ZOE! HAMMIE!
KIRKMAN & SCOTT
CAN'T YOU TWO JUST HAVE A NORMAL CONVERSATION WITHOUT INSULTS AND TAUNTS?
HE'S MY BROTHER. INSULTS AND TAUNTS ARE OUR NORMAL CONVERSATION.

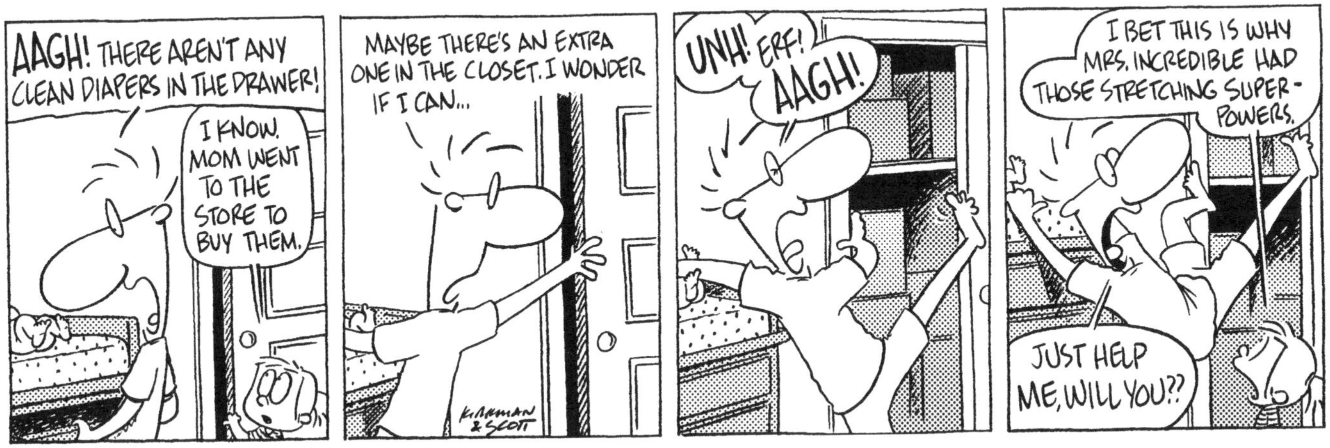
AAGH! THERE AREN'T ANY CLEAN DIAPERS IN THE DRAWER!
I KNOW. MOM WENT TO THE STORE TO BUY THEM.
MAYBE THERE'S AN EXTRA ONE IN THE CLOSET. I WONDER IF I CAN...
KIRKMAN & SCOTT
UNH! ERF! AAGH!
I BET THIS IS WHY MRS. INCREDIBLE HAD THOSE STRETCHING SUPER-POWERS.
JUST HELP ME, WILL YOU??

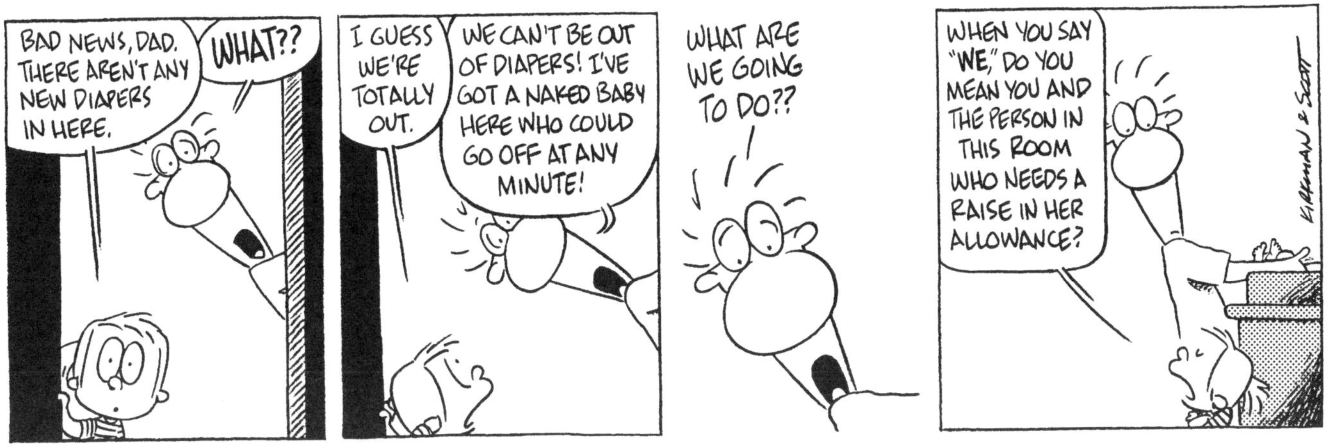
BAD NEWS, DAD. THERE AREN'T ANY NEW DIAPERS IN HERE.
WHAT??
I GUESS WE'RE TOTALLY OUT.
WE CAN'T BE OUT OF DIAPERS! I'VE GOT A NAKED BABY HERE WHO COULD GO OFF AT ANY MINUTE!
WHAT ARE WE GOING TO DO??
WHEN YOU SAY "WE," DO YOU MEAN YOU AND THE PERSON IN THIS ROOM WHO NEEDS A RAISE IN HER ALLOWANCE?
KIRKMAN & SCOTT

OKAY ZOE, WE NEED TO COME UP WITH SOME KIND OF TEMPORARY DIAPER FOR WREN UNTIL MOM GETS HOME FROM THE STORE.

RIGHT!

LOOK FOR SOMETHING ABSORBENT AND A WAY TO FASTEN IT TO HER.

GOT IT!

COTTON BALLS AND DUCT TAPE!

OKAY. YOU HOLD HER WHILE I LOOK.

BUT A SHINY SILVER DIAPER MADE OUT OF THIS STUFF WOULD BE SO COOL!

THERE, THAT OUGHT TO HOLD HER FOR A WHILE.

THAT LOOKS GREAT!

SLAM!

HEY! I THINK MOM'S HOME!

WAIT! MAYBE WE SHOULD KEEP THIS—

MOM! WREN RAN OUT OF DIAPERS SO DADDY AND ME MADE A REALLY COOL ONE OUT OF STUFF WE FOUND AROUND THE HOUSE!

KIRKMAN & SCOTT

—A SECRET.

TOO LATE I BROUGHT THE VIDEO CAMERA.

WELL, I HAVE TO ADMIT THIS SHOWS A LOT OF IMAGINATION.

I DIDN'T KNOW IT WAS POSSIBLE TO MAKE A DIAPER OUT OF A MAXI-PAD, A DISHTOWEL AND TWO HAIR SCRUNCHIES.

YOU NEVER KNOW WHAT YOU CAN DO UNTIL THE ADRENALINE TAKES OVER.

KIRKMAN & SCOTT

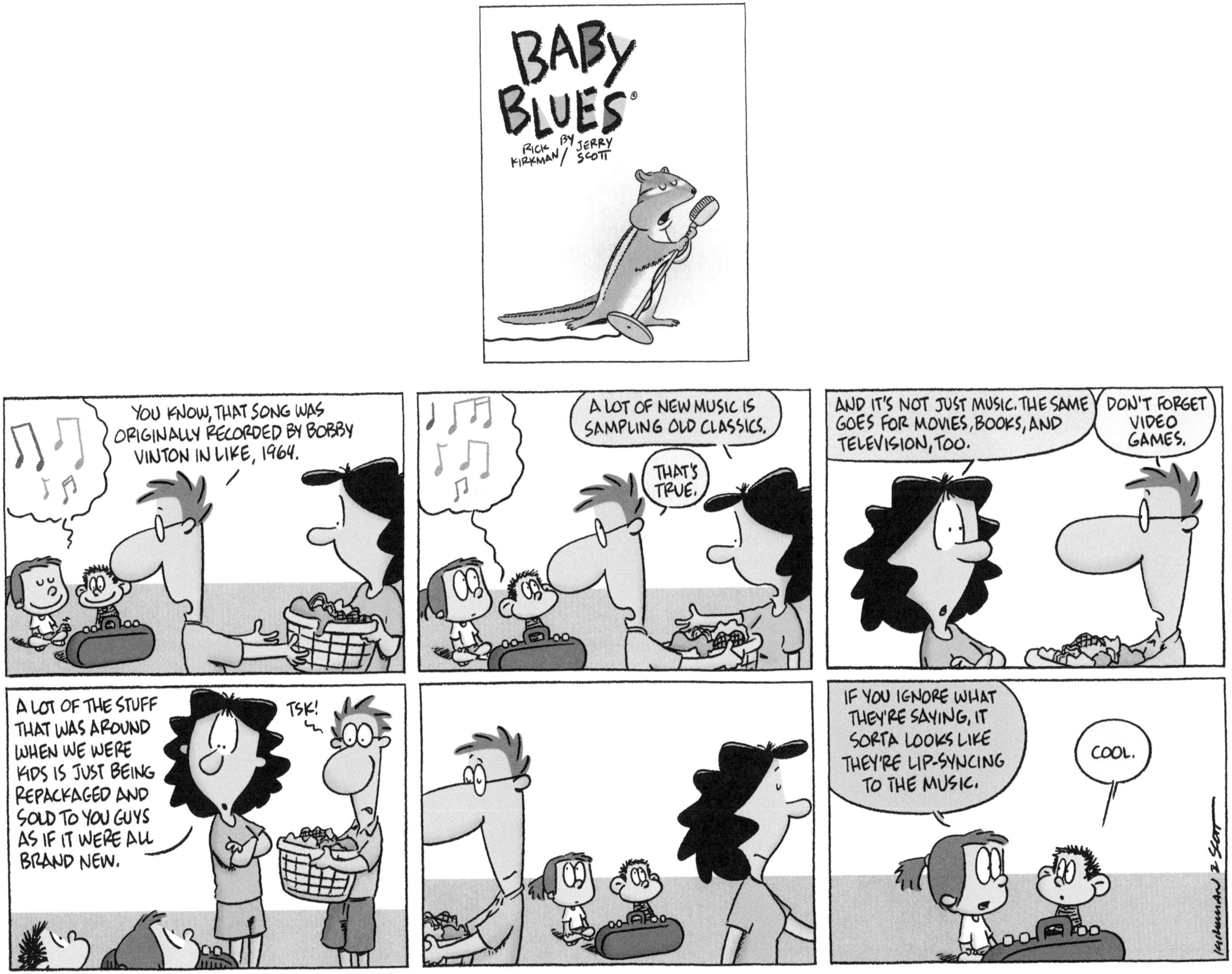
BABY BLUES®
BY RICK KIRKMAN / JERRY SCOTT
YOU KNOW, THAT SONG WAS ORIGINALLY RECORDED BY BOBBY VINTON IN LIKE, 1964.
A LOT OF NEW MUSIC IS SAMPLING OLD CLASSICS.
THAT'S TRUE.
AND IT'S NOT JUST MUSIC. THE SAME GOES FOR MOVIES, BOOKS, AND TELEVISION, TOO.
DON'T FORGET VIDEO GAMES.
A LOT OF THE STUFF THAT WAS AROUND WHEN WE WERE KIDS IS JUST BEING REPACKAGED AND SOLD TO YOU GUYS AS IF IT WERE ALL BRAND NEW.
TSK!
IF YOU IGNORE WHAT THEY'RE SAYING, IT SORTA LOOKS LIKE THEY'RE LIP-SYNCING TO THE MUSIC.
COOL.
KIRKMAN & SCOTT

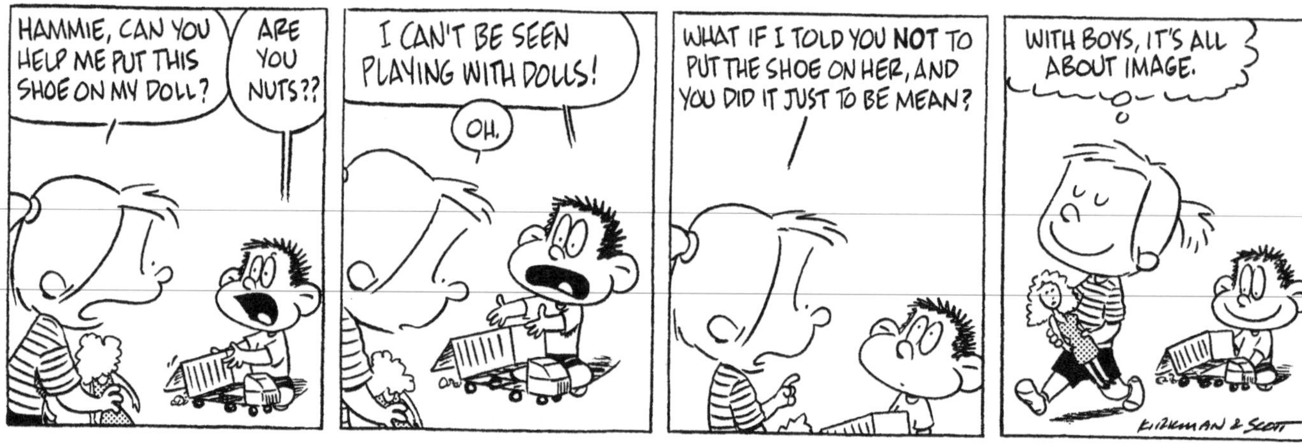

HAMMIE, CAN YOU HELP ME PUT THIS SHOE ON MY DOLL?
ARE YOU NUTS??
I CAN'T BE SEEN PLAYING WITH DOLLS!
OH.
WHAT IF I TOLD YOU NOT TO PUT THE SHOE ON HER, AND YOU DID IT JUST TO BE MEAN?
WITH BOYS, IT'S ALL ABOUT IMAGE.
KIRKMAN & SCOTT

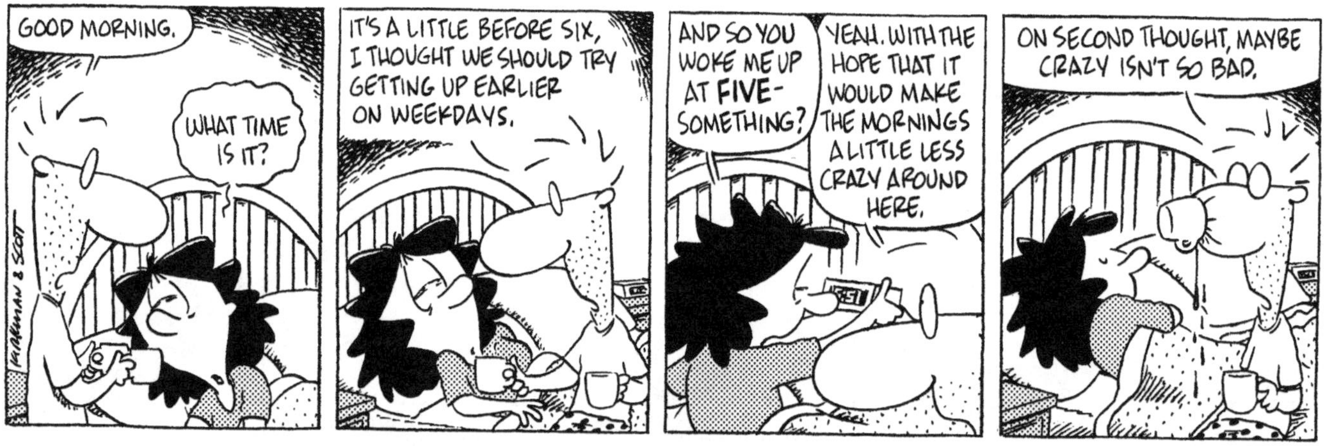

GOOD MORNING.
WHAT TIME IS IT?
KIRKMAN & SCOTT
IT'S A LITTLE BEFORE SIX, I THOUGHT WE SHOULD TRY GETTING UP EARLIER ON WEEKDAYS.
AND SO YOU WOKE ME UP AT FIVE-SOMETHING?
YEAH. WITH THE HOPE THAT IT WOULD MAKE THE MORNINGS A LITTLE LESS CRAZY AROUND HERE.
ON SECOND THOUGHT, MAYBE CRAZY ISN'T SO BAD.

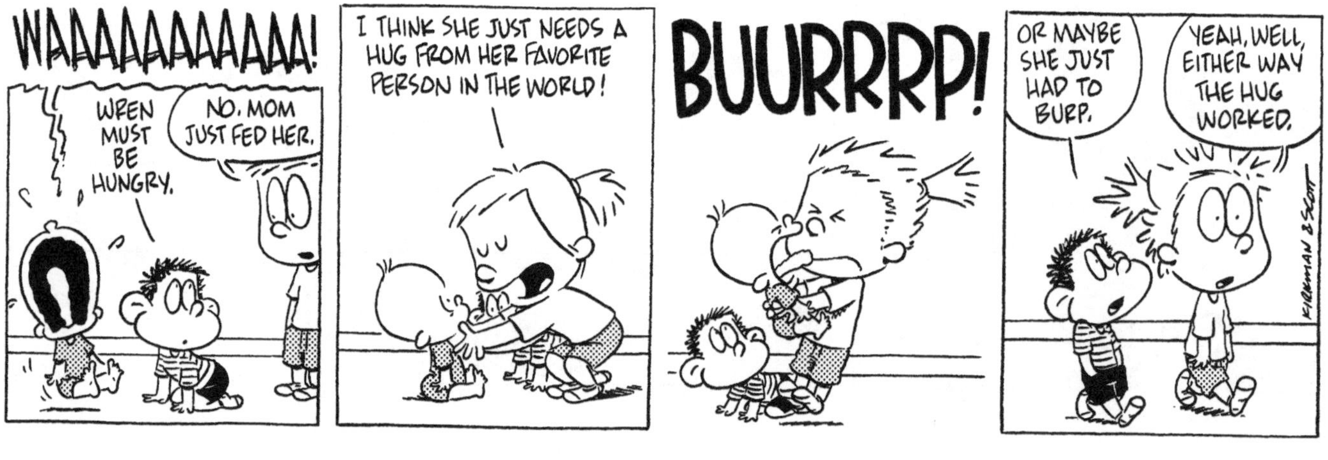

WAAAAAAAAAAA!
WREN MUST BE HUNGRY.
NO. MOM JUST FED HER.
I THINK SHE JUST NEEDS A HUG FROM HER FAVORITE PERSON IN THE WORLD!
BUURRRP!
OR MAYBE SHE JUST HAD TO BURP.
YEAH, WELL, EITHER WAY THE HUG WORKED.
KIRKMAN & SCOTT

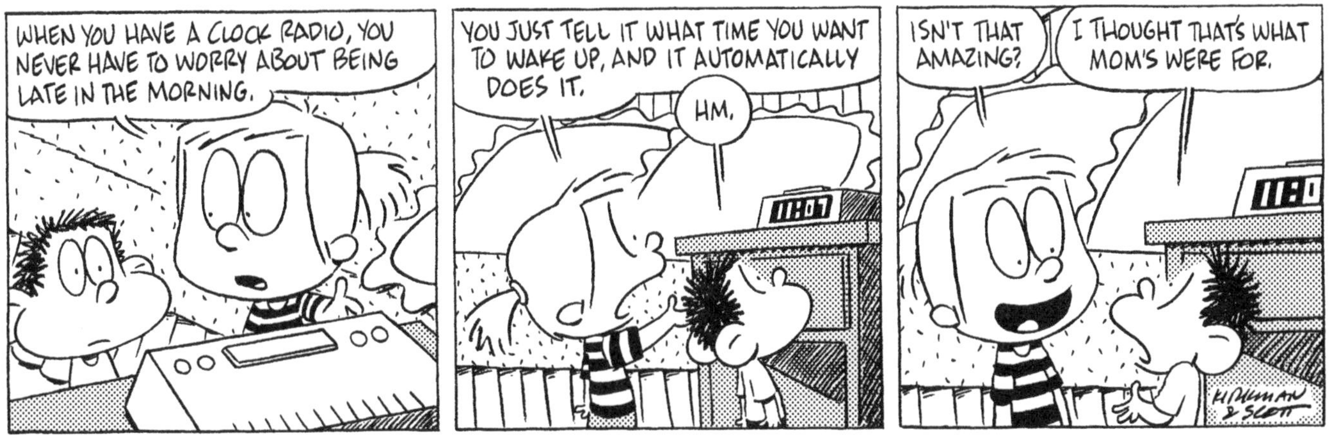
WHEN YOU HAVE A CLOCK RADIO, YOU NEVER HAVE TO WORRY ABOUT BEING LATE IN THE MORNING.
YOU JUST TELL IT WHAT TIME YOU WANT TO WAKE UP, AND IT AUTOMATICALLY DOES IT.
HM.
11:07
ISN'T THAT AMAZING?
I THOUGHT THAT'S WHAT MOM'S WERE FOR.
KIRKMAN & SCOTT

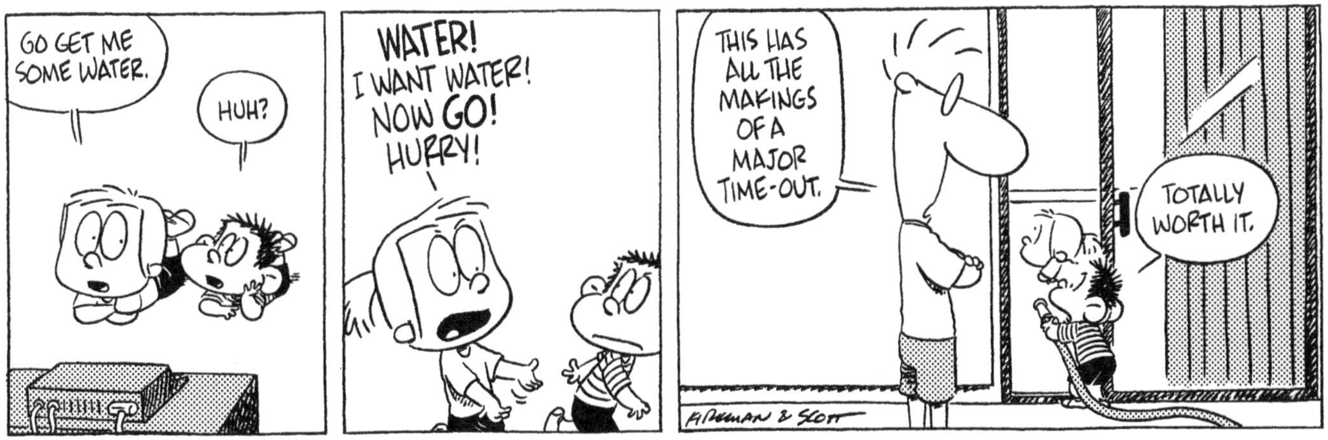
GO GET ME SOME WATER.
HUH?
WATER! I WANT WATER! NOW GO! HURRY!
THIS HAS ALL THE MAKINGS OF A MAJOR TIME-OUT.
TOTALLY WORTH IT.
KIRKMAN & SCOTT

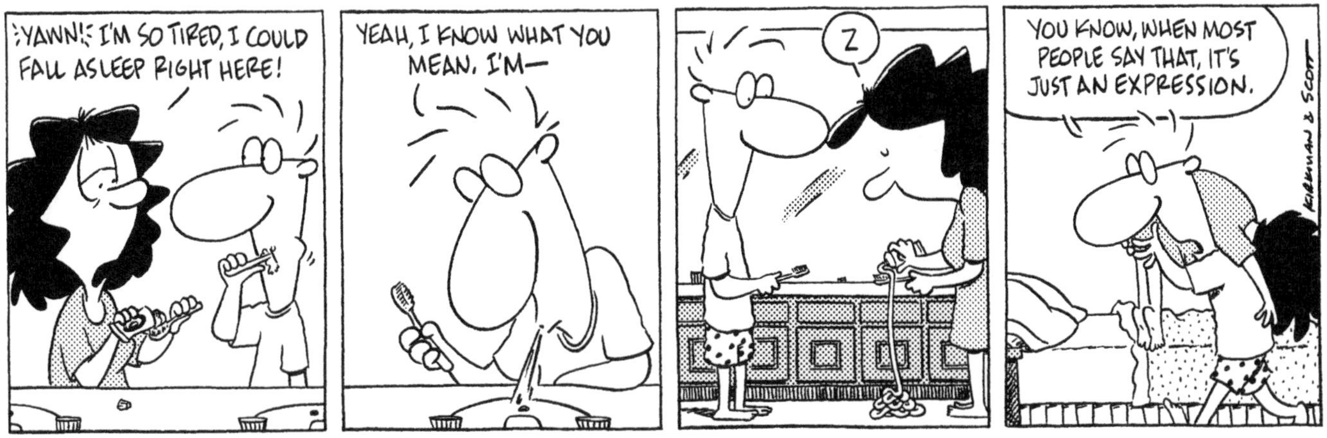
YAWN! I'M SO TIRED, I COULD FALL ASLEEP RIGHT HERE!
YEAH, I KNOW WHAT YOU MEAN. I'M—
Z
YOU KNOW, WHEN MOST PEOPLE SAY THAT, IT'S JUST AN EXPRESSION.
KIRKMAN & SCOTT

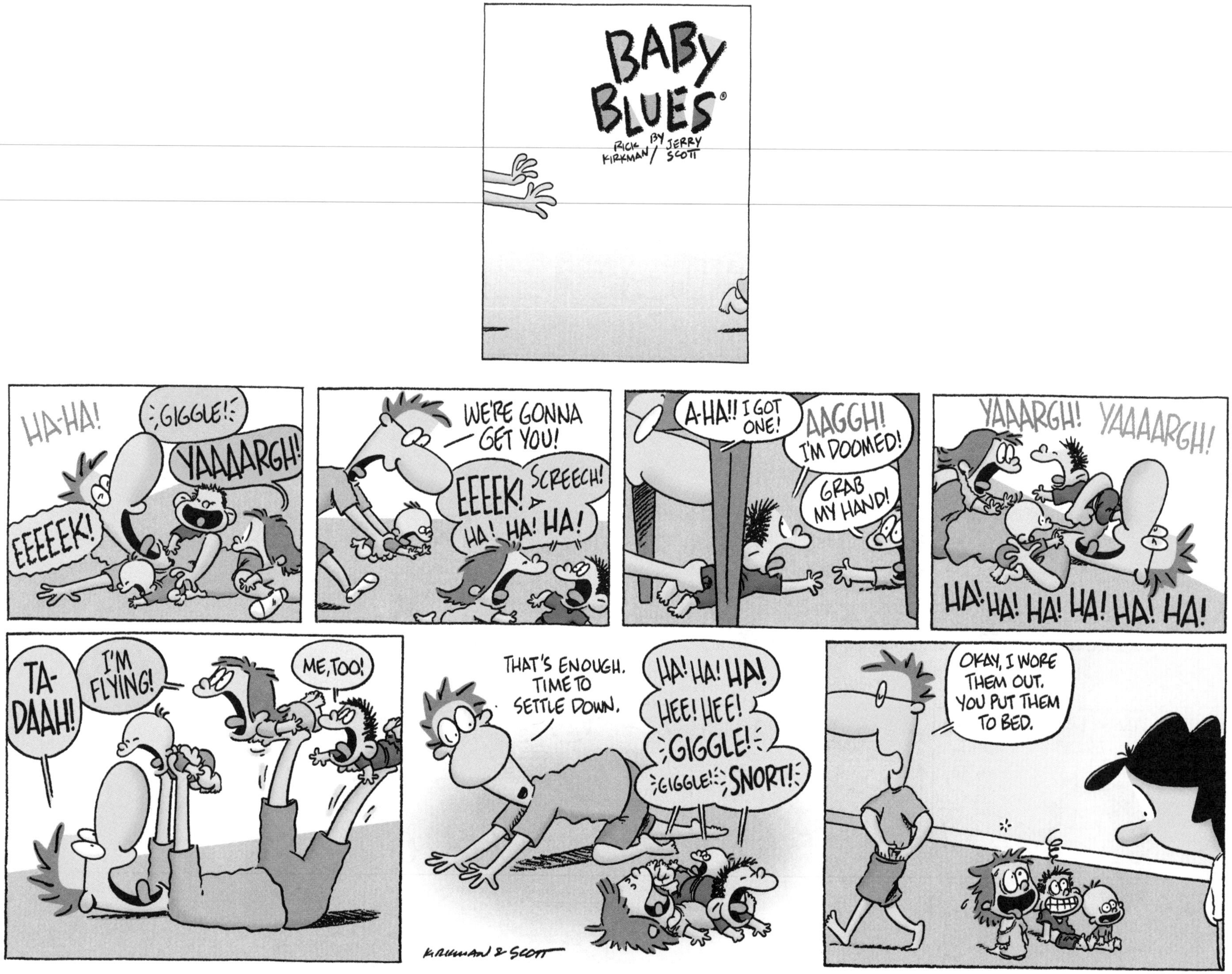
BABY BLUES®
BY RICK KIRKMAN / JERRY SCOTT
HA-HA!
GIGGLE!
YAAAARGH!
EEEEEK!
WE'RE GONNA GET YOU!
EEEEK!
SCREECH!
HA! HA! HA!
A-HA!! I GOT ONE!
AAGGH! I'M DOOMED!
GRAB MY HAND!
YAAARGH!
YAAAARGH!
HA! HA! HA! HA! HA! HA!
TA-DAAH!
I'M FLYING!
ME, TOO!
THAT'S ENOUGH. TIME TO SETTLE DOWN.
HA! HA! HA!
HEE! HEE!
GIGGLE!
GIGGLE!
SNORT!
KIRKMAN & SCOTT
OKAY, I WORE THEM OUT. YOU PUT THEM TO BED.

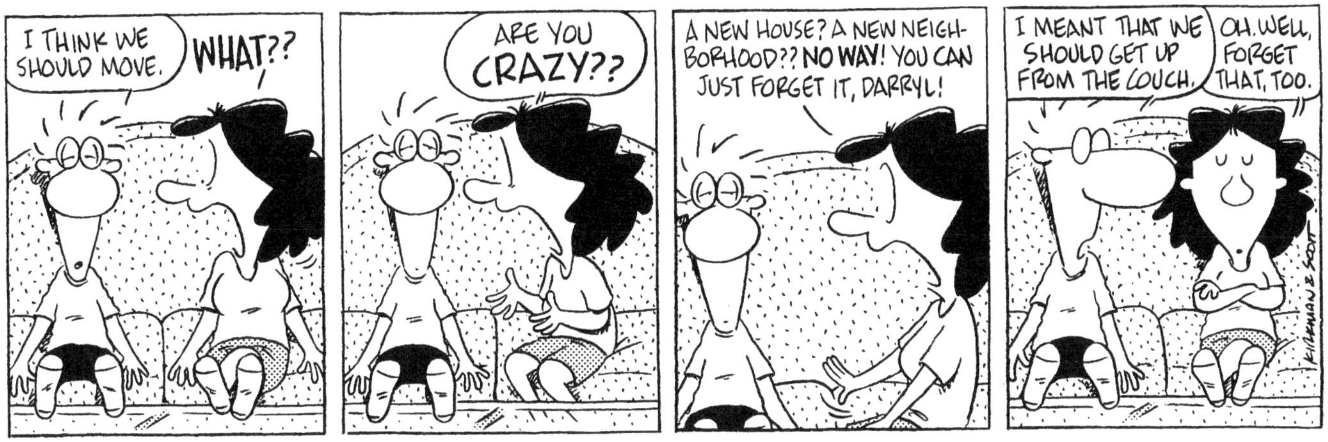
I THINK WE SHOULD MOVE.
WHAT??
ARE YOU CRAZY??
A NEW HOUSE? A NEW NEIGHBORHOOD?? NO WAY! YOU CAN JUST FORGET IT, DARRYL!
I MEANT THAT WE SHOULD GET UP FROM THE COUCH.
OH. WELL, FORGET THAT, TOO.
KIRKMAN & SCOTT

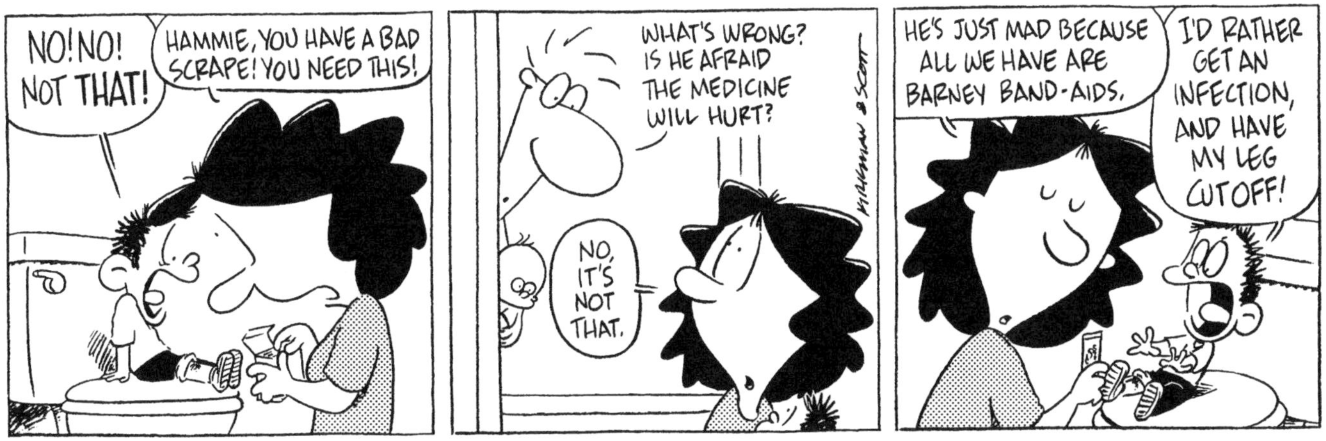
NO! NO! NOT THAT!
HAMMIE, YOU HAVE A BAD SCRAPE! YOU NEED THIS!
WHAT'S WRONG? IS HE AFRAID THE MEDICINE WILL HURT?
NO, IT'S NOT THAT.
KIRKMAN & SCOTT
HE'S JUST MAD BECAUSE ALL WE HAVE ARE BARNEY BAND-AIDS.
I'D RATHER GET AN INFECTION, AND HAVE MY LEG CUT OFF!

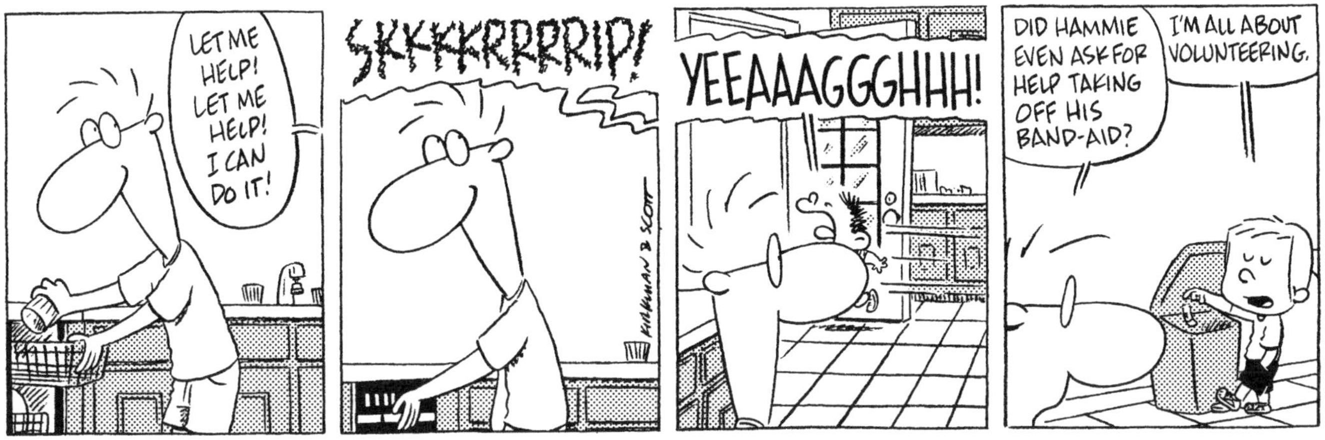
LET ME HELP! LET ME HELP! I CAN DO IT!
SKKKKRRRRRIP!
KIRKMAN & SCOTT
YEEAAAGGGHHH!
DID HAMMIE EVEN ASK FOR HELP TAKING OFF HIS BAND-AID?
I'M ALL ABOUT VOLUNTEERING.

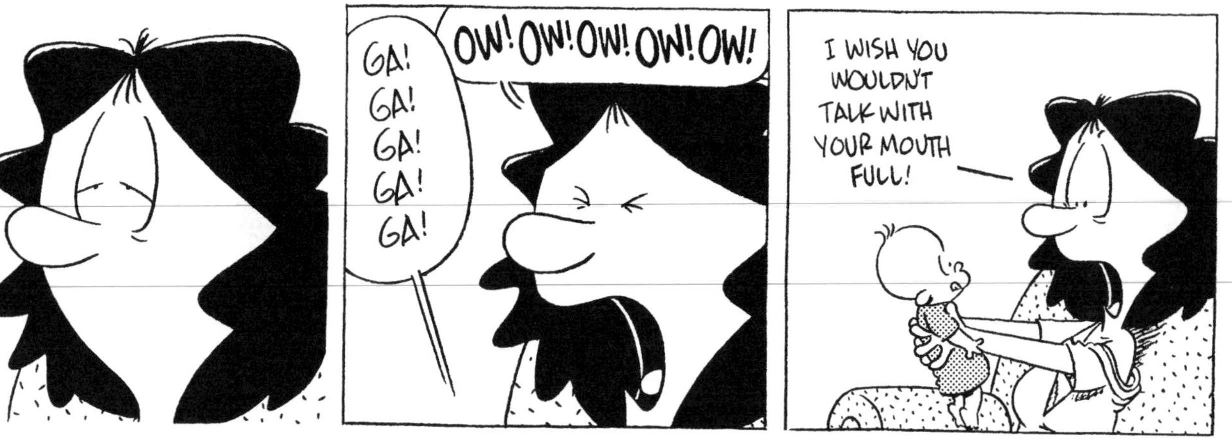
GA!
GA!
GA!
GA!
GA!
OW! OW! OW! OW! OW!
I WISH YOU WOULDN'T TALK WITH YOUR MOUTH FULL!

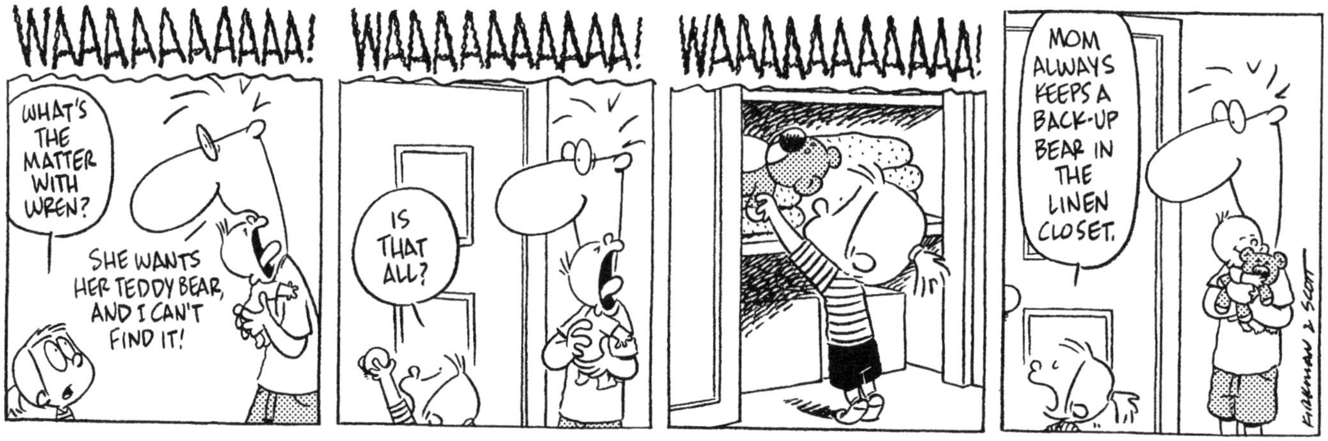
WAAAAAAAAAA!
WHAT'S THE MATTER WITH WREN?
SHE WANTS HER TEDDY BEAR, AND I CAN'T FIND IT!
WAAAAAAAAAA!
IS THAT ALL?
WAAAAAAAAAAA!
MOM ALWAYS KEEPS A BACK-UP BEAR IN THE LINEN CLOSET.
KIRKMAN & SCOTT

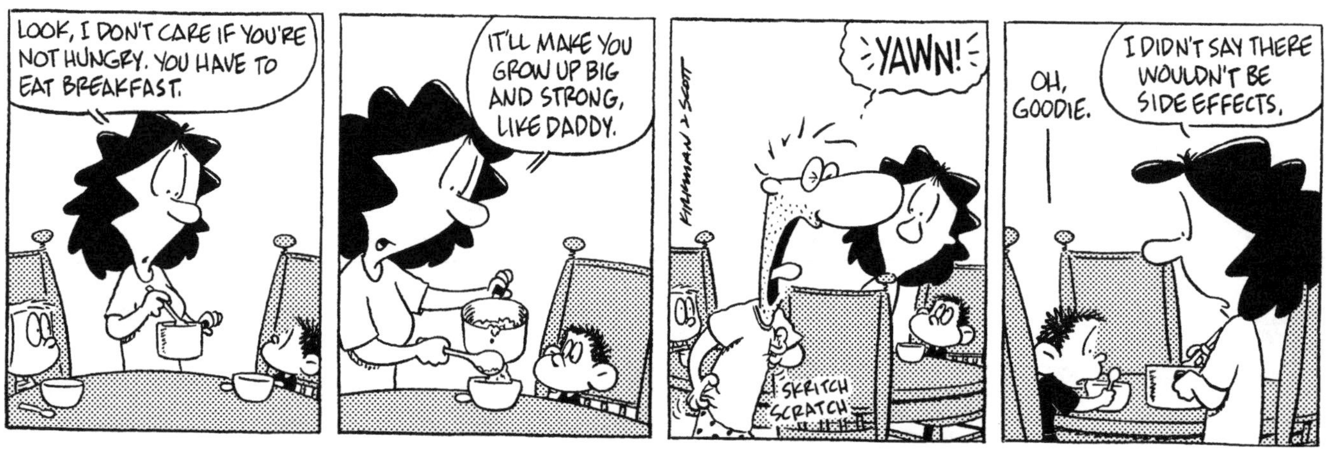
LOOK, I DON'T CARE IF YOU'RE NOT HUNGRY. YOU HAVE TO EAT BREAKFAST.
IT'LL MAKE YOU GROW UP BIG AND STRONG, LIKE DADDY.
KIRKMAN & SCOTT
YAWN!
SKRITCH SCRATCH
OH, GOODIE.
I DIDN'T SAY THERE WOULDN'T BE SIDE EFFECTS.

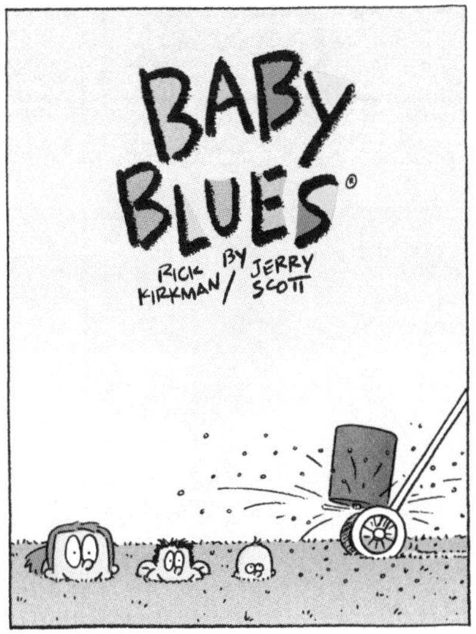
BABY BLUES®
BY RICK KIRKMAN / JERRY SCOTT

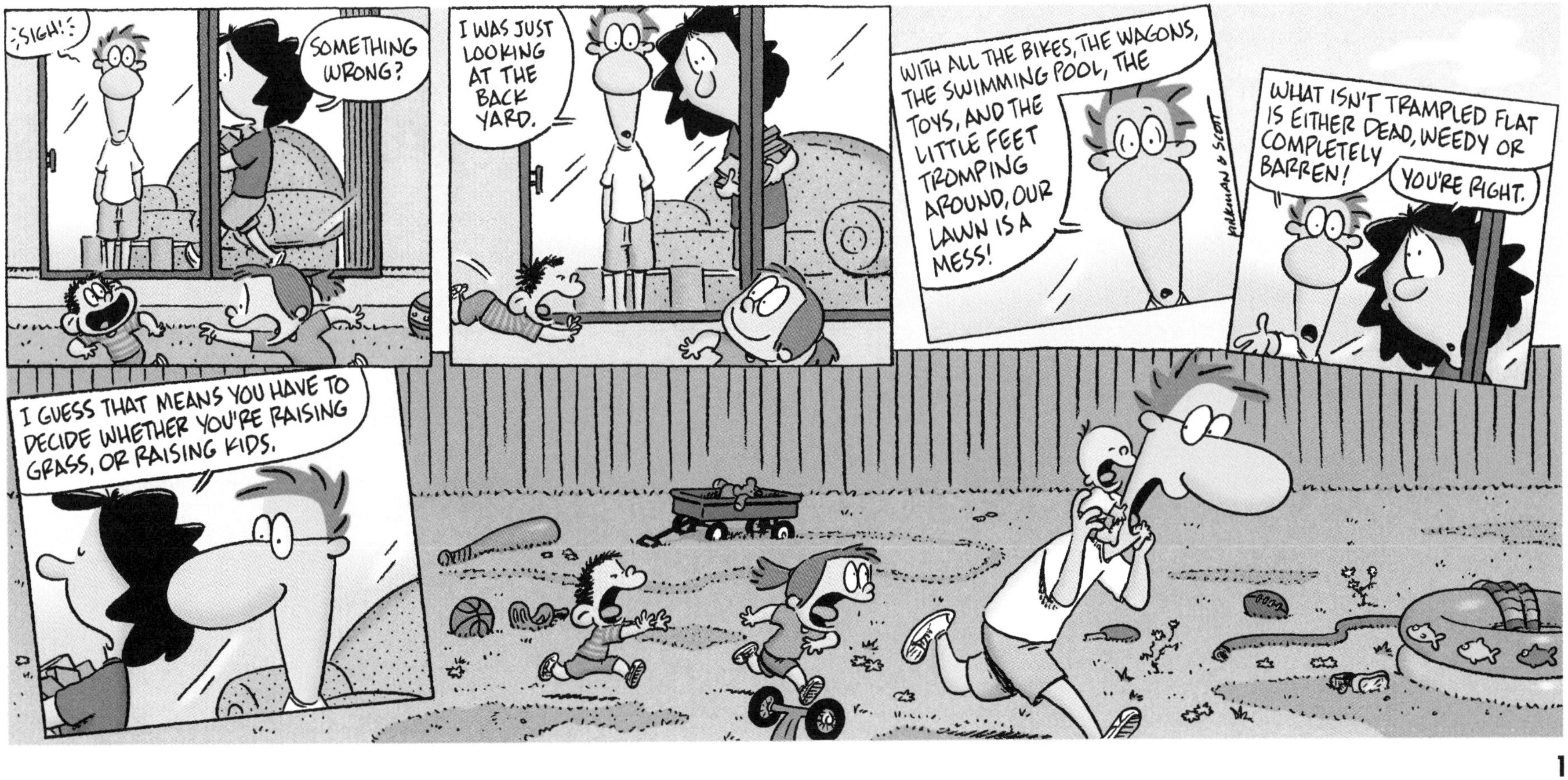
SIGH!
SOMETHING WRONG?
I WAS JUST LOOKING AT THE BACK YARD.
WITH ALL THE BIKES, THE WAGONS, THE SWIMMING POOL, THE TOYS, AND THE LITTLE FEET TROMPING AROUND, OUR LAWN IS A MESS!
WHAT ISN'T TRAMPLED FLAT IS EITHER DEAD, WEEDY OR COMPLETELY BARREN!
YOU'RE RIGHT.
I GUESS THAT MEANS YOU HAVE TO DECIDE WHETHER YOU'RE RAISING GRASS, OR RAISING KIDS.

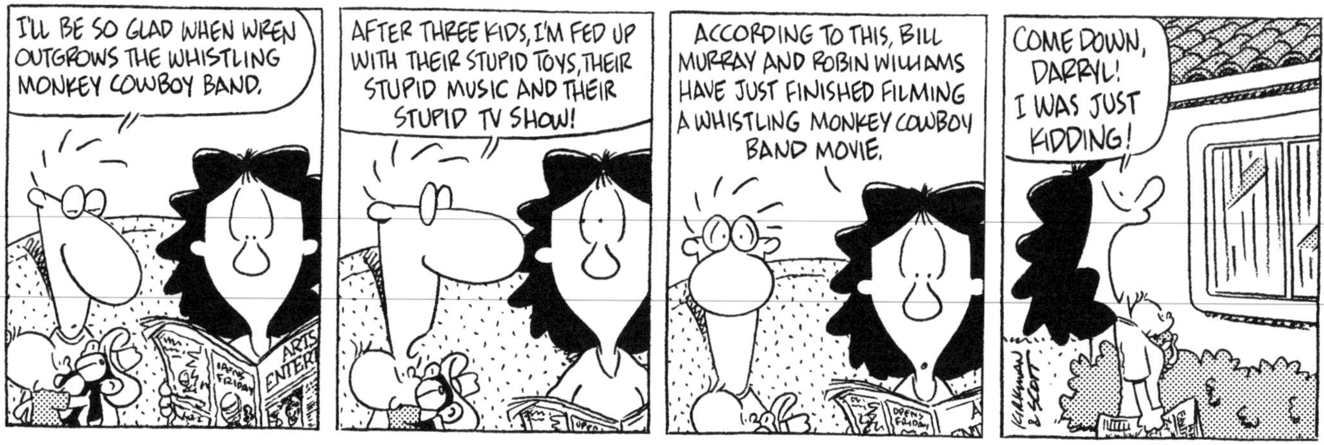
I'LL BE SO GLAD WHEN WREN OUTGROWS THE WHISTLING MONKEY COWBOY BAND.
AFTER THREE KIDS, I'M FED UP WITH THEIR STUPID TOYS, THEIR STUPID MUSIC AND THEIR STUPID TV SHOW!
ACCORDING TO THIS, BILL MURRAY AND ROBIN WILLIAMS HAVE JUST FINISHED FILMING A WHISTLING MONKEY COWBOY BAND MOVIE.
COME DOWN, DARRYL! I WAS JUST KIDDING!

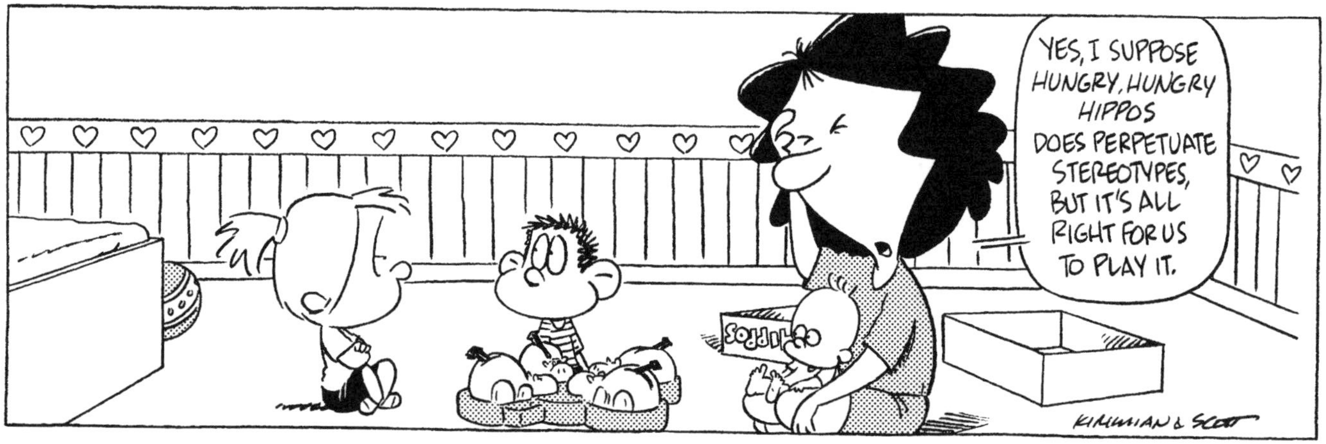
YES, I SUPPOSE HUNGRY, HUNGRY HIPPOS DOES PERPETUATE STEREOTYPES, BUT IT'S ALL RIGHT FOR US TO PLAY IT.
KIRKMAN & SCOTT

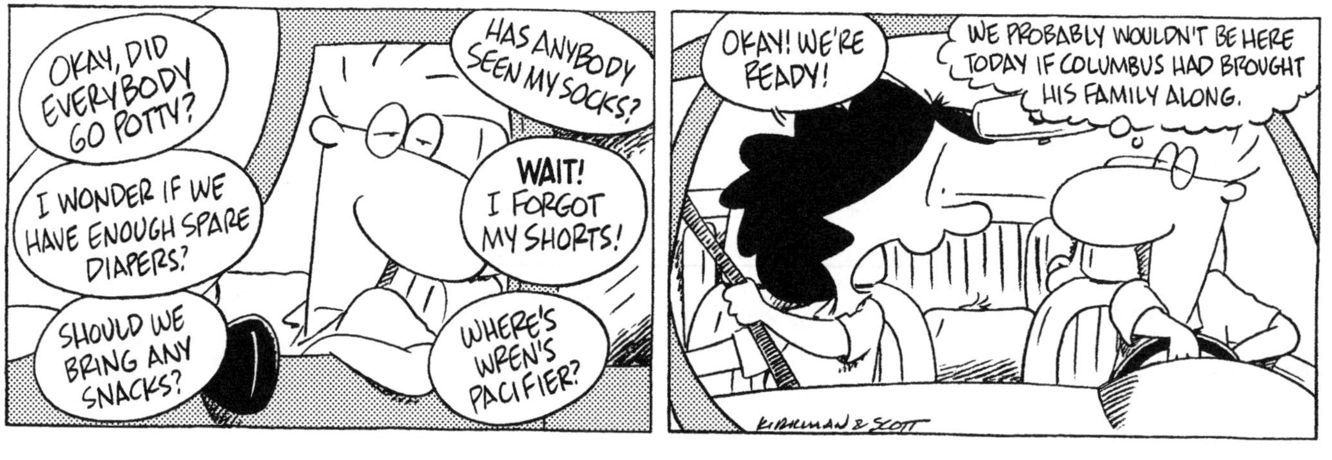
OKAY, DID EVERYBODY GO POTTY?
HAS ANYBODY SEEN MY SOCKS?
I WONDER IF WE HAVE ENOUGH SPARE DIAPERS?
WAIT! I FORGOT MY SHORTS!
SHOULD WE BRING ANY SNACKS?
WHERE'S WREN'S PACIFIER?
OKAY! WE'RE READY!
WE PROBABLY WOULDN'T BE HERE TODAY IF COLUMBUS HAD BROUGHT HIS FAMILY ALONG.
KIRKMAN & SCOTT

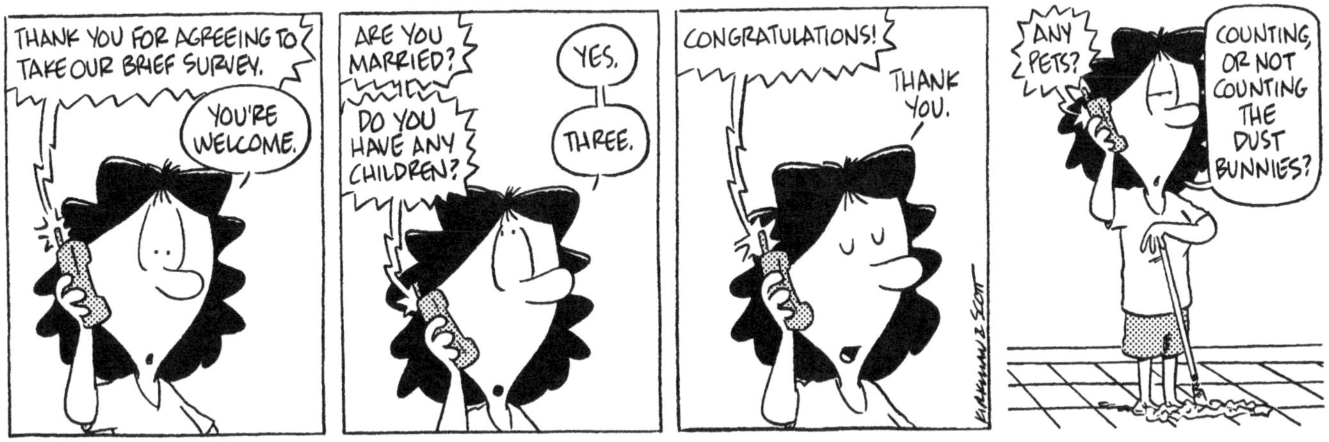
THANK YOU FOR AGREEING TO TAKE OUR BRIEF SURVEY.
YOU'RE WELCOME.
ARE YOU MARRIED?
YES.
DO YOU HAVE ANY CHILDREN?
THREE.
CONGRATULATIONS!
THANK YOU.
ANY PETS?
COUNTING, OR NOT COUNTING THE DUST BUNNIES?

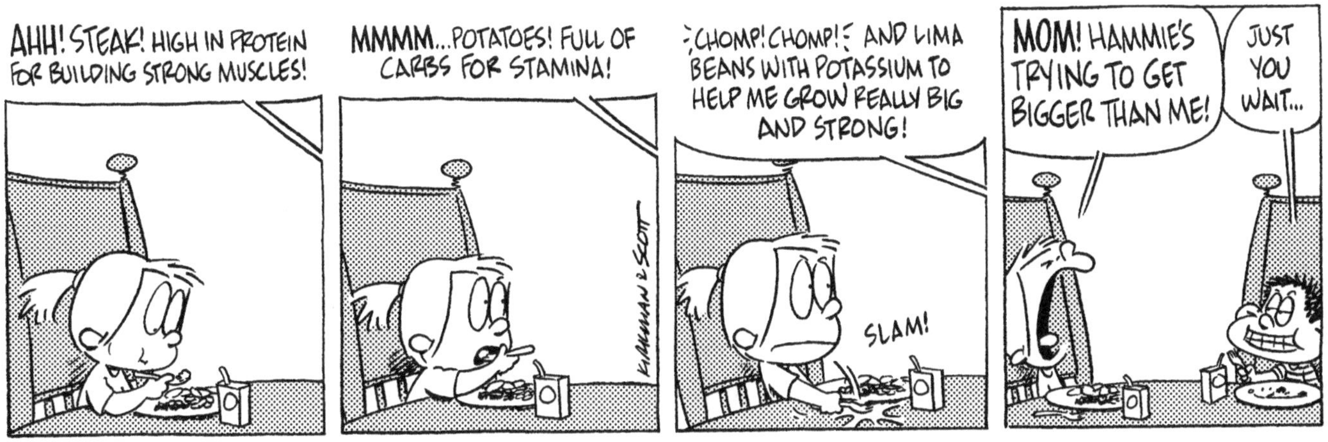
AHH! STEAK! HIGH IN PROTEIN FOR BUILDING STRONG MUSCLES!
MMMM...POTATOES! FULL OF CARBS FOR STAMINA!
CHOMP! CHOMP! AND LIMA BEANS WITH POTASSIUM TO HELP ME GROW REALLY BIG AND STRONG!
SLAM!
MOM! HAMMIE'S TRYING TO GET BIGGER THAN ME!
JUST YOU WAIT...

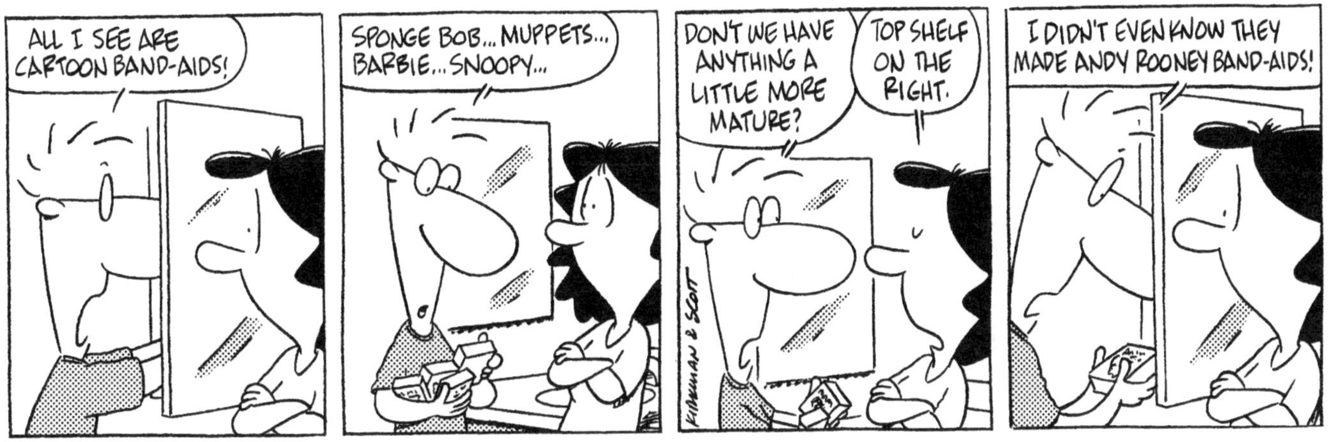
ALL I SEE ARE CARTOON BAND-AIDS!
SPONGE BOB... MUPPETS... BARBIE... SNOOPY...
DON'T WE HAVE ANYTHING A LITTLE MORE MATURE?
TOP SHELF ON THE RIGHT.
I DIDN'T EVEN KNOW THEY MADE ANDY ROONEY BAND-AIDS!

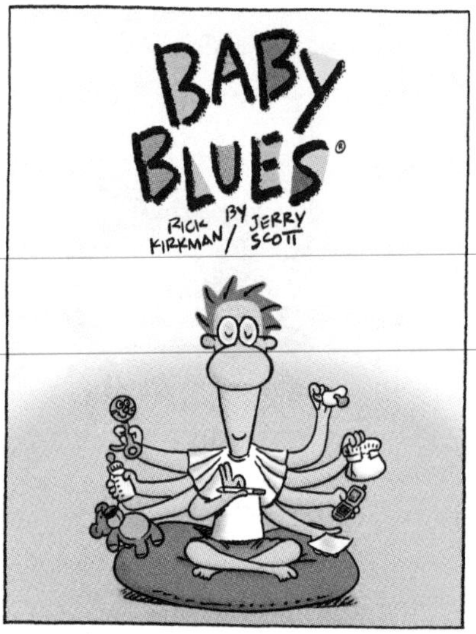
BABY BLUES®
RICK KIRKMAN / BY JERRY SCOTT

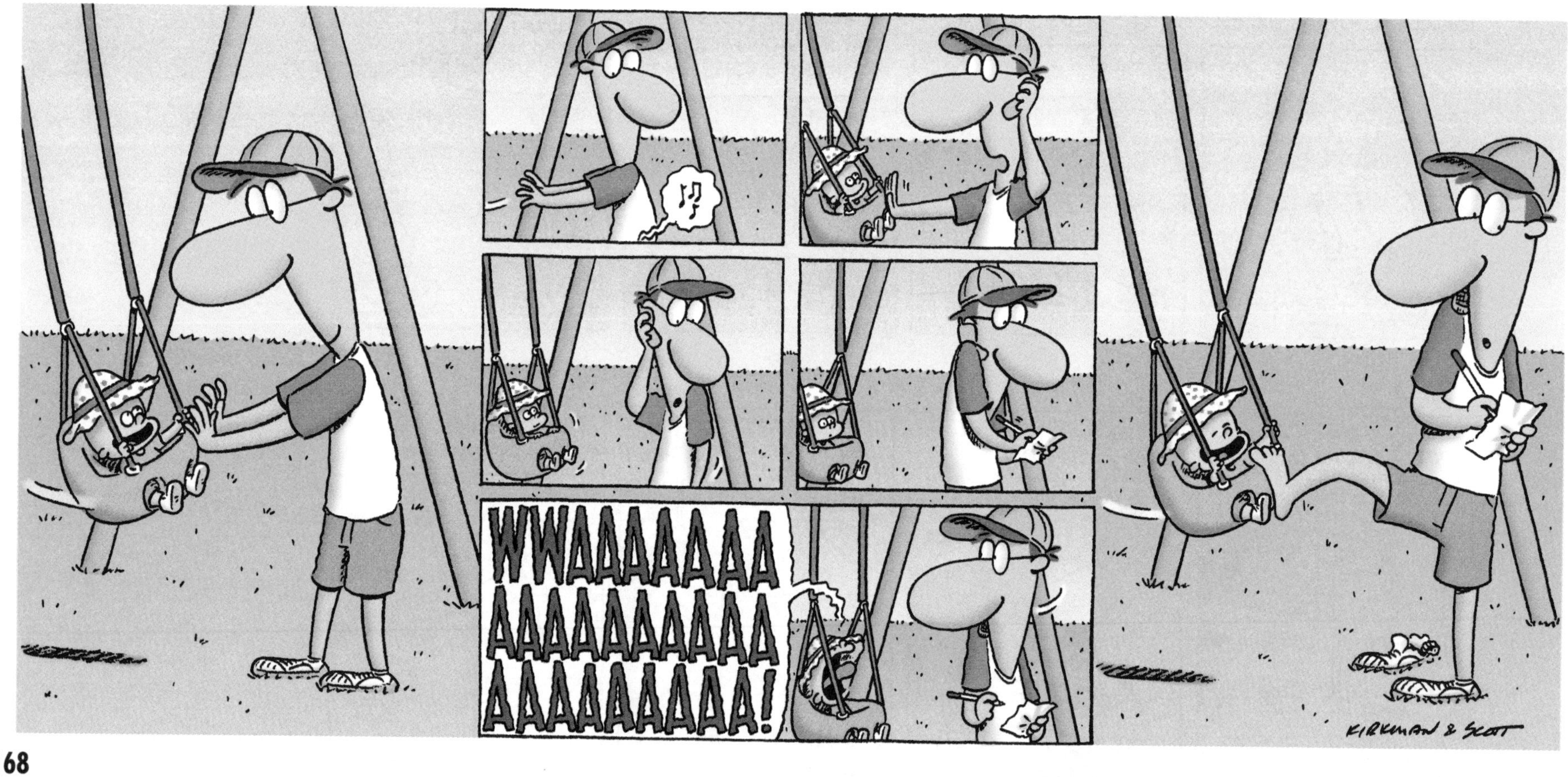
WWAAAAAAAA AAAAAAAAAA AAAAAAAAA!
KIRKMAN & SCOTT

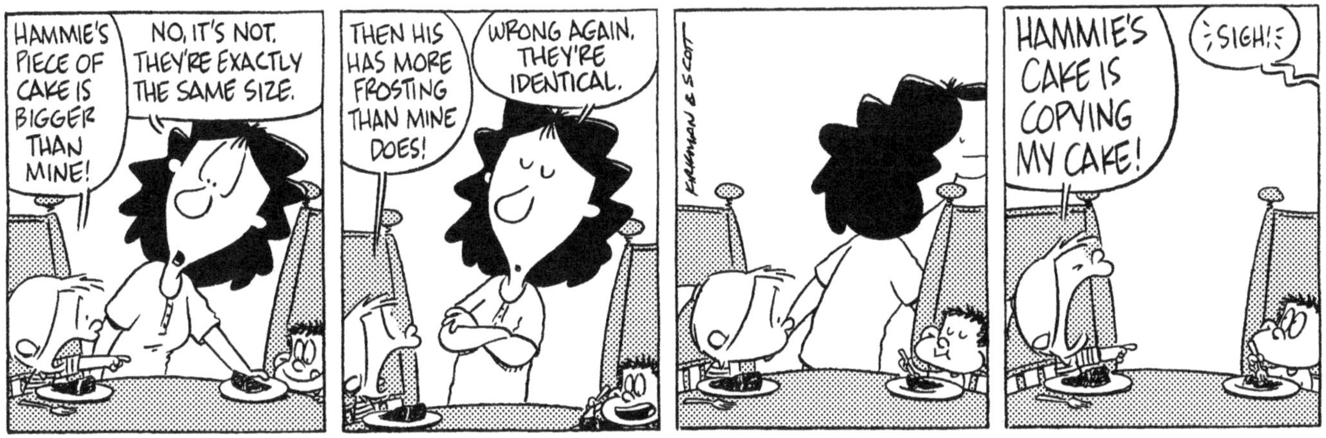
HAMMIE'S PIECE OF CAKE IS BIGGER THAN MINE!
NO, IT'S NOT. THEY'RE EXACTLY THE SAME SIZE.
THEN HIS HAS MORE FROSTING THAN MINE DOES!
WRONG AGAIN. THEY'RE IDENTICAL.
KIRKMAN & SCOTT
HAMMIE'S CAKE IS COPYING MY CAKE!
SIGH!

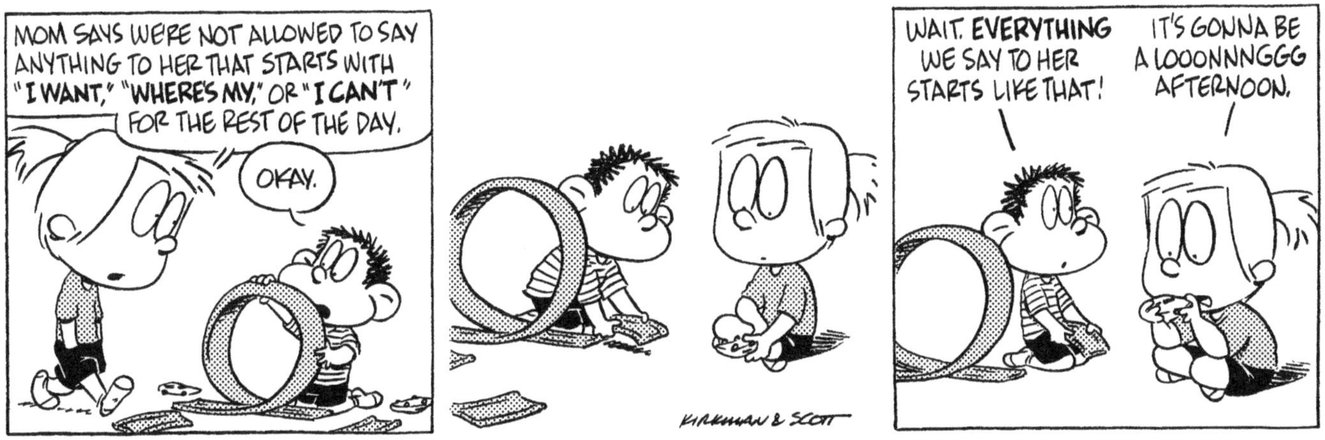
MOM SAYS WE'RE NOT ALLOWED TO SAY ANYTHING TO HER THAT STARTS WITH "I WANT," "WHERE'S MY," OR "I CAN'T" FOR THE REST OF THE DAY.
OKAY.
KIRKMAN & SCOTT
WAIT. EVERYTHING WE SAY TO HER STARTS LIKE THAT!
IT'S GONNA BE A LOOONNNGGG AFTERNOON.

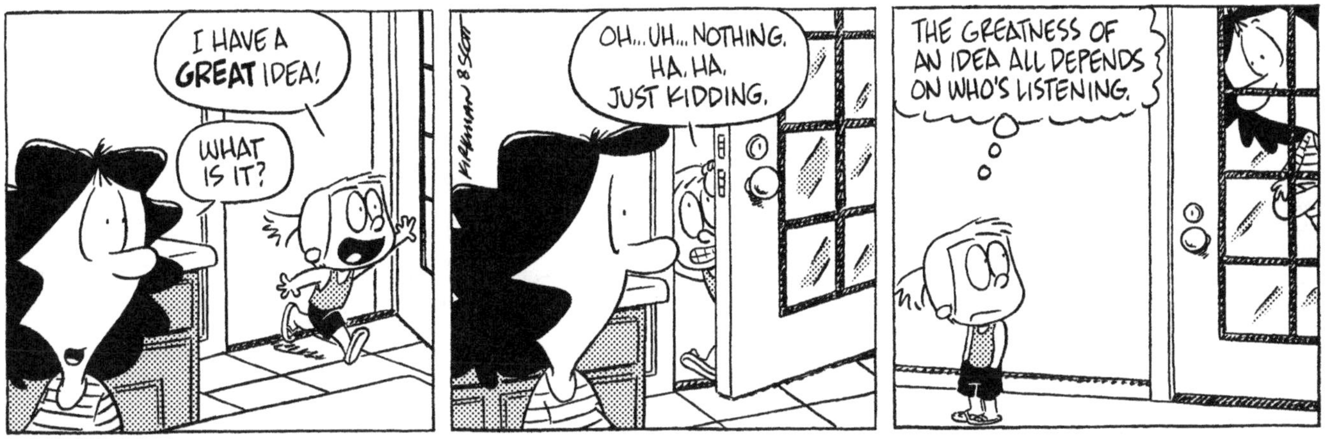
I HAVE A GREAT IDEA!
WHAT IS IT?
KIRKMAN & SCOTT
OH... UH... NOTHING. HA. HA. JUST KIDDING.
THE GREATNESS OF AN IDEA ALL DEPENDS ON WHO'S LISTENING.

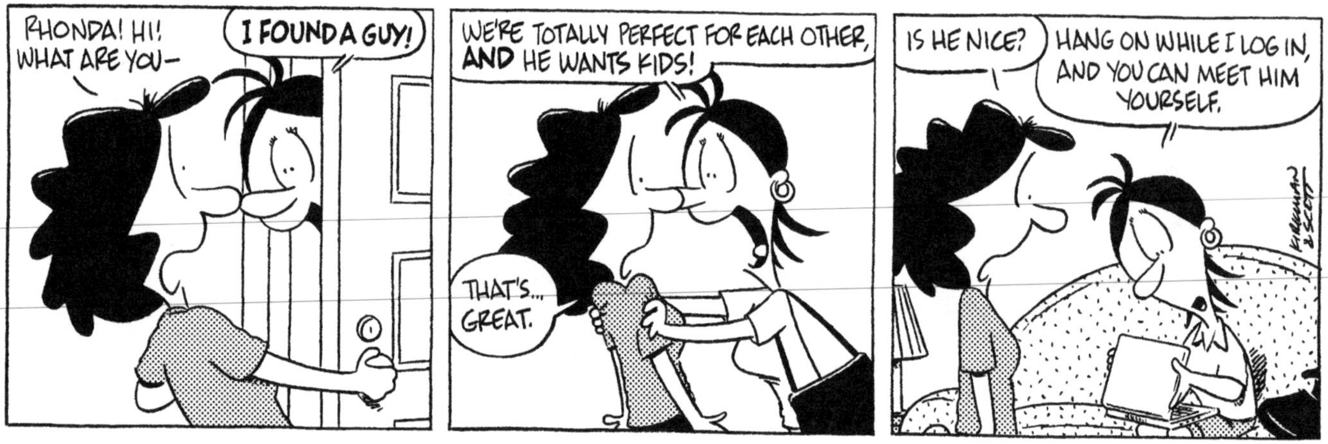
RHONDA! HI! WHAT ARE YOU—
I FOUND A GUY!
WE'RE TOTALLY PERFECT FOR EACH OTHER, AND HE WANTS KIDS!
THAT'S... GREAT.
IS HE NICE?
HANG ON WHILE I LOG IN, AND YOU CAN MEET HIM YOURSELF.
KIRKMAN & SCOTT

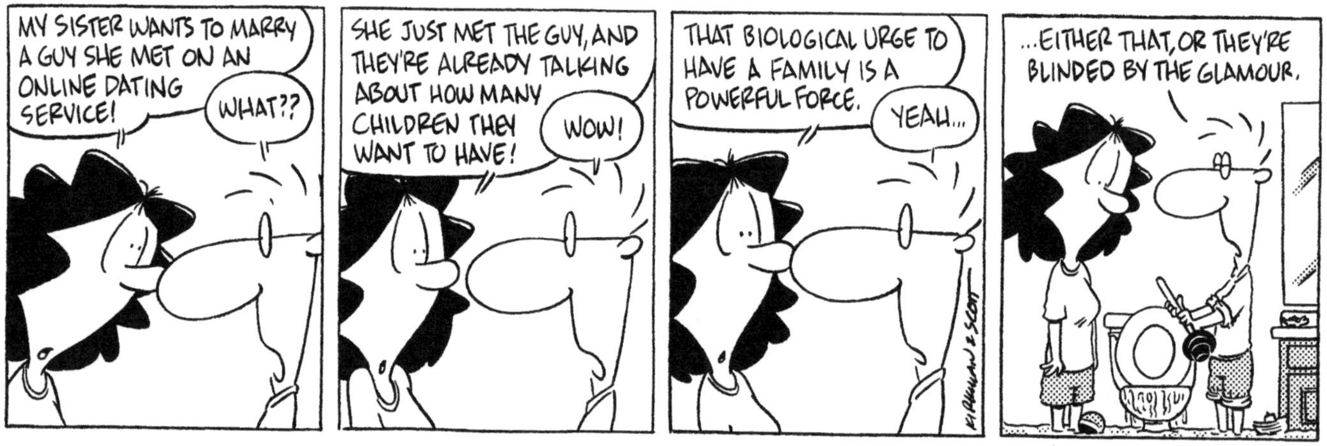
MY SISTER WANTS TO MARRY A GUY SHE MET ON AN ONLINE DATING SERVICE!
WHAT??
SHE JUST MET THE GUY, AND THEY'RE ALREADY TALKING ABOUT HOW MANY CHILDREN THEY WANT TO HAVE!
WOW!
THAT BIOLOGICAL URGE TO HAVE A FAMILY IS A POWERFUL FORCE.
YEAH...
KIRKMAN & SCOTT
...EITHER THAT, OR THEY'RE BLINDED BY THE GLAMOUR.

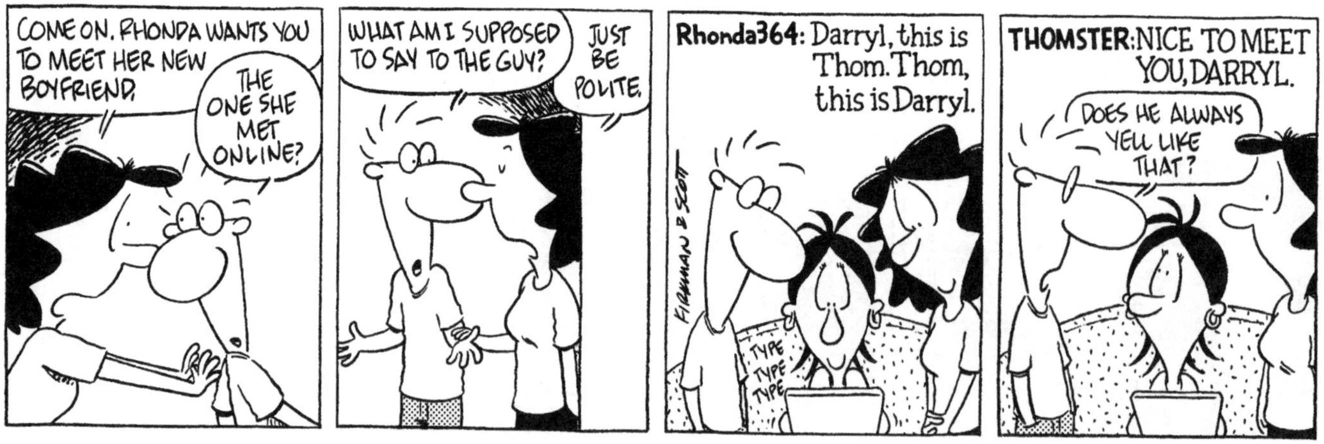
COME ON. RHONDA WANTS YOU TO MEET HER NEW BOYFRIEND.
THE ONE SHE MET ONLINE?
WHAT AM I SUPPOSED TO SAY TO THE GUY?
JUST BE POLITE.
Rhonda364: Darryl, this is Thom. Thom, this is Darryl.
KIRKMAN & SCOTT
TYPE TYPE TYPE
THOMSTER: NICE TO MEET YOU, DARRYL.
DOES HE ALWAYS YELL LIKE THAT?

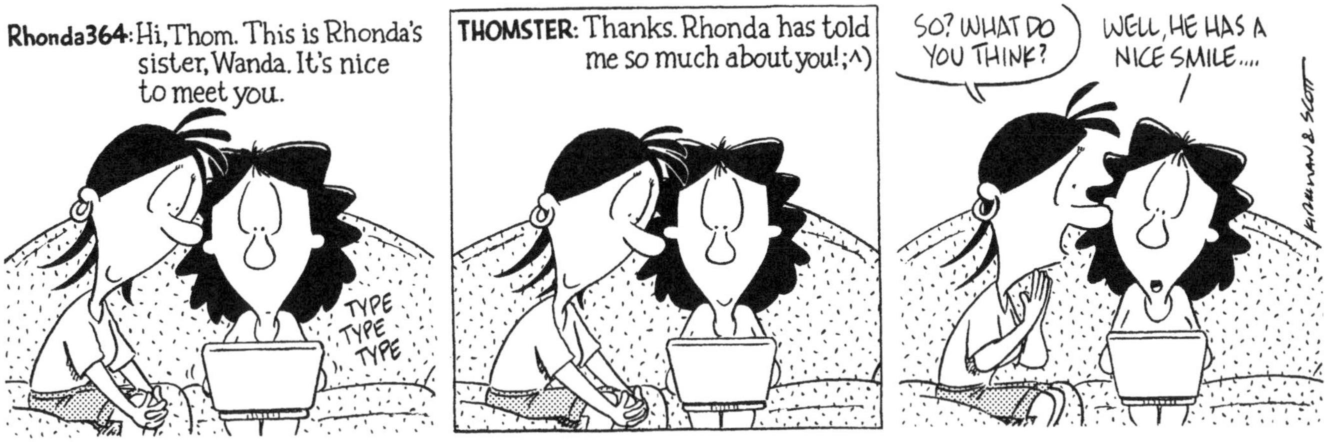
Rhonda364: Hi, Thom. This is Rhonda's sister, Wanda. It's nice to meet you.
TYPE TYPE TYPE
THOMSTER: Thanks. Rhonda has told me so much about you! ;^)
SO? WHAT DO YOU THINK?
WELL, HE HAS A NICE SMILE....
KIRKMAN & SCOTT

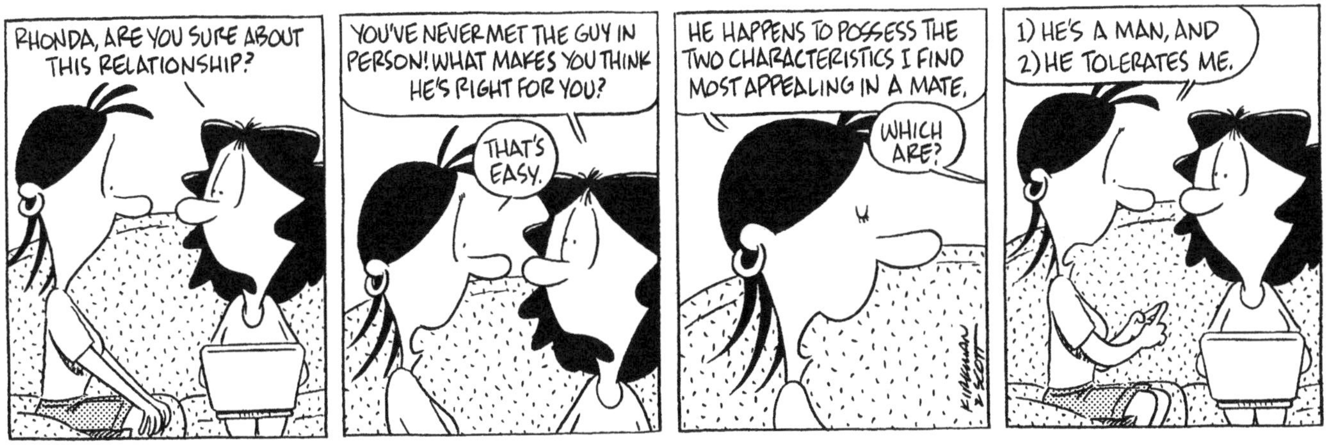
RHONDA, ARE YOU SURE ABOUT THIS RELATIONSHIP?
YOU'VE NEVER MET THE GUY IN PERSON! WHAT MAKES YOU THINK HE'S RIGHT FOR YOU?
THAT'S EASY.
HE HAPPENS TO POSSESS THE TWO CHARACTERISTICS I FIND MOST APPEALING IN A MATE.
WHICH ARE?
KIRKMAN & SCOTT
1) HE'S A MAN, AND
2) HE TOLERATES ME.

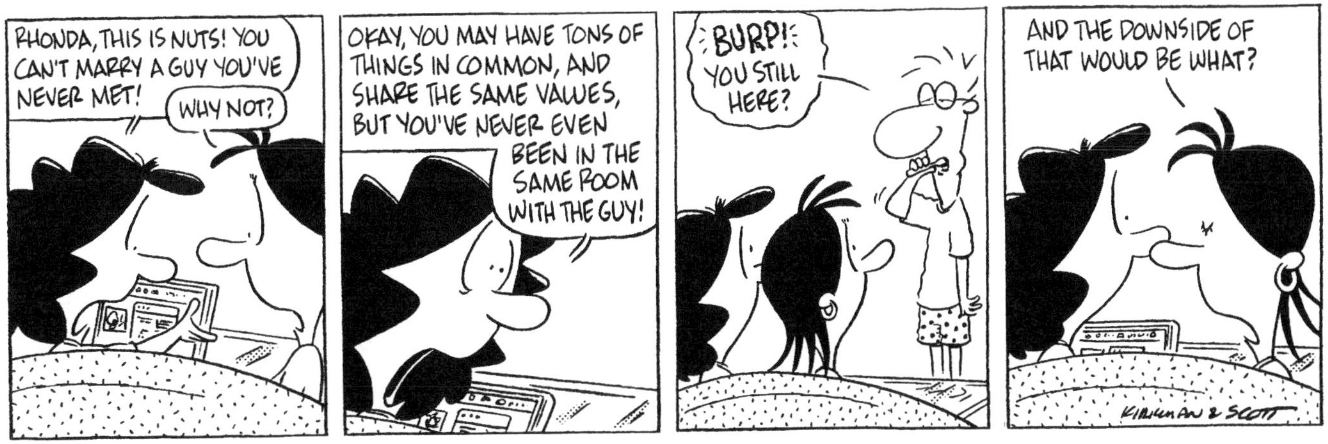
RHONDA, THIS IS NUTS! YOU CAN'T MARRY A GUY YOU'VE NEVER MET!
WHY NOT?
OKAY, YOU MAY HAVE TONS OF THINGS IN COMMON, AND SHARE THE SAME VALUES, BUT YOU'VE NEVER EVEN BEEN IN THE SAME ROOM WITH THE GUY!
BURP!
YOU STILL HERE?
AND THE DOWNSIDE OF THAT WOULD BE WHAT?
KIRKMAN & SCOTT

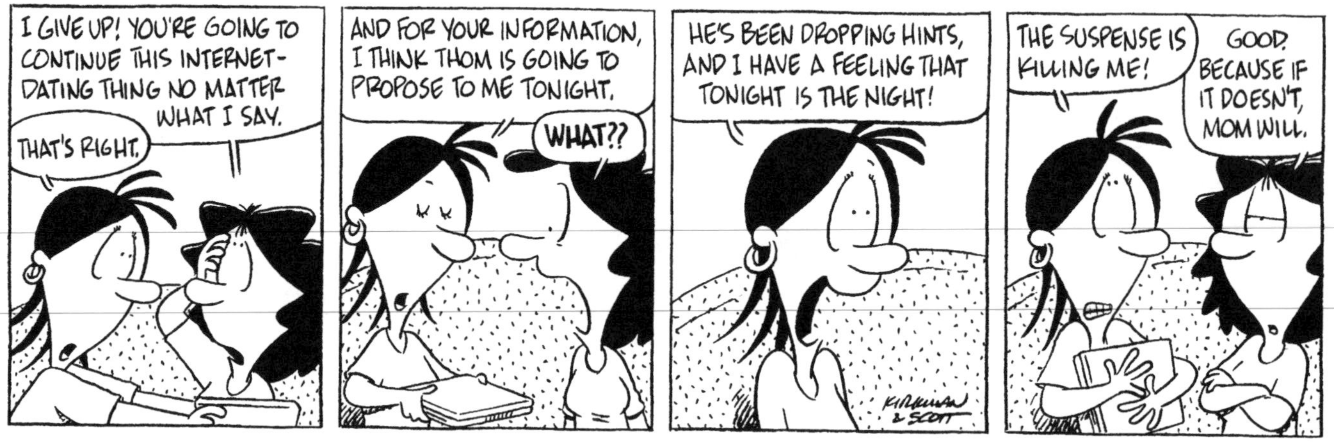
I GIVE UP! YOU'RE GOING TO CONTINUE THIS INTERNET-DATING THING NO MATTER WHAT I SAY.
THAT'S RIGHT.
AND FOR YOUR INFORMATION, I THINK THOM IS GOING TO PROPOSE TO ME TONIGHT.
WHAT??
HE'S BEEN DROPPING HINTS, AND I HAVE A FEELING THAT TONIGHT IS THE NIGHT!
KIRKMAN & SCOTT
THE SUSPENSE IS KILLING ME!
GOOD. BECAUSE IF IT DOESN'T, MOM WILL.

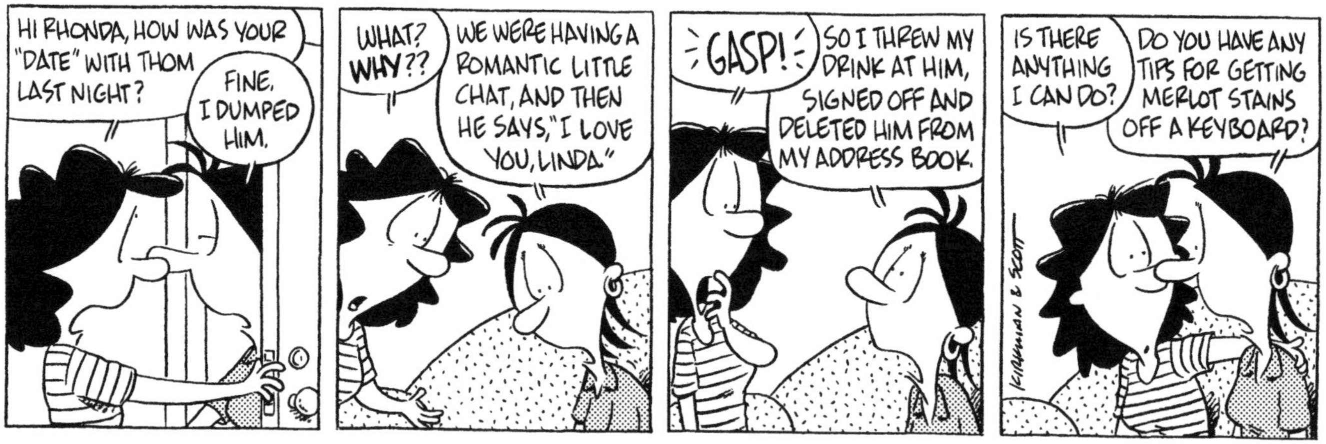
HI RHONDA, HOW WAS YOUR "DATE" WITH THOM LAST NIGHT?
FINE. I DUMPED HIM.
WHAT? WHY??
WE WERE HAVING A ROMANTIC LITTLE CHAT, AND THEN HE SAYS, "I LOVE YOU, LINDA."
GASP!
SO I THREW MY DRINK AT HIM, SIGNED OFF AND DELETED HIM FROM MY ADDRESS BOOK.
KIRKMAN & SCOTT
IS THERE ANYTHING I CAN DO?
DO YOU HAVE ANY TIPS FOR GETTING MERLOT STAINS OFF A KEYBOARD?

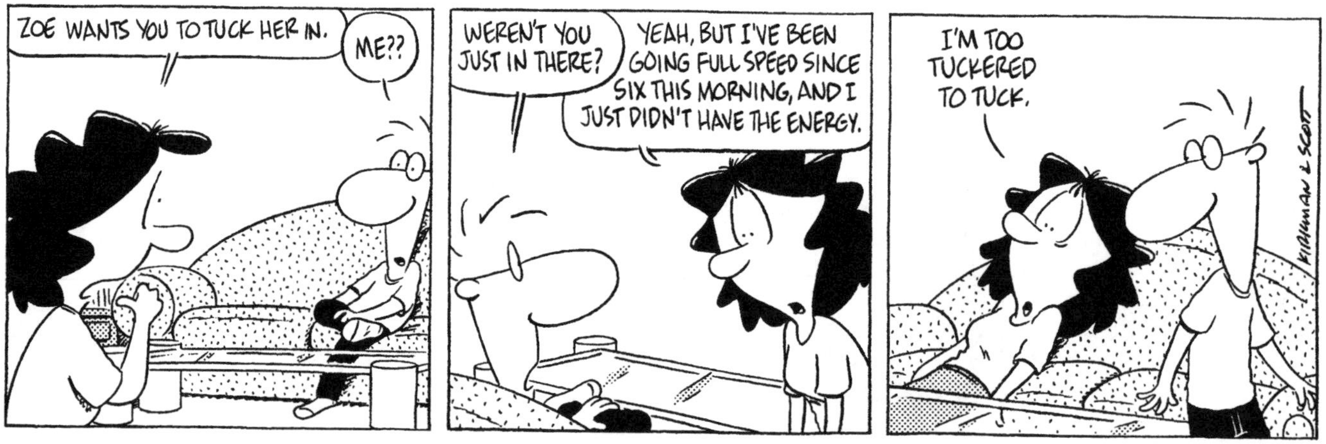
ZOE WANTS YOU TO TUCK HER IN.
ME??
WEREN'T YOU JUST IN THERE?
YEAH, BUT I'VE BEEN GOING FULL SPEED SINCE SIX THIS MORNING, AND I JUST DIDN'T HAVE THE ENERGY.
I'M TOO TUCKERED TO TUCK.
KIRKMAN & SCOTT

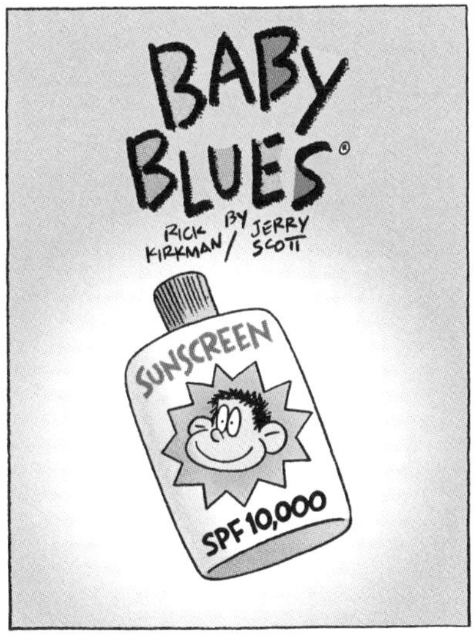
BABY BLUES®
BY RICK KIRKMAN / JERRY SCOTT
SUNSCREEN
SPF 10,000

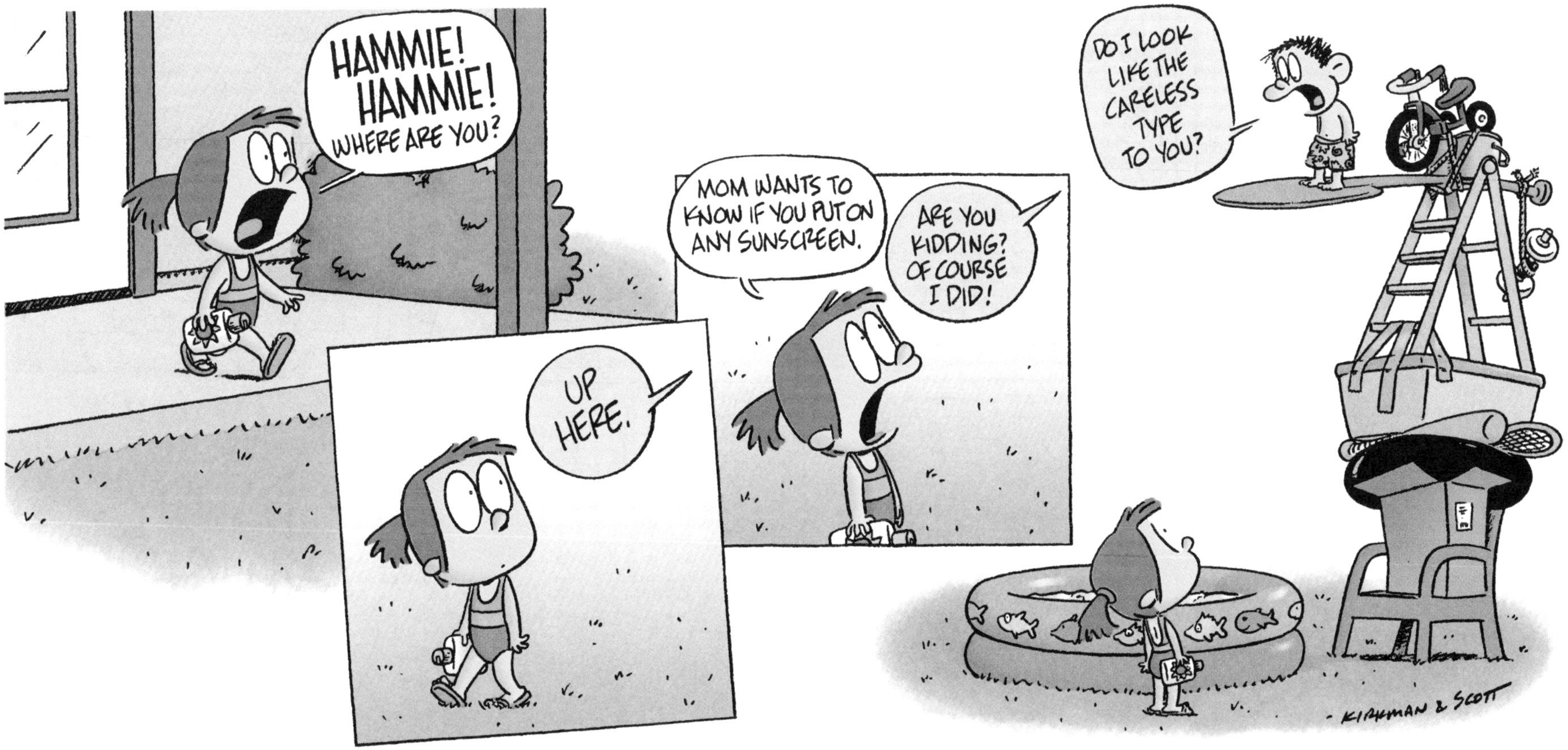
HAMMIE! HAMMIE! WHERE ARE YOU?
UP HERE.
MOM WANTS TO KNOW IF YOU PUT ON ANY SUNSCREEN.
ARE YOU KIDDING? OF COURSE I DID!
DO I LOOK LIKE THE CARELESS TYPE TO YOU?
KIRKMAN & SCOTT

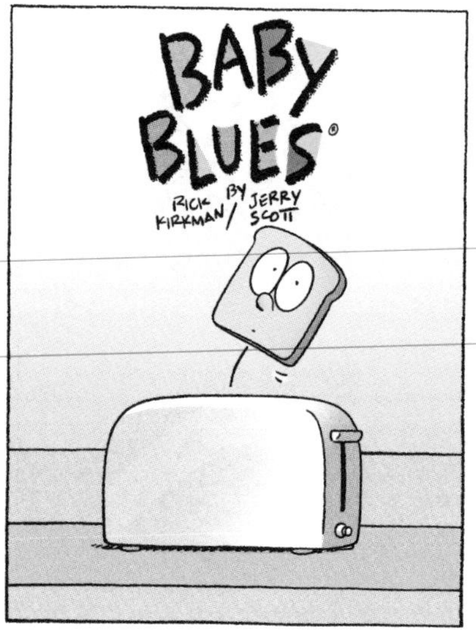
BABY BLUES®
RICK KIRKMAN / BY JERRY SCOTT

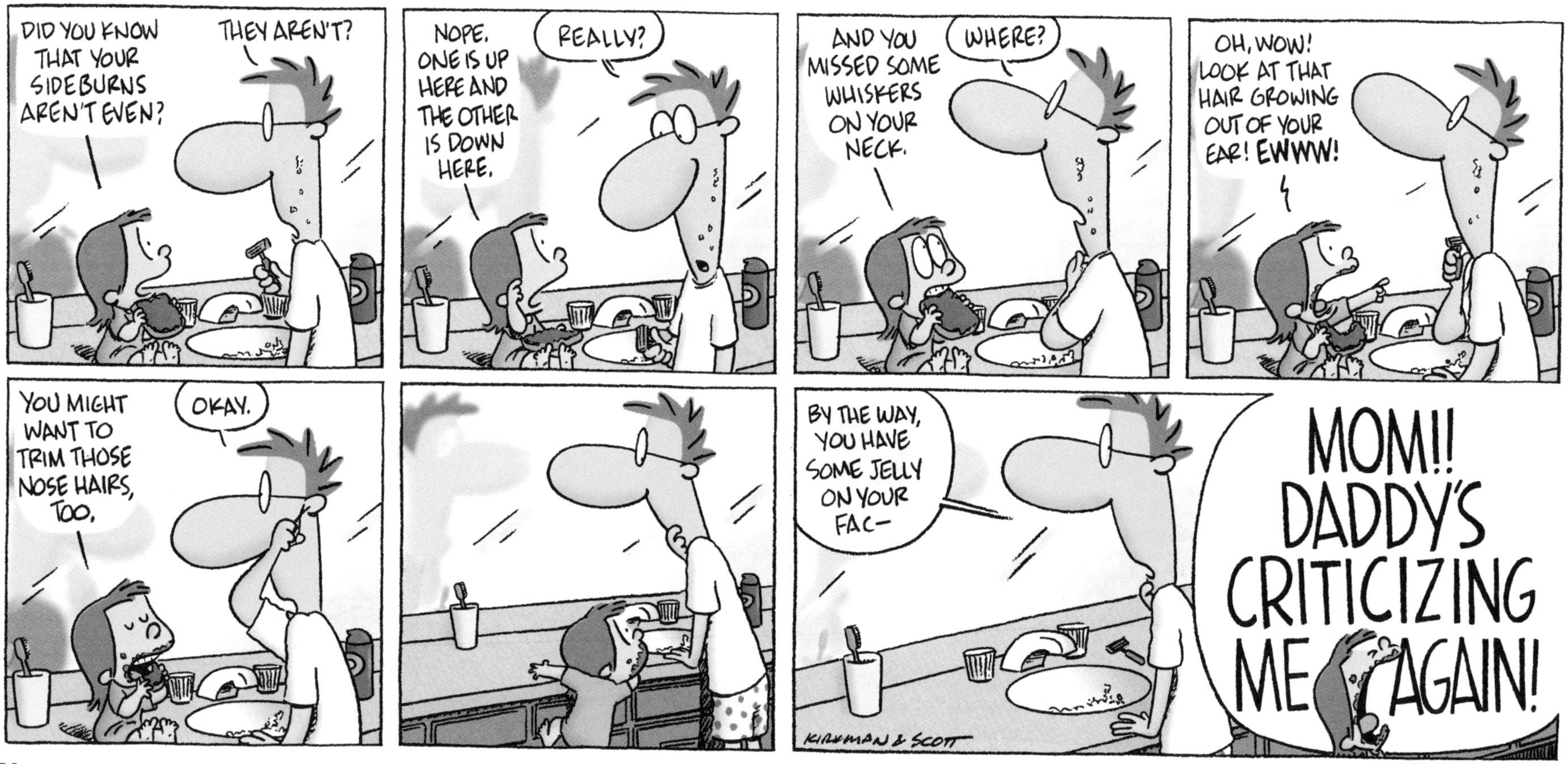
DID YOU KNOW THAT YOUR SIDEBURNS AREN'T EVEN?
THEY AREN'T?
NOPE. ONE IS UP HERE AND THE OTHER IS DOWN HERE.
REALLY?
AND YOU MISSED SOME WHISKERS ON YOUR NECK.
WHERE?
OH, WOW! LOOK AT THAT HAIR GROWING OUT OF YOUR EAR! EWWW!
YOU MIGHT WANT TO TRIM THOSE NOSE HAIRS, TOO.
OKAY.
BY THE WAY, YOU HAVE SOME JELLY ON YOUR FAC—
MOM!! DADDY'S CRITICIZING ME AGAIN!
KIRKMAN & SCOTT

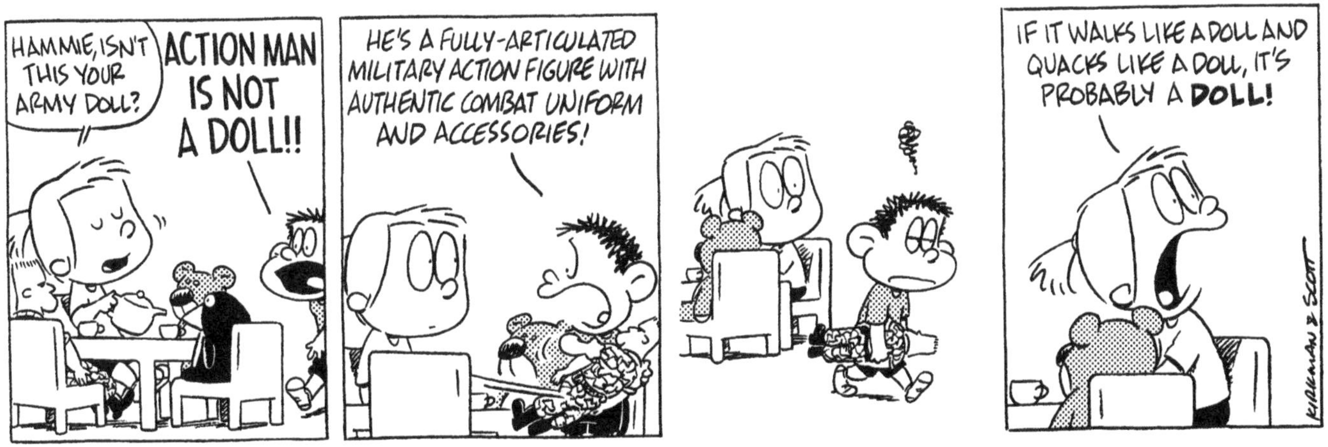
HAMMIE, ISN'T THIS YOUR ARMY DOLL?
ACTION MAN IS NOT A DOLL!!
HE'S A FULLY-ARTICULATED MILITARY ACTION FIGURE WITH AUTHENTIC COMBAT UNIFORM AND ACCESSORIES!
IF IT WALKS LIKE A DOLL AND QUACKS LIKE A DOLL, IT'S PROBABLY A **DOLL!**
KIRKMAN & SCOTT

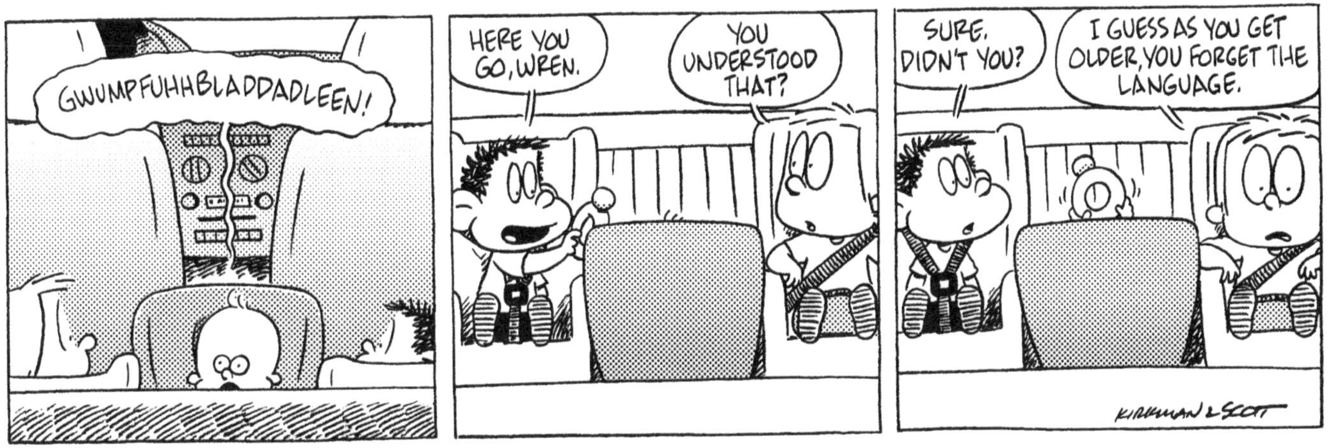
GWUMPFUHHBLADDADLEEN!
HERE YOU GO, WREN.
YOU UNDERSTOOD THAT?
SURE. DIDN'T YOU?
I GUESS AS YOU GET OLDER, YOU FORGET THE LANGUAGE.
KIRKMAN & SCOTT

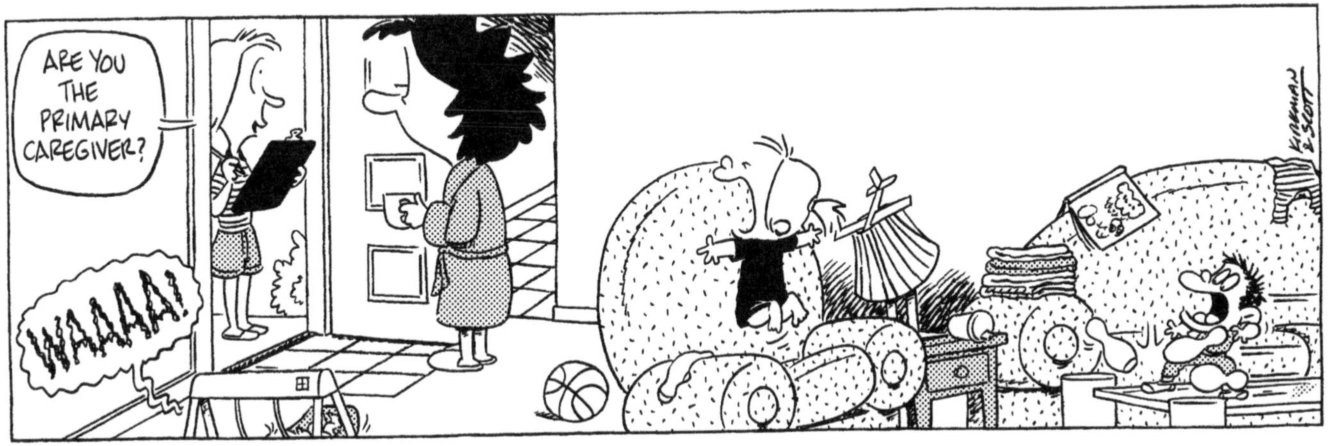
ARE YOU THE PRIMARY CAREGIVER?
WAAAA!
KIRKMAN & SCOTT

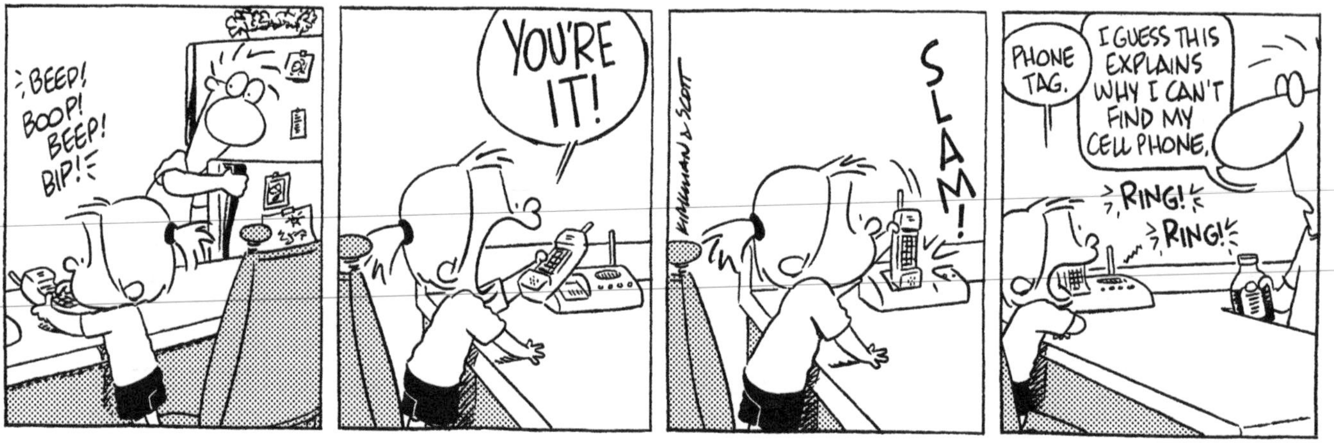

BEEP! BOOP! BEEP! BIP!
YOU'RE IT!
SLAM!
KIRKMAN & SCOTT
PHONE TAG.
I GUESS THIS EXPLAINS WHY I CAN'T FIND MY CELL PHONE.
RING! RING!

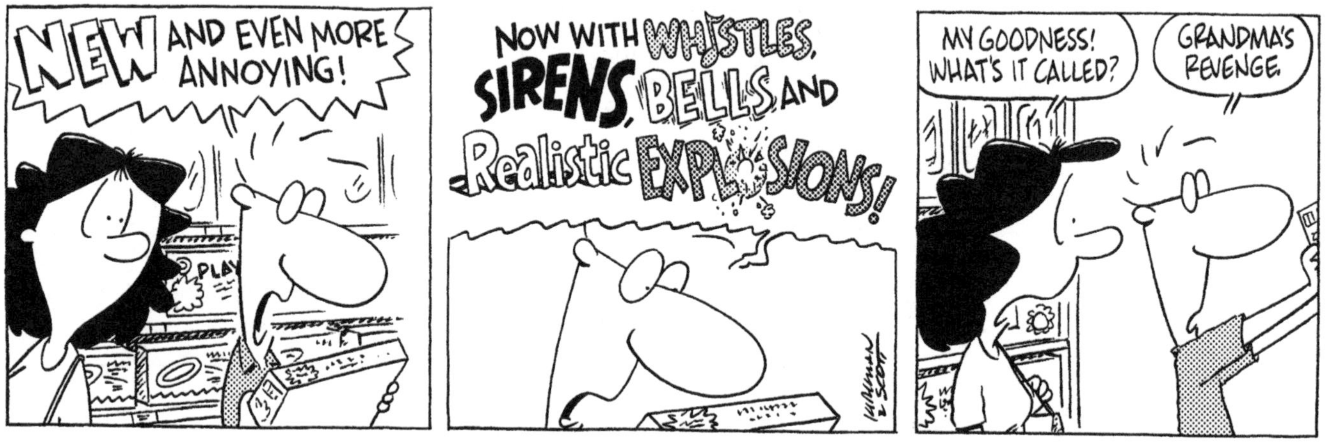

NEW AND EVEN MORE ANNOYING!
NOW WITH WHISTLES, SIRENS, BELLS AND Realistic EXPLOSIONS!
KIRKMAN & SCOTT
MY GOODNESS! WHAT'S IT CALLED?
GRANDMA'S REVENGE.

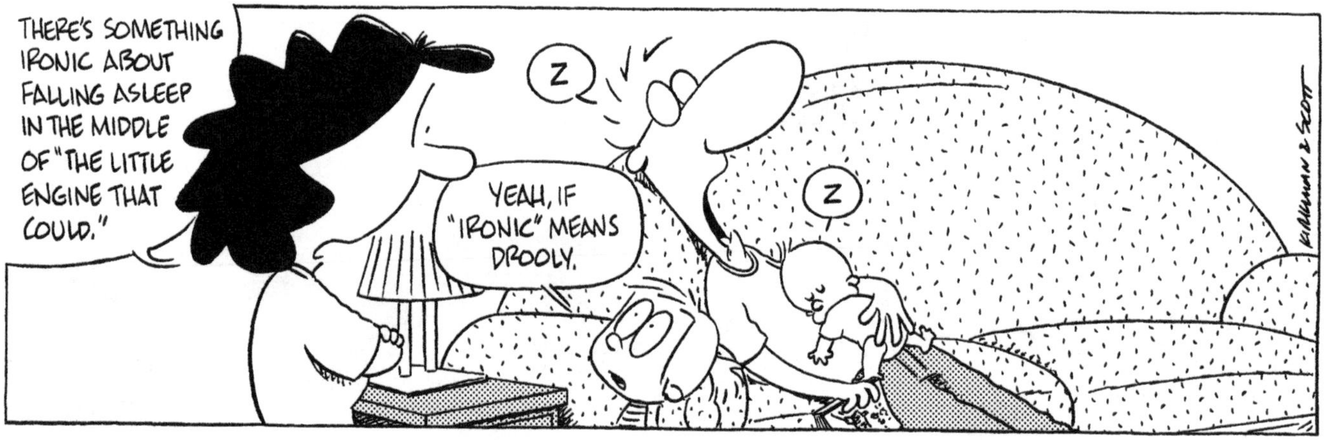

THERE'S SOMETHING IRONIC ABOUT FALLING ASLEEP IN THE MIDDLE OF "THE LITTLE ENGINE THAT COULD."
Z
Z
YEAH, IF "IRONIC" MEANS DROOLY.
KIRKMAN & SCOTT

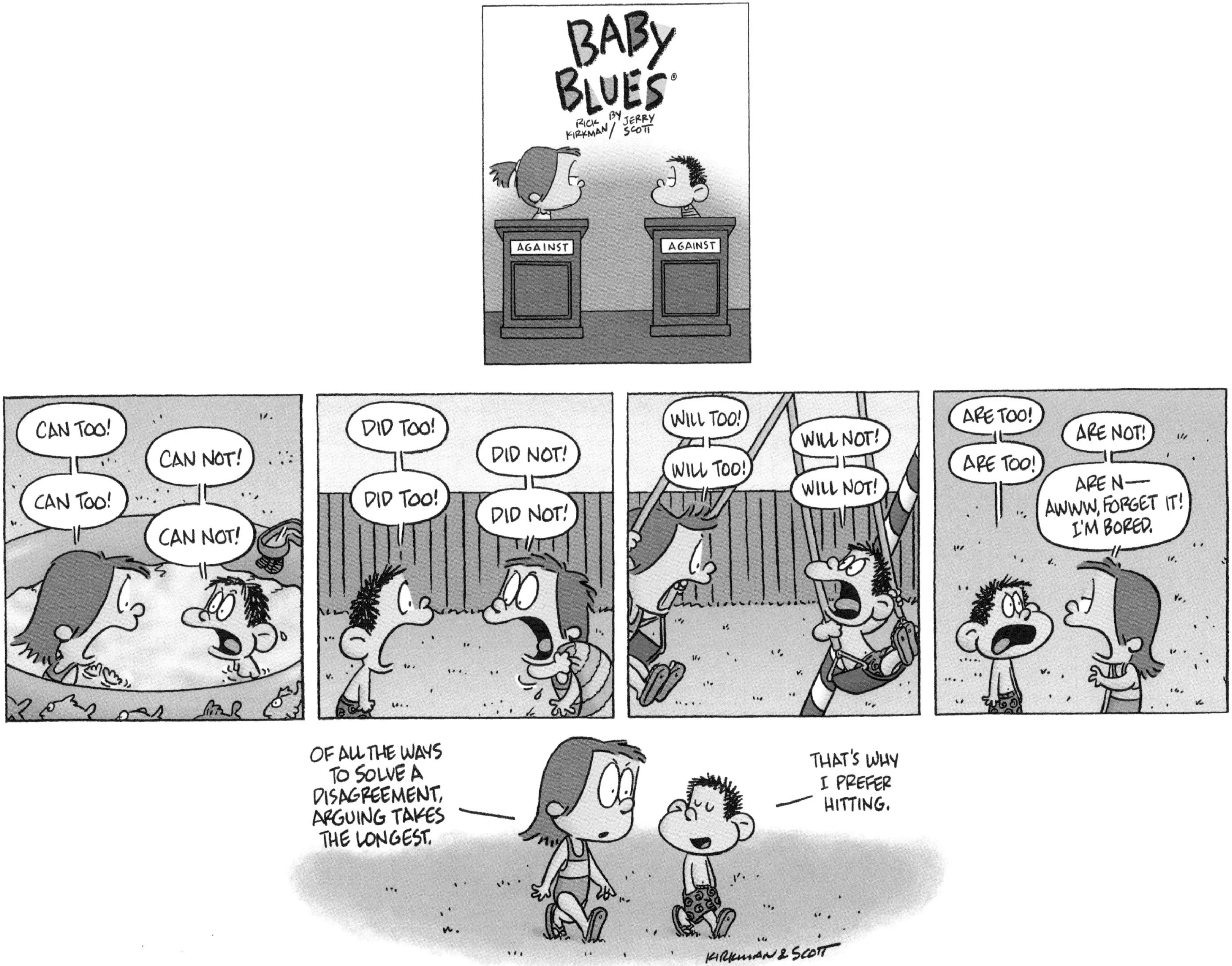
BABY BLUES®
BY RICK KIRKMAN / JERRY SCOTT
AGAINST
AGAINST
CAN TOO!
CAN NOT!
CAN TOO!
CAN NOT!
DID TOO!
DID NOT!
DID TOO!
DID NOT!
WILL TOO!
WILL NOT!
WILL TOO!
WILL NOT!
ARE TOO!
ARE NOT!
ARE TOO!
ARE N— AWWW, FORGET IT! I'M BORED.
OF ALL THE WAYS TO SOLVE A DISAGREEMENT, ARGUING TAKES THE LONGEST.
THAT'S WHY I PREFER HITTING.
KIRKMAN & SCOTT

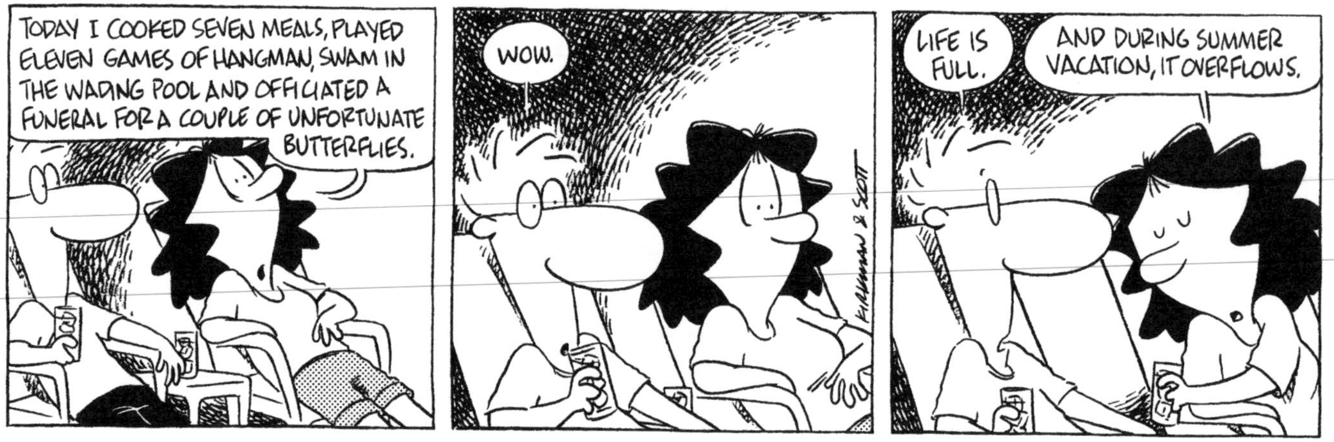
TODAY I COOKED SEVEN MEALS, PLAYED ELEVEN GAMES OF HANGMAN, SWAM IN THE WADING POOL AND OFFICIATED A FUNERAL FOR A COUPLE OF UNFORTUNATE BUTTERFLIES.
WOW.
LIFE IS FULL.
AND DURING SUMMER VACATION, IT OVERFLOWS.
KIRKMAN & SCOTT

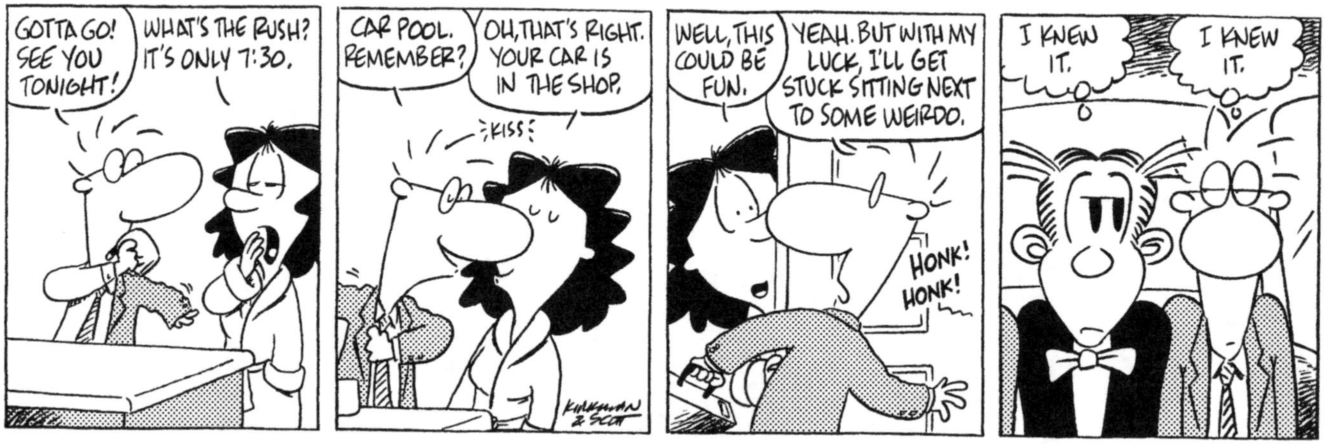
GOTTA GO! SEE YOU TONIGHT!
WHAT'S THE RUSH? IT'S ONLY 7:30.
CAR POOL. REMEMBER?
OH, THAT'S RIGHT. YOUR CAR IS IN THE SHOP.
KISS
KIRKMAN & SCOTT
WELL, THIS COULD BE FUN.
YEAH. BUT WITH MY LUCK, I'LL GET STUCK SITTING NEXT TO SOME WEIRDO.
HONK! HONK!
I KNEW IT.
I KNEW IT.

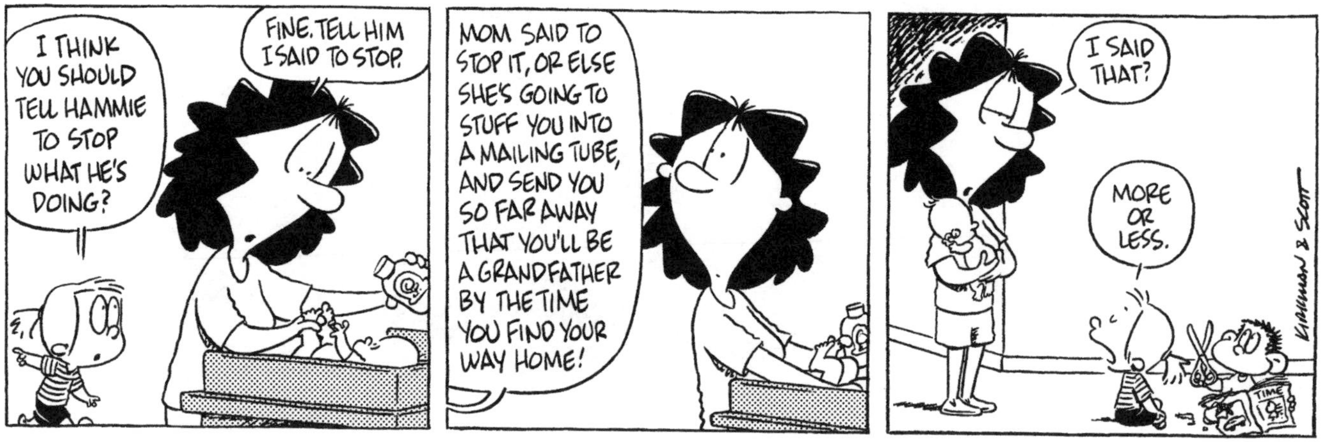
I THINK YOU SHOULD TELL HAMMIE TO STOP WHAT HE'S DOING?
FINE. TELL HIM I SAID TO STOP.
MOM SAID TO STOP IT, OR ELSE SHE'S GOING TO STUFF YOU INTO A MAILING TUBE, AND SEND YOU SO FAR AWAY THAT YOU'LL BE A GRANDFATHER BY THE TIME YOU FIND YOUR WAY HOME!
I SAID THAT?
MORE OR LESS.
KIRKMAN & SCOTT

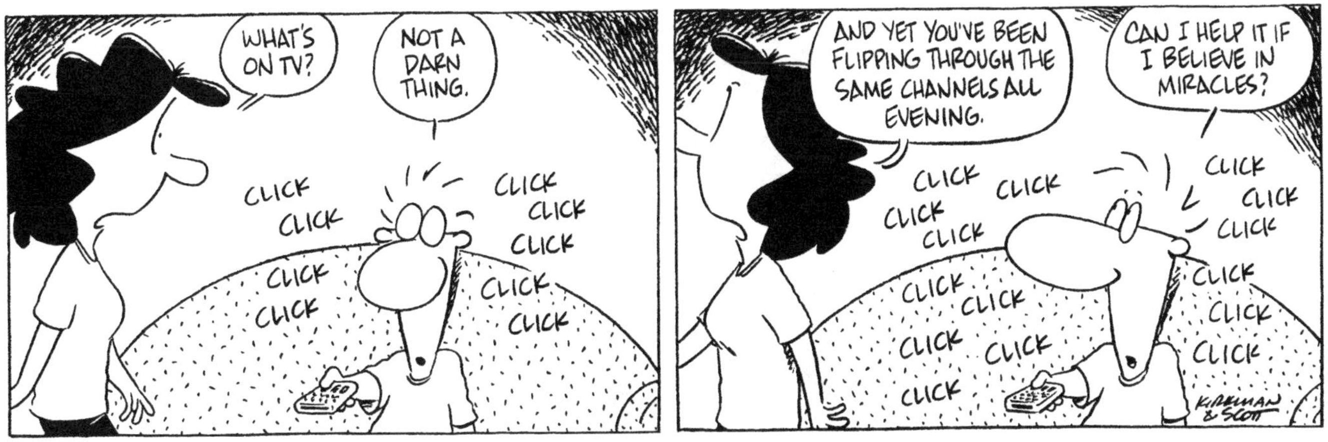
WHAT'S ON TV?
NOT A DARN THING.
CLICK CLICK CLICK CLICK CLICK CLICK CLICK CLICK CLICK CLICK
AND YET YOU'VE BEEN FLIPPING THROUGH THE SAME CHANNELS ALL EVENING.
CAN I HELP IT IF I BELIEVE IN MIRACLES?
CLICK CLICK CLICK CLICK CLICK CLICK CLICK CLICK CLICK CLICK CLICK CLICK CLICK CLICK
KIRKMAN & SCOTT

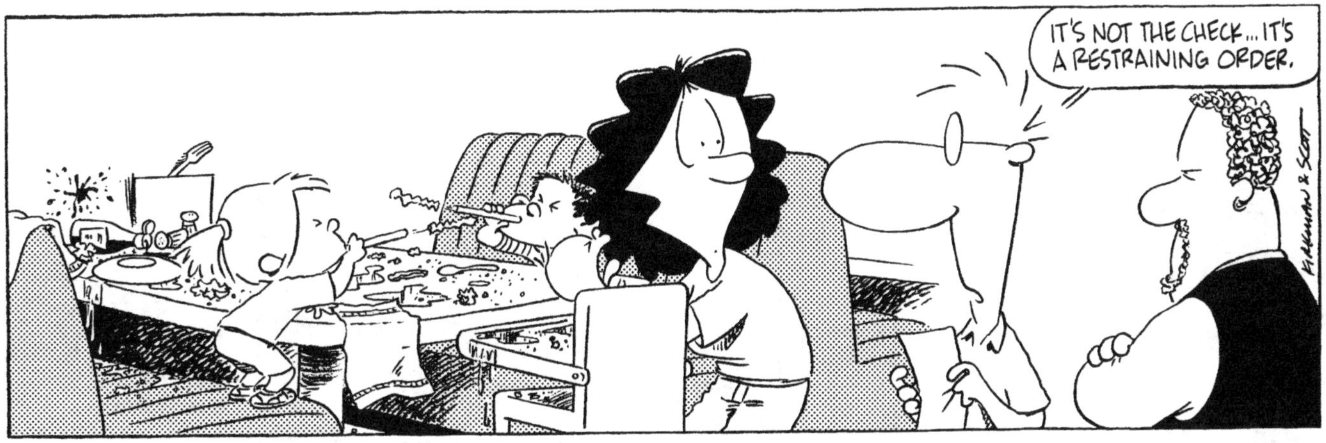
IT'S NOT THE CHECK... IT'S A RESTRAINING ORDER.
KIRKMAN & SCOTT

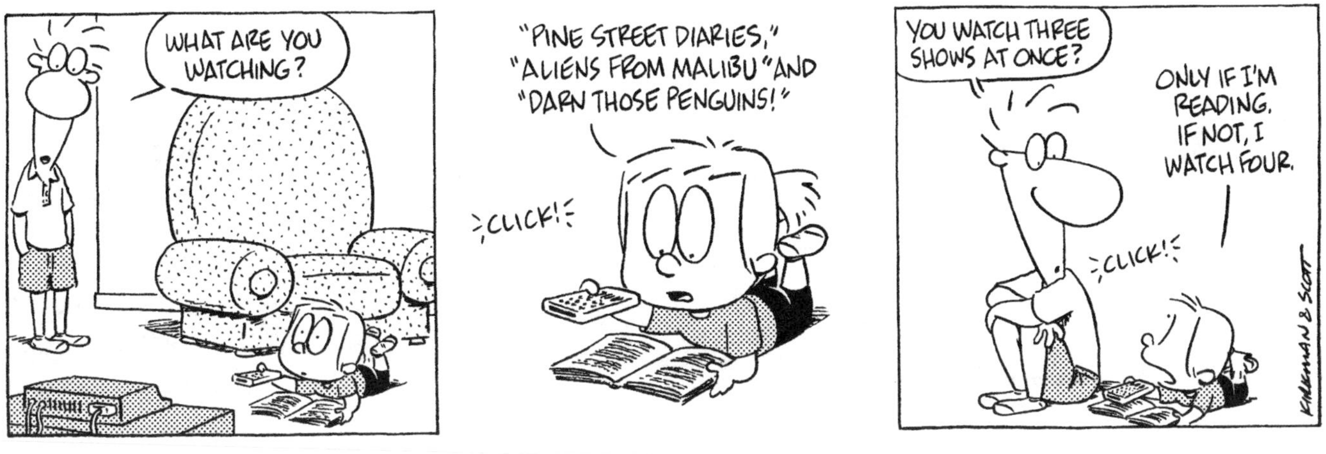
WHAT ARE YOU WATCHING?
"PINE STREET DIARIES," "ALIENS FROM MALIBU" AND "DARN THOSE PENGUINS!"
CLICK!
YOU WATCH THREE SHOWS AT ONCE?
ONLY IF I'M READING. IF NOT, I WATCH FOUR.
CLICK!
KIRKMAN & SCOTT

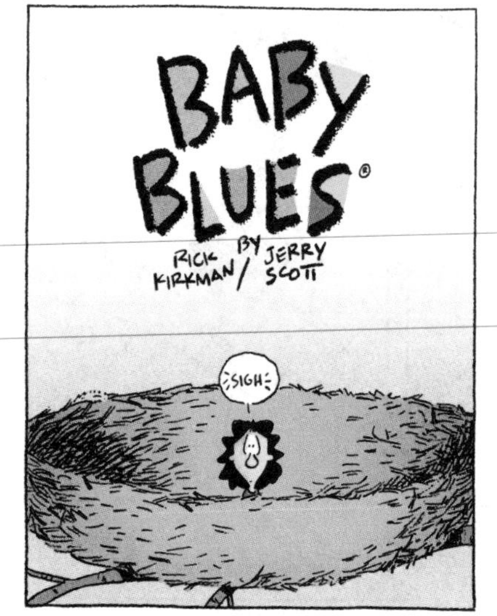
BABY BLUES®
BY RICK KIRKMAN / JERRY SCOTT
SIGH

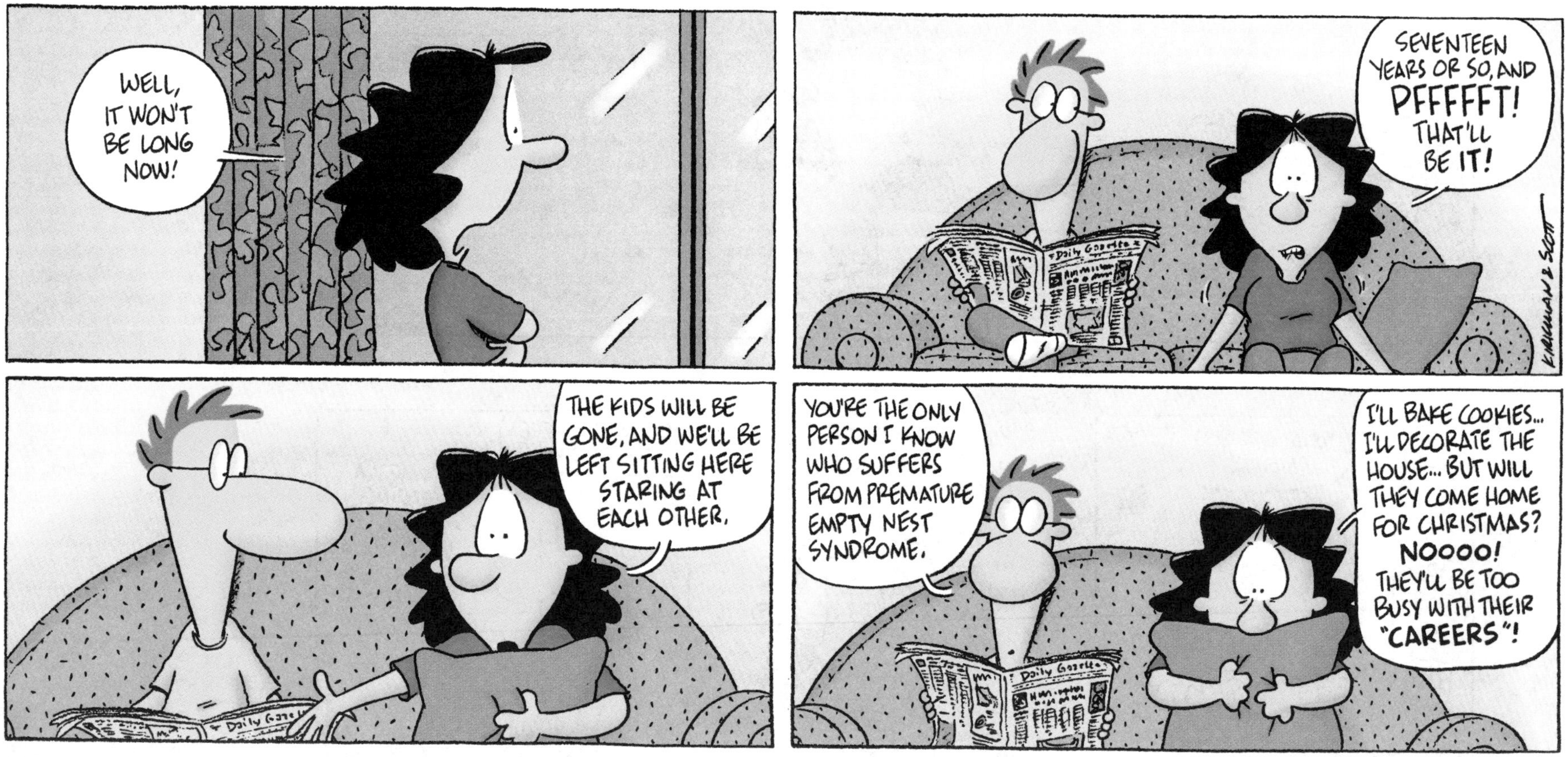
WELL, IT WON'T BE LONG NOW!
SEVENTEEN YEARS OR SO, AND PFFFFFT! THAT'LL BE IT!
KIRKMAN & SCOTT
THE KIDS WILL BE GONE, AND WE'LL BE LEFT SITTING HERE STARING AT EACH OTHER.
YOU'RE THE ONLY PERSON I KNOW WHO SUFFERS FROM PREMATURE EMPTY NEST SYNDROME.
I'LL BAKE COOKIES... I'LL DECORATE THE HOUSE... BUT WILL THEY COME HOME FOR CHRISTMAS? NOOOO! THEY'LL BE TOO BUSY WITH THEIR "CAREERS"!

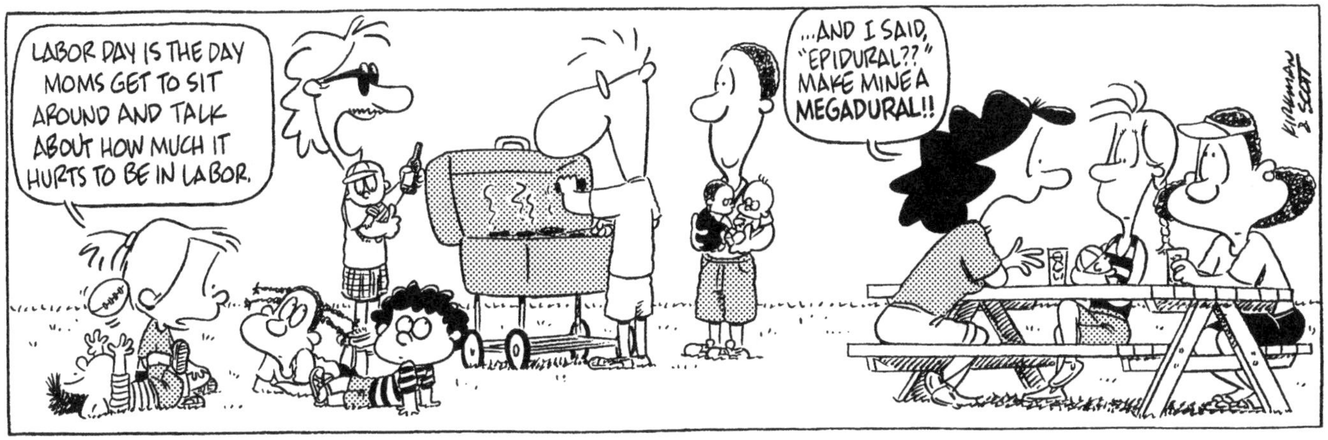
LABOR DAY IS THE DAY MOMS GET TO SIT AROUND AND TALK ABOUT HOW MUCH IT HURTS TO BE IN LABOR.
...AND I SAID, "EPIDURAL??" MAKE MINE A MEGADURAL!!
KIRKMAN & SCOTT

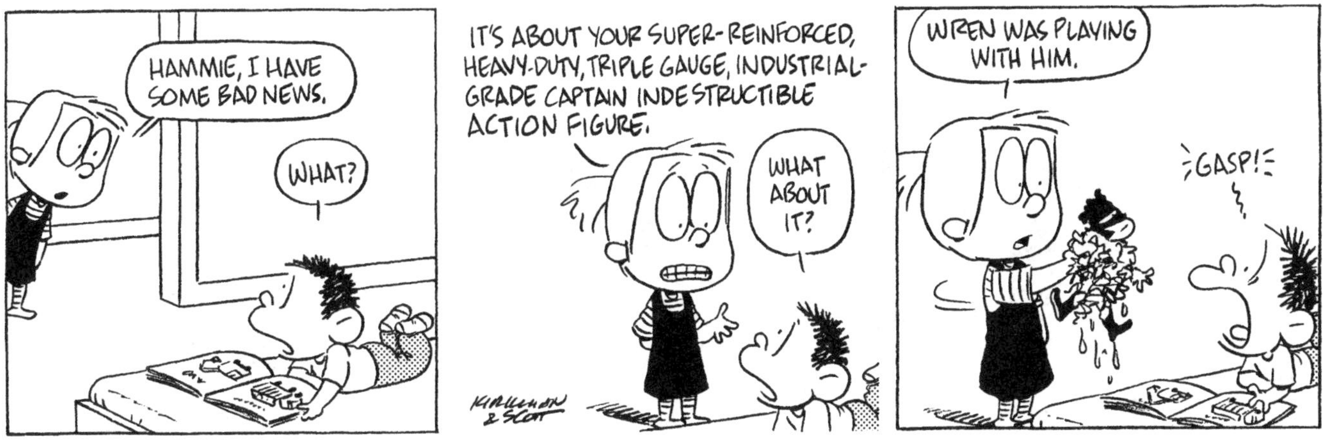
HAMMIE, I HAVE SOME BAD NEWS.
WHAT?
IT'S ABOUT YOUR SUPER-REINFORCED, HEAVY-DUTY, TRIPLE GAUGE, INDUSTRIAL-GRADE CAPTAIN INDESTRUCTIBLE ACTION FIGURE.
WHAT ABOUT IT?
KIRKMAN & SCOTT
WREN WAS PLAYING WITH HIM.
GASP!

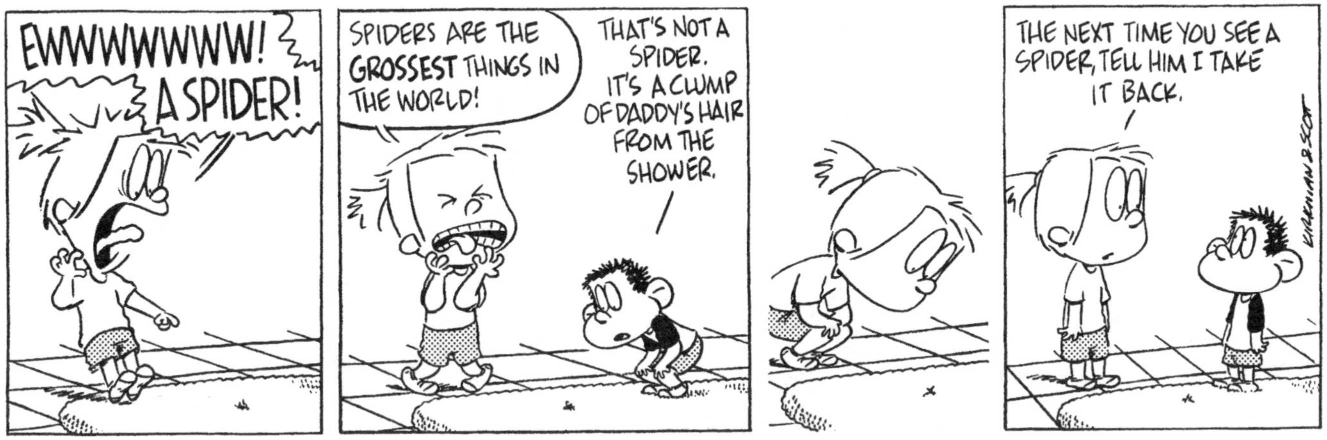
EWWWWWWW! A SPIDER!
SPIDERS ARE THE GROSSEST THINGS IN THE WORLD!
THAT'S NOT A SPIDER. IT'S A CLUMP OF DADDY'S HAIR FROM THE SHOWER.
THE NEXT TIME YOU SEE A SPIDER, TELL HIM I TAKE IT BACK.
KIRKMAN & SCOTT

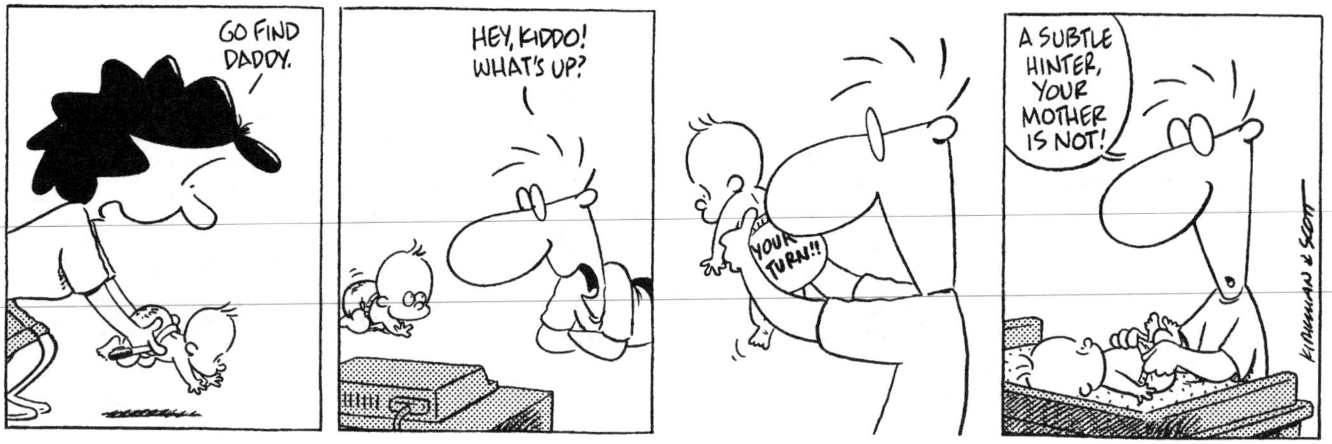
GO FIND DADDY.
HEY, KIDDO! WHAT'S UP?
YOUR TURN!!
A SUBTLE HINTER, YOUR MOTHER IS NOT!
KIRKMAN & SCOTT

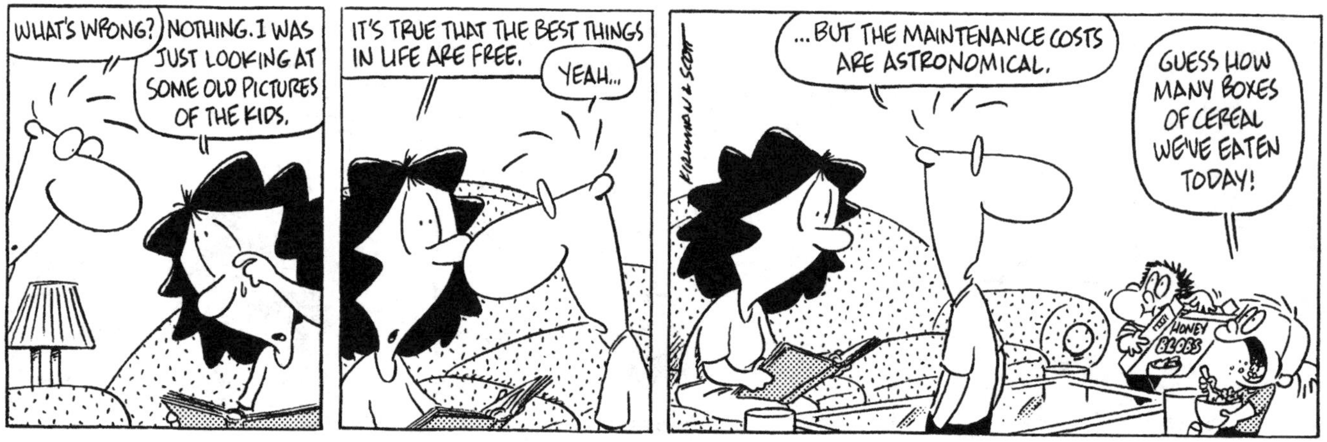
WHAT'S WRONG?
NOTHING. I WAS JUST LOOKING AT SOME OLD PICTURES OF THE KIDS.
IT'S TRUE THAT THE BEST THINGS IN LIFE ARE FREE.
YEAH...
KIRKMAN & SCOTT
...BUT THE MAINTENANCE COSTS ARE ASTRONOMICAL.
GUESS HOW MANY BOXES OF CEREAL WE'VE EATEN TODAY!
HONEY BLOBS

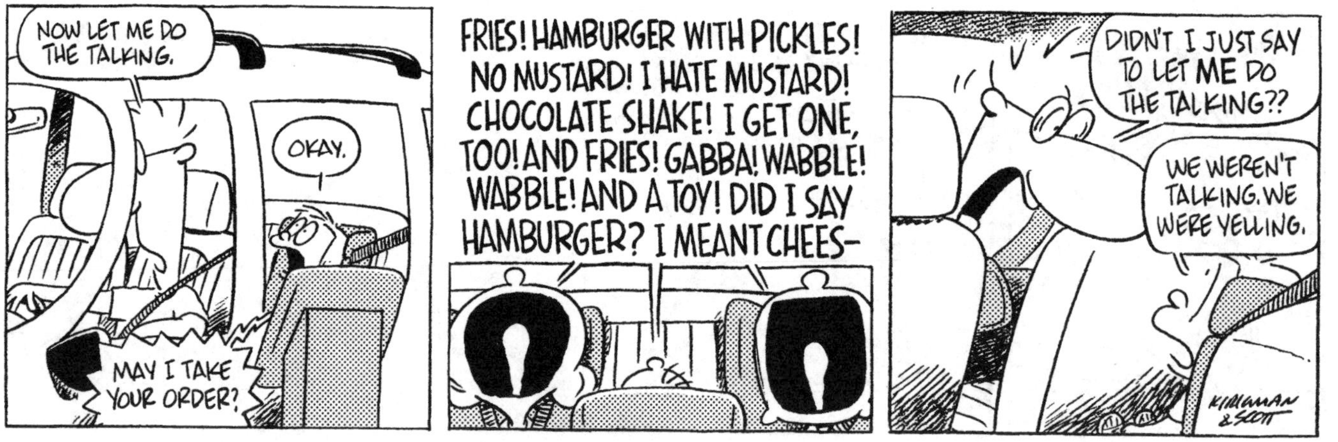
NOW LET ME DO THE TALKING.
OKAY.
MAY I TAKE YOUR ORDER?
FRIES! HAMBURGER WITH PICKLES! NO MUSTARD! I HATE MUSTARD! CHOCOLATE SHAKE! I GET ONE, TOO! AND FRIES! GABBA! WABBLE! WABBLE! AND A TOY! DID I SAY HAMBURGER? I MEANT CHEES–
DIDN'T I JUST SAY TO LET ME DO THE TALKING??
WE WEREN'T TALKING. WE WERE YELLING.
KIRKMAN & SCOTT

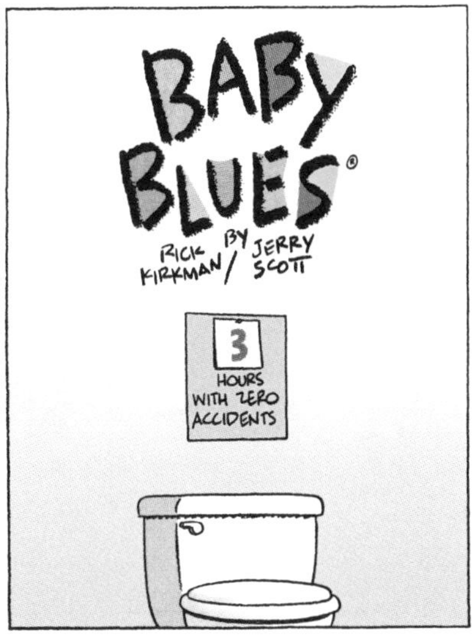
BABY BLUES®
BY RICK KIRKMAN / JERRY SCOTT
3 HOURS WITH ZERO ACCIDENTS

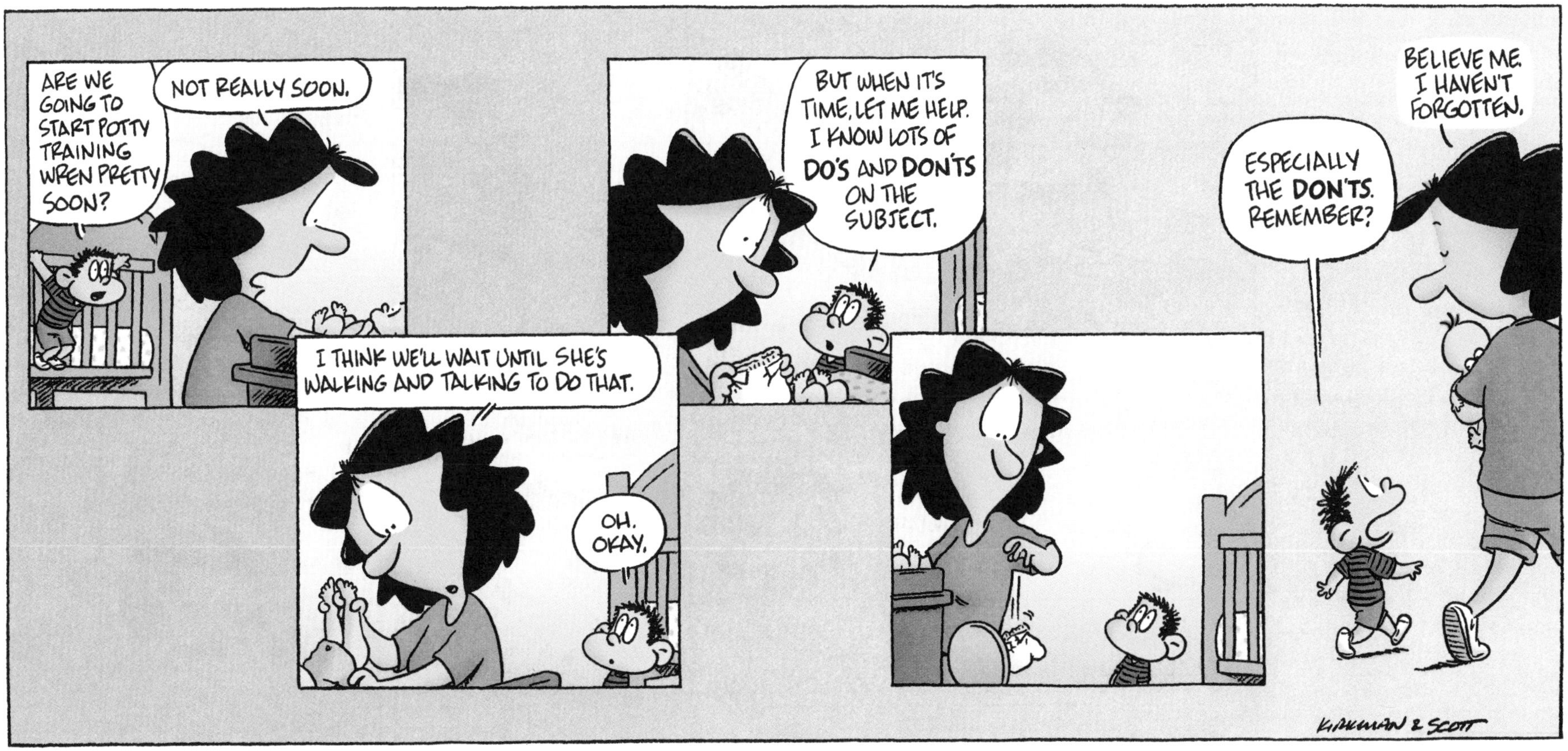
ARE WE GOING TO START POTTY TRAINING WREN PRETTY SOON?
NOT REALLY SOON.
BUT WHEN IT'S TIME, LET ME HELP. I KNOW LOTS OF DO'S AND DON'TS ON THE SUBJECT.
I THINK WE'LL WAIT UNTIL SHE'S WALKING AND TALKING TO DO THAT.
OH. OKAY.
ESPECIALLY THE DON'TS. REMEMBER?
BELIEVE ME. I HAVEN'T FORGOTTEN.
KIRKMAN & SCOTT

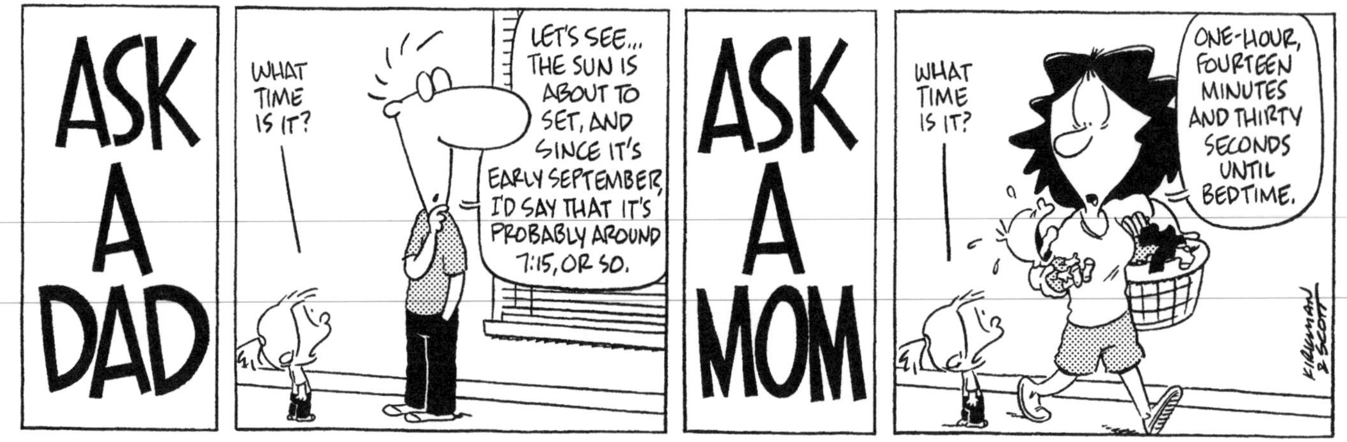
ASK A DAD
WHAT TIME IS IT?
LET'S SEE... THE SUN IS ABOUT TO SET, AND SINCE IT'S EARLY SEPTEMBER, I'D SAY THAT IT'S PROBABLY AROUND 7:15, OR SO.
ASK A MOM
WHAT TIME IS IT?
ONE-HOUR, FOURTEEN MINUTES AND THIRTY SECONDS UNTIL BEDTIME.
KIRKMAN & SCOTT

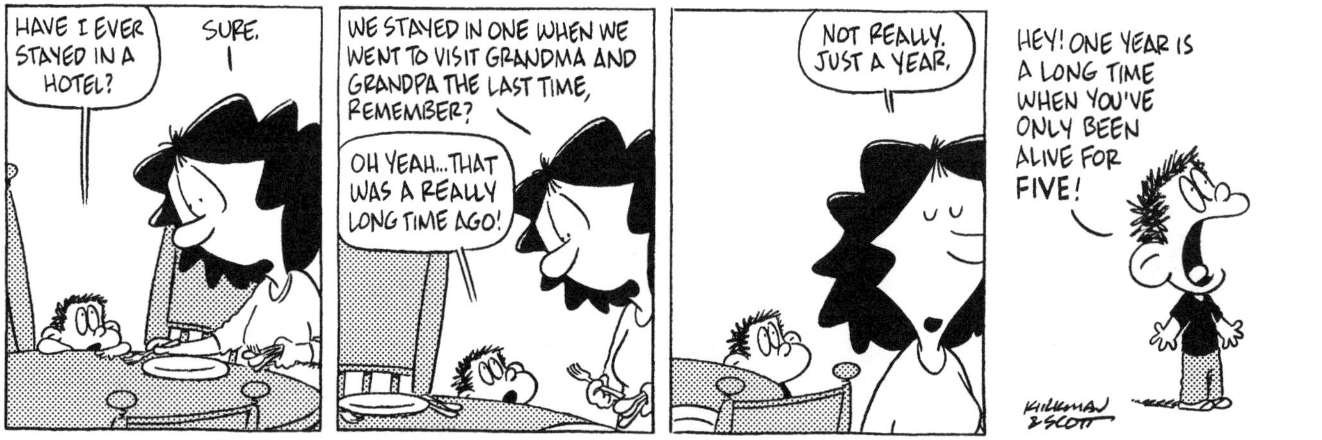
HAVE I EVER STAYED IN A HOTEL?
SURE.
WE STAYED IN ONE WHEN WE WENT TO VISIT GRANDMA AND GRANDPA THE LAST TIME, REMEMBER?
OH YEAH...THAT WAS A REALLY LONG TIME AGO!
NOT REALLY. JUST A YEAR.
HEY! ONE YEAR IS A LONG TIME WHEN YOU'VE ONLY BEEN ALIVE FOR FIVE!
KIRKMAN & SCOTT

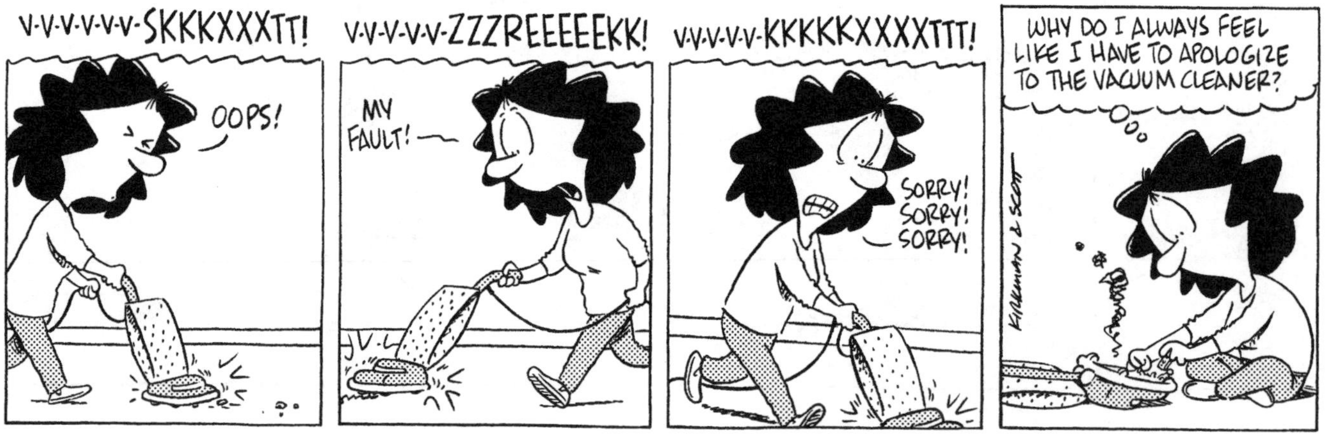
V-V-V-V-V-V-SKKKXXXTT!
OOPS!
V-V-V-V-V-ZZZREEEEEKK!
MY FAULT!
V-V-V-V-V-KKKKKXXXXTTT!
SORRY! SORRY! SORRY!
WHY DO I ALWAYS FEEL LIKE I HAVE TO APOLOGIZE TO THE VACUUM CLEANER?
KIRKMAN & SCOTT

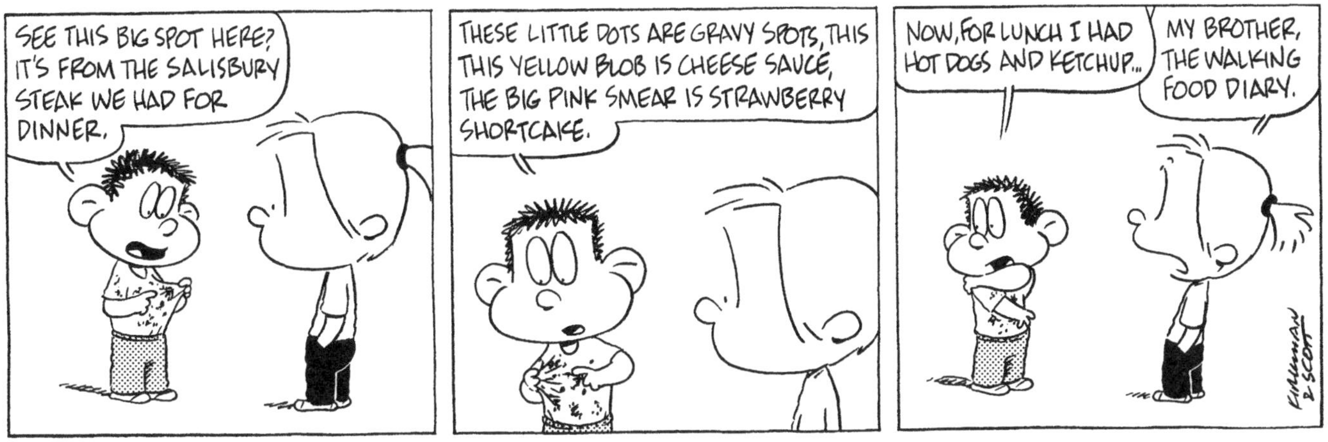
SEE THIS BIG SPOT HERE? IT'S FROM THE SALISBURY STEAK WE HAD FOR DINNER.
THESE LITTLE DOTS ARE GRAVY SPOTS, THIS THIS YELLOW BLOB IS CHEESE SAUCE, THE BIG PINK SMEAR IS STRAWBERRY SHORTCAKE.
NOW, FOR LUNCH I HAD HOT DOGS AND KETCHUP...
MY BROTHER, THE WALKING FOOD DIARY.
KIRKMAN & SCOTT

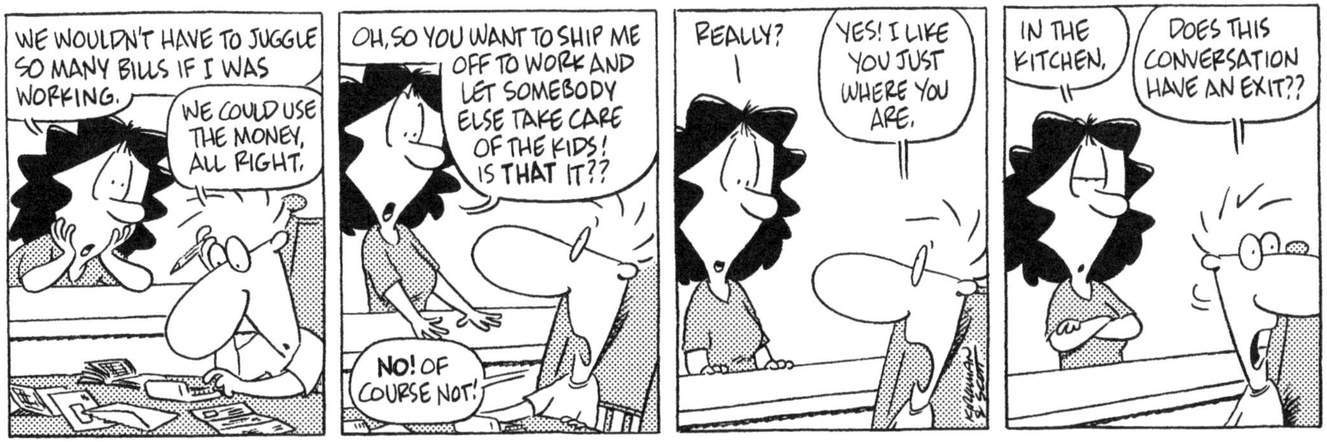
WE WOULDN'T HAVE TO JUGGLE SO MANY BILLS IF I WAS WORKING.
WE COULD USE THE MONEY, ALL RIGHT.
OH, SO YOU WANT TO SHIP ME OFF TO WORK AND LET SOMEBODY ELSE TAKE CARE OF THE KIDS! IS **THAT** IT??
NO! OF COURSE NOT!
REALLY?
YES! I LIKE YOU JUST WHERE YOU ARE.
IN THE KITCHEN.
DOES THIS CONVERSATION HAVE AN EXIT??

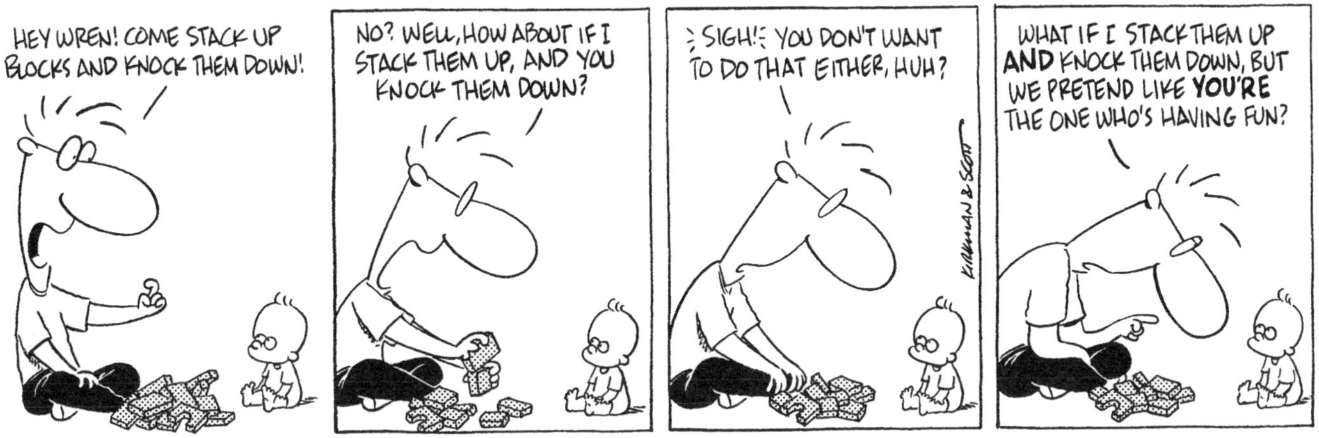
HEY WREN! COME STACK UP BLOCKS AND KNOCK THEM DOWN!
NO? WELL, HOW ABOUT IF I STACK THEM UP, AND YOU KNOCK THEM DOWN?
SIGH! YOU DON'T WANT TO DO THAT EITHER, HUH?
WHAT IF I STACK THEM UP **AND** KNOCK THEM DOWN, BUT WE PRETEND LIKE **YOU'RE** THE ONE WHO'S HAVING FUN?
KIRKMAN & SCOTT

BABY BLUES
RICK BY JERRY
KIRKMAN/ SCOTT

OKAY. SO THE CHICKEN IS LONELY, RIGHT?

THE LONELY LITTLE CHICKEN

HE DECIDES TO GO AROUND ASKING DIFFERENT ANIMALS IF THEY WANT TO BE HIS FRIEND.

FLIP! FLIP! FLIP!

THE LONELY LITTLE CHICKEN

...AND SO BLAH-DE-BLAH-DE-BLAH... SOME STUFF HAPPENS, THEN SOME MORE STUFF HAPPENS, AND THE CHICKEN LIVES HAPPILY EVER AFTER, OR WHATEVER. THE END.

FLIP! FLIP! FLIP! FLIP! FLIP! FLIP!

THE LONELY LITTLE CHICKEN

FLIP! FLIP! FLIP! FLIP!

FUMP!

I THINK I LIKED THE MOVIE BETTER.

ME, TOO. THE BOOK DIDN'T SEEM TO HAVE AS MUCH DETAIL.

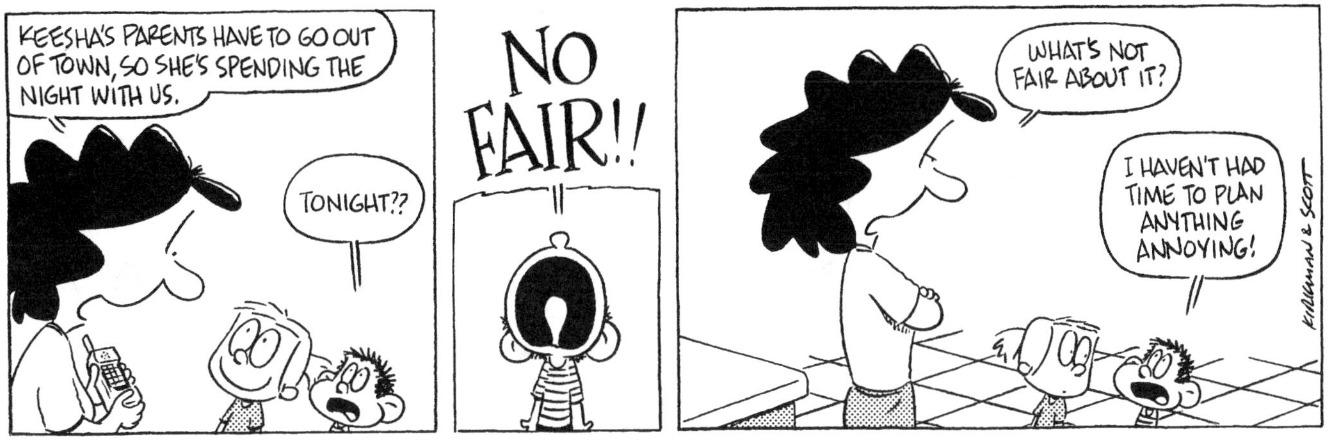
KEESHA'S PARENTS HAVE TO GO OUT OF TOWN, SO SHE'S SPENDING THE NIGHT WITH US.
TONIGHT??
NO FAIR!!
WHAT'S NOT FAIR ABOUT IT?
I HAVEN'T HAD TIME TO PLAN ANYTHING ANNOYING!
KIRKMAN & SCOTT

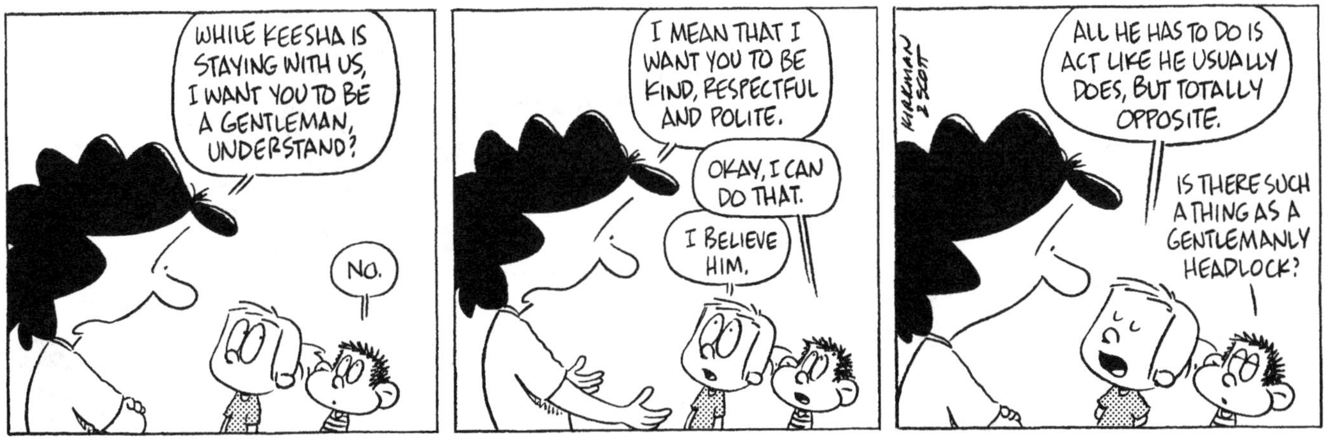
WHILE KEESHA IS STAYING WITH US, I WANT YOU TO BE A GENTLEMAN, UNDERSTAND?
NO.
I MEAN THAT I WANT YOU TO BE KIND, RESPECTFUL AND POLITE.
OKAY, I CAN DO THAT.
I BELIEVE HIM.
KIRKMAN & SCOTT
ALL HE HAS TO DO IS ACT LIKE HE USUALLY DOES, BUT TOTALLY OPPOSITE.
IS THERE SUCH A THING AS A GENTLEMANLY HEADLOCK?

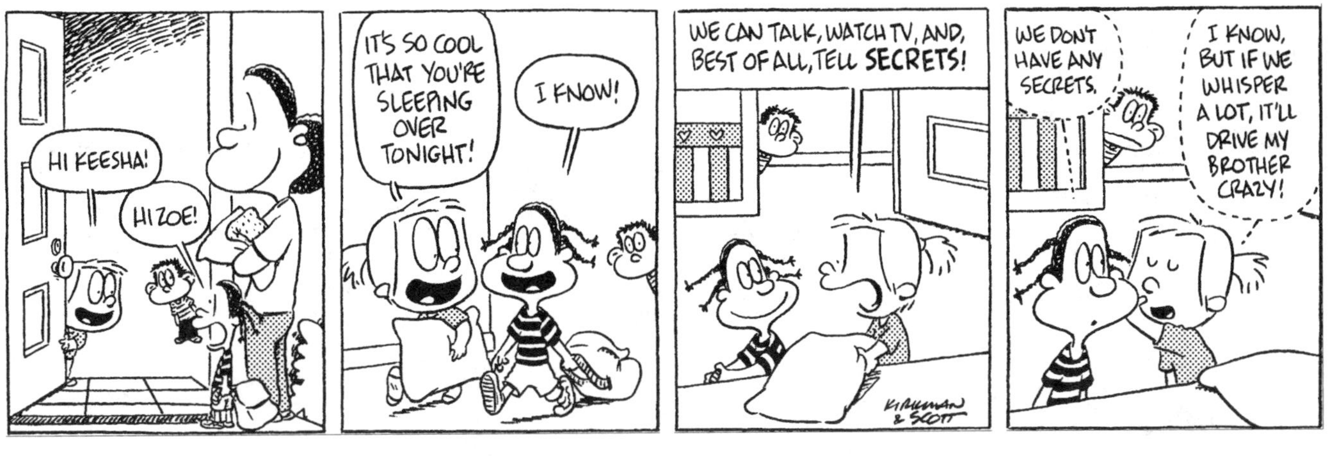
HI KEESHA!
HI ZOE!
IT'S SO COOL THAT YOU'RE SLEEPING OVER TONIGHT!
I KNOW!
WE CAN TALK, WATCH TV, AND, BEST OF ALL, TELL SECRETS!
KIRKMAN & SCOTT
WE DON'T HAVE ANY SECRETS.
I KNOW, BUT IF WE WHISPER A LOT, IT'LL DRIVE MY BROTHER CRAZY!

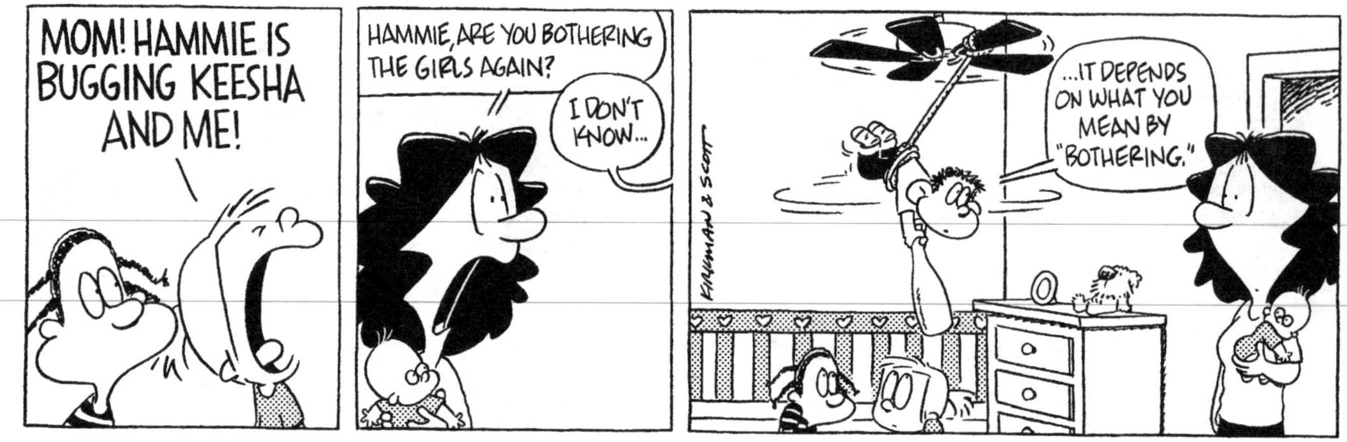
MOM! HAMMIE IS BUGGING KEESHA AND ME!
HAMMIE, ARE YOU BOTHERING THE GIRLS AGAIN?
I DON'T KNOW...
...IT DEPENDS ON WHAT YOU MEAN BY "BOTHERING."
KIRKMAN & SCOTT

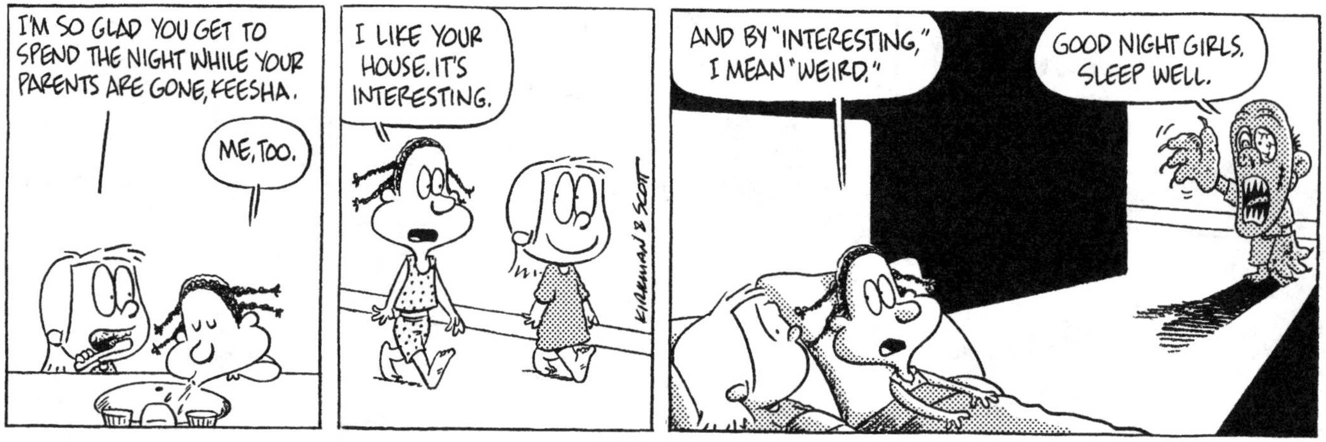
I'M SO GLAD YOU GET TO SPEND THE NIGHT WHILE YOUR PARENTS ARE GONE, KEESHA.
ME, TOO.
I LIKE YOUR HOUSE. IT'S INTERESTING.
KIRKMAN & SCOTT
AND BY "INTERESTING," I MEAN "WEIRD."
GOOD NIGHT GIRLS. SLEEP WELL.

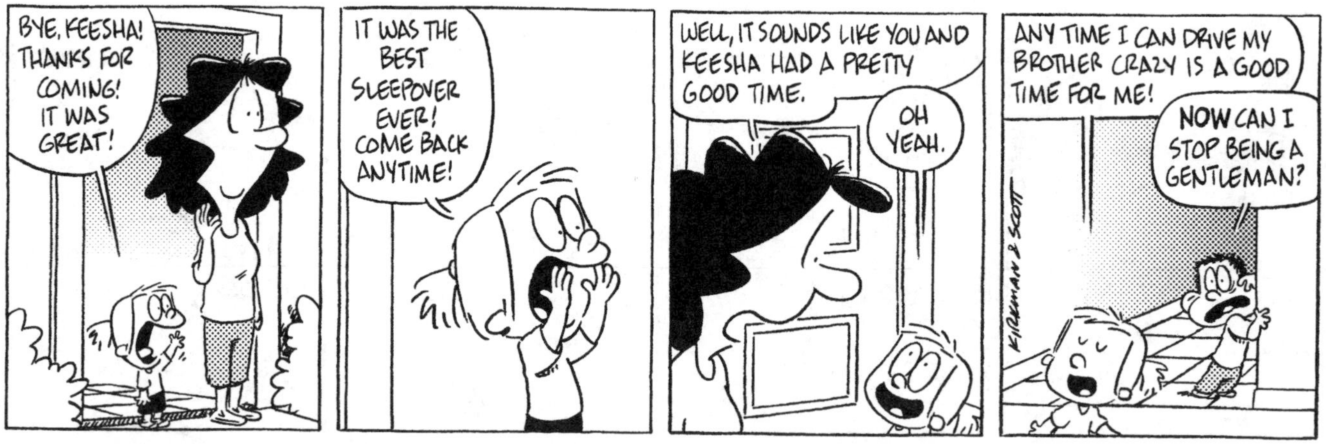
BYE, KEESHA! THANKS FOR COMING! IT WAS GREAT!
IT WAS THE BEST SLEEPOVER EVER! COME BACK ANYTIME!
WELL, IT SOUNDS LIKE YOU AND KEESHA HAD A PRETTY GOOD TIME.
OH YEAH.
ANY TIME I CAN DRIVE MY BROTHER CRAZY IS A GOOD TIME FOR ME!
NOW CAN I STOP BEING A GENTLEMAN?
KIRKMAN & SCOTT

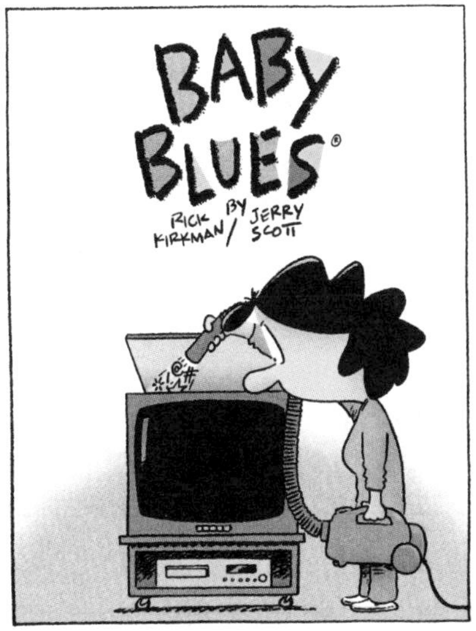
BABY BLUES®
BY RICK KIRKMAN / JERRY SCOTT

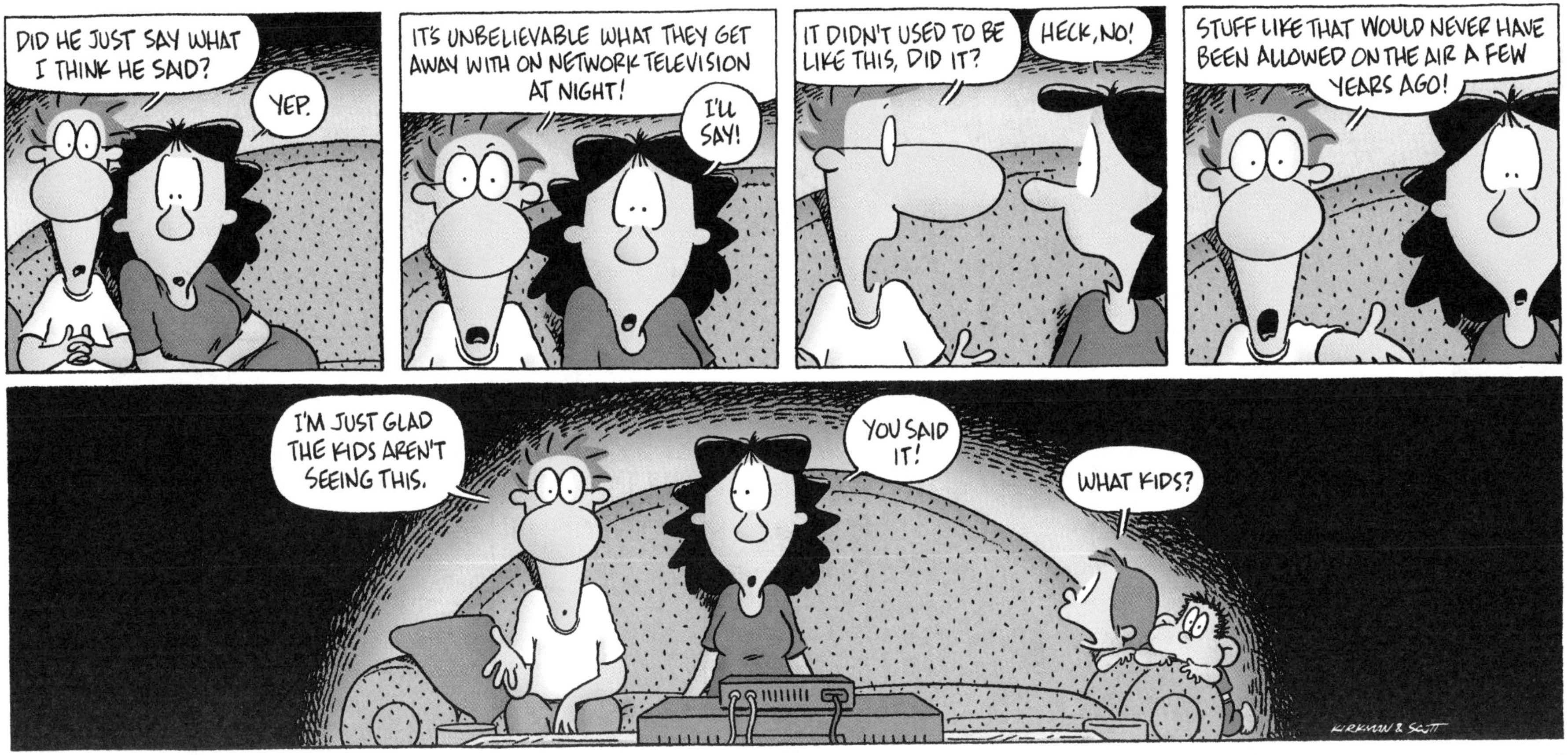
DID HE JUST SAY WHAT I THINK HE SAID?
YEP.
IT'S UNBELIEVABLE WHAT THEY GET AWAY WITH ON NETWORK TELEVISION AT NIGHT!
I'LL SAY!
IT DIDN'T USED TO BE LIKE THIS, DID IT?
HECK, NO!
STUFF LIKE THAT WOULD NEVER HAVE BEEN ALLOWED ON THE AIR A FEW YEARS AGO!
I'M JUST GLAD THE KIDS AREN'T SEEING THIS.
YOU SAID IT!
WHAT KIDS?
KIRKMAN & SCOTT

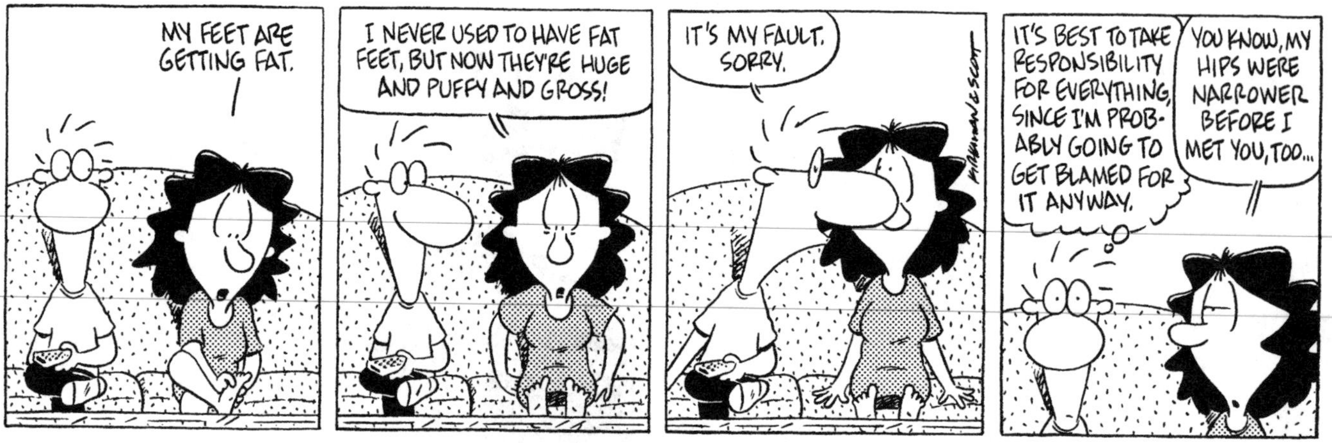
MY FEET ARE GETTING FAT.
I NEVER USED TO HAVE FAT FEET, BUT NOW THEY'RE HUGE AND PUFFY AND GROSS!
IT'S MY FAULT. SORRY.
IT'S BEST TO TAKE RESPONSIBILITY FOR EVERYTHING, SINCE I'M PROBABLY GOING TO GET BLAMED FOR IT ANYWAY.
YOU KNOW, MY HIPS WERE NARROWER BEFORE I MET YOU, TOO...

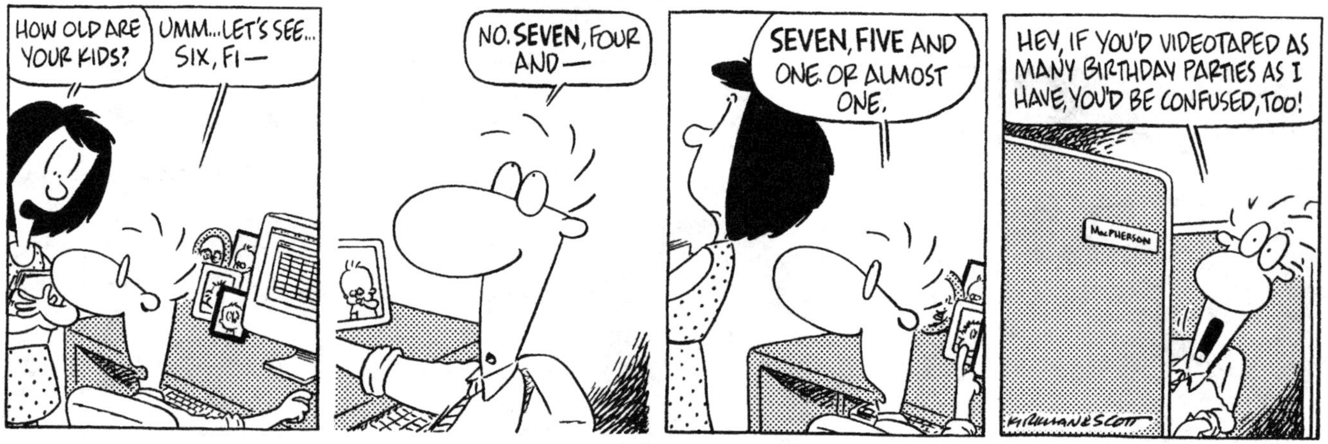
HOW OLD ARE YOUR KIDS?
UMM... LET'S SEE... SIX, FI—
NO. SEVEN, FOUR AND—
SEVEN, FIVE AND ONE. OR ALMOST ONE.
HEY, IF YOU'D VIDEOTAPED AS MANY BIRTHDAY PARTIES AS I HAVE, YOU'D BE CONFUSED, TOO!
MacPHERSON

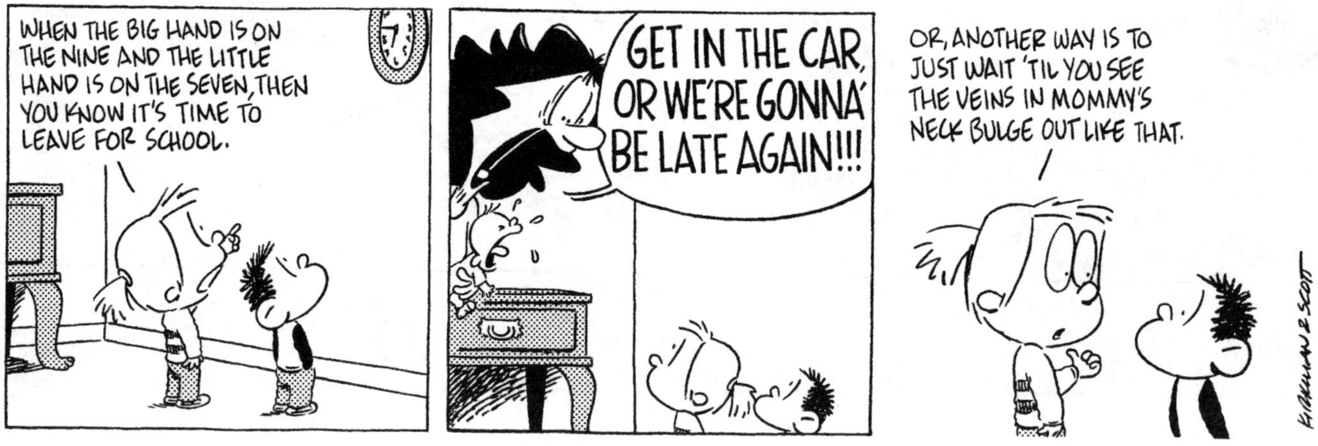
WHEN THE BIG HAND IS ON THE NINE AND THE LITTLE HAND IS ON THE SEVEN, THEN YOU KNOW IT'S TIME TO LEAVE FOR SCHOOL.
GET IN THE CAR, OR WE'RE GONNA' BE LATE AGAIN!!!
OR, ANOTHER WAY IS TO JUST WAIT 'TIL YOU SEE THE VEINS IN MOMMY'S NECK BULGE OUT LIKE THAT.

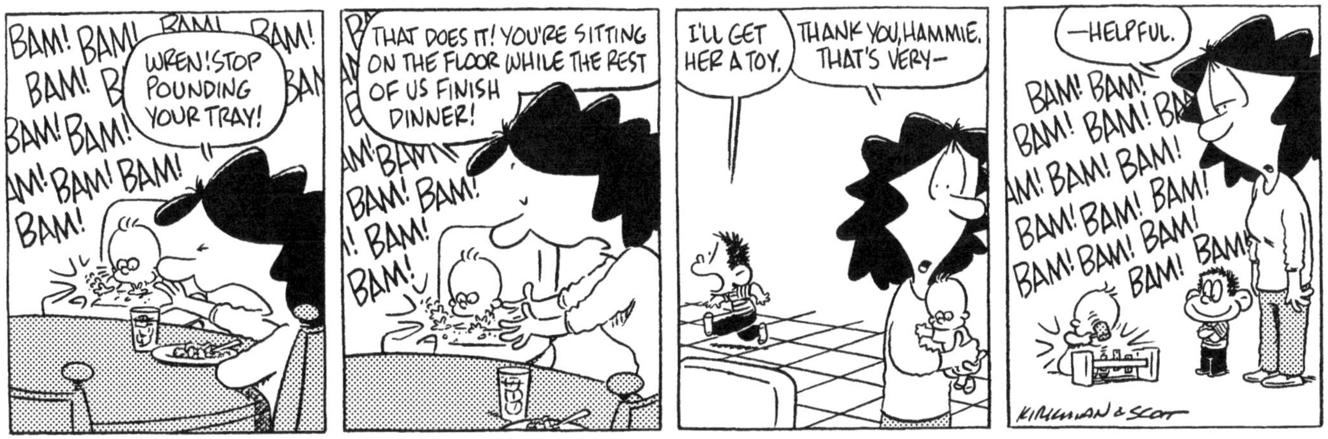
BAM! BAM! BAM! BAM! BAM! BAM! BAM! BAM! BAM! BAM! BAM! BAM! BAM!
WREN! STOP POUNDING YOUR TRAY!
THAT DOES IT! YOU'RE SITTING ON THE FLOOR WHILE THE REST OF US FINISH DINNER!
BAM! BAM! BAM! BAM! BAM!
I'LL GET HER A TOY.
THANK YOU, HAMMIE. THAT'S VERY—
—HELPFUL.
BAM! BAM! BAM! BAM! BAM! BAM! BAM! BAM! BAM! BAM! BAM! BAM! BAM! BAM! BAM!
KIRKMAN & SCOTT

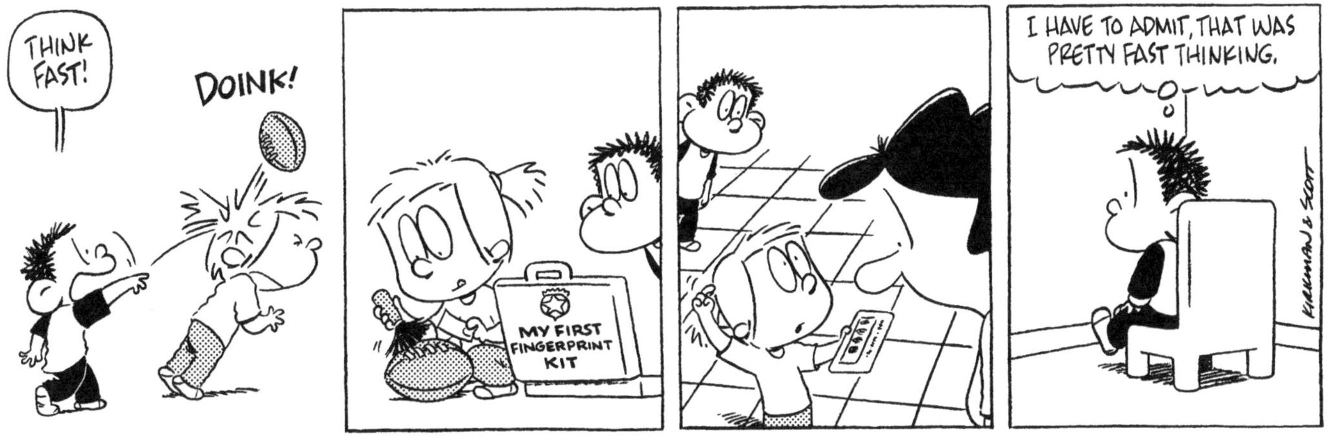
THINK FAST!
DOINK!
MY FIRST FINGERPRINT KIT
I HAVE TO ADMIT, THAT WAS PRETTY FAST THINKING.
KIRKMAN & SCOTT

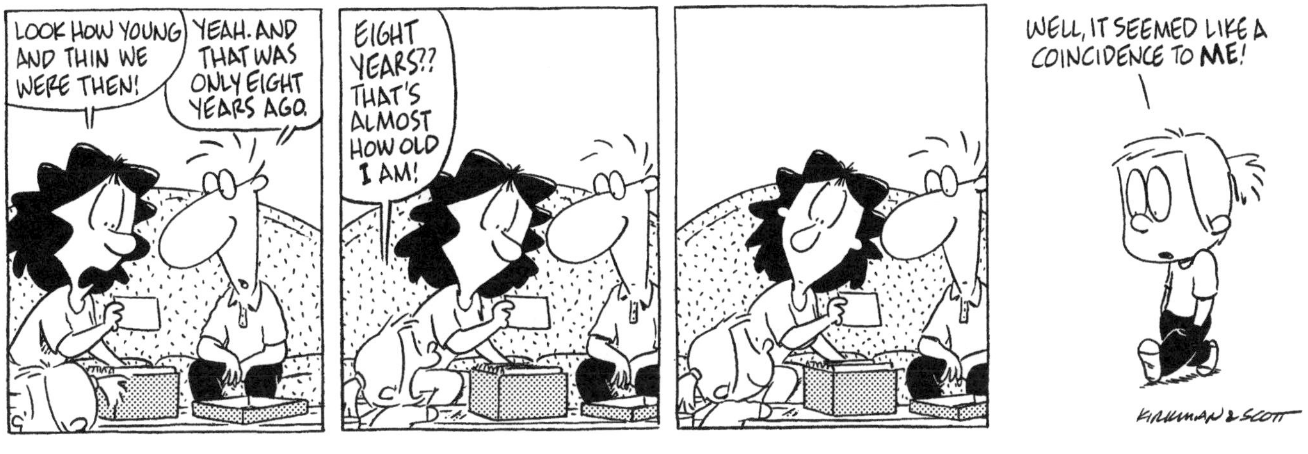
LOOK HOW YOUNG AND THIN WE WERE THEN!
YEAH. AND THAT WAS ONLY EIGHT YEARS AGO.
EIGHT YEARS?? THAT'S ALMOST HOW OLD I AM!
WELL, IT SEEMED LIKE A COINCIDENCE TO ME!
KIRKMAN & SCOTT

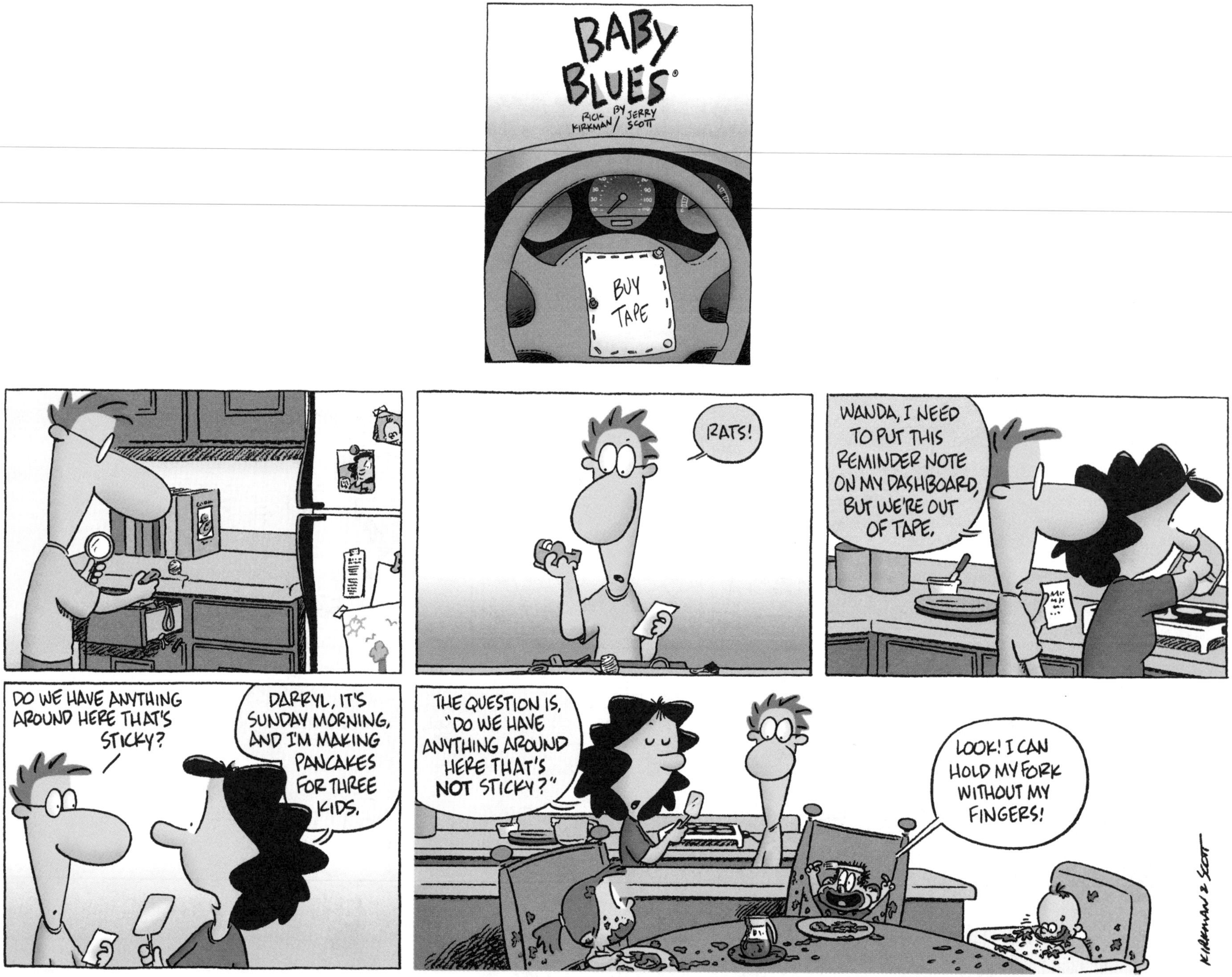
BABY BLUES®
BY RICK KIRKMAN / JERRY SCOTT
BUY TAPE
RATS!
WANDA, I NEED TO PUT THIS REMINDER NOTE ON MY DASHBOARD, BUT WE'RE OUT OF TAPE.
DO WE HAVE ANYTHING AROUND HERE THAT'S STICKY?
DARRYL, IT'S SUNDAY MORNING, AND I'M MAKING PANCAKES FOR THREE KIDS.
THE QUESTION IS, "DO WE HAVE ANYTHING AROUND HERE THAT'S NOT STICKY?"
LOOK! I CAN HOLD MY FORK WITHOUT MY FINGERS!
KIRKMAN & SCOTT

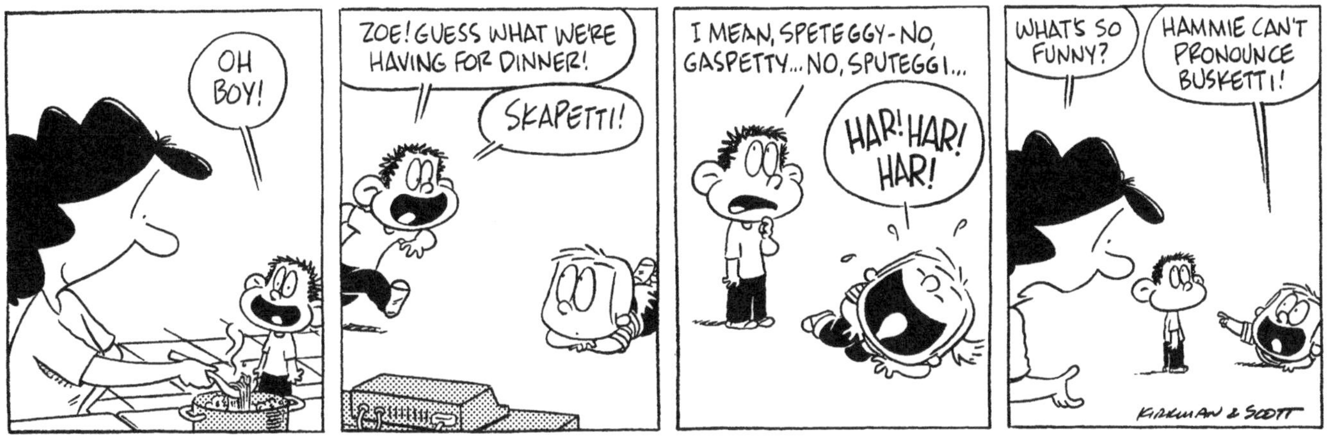
OH BOY!
ZOE! GUESS WHAT WE'RE HAVING FOR DINNER!
SKAPETTI!
I MEAN, SPETEGGY- NO, GASPETTY... NO, SPUTEGGI...
HAR! HAR! HAR!
WHAT'S SO FUNNY?
HAMMIE CAN'T PRONOUNCE BUSKETTI!
KIRKMAN & SCOTT

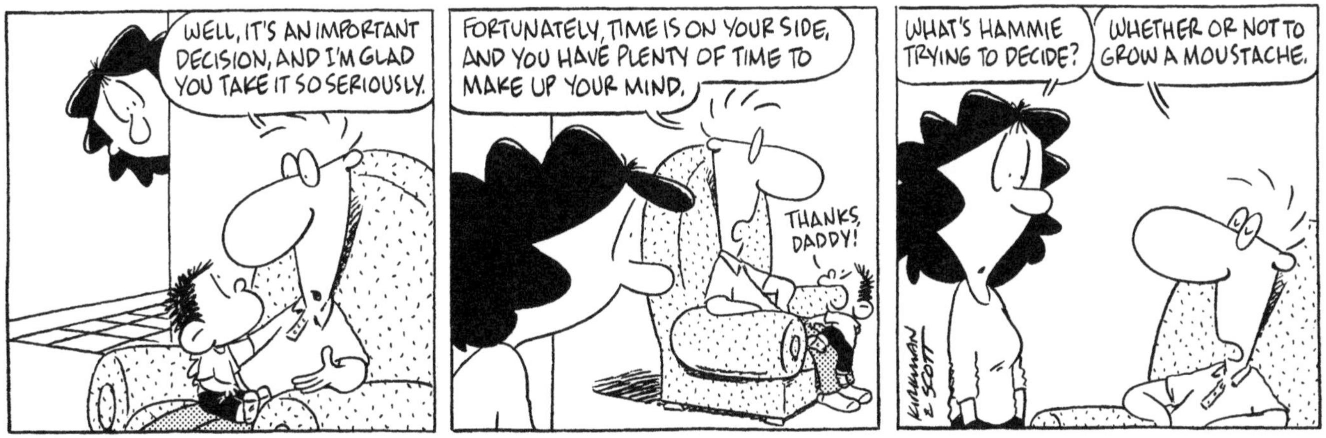
WELL, IT'S AN IMPORTANT DECISION, AND I'M GLAD YOU TAKE IT SO SERIOUSLY.
FORTUNATELY, TIME IS ON YOUR SIDE, AND YOU HAVE PLENTY OF TIME TO MAKE UP YOUR MIND.
THANKS, DADDY!
KIRKMAN & SCOTT
WHAT'S HAMMIE TRYING TO DECIDE?
WHETHER OR NOT TO GROW A MOUSTACHE.

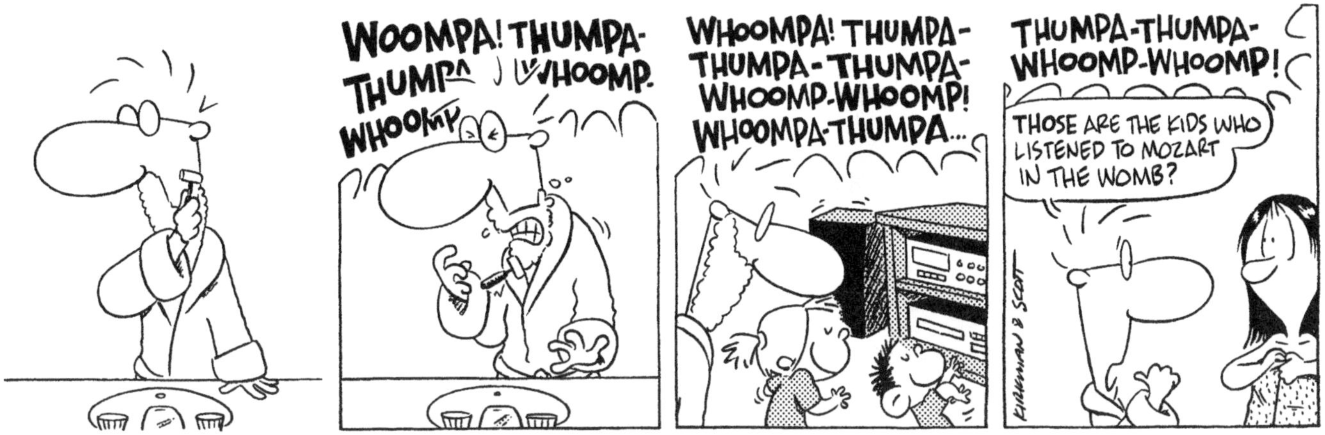
WOOMPA! THUMPA-
WHOOMP.
WHOOMPA! THUMPA-THUMPA-THUMPA-THUMPA-WHOOMP-WHOOMP! WHOOMPA-THUMPA...
KIRKMAN & SCOTT
THUMPA-THUMPA-WHOOMP-WHOOMP!
THOSE ARE THE KIDS WHO LISTENED TO MOZART IN THE WOMB?

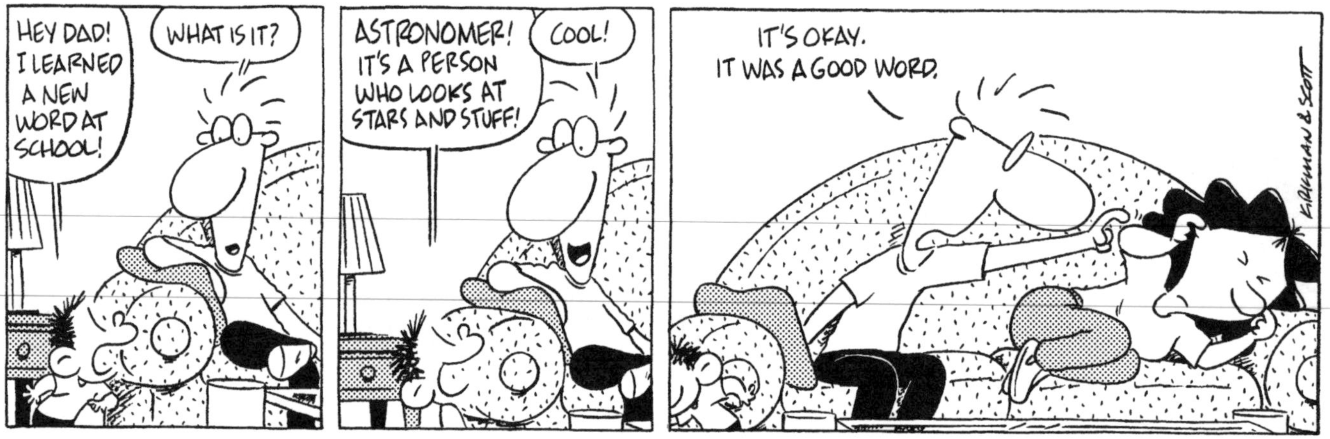
HEY DAD! I LEARNED A NEW WORD AT SCHOOL!
WHAT IS IT?
ASTRONOMER! IT'S A PERSON WHO LOOKS AT STARS AND STUFF!
COOL!
IT'S OKAY. IT WAS A GOOD WORD.
KIRKMAN & SCOTT

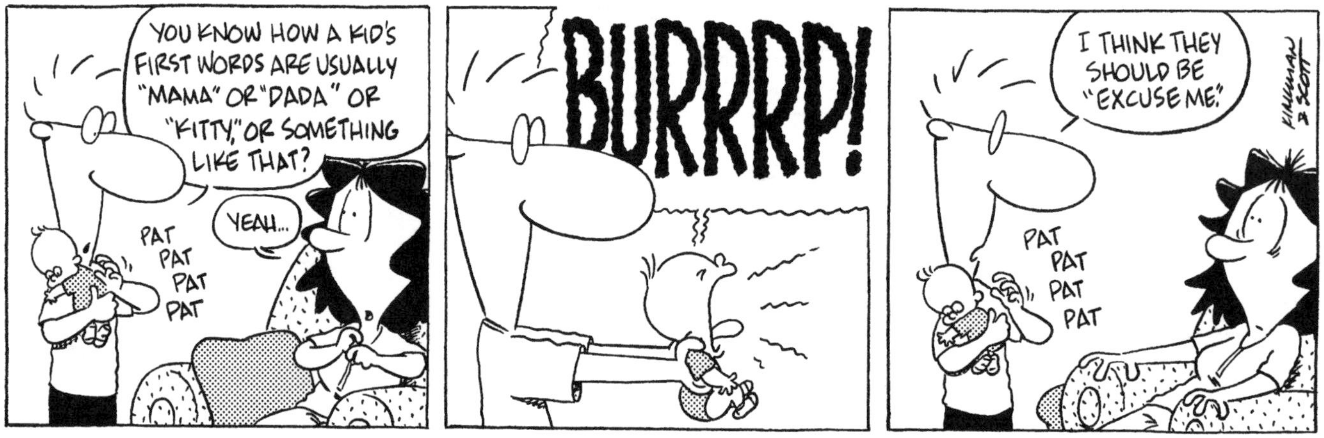
YOU KNOW HOW A KID'S FIRST WORDS ARE USUALLY "MAMA" OR "DADA" OR "KITTY," OR SOMETHING LIKE THAT?
YEAH...
PAT PAT PAT PAT
BURRRP!
I THINK THEY SHOULD BE "EXCUSE ME."
PAT PAT PAT PAT
KIRKMAN & SCOTT

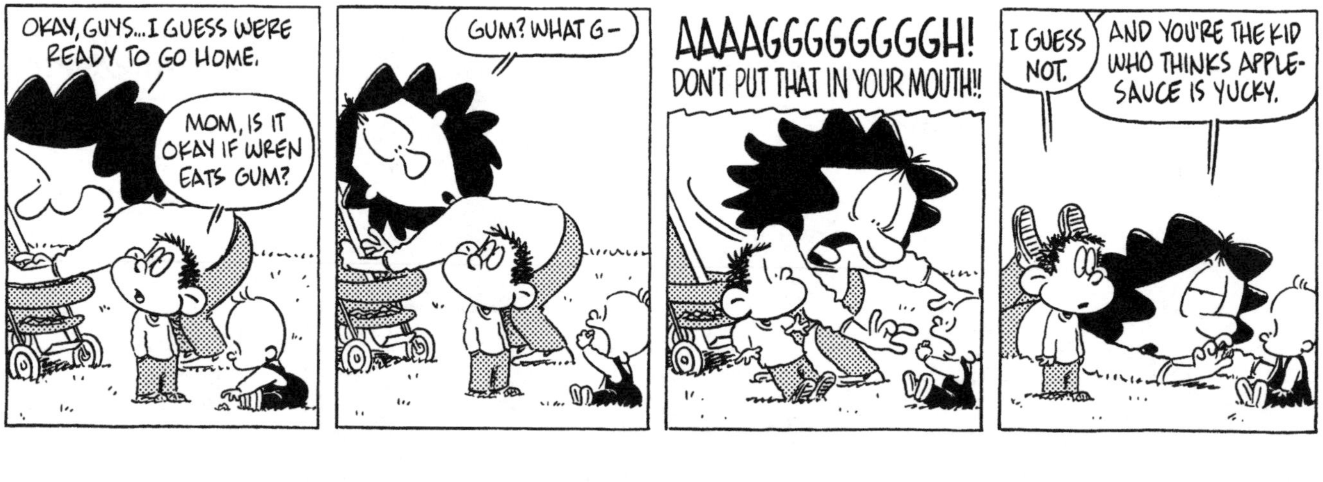
OKAY, GUYS...I GUESS WE'RE READY TO GO HOME.
MOM, IS IT OKAY IF WREN EATS GUM?
GUM? WHAT G–
AAAAGGGGGGGGH! DON'T PUT THAT IN YOUR MOUTH!!
I GUESS NOT.
AND YOU'RE THE KID WHO THINKS APPLE-SAUCE IS YUCKY.

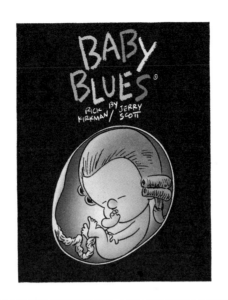

BABY BLUES®
by RICK KIRKMAN / JERRY SCOTT

MOZART?

MM-HMM.

WHEN MY FIRST BABY WAS BORN, MY PLAN WAS FOR HER TO PLAY THE PIANO AND BE FLUENT IN AT LEAST TWO LANGUAGES BY THE AGE OF FIVE.

WOW!

THEN WHEN I HAD MY SECOND BABY, I WAS A LITTLE MORE REALISTIC.

OH?

YEAH. I SCALED BACK MY EXPECTATIONS TO JUST READING AND WRITING BY AGE FIVE.

INTERESTING. AND WITH YOUR THIRD?

POTTY-TRAINED AND WEANED BY THE TIME SHE GRADUATES FROM COLLEGE.

BBTHHHHHHH!

KIRKMAN & SCOTT

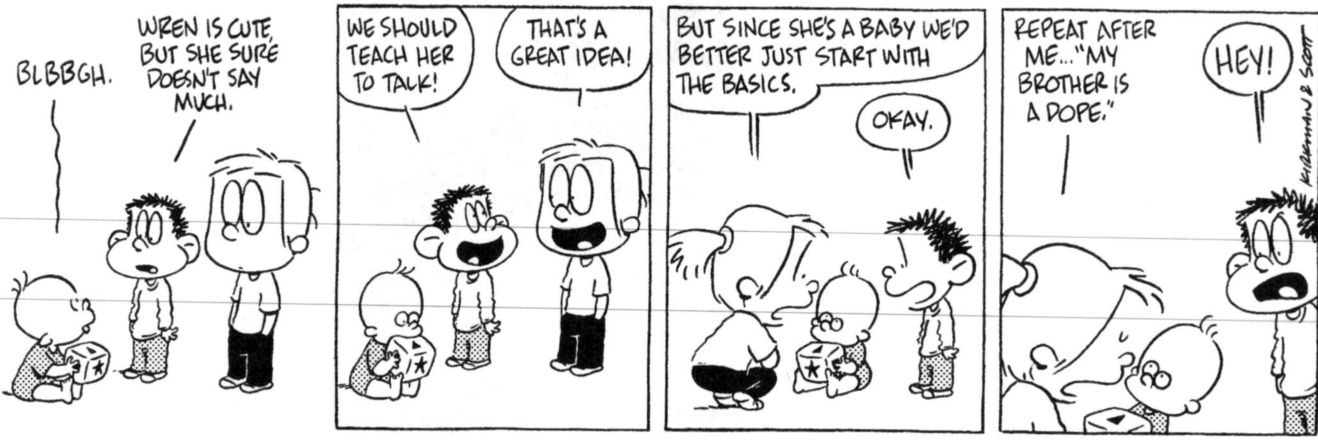
BLBBGH.
WREN IS CUTE, BUT SHE SURE DOESN'T SAY MUCH.
WE SHOULD TEACH HER TO TALK!
THAT'S A GREAT IDEA!
BUT SINCE SHE'S A BABY WE'D BETTER JUST START WITH THE BASICS.
OKAY.
REPEAT AFTER ME..."MY BROTHER IS A DOPE."
HEY!
KIRKMAN & SCOTT

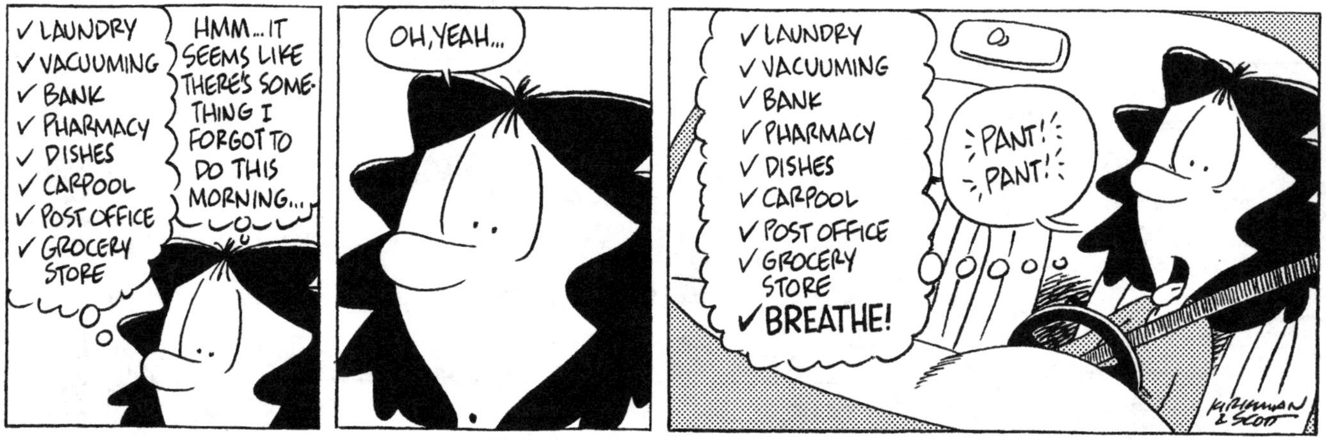
✓ LAUNDRY ✓ VACUUMING ✓ BANK ✓ PHARMACY ✓ DISHES ✓ CARPOOL ✓ POST OFFICE ✓ GROCERY STORE
HMM... IT SEEMS LIKE THERE'S SOMETHING I FORGOT TO DO THIS MORNING...
OH, YEAH...
✓ LAUNDRY ✓ VACUUMING ✓ BANK ✓ PHARMACY ✓ DISHES ✓ CARPOOL ✓ POST OFFICE ✓ GROCERY STORE ✓ BREATHE!
PANT! PANT!
KIRKMAN & SCOTT

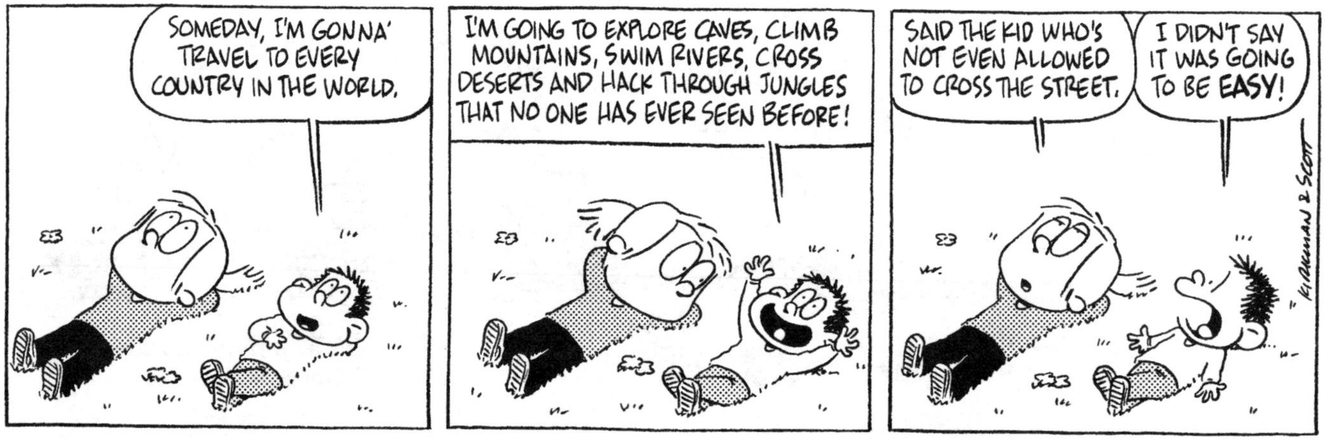
SOMEDAY, I'M GONNA' TRAVEL TO EVERY COUNTRY IN THE WORLD.
I'M GOING TO EXPLORE CAVES, CLIMB MOUNTAINS, SWIM RIVERS, CROSS DESERTS AND HACK THROUGH JUNGLES THAT NO ONE HAS EVER SEEN BEFORE!
SAID THE KID WHO'S NOT EVEN ALLOWED TO CROSS THE STREET.
I DIDN'T SAY IT WAS GOING TO BE EASY!
KIRKMAN & SCOTT

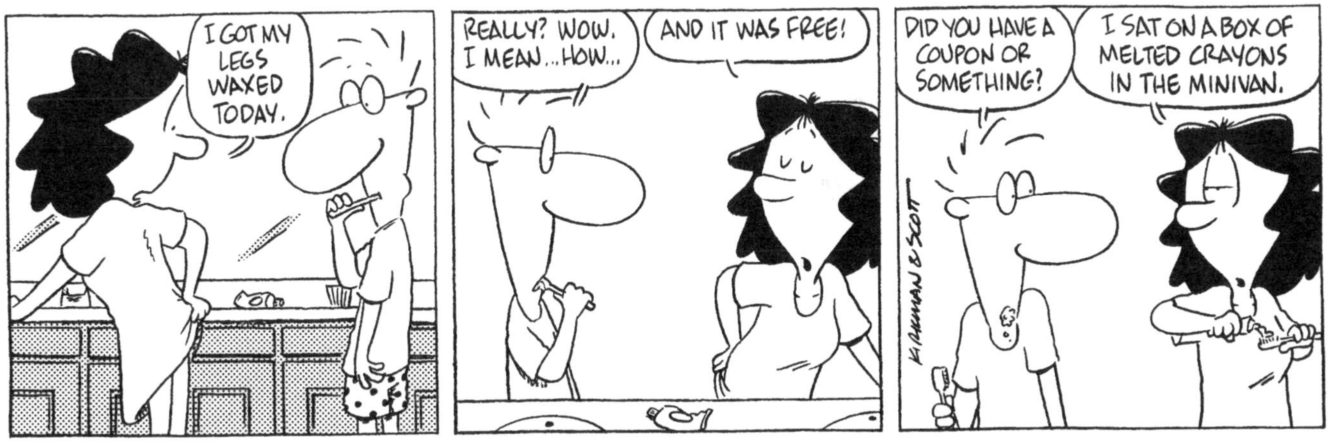
I GOT MY LEGS WAXED TODAY.
REALLY? WOW. I MEAN...HOW...
AND IT WAS FREE!
DID YOU HAVE A COUPON OR SOMETHING?
I SAT ON A BOX OF MELTED CRAYONS IN THE MINIVAN.
KIRKMAN & SCOTT

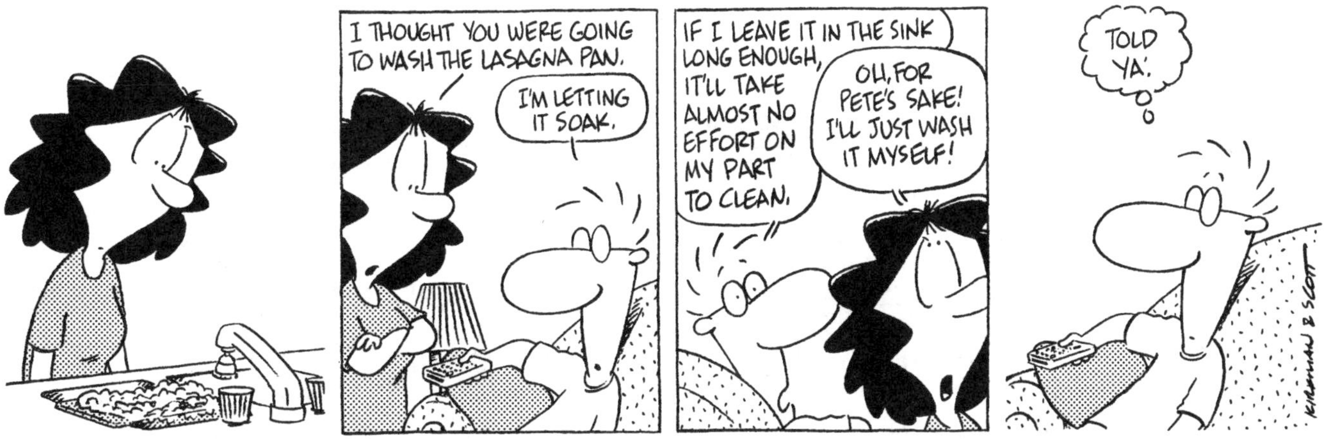
I THOUGHT YOU WERE GOING TO WASH THE LASAGNA PAN.
I'M LETTING IT SOAK.
IF I LEAVE IT IN THE SINK LONG ENOUGH, IT'LL TAKE ALMOST NO EFFORT ON MY PART TO CLEAN.
OH, FOR PETE'S SAKE! I'LL JUST WASH IT MYSELF!
TOLD YA.
KIRKMAN & SCOTT

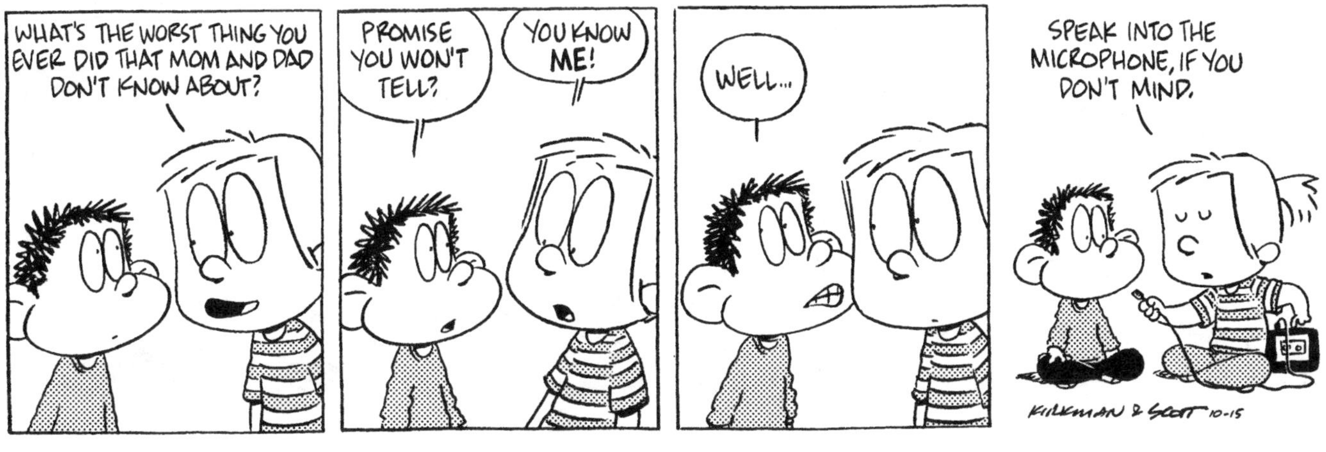
WHAT'S THE WORST THING YOU EVER DID THAT MOM AND DAD DON'T KNOW ABOUT?
PROMISE YOU WON'T TELL?
YOU KNOW **ME**!
WELL...
SPEAK INTO THE MICROPHONE, IF YOU DON'T MIND.
KIRKMAN & SCOTT 10-15

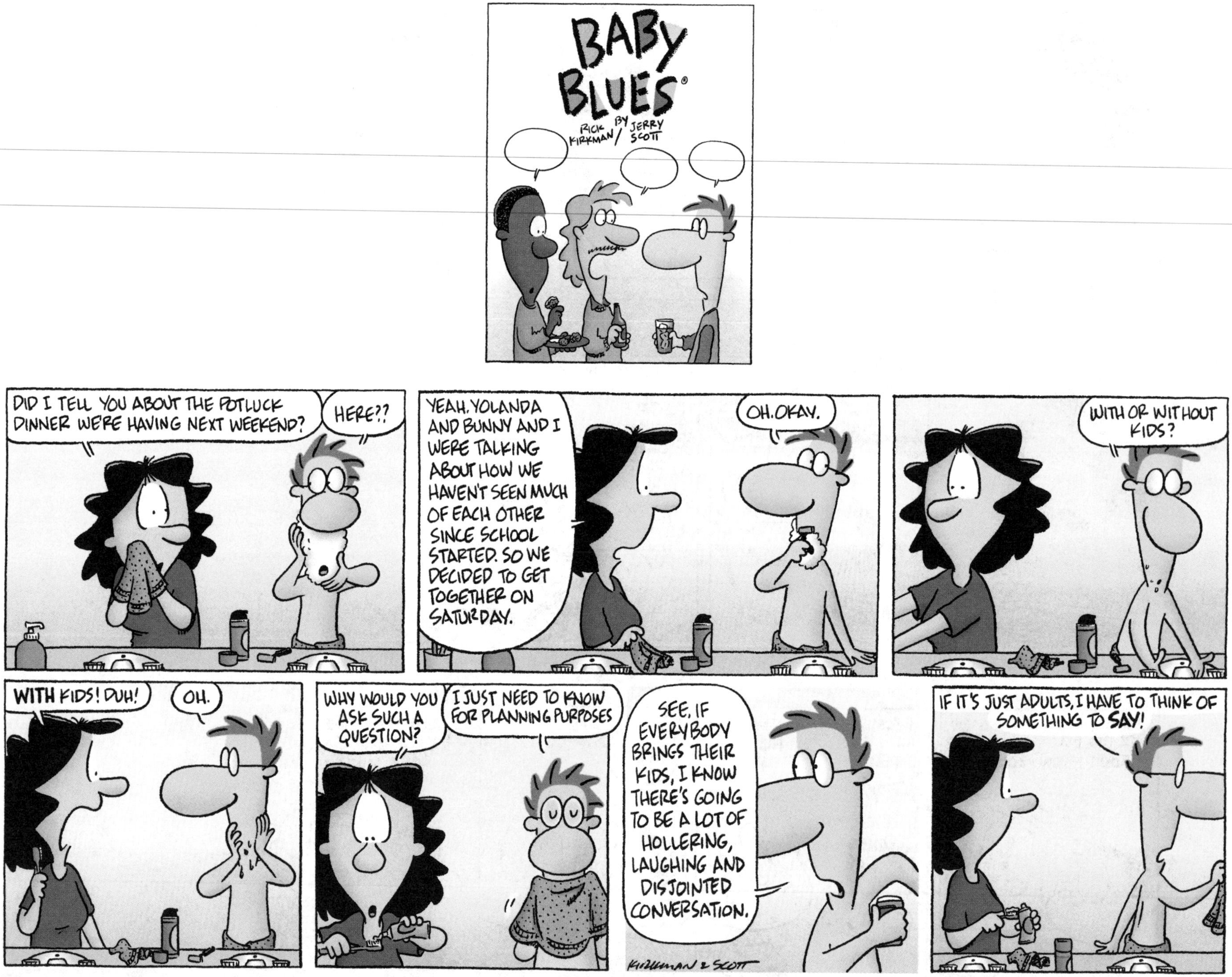
BABY BLUES®
RICK KIRKMAN / BY JERRY SCOTT
DID I TELL YOU ABOUT THE POTLUCK DINNER WE'RE HAVING NEXT WEEKEND?
HERE??
YEAH. YOLANDA AND BUNNY AND I WERE TALKING ABOUT HOW WE HAVEN'T SEEN MUCH OF EACH OTHER SINCE SCHOOL STARTED. SO WE DECIDED TO GET TOGETHER ON SATURDAY.
OH. OKAY.
WITH OR WITHOUT KIDS?
WITH KIDS! DUH!
OH.
WHY WOULD YOU ASK SUCH A QUESTION?
I JUST NEED TO KNOW FOR PLANNING PURPOSES
SEE, IF EVERYBODY BRINGS THEIR KIDS, I KNOW THERE'S GOING TO BE A LOT OF HOLLERING, LAUGHING AND DISJOINTED CONVERSATION.
IF IT'S JUST ADULTS, I HAVE TO THINK OF SOMETHING TO SAY!
KIRKMAN & SCOTT

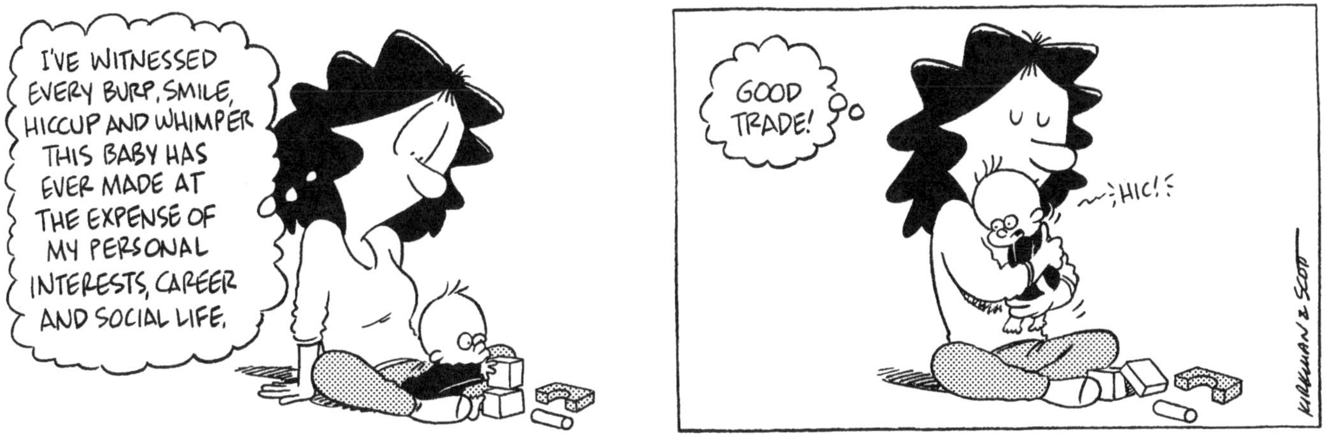
I'VE WITNESSED EVERY BURP, SMILE, HICCUP AND WHIMPER THIS BABY HAS EVER MADE AT THE EXPENSE OF MY PERSONAL INTERESTS, CAREER AND SOCIAL LIFE.
GOOD TRADE!
HIC!
KIRKMAN & SCOTT

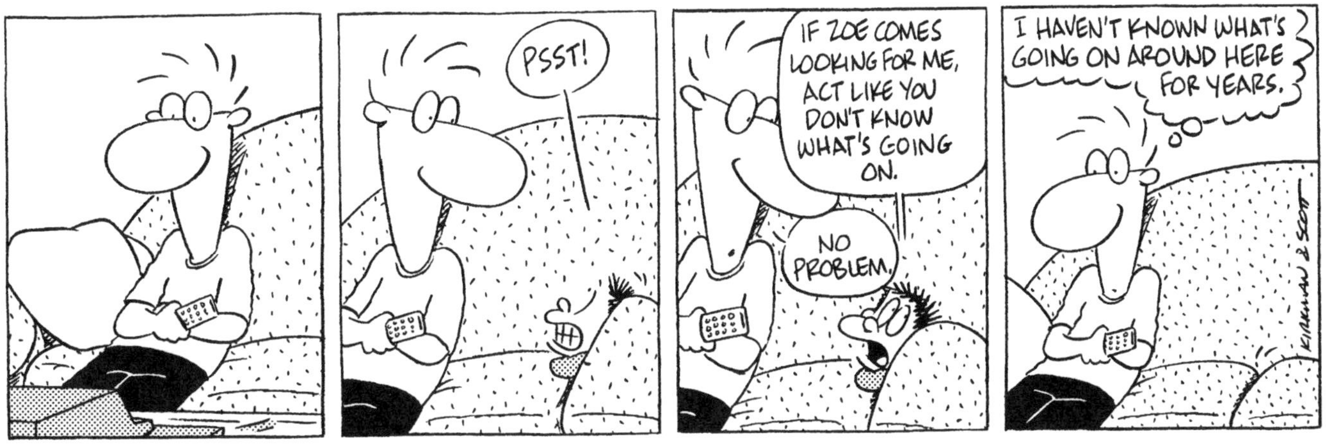
PSST!
IF ZOE COMES LOOKING FOR ME, ACT LIKE YOU DON'T KNOW WHAT'S GOING ON.
NO PROBLEM.
I HAVEN'T KNOWN WHAT'S GOING ON AROUND HERE FOR YEARS.
KIRKMAN & SCOTT

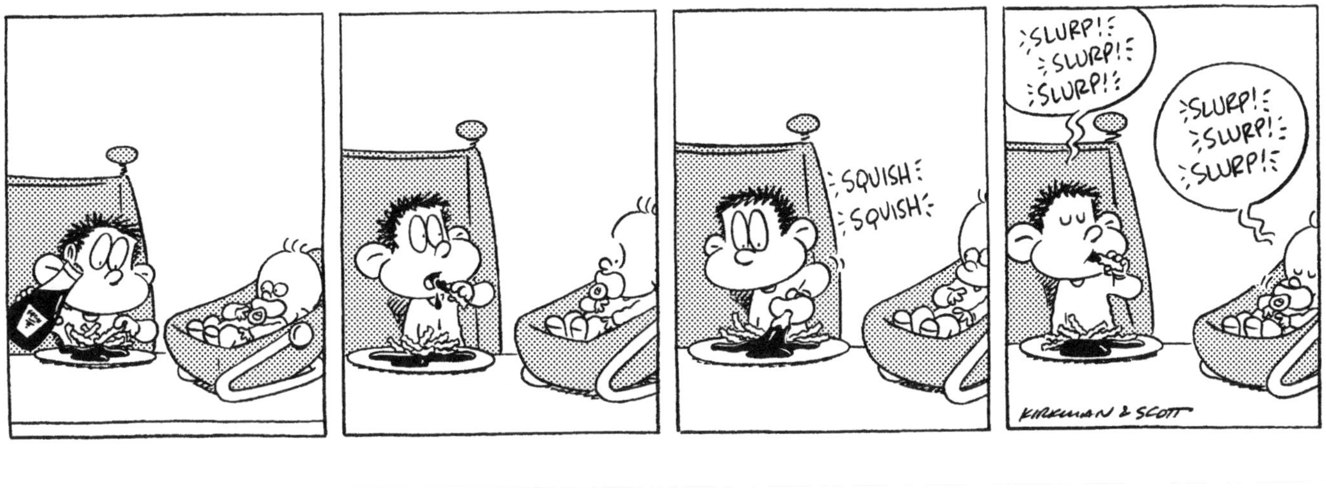
SQUISH
SQUISH
SLURP! SLURP! SLURP!
SLURP! SLURP! SLURP!
KIRKMAN & SCOTT

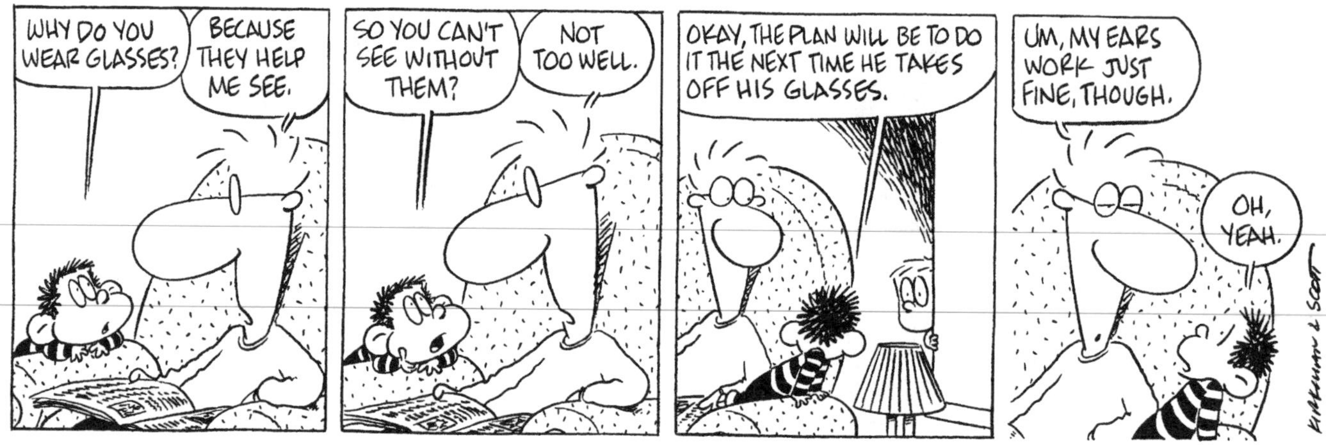
WHY DO YOU WEAR GLASSES?
BECAUSE THEY HELP ME SEE.
SO YOU CAN'T SEE WITHOUT THEM?
NOT TOO WELL.
OKAY, THE PLAN WILL BE TO DO IT THE NEXT TIME HE TAKES OFF HIS GLASSES.
UM, MY EARS WORK JUST FINE, THOUGH.
OH, YEAH.
KIRKMAN & SCOTT

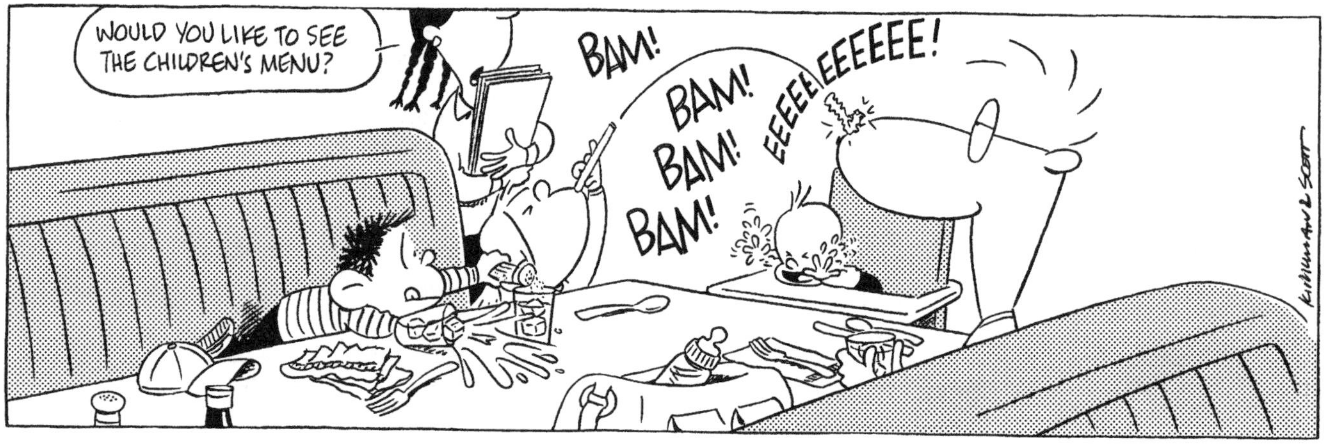
WOULD YOU LIKE TO SEE THE CHILDREN'S MENU?
BAM!
BAM! BAM! BAM!
EEEEEEEEEEE!
KIRKMAN & SCOTT

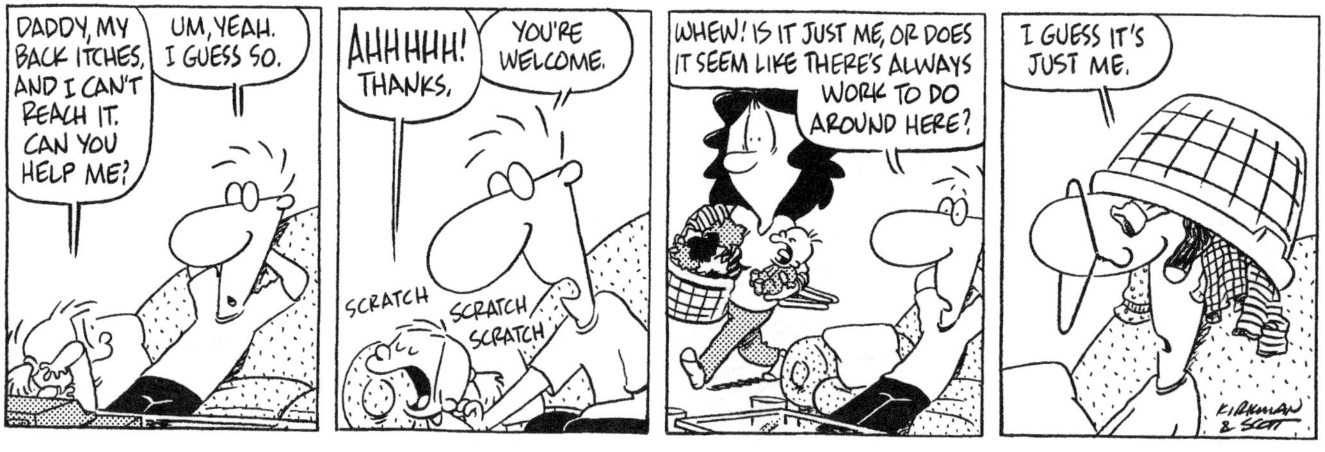
DADDY, MY BACK ITCHES, AND I CAN'T REACH IT. CAN YOU HELP ME?
UM, YEAH. I GUESS SO.
AHHHHH! THANKS.
YOU'RE WELCOME.
SCRATCH
SCRATCH SCRATCH
WHEW! IS IT JUST ME, OR DOES IT SEEM LIKE THERE'S ALWAYS WORK TO DO AROUND HERE?
I GUESS IT'S JUST ME.
KIRKMAN & SCOTT

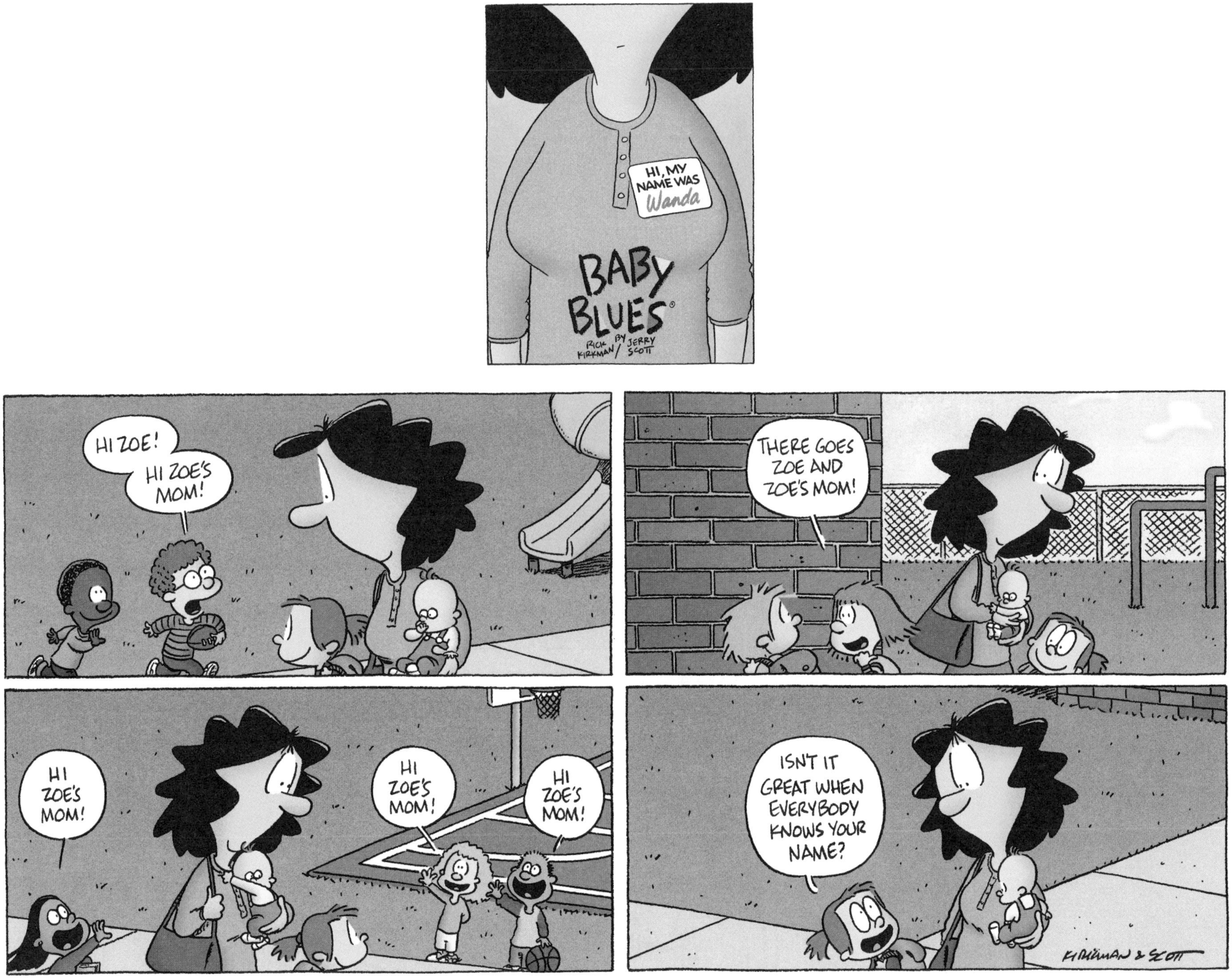
HI, MY NAME WAS Wanda
BABY BLUES
BY RICK KIRKMAN / JERRY SCOTT
HI ZOE!
HI ZOE'S MOM!
THERE GOES ZOE AND ZOE'S MOM!
HI ZOE'S MOM!
HI ZOE'S MOM!
HI ZOE'S MOM!
ISN'T IT GREAT WHEN EVERYBODY KNOWS YOUR NAME?
KIRKMAN & SCOTT

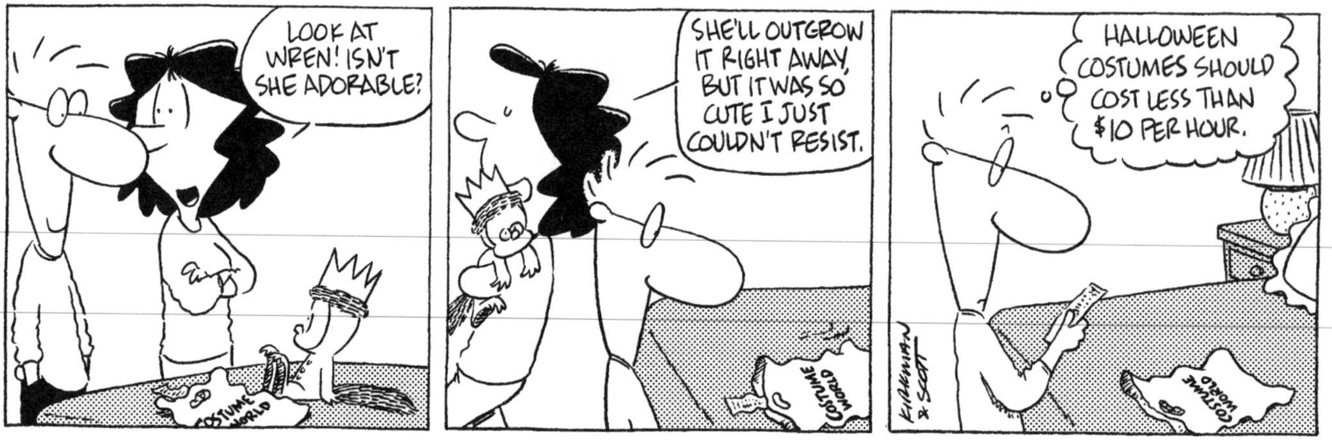
LOOK AT WREN! ISN'T SHE ADORABLE?
COSTUME WORLD
SHE'LL OUTGROW IT RIGHT AWAY, BUT IT WAS SO CUTE I JUST COULDN'T RESIST.
HALLOWEEN COSTUMES SHOULD COST LESS THAN $10 PER HOUR.
KIRKMAN & SCOTT

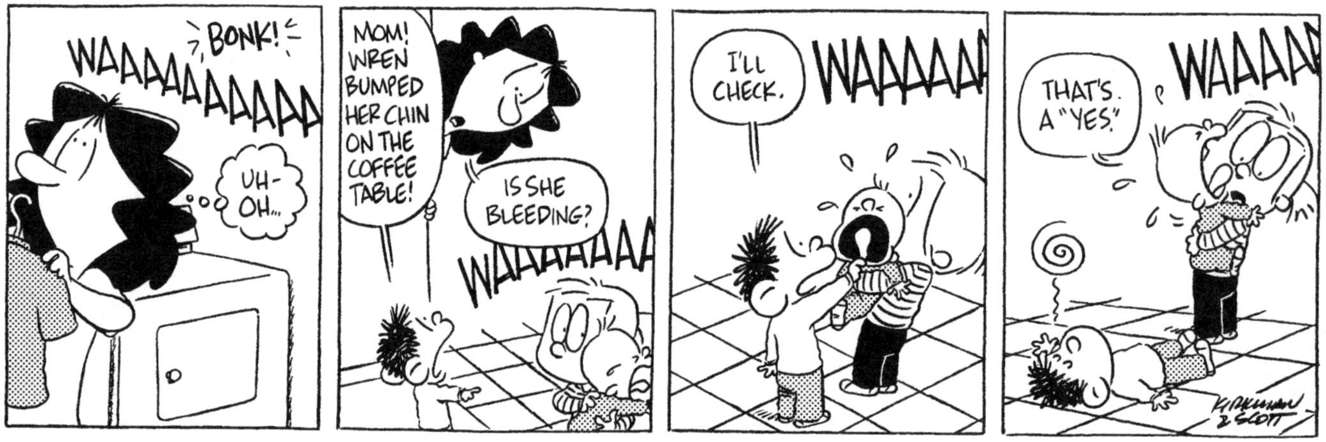
BONK!
WAAAAAAAAAAA
UH-OH...
MOM! WREN BUMPED HER CHIN ON THE COFFEE TABLE!
IS SHE BLEEDING?
WAAAAAAA
I'LL CHECK.
WAAAAAA
THAT'S A "YES."
WAAAA
KIRKMAN & SCOTT

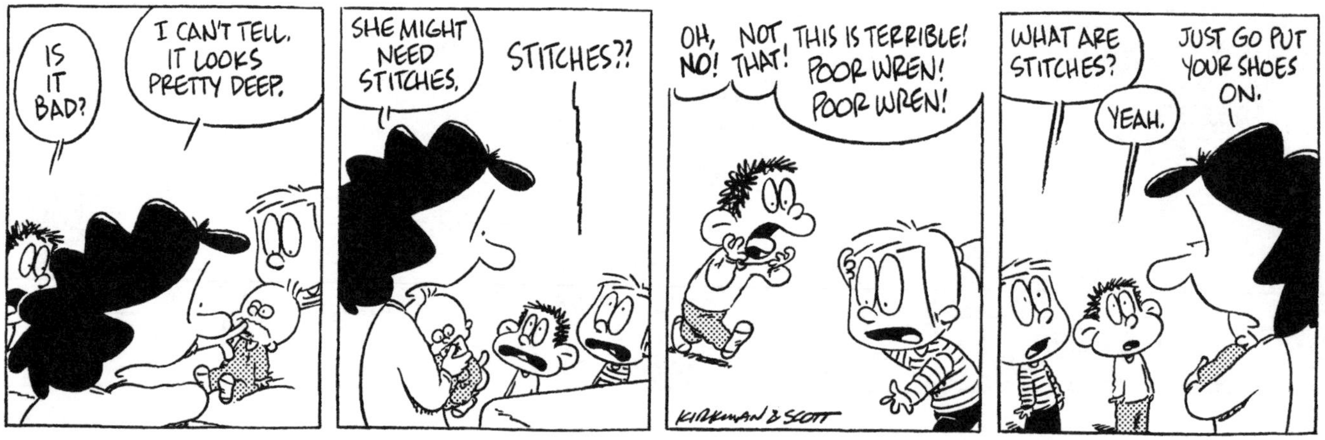
IS IT BAD?
I CAN'T TELL. IT LOOKS PRETTY DEEP.
SHE MIGHT NEED STITCHES.
STITCHES??
OH, NO!
NOT THAT!
THIS IS TERRIBLE! POOR WREN! POOR WREN!
KIRKMAN & SCOTT
WHAT ARE STITCHES?
YEAH.
JUST GO PUT YOUR SHOES ON.

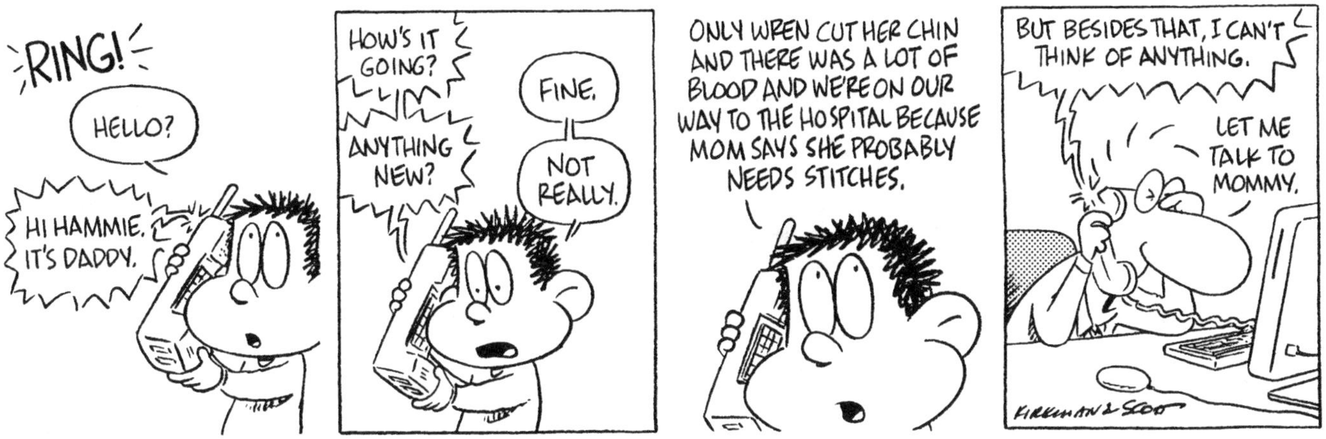
RING!
HELLO?
HI HAMMIE. IT'S DADDY.
HOW'S IT GOING?
FINE.
ANYTHING NEW?
NOT REALLY.
ONLY WREN CUT HER CHIN AND THERE WAS A LOT OF BLOOD AND WE'RE ON OUR WAY TO THE HOSPITAL BECAUSE MOM SAYS SHE PROBABLY NEEDS STITCHES.
BUT BESIDES THAT, I CAN'T THINK OF ANYTHING.
LET ME TALK TO MOMMY.
KIRKMAN & SCOTT

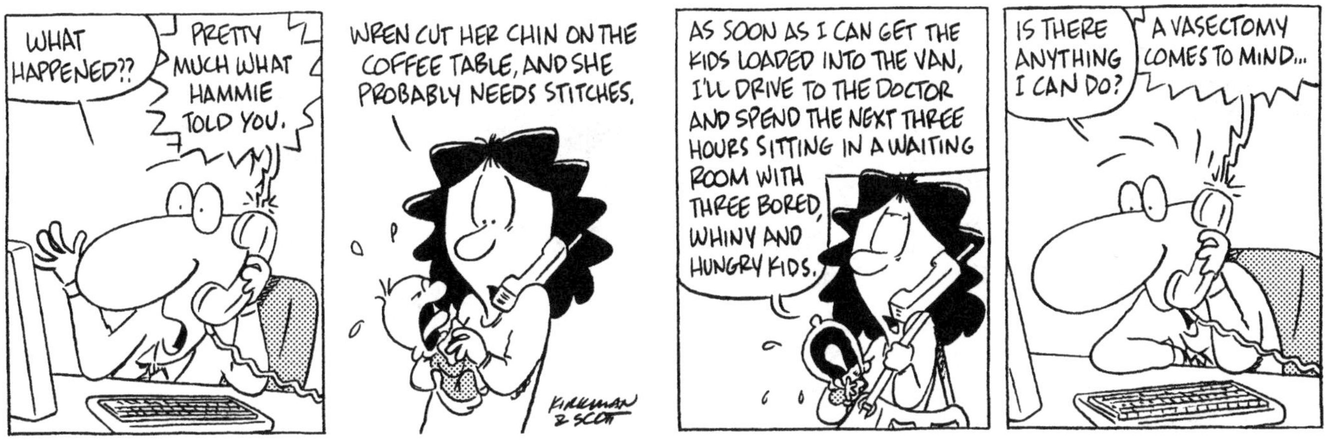
WHAT HAPPENED??
PRETTY MUCH WHAT HAMMIE TOLD YOU.
WREN CUT HER CHIN ON THE COFFEE TABLE, AND SHE PROBABLY NEEDS STITCHES.
KIRKMAN & SCOTT
AS SOON AS I CAN GET THE KIDS LOADED INTO THE VAN, I'LL DRIVE TO THE DOCTOR AND SPEND THE NEXT THREE HOURS SITTING IN A WAITING ROOM WITH THREE BORED, WHINY AND HUNGRY KIDS.
IS THERE ANYTHING I CAN DO?
A VASECTOMY COMES TO MIND...

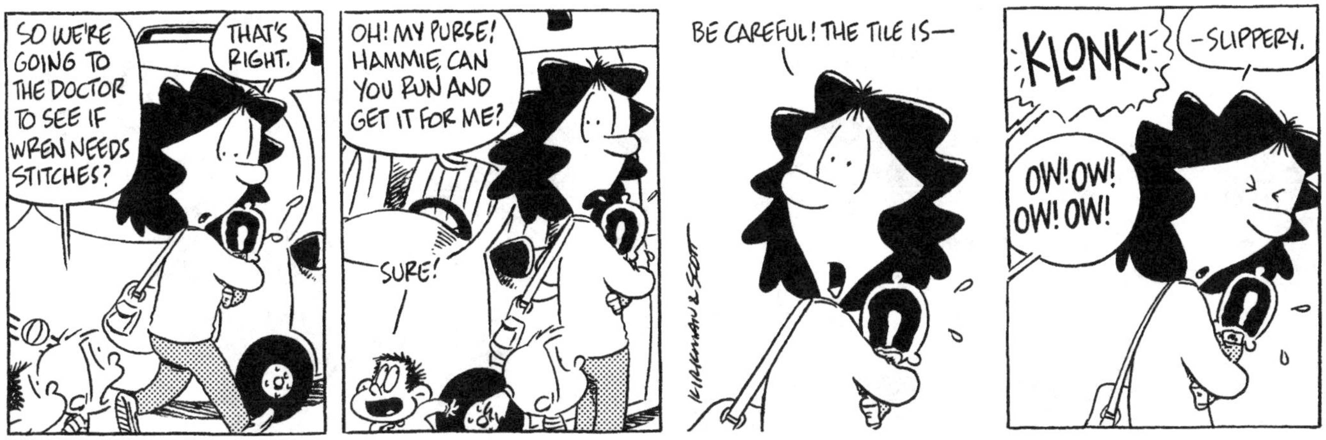
SO WE'RE GOING TO THE DOCTOR TO SEE IF WREN NEEDS STITCHES?
THAT'S RIGHT.
OH! MY PURSE! HAMMIE, CAN YOU RUN AND GET IT FOR ME?
SURE!
BE CAREFUL! THE TILE IS—
KIRKMAN & SCOTT
KLONK!
–SLIPPERY.
OW! OW! OW! OW!

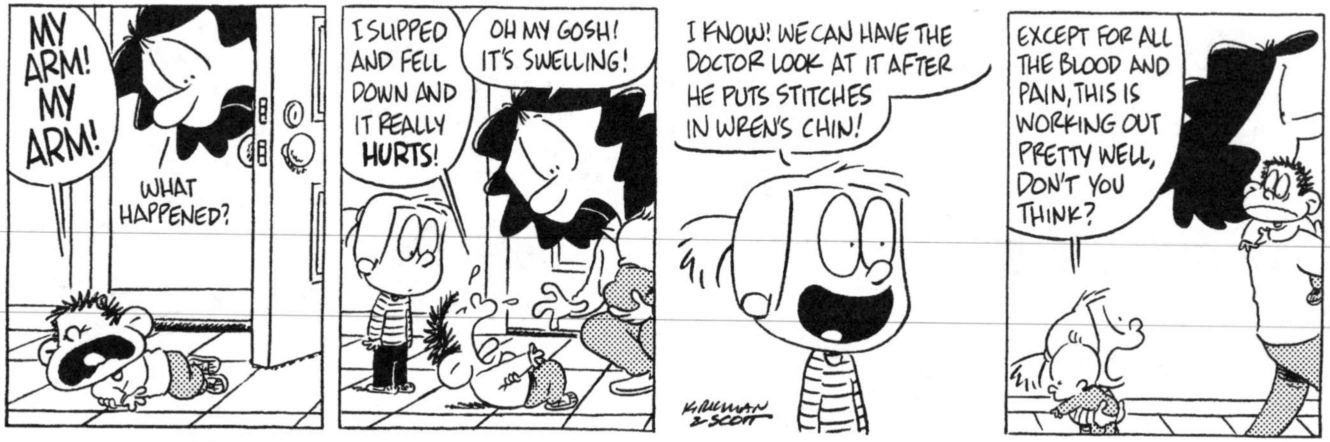
MY ARM! MY ARM!
WHAT HAPPENED?
I SLIPPED AND FELL DOWN AND IT REALLY HURTS!
OH MY GOSH! IT'S SWELLING!
I KNOW! WE CAN HAVE THE DOCTOR LOOK AT IT AFTER HE PUTS STITCHES IN WREN'S CHIN!
KIRKMAN & SCOTT
EXCEPT FOR ALL THE BLOOD AND PAIN, THIS IS WORKING OUT PRETTY WELL, DON'T YOU THINK?

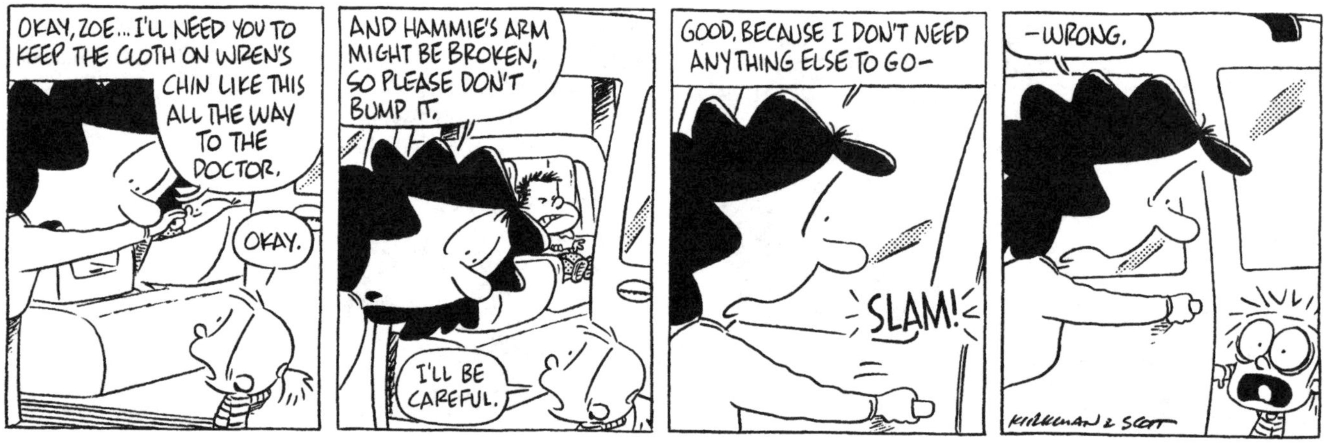
OKAY, ZOE... I'LL NEED YOU TO KEEP THE CLOTH ON WREN'S CHIN LIKE THIS ALL THE WAY TO THE DOCTOR.
OKAY.
AND HAMMIE'S ARM MIGHT BE BROKEN, SO PLEASE DON'T BUMP IT.
I'LL BE CAREFUL.
GOOD, BECAUSE I DON'T NEED ANYTHING ELSE TO GO—
SLAM!
—WRONG.
KIRKMAN & SCOTT

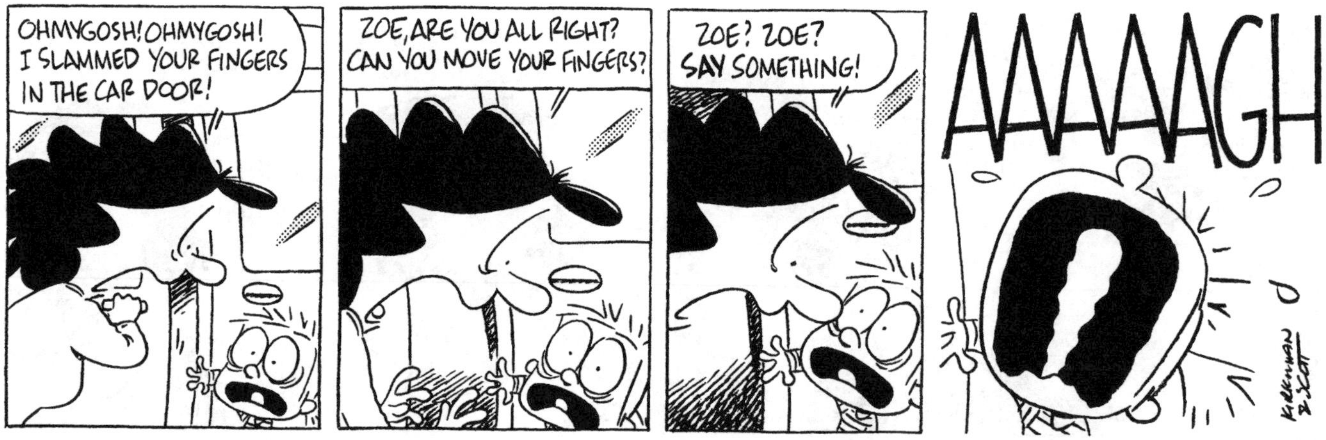
OHMYGOSH! OHMYGOSH! I SLAMMED YOUR FINGERS IN THE CAR DOOR!
ZOE, ARE YOU ALL RIGHT? CAN YOU MOVE YOUR FINGERS?
ZOE? ZOE? SAY SOMETHING!
AAAAAAGH
KIRKMAN & SCOTT

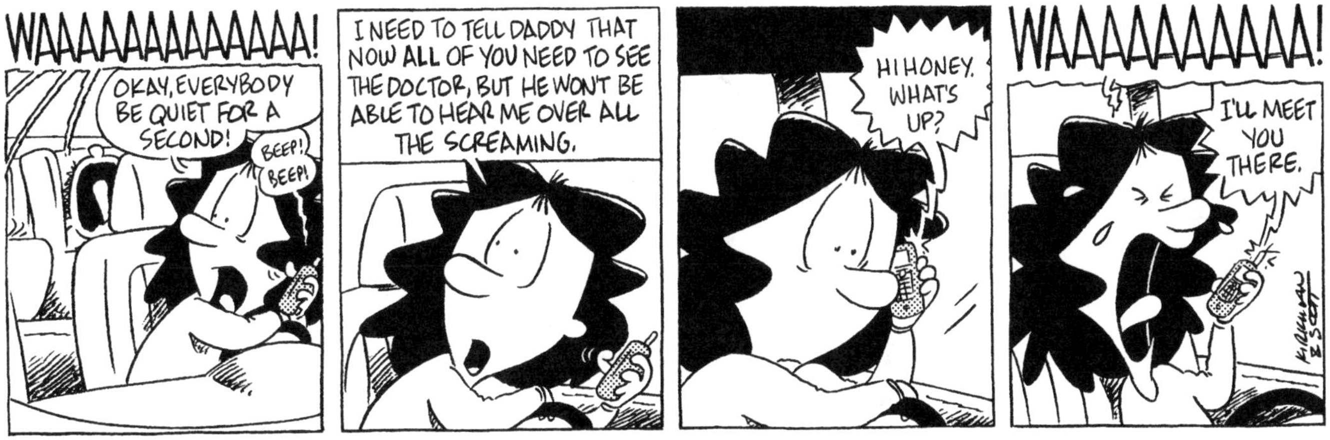
WAAAAAAAAAAAAA!
OKAY, EVERYBODY BE QUIET FOR A SECOND!
BEEP! BEEP!
I NEED TO TELL DADDY THAT NOW ALL OF YOU NEED TO SEE THE DOCTOR, BUT HE WON'T BE ABLE TO HEAR ME OVER ALL THE SCREAMING.
HI HONEY. WHAT'S UP?
WAAAAAAAAAA!
I'LL MEET YOU THERE.

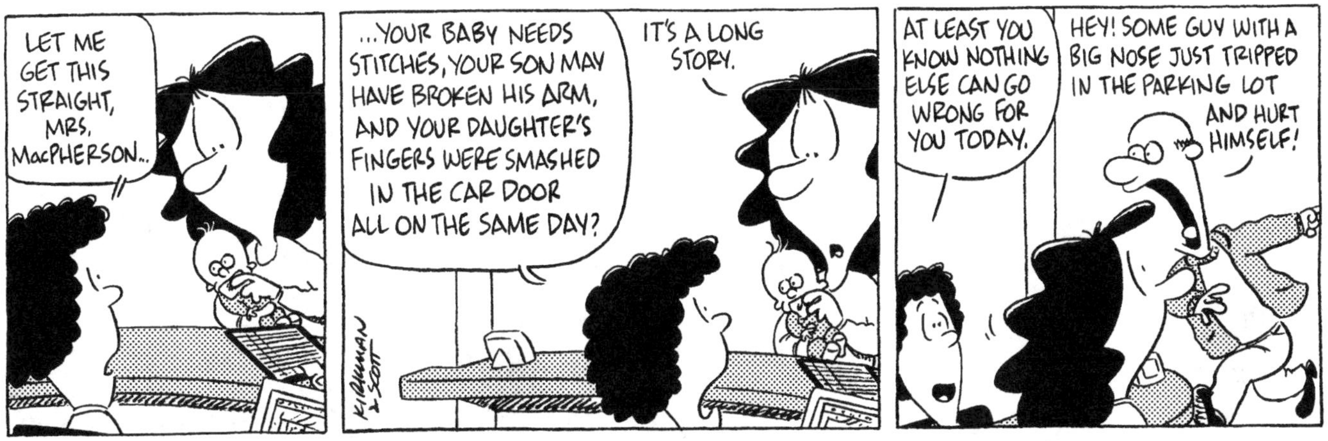
LET ME GET THIS STRAIGHT, MRS. MacPHERSON...
...YOUR BABY NEEDS STITCHES, YOUR SON MAY HAVE BROKEN HIS ARM, AND YOUR DAUGHTER'S FINGERS WERE SMASHED IN THE CAR DOOR ALL ON THE SAME DAY?
IT'S A LONG STORY.
AT LEAST YOU KNOW NOTHING ELSE CAN GO WRONG FOR YOU TODAY.
HEY! SOME GUY WITH A BIG NOSE JUST TRIPPED IN THE PARKING LOT AND HURT HIMSELF!

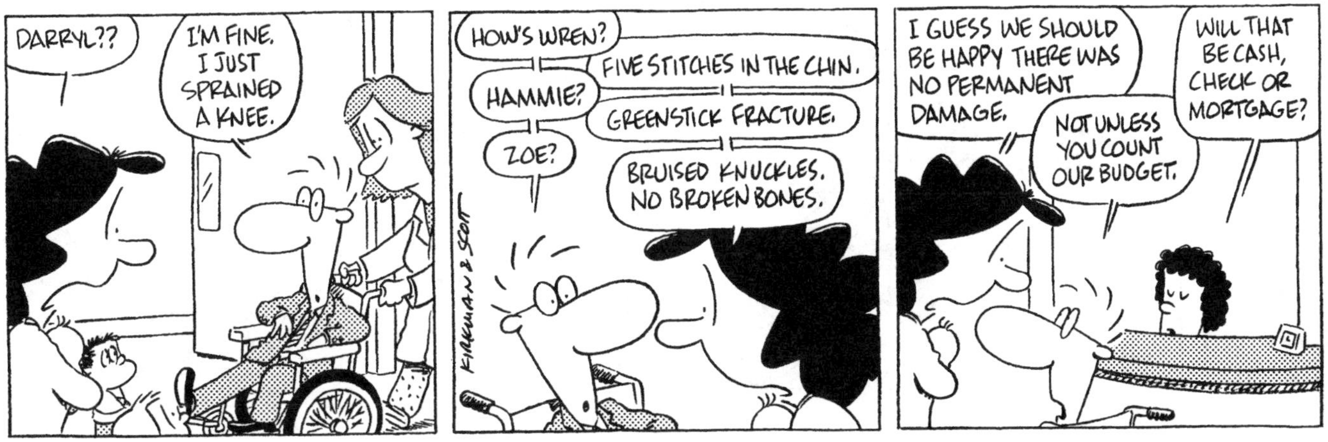
DARRYL??
I'M FINE. I JUST SPRAINED A KNEE.
HOW'S WREN?
FIVE STITCHES IN THE CHIN.
HAMMIE?
GREENSTICK FRACTURE.
ZOE?
BRUISED KNUCKLES. NO BROKEN BONES.
I GUESS WE SHOULD BE HAPPY THERE WAS NO PERMANENT DAMAGE.
NOT UNLESS YOU COUNT OUR BUDGET.
WILL THAT BE CASH, CHECK OR MORTGAGE?

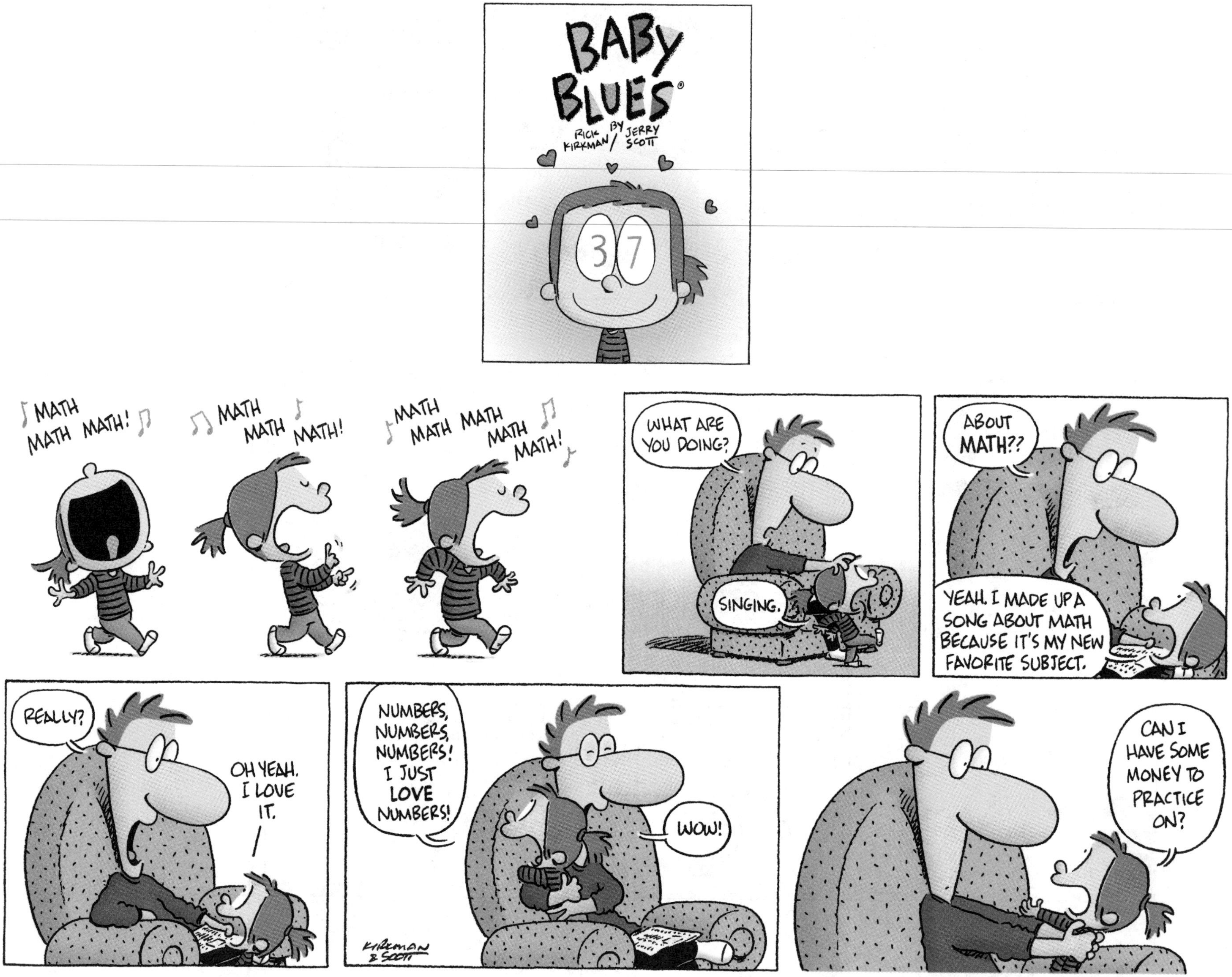
BABY BLUES®
BY RICK KIRKMAN / JERRY SCOTT
37
MATH MATH MATH!
MATH MATH MATH!
MATH MATH MATH MATH MATH!
WHAT ARE YOU DOING?
SINGING.
ABOUT MATH??
YEAH. I MADE UP A SONG ABOUT MATH BECAUSE IT'S MY NEW FAVORITE SUBJECT.
REALLY?
OH YEAH. I LOVE IT.
NUMBERS, NUMBERS, NUMBERS! I JUST LOVE NUMBERS!
WOW!
KIRKMAN & SCOTT
CAN I HAVE SOME MONEY TO PRACTICE ON?

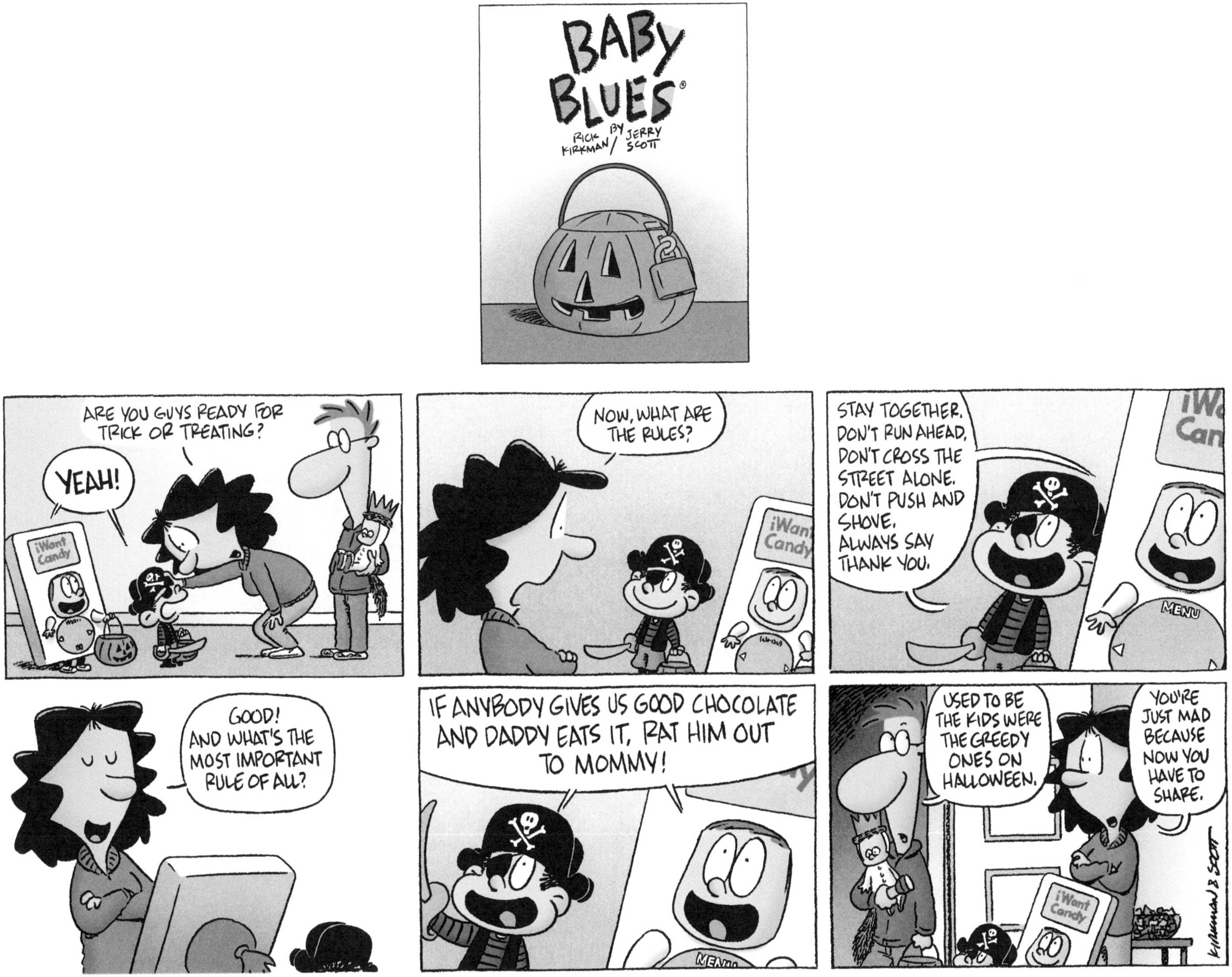

BABY BLUES®
BY RICK KIRKMAN / JERRY SCOTT
ARE YOU GUYS READY FOR TRICK OR TREATING?
YEAH!
iWant Candy
NOW, WHAT ARE THE RULES?
STAY TOGETHER. DON'T RUN AHEAD. DON'T CROSS THE STREET ALONE. DON'T PUSH AND SHOVE. ALWAYS SAY THANK YOU.
MENU
GOOD! AND WHAT'S THE MOST IMPORTANT RULE OF ALL?
IF ANYBODY GIVES US GOOD CHOCOLATE AND DADDY EATS IT, RAT HIM OUT TO MOMMY!
USED TO BE THE KIDS WERE THE GREEDY ONES ON HALLOWEEN.
YOU'RE JUST MAD BECAUSE NOW YOU HAVE TO SHARE.
KIRKMAN & SCOTT

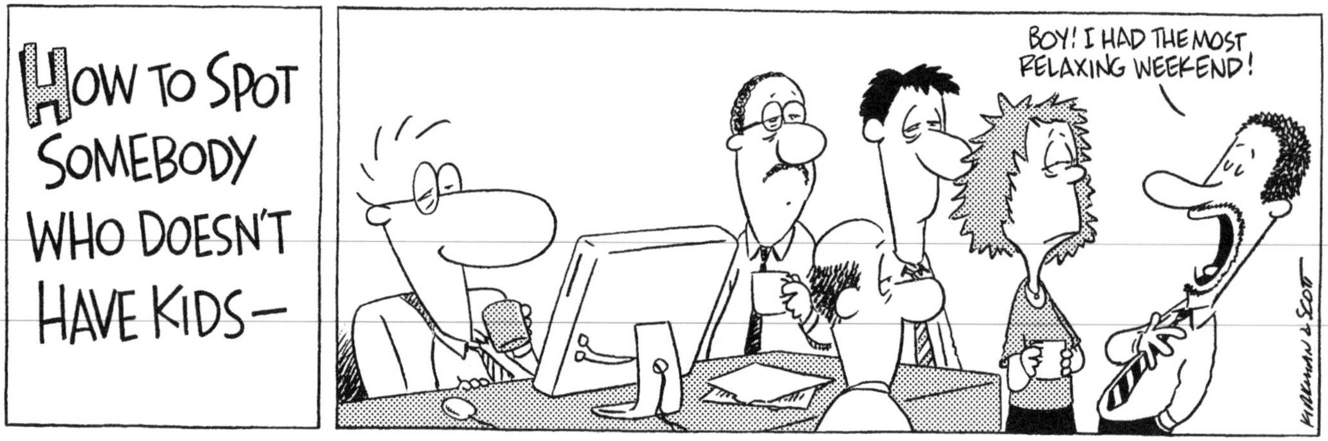
HOW TO SPOT SOMEBODY WHO DOESN'T HAVE KIDS—
BOY! I HAD THE MOST RELAXING WEEKEND!
KIRKMAN & SCOTT

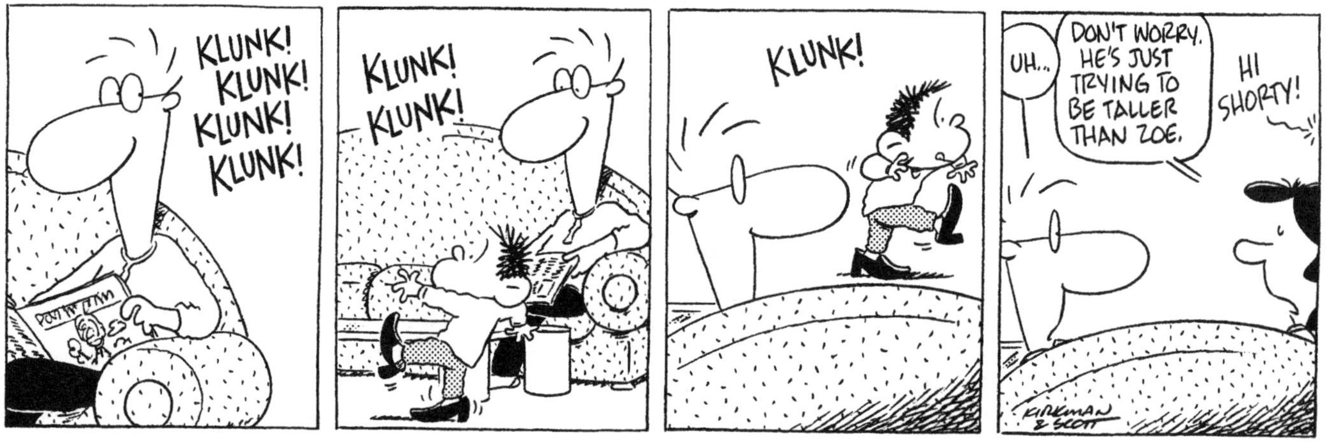
KLUNK! KLUNK! KLUNK! KLUNK!
KLUNK! KLUNK!
KLUNK!
UH...
DON'T WORRY. HE'S JUST TRYING TO BE TALLER THAN ZOE.
HI SHORTY!
KIRKMAN & SCOTT

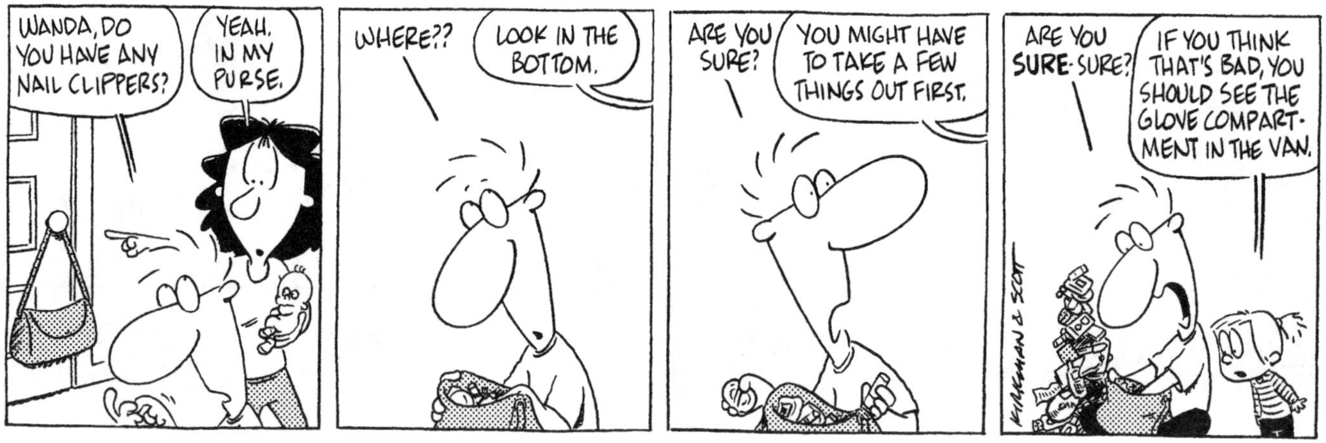
WANDA, DO YOU HAVE ANY NAIL CLIPPERS?
YEAH. IN MY PURSE.
WHERE??
LOOK IN THE BOTTOM.
ARE YOU SURE?
YOU MIGHT HAVE TO TAKE A FEW THINGS OUT FIRST.
ARE YOU SURE-SURE?
IF YOU THINK THAT'S BAD, YOU SHOULD SEE THE GLOVE COMPARTMENT IN THE VAN.
KIRKMAN & SCOTT

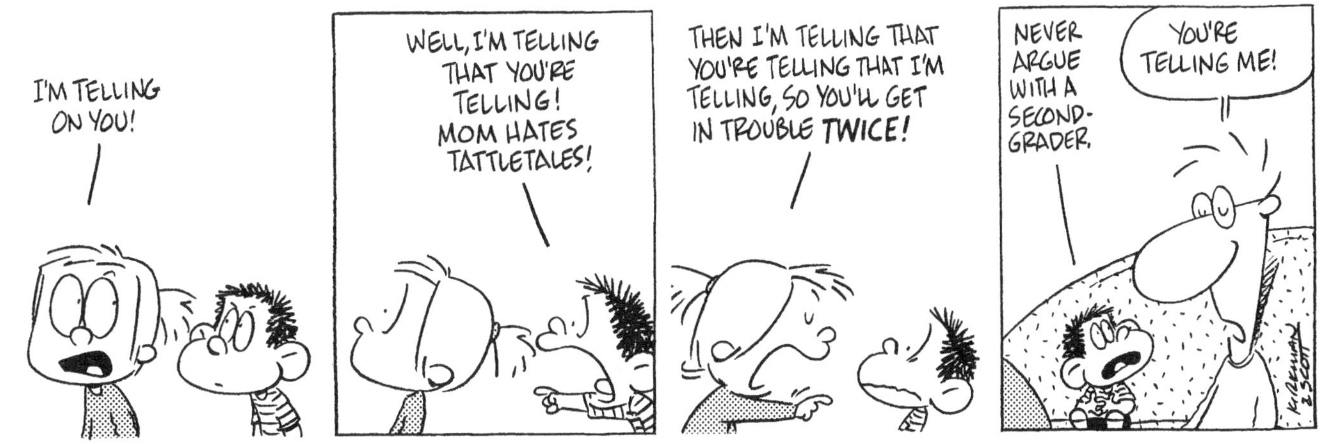
I'M TELLING ON YOU!
WELL, I'M TELLING THAT YOU'RE TELLING! MOM HATES TATTLETALES!
THEN I'M TELLING THAT YOU'RE TELLING THAT I'M TELLING, SO YOU'LL GET IN TROUBLE TWICE!
NEVER ARGUE WITH A SECOND-GRADER.
YOU'RE TELLING ME!

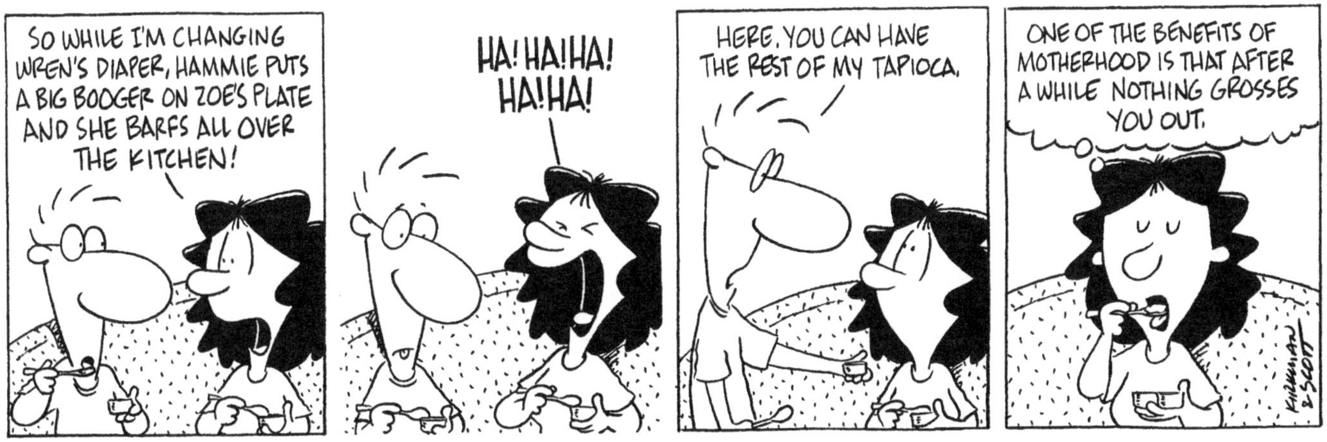
SO WHILE I'M CHANGING WREN'S DIAPER, HAMMIE PUTS A BIG BOOGER ON ZOE'S PLATE AND SHE BARFS ALL OVER THE KITCHEN!
HA! HA! HA! HA! HA!
HERE. YOU CAN HAVE THE REST OF MY TAPIOCA.
ONE OF THE BENEFITS OF MOTHERHOOD IS THAT AFTER A WHILE NOTHING GROSSES YOU OUT.

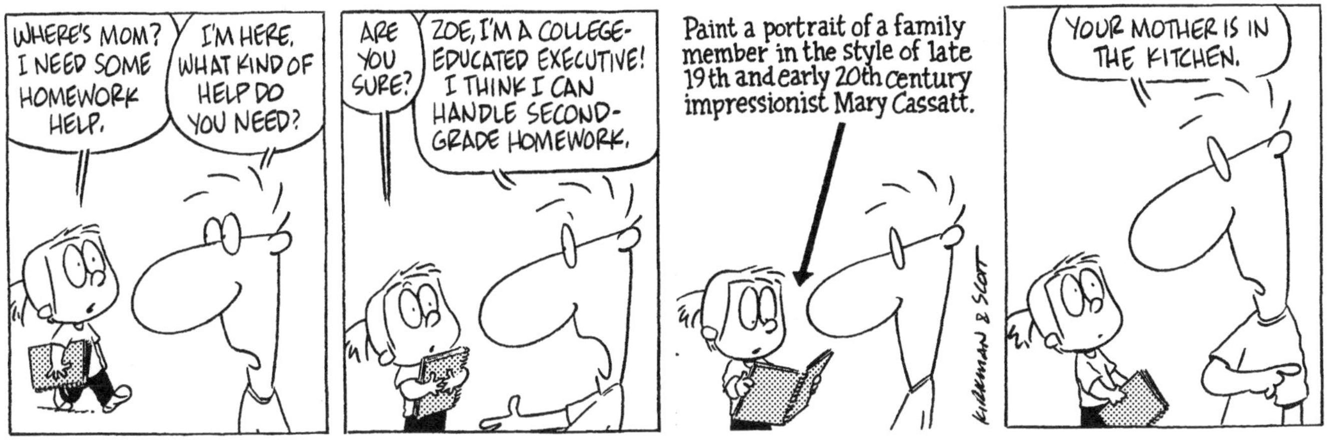
WHERE'S MOM? I NEED SOME HOMEWORK HELP.
I'M HERE. WHAT KIND OF HELP DO YOU NEED?
ARE YOU SURE?
ZOE, I'M A COLLEGE-EDUCATED EXECUTIVE! I THINK I CAN HANDLE SECOND-GRADE HOMEWORK.
Paint a portrait of a family member in the style of late 19th and early 20th century impressionist Mary Cassatt.
YOUR MOTHER IS IN THE KITCHEN.

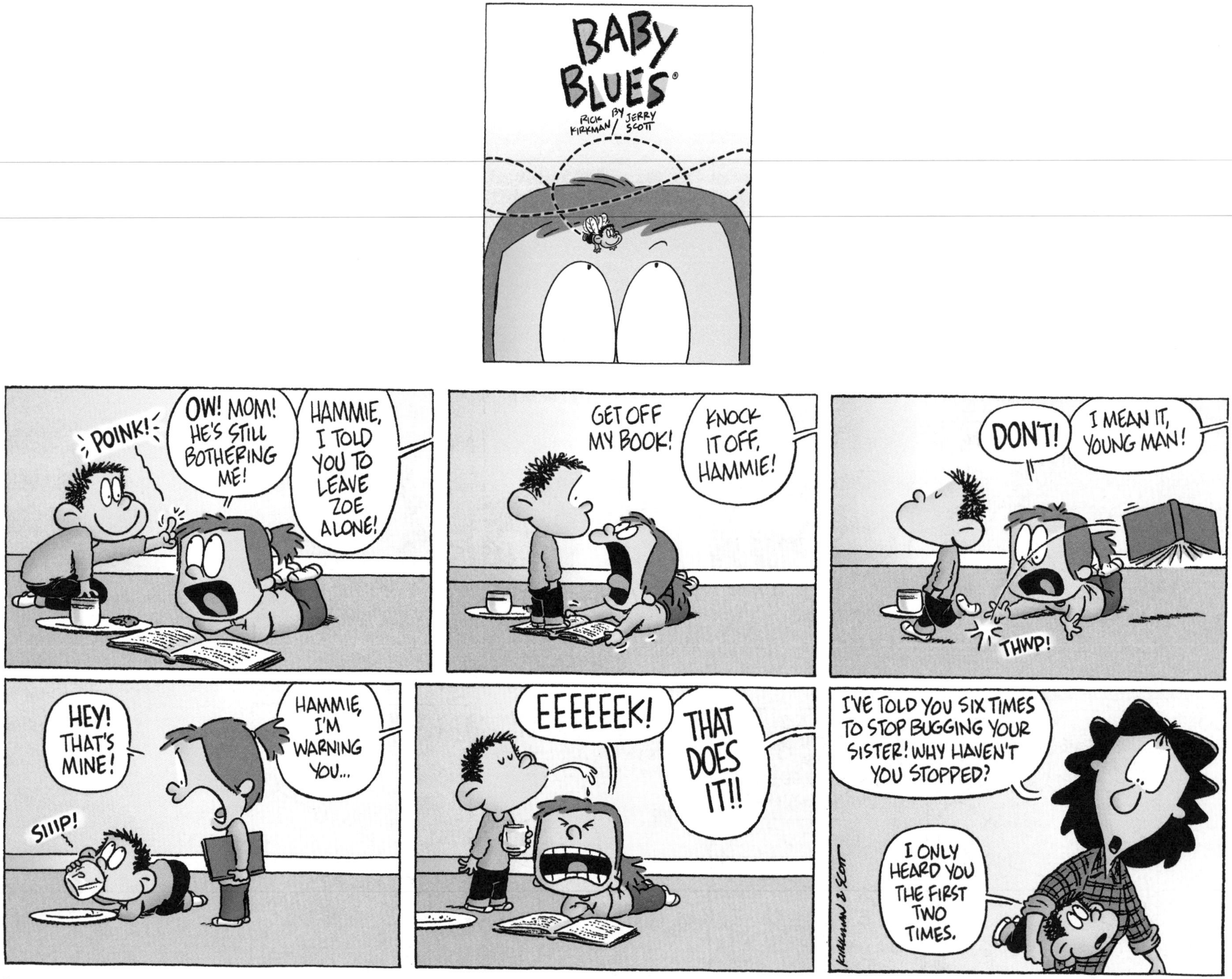
BABY BLUES®
RICK KIRKMAN / BY JERRY SCOTT
POINK!
OW! MOM! HE'S STILL BOTHERING ME!
HAMMIE, I TOLD YOU TO LEAVE ZOE ALONE!
GET OFF MY BOOK!
KNOCK IT OFF, HAMMIE!
DON'T!
I MEAN IT, YOUNG MAN!
THWP!
HEY! THAT'S MINE!
HAMMIE, I'M WARNING YOU...
SIIIP!
EEEEEEK!
THAT DOES IT!!
I'VE TOLD YOU SIX TIMES TO STOP BUGGING YOUR SISTER! WHY HAVEN'T YOU STOPPED?
I ONLY HEARD YOU THE FIRST TWO TIMES.
KIRKMAN & SCOTT

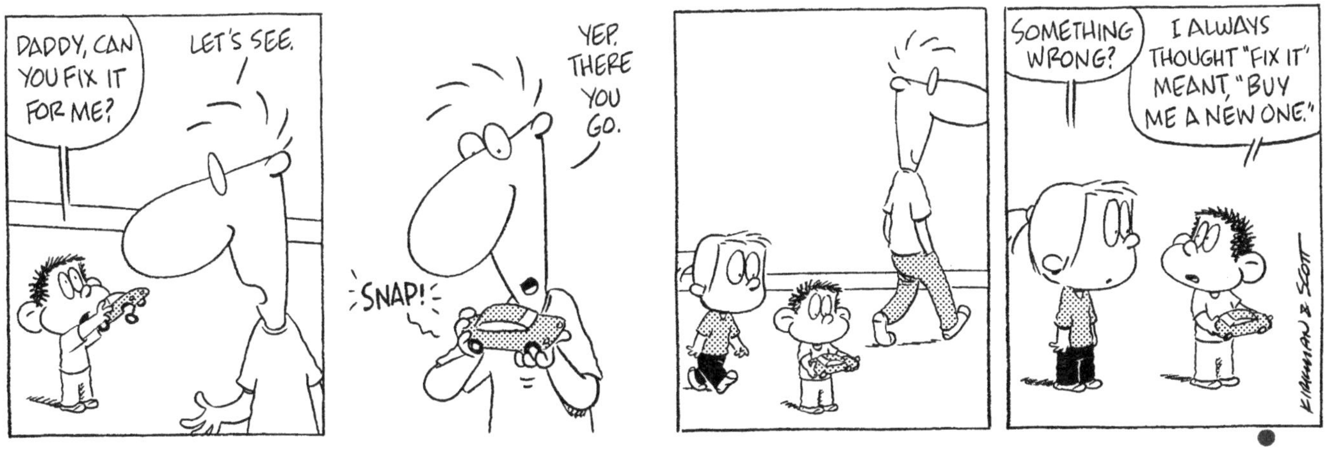
DADDY, CAN YOU FIX IT FOR ME?
LET'S SEE.
SNAP!
YEP. THERE YOU GO.
SOMETHING WRONG?
I ALWAYS THOUGHT "FIX IT" MEANT, "BUY ME A NEW ONE."
KIRKMAN & SCOTT

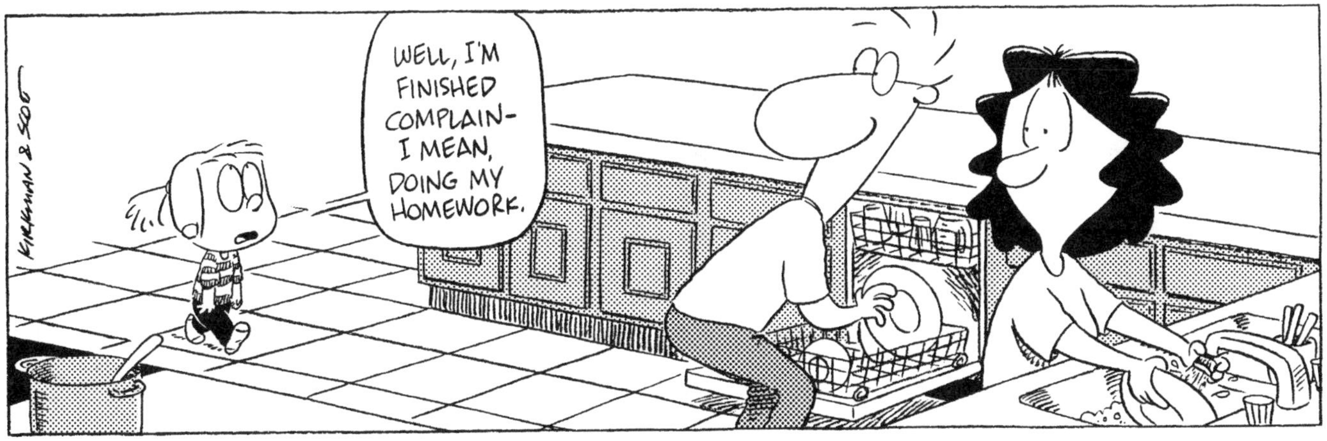
KIRKMAN & SCOTT
WELL, I'M FINISHED COMPLAIN- I MEAN, DOING MY HOMEWORK.

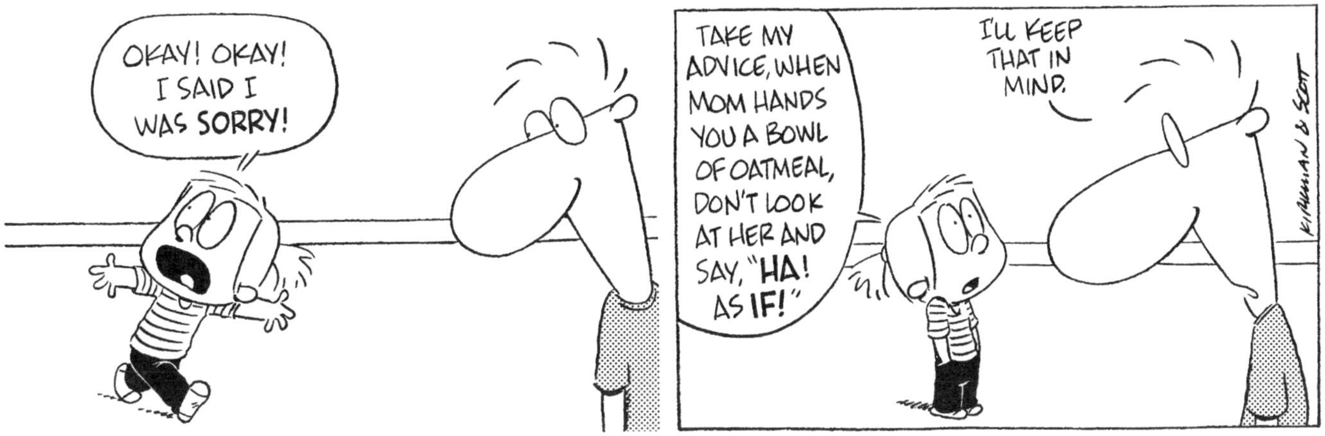
OKAY! OKAY! I SAID I WAS SORRY!
TAKE MY ADVICE, WHEN MOM HANDS YOU A BOWL OF OATMEAL, DON'T LOOK AT HER AND SAY, "HA! AS IF!"
I'LL KEEP THAT IN MIND.
KIRKMAN & SCOTT

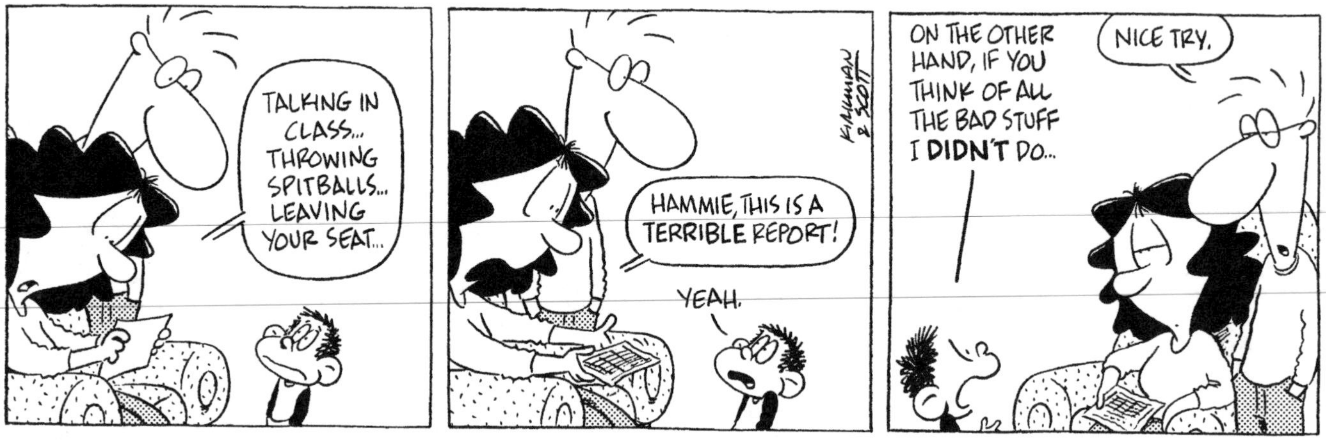
TALKING IN CLASS... THROWING SPITBALLS... LEAVING YOUR SEAT...
HAMMIE, THIS IS A TERRIBLE REPORT!
YEAH.
KIRKMAN & SCOTT
ON THE OTHER HAND, IF YOU THINK OF ALL THE BAD STUFF I **DIDN'T** DO...
NICE TRY.

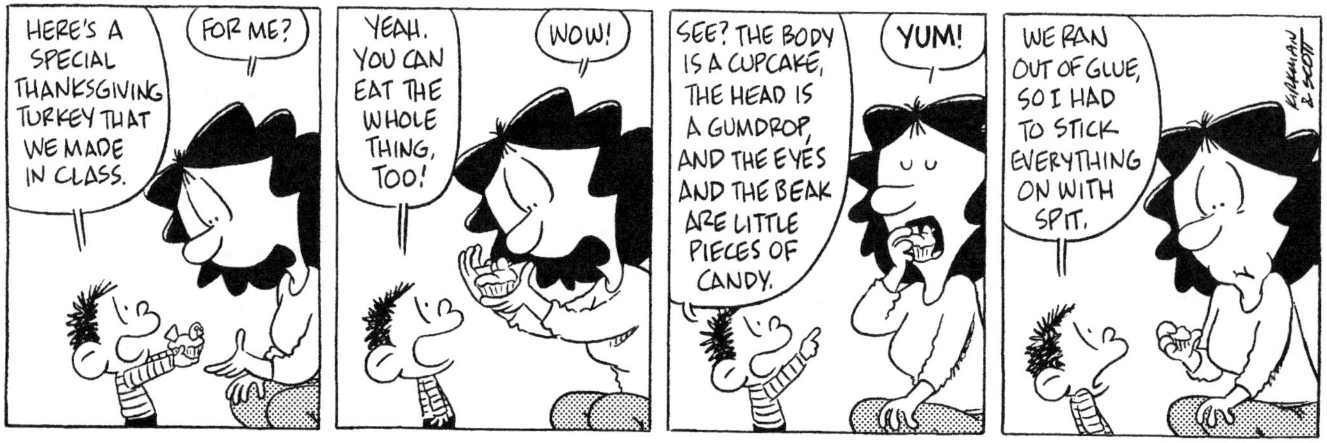
HERE'S A SPECIAL THANKSGIVING TURKEY THAT WE MADE IN CLASS.
FOR ME?
YEAH. YOU CAN EAT THE WHOLE THING, TOO!
WOW!
SEE? THE BODY IS A CUPCAKE, THE HEAD IS A GUMDROP, AND THE EYES AND THE BEAK ARE LITTLE PIECES OF CANDY.
YUM!
WE RAN OUT OF GLUE, SO I HAD TO STICK EVERYTHING ON WITH SPIT.
KIRKMAN & SCOTT

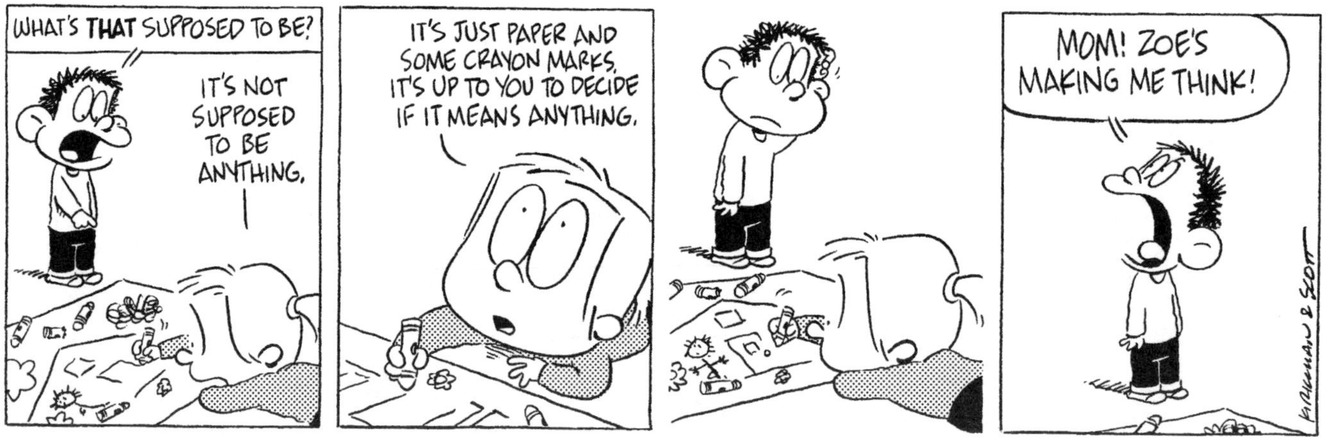
WHAT'S **THAT** SUPPOSED TO BE?
IT'S NOT SUPPOSED TO BE ANYTHING.
IT'S JUST PAPER AND SOME CRAYON MARKS. IT'S UP TO YOU TO DECIDE IF IT MEANS ANYTHING.
MOM! ZOE'S MAKING ME THINK!
KIRKMAN & SCOTT

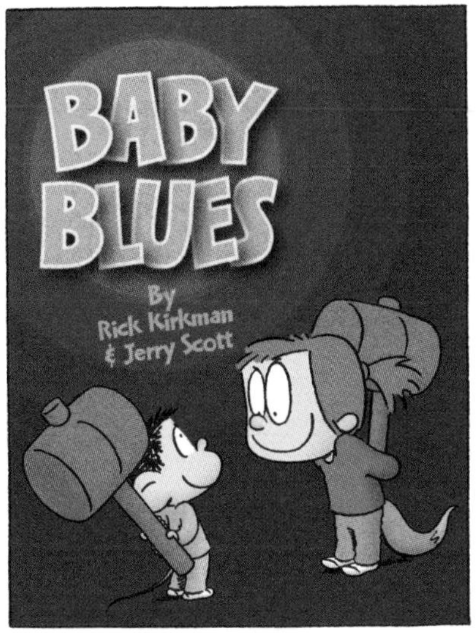
BABY BLUES
By
Rick Kirkman
& Jerry Scott

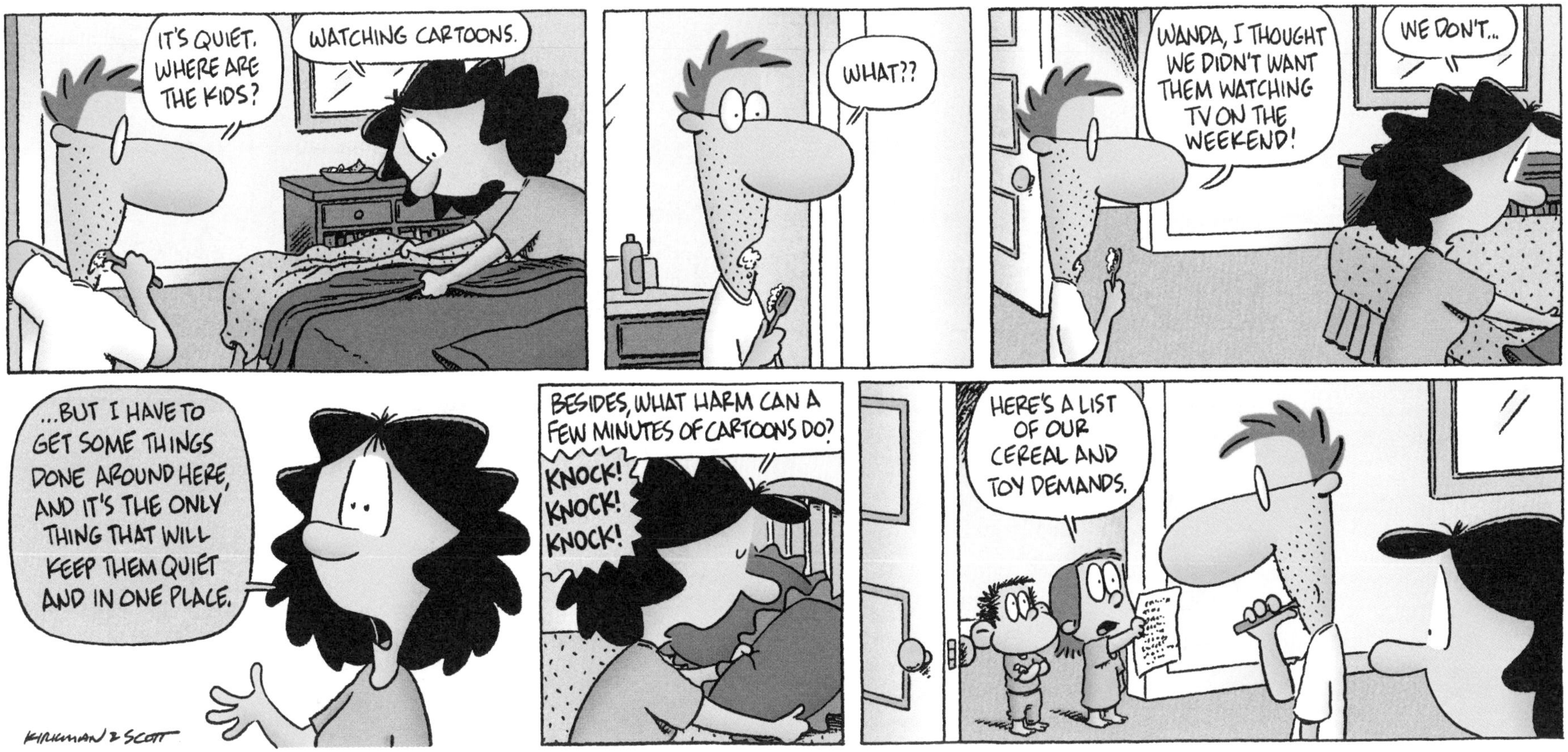
IT'S QUIET. WHERE ARE THE KIDS?
WATCHING CARTOONS.
WHAT??
WANDA, I THOUGHT WE DIDN'T WANT THEM WATCHING TV ON THE WEEKEND!
WE DON'T...
...BUT I HAVE TO GET SOME THINGS DONE AROUND HERE, AND IT'S THE ONLY THING THAT WILL KEEP THEM QUIET AND IN ONE PLACE.
KIRKMAN & SCOTT
BESIDES, WHAT HARM CAN A FEW MINUTES OF CARTOONS DO?
KNOCK! KNOCK! KNOCK!
HERE'S A LIST OF OUR CEREAL AND TOY DEMANDS.

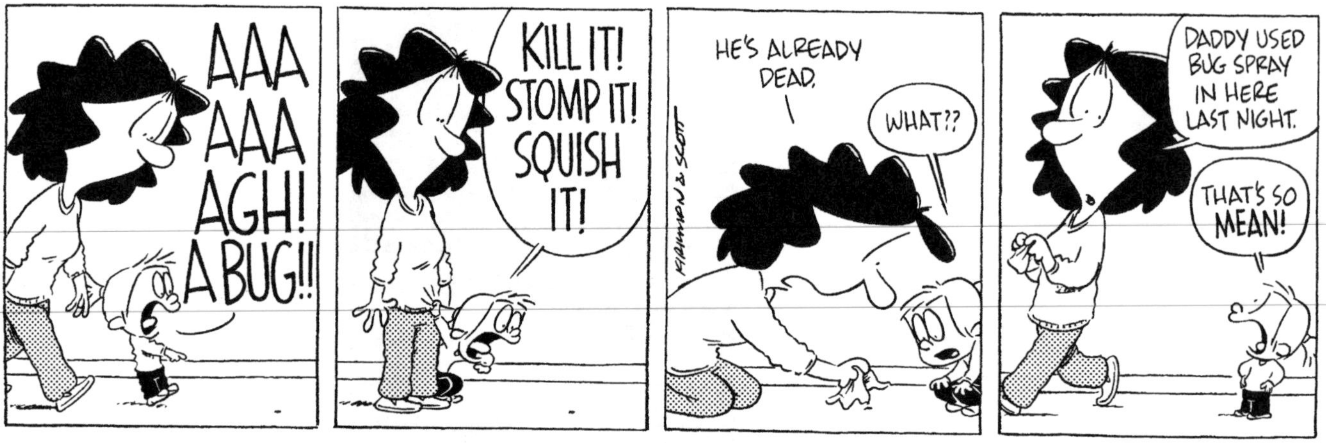
AAA AAA AGH! A BUG!!
KILL IT! STOMP IT! SQUISH IT!
KIRKMAN & SCOTT
HE'S ALREADY DEAD.
WHAT??
DADDY USED BUG SPRAY IN HERE LAST NIGHT.
THAT'S SO MEAN!

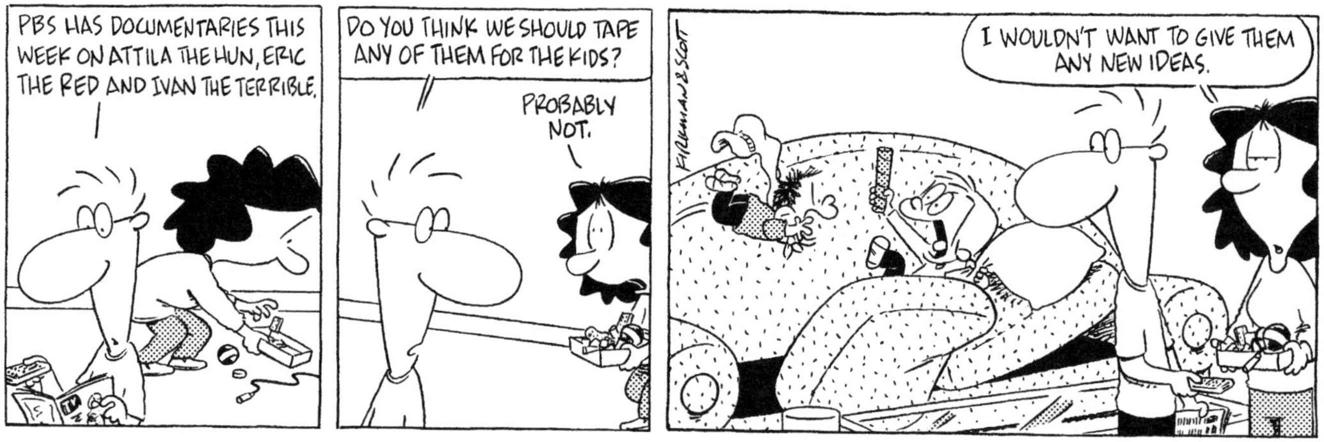
PBS HAS DOCUMENTARIES THIS WEEK ON ATTILA THE HUN, ERIC THE RED AND IVAN THE TERRIBLE.
DO YOU THINK WE SHOULD TAPE ANY OF THEM FOR THE KIDS?
PROBABLY NOT.
KIRKMAN & SCOTT
I WOULDN'T WANT TO GIVE THEM ANY NEW IDEAS.

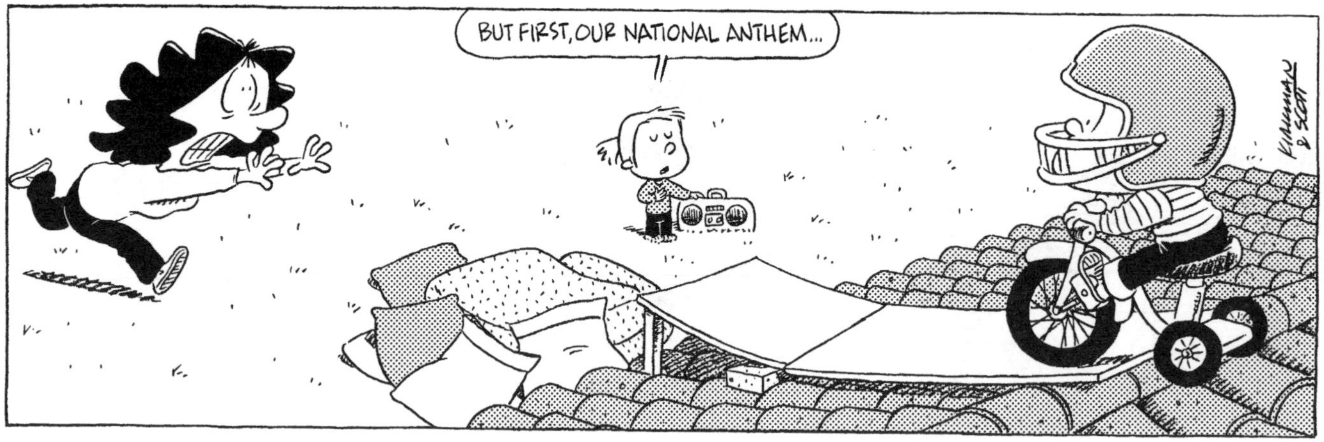
BUT FIRST, OUR NATIONAL ANTHEM...
KIRKMAN & SCOTT

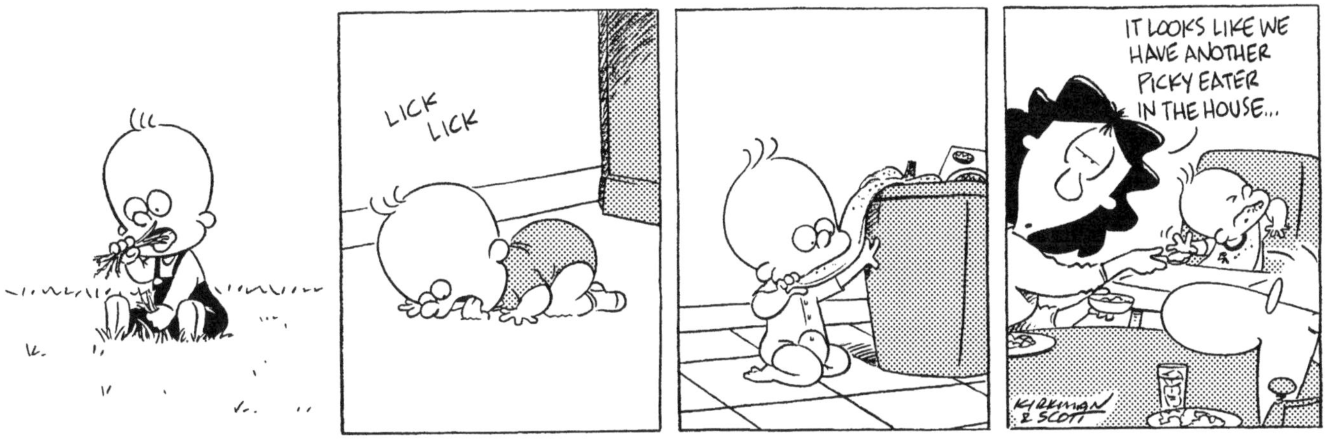
LICK LICK
IT LOOKS LIKE WE HAVE ANOTHER PICKY EATER IN THE HOUSE...
KIRKMAN & SCOTT

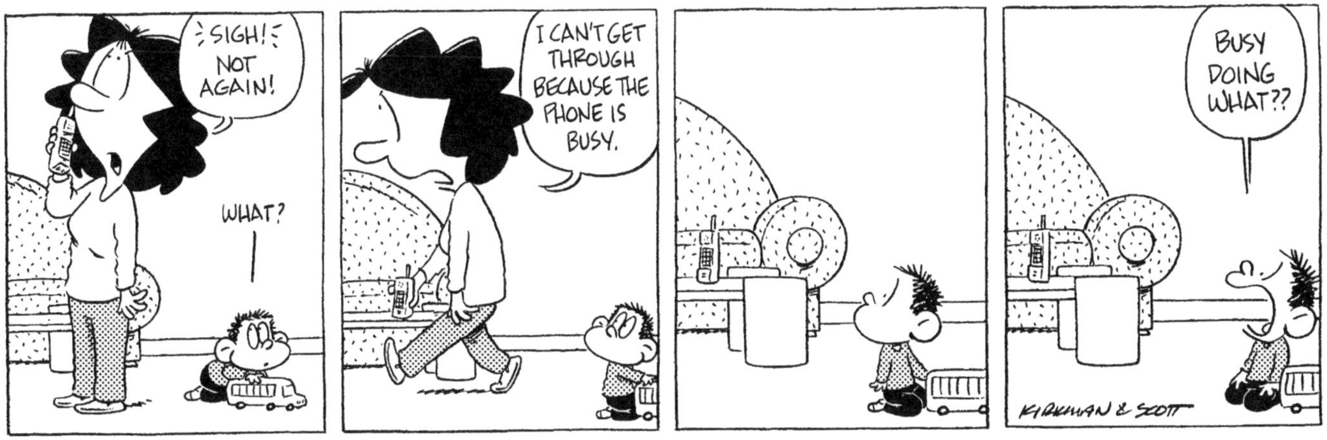
SIGH! NOT AGAIN!
WHAT?
I CAN'T GET THROUGH BECAUSE THE PHONE IS BUSY.
BUSY DOING WHAT??
KIRKMAN & SCOTT

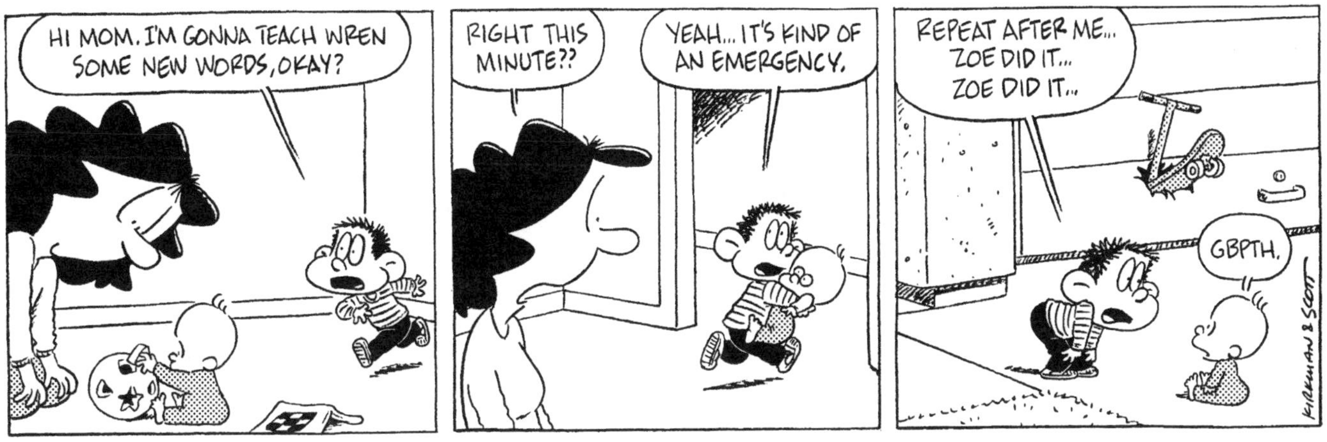
HI MOM. I'M GONNA TEACH WREN SOME NEW WORDS, OKAY?
RIGHT THIS MINUTE??
YEAH... IT'S KIND OF AN EMERGENCY.
REPEAT AFTER ME... ZOE DID IT... ZOE DID IT...
GBPTH.
KIRKMAN & SCOTT

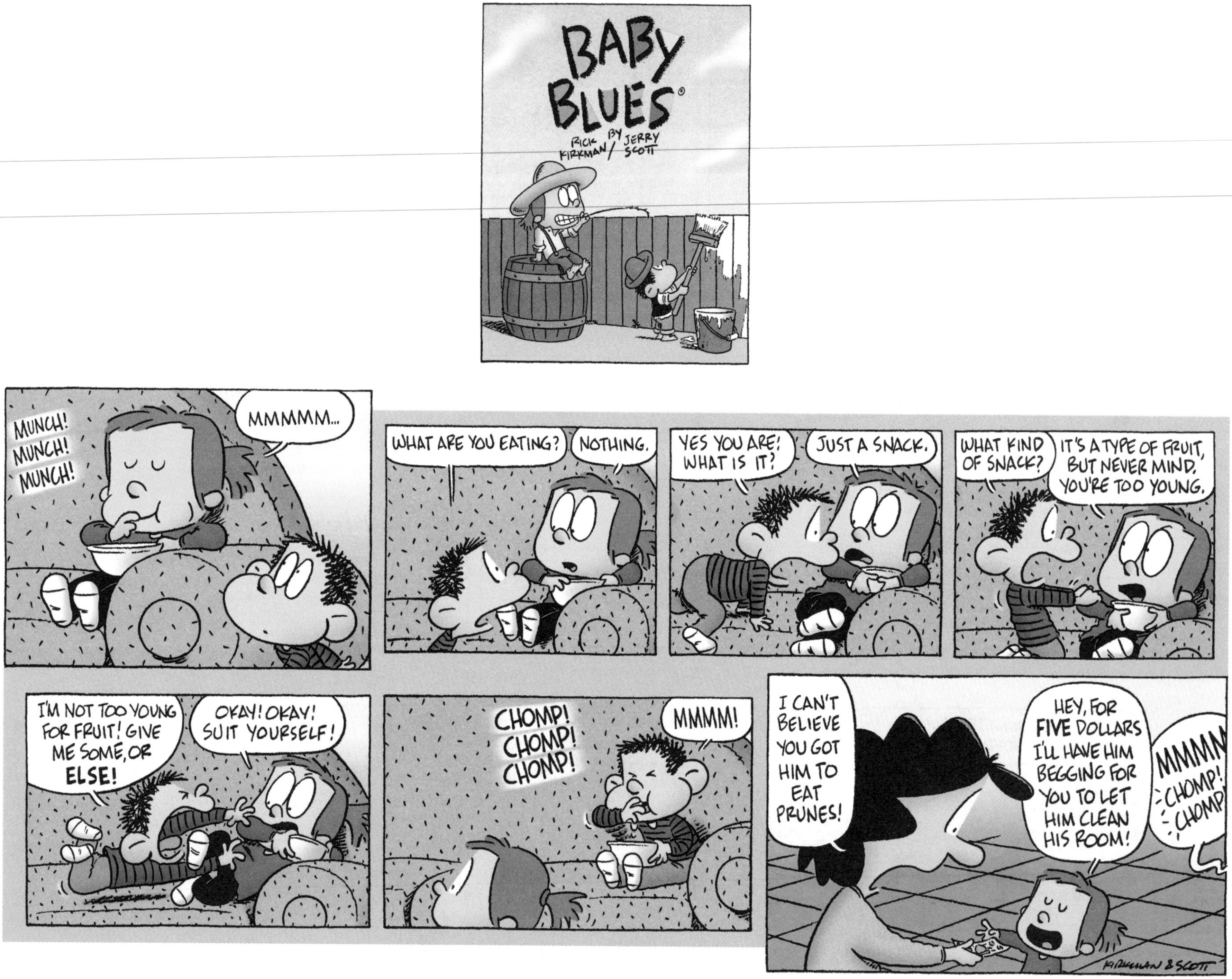

BABY BLUES®
BY RICK KIRKMAN / JERRY SCOTT
MUNCH! MUNCH! MUNCH!
MMMMM...
WHAT ARE YOU EATING?
NOTHING.
YES YOU ARE! WHAT IS IT?
JUST A SNACK.
WHAT KIND OF SNACK?
IT'S A TYPE OF FRUIT, BUT NEVER MIND. YOU'RE TOO YOUNG.
I'M NOT TOO YOUNG FOR FRUIT! GIVE ME SOME, OR ELSE!
OKAY! OKAY! SUIT YOURSELF!
CHOMP! CHOMP! CHOMP!
MMMM!
I CAN'T BELIEVE YOU GOT HIM TO EAT PRUNES!
HEY, FOR FIVE DOLLARS I'LL HAVE HIM BEGGING FOR YOU TO LET HIM CLEAN HIS ROOM!
CHOMP! CHOMP!
KIRKMAN & SCOTT

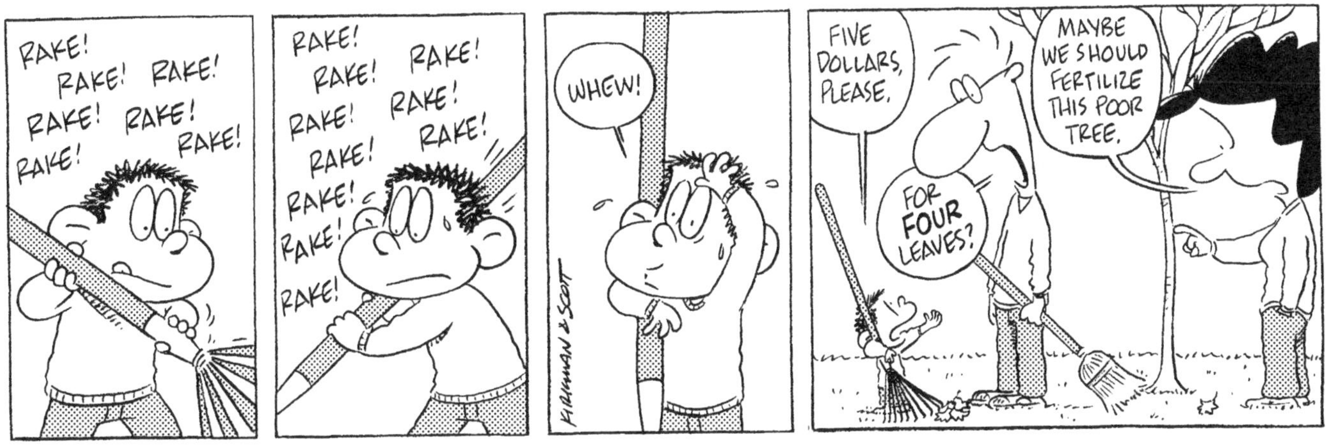
RAKE! RAKE! RAKE! RAKE! RAKE! RAKE! RAKE!
RAKE! RAKE! RAKE! RAKE! RAKE! RAKE! RAKE! RAKE! RAKE!
WHEW!
KIRKMAN & SCOTT
FIVE DOLLARS, PLEASE.
FOR FOUR LEAVES?
MAYBE WE SHOULD FERTILIZE THIS POOR TREE.

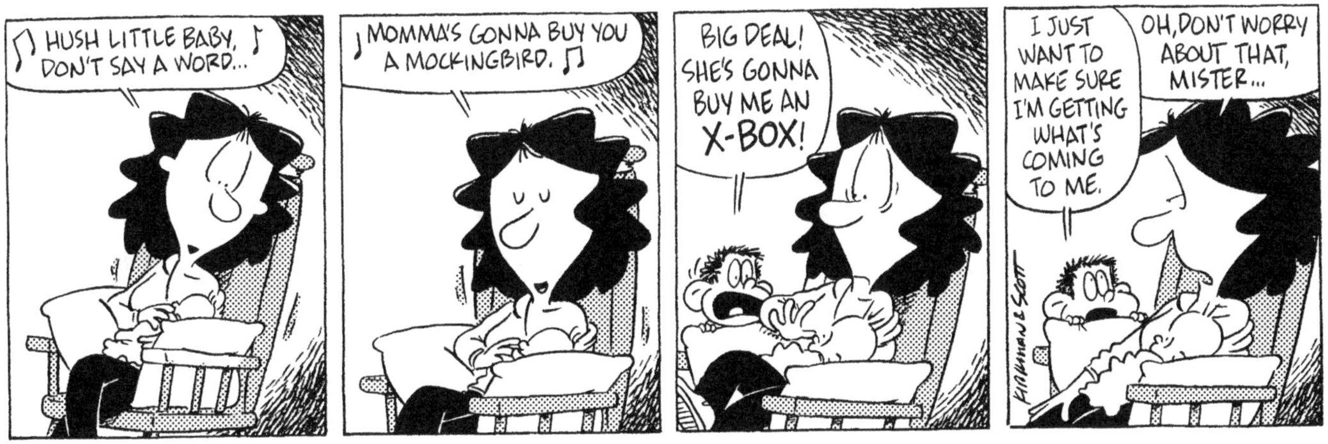
HUSH LITTLE BABY, DON'T SAY A WORD...
MOMMA'S GONNA BUY YOU A MOCKINGBIRD.
BIG DEAL! SHE'S GONNA BUY ME AN X-BOX!
I JUST WANT TO MAKE SURE I'M GETTING WHAT'S COMING TO ME.
OH, DON'T WORRY ABOUT THAT, MISTER...
KIRKMAN & SCOTT

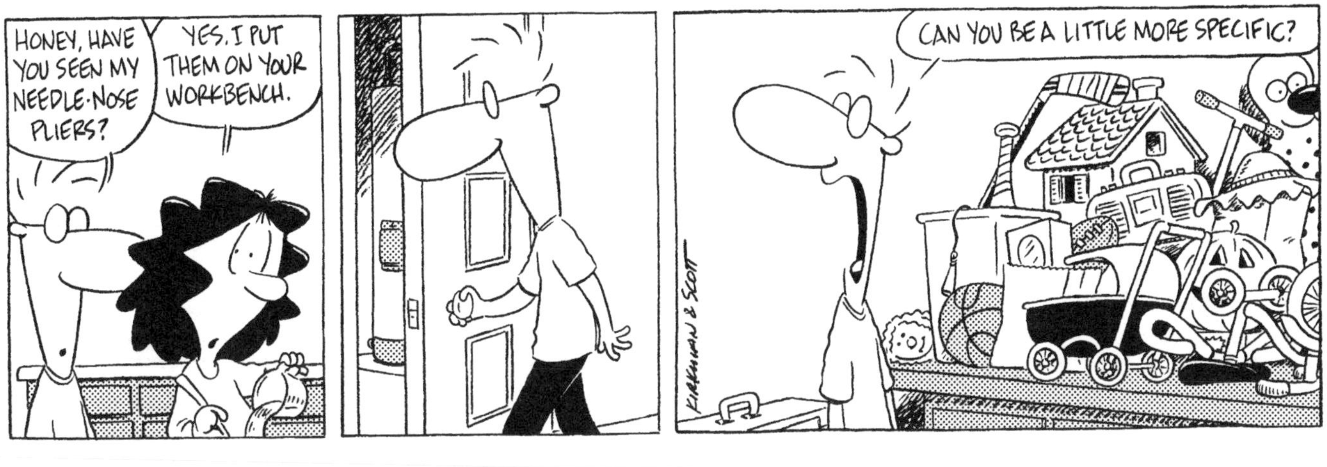
HONEY, HAVE YOU SEEN MY NEEDLE-NOSE PLIERS?
YES. I PUT THEM ON YOUR WORKBENCH.
KIRKMAN & SCOTT
CAN YOU BE A LITTLE MORE SPECIFIC?

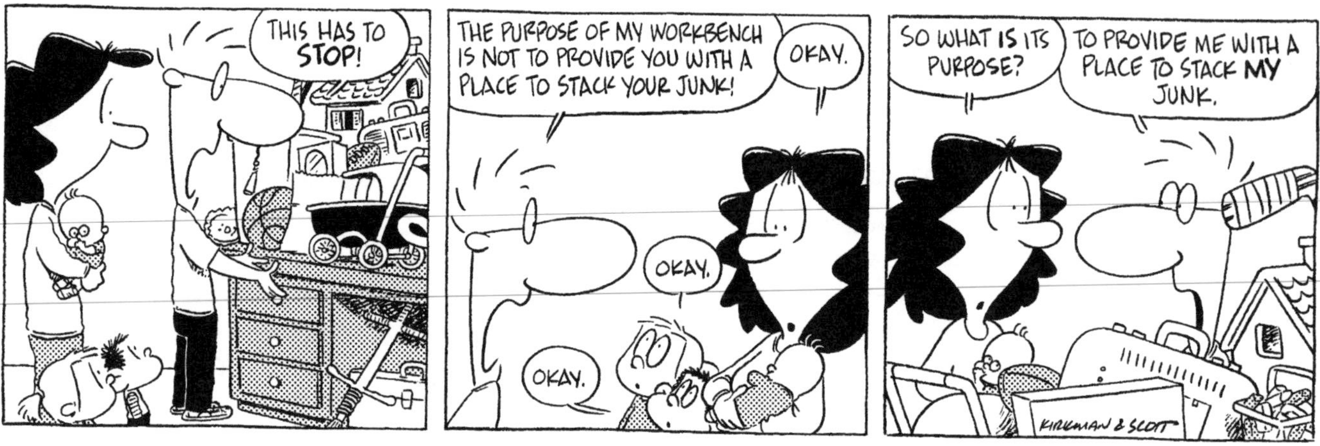
THIS HAS TO STOP!
THE PURPOSE OF MY WORKBENCH IS NOT TO PROVIDE YOU WITH A PLACE TO STACK YOUR JUNK!
OKAY.
OKAY.
OKAY.
SO WHAT IS ITS PURPOSE?
TO PROVIDE ME WITH A PLACE TO STACK MY JUNK.
KIRKMAN & SCOTT

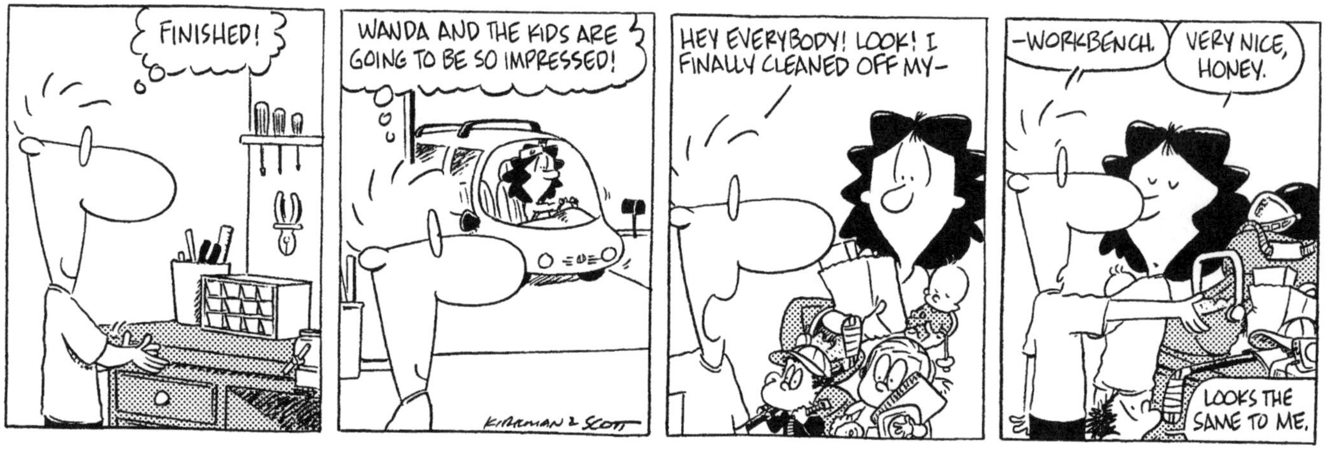
FINISHED!
WANDA AND THE KIDS ARE GOING TO BE SO IMPRESSED!
KIRKMAN & SCOTT
HEY EVERYBODY! LOOK! I FINALLY CLEANED OFF MY-
-WORKBENCH.
VERY NICE, HONEY.
LOOKS THE SAME TO ME.

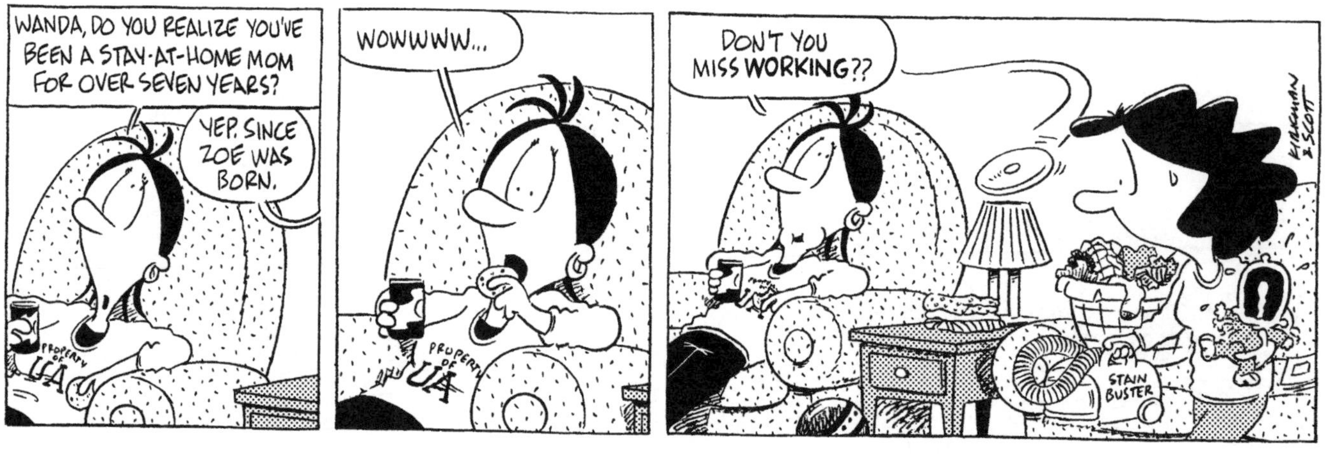
WANDA, DO YOU REALIZE YOU'VE BEEN A STAY-AT-HOME MOM FOR OVER SEVEN YEARS?
YEP. SINCE ZOE WAS BORN.
WOWWWW...
DON'T YOU MISS WORKING??
KIRKMAN & SCOTT

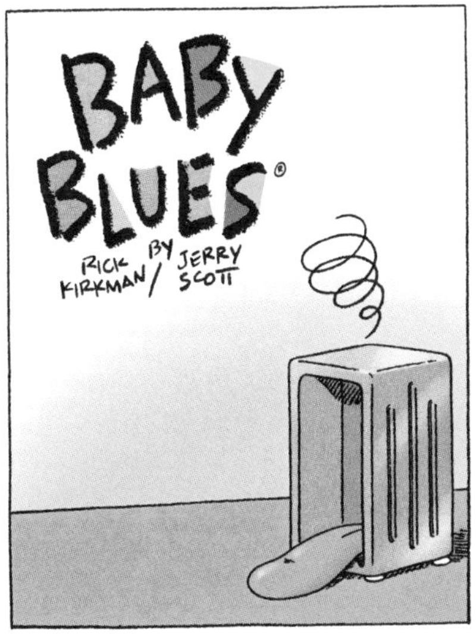
BABY BLUES®
BY
RICK KIRKMAN / JERRY SCOTT

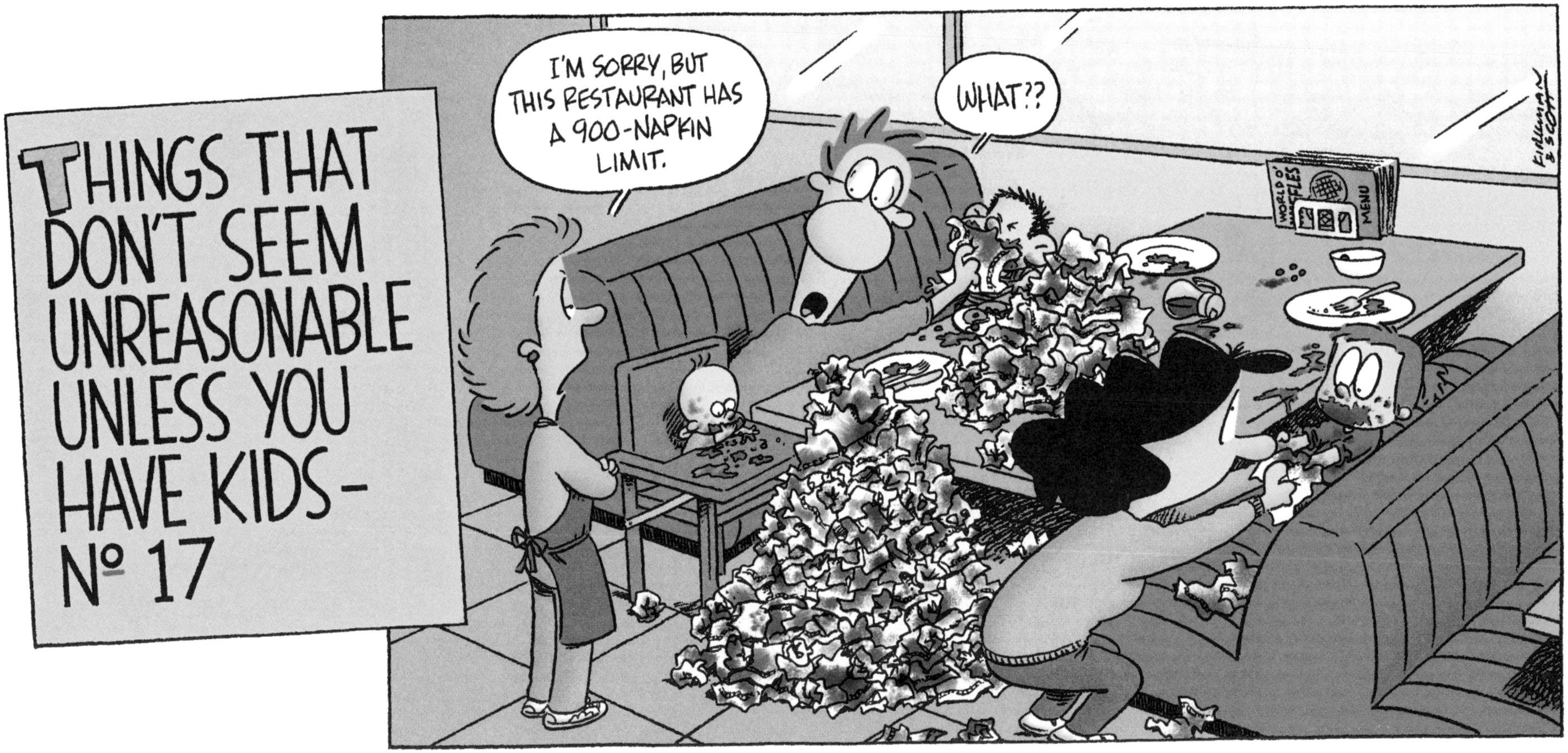
THINGS THAT DON'T SEEM UNREASONABLE UNLESS YOU HAVE KIDS– № 17
I'M SORRY, BUT THIS RESTAURANT HAS A 900-NAPKIN LIMIT.
WHAT??
KIRKMAN & SCOTT
MENU

WHEN ZOE WAS A BABY, WE SPOON-FED HER EVERY MEAL.

YEP.

WITH HAMMIE, WE MONITORED EVERY BITE, BUT WE LET HIM FEED HIMSELF.

UH-HUH.

AND NOW WITH WREN, I JUST TOSS TINY BITS OF FOOD ON HER TRAY, AND LET HER DO THE REST.

SO ARE YOU AFRAID WE'RE NOT GIVING THE THIRD BABY ENOUGH ATTENTION?

NO, I THINK WE WASTED A LOT OF EFFORT ON THE FIRST TWO.

I CAN'T FIND MY BACKPACK!

WHO TOOK MY BACKPACK??

SOMEBODY STOLE MY BACKPACK!

WHOOPS!

THUD!

WHAT HAPPENED?

I TRIPPED OVER MY BACKPACK.

KIRKMAN & SCOTT

ZOE, I NEED YOU AND HAMMIE TO DO ME A BIG FAVOR.

WHAT?

I'M EXPECTING AN IMPORTANT PHONE CALL, SO I DON'T WANT TO HEAR ANY FIGHTING OUT HERE.

OKAY.

THANKS.

SURE.

KIRKMAN & SCOTT

WHAT DID MOM SAY?

SHE WANTS US TO HAVE A NICE, QUIET FIGHT.

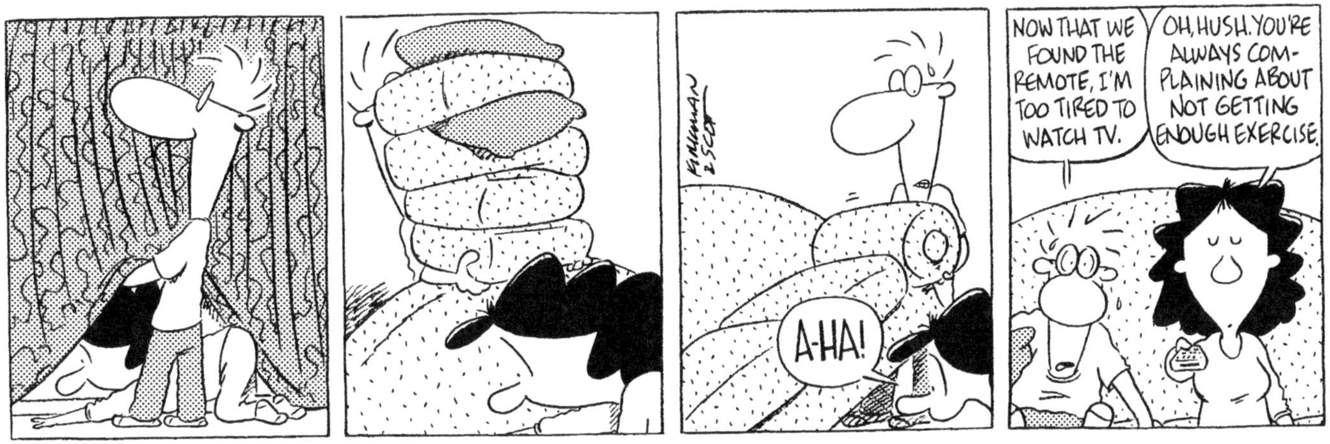
A-HA!
NOW THAT WE FOUND THE REMOTE, I'M TOO TIRED TO WATCH TV.
OH, HUSH. YOU'RE ALWAYS COMPLAINING ABOUT NOT GETTING ENOUGH EXERCISE.

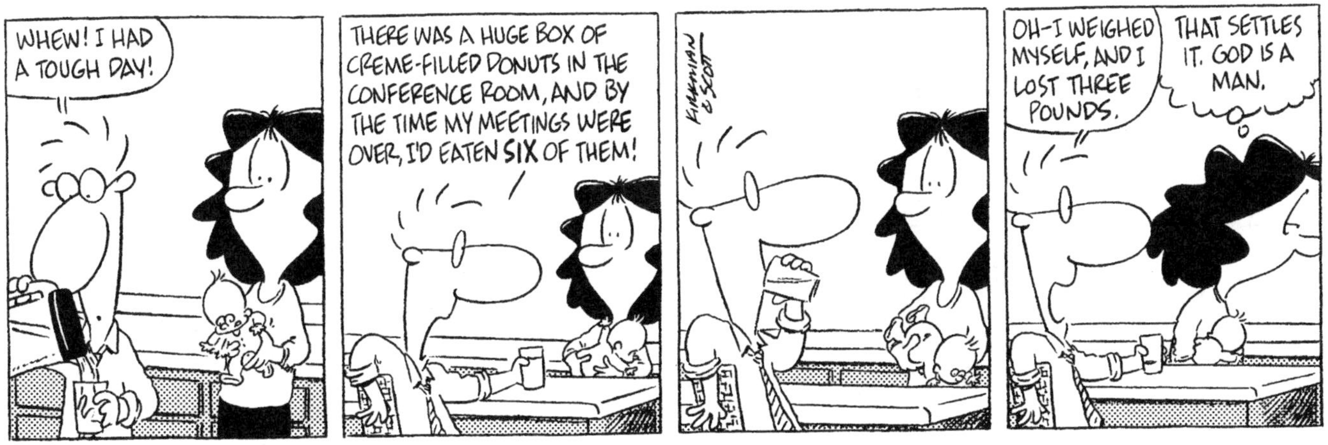
WHEW! I HAD A TOUGH DAY!
THERE WAS A HUGE BOX OF CREME-FILLED DONUTS IN THE CONFERENCE ROOM, AND BY THE TIME MY MEETINGS WERE OVER, I'D EATEN SIX OF THEM!
OH—I WEIGHED MYSELF, AND I LOST THREE POUNDS.
THAT SETTLES IT. GOD IS A MAN.

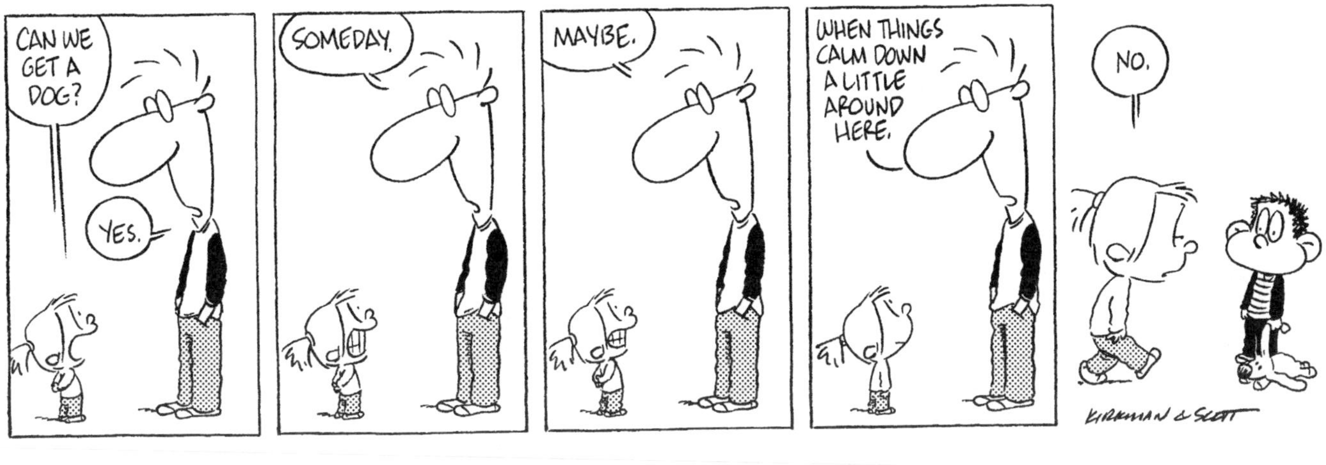
CAN WE GET A DOG?
YES.
SOMEDAY.
MAYBE.
WHEN THINGS CALM DOWN A LITTLE AROUND HERE.
NO.
KIRKMAN & SCOTT

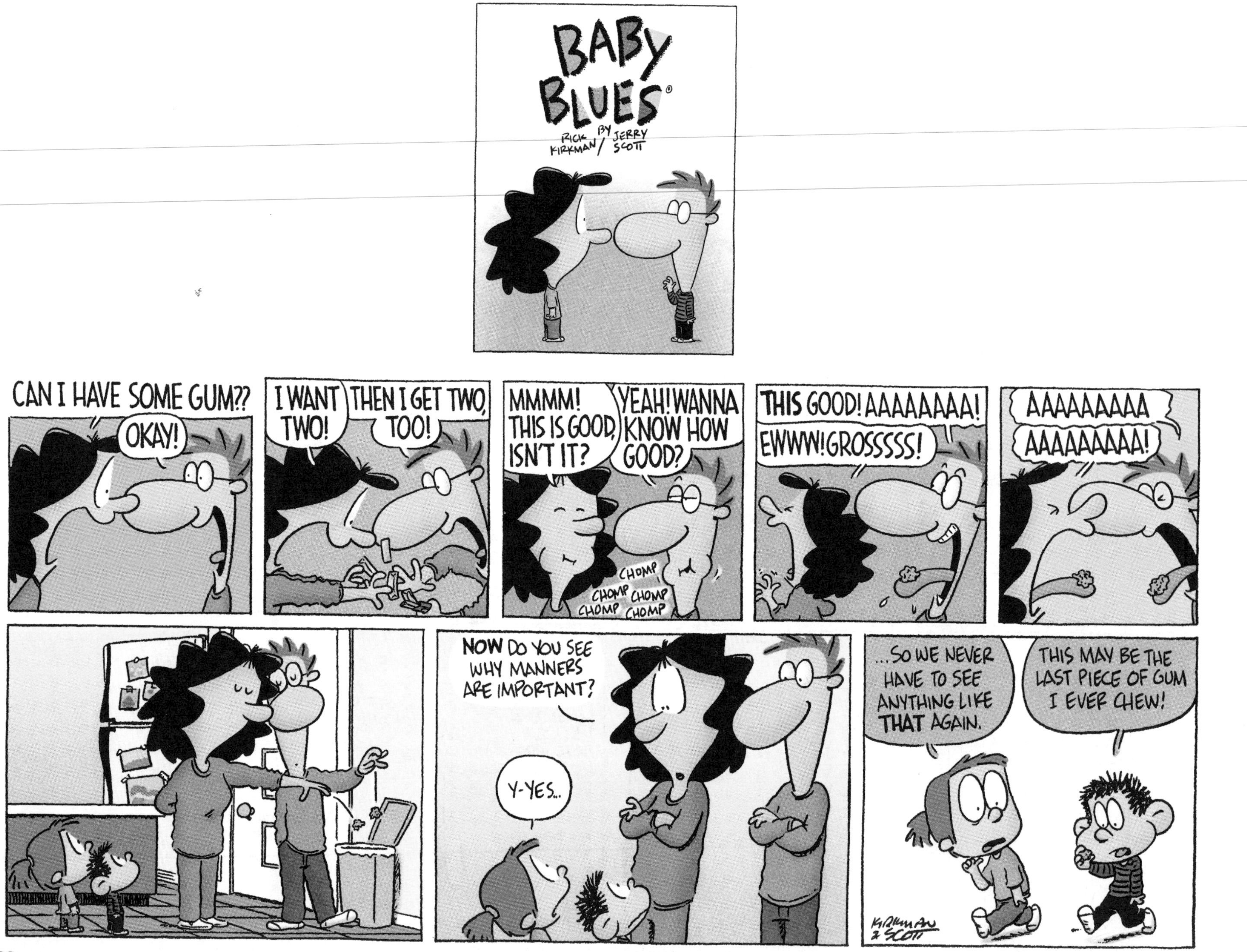
BABY BLUES®
BY RICK KIRKMAN / JERRY SCOTT
CAN I HAVE SOME GUM??
OKAY!
I WANT TWO!
THEN I GET TWO, TOO!
MMMM! THIS IS GOOD, ISN'T IT?
YEAH! WANNA KNOW HOW GOOD?
CHOMP
CHOMP
CHOMP
CHOMP
CHOMP
THIS GOOD! AAAAAAAA!
EWWW! GROSSSSS!
AAAAAAAAA
AAAAAAAAA!
NOW DO YOU SEE WHY MANNERS ARE IMPORTANT?
Y-YES...
...SO WE NEVER HAVE TO SEE ANYTHING LIKE THAT AGAIN.
THIS MAY BE THE LAST PIECE OF GUM I EVER CHEW!
KIRKMAN & SCOTT

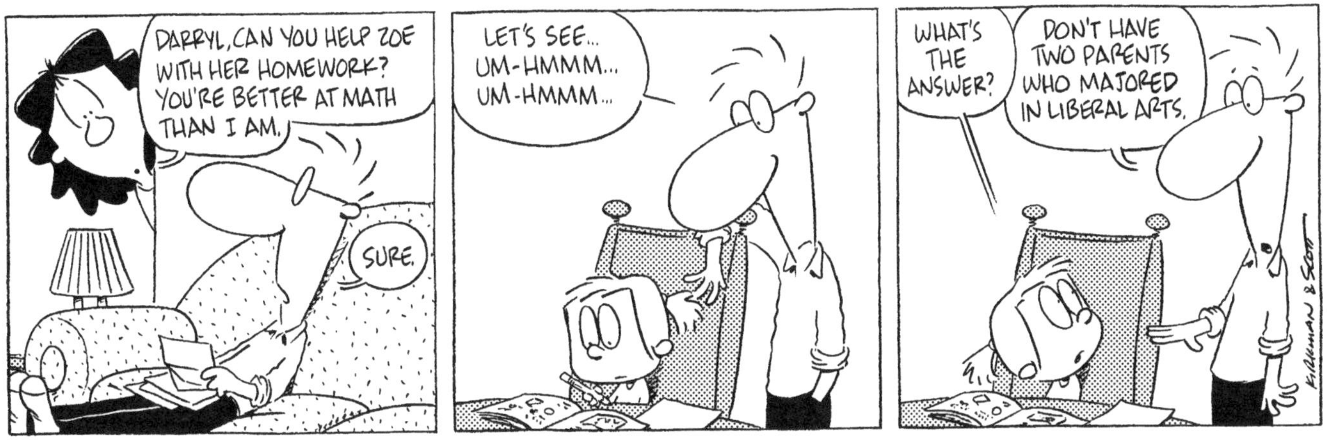
DARRYL, CAN YOU HELP ZOE WITH HER HOMEWORK? YOU'RE BETTER AT MATH THAN I AM.
SURE.
LET'S SEE... UM-HMMM... UM-HMMM...
WHAT'S THE ANSWER?
DON'T HAVE TWO PARENTS WHO MAJORED IN LIBERAL ARTS.

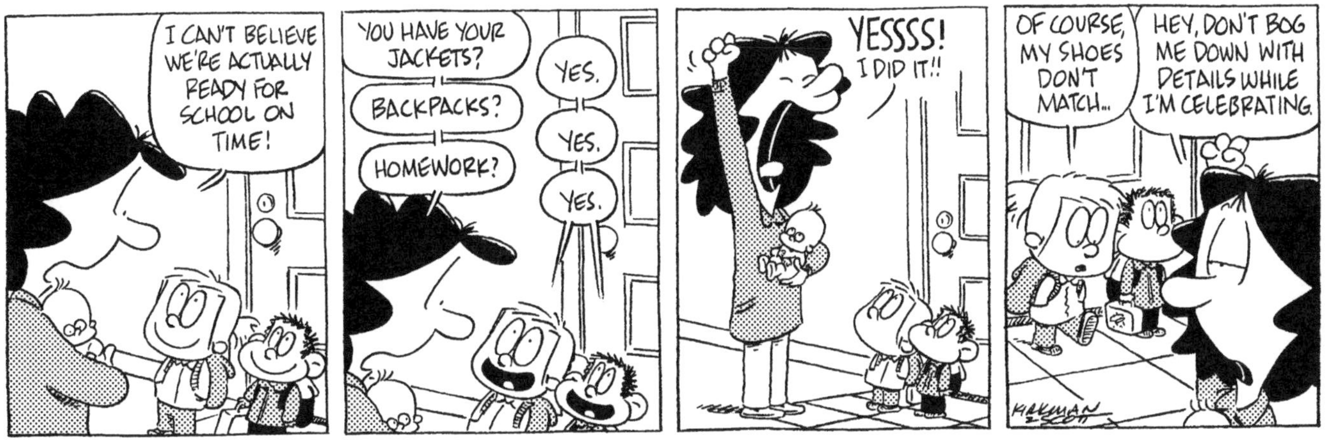
I CAN'T BELIEVE WE'RE ACTUALLY READY FOR SCHOOL ON TIME!
YOU HAVE YOUR JACKETS?
YES.
BACKPACKS?
YES.
HOMEWORK?
YES.
YESSSS! I DID IT!!
OF COURSE, MY SHOES DON'T MATCH...
HEY, DON'T BOG ME DOWN WITH DETAILS WHILE I'M CELEBRATING.

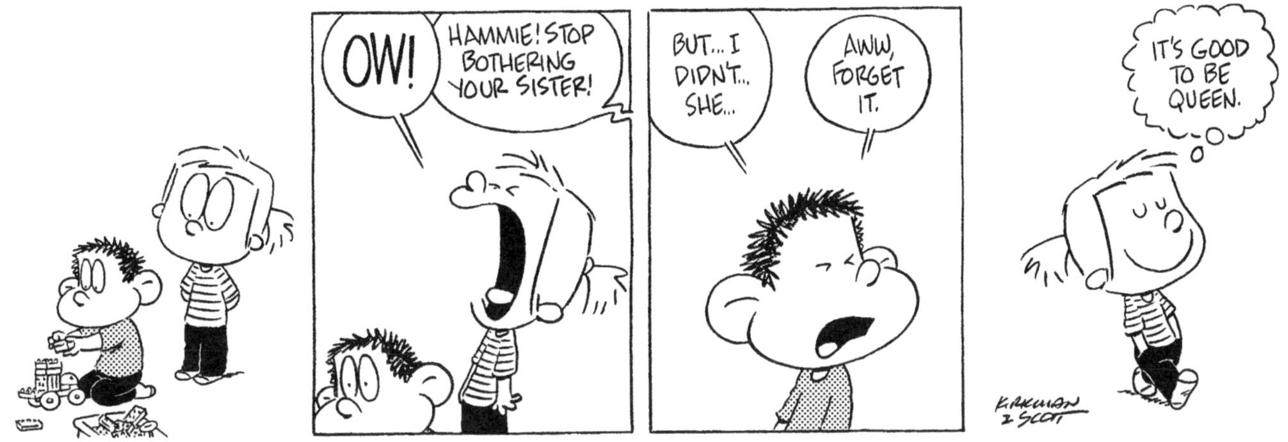
OW!
HAMMIE! STOP BOTHERING YOUR SISTER!
BUT... I DIDN'T... SHE...
AWW, FORGET IT.
IT'S GOOD TO BE QUEEN.

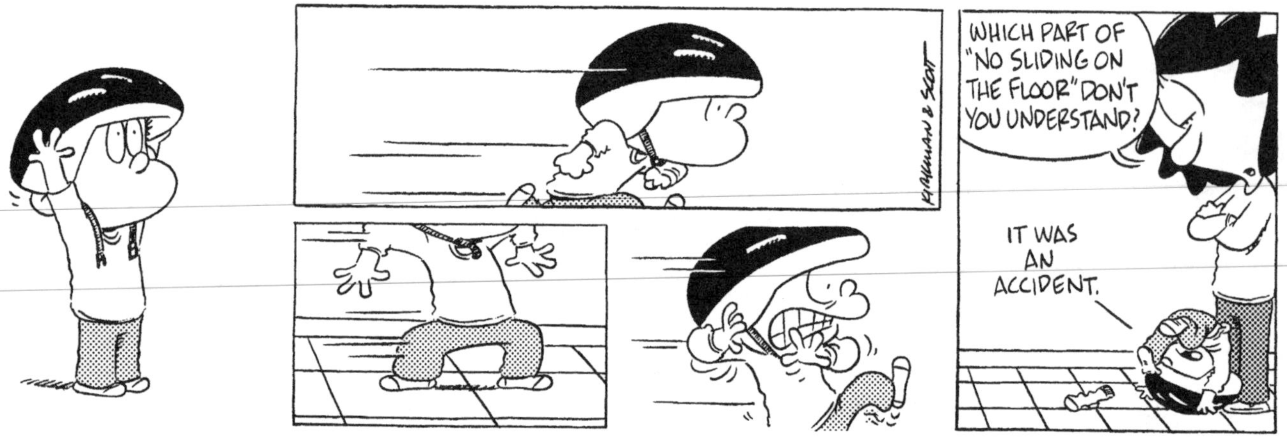
WHICH PART OF "NO SLIDING ON THE FLOOR" DON'T YOU UNDERSTAND?
IT WAS AN ACCIDENT.

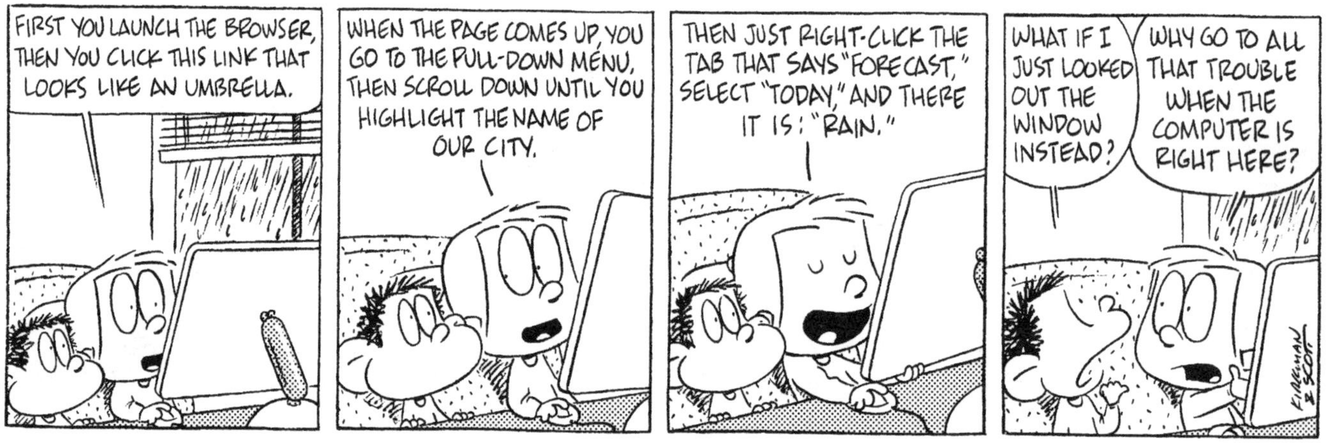
FIRST YOU LAUNCH THE BROWSER, THEN YOU CLICK THIS LINK THAT LOOKS LIKE AN UMBRELLA.
WHEN THE PAGE COMES UP, YOU GO TO THE PULL-DOWN MENU, THEN SCROLL DOWN UNTIL YOU HIGHLIGHT THE NAME OF OUR CITY.
THEN JUST RIGHT-CLICK THE TAB THAT SAYS "FORECAST," SELECT "TODAY," AND THERE IT IS: "RAIN."
WHAT IF I JUST LOOKED OUT THE WINDOW INSTEAD?
WHY GO TO ALL THAT TROUBLE WHEN THE COMPUTER IS RIGHT HERE?

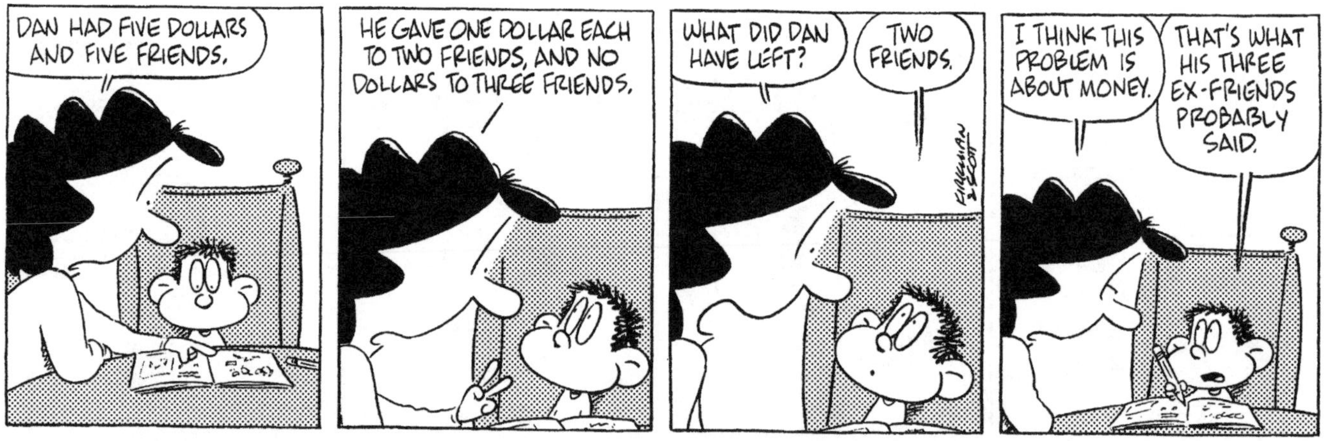
DAN HAD FIVE DOLLARS AND FIVE FRIENDS.
HE GAVE ONE DOLLAR EACH TO TWO FRIENDS, AND NO DOLLARS TO THREE FRIENDS.
WHAT DID DAN HAVE LEFT?
TWO FRIENDS.
I THINK THIS PROBLEM IS ABOUT MONEY.
THAT'S WHAT HIS THREE EX-FRIENDS PROBABLY SAID.

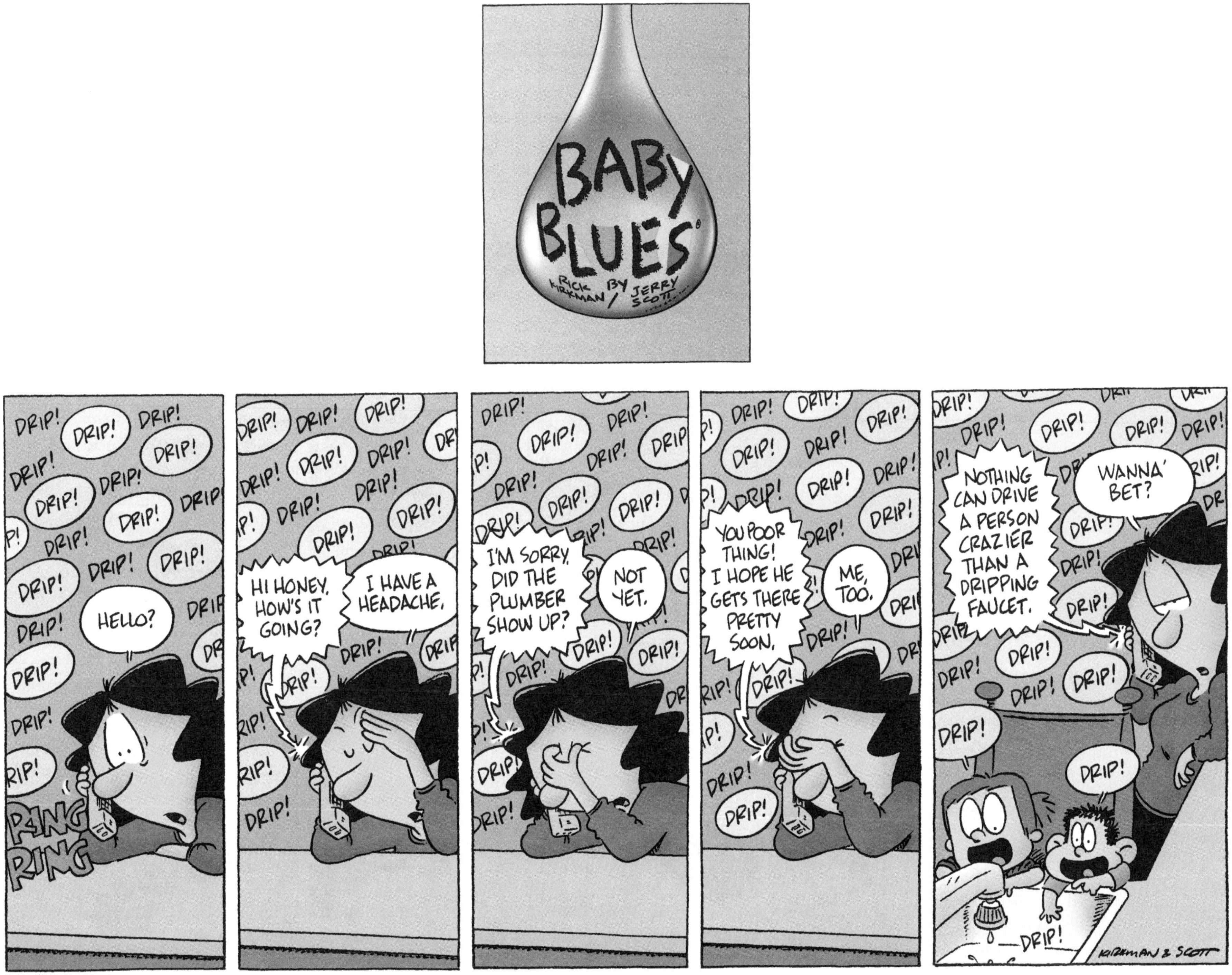
BABY BLUES®
BY RICK KIRKMAN / JERRY SCOTT
HELLO?
RING RING
HI HONEY. HOW'S IT GOING?
I HAVE A HEADACHE.
I'M SORRY. DID THE PLUMBER SHOW UP?
NOT YET.
YOU POOR THING! I HOPE HE GETS THERE PRETTY SOON.
ME, TOO.
NOTHING CAN DRIVE A PERSON CRAZIER THAN A DRIPPING FAUCET.
WANNA' BET?
DRIP!
KIRKMAN & SCOTT

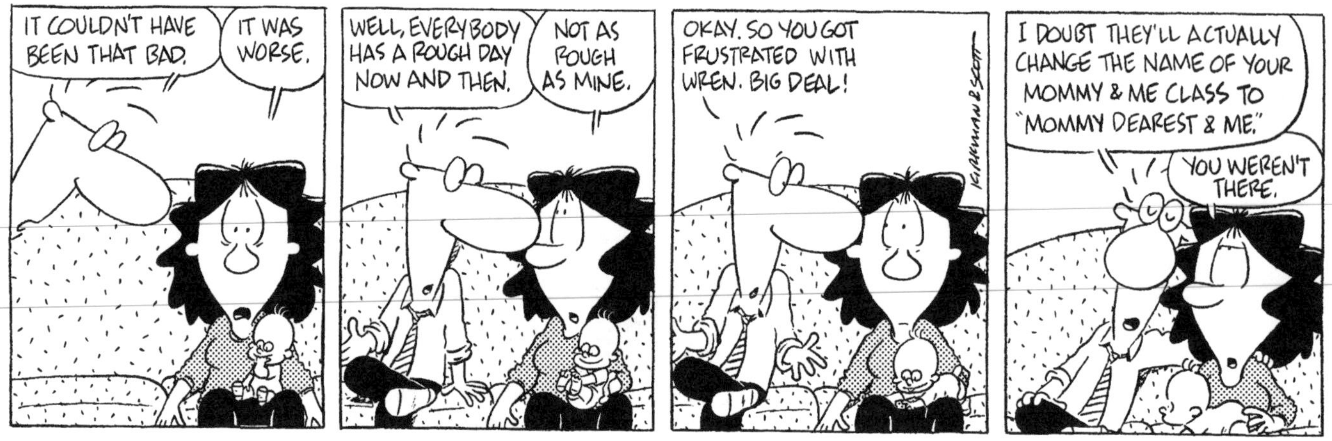
IT COULDN'T HAVE BEEN THAT BAD.
IT WAS WORSE.
WELL, EVERYBODY HAS A ROUGH DAY NOW AND THEN.
NOT AS ROUGH AS MINE.
OKAY. SO YOU GOT FRUSTRATED WITH WREN. BIG DEAL!
KIRKMAN & SCOTT
I DOUBT THEY'LL ACTUALLY CHANGE THE NAME OF YOUR MOMMY & ME CLASS TO "MOMMY DEAREST & ME."
YOU WEREN'T THERE.

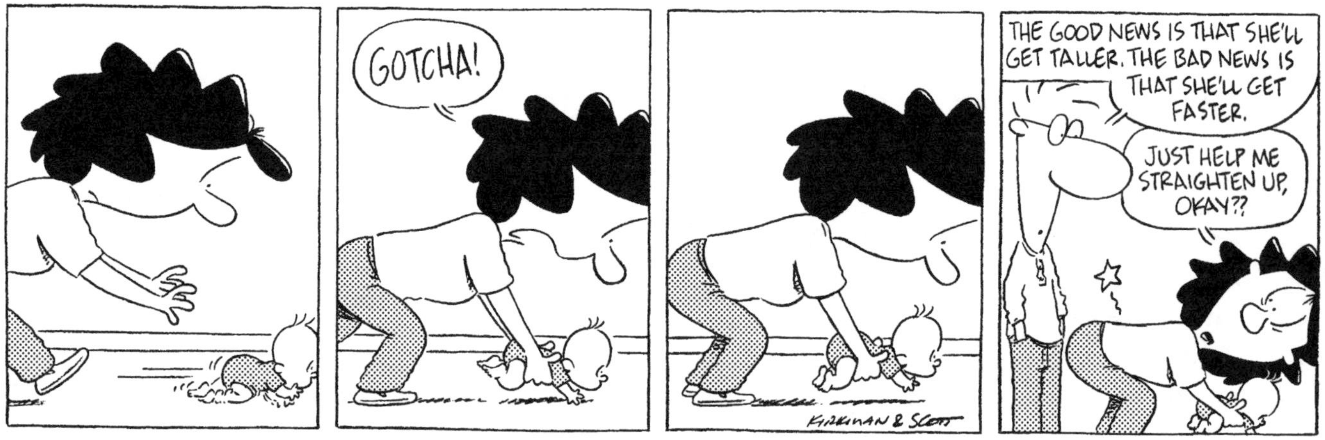
GOTCHA!
KIRKMAN & SCOTT
THE GOOD NEWS IS THAT SHE'LL GET TALLER. THE BAD NEWS IS THAT SHE'LL GET FASTER.
JUST HELP ME STRAIGHTEN UP, OKAY??

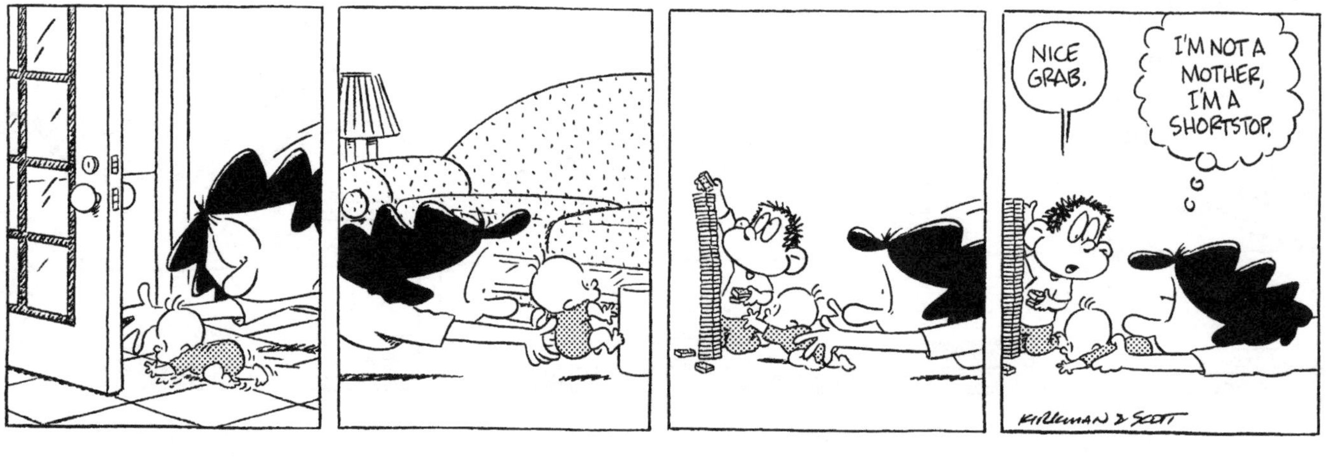
NICE GRAB.
I'M NOT A MOTHER, I'M A SHORTSTOP.
KIRKMAN & SCOTT

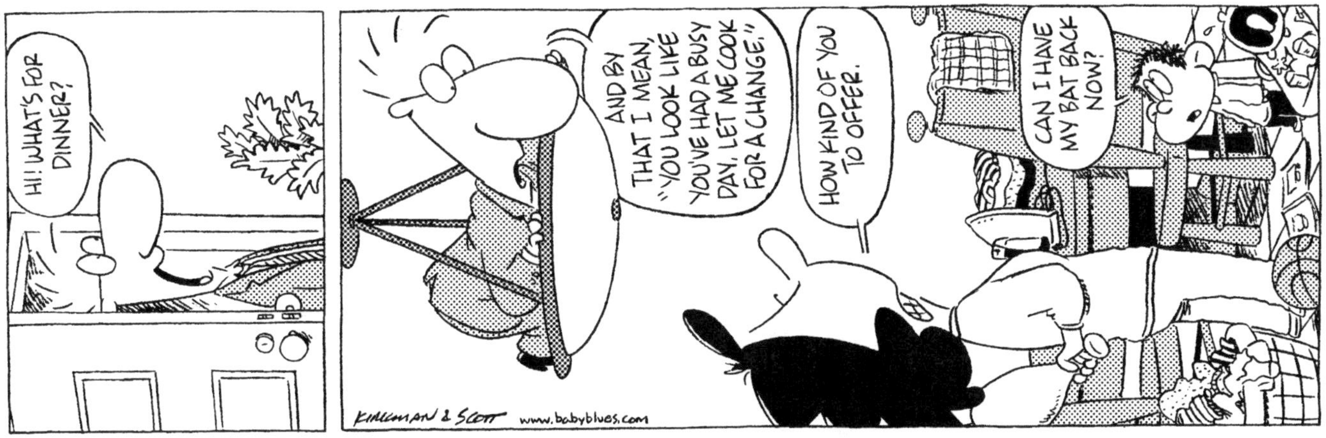
HI! WHAT'S FOR DINNER?
AND BY THAT I MEAN, "YOU LOOK LIKE YOU'VE HAD A BUSY DAY. LET ME COOK FOR A CHANGE."
HOW KIND OF YOU TO OFFER.
CAN I HAVE MY BAT BACK NOW?
KIRKMAN & SCOTT www.babyblues.com

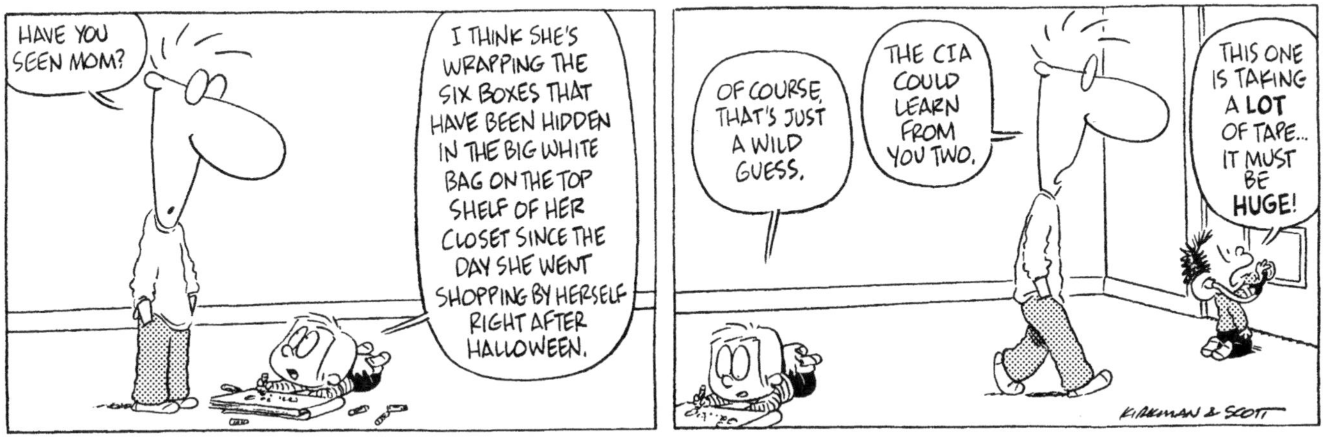
HAVE YOU SEEN MOM?
I THINK SHE'S WRAPPING THE SIX BOXES THAT HAVE BEEN HIDDEN IN THE BIG WHITE BAG ON THE TOP SHELF OF HER CLOSET SINCE THE DAY SHE WENT SHOPPING BY HERSELF RIGHT AFTER HALLOWEEN.
OF COURSE, THAT'S JUST A WILD GUESS.
THE CIA COULD LEARN FROM YOU TWO.
THIS ONE IS TAKING A LOT OF TAPE.. IT MUST BE HUGE!
KIRKMAN & SCOTT

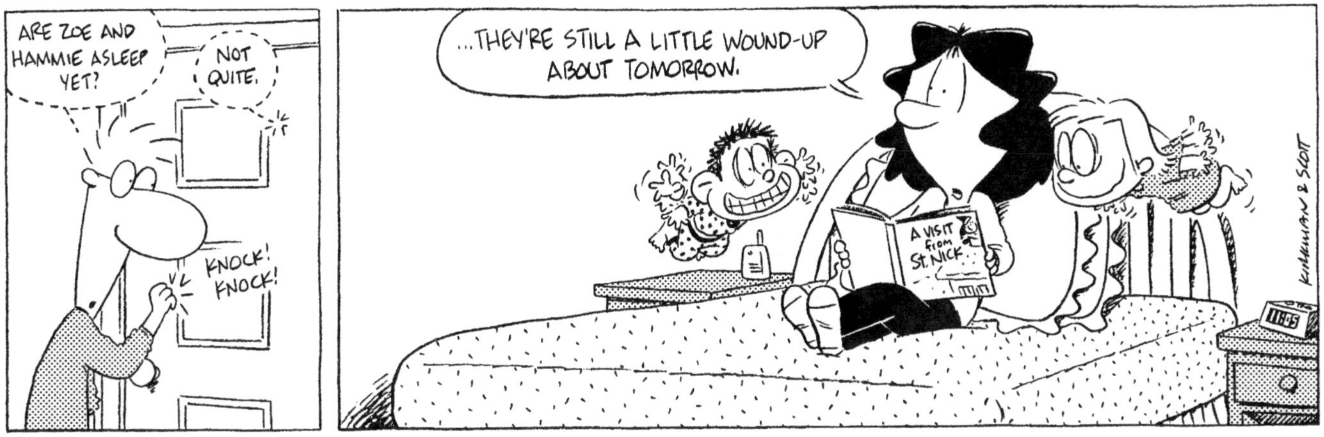
ARE ZOE AND HAMMIE ASLEEP YET?
NOT QUITE.
KNOCK! KNOCK!
...THEY'RE STILL A LITTLE WOUND-UP ABOUT TOMORROW.
A VISIT from ST. NICK
KIRKMAN & SCOTT

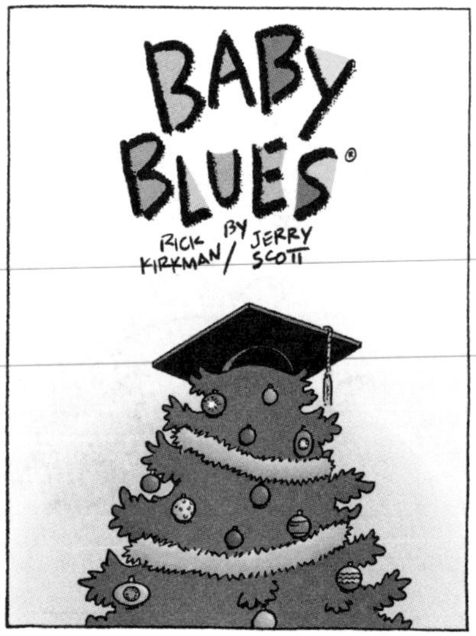
BABY BLUES®
BY RICK KIRKMAN / JERRY SCOTT

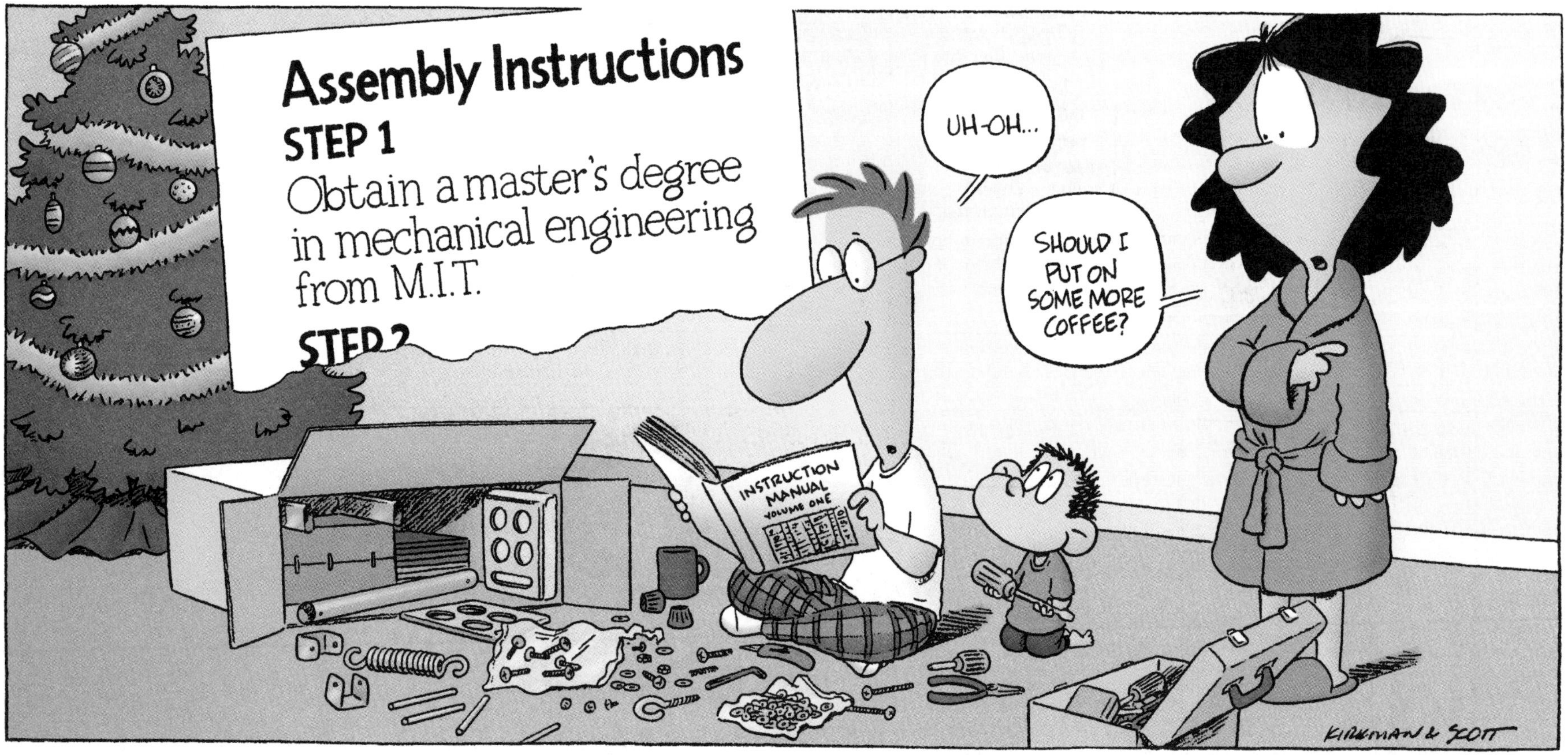
Assembly Instructions
STEP 1
Obtain a master's degree in mechanical engineering from M.I.T.
STEP 2
UH-OH...
SHOULD I PUT ON SOME MORE COFFEE?
INSTRUCTION MANUAL VOLUME ONE
KIRKMAN & SCOTT

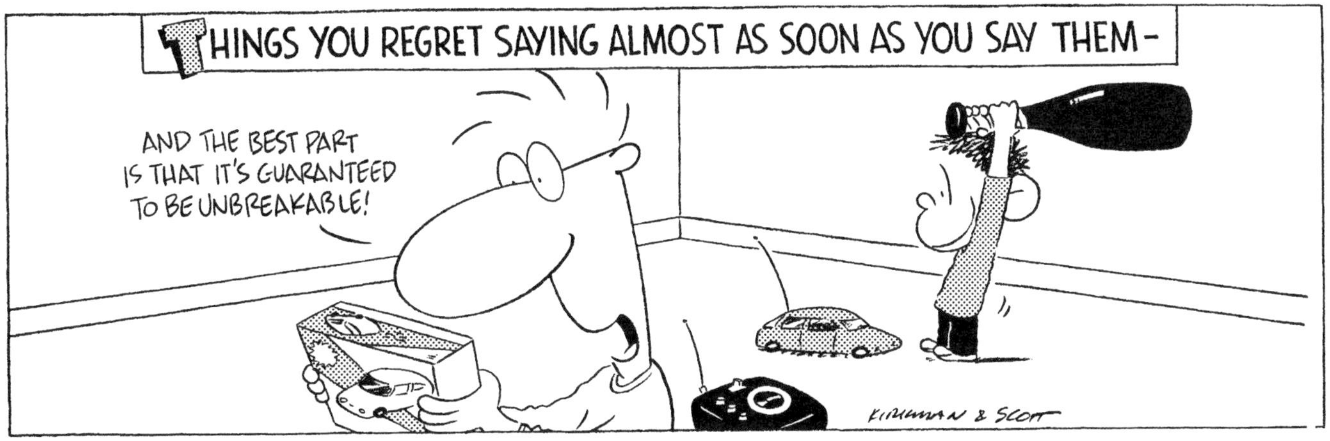
THINGS YOU REGRET SAYING ALMOST AS SOON AS YOU SAY THEM-
AND THE BEST PART IS THAT IT'S GUARANTEED TO BE UNBREAKABLE!
KIRKMAN & SCOTT

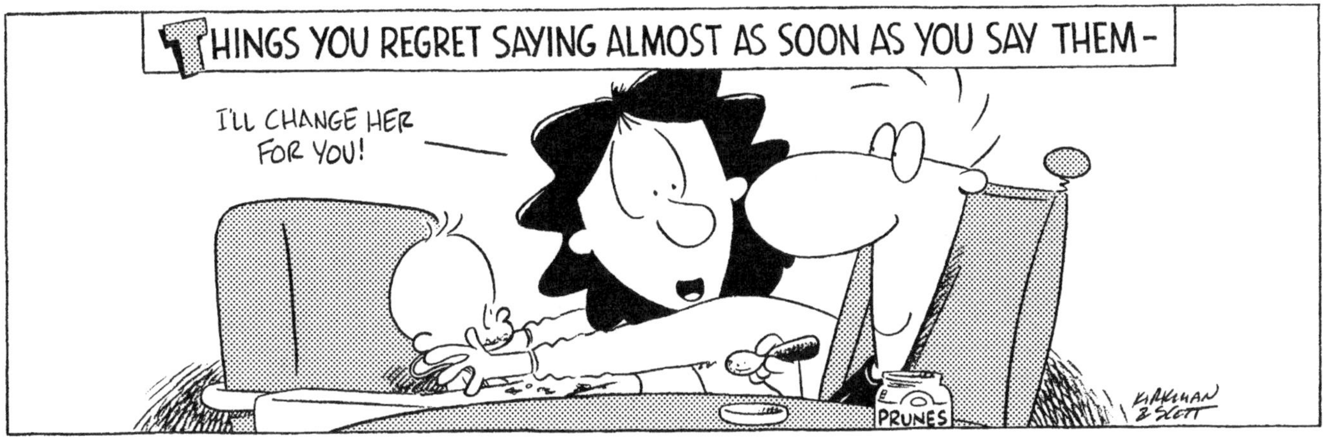
THINGS YOU REGRET SAYING ALMOST AS SOON AS YOU SAY THEM-
I'LL CHANGE HER FOR YOU!
PRUNES
KIRKMAN & SCOTT

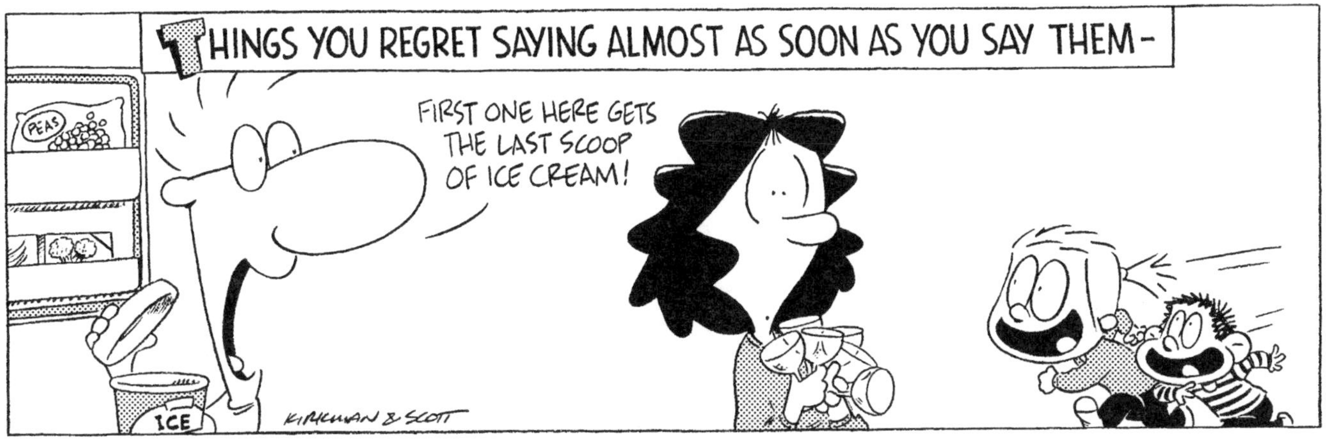
THINGS YOU REGRET SAYING ALMOST AS SOON AS YOU SAY THEM-
FIRST ONE HERE GETS THE LAST SCOOP OF ICE CREAM!
PEAS
ICE
KIRKMAN & SCOTT

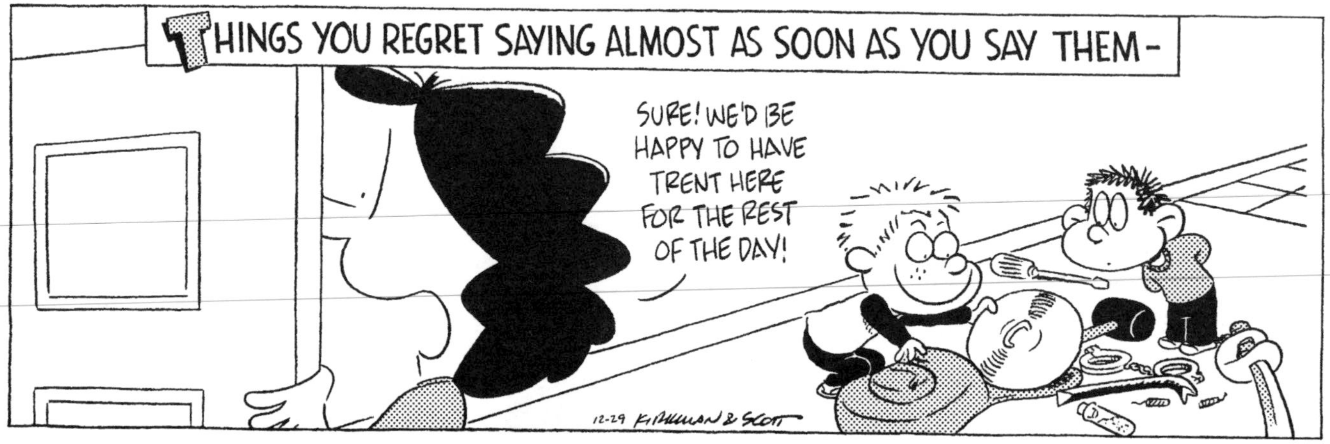
THINGS YOU REGRET SAYING ALMOST AS SOON AS YOU SAY THEM-
SURE! WE'D BE HAPPY TO HAVE TRENT HERE FOR THE REST OF THE DAY!
12-29 KIRKMAN & SCOTT

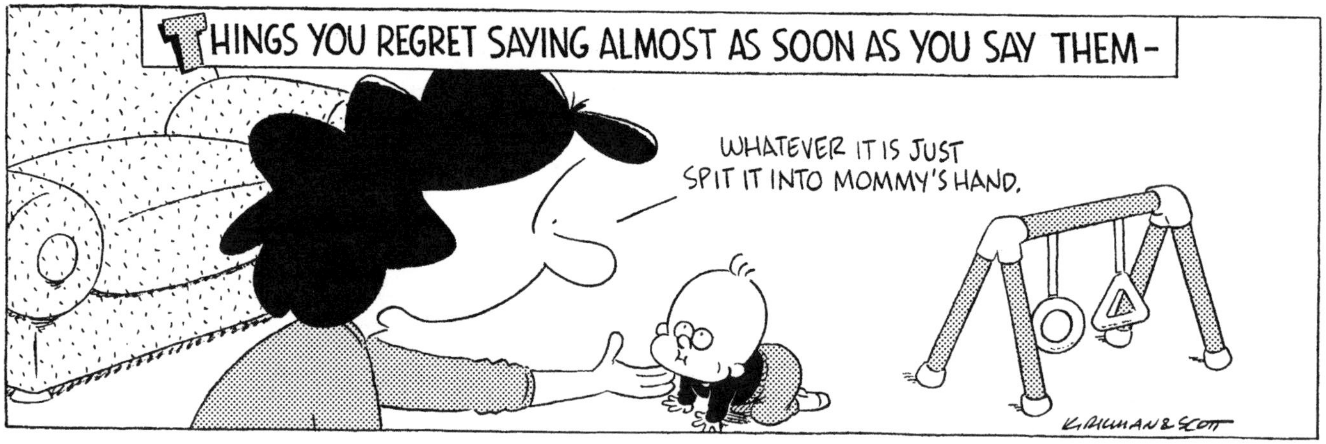
THINGS YOU REGRET SAYING ALMOST AS SOON AS YOU SAY THEM-
WHATEVER IT IS JUST SPIT IT INTO MOMMY'S HAND.
KIRKMAN & SCOTT

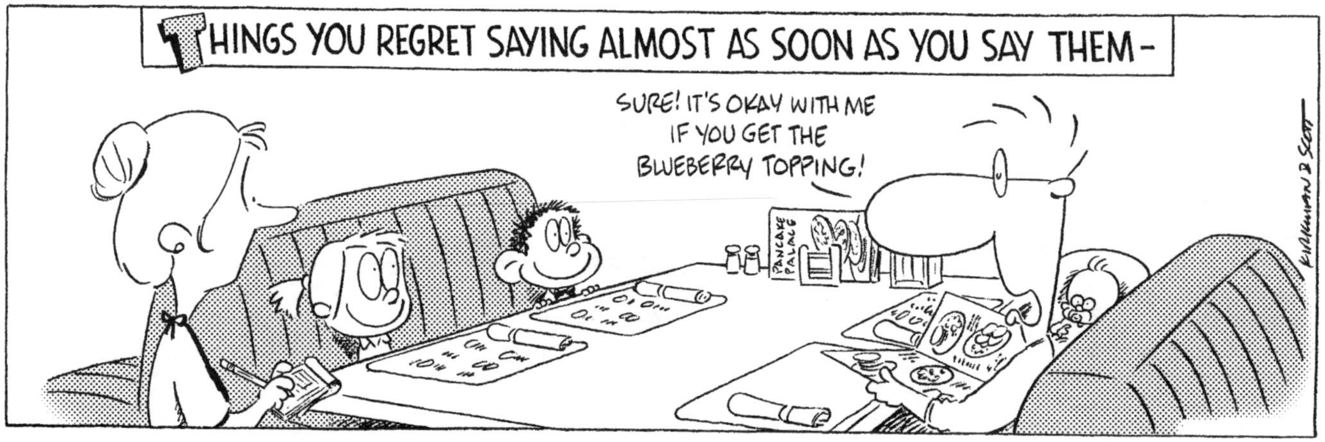
THINGS YOU REGRET SAYING ALMOST AS SOON AS YOU SAY THEM-
SURE! IT'S OKAY WITH ME IF YOU GET THE BLUEBERRY TOPPING!
PANCAKE PALACE
KIRKMAN & SCOTT

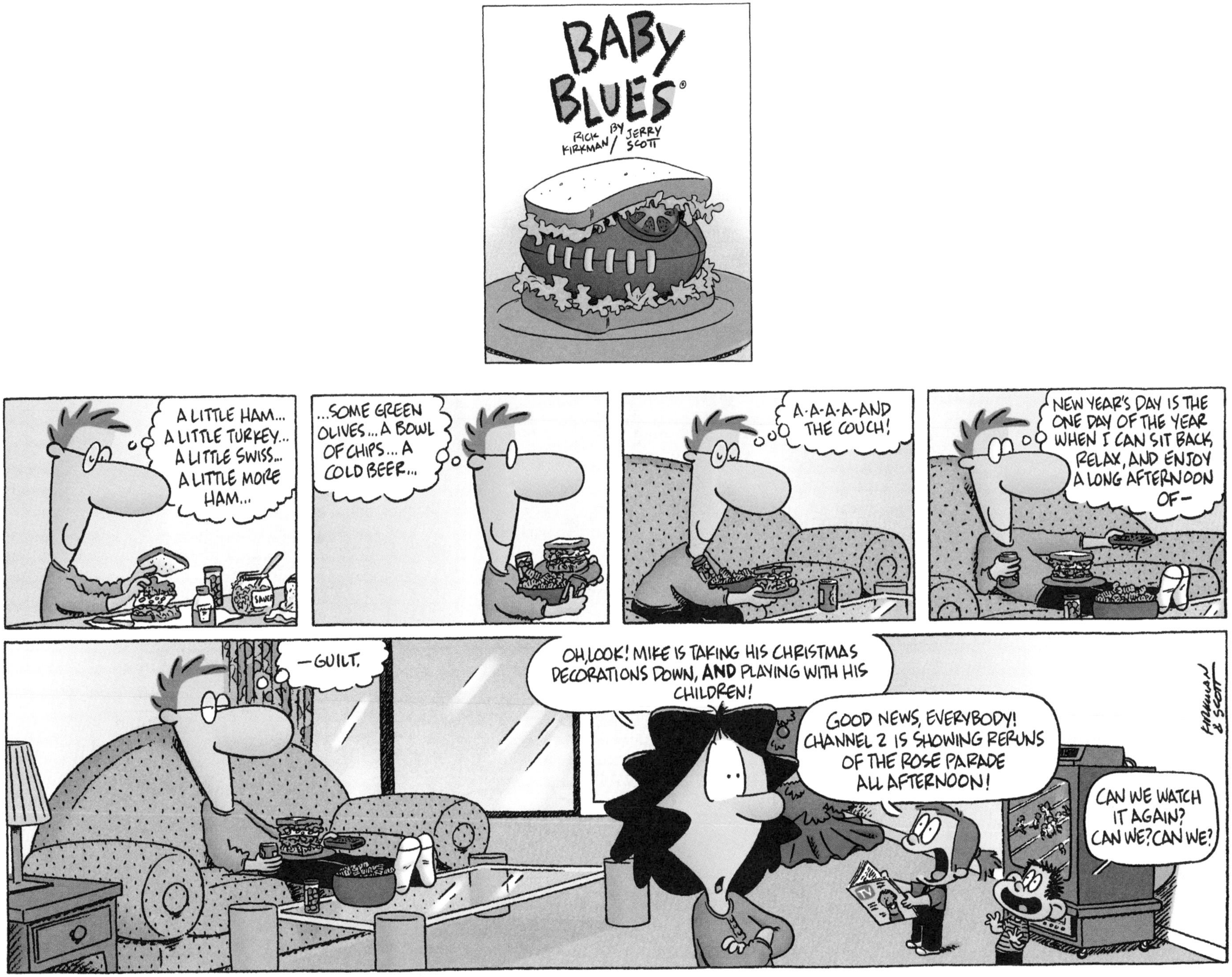
BABY BLUES®
BY RICK KIRKMAN / JERRY SCOTT
A LITTLE HAM... A LITTLE TURKEY... A LITTLE SWISS... A LITTLE MORE HAM...
...SOME GREEN OLIVES... A BOWL OF CHIPS... A COLD BEER...
A-A-A-A-AND THE COUCH!
NEW YEAR'S DAY IS THE ONE DAY OF THE YEAR WHEN I CAN SIT BACK, RELAX, AND ENJOY A LONG AFTERNOON OF—
—GUILT.
OH, LOOK! MIKE IS TAKING HIS CHRISTMAS DECORATIONS DOWN, AND PLAYING WITH HIS CHILDREN!
GOOD NEWS, EVERYBODY! CHANNEL 2 IS SHOWING RERUNS OF THE ROSE PARADE ALL AFTERNOON!
CAN WE WATCH IT AGAIN? CAN WE? CAN WE?
KIRKMAN & SCOTT

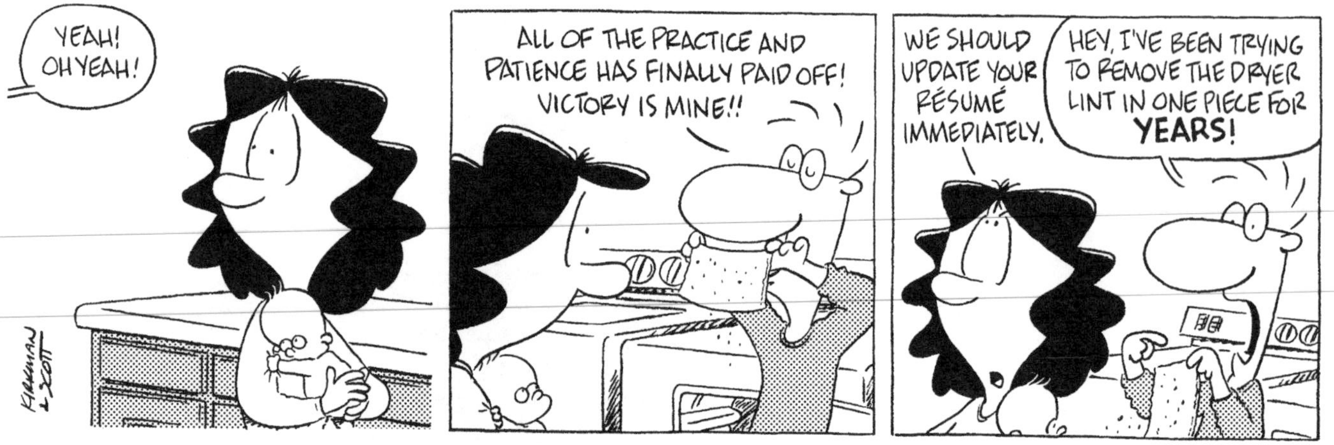
YEAH! OH YEAH!
ALL OF THE PRACTICE AND PATIENCE HAS FINALLY PAID OFF! VICTORY IS MINE!!
WE SHOULD UPDATE YOUR RÉSUMÉ IMMEDIATELY.
HEY, I'VE BEEN TRYING TO REMOVE THE DRYER LINT IN ONE PIECE FOR **YEARS**!
KIRKMAN & SCOTT

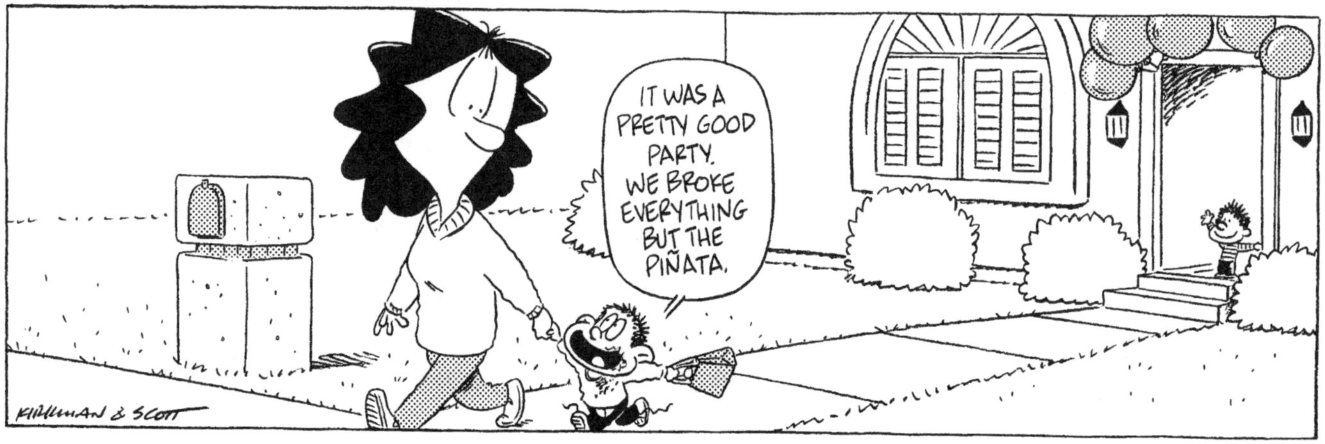
IT WAS A PRETTY GOOD PARTY. WE BROKE EVERYTHING BUT THE PIÑATA.
KIRKMAN & SCOTT

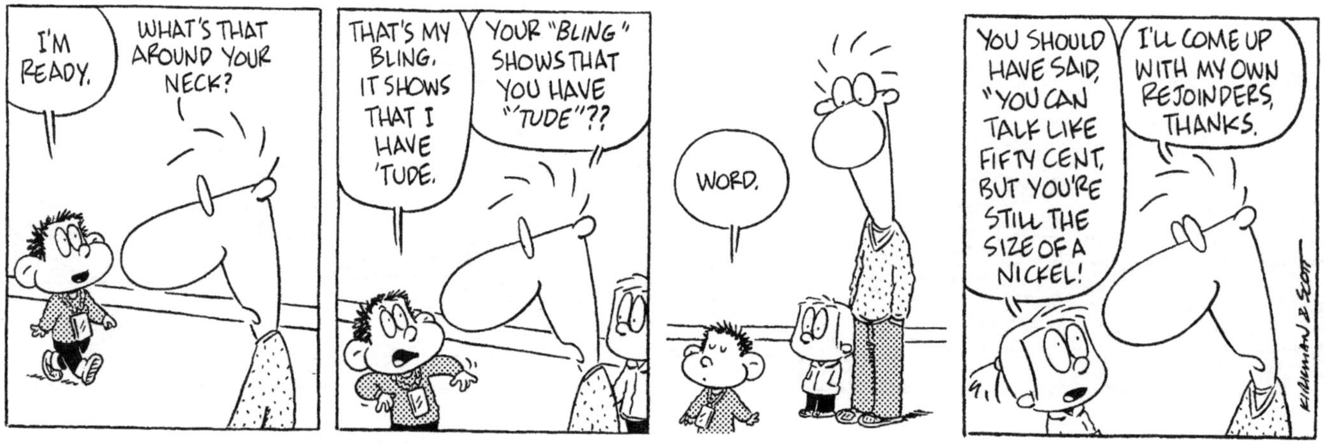
I'M READY.
WHAT'S THAT AROUND YOUR NECK?
THAT'S MY BLING. IT SHOWS THAT I HAVE 'TUDE.
YOUR "*BLING*" SHOWS THAT YOU HAVE "*'TUDE*"??
WORD.
YOU SHOULD HAVE SAID, "YOU CAN TALK LIKE FIFTY CENT, BUT YOU'RE STILL THE SIZE OF A NICKEL!
I'LL COME UP WITH MY OWN REJOINDERS, THANKS.
KIRKMAN & SCOTT

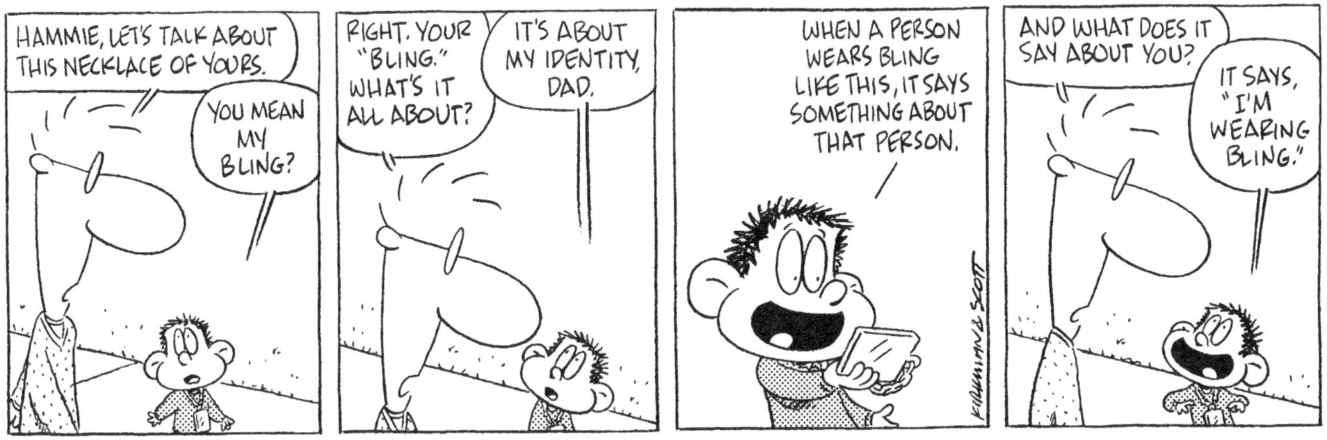
HAMMIE, LET'S TALK ABOUT THIS NECKLACE OF YOURS.
YOU MEAN MY BLING?
RIGHT. YOUR "BLING." WHAT'S IT ALL ABOUT?
IT'S ABOUT MY IDENTITY, DAD.
WHEN A PERSON WEARS BLING LIKE THIS, IT SAYS SOMETHING ABOUT THAT PERSON.
AND WHAT DOES IT SAY ABOUT YOU?
IT SAYS, "I'M WEARING BLING."

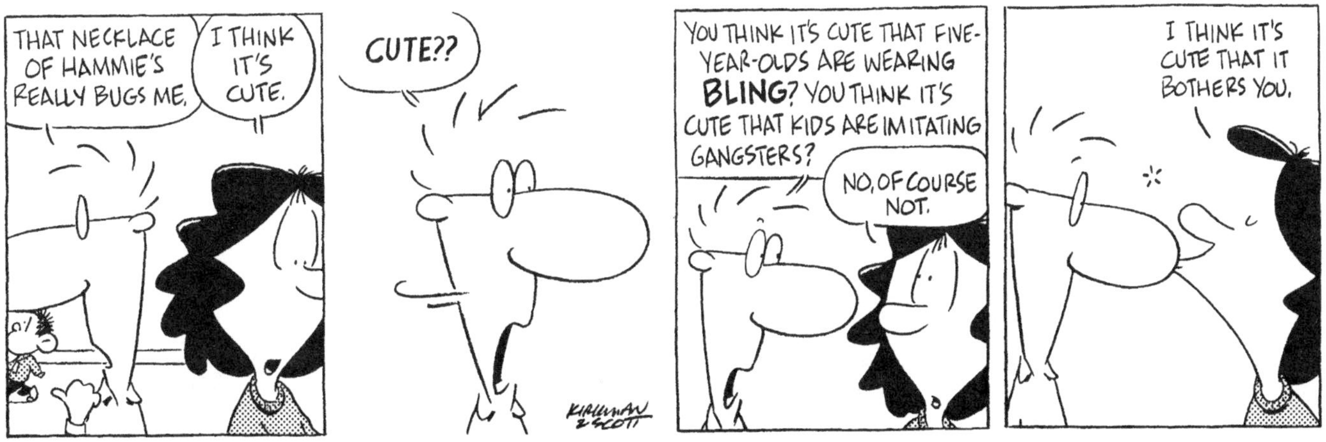
THAT NECKLACE OF HAMMIE'S REALLY BUGS ME.
I THINK IT'S CUTE.
CUTE??
YOU THINK IT'S CUTE THAT FIVE-YEAR-OLDS ARE WEARING BLING? YOU THINK IT'S CUTE THAT KIDS ARE IMITATING GANGSTERS?
NO, OF COURSE NOT.
I THINK IT'S CUTE THAT IT BOTHERS YOU.

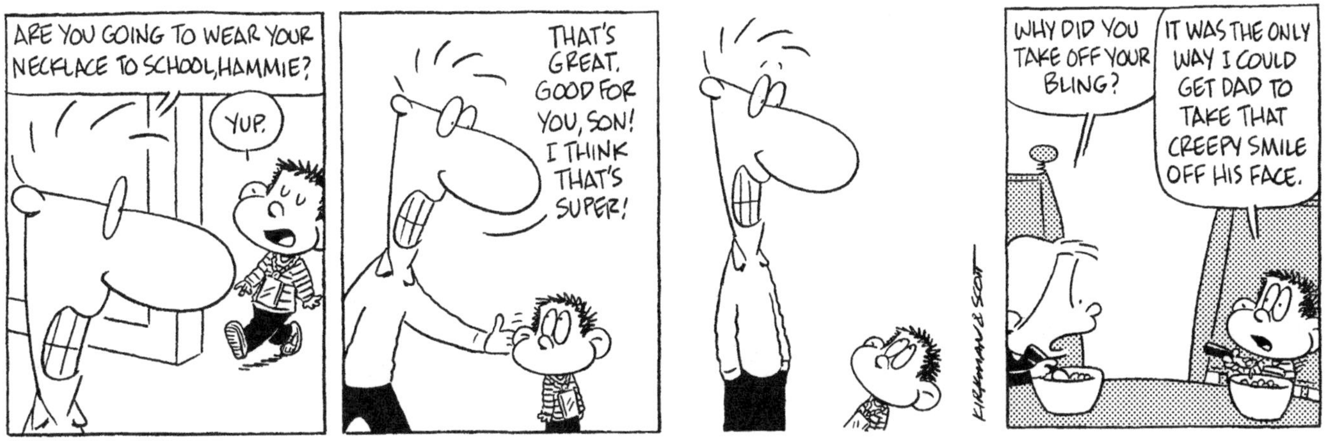
ARE YOU GOING TO WEAR YOUR NECKLACE TO SCHOOL, HAMMIE?
YUP.
THAT'S GREAT. GOOD FOR YOU, SON! I THINK THAT'S SUPER!
WHY DID YOU TAKE OFF YOUR BLING?
IT WAS THE ONLY WAY I COULD GET DAD TO TAKE THAT CREEPY SMILE OFF HIS FACE.

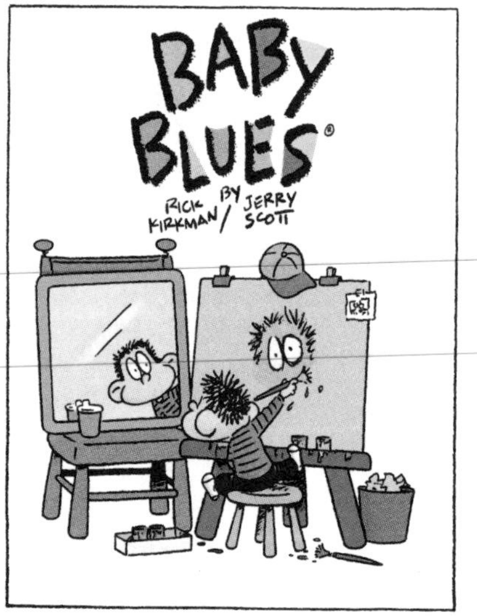
BABY BLUES®
BY RICK KIRKMAN / JERRY SCOTT

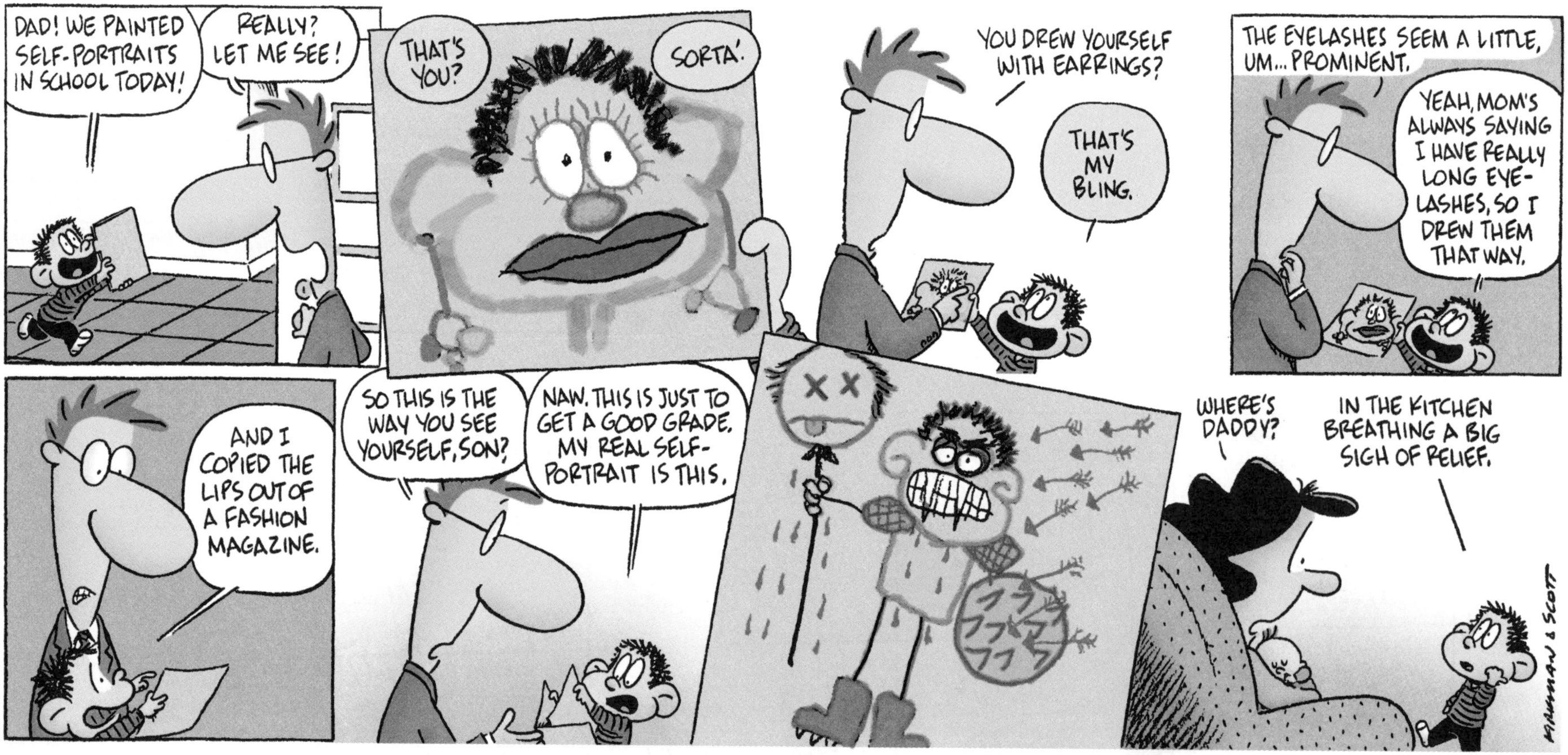
DAD! WE PAINTED SELF-PORTRAITS IN SCHOOL TODAY!
REALLY? LET ME SEE!
THAT'S YOU?
SORTA.
YOU DREW YOURSELF WITH EARRINGS?
THAT'S MY BLING.
THE EYELASHES SEEM A LITTLE, UM... PROMINENT.
YEAH, MOM'S ALWAYS SAYING I HAVE REALLY LONG EYE-LASHES, SO I DREW THEM THAT WAY.
AND I COPIED THE LIPS OUT OF A FASHION MAGAZINE.
SO THIS IS THE WAY YOU SEE YOURSELF, SON?
NAW. THIS IS JUST TO GET A GOOD GRADE. MY REAL SELF-PORTRAIT IS THIS.
WHERE'S DADDY?
IN THE KITCHEN BREATHING A BIG SIGH OF RELIEF.
KIRKMAN & SCOTT

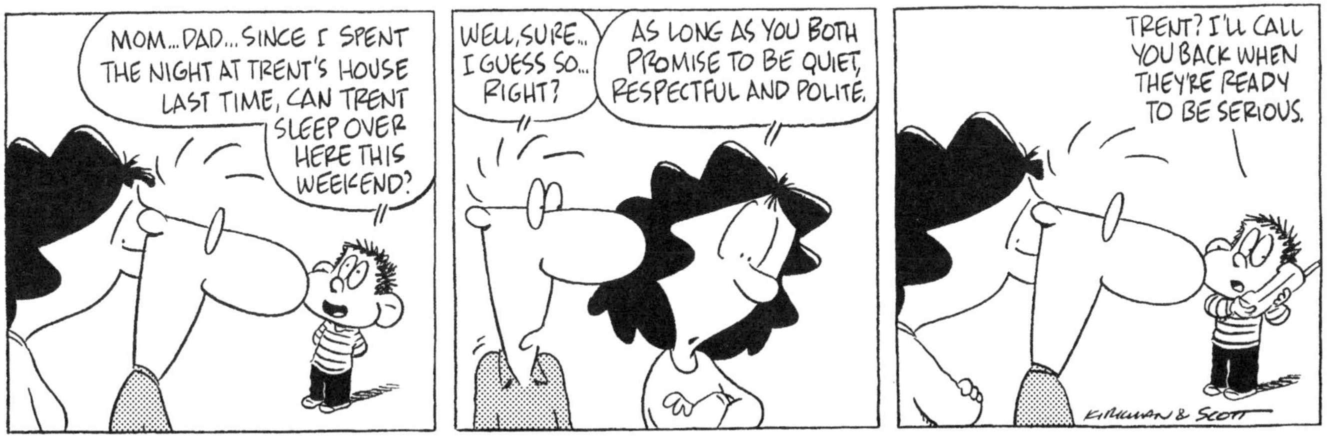
MOM...DAD...SINCE I SPENT THE NIGHT AT TRENT'S HOUSE LAST TIME, CAN TRENT SLEEP OVER HERE THIS WEEKEND?
WELL, SURE... I GUESS SO... RIGHT?
AS LONG AS YOU BOTH PROMISE TO BE QUIET, RESPECTFUL AND POLITE.
TRENT? I'LL CALL YOU BACK WHEN THEY'RE READY TO BE SERIOUS.
KIRKMAN & SCOTT

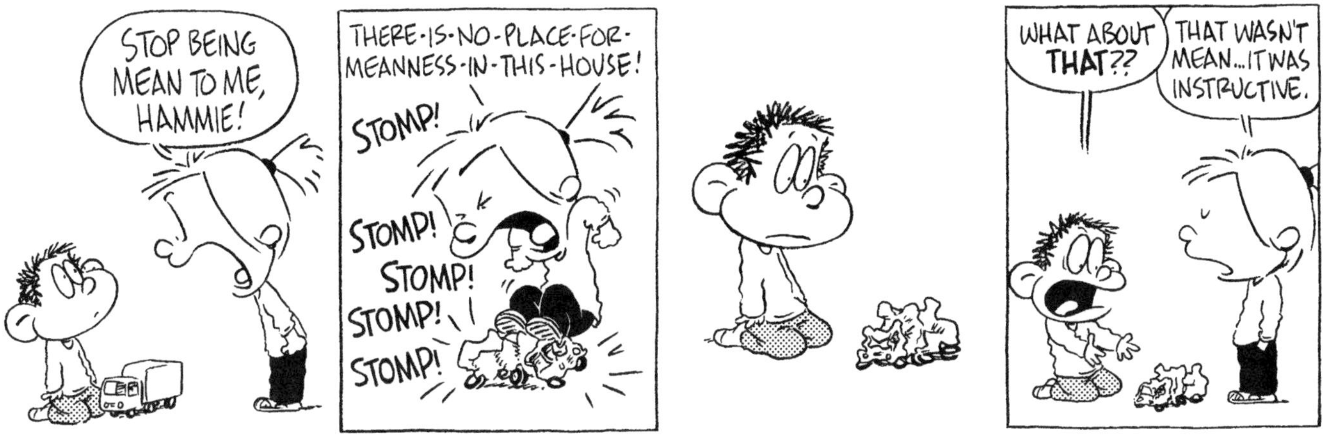
STOP BEING MEAN TO ME, HAMMIE!
THERE-IS-NO-PLACE-FOR-MEANNESS-IN-THIS-HOUSE!
STOMP!
STOMP!
STOMP!
STOMP!
STOMP!
WHAT ABOUT THAT??
THAT WASN'T MEAN...IT WAS INSTRUCTIVE.

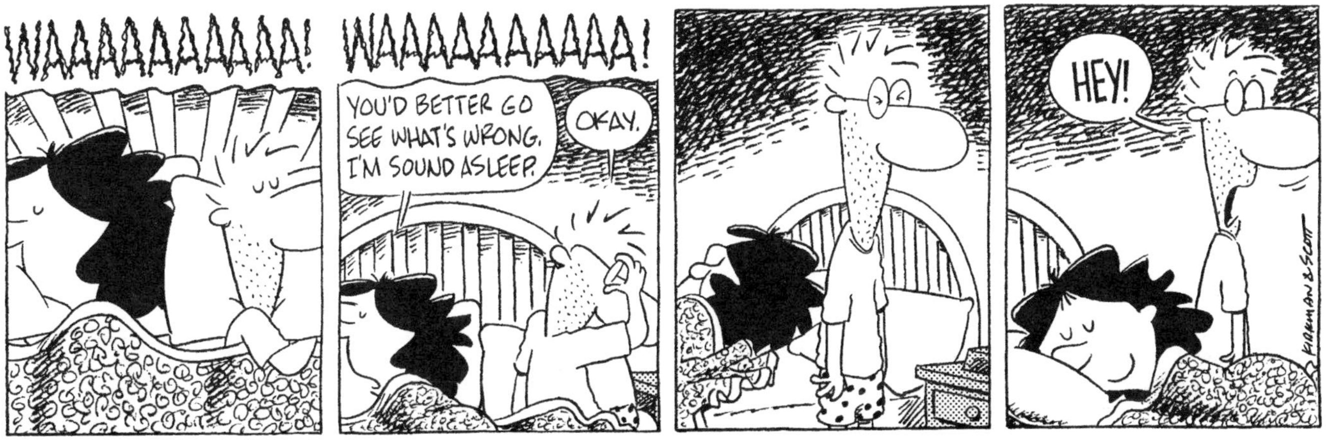
WAAAAAAAAAA!
WAAAAAAAAAA!
YOU'D BETTER GO SEE WHAT'S WRONG. I'M SOUND ASLEEP.
OKAY.
HEY!
KIRKMAN & SCOTT

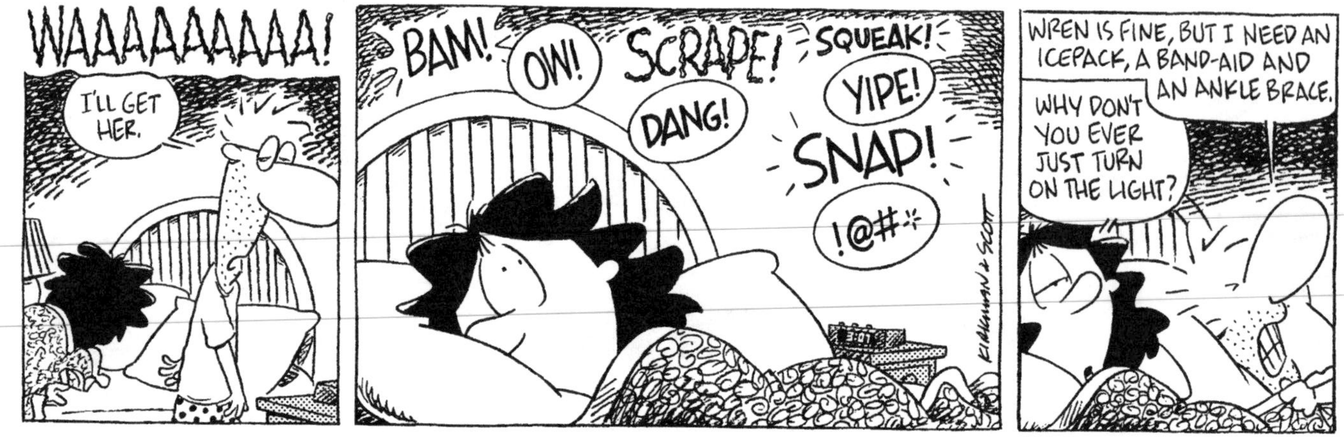
WAAAAAAAAA!
I'LL GET HER.
BAM!
OW!
SCRAPE!
SQUEAK!
DANG!
YIPE!
SNAP!
!@#*
WREN IS FINE, BUT I NEED AN ICEPACK, A BAND-AID AND AN ANKLE BRACE.
WHY DON'T YOU EVER JUST TURN ON THE LIGHT?

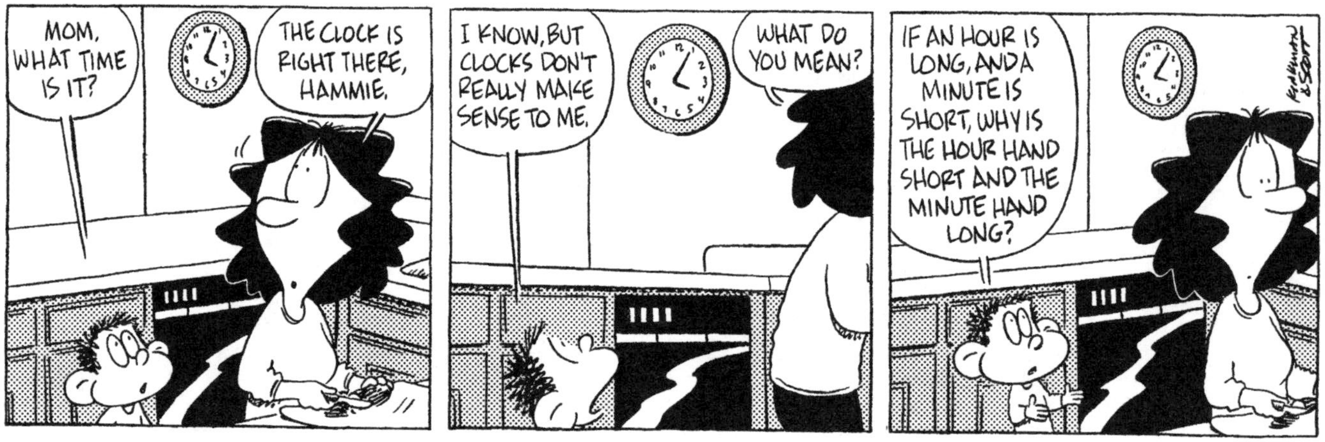
MOM, WHAT TIME IS IT?
THE CLOCK IS RIGHT THERE, HAMMIE.
I KNOW, BUT CLOCKS DON'T REALLY MAKE SENSE TO ME.
WHAT DO YOU MEAN?
IF AN HOUR IS LONG, AND A MINUTE IS SHORT, WHY IS THE HOUR HAND SHORT AND THE MINUTE HAND LONG?

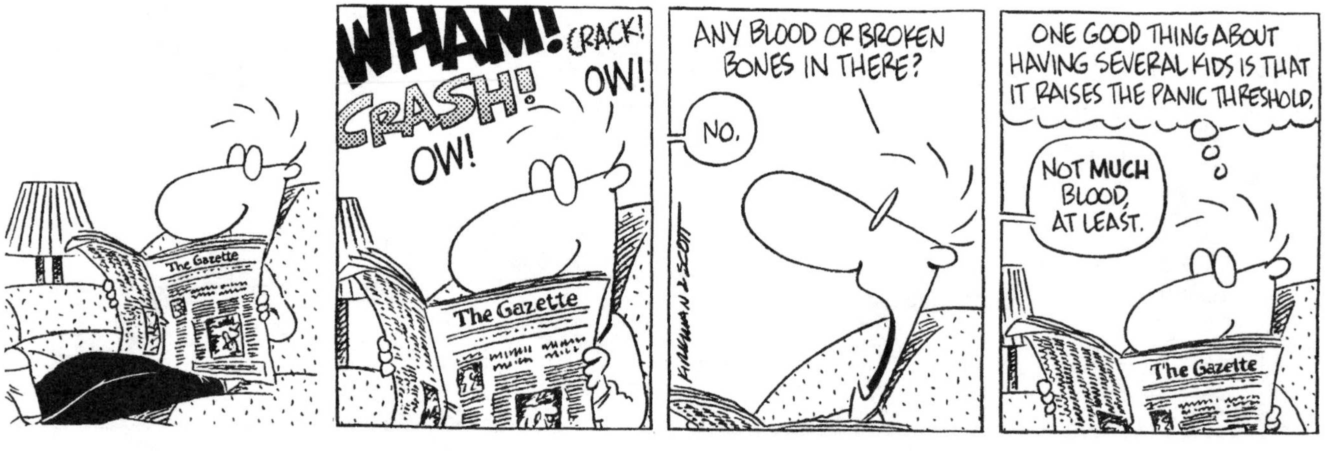
The Gazette
WHAM!
CRACK!
CRASH!
OW!
OW!
The Gazette
ANY BLOOD OR BROKEN BONES IN THERE?
NO.
ONE GOOD THING ABOUT HAVING SEVERAL KIDS IS THAT IT RAISES THE PANIC THRESHOLD.
NOT MUCH BLOOD, AT LEAST.
The Gazette

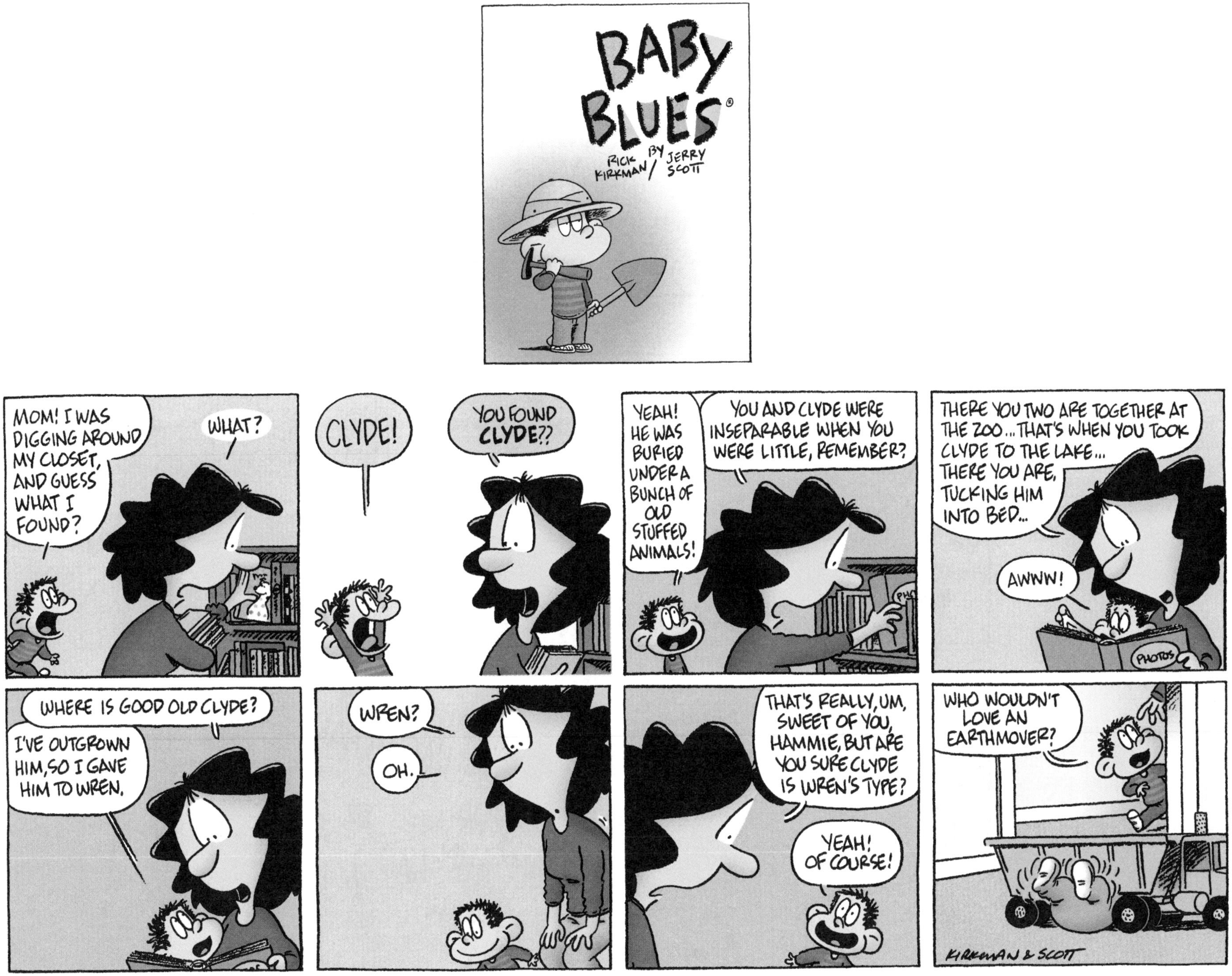
BABY BLUES®
BY RICK KIRKMAN / JERRY SCOTT
MOM! I WAS DIGGING AROUND MY CLOSET, AND GUESS WHAT I FOUND?
WHAT?
CLYDE!
YOU FOUND CLYDE??
YEAH! HE WAS BURIED UNDER A BUNCH OF OLD STUFFED ANIMALS!
YOU AND CLYDE WERE INSEPARABLE WHEN YOU WERE LITTLE, REMEMBER?
THERE YOU TWO ARE TOGETHER AT THE ZOO... THAT'S WHEN YOU TOOK CLYDE TO THE LAKE... THERE YOU ARE, TUCKING HIM INTO BED...
AWWW!
PHOTOS
WHERE IS GOOD OLD CLYDE?
I'VE OUTGROWN HIM, SO I GAVE HIM TO WREN.
WREN?
OH.
THAT'S REALLY, UM, SWEET OF YOU, HAMMIE, BUT ARE YOU SURE CLYDE IS WREN'S TYPE?
YEAH! OF COURSE!
WHO WOULDN'T LOVE AN EARTHMOVER?
KIRKMAN & SCOTT

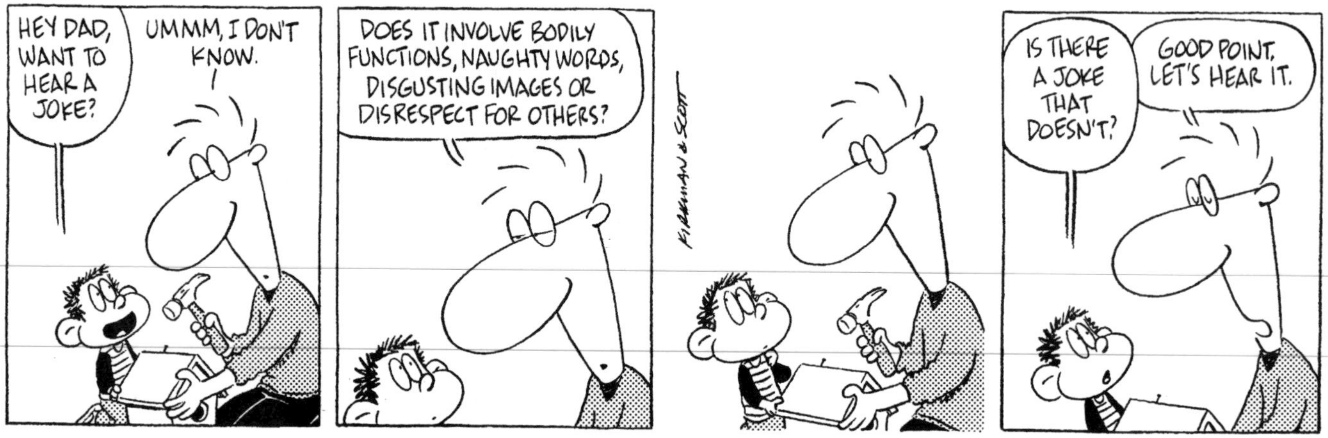
HEY DAD, WANT TO HEAR A JOKE?
UMMM, I DON'T KNOW.
DOES IT INVOLVE BODILY FUNCTIONS, NAUGHTY WORDS, DISGUSTING IMAGES OR DISRESPECT FOR OTHERS?
KIRKMAN & SCOTT
IS THERE A JOKE THAT DOESN'T?
GOOD POINT. LET'S HEAR IT.

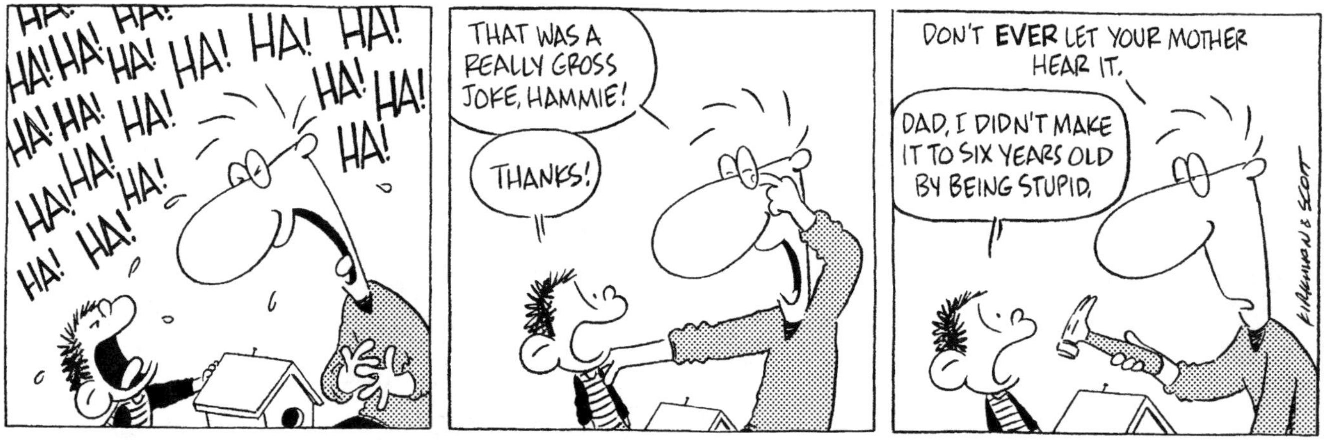
HA! HA! HA! HA! HA! HA! HA! HA! HA! HA! HA! HA! HA! HA! HA! HA! HA! HA! HA! HA!
THAT WAS A REALLY GROSS JOKE, HAMMIE!
THANKS!
DON'T **EVER** LET YOUR MOTHER HEAR IT.
DAD, I DIDN'T MAKE IT TO SIX YEARS OLD BY BEING STUPID.
KIRKMAN & SCOTT

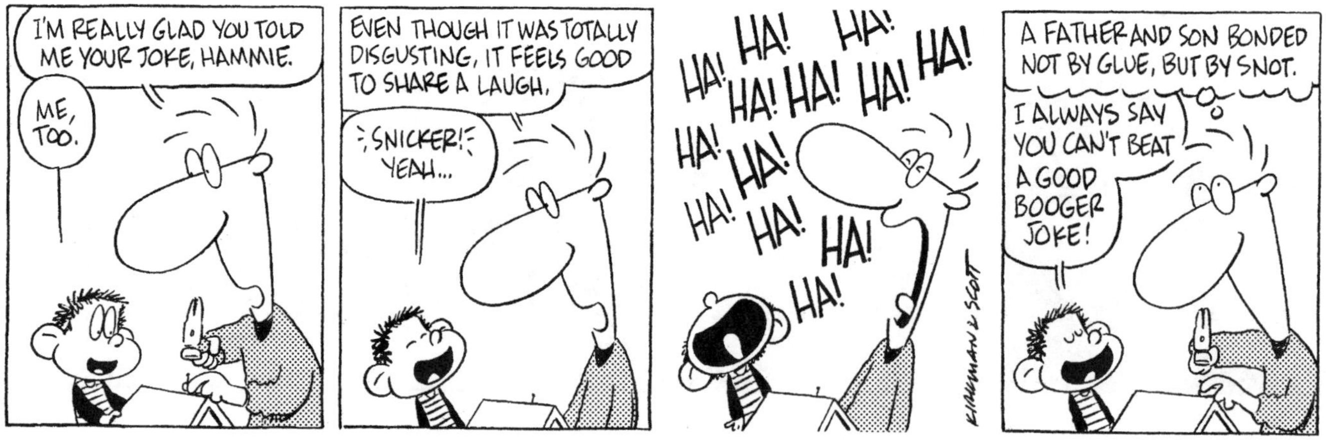
I'M REALLY GLAD YOU TOLD ME YOUR JOKE, HAMMIE.
ME, TOO.
EVEN THOUGH IT WAS TOTALLY DISGUSTING, IT FEELS GOOD TO SHARE A LAUGH.
SNICKER! YEAH...
HA! HA! HA! HA! HA! HA! HA! HA! HA! HA! HA! HA! HA! HA!
KIRKMAN & SCOTT
A FATHER AND SON BONDED NOT BY GLUE, BUT BY SNOT.
I ALWAYS SAY YOU CAN'T BEAT A GOOD BOOGER JOKE!

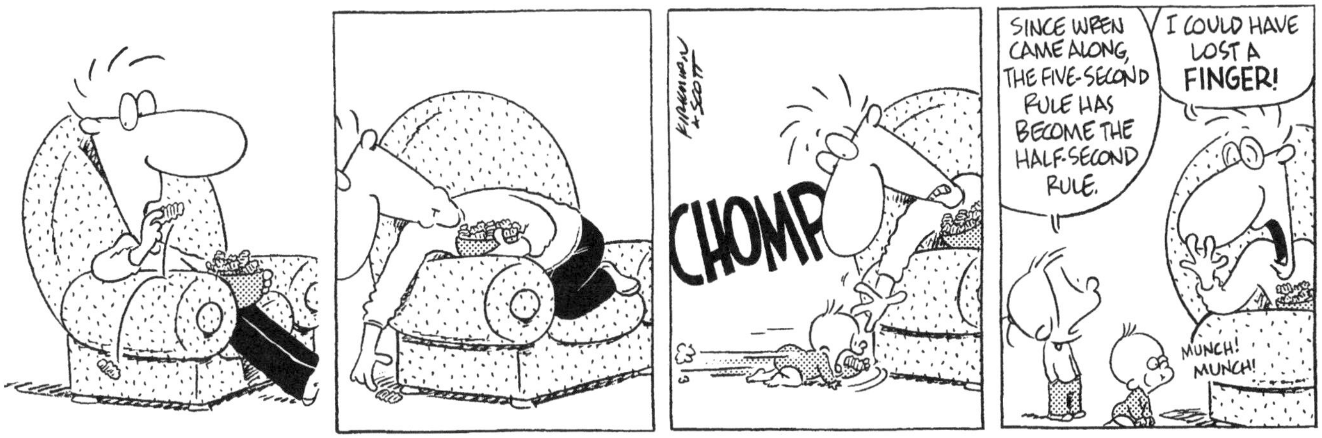
KIRKMAN & SCOTT
CHOMP
SINCE WREN CAME ALONG, THE FIVE-SECOND RULE HAS BECOME THE HALF-SECOND RULE.
I COULD HAVE LOST A FINGER!
MUNCH! MUNCH!

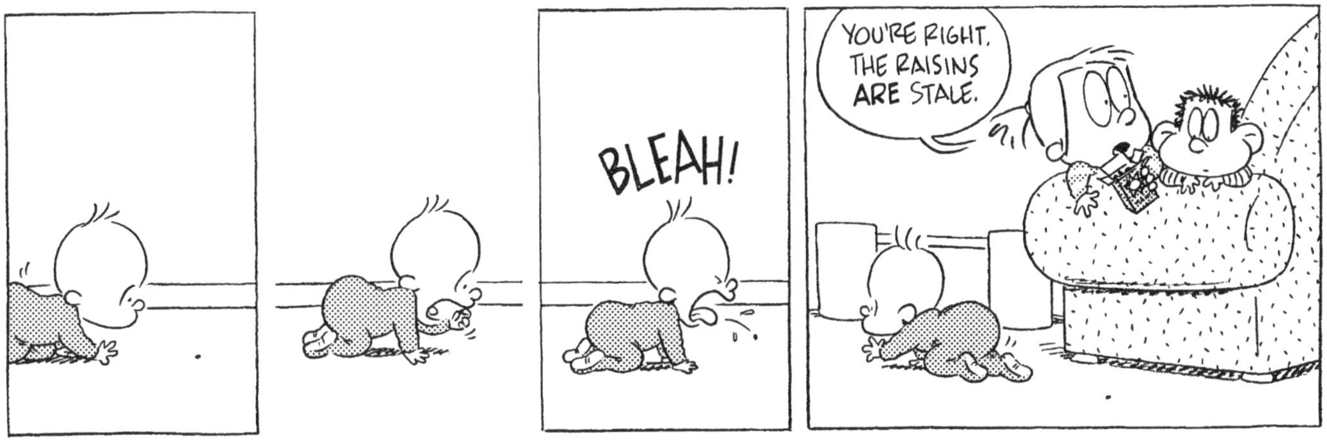
BLEAH!
YOU'RE RIGHT. THE RAISINS ARE STALE.

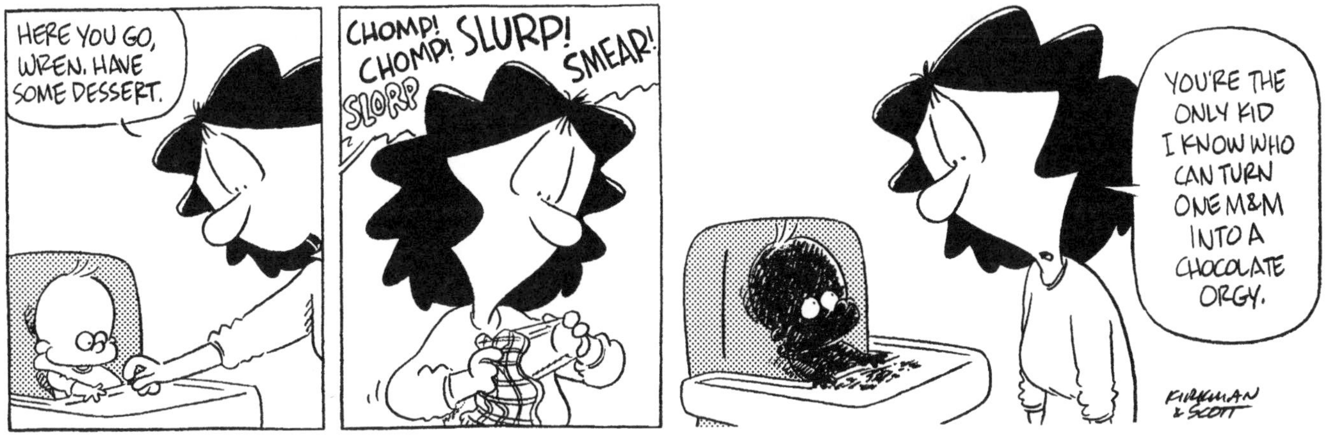
HERE YOU GO, WREN. HAVE SOME DESSERT.
CHOMP! CHOMP!
SLURP!
SMEAR!
SLORP
YOU'RE THE ONLY KID I KNOW WHO CAN TURN ONE M&M INTO A CHOCOLATE ORGY.
KIRKMAN & SCOTT